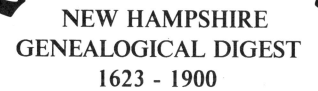

# NEW HAMPSHIRE
# GENEALOGICAL DIGEST
# 1623 - 1900

## Volume 1

Compiled By Glenn C. Towle

## HERITAGE BOOKS, INC.

Published 1989 By

**HERITAGE BOOKS, INC.**
1540E Pointer Ridge Place, Bowie, Maryland 20716
(301)-390-7709

ISBN 1-55613-174-7

A Catalog Listing Hundreds Of Titles On
Genealogy, History, and Americana
Available Free Upon Request

# INTRODUCTION

Welcome to a new series of books offering valuable, but heretofore difficult to locate, genealogical information. Old histories and gazetteers contain many biographical sketches and family histories in addition to information covering the counties and towns; however, few of these books originally contained an every-name or place index. To create an index and reprint even one of these large books would take considerable effort and expense, resulting in an extremely expensive reference tool. To make this information available at an affordable cost, this Digest was created.

This initial volume contains abstracted biographies, presented in a compact and precise format, from seven out of print or hard to find works concerning New Hampshire. (See Bibliography.)

This Digest is not an every name index for the books abstracted, but rather a biographical overview of the material contained therein. Lists of early settlers, rosters of voters/petitioners, military muster rolls, and the like were not included because a name has limited use in proving family connections. Individuals with accompanying biographical data (such as: dates of birth/marriage and/or names of parents, spouses, or children) are included because a family setting has been established.

To use this Digest look for the male surname(s) you are researching. Find the male as a subject of a sketch, or as the father or son included in another sketch; check the cross-index to find where he may be listed as a spouse. To find a female, look under her husband's or father's surnames for a listing; check the cross-index for additional (hidden) references.

Below is a sample entry and an explanation of how to interpret it:

PARSONS,
| | |
|---|---|
| Hezekiah; b1752 s/o Capt Hezekiah & Sarah Abbe Chapin; | subject; birth and parents; |
| m1775 Margaret Kibbee d/o Isaac & Mary Terry of Enfield | marriage(s); |
| CT; liv Enfield CT, Colebrook NH; ch Hezekiah b1776 m Polly (Mary) Bevins, Abdiel b1779, George b1781, Samuel Burt | principle residences; children and their spouses; |
| b1783, Jeremiah b1787; NH-0005-627 | reference to source |

The above abstract may be found on page 189 column 2. The surname Parsons is listed once, then the males are listed alphabetically by given name. Although this causes generations within a family to become jumbled, individual members are more easily located. Both parents are listed when known, the mother's maiden name being included when possible. Grandparent's names are included when there is not enough information to justify an independent listing. In many instances a place of residence is included with the parents' names; this typically refers to the place of birth of the subject. When the place of birth is not given or the parents lived in many places, this reference may be omitted. Parents of spouses are listed; residence is included following above guidelines. A year of birth for the spouse is included when known. A spouse's grandparents will be included here, in the same case as the subject's grandparents. This information will be repeated for more than one wife. The next section lists principle residences of the subject. There are many towns in different states bearing the same name. When known, the state is shown after the town or a string of towns in the same state are connected by ampersands (&). A town name followed only by a comma had no state reference in the original and assumptions were not made as to the location. If no place of birth for the subject is referenced with the parents' names, the first town listed here may be it. Places of residence during childhood years as well as educational years are not included unless the subject spent part of his adult life there. The last section of a biographical sketch contains the names of the subject's children including years of birth and spouses when known. Dates of marriage are included here only when an independent reference was not needed. Children listed as having died young passed away when less than twenty years of age, on the assumption that they did not acheive adult-like status. The sketch ends with a reference to the original title.

The original titles used in this Digest are found in the Bibliography which follows the introduction. The abbreviations used are straight forward; a listing follows the Bibliography. A cross-index of every name not listed alphabetically begins on page 277.

This Digest was not intended to replace the books from which the information was garnered, but to make those original works more useful. These books are, for the most part, out of print. If you are unable to locate a copy for purchase from antiquarian book dealers, try the inter-library loan system. Due to age, many of the original works are not available for public inspection though photocopies of appropriate passages should be obtainable.

Much care has been taken to make the Digest an accurate reproduction of material. Despite great effort (which included two complete checks for errors), the possibility for inaccuracies exists in a compilation of this magnitude. To make this publication more accurate, in the case of a second printing, please address typographical and content errors to the editor care of the publisher. The Digest will not be changed to correct errors found in the original books, because we are unable to verify claims of inaccuracy. This does not discount the validity of these claims nor the need for accurate information to be published. It is more appropriate for this information to be brought to the attention of the public through surname and/or appropriate genealogical periodicals. This information will then be indexed in the Genealogical Periodical Annual Index, published by Heritage Books, Inc. and will be available to all genealogists.

This Digest series was created to release vast stores of information which have been locked up in hard to find and out of print works. It was not designed to replace these valuable books, but to make them more useful. I hope everyone with New Hampshire natives in their family tree can make much use of this and subsequent volumes. I also hope that this series will create enough interest in New

Hampshire and New England genealogy that some of the
books used to create these Digests may eventually be
reprinted in their original glory.

                              GLENN C. TOWLE, Editor
                              June, 1986

# BIBLIOGRAPHY

A listing of books used in compiling this Digest is found below. Each data entry is concluded with a code which looks like: NH-0003-247. NH stands for New Hampshire, 0003 stands for book three as listed below, and 247 stands for the page number. The page number indicates the page on which information begins, many of the entries occupying several pages of the original work.

1) CLARKE, John B., ed. Sketches of Successful New Hampshire Men. Manchester: John B. Clarke, 1882.

2) HURD, D. Hamilton, ed. History of Hillsborough County, New Hampshire. Philadelphia: J. W. Lewis & Co., 1885.

3) HURD, D. Hamilton, ed. History of Rockingham and Strafford Counties, New Hampshire, with Biographical Sketches of Many of its Pioneers and Prominent Men. Philadelphia: . W. Lewis & Co., 1882.

4) HURD, D. Hamilton, ed. History of Merrimack and Belknap Counties, New Hampshire. Philadelphia: J. W. Lewis & Co., 1888.

5) --- History of Coos County, New Hampshire. 1888. Reprint. Somersworth: New Hampshire Publishing Company, 1972.

6) MERRILL, Georgia Drew, ed. History of Carroll County, New Hampshire. 1889. Reprint. Somersworth: New Hampshire Publishing Company, 1971.

7) CHILD, Hamilton, ed. Gazetteer of Grafton County, New Hampshire, 1709-1886. Syracuse, NY: Hamilton Child, 1886.

## ABBREVIATIONS

| | | | | |
|---|---|---|---|---|
| AM | - Master of Arts | | gs/o | - grandson of |
| b | - born | | Hon | - Honorable |
| bapt | - baptised | | Jr | - Junior |
| bc | - born circa | | liv | - lived in |
| bro/o | - brother of | | Lt | - Lieutenant |
| c | - circa | | m | - married |
| Capt | - Captain | | MA | - Master of Arts |
| ch | - children | | Maj | - Major |
| ch/o | - children of | | mc | - married circa |
| Col | - Colonel | | MD | - medical doctor |
| d | - died | | Mr | - Mister |
| d/o | - daughter of | | Mrs | - Misses |
| dau | - daughter | | N | - north |
| DD | - Doctor of Divinity | | Pres | - President |
| Dea | - Deacon | | Prof | - professor |
| Dr | - Doctor | | Rev | - Reverend |
| d/o | - daughter of | | S | - south |
| E | - east | | sis/o | - sister of |
| Eld | - Elder | | Sr | - Senior |
| Esq | - Esquire | | s/o | - son of |
| gd/o | - granddaughter of | | W | - west |
| Gen | - General | | wid/o | - widow of |
| Gov | - Governor | | --- | name not given |

States are abbreviated using modern two letter postal codes.

Foreign countries are abbreviated using three letter capitalized codes such as GER - Germany; HOL - Holland; FRA - France; ENG - England; SCO - Scotland; CAN(CND) - Canada; IRE - Ireland; etc.

## -A-

ABBOTT,

Hon Alson B; b1844 s/o William & Sarah J of Greenfield; m1873 Sarah Morgan d/o James; liv Andover MA, Glen Falls; NH-0002-339

Carl; b1859 s/o Prof George N & Mary Ladd of Newbury VT gs/o James ggs/o Bancroft gggs/o James ggggs/o William gggggs/o George of Andover MA; liv Newbury & Gorham NH; NH-0005-239

Daniel; b1834 s/o Moses & Sarah Bliss of Rumney; m1859 Caroline M Phillips; ch Charles W b1860, George B b1863, Caroline E b1868, Elizabeth b1874; NH-0007-605

Darius; s/o Paul & Naomi Cart of Hillsboro NH gs/o Darius; m Betsey Prescott & m Mrs Bean & m Nancy Huckins; ch Parker P m Harriet C Smythe, 2 others; NH-0007-130

George; d1681; m1647 Hannah Chandler; liv Yorkshire ENG, Andover MA; ch Nathaniel m Dorcas Hibbert; NH-0006-898

George W; m Phebe J Graves d/o Abram & --- Dennett of Canaan; ch Sewall W Esq; NH-0006-440

Hiram Calvin; b1812 s/o Jeremiah & Mary Smith; m1846 Laura A Chase d/o Judge Jonathan T & m1876 Margaret T Hall d/o Jonathan & Lydia Carlton gd/o Ebenezer L D of Bartlett; liv Conway NH; ch/o Laura - Fanny C, Ann M, William Myron, Marion; NH-0006-898

J Stephens; b1804; m1829 Grace Wiggin b1806 d/o Sherburne & Margaret Sargent; liv Albany ME, Concord NH; ch Edward Augustus, Margaret Ann, Joseph Henry, Francis Lewis, Mary; NH-0004-142

Jeremiah; s/o Nathaniel & Penelope Ballard; m Elizabeth Stickney d/o C Thomas of Concord; liv Conway NH; ch Jeremiah m Mary Smith; NH-0006-898

Jeremiah; s/o Jeremiah & Elizabeth Stickney of Conway NH; m

ABBOTT (continued)

Mary Smith of Biddeford ME; liv Saco, Conway; ch Hiram Calvin b1812 m Laura A Chase & m Margaret T Hall, John, William S, Horace, Osgood, Ellen, Elizabeth, Mary; NH-0006-898

Joseph; s/o Nathaniel; m Affie Brainard d/o Daniel; liv Rumney NH; ch Moses b1805 m Sarah Bliss, 1 son, 3 dau; NH-0007-605

Moses; m Lucia Eastman d/o Moses & Sally Smith; liv Bath; ch Chester; NH-0007-137

Moses; b1805 s/o Joseph & Affie Brainard of Rumney; m Sarah Bliss; liv Rumney NH; ch Caroline S m Ira Avery, Harriet dy, Joseph b1831, Daniel b1834 m Caroline M Phillips, Sylvester D b1838, Thomas dy; NH-0007-605

Parker P; s/o Darius; m Harriet C Smythe; liv Ashland NH; ch Elmer E; NH-0007-130

Samuel; m Mrs Ann Wallace; liv Andover MA, Bennington; ch Sarah m --- Dodge; NH-0002-287

William; m Hannah Bailey; liv Greenfield NH, Andover MA; ch 13; NH-0002-344

William; m1801 Rebecca Bailey; liv Andover MA, Concord NH; ch William b1801, Isaac b1803, Rebecca b1806, Moses B b1815, Phebe E b1817 m Joseph S Lund; NH-0004-154

William; b1801 s/o William & Rebecca Bailey; m Desdemonia Fisk Watkins of Warner NH & m Mrs Betsy Jones Davis of Warner NH & m Mrs Vasta Morrison Dolby of Pembroke NH wid/o Albert T; liv Billerica MA, Concord NH; NH-0004-154

ACKERMAN,

John; s/o Peter of Rye NH; m Abigail Gray of Farmington NH; liv Alexandria NH; ch Shem G m Joanna W Clark; NH-0007-119

Peter; s/o Phineas & Sarah Allad; m Betsey Scruten of Strafford NH; ch Peter T m Emma J Berry, 9 others, NH-0007-119

Peter; m Rachel Lock & m Harriet Marden; liv Rye NH;

ACKERMAN (continued)
ch/o ? - John m Abigail Gray,
5 others; NH-0007-119
Peter T; s/o Peter & Betsey
Scruten; m Emma J Berry; liv
Alexandria NH; ch Peter,
Etta, Enoch, Arthur, Clark,
Oren; NH-0007-119
Phineas W; m Elizabeth Bailey
d/o Daniel & Susan Chesley;
liv Alexandria NH; ch Charles
O, Lydia O; NH-0007-119
Shem G; s/o John & Abigail Gray
of Alexandria; m Joanna W
Clark d/o Samuel & Betsey
Rollins of Dorchester; liv
Alexandria NH; ch William C,
John L, Fred H, Abbie G,
George W; NH-0007-119
ADAMS,
Dr Charles; b1782 s/o Jesse &
Miriam Richardson of Brook-
field MA; m1809 Sarah Mc-
Allister d/o James & Sara
McClary of Antrim; liv Brook-
field MA, Antrim NH; ch Hon
Charles Jr AM b1810 m Eliza
Cummings; NH-0001-279
Hon Charles Jr AM; b1810 s/o Dr
Charles & Sarah McAllister;
m1834 Eliza Cummings d/o Hon
Joseph of Ware MA; liv Antrim
NH, Petersham MA, N Brook-
field; ch Charles Woodburn,
George Arthur, John Quincy,
Ellen Eliza d1866 m Frank
Smith; NH-0001-279
Francis Page; m Susan P Brown
d/o Adam & Susan Plummer of
Wolfeborough NH; liv Newfield
ME, Boston; ch Adam B d1887,
Samuel C, Fanny Isabelle; NH-
0006-385
George H; b1851 s/o Isaac L &
Louisa C Blair of Campton NH
gs/o Walter Blair; liv
Plymouth; NH-0007-112.17
Henry; s/o William of Devon ENG
d1646; liv Braintree MA; ch
Edward, Joseph b1626 m
Abigail Baxter; NH-0001-278
Henry; liv Devonshire ENG,
Braintree MA; ch Joseph, 7
sons; NH-0002-123
Ira H MD; b1846; m Louise S
Perley of Lempster NH; liv
Pomfret VT, Hooksett & Derry
Depot NH; ch 2; NH-0004-375
Jesse; s/o Abraham of Brook-
field MA; m Miriam Richard-
son; liv Brookfield MA; ch Dr

ADAMS (continued)
Charles b1782 m Sarah Mc-
Allister; NH-0001-279
Dea John; s/o Joseph; m Susanna
Boylston of Brookline MA; ch
Pres John b1735; NH-0001-279
Pres John; b1735 s/o Dea John &
Susanna Boylston; ch Pres
John Quincy; NH-0001-279
Rev John R; b1790 s/o John of
Stratham NH; m1815 Mary Lane
& m1867 Sarah W Treadwell d/o
Capt Charles & Elizabeth; liv
Greenland; ch/o Mary - 6; NH-
0003-306
Pres John Quincy; s/o Pres
John; ch Hon Charles Francis;
NH-0001-279
Joseph; s/o Henry; ch Edward;
NH-0002-123
Joseph; b1626 s/o Henry of
Braintree MA; m Abigail
Baxter; ch Joseph b1654; NH-
0001-278
Joseph; b1654 s/o Joseph &
Abigail Baxter; ch Dea John m
Susanna Boylston, 1 son; NH-
0001-279
Phinehas; s/o Phinehas gs/o
John ggs/o Eleazer gggs/o
John; m1811 Sarah W Barber of
Holliston MA; liv Waltham &
Cambridge MA, Nashua NH,
Walpole; ch Hon Phinehas Jr
b1814 m Elizabeth P Simpson,
Sarah Ann b1816 m E B Hammond
MD of Nashua, Eliza P b1820 m
Ira Stone, Mary Jane b1822 m
James Buncher, 2 sons, 4
dau; NH-0001-166, NH-0002-123
Hon Phinehas Jr; b1814 s/o
Phinehas & Sarah W Barber;
m1839 Elizabeth P Simpson d/o
Dea Samuel of Deerfield NH
gd/o Maj John; liv Medway &
Lowell MA, Hooksett, Pitts-
field & Manchester NH; ch
Elizabeth b1842 m Col Daniel
C Gould of Manchester NH s/o
Dea Daniel, Phinehas III
b1844 m Anna P Morrison of
Belfast ME; NH-0001-166, NH-
0002-123
Samuel; s/o Samuel; m Dorcas
Hall of Carlisle MA; ch Jonas
J m Betsey Foster of Tewks-
bury MA & m Mrs Sarah A
Preston d/o Thomas Perkins &
Hannah P McCoy Perkins; NH-
0007-558
William; m1744 Mary Spears; liv

ADAMS (continued)
W Dunstable; ch William; NH-0002-437

AIKEN,
Andrew; m Margaret ---; ch Elizabeth, Mary, Margaret b1783, James; NH-0002-382

Capt Benjamin; bro/o Luke; m twice; liv Wentworth; ch John J, 9 others; NH-0007-575

Edward; liv IRE, Londonderry; ch Nathaniel, James, William; NH-0002-375

Herrick; b1797 s/o Matthew & Sally Hackett; m1830 Ann Matilda Bradley d/o Isaac of Dracut MA; liv Dracut MA, Franklin NH; ch Walter b1831 m Susan Colby & m Mary Dodge, Jonas Bradley b1833 m Helen M Scribner & m Addie G Proctor, James Hackett b1835, Francis Herrick b1843 m1865 Hannah A Colby of Hill NH, Charles Lowe b1845 m Isabella Burleigh of Thornton; NH-0004-326

John; s/o William of Deering NH; ch Electa m David Wilson of Deering, Joseph, Calvin, William, Martha, Relief, Luther, Harriett, Rebecca, Jane; NH-0002-375

John s/o Thomas of Deering NH; ch Elmira, Cyrus, Caroline, Hermon, Fanny, James; NH-0002-375

Jonas Bradley; b1833 s/o Herrick & Ann Matilda Bradley, m1864 Helen M Scribner of Franklin & m Addie G Proctor of Northfield VT; ch/o Helen - Alice Matilda dy; ch/o Addie - Mary Louisa b1867, Charles Wilson b1869, George Proctor b1873 dy; NH-0004-326

Matthew; b1776 s/o Thomas gs/o Nathaniel ggs/o Edward; m Sally Hackett of Portsmouth NH; liv Derry & Pelham NH; ch James Gilman b1795, Herrick b1797 m Ann Matilda Bradley, Sally b1799 m Phineas Stevens, Emma b1802 m David Hamblett of Manchester NH, Alfred b1804; NH-0004-326

Nathaniel; s/o Edward; ch Edward, John, James, Thomas, William; NH-0002-375

Thomas, s/o Nathaniel; liv

AIKEN (continued)
Deering NH; ch John; NH-0002-375

Walter; b1831 s/o Herrick & Ann Matilda Bradley; m1853 Susan Colby of Warner & m1867 Mary Dodge of Hampton Falls; liv Franklin NH; ch/o Susan - James b1854, Frederick b1855; NH-0004-326

William; s/o Nathaniel; liv Deering NH; ch John; NH-0002-375

AINSWORTH,
Calvin Jr; b1807; m Eliza Bellows sis/o Hon Henry A & William J & m Mrs Letitia Stinson White; liv Littleton, Concord, Madison WI; NH-0007-102

ALBEE,
Alexander; liv Chesterfield NH, Littleton; ch Joseph, 8 others; NH-0007-555

ALBIN,
John Henry; b1843 s/o John & Emily White of W Randolph VT; m1872 Georgie A Modica of Henniker; liv Concord & Henniker NH; ch Henry A b1875, Edith G b1878; NH-0004-26

ALCOCK,
James; s/o Robert & ?; m Polly Stuart; ch Nancy m Daniel Brown, Henry m Charlotte Cheney, James M m Caroline McCoy, Mary m Freeman Dow, Aura m William French, Clarissa m Joel Bullard, Charles m Nancy J Parker; NH-0002-383

Joseph; s/o Robert & ?; m Lucy Hobson; ch Elbridge, Harriet, Joseph; NH-0002-383

Mansil; s/o Robert & ?; m Lucy Bradford & m ?; ch/o Lucy - Mansil m Lucy Brown, Cyrus, Clara m John Tandy, Timothy m Kate Howe, Robert, Luke m Mahala White, John m Hannah Baldwin, Lucy m Jonathan Ellsworth, Sally m Peter Whitaker, Baxter, Alver, Frederick m Eliza Putney; NH-0002-383

Robert; m Elizabeth Marong & m Elizabeth Currier & m Mary Currier; liv London, Marblehead & Salem MA, Weare & Deering NH; ch/o ? Mansil m

ALCOCK (continued)
Lucy Bradford & m ?, Robert m
--- Codman sis/o Peter & m
--- Blainer & m --- Grant,
Elizabeth, John m Mattie
Shearer, James m Polly Stuart
& m Mrs Taylor, Benjamin m
--- Page & m ?, Joseph m Lucy
Hobson, Samuel m Betsy Chad-
wick, William m Ruth Gerry &
m Judith Colby & m Theresa
Howe, Betsy m --- Tennant,
Nancy m Samuel Kimball, Sally
m --- Goodwin, Ann, 2 dy; NH-
0002-383
Robert; s/o Robert & ?; m ---
Codman sis/o Peter & m ---
Blainer & m --- Grant; ch/o
Codman - William, Betsy m
Jonathan Danforth, Ruth m
Peter Codman, Grace; ch/o
Blainer - Robert m Clarissa
Flanders & m Mary Tarleton,
Stephen m Sally Wilson & m
--- Pope, Christopher m ---
Flanders; NH-0002-383
Samuel; s/o Robert & ?; m Betsy
Chadwick; ch Marony dy,
Marony dy, Elizabeth m Milton
McCoy, Ira A m Josette Alcock
Appleton; NH-0002-383
William; s/o Robert & ?; m Ruth
Gerry & m Judith Colby & m
Theresa Howe; ch/o Ruth -
William H m Almira A Smiley;
ch/o Judith - Ora m John
Ellingwood, Harriet m Gideon
Page, Jane m Wilson Campbell,
2 dy; ch/o Theresa - Irene,
Cyrus H m --- Brown; NH-0002-
383
ALDRICH,
Alpheus; s/o Mark & Lydia
Terry; m Isabel Amy; ch
Schuyler H, Samuel, Mark; NH-
0005-621
Charles; s/o Mark & Lydia
Terry; m Lydia Hathorn; ch
Charles S; NH-0005-621
David; b1806; m Mary Quimby d/o
Rev Joshua; liv Franconia,
Lisbon NH; ch 5; NH-0007-454
Edgar; b1848 s/o Ephraim C &
Adaline B Haynes of Pittsburg
NH; m1872 Louise M Remick d/o
Samuel & Sophia Cushman; liv
Pittsburg & Littleton & Cole-
brook NH; ch Florence M
b1874, Fred b1878; NH-0005-
254, NH-0007-112.2
George; s/o Jonathan & Dorothy

ALDRICH (continued)
Drake of Grafton; m Elsie
Reed: ch Maria, Elsie m ---
Watson, Mary, 7 others; NH-
0007-283
George; b1796 s/o Mark & Lydia
Terry; m Sarah Morrison; ch
Mahala m Hezekiah B Parsons;
NH-0005-621
Hosea; s/o Mark & Lydia Terry;
m Electa Barnes; ch Ezra,
Melinda, Persis m Charles
Huntoon; NH-0005-621
Mark; b1769; m Lydia Terry; liv
Shutesbury MA, Columbia; ch
Mark Jr m Polly Lovering,
George b1796 m Sarah
Morrison, Artemas m Keziah
Rowe of Eddington ME,
Aurilla, Alpheus m Isabel
Amy, Jonathan Northum, Hosea
b1804 m Electa Barnes, Jacob
Terry, Lydia m Samuel Mc-
Mahon, Horatio Nelson m
Adaline French, Mary Tevey m
--- Nichols, Charles m Lydia
Hathorn; NH-0005-613 & 621
ALEXANDER,
Enoch; b1771 s/o Samuel & Mary
Bornton; m1797 Miriam Colby
d/o Willoughby of Bow; ch
Betsey, Samuel, Philip C,
Sarah, Miriam, Capt Enoch
b1810 m Lois P Hadley, Eli, J
G, Willoughby C, Adaline; NH-
0004-287
Capt Enoch; b1810 s/o Enoch &
Miriam Colby; m Lois P Hadley
d/o Amos & Sarah Colby; liv
Bow; NH-0004-287
James G; b1815 s/o Enoch &
Merriam Colby; m1841 Aurelia
Veasey b1816; ch Charles H
b1844 m1870 Sarah Abby Marsh;
NH-0004-286
Philip C; b1804 s/o Enoch
Merriam Colby; m1828 Mary A
Taylor b1808; ch George
Warren b1829 m Harriet Apple-
ton, Elvira S b1830 m1854
John C Morrison, Rosantha A
b1832 m1855 Asa Strong, Sarah
R b1834 m1854 James N Wright,
Merriam A b1836 m1857 Horatio
B Shoals, Lois P b1840 m
Justus Lyman, Dolly T b1842
m1872 Zediah Cooley, Ella J
b1850 m1868 Oscar Ward, Edwin
F b1850, Nettie Mark b1854;
NH-0004-286

ALEXANDER (continued)
Samuel; b1730; liv Londonderry
& Bow NH; ch Martha b1760
m1783 Jonathan Colby, William
m Polly Putney of Dunbarton,
Enoch b1771 m Merriam Colby,
Polly m James White; NH-0004-
285
Samuel; b1731; m Mary Bornton;
liv Derry & Bow NH; ch Enoch
b1771 m Miriam Colby,
William, Mary, Pattie; NH-
0004-287
Samuel b1800 s/o Enoch &
Merriam Colby; m1825 Mary
Nutt b1797; ch Eliza Jane
b1826 m1856 Allen T Hubbard,
Mary A b1829 m1853 C Waterman
Pratt, J Bordman b1834 m1870
Mary Nyland, S Judson b1837;
NH-0004-286
Willaby C; b1818 s/o Enoch &
Merriam Colby; m1848 Sarah
Ann Blood b1826; ch Edwin G
b1849; NH-0004-286
ALGER,
Asa; b1796 s/o Edmund & Huldah
Lothrop; m Abigail Sawyer d/o
Capt Josiah & Susanna Green;
liv Eaton PQ, Bridgewater MA;
ch Emily m William Lindsey,
Horace, Henry, Ruth, Lyman
Willis b1831 m Marian Wallace
Loomis, Persis m Eben
Goodwin; NH-0005-683
Edmund; b1763 s/o Joseph of
Bridgewater MA; m Huldah
Lothrop; liv Eaton PQ; ch Asa
b1796, 4 sons; NH-0005-683
Israel; liv Bridgewater; ch
Joseph, 4 sons; NH-0005-683
Joseph; s/o Joseph; liv Bridge-
water MA; ch Edmund b1763 m
Huldah Lothrop; NH-0005-683
Lyman Willis; b1831 s/o Asa &
Abigail Sawyer; m1856 Marion
Wallace Loomis d/o Gen Lewis
& Rispah Beach; liv Eaton PQ,
N Stratford & Colebrook & W
Stewartstown NH; NH-0005-683
Thomas; m Elizabeth Packard;
liv Taunton MA; ch Israel;
NH-0005-683
ALLARD,
---; m Judith Fall d/o Samuel
of Bartlett; ch Samuel,
Joseph; NH-0006-916
David; liv New Durham, Eaton;
ch Capt Job; NH-0006-793
ALLEN,
Abijah; s/o Abijah b1776; m

ALLEN (continued)
Adaline Cox of Holderness;
liv Littleton NH; ch Charles
R m Sophia Harriman, Alice I
m George L Flanders; NH-0007-
486
Rev Frank Houghton; m1883
Harriet Augusta; liv Shrews-
bury MA; ch Harold Bickford
b1884; NH-0004-442
AMBROSE,
Samuel; bc1771; liv Sandwich
Centre NH; ch Jesse, Merritt,
1 dau m Caleb Marston, 1 dau
m Rev Elias Hutchins; NH-
0006-671
AMES,
Charles J; b1838 s/o James &
Joanna Hayford; m Mary H
Flood; liv Tamworth NH; ch
Charles J b1864 m Kitty
Hauft, W H b1868; NH-0006-774
Daniel H; s/o Caleb; m Mary M
Batchelder & m Anna B Cheney
d/o Alonzo & Theodate of
Boston MA; liv Ashland NH; ch
4; NH-0007-125
David; m Mary Penniman; liv
Braintree MA, Cardigan NH; ch
David b1726 m Irene Waldo,
John, Elijah; NH-0004-212
David; b1726 s/o David & Mary
Penniman; m Irene Waldo b1738
of Scotland CT; liv Norwich &
Killingsley CT; ch Thaddeus
b1755 m Judy Clark, John
b1756, David b1758 m Ruth
Anin, Nathaniel b1761 m Sally
Anin, Susanna b1763 m Joseph
Daniels, Abigail b1766 m
Nathaniel Briggs, Anna b1769
m Peter Perkins, Jesse b1772
m Patty Howard, Ebenezer
b1775 m Chloe Osborn; NH-
0004-212
David; b1749 s/o Samuel &
Hannah Daloff of Canterbury;
m Phebe Hoyt d/o Thomas; liv
Canterbury; ch Samuel b1784 m
Myra Ayres, Ruth b1797 m
Benjamin Kimball, 2 sons, 6
dau; NH-0004-144 & 231
Henry George; b1830 s/o Jason
Howard MD & Clara George; m
Mary Graves Stoddard of Perry
NY; ch Clara George b1860,
Henry Stoddard b1861; NH-
0004-212
James; m Comfort Masten; liv
New Market NH; ch 1 son m
Sarah Burleigh d/o William &

AMES (continued)
Sarah, 7 others; NH-0007-125
James; b1810; m Joanna Hayford of Tamworth NH; liv Tamworth NH; ch Charles J b1838 m Mary H Flood, James, Asa m Rowena Hatch, Elizabeth m David Hayford; NH-0006-774
Jason Howard MD; b1796 s/o Jesse & Patty Howard; m1827 Clara George b1798 of Warner NH; liv Fairlee VT, Bradford & Warner NH; ch George b1828 dy, Henry George b1830 m Mary G Stoddard, Martha Jane b1832 m Bartlett G Cilley; NH-0004-198 & 212
Jesse; b1772 s/o David & Irene Waldo; m Patty Howard of Munson MA; ch Jason Howard MD b1796 m Clara George, Polly, Pamelia, Roxanna M, Ruth, Cynthia, Martha L, Lyman D, Loren J; NH-0004-212
Lorenzo; b1814 s/o Samuel & Myra Ayres of Canterbury NH; m1852 Lydia Page d/o Hon Ezekiel Morrill of Canterbury; liv Boston MA, Concord & Canterbury NH, Albany NY; ch Samuel Patten b1865, 3 others; NH-0004-231
Samuel; bc1723; m Hannah Daloff bc1728; liv Canterbury; ch David b1749 m Phebe Hoyt, 3 others; NH-0004-144 & 231
Samuel; b1784 s/o David & Phoebe Hoyt of Canterbury; m Myra Ayres d/o Jonathan of Canterbury; liv Canterbury NH; ch Lorenzo b1814, Samuel F, Jeremiah F; NH-0004-231
Ens Stephen; m1731 Jane Robbins; liv Groton MA, W Dunstable; ch Jonathan, David; NH-0002-437
AMORY,
William; b1804 s/o Thomas C & Hannah R Linzee of Boston MA; m1833 Anna P G Sears d/o David of Boston MA; liv Boston MA & Nashua NH; ch 6; NH-0001-151
AMSDEN,
Charles Hubbard; b1848 s/o Henry & Mary Muzzey; m1870 Helen A Brown d/o David A & Martha A Daggett of Penacook; liv Boscawen; ch Henry Hubbard b1872, Mary Ardelle b1878 dy; NH-0004-158

AMSDEN (continued)
Henry; b1816 s/o Hubbard & Annie Saunders; m1840 Mary Muzzey of New Ipswich NH; ch George Henry b1841, Charles Hubbard b1846 dy, Charles Hubbard b1848, Edward b1853 dy; NH-0004-158
Hubbard; b1790 s/o Jonas & Hannah Rice; m1814 Annie Saunders of Mason NH; ch Henry b1816 m Mary Muzzey, 1 other; NH-0004-158
Isaac; m1654 Frances Perriman; liv Cambridge MA; ch Isaac b1655 m Jane Rutter, 1 other; NH-0004-158
Isaac; b1655 s/o Isaac & Frances Perriman of Cambridge MA; m1677 Jane Rutter; ch John b1683 m Hannah Howe, 2 sons; NH-0004-158
Jesse; b1729 s/o John & Hannah Howe; m1748 Bettie Ball of Southborough; liv Southborough MA; ch Jonas b1749 m Hannah Rice, 11 others; NH-0004-158
John; b1683 s/o Isaac & Jane Rutter; m Hannah Howe b1688 d/o Isaac & Frances Woods of Marlborough MA; liv Marlborough & Southborough MA; ch Jesse b1729 m Bettie Ball, 11 others; NH-0004-158
Jonas; b1749 s/o Jesse & Bettie Ball of Southborough MA; m1770 Hannah Rice; ch Hubbard b1790 m Annie Saunders; NH-0004-158
Dr William; b1796; m1828 Mary Cook d/o Maj James of Lyme; liv Henniker & Lyme NH; ch George P, 3 sons, 1 dau; NH-0007-522
ANDERSON,
William; m Margaret Clark; ch Margaret m Craig Muzzey of Weare, Eliza m Reuben Loveren; NH-0002-382
APPLEBEE,
Benjamin; liv RI, Franconia, Easton; ch Justice, Emer, James, David, Minot m Rhoda Howland, 3 others; NH-0007-270
Minot; s/o Benjamin; m Rhoda Howland; liv Franconia, Easton; ch Jerome, Lydia, Sally, Mary, George H, David H; NH-0007-270

APPLEBEE (continued)
Nathan; b1792; m Amarintha Bemis of Brattleboro VT & m Ruby Farnum of Lisbon; liv Littleton NH; ch/o Amarintha - 8; ch/o Ruby - Emeline m George Abbott, Warren, Annette m Aaron Fisher; NH-0007-485

APPLETON,
Rev Joseph; b1751; m1777 Mary Hook d/o Jacob of Kingston; liv N Brookfield MA; ch Hon William b1786; NH-0003-378

ARMINGTON,
Willard N; b1850; liv Waterford VT, Whitefield; NH-0005-237

ASH,
David; liv ENG, Lisbon; ch Reuben b1807; NH-0007-516

ATHERTON,
Charles H; s/o Hon Joshua; ch Hon Charles G; NH-0001-81
Charles Humphrey; s/o Joshua of Amherst NH; liv Amherst; NH-0002-10
Hon Joshua; ch Rebecca m Dr Matthew Spaulding, Charles H; NH-0001-81
Hon Joshua; b1737; liv Harvard MA, Litchfield, Merrimack, Amherst; NH-0002-9
Samuel; liv Dalton NH; ch Nathaniel b1809; NH-0005-520

ATKINSON,
Daniel C; bc1784 s/o Simeon & Phebe Clark of Boscawen NH; m Mahala Tilton & m Mehetable Tilton sis/o Mahala; liv Sanbornton Bridge NH; NH-0004-701
John; liv Buton ME, Eaton NH; ch Samuel m --- March d/o John, Sally m Joseph Snow, Isaac, Joseph, Kindsman, King; NH-0006-793

ATWOOD,
Charles D; b1847 s/o David & Julia of Landaff; m Emma Clough d/o Ephraim & Lucinda; liv Bath NH; ch 3 sons, 1 dau; NH-0007-146
John; s/o Moses of Alexandria; m Elizabeth Corliss; ch George, Mary, Elizabeth, John W m Susan Bailey; NH-0007-116
Rev John; b1795; m1826 Lydia Dodge d/o Dea Solomon; liv Nottingham West, New Boston, Hillsborough; ch Lydia D, Sarah E m John L Blair, John

ATWOOD (continued)
B dy, Roger W m Emily Larcom of Beverly MA, Ann J m Rev J L A Fish, Mary F, Solomon D m Flora A Dodge of Francestown, John H dy; NH-0002-601
John W; s/o John & Elizabeth Corliss; m Susan Bailey d/o Daniel & Susan Cheley; ch Ella F, Emma, William I, 1 other; NH-0007-116

AUSTIN,
Hope; liv Shelburne NH; ch Mary, Judith, Lydia m Samuel Wheeler, Hannah m Samuel Wheeler, James m Sally Lary; NH-0005-871
James; s/o Hope; m Sally Lary d/o Joseph Jr of Gilead; liv Shelburne NH; ch John, Caverno, Dearborn m Rose Coffin; NH-0005-871

AVERILL,
Calvin; b1788 s/o Ebenezer & Anna Johnson; m1814 Eunice Spalding d/o Oliver & Eunice Brown; liv Milford; ch Clinton Spalding b1827 m Catherine Frances Hutchinson; NH-0002-579
Clinton Spalding; b1827 s/o Calvin & Eunice Spalding; m1852 Catherine Frances Hutchinson d/o Dr Jonas of Milford; liv Marietta OH, Milford NH; ch 1 dy; NH-0002-579
Ebenezer; liv Topsfield MA, Milford NH; ch Ruth, Ebenezer b1752 m Anna Johnson, David, Elijah, Moses; NH-0002-579
Ebenezer, b1752 s/o Ebenezer; m Anna Johnson b1755; liv Milford; ch James b1778, Elijah b1781, Eben b1783, Luther b1786, Calvin b1788, Aladan, Nancy m John Leavitt of Amherst, Alma m Daniel Johnson & m Benjamin Barker of Milford; NH-0002-579

AVERY,
Alonzo; b1851 s/o Joseph & Johanna Hill of Ellsworth; m1875 Ella J Fales d/o William W Sr & Mary A Guild; liv Rumney NH; ch 3; NH-0007-613
Augustine Decatur; b1814 s/o Samuel & Mary Moody Clark of Wolfeborough; m1854 Sarah Elizabeth Libby d/o Dudley

AVERY (continued)
Leavitt & Sarah Ann Wiggin of Wolfeborough; liv Wolfeborough NH; ch Mary Elizabeth b1855 dy, Dudley Libby b1857 dy, Samuel Augustine b1860 dy, Samuel b1862, Belle b1866; NH-0006-373
Gardner; b1848 s/o Daniel; m1873 Laura J Fales d/o William W Sr; liv Rumney NH; ch Mary Ella b1874; NH-0007-613
James; b1620 s/o Christopher; m1643 Joanna Greenslade of Boston; liv ENG, New London CT; ch John b1654; NH-0006-373
John; m Bridget ---; liv Stratham; ch Daniel, Joshua b1740 m Hannah Clark, Josiah b1740; NH-0006-373
Joseph Lorenzo; b1817 s/o Samuel & Mary Moody Clark of Wolfeborough; m1857 Helen Maria Libby d/o Dudley Leavitt & Sarah Ann Wiggin of Wolfeborough; liv Wolfeborough NH; ch Joseph William b1867 dy, Joseph Clifton b1874; NH-0006-373
Joshua; b1740 s/o John & Bridget of Stratham; m1768 Hannah Clark b1747; liv Stratham; ch Samuel b1785 m Mary Moody Clark; NH-0006-373
Roland A; s/o Jasper E & Mary R Willey; m Rosa J Dow; liv Plymouth NH; ch 3 dau; NH-0007-597
Samuel; b1785 s/o Joshua & Hannah Clark of Stratham; m1814 Mary Moody Clark b1795 d/o Joseph & Comfort Weeks of Greenland NH; liv Wolfeborough NH; ch Augustine Decatur b1814 m Sarah Elizabeth Libby, Joseph Lorenzo b1817 m Helen Maria Libby, Anne Eliza b1819 m Rev Leander Thompson; NH-0006-373
AYER,
Hon Benjamin Franklin; b1825 s/o Robert & Louisa Sanborn of Kingston; liv Manchester NH; NH-0002-34
Hon Richard H; b1778; m --- Green d/o Peter Esq of Concord; liv Concord & Dunbarton & Hooksett & Manchester NH; ch Susan R m Dr

AYER (continued)
Enoch B Barnes, Mary G m Dr Amos G Gale; NH-0004-384
Hon Samuel H; b1819; liv Eastport ME, Concord, Hillsborough, Manchester NH; NH-0002-13
AYERS,
Augustine R; m1873 Clara Maria Kimball d/o Hon John & Maria H Philips; liv Concord NH; ch Ruth Ames, John Kimball, Helen McGregor, Joseph Sherburne & Josiah Phillips, Augustine Haines; NH-0001-92, NH-0004-146

-B-

BACHELDER,
Abraham Esq; s/o Jethro Sr; liv Canterbury; ch Abraham Jr b1744 m Anna Judkins; NH-0004-499
Abraham Jr; b1744 s/o Abraham Esq of Canterbury; m1772 Anna Judkins b1750; ch Nathan b1773, Abraham b1775, Josiah b1775, Hannah b1776, Josiah b1779, Philip b1781, James b1783, John b1785, Sally, Jonathan b1790 m Lois Wells, Judith; NH-0004-499
Capt Abraham; m Betsy Bachelder b1759; ch Smith b1785, Zephaniah b1786 m Mary Eastman, Olive b1788, Nathaniel b1790, Gardner b1792 m Clarisa Bradley & m Nancy Young, Betsy b1793, Asa b1795 m Rachel True, Lois b1797, Enoch W b1798, Joseph b1800, Clarisa b1802; NH-0004-499
Abraham G; s/o Zephaniah & Mary Eastman; m Rebecca Fifield; ch Fred, Frank, Charles, Asa C m Jennie Badger, Frank; NH-0004-499
Abram; s/o Gardner & ?; m --- Whitney; ch Ivy; NH-0004-499
Alfred P; s/o Joseph P & Elvira A Whitney; m Nellie M Brown of Canterbury; ch Ernest L; NH-0004-510
Asa; s/o Abraham G & Rebecca Fifield; m Jennie Badger; ch Edwin, Emory, Kate, Genette,

BACHELDER (continued)
Lillian; NH-0004-499
Asa; b1795 s/o Capt Abraham &
Betsy Bachelder; m Rachel
True; ch Augustine, Abram,
Roscoe G, Ancie m Joseph
Wiggin, 3 dy; NH-0004-499
Benjamin; s/o Jonathan & Lois
Wells; m Mary E Bachelder of
Meredith NH; liv Loudon
Centre NH; ch Marta E, John;
NH-0004-499
Cyrus; s/o Thomas gs/o Abraham
Jr; liv Loudon; ch James K P,
Georgia m Rev Warren Apple-
bee; NH-0004-499
Dea David; s/o Josiah of
Hampton Falls; liv Hampton
Falls; ch Josiah b1767; NH-
0004-499
Dea Ebenezer; s/o Dea Nathaniel
Jr of Hampton; liv E
Kingston; ch Maj Nathan Esq
b1734 m Margaret Bean,
Richard b1736, Nathaniel
b1740; NH-0004-499
Gardner; b1792 s/o Capt Abraham
& Betsy Bachelder; m Clarisa
Bradley & m Nancy Young; ch/o
? - Nathaniel S, Emory B,
Judith, Stephen, William,
Abby, Henry F m Lydia S
Rogers, William, Winthrop,
Abram m --- Whitney; NH-0004-
499
Dea Harmon E; s/o Zaphaniah &
Mary Eastman; m Clarisa San-
born; liv Loudon; ch 1 dau m
Samuel M True; NH-0004-499
Henry F; s/o Gardner & ?; m
Lydia S Rogers; liv Loudon;
ch Marion m Fred Lawrence,
Emma m Frank E Robinson,
Hellen; NH-0004-499
Jethro Sr; s/o Dea Nathaniel Jr
of Hampton; ch Abraham Esq,
Jethro Jr b1723 m Abigail
Lovering; NH-0004-499
Jethro Jr; b1723 s/o Jethro Sr;
m Abigail Lovering; ch
William, Abram, Jethro,
Daniel, Libby, Nathaniel,
Jacob, Aaron; NH-0004-499
Jonathan; b1790 s/o Abraham Jr
& Anna Judkins; m Lois Wells;
ch Abraham, Mary Ann, Stephen
W, True, William T, Nathan,
Nancy G, Sarah S, Hannah E, H
John, John, Benjamin m Mary E
Bachelder; NH-0004-499
Joseph; m Sally Knowles d/o

BACHELDER (continued)
Joseph & Sarah Locke; liv
Andover NH; ch William A; NH-
0004-546
Joseph; b1800 s/o Capt Abraham
of Loudon; m Hannah H Hill;
ch John Q A b1826 m Eliza J
Sanborn d/o Edmund, Otis H
b1828 m Maria Howard of
Lawrence MA, Clarissa b1830 m
Cyrus T Bachelder, Joseph P
b1835 m Elvira A Whitney,
Elvira A b1839, Roseltha
b1845 dy; NH-0004-510
Joseph P; b1835 s/o Joseph &
Hannah H Hill; m Elvira A
Whitney; ch Alfred P m Nellie
M Brown; NH-0004-519
Josiah; s/o Dea Nathaniel Jr of
Hampton; liv Hampton Falls;
ch Dea David; NH-0004-499
Libbe; ch Nabby b1779, Peter
b1781, Dolly b1784, Polly
b1786, Sukey b1790, Manly
b1793, Betsey b1793; NH-0004-
499
Maj Nathan Esq; b1734 s/o Dea
Ebenezer of E Kingston; m1756
Margaret Bean; liv Loudon
Ridge; ch Richard b1756,
Phineas b1760, William b1762,
Joseph b1764, Ebenezer b1769,
Dolly b1772, Josiah b1775;
NH-0004-499
Nathaniel Sr; gs/o Rev Stephen
Bachilor; liv Hampton; ch Dea
Nathaniel Jr; NH-0004-499
Dea Nathaniel Jr; s/o Nathaniel
Sr of Hampton; liv Hampton;
ch Josiah, Dea Ebenezer,
Jethro; NH-0004-499
Nathaniel; ch Betty b1783,
Sally b1784, Fanny b1784,
True b1794; NH-0004-499
William; s/o Richard gs/o Maj
Nathan Esq of Loudon Ridge; m
Mary Sargent of Canterbury
NH; ch Mary E, Jeremiah,
Nettie P, William N, Sarah A,
Park B; NH-0004-499
William; ch James b1784, John
b1786, William Jr b1791,
Hazen b1793; NH-0004-499
William A; s/o Josiah & Sally
Knowles of Andover NH; ch
Nahum; NH-0004-546
Zephaniah; b1786 s/o Capt
Abraham & Betsy Bachelder; m
Mary Eastman; ch Dea Harmon E
m Clarisa Sanborn, Abraham G
m Rebecca Fifield, Mary,

BACHELDER (continued)
Arvilla, Genette m William T
Wheeler, Martha, Louisa; NH-
0004-499
BACHILER,
Nathaniel; s/o Rev Stephen; m
Deborah Smith & m Wid Mary
Wyman & m Elizabeth ---; ch/o
Deborah - Deborah, Nathaniel,
Ruth, Esther, Abigail, Jane,
Stephen, Benjamin, Stephen;
ch/o Mary - Mercy, Mary,
Samuel, Jonathan, Thomas,
Theodata, Joseph, Mary; NH-
0003-331
Rev Stephen; b1561; m 4 times;
liv ENG, Lynn & Ipswich MA,
Hampton & Portsmouth NH; ch
Theodata, Deborah, Nathaniel
m Deborah Smith & m Mary
Wyman & m Elizabeth ---,
Francis, Stephen, 1 son, 1
dau; NH-0003-331
BACHILOR,
Rev Stephen; m 2 & m Mary ---;
liv ENG, HOLLAND, Lynn &
Newbury MA; ch Theodate m
Christopher Hussey, Nathaniel
d1710 m 3; NH-0004-499
BACON,
Dea Abner; liv Putney; ch Asa
b1796 m Roxana M Perry,
Timothy R; NH-0007-356
Asa; b1796 s/o Dea Abner of
Putney; m Roxana M Perry; liv
Haverhill NH; ch Caroline M,
Fayette; NH-0007-356
Timothy R; s/o Dea Abner of
Putney; liv Haverhill NH; ch
Abner, Elmore C, Sumner P,
Lusena m T C Haynes, Mary m
Moses Meader, Caroline E m E
Haywood, Martha m C M
Carleton; NH-0007-356
BADGER,
John; bro/o Joseph & Eliphalet;
m Mary McFarland of SCO; liv
ENG, Nottingham; ch David,
Robert, Mary m David Cram,
Betsey dy; NH-0002-508
John; s/o Giles & Elizabeth
Greenleaf of Newbury MA; m
Elizabeth ---; ch John Jr m
Rebecca Browne; NH-0001-137
John Jr; s/o John & Elizabeth
--- of Newbury MA; m Rebecca
Browne; ch Joseph m Hannah
Peaslee; NH-0001-137
Joseph; s/o John Jr & Rebecca
Browne of Newbury MA; m
Hannah Peaslee; ch Gen Joseph

BADGER (continued)
m Hannah Pearson; NH-0001-137
Gen Joseph; s/o Joseph & Hannah
Peaslee of Haverhill MA; m
Hannah Pearson; liv Haverhill
MA, Gilmanton NH; ch Judith
m Dr William Cogswell; NH-
0001-137
Gen Joseph; b1722; liv Gilman-
ton NH, Haverhill MA; ch Hon
Joseph Jr b1746 m --- Parsons
d/o Rev William; NH-0001-312
Stephen C; m Sophronia Evans of
Warner; liv Warner & New
London & Concord NH; NH-0004-
441
Hon William; b1779 s/o Hon
Joseph gs/o Gen Joseph; m
Martha Smith d/o Rev Isaac of
Gilmanton & m1814 Hannah
Pearson Cogswell d/o Dr
William & Judith Badger of
Atkinson; liv Gilmanton &
Belmont NH; ch/o Smith - 1
son, 1 dau; ch/o Hannah -
Col Joseph, Capt William; NH-
0001-177, NH-0004-703 & 718
BAER,
Bernhard; m1872 Annie Wentworth
Stackpole d/o Lorenzo &
Elvira C Wentworth wid/o
Joshua H Lane of NJ; liv
Rollinsford; ch Lorenzo E
b1876; NH-0003-680
BAILEY,
Abel; b1806 s/o Richard; m1829
Alfreda Foster & m1844 Eliza-
beth Foot; liv Groton NH;
ch/o Alfreda - 5 sons, 4 dau;
ch/o Elizabeth - Abel,
Charles, George W b1849 m
Abbie E Brown, Elias F,
Ladena m John Byer, Effie m
Ira Cummings; NH-0007-293
Benjamin; b1790 s/o Solomon;
m1810 Ruth Eastman; ch Mary
Jane, Phebe, Timothy E b1829
m Susan G Cochran; NH-0007-
589
Daniel; liv Marlborough MA,
Hollis NH; ch Joel, Andrew,
Daniel Jr; NH-0002-437
Edwin M; m Luella Marshall d/o
Nathan Richardson & Abigail
Hawks of Bradford NH; ch
Georgia, Florence; NH-0004-
206
George W; b1849 s/o Abel &
Elizabeth Foot; m1868 Abbie E
Brown d/o John S & Anna
Robinson; ch Frankie I,

BAILEY (continued)
Mabel; NH-0007-293
Rev Jacob; m Sarah (Sally)
Weeks d/o Dr John & Martha
Wingate; liv Pownalborough
ME, Annapolis NS; ch Charles
Percy, Rebecca L, Charlotte
M, Thomas H, William G,
Elizabeth A; NH-0005-379
James A; b1827; m Adaline Chase
& m Martha Chase & m Mary
Felch & m Louisa C Barrett
Brown; liv Lyman, Lisbon NH;
ch/o ? - Debbie M; NH-0007-
457
Jonathan MD; b1784; m1816
Elizabeth Fifield b1792 d/o
Col Joseph & Elizabeth San-
born; liv Weare & E Kingston
NH; ch Albon W, 2 others; NH-
0003-189
Joshua; bc1738; m Anna --- & m
Sarah ---; liv ENG, MA,
Hopkinton NH; ch/o Anna -
John b1769, Joshua b1770,
Elijah b1773, Betty b1780,
Rachel b1782, Esther b1785;
NH-0004-407
Oliver; b1797 s/o Capt Oliver &
Mary Thompson of Dunbarton
NH; m1821 Jane Mills d/o
James & Jane Fulton of Dun-
barton NH & m1850 Mary D
Ryder d/o Ezekiel & Betsey of
Dunbarton; liv Dunbarton;
ch/o Jane - 1 dau dy, Oliver,
James M, 1 son; ch/o Mary -
George dy; NH-0004-307
Solomon; liv Plymouth NH; ch
Mary Jane, Henry, Roxa m
James Stevens, Benjamin b1790
m Ruth Eastman, 3 dau, 1 son;
NH-0007-589
Thomas; ch Thomas, Eaton, David
m Mary Chase, Nathan m Phebe
Peasley, Enos m Judith White,
Willard m Betsy Fulton, Hiram
m Mary Manahan, Lydia m ---
Walker, Mary m Robert Fulton,
Mehitable m Alexander Wilson,
Nancy m Stephen Manahan; NH-
0002-377
Timothy E; b1829 s/o Benjamin &
Ruth Eastman; m1855 Susan G
Cochran of Plymouth; liv Ply-
mouth NH; ch Mary Ann m
Perley M Johnson, George E,
Charles, William C, Herbert
E, Lizzie A; NH-0007-589
BAKER,
Aaron W; b1796 s/o James &

BAKER (continued)
Judith Whittemore of Bow;
m1825 Nancy Dustin b1801 of
Concord; liv Bow; ch Francis
M b1826 dy, Rufus b1831 m1858
Lucy S Cutter b1833 of Somer-
ville MA, John B b1834 m
Sarah J Locke, Henry M b1841;
NH-0004-286
Alpheus; m Nancy Slapp d/o
Simon gd/o Maj John; liv
Montville CT, Lebanon NH; ch
Alpheus W b1834; NH-0007-425
Andrew; s/o Joseph; m Anna
Knowlton; liv Holderness; ch
James m Jane Smith, Andrew K,
Stephen, Ebenezer, Col
Nathan, Joseph m Hannah
Piper, 3 dau; NH-0007-125
Andrew; s/o James & Jane Smith;
m Sarah Mudgett of New
Hampton; ch James S m Arabel
A Simonds d/o Arad &
Sophronia Drew, 2 sons; NH-
0007-125
Benjamin; liv Epping; ch
William, Benjamin; NH-0007-
204
Benjamin; b1776 s/o Hon Moses &
Deborah Davis; m --- Wyatt
d/o Dean Daniel of Campton;
liv Candia; ch Mary m John
Keniston, Eliza m Samuel
Keniston; NH-0007-203
Caleb; liv RI, Franconia,
Bethlehem NH; ch Reuben, 10
others; NH-0007-167
David; b1784 s/o Thomas of Lyme
NH; liv Vershire & Thetford
VT; ch Francis W m Sarah F
Hewes d/o Sylvanus, 2 sons, 1
dau; NH-0007-535
Col Davis; b1791 s/o Col Moses
& Molly Wyatt of Campton;
m1814 Hannah Church; liv
Campton NH; ch Deborah Davis
m George W Keniston, Walter
Wyatt m Elizabeth L Noyes,
Davis m Statira Spencer,
Hannah m Gardner Spencer,
Freeman m Sarah L Noyes & m
Ellen M Case, Elihu Church m
Adeline A Parker, S C, Henry
Woodward, Henrietta m
Jeremiah Leavitt, Edward
Payson m Leora A Parker,
Moses Rogers; NH-0007-204
Hosea Swett; b1797 s/o Timothy
& Catharine Healy of Stoddard
NH; m1821 Fanny Huntington
b1801 d/o Hezekiah & Esther

BAKER (continued)
Slade of Hanover; liv Haverhill NH; ch Royal Huntington b1812, Peyton Randolph b1826, Solon Healy b1827 dy, Solon Healy b1829, Fanny Maria b1831, Oliver Harrison b1834; NH-0007-380

James; s/o Andrew & Anna Knowlton; m Jane Smith d/o Samuel & Peggy Smith; ch Samuel S m Avis Drew of Ashland, Daniel S m Henrietta A Elkins & m Edna M Smith d/o Jeremiah & Mahala Veasie of Laconia, Frances O m Paul Perkins, Andrew m Sarah Mudgett; NH-0007-125

James; s/o Joseph; m Judith Whittemore of Pembroke; liv Bow; ch Aaron W b1796 m Nancy Dustin, 5 others; NH-0004-286

John B; b1834 s/o Aaron W & Nancy Dustin of Bow; m1865 Sarah J Locke of E Concord; liv Bow; ch Rufus Henry b1870, John Perley b1871 dy; NH-0004-286

Joseph; liv ENG, Nottingham NH, Holderness; ch Andrew m Anna Knowlton, 1 dau m John Shaw, 1 dau m Levi Drew; NH-0007-125

Joseph; b1740 s/o Capt Joseph; liv Bow; ch James m Judith Whittemore, 9 others; NH-0004-286

Joseph; s/o Andrew & Anna Knowlton; m Hannah Piper; liv Holderness; ch Stephen Chase b1821, 4 sons, 4 dau; NH-0007-125

Hon Moses; b1738 s/o Benjamin & Ruth True of Epping; m1758 Deborah Davis d/o Ephraim; liv Chester, Campton; ch Mary b1760 m Rev Selden Church & m Moody Cook, Col Moses b1769 m Molly Wyatt, Benjamin b1776 m --- Wyatt; NH-0007-203

Col Moses; b1769 s/o Moses & Deborah Davis; m1789 Molly Wyatt; liv Campton NH; ch Levi, Col Davis b1791 m Hannah Church, Hannah m Samuel Marsh, Moses m Polly Dearborn, Polly m Gilman R Taylor, Rebecca m Coffin Cook, Lois m William H Blair, Clarissa m Zebedee Cook, Caroline m John Buckman; NH-

BAKER (continued)
0006-204
Peyton Randolph; b1826 s/o Hosea Swett & Fanny Huntington of Haverhill NH; liv ME; ch Oliver Randolph; NH-0007-380

Royal Huntington; b1812 s/o Hosea Swett & Fanny Huntington of Haverhill NH; liv E Haverhill; ch Martha M, Solon H; NH-0007-380

Thomas; liv Lyme NH; ch Daniel, David b1784, Thomas, Edward C, Samuel; NH-0007-535

BALCH,
Col Charles Edward; b1834 s/o Mason & Hannah Holt; m1867 Emeline R Brooks d/o Rev Nahum of Bath ME; liv Francestown & Manchester NH; NH-0001-113, NH-0002-133

Mark; b1820 s/o William & Abigail Johnson; m1850 Laurilla H Farnham d/o Peter F & Lucy H of Francestown; liv Manchester, Francestown; NH-0002-300

Mason; m Hannah Holt d/o Joshua of Greenland NH; liv Francestown NH; ch Col Charles Edward b1834; NH-0001-113

William; m Abigail Johnson; liv Francestown, New Boston NH, Redding MA; ch Mark b1820 m Laurilla H Farnham; NH-0002-300

BALDWIN,
Edmund; s/o William Lothrop & Maria Jane Holmes; m Flora Madison; liv Stratford NH; ch Bertie Edith, Janie Holmes; NH-0005-776

Elisha; b1788 s/o Jabez & Judith Brace; m Huldah Alger d/o Edmund & Huldan Lothrop of W Bridgewater MA; liv Stratford NH; ch Elisha Alger b1818, William Lothrop b1820 m Maria Jane Holmes, John Brace b1822, Edmund Willis b1825, Jedediah Miller b1827, Lucinda Annette b1829 m Jabez B Alger, Lucia Annette b1833 m Robert R Thompson; NH-0005-776

Jabez; b1733; m1770 Judith Brace; liv Newton CT, Stratford NH; ch Nathan m Kate Schoff & m Susan Bundy, John, Lucinda, Lucia, Marcia,

BAKER (continued)

Elisha b1788 m Huldah Alger, Charlotte b1792 m Enos Alger; NH-0005-776

Samuel; b1802 s/o Isaac & Bethia Poole gs/o Col Nahum & Martha Low of Amherst; m 1830 Betsey G Bell d/o Hugh & Nancy Wilson of Francestown, & m1871 Mrs Martha Gregg Lear of Manchester & m1882 Mrs Margaret Temple Peaslee of Nashua; liv Bennington; ch/o Betsey 2 sons, 5 dau; NH-0002-288

William Lothrop; b1820 s/o Elisha & Huldah Alger of Stratford NH; m1850 Maria Jane Holmes b1822 d/o John & Sarah Towne of Colebrook; liv Bloomfield; ch Edmund William m Flora Madison, John Holmes, Mary Annette dy, Mira Agnes dy, Isabella Sarah dy, Jane Maria dy; NH-0005-776

BALL,

Ebenezer; liv Concord MA, Hollis NH; ch Ebenezer, Nathaniel, William, John; NH-0002-437

Elisha P; liv Lyme NH; ch Dea Samuel F m1863 Laura A Gordon d/o Cyrus; NH-0007-545

Capt George T; b1809 s/o Samuel S & Mary Muchmore of Portsmouth NH; m Laurinda Mason d/o Daniel of Rye & m Sarah A Furber of Newington; liv Greenland NH; ch/o Laurinda - Arthur P, 3 others; NH-0003-310

BALLOU,

Hiram P; s/o John & Tirzah Evans; m Sarah Heath of New Hampton; liv Bristol NH; ch Arthur W, Minnie E; NH-0007-190

Hosea; s/o Oliver; m Cynthia P Sanborn d/o Joseph & Sarah Parsons; liv Alexandria NH; ch Charlotte A, Ellen Burpee, Luisde F, 4 others; NH-0007-118

John; b1807 s/o Oliver & ?; m Tirzah Evans; liv Hanover, Alexandria; ch Hiram P m Sarah Heath, 6 others; NH-0007-190

Oliver; s/o Oliver m --- Tiffany & m Mary Simons of Alexandria; liv Providence

BALLOU (continued)

RI, Enfield, Hanover, Alexandria; ch/o ? - Horace m Mary Simons d/o Caleb & Louis Phelps, Hosea m Cynthia P Sanburn, John b1807 m Tirzah Evans, 13 others; NH-0007-119 & 190

BANFIELD,

Tobias; liv Portsmouth, Wolfeborough; ch Joseph, Everett C, Joshua, Nathaniel, Ira; NH-0006-311

BARKER,

Addison P; m Susan A Brown of N Woodstock NH; liv Island Falls ME; ch Addison P m Minnie E Young d/o Louis A & Lucy M; NH-0007-214

Albert; b1820; m1852 Nancy A Irish d/o Hon Stephen of Stowe ME & m1870 Mrs Lucinda E Dinsmore wid/o Wilbur F d/o Rev Beniah Bean; liv Rumford & Waterford ME, Colebrook NH; ch/o Nancy - Lilla, 3 others; NH-0005-248

David Jr; b1797 s/o Col David of Stratham; liv Rochester; NH-0003-603

Francisco Weston; b1846 s/o John & Selina Little of Lovell ME; m1872 Lucretia M Marston of Effingham; liv Effingham NH; ch Kate E b1873; NH-0006-556

George; s/o Levi & Mary Wiggin; m Mary Piper; ch Mary A, Albion, Caroline, George M, Louisa, John H, Thomas, Levi, 2 others; NH-0003-548

Gilman; b1808 s/o Noah & Deborah Gilman; m1839 Emeline Smith d/o Dea Daniel of Brentwood & m1853 Lucy Ann Russell d/o Thomas K of Brentwood; liv Exeter; ch/o Emeline - Sarah b1842 m William C Marble, Annie E b1846, William G b1849 m Alice Amadon; ch/o Lucy - Arthur C b1858, Charles W b1863; NH-0003-296

Hiram; b1815 s/o John & Sally Davis; m1838 Maria Hayes d/o Reuben & Patience Hayes of New Durham; liv Farmington; ch 4 dy, Clara, Martha C, Hiram H; NH-0003-630

John; liv Epping, Stratham; m twice; ch/o first - John

BARKER (continued)
b1762 m Sally Davis, 4 dau; ch/o second - 1 dau; NH-0003-630

John; b1762 s/o John; m Sally Davis b1780 d/o Eleazer of Alton NH; liv Epping NH, New Durham; ch Mercy m Ephraim Mallard of Laconia, John, Dudley, Eleazer D, Sarah D m Gilman Cooper of Wolfeboro, 1 dy, Hiram b1815, Eleazer D; NH-0003-630

Josiah H; b1810 s/o Samuel & Dolly Blake; m1834 Adeline Godfrey d/o Capt James & Theodate; liv Boston & Melrose MA; ch Theodate, Anna T b1840 m R H Shelton; NH-0003-330

Dr Lemuel; s/o Lemuel & Mary; m1826 Sarah Richardson d/o Hon William M; liv Chester, Great Falls, Boston; NH-0003-147

Levi; b1769 s/o Ezra b1720; m Mary Wiggin & m Mehitable Clark; liv Stratham; ch/o Mary - Mark, George m Mary Piper, Mary m Capt George Lane, Elizabeth m Edmond J Lane, Nancy, Ezra b1803, Abby, Martha J; NH-0003-548

Noah; b1763; m1789 Mary Philbrook & m1800 Deborah Gilman b1773; liv Exeter; ch/o Mary - Josiah b1790, Benjamin b1792, Noah b1794, Lydia b1796, John b1798; ch/o Deborah - Mary G b1801 m John Scamon of Stratham, 3 dy; Gilman b1808 m Emeline Smith & m Lucy Ann Russell; Susannah G b1810 m Nathaniel Shute of Exeter, Deborah b1812, William b1815; NH-0003-296

Samuel; b1780; m Dolly Blake d/o Jethro; liv Ipswich MA, Hampton NH; ch Betsey, Josiah H b1810 m Adeline Godfrey, Sarah, Eliza A, Samuel, Polly, Abby, James; NH-0003-329

William G; b1849 s/o Gilman & Emeline Smith of Exeter; m Alice Amadon of Bellows Falls VT; ch Lucy, William, Edith; NH-0003-296

BARNARD,
Daniel; b1827 s/o Thomas &

BARNARD (continued)
Phebe Eastman of Orange; m1854 Amelia Morse d/o Rev William & Sophronia of Chelmsford MA; liv Orange & Franklin NH; ch William Morse, James Ellery, Charles Daniel, Frank Eugene, Emma Sophronia m Capt Samuel Pray of Portsmouth NH, Mary Amelia; NH-0001-304, NH-0004-31

Edmund; b1813 s/o Reuben & Huldah Eaton of Ware NH; m1842 Sarah Luflin d/o Edward & Phebe Burnham; liv Dunbarton, Hebron NH; ch Lucy M (adopted); NH-0007-389

John; s/o John of Ipswich ENG; ch Jonathan, Samuel; NH-0004-31

John F; s/o Jonathan & Sarah Currier; m1861 Maria H Barnard of Haverhill MA; liv Contoocook; ch John Arthur, Charles Currier; NH-0004-414e

Thomas; b1782 s/o Charles of Warner gs/o Jonathan; m Ruth Eastman of Hopkinton & Phebe sis/o Ruth; liv Warner & Orange NH; ch/o Phebe - Hon Daniel b1827 m Amelia Morse & 6 sons & 1 dau; NH-0001-304, NH-0004-31

BARNES,
Lt Amos; b1757; m1789 Polly Eastman d/o John; liv Groton MA, Concord & Conway NH; ch John, Polly m Jonathan Seavey, Richard E, Sally m Nathan Chandler, Abiah, Alonzo W, Albert; NH-0006-849

David; s/o Reuben; liv Merrimack; ch Charles, Sarah, Willie, Almira, Ella Etta, Frank; NH-0002-542

John; ch Edgar, Clinton, Fred, Lillian, Addie, Nellie; NH-0002-542

Dr Joseph; bro/o Lt Thomas; liv Merrimack; ch Lt Reuben; NH-0002-542

Joseph; ch Charles, Hiram, 2 dau; NH-0002-542

Lt Reuben; s/o Dr Joseph; ch Reuben, Joseph, Samuel, John, Sally dy, Eleanor, Joanna m Henry Fretts, Polly; NH-0002-542

Reuben; s/o Lt Reuben; ch Hannah m Ira Mears, Rebecca

BARNES (continued)
dy, Ann m Nelson Longa, Lucy, Dolly m Solomon Barron & m 1 other, James dy, David, John, Joel, Eliza R, Lavinia; NH-0002-542

Royal D; b1854 s/o Warren M; liv Litchfield; NH-0002-496

Samuel; s/o Lt Reuben; ch Betsy m John Connary of Milford & m --- Goodwin, Samuel, Solomon, Jane m Elijah Leech of Milford, Amanda m Moses Pinghram of Deering, Hannah m Morrison Sanderson, Nancy m Joseph Day of Derry; NH-0002-542

Silas Parker; liv London; ch Benjamin, Samuel m Sally Lund, Sally m Robert McKeen, Alice, Wheeler m Nancy Gay, Hannah m Charles Craft, Silas m Oliver Chatman, Rodney, Mary E m Samuel Cutler, John m Clarissa Grover, Harriet m Charles Martin; NH-0002-384

Lt Thomas; bro/o Dr Joseph; liv Merrimack; ch 4 sons, 5 dau; NH-0002-542

Dr W R; b1854; m1883 Olive E Vance of Albany VT; liv Chelsea VT, Lyme NH; NH-0007-524

Wheeler; s/o Silas Parker; m Nancy Gay; ch Climenia, George m Carrie Spencer, Sarah m George King, Charles m Nelly A Collins, Mary m Peter Rumrill, Edward, Frank, John m Ann Wilson; NH-0002-384

BARNEY,
Aaron; s/o Cyril; m Sarah Kimball; liv Grafton NH; ch Cyril H, Alcena H, Charles m Mrs Phebe A Brown d/o Ezra T & Elmira Kimball Gifford; NH-0007-280

Cyril; s/o Aaron gs/o Aaron; m Polly Kilton & m Sarah Martin; ch Jarvis m Jane Scotney, Aaron m Sarah Kimball, 4 others; NH-0007-280

Hiram; s/o Jarvis & Fanny Williams; m Andalucia P Smith; liv Grafton NH; ch Fred W, Fannie M, Eddie; NH-0007-280

Jarvis; s/o Aaron; m Fanny Williams; ch Samuel W m Caroline Whitney, Hiram m

BARNEY (continued)
Andalucia P Smith; NH-0007-280

Jarvis; s/o Cyril; m Jane Scotney d/o Francis & Elizabeth Hickey; liv Grafton NH; ch Frank E, Alice J, Fred W, Clarence E; NH-0007-280

Jedediah; s/o John & Anna Smith gs/o Aaron; m Melaney Williams & m Eunice Blackman & m Nancy Davis; ch/o ? - Lafayette T m Victoria Cole, 7 others; NH-0007-280

Jesse; s/o John & Nancy Martin; m Elvira Hale d/o Simeon & Jane Williams; ch William H, George S, Jennie S, Nellie M; NH-0007-280

John; s/o Jabez & --- Barney gs/o Aaron; m Nancy Martin; ch Jesse m Elvira Hale, 7 others; NH-0007-280

Lafayette T; s/o Jedediah; m Victoria Cole d/o Richard & Sylvia Dwiner; liv Grafton NH; ch Harlan W, Eva J, Almond H, Grover L; NH-0007-280

Samuel W; s/o Jarvis & Fanny Williams; m Caroline Whitney d/o Jeremiah & Mary Wiggins; liv Grafton NH; ch Albina M, Flora E; NH-0007-280

BARRETT,
Hon James J; b1823 s/o Joseph & Mary Kenney of Bethlehem; m1845 Lydia Smith d/o Isaac of Brownington VT; liv Littleton NH; ch George W b1846 m Ella M Taylor, Alice E b1851 dy, Allien J b1857 m Ida M Whitcher; NH-0007-503

Joseph; s/o Thornton; m Mary Kenney d/o William of Bethlehem liv Winchendon MA, Bethlehem NH; ch Joseph K, Hon James J b1823 m Lydia Smith, Sally m --- Bowles, 2 others; NH-0007-165 & 503

BARRON,
Benjamin; b1755; m1784 Abigail Varnum of Dracut MA; liv Woodstock NH; ch Benjamin M b1785 m Laura Walker, John V b1787, Abigail b1789, Oliver b1791, DeLafayette b1793, Hannah b1795, Martha b1797; NH-0007-642

Benjamin M; b1785 s/o Benjamin & Abigail Varnum of Wood-

BARRON (continued)
stock; m Laura Walker; liv
Woodstock NH; ch Lovina
b1820, Benjamin M b1822,
Betsey b1824, Hiram b1827,
Abigail b1830, Lula A b1835 m
Josiah Tourtillotte, Rachel
b1837; NH-0007-642
Solomon; m Dolly d/o Reuben;
liv Merrimack; ch Sarah m
Charles Longa, John, Clarence
dy, Daniel; NH-0002-542
BARROWS,
Jacob; liv Hanover, Dalton NH;
ch Urial; NH-0005-526
BARSTOW,
William; s/o Michael; m Abigail
Townsend of Chester; ch 9;
NH-0007-574
BARTLETT,
Hon Charles Henry; b1833 s/o
John & Sarah J Sanborn of
Sunapee NH; m1858 Hannah M
Eastman of Croydon NH; liv
Sunapee, Wentworth & Man-
chester NH; ch Charles Leslie
dy & Carrie Bell; NH-0001-33,
NH-0002-32, NH-0007-112.25
Daniel; s/o John & Hepzibath
Stevens of Deering; m Abigail
Stevens & m Elinor Stevens &
m Hope White; ch/o ? Solomon
dy, John m Anna Lock, Daniel
m Anna Loveren, Abigail m
Reuben Loveren, Dorothy,
Josiah m Mary Gove,
Kerenhappuch m Stephen
Rowell, Erastus Harvey m
Sarah Chase, Elinor m Parker
Bartlett; NH-0002-379
David; s/o David & Johanna
Hazelton; m Eunice Marsh d/o
Edmond & Eunice Cook; ch
Gardner S m Rebecca S
Burrows, 7 others; NH-0007-
215
David R; b1812 s/o Stephen &
Mary Ramsey of Plymouth; m
Louisa Frances Brown of N
Hampton; liv Plymouth NH; ch
Stephen R, George A, Mary F m
George Redlow, Elsie, Luella
R; NH-0007-589
Enoch; s/o Hon Bradbury of
Nottingham; liv Epping,
Lawrence MA; NH-0003-29
Frederic; b1815 s/o Ichabod C &
Anne S Barlett; m1845 ?; liv
Bristol; ch 4; NH-0007-69
Gardner S; s/o David & Eunice
Marsh; m Rebecca S Burrows

BARTLETT (continued)
d/o George & Lydia of Brad-
ford MA; ch David G, Martha
P; NH-0007-215
George; s/o Solomon & Anna
Stevens; m Polly Simons; ch
Enoch H m Huldah Sleeper,
Solomon, Ira; NH-0002-379
Ichabod Colby; s/o Levi; m1801
Ann Sleeper; liv Boscawan &
Salisbury & Bristol NH; ch
Mary b1802 m William M Lewis
of Bristol, Jane b1804, Levi
b1807, Frederick b1808 dy,
Gustavus b1810, Anna b1812 m
Jonas Minot of Bristol,
Frederick b1815; NH-0007-184
Jacob; bro/o John; m ---
Sargent; liv Deering; ch
Sarah m Benjamin Gillingham,
Stephen m Phebe Whitaker,
Abigail m Samuel Balch,
Joshua m Patty Chase, Jacob m
Catherine Hall, Martha m
Jonathan Gove, Hannah, Alice,
Betsy m Manly Peasley, Fanny
m Gilliman George; NH-0002-
386
James; b1792 s/o Dr Joseph of
Salisbury; liv Durham, Dover;
NH-0003-601
John; m Hepzibath Stevens; liv
Deering; ch Solomon m Anna
Stevens, John Jr m Mary
Simons, Daniel m Abigail
Stevens & m Elinor Stevens &
m Hope White, Lydia m John
Simons, Hepzibath dy; NH-
0002-378
John; s/o Solomon & Anna
Stevens; m Sarah J Sanborn;
liv Sunapee NH; ch Hon
Charles Henry b1833, Solomon,
Joseph S, John Z, George H,
dau m Thomas P Smith, dau m
John Felch; NH-0001-33, NH-
0002-32 & 378
John; s/o Daniel & ?; m Anna
Lock; ch Abigail, Benjamin L;
NH-0002-379
Jonathan; m Hannah Peaslee d/o
Maj Jacob & Martha Chellis of
Kingston; ch James M, 7
others; NH-0003-382
Joseph MD; b1751; m1773 Hannah
Colcord of Kingston; liv
Amesbury MA, Salisbury NH; ch
Joseph MD, Samuel C b1780 m
Eleanor Pettengill, Hon
Ichabod AM b1786, Peter MD
b1788 m1816 Ann Pettingill,

BARTLETT (continued)
Hon James AM b1792, Daniel b1795; NH-0004-616
Joseph; b1762; m Ann Witherell of Kingston MA; liv Portsmouth; NH-0003-19
Dr Josiah; b1728 s/o Stephen gs/o Richard ggs/o Richard; m1754 Mary Bartlett of Newton; liv Kingston; ch Dr Levi b1763, 11 others; NH-0003-377
Levi; b1793 s/o Joseph of Warner NH; m1815 Hannah Kelly d/o Rev William of Warner; ch William K m Harriet N Walker d/o Nathan, Lavinia K m Dr Dana D Davis; NH-0004-676
Levi S; b1811 s/o Dr Levi; m Aroline E Sanborn d/o Moses; liv Kingston; NH-0003-377
Parker; s/o Stepehen & Phebe Whitaker; m Eleanor Bartlett; ch Rotheous E m Emma J Merril, Rosilla A m Parker Craig, Erastus H m Jennie Orne, Ai m Allie Jones, Sarah m Edwin Rice; NH-0002-386
Samuel Colcord; b1780 s/o Joseph MD & Hannah Colcord; m1810 Eleanor Petti(e)ngill; liv Salisbury NH; ch Rev Joseph AM b1816, William Henry b1827, Samuel; NH-0004-10 & 617
Simeon; bro/o Gov Josiah of Kingston NH; liv Warner NH, Amesbury MA; ch Joseph, Richard, Simeon; NH-0004-676
Solomon; s/o John & Hepzibath Stevens of Deering; m Anna Stevens; ch Hepzibath m Jonathan Straw, Nancy m --- Putney, Abigail m --- Putney, Sarah m Ebenezer Lock, Mary m Jesse Brown, John m Sarah Sanborn, Solomon m Hannah Hadlock & m Lucy Lock, Esther m Benjamin Loveren, Rebecca m Jesse Collins, George m Polly Simons, Irena m Stephen Rowell, Greeley m Sarah Ann Gove; NH-0002-378
Stephen; s/o Jacob & --- Sargent; m Phebe Whitaker; ch Phebe, Relief m Willard Cory, Almira m Elijah Mason, Hannah, Parker m Eleanor Bartlett, Fanny m Hugh Craig, Stephen m Edna Craig, Oliver H P m Loisa Morse; NH-0002-

BARTLETT (continued)
386
Stephen; m Elizabeth Barnard; liv MA, Plymouth NH; ch Sargent, Joseph, Elizabeth m Samuel Dearborn, Stephen b1786 m Mary Ramsey, David b1795; NH-0007-589
Stephen; b1786 s/o Stephen & Elizabeth Barnard; m1811 Mary Ramsey; liv Plymouth NH; ch David R b1812 m Louisa Frances Brown; NH-0007-589
BARTON,
Aaron; b1808; liv Croydon & Piermont NH; ch Albert, Aaron Jr; NH-0007-575
Bezaleel; b1722 s/o Samuel & Elizabeth Bellows; m1747 Phebe Carlton; liv Sutton & Royalton MA; ch Phebe, Bezaleel, Benjamin, Peter b1763 m Hepsibeth Baker; NH-0001-52
Bezaleel; b1794 s/o Peter & Hepsibeth Baker; m Hannah Powers; ch Levi Winter b1818 m Mary A Pike; NH-0001-52
Charles C; b1821 s/o William & Mary A C Frost of Stratham NH; m1850 Dorcas Libbey d/o James of Ossipee NH; liv Lowell MA, N Hampton NH; ch Charles L, James W, George E; NH-0003-423
Hon Levi Winter; b1818 s/o Bezaleel 2nd & Hannah Powers; mc1839 Mary A Pike of Newport NH & m1852 Lizzie F Jewett of Hollis NH; liv Croydon & Canaan NH; ch Col Ira McL, Herbert J b1853 m Sarah L Dodge, Florence F, Natt L & Jesse M; NH-0001-50
Peter; b1763 s/o Bezaleel & Phebe Carlton; m1789 Hepsibeth Baker; liv Sutton MA, Croydon & Sunapee NH; NH-0001-52
Samuel; b1691; m1715 Elizabeth Bellows; liv Framingham MA; ch Bezaleel b1722 m Phebe Carlton; NH-0001-52
William; m Mary A C Frost; ch William, Charles C b1821 m Dorcas Libbey, Mary A C; NH-0003-423
BASSETT,
John; s/o Rev John?; m1757 Sarah Shepard d/o Thomas gd/o Jacob & Mercy; liv Sharon MA,

BASSETT (continued)
Goffstown NH; ch Thomas m
Susanna McGregor, 9 others;
NH-0003-380
Thomas; s/o John & Sarah
Shepard; m Susanna McGregor;
liv Atkinson NH, Deerfield,
Londonderry; ch Dr Thomas
b1797 m Miranda Spofford,
David, 3 others; NH-0003-380
Dr Thomas; b1797 s/o Thomas &
Susanna McGregor; m1828
Miranda Spofford d/o Samuel &
gd/o Maj Jacob Peaslee; liv
Kingston; NH-0003-380
BATCHELDER,
Abraham; b1750; m Nabby ---
b1752; liv Northwood NH; ch
Nathaniel b1786 m Patience
Page; NH-0004-867
Amos MD; b1811 s/o Amos M &
Sally Stoker; m1837 Rebecca H
Atwood of Pelham; liv Pelham
NH; NH-0003-190
Benjamin; b1673 s/o Nathaniel
Sr; m1696 Susanna Page; liv
Hampton Falls; ch Susanna
m1738 Ebenezer Webster, 12
others; NH-0003-190 & 345
Caleb; s/o Simeon & Mary Martin
of Bridgewater; m Hannah
Moses; ch Simeon m Ann Banks
d/o Joseph & Fanny James of
Newport RI; NH-0007-130
David; b1736 s/o Josiah & Sarah
Page; m Sarah Sweatt & m Mary
Emery b1741; liv Hampton
Falls; ch/o Sarah - Sarah,
Elisha, Elizabeth, Joshua,
Hannah; ch/o Mary - Mary,
Lydia, Anna, Rhoda, Reuben
b1777 m Betsey Tilton, Dolly,
Moses b1782 m Abigail Drake,
Abigail; NH-0003-349 & 350
Dearborn; b1810 s/o Samuel &
Sarah Dearborn of Hampton NH;
m1833 Mary Jenness d/o Thomas
& m1841 Abby O Jenness sis/o
Mary; ch/o Mary - Fidelia F,
3 others; ch/o Abby - Dorinda
A, Sarah M, Susan E dy,
Samuel D, George H, Charles
Joseph b1858, Frank P; NH-
0003-331
Emery; b1812 s/o Reuben &
Betsey Tilton; m Dorothy A
Dearborn b1817 d/o Simon N of
Hampton NH; liv Hampton
Falls; ch Charles E, Annah E
m Homer B Cram of Amesbury
MA, John A, Ellen P m Irving

BATCHELDER (continued)
H Lamprey of Charlestown MA,
Abby C m Cyrus L Brown of
Pittsfield NH, David F, Mary
L; NH-0003-350
James; b1795 s/o John & Molly
Cotton of N Hampton; m1815
Sally Batchelder d/o John &
mc1822 Elizabeth Batchelder
sis/o Sally; liv N Hampton;
ch/o Sally - John, Sarah
Jane; ch/o Elizabeth - Almira
m Sheridan Jenness of Rye,
James, Ambrose, Emily m J S
Bancroft of MA, Mary A, Ann
Maria m George A Hill, Warren
C, Albert; NH-0003-420
John; b1757; m1780 Molly Cotton
b1762; liv N Hampton; ch
Abigail D, Sarah B, Mary,
Sally, Charlotte, James b1795
m Sally Batchelder & m Eliza-
beth Batchelder, Patty,
Jeremiah, Asenath, Thomas,
John; NH-0003-420
John T; b1829 s/o Moses &
Abigail Drake; m1872 Emma
Davis b1845 d/o Horace Miles
& Seviah of Patton ME; liv
Hampton Falls; ch Nathaniel
M, Alice G, Abbie E, Mary A,
Sarah L; NH-0003-349
John W; m Mehitable Noyes d/o
Timothy; liv Meredith, Whit-
field, Lisbon NH; ch Austin
J, 1 dau m Jasper S Young, 1
dau m David B Hildreth; NH-
0007-454
Josiah; b1695 s/o Nathaniel &
Elizabeth Foss; m Sarah Page
b1698; ch Josiah, Elisha,
Sarah, Nathaniel, Reuben,
David b1736 m Sarah Sweatt &
m Mary Emery; NH-0003-349
Levi; b1765 s/o Nathaniel; m
Deborah Ward; ch Samuel b1786
m Sarah Dearborn, Cotton; NH-
0003-331
Moses; b1782 s/o Daniel & Mary
Emery; m1809 Abigail Drake
b1784 d/o Samuel of Hampton
NH; ch Josiah, Mary, Samuel,
Aaron, Nancy, Moses E, Eliza-
beth, John T b1829 m Emma
Davis; NH-0003-349
Nathaniel Sr; gs/o Stephen; ch
Benjamin m Susanna Page; NH-
0003-190
Nathaniel; s/o Stephen; m1656
Deborah Smith & m ?; ch/o
Deborah - Nathaniel b1659 m

BATCHELDER (continued)
   Elizabeth Foss, 8 others; ch/o ? - 8; NH-0003-349
   Nathaniel; b1659 s/o Nathaniel & Deborah Smith; m Elizabeth Foss; liv Hampton Falls; ch Nathaniel, Deborah, John, Josiah b1695 m Sarah Page, Jethro, Nathan, Phineas, Elizabeth; NH-0003-349
   Nathaniel; b1786 s/o Abraham & Nabby of Northwood NH; m Patience Page; ch Betsey m Simeon D Pease; NH-0004-867
   Reuben; b1777 s/o David & Mary Emery of Hampton Falls; m Betsey Tilton; liv Hampton Falls; ch David, Lucy, Emery b1812 m Dorothy A Dearborn, Rhoda, Dolly, John, Nathaniel; NH-0003-350
   Samuel; b1786 s/o Levi & Deborah Ward; m1810 Sarah Dearborn b1790 d/o Joseph F & Mary Nudd of Hampton gd/o Simon Nudd; liv Hampton NH; ch Dearborn b1810 m Mary Jenness & m Abby O Jenness, Alfred C, Thomas W, Deborah A, Mary Ann b1822, Sandborn dy, Sarah F; NH-0003-331
   Ward C; liv Orford, Warren NH; ch Elsie m --- French, Reuben, 6 others; NH-0007-635
BATCHELLOR,
   Albert Stillman; b1850 s/o Stillman & Mary Jane Smith of Bethlehem NH; m1880 Harriet A Copeland; liv Littleton; ch 1 son, 1 dau; NH-0007-112
BATTELLE,
   Ebenezer; m Prudence Draper; ch Lucy m Eleazer Everett; NH-0002-301
BEACHAM,
   Asa; b1809 s/o Richard & Hannah of Ossipee NH; m Aphia Canney & m1845 Abigail Ann Caroline Quarles; liv Ossipee NH; ch/o Aphia - George, Eunice C m Elisha P Allen, Annie A; NH-0006-622
   George A; b1826 s/o Asa & Aphia Canney; m Mary Frances Canney d/o Moses B & Mary Abbott of Salem MA; ch Howard Arthur; NH-0006-528
   Richard; m --- Wadleigh; liv London ENG, Ossipee NH; ch Richard m --- Pitman, Hannah m Benjamin Gilman of Brook-

BEACHAM (continued)
   field, Mary Joseph Peery; NH-0006-622
   Richard; s/o Richard & --- Wadleigh; m --- Pitman; ch Asa, Richard, Moses, Simon, John C, Sally, Betsey m James Canney, Hannah m Theodore Thompson of Tuftonborough, Sabrina m Washington Thompson, Joanna m Hiram Thompson; NH-0006-622
BEAN,
   Abraham; b1789 s/o John; m1810 Sally Clough d/o Ezekiel & Mary A Sanborn of Loudon; liv Loudon & Concord NH; ch Mary Ann b1812 m Herman Sanborn of Boscawen, Sarah Jane b1818 m John L Tallant of Canterbury; NH-0004-159
   Benjamin; liv Brentwood, Moultonborough, Tuftonborough; ch Jonathan, James, Josiah; NH-0006-441
   Hon Benning Moulton; b1782 s/o Moody; m .? & m Lydia Adams; liv Moultonborough NH; ch 1 dau m Josiah C Sturtevant, 9 others; NH-0006-404
   Ira A; bc1799; m Eliza Hoit d/o Gen Daniel of Sandwich; liv Sandwich NH, OH; NH-0006-244
   James; s/o John; m1697 Sarah Bradley; liv Kingston; ch Benjamin b1699, Margaret b1702, Joseph b1704 m Miriam Folsom, Jeremy b1707, Samuel bc1710, Catherine b1714; NH-0003-377
   Rev James Morey; b1833 ggs/o Sinclair; m Mary Trussell; liv Salisbury NH; NH-0004-616
   John; liv SCO, Exeter; ch John b1661 dy, Daniel, Samuel, John b1668, Margaret, James m Sarah Bradley, Jeremy b1675, Elizabeth; NH-0003-377
   Rev John Wesley; b1836 bro/o Rev James Morey; m ? & m Sarah B Saunders of Grafton; liv Salisbury NH; NH-0004-616
   Joseph; s/o Joseph; m Betsey Fifield; liv Kington, Salisbury; NH-0004-616
   Joseph; b1704 s/o James & Sarah Bradley; m1734 Miriam Folsom; liv Kingston; ch Joseph Jr b1738, Nathaniel b1739, Mary b1741, Jonathan b1743, Daniel b1745, Folsom b1747, Miriam

BEAN (continued)
b1749; NH-0003-377
Moody; liv Brentwood & Moulton-
borough NH; ch Moody, David,
Jonathan, Hon Benning Moulton
b1782 m ? & m Lydia Adams,
Samuel, Josiah; NH-0006-404
Sinclair; m1739 Shuah Fifield;
liv Brentwood, Salisbury; NH-
0004-616
BEANE,
William P; b1798 s/o William; m
Sophronia Smith of Lancaster;
liv Lisbon NH; ch 7; NH-0007-
456
BECKFORD,
Benjamin P; d1867 s/o Henry S &
Mary Ann Perry; m Mary E
Emerson of Salem NH; ch
Roxana; NH-0007-286
Henry S; s/o Capt David & Sally
Edmonds of Salem MA; m Mary
Ann Perry; ch Benjamin P m
Mary E Emerson; NH-0007-286
BEDEE,
Daniel S; m Laura E Ela d/o
Joseph & Sally Miller; ch
Nellie m James W Horn; NH-
0004-866
BEDEL,
Col Hazen; b1818 s/o Timothy &
Mary Hunt; m1847 Ann S
Lombard d/o Dr Lyman; liv
Lancaster & Colebrook NH; ch
Ellen dy, Lyman L dy, Alice,
Isabel L dy, Hazen, Mary; NH-
0005-637
John; b1822 s/o Gen Moody;
m1853 Mary Augusta Bourns d/o
Hon Jesse of Nashua; liv Bath
NH; ch 7; NH-0007-66
Timothy; b1737; m Elizabeth ---
& m Mary Hunt of Bath; liv
Salem & Haverhill NH; ch/o
Elizabeth - Moody b1764; ch/o
Mary - Col Hazen b1818 m Ann
S Lombard, 8 others; NH-0005-
637
BEDELL,
Amos; b1774; m1818 Mrs Nancy
Smith; liv Bath NH; ch Martha
m Abraham Little, B N b1824
m1854 Sarah A Spaulding; NH-
0007-517
Charles W; b1839 s/o Timothy; m
Mary Pennock of Lisbon; liv
Bath, Littleton NH; NH-0007-
502
BEEDE,
Aaron; bc1860 s/o Aaron & Mary
McGaffey of Sandwich; liv ME;

BEEDE (continued)
NH-0006-254
Judge Daniel; b1729 s/o Eli;
m1750 Patience Prescott &
m1795 Dorothy Ethridge wid/o
Capt Nathaniel; liv E
Kingston, Gilmanton, Sandwich
NH; ch/o Patience - Nathan
b1750, Daniel b1752, Aaron
b1754, Elijah b1757, Joshua
b1760, Sarah b1762 m Joseph
Varney, Mary b1764 m Richard
Varney, Cyrus b1766, Martha
b1770 m Stephen Hoag, Phebe
b1771 m John Purington, Lydia
b1773 m Samuel Tibbetts,
Patience b1777 m Barzilla
Hines; NH-0006-667
Daniel; b1804 s/o Eli & Ruth
Peaslee; m1834 Ann Elizabeth
Folsom d/o John of Epping; ch
Susan L b1836 m Andrew Phil-
brick of Danville, George F
b1838 m Ruth Nichols; NH-
0003-298
Eli; m Mehitable Sleeper; liv
Isle of Jersey; ch Hezekiah,
Daniel, Thomas, Jonathan
b1734 m Anna Sleeper & m
Susannah Hoag, Elizabeth, 1
other; NH-0003-298
Eli; b1777 s/o Jonathan & Anna
Sleeper; m1800 Ruth Peaslee;
ch Jonathan b1802 m1842
Ezubah Leishure, Daniel b1804
m Ann Elizabeth Folsom, Eli
b1806 m Miriam Huntington & m
Elizabeth Huntington, Mary
b1808; NH-0003-298
Eli; b1806 s/o Eli & Ruth Peas-
lee; m1834 Miriam Huntington
& m1846 Elizabeth Huntington
b1822 sis/o Miram; liv S
Hampton NH; ch/o Miriam -
Ruth Ann b1835, Phebe b1838,
Lindley M b1840, Mary Ellen
b1843; ch/o Elizabeth - Anna
M b1848, Almira B b1850,
Daniel S b1852, Charles
b1854, John J b1856, Lillie H
b1863; NH-0003-298
George F; b1838 s/o Daniel &
Ann Elizabeth Folsom; m1863
Ruth P Nichols b1839 d/o John
& Sarah of Winslow ME; ch
William b1864, Annie E b1866,
Louis A b1868, George E
b1870, Mary Alice b1874,
Augustine b1876, Charles C
b1877, Abbie S b1880; NH-
0003-298

BEEDE (continued)
Jonathan; liv Poplin & Sandwich NH; ch Samuel m --- Crosby, Mary, Sarah, Annie, Mehitable; NH-0006-730
Jonathan; b1734 s/o Eli & Mehitable Sleeper; m Anna Sleeper b1736 & m Susannah Hoag; ch/o Anna - Ruth b1759, Jonathan b1760, Naomi b1763, Mary b1764, Huldah b1767, Hannah b1769, John b1771, Moses b1773, Abraham b1775, Eli b1777 m Ruth Peaslee; NH-0003-298

BELKNAP,
Burke; m Helen Hawkes d/o David Knowlton & Susan Straw; liv Newport, Lawrence MA; ch Lawrence; NH-0004-204

BELL,
Charles Henry; b1823 s/o Gov John & Persis Thom of Chester; liv Chester, Great Falls, Exeter; NH-0003-35
Hugh; b1771 s/o Abigail Ketterage of Andover MA; m Nancy Wilson d/o Capt David & Sarah C of Deering; ch Betsey m Samuel Baldwin, Nancy m --- Jameson of Antrim & 6 others; NH-0002-287
Jacob; b1795; m Laura Bartlett d/o Dr Ezra gd/o Gov Josiah; liv Haverhill NH; ch Jacob LeRoy b1839 m Sarah E Fling & m Harriet Weeks d/o Moses of Haverhill, 3 sons; NH-0007-354
James; s/o Gov Samuel; m Judith Upham; liv Exeter; NH-0004-702
James; b1804 s/o Hon Samuel of Francestown; liv Gilmanton, Exeter; NH-0003-32
John MD; b1831 s/o Gov Samuel of Chester NH; liv Kingston & Derry & Dover & Manchester NH; NH-0003-850
Joseph; b1787 s/o Joseph & Mary Houston of Bradford NH; m Catharine Olcott d/o Mills of Hanover; liv Haverhill, Boston; ch 1 son, 2 dau; NH-0007-82
Louis; b1837 s/o Hon Samuel of Chester; liv Farmington; NH-0003-601
Samuel; b1770 s/o Hon John of Londonderry; m --- Dana d/o Hon Samuel of Amherst; liv

BELL (continued)
Francestown, Chester; NH-0003-26
Hon Samuel LLD; m d/o Samuel Dana of Antrim NH; liv Francestown; ch Samuel Dana b1798; NH-0002-17
Samuel Dana; b1798 s/o Hon Samuel LLD; liv Exeter, Concord, Manchester, Chester; NH-0002-17, NH-0003-26

BELLOWS,
Henry Adams; b1805 s/o Joseph of Walpole NH; m1836 Catharine Bellows of Walpole NH; liv Concord, Littleton; ch Josiah, John Adams, Stella m Charles P Sanborn Esq of Concord, Fanny m Charles P Sanborn Esq of Concord; NH-0007-101
William Joseph; b1817; m1847 Caroline Bullard d/o Samson; liv Rockingham VT, Haverhill, Concord, Littleton; NH-0007-108

BENNETT,
Jeremiah; liv Loudon NH; ch William, Betsey, Elsa, Sally, Rachel, Jeremiah, Leavitt, Mary, Amos; NH-0004-508
John E; m Hannah Welch; liv Wolfeborough & Tuftonborough NH; ch James A b1847; NH-0006-442

BENTON,
Charles; b1819 s/o Reuben; m Elizabeth L Barker of Windsor VT; ch Martha E, Adaline F, Lizzie F, Achsa A, Charles F, Laura M, Annie O, Frank A, Marjorie; NH-0007-325
Colbee C; b1805 s/o William; m1841 Susan A Wright of Norwich; liv Langdon & Lebanon NH; ch Ellen W, Sarah P, John W, Jennie A; NH-0007-426
Hon Jacob; b1874 s/o Samuel Slade & Esther Prouty of Waterford VT; m1860 Louisa Dwight Dow d/o Gen Neal of Portland ME; liv Lancaster NH; NH-0005-217
Reuben; liv Norwich VT, Hanover NH; ch George, Charles b1819 m Elizabeth L Barker, 7 others; NH-0007-325

BERRY,
Rev Augustus; b1824 s/o Washington & Maria Dale;

BERRY (continued)
m1853 Dora Richardson Snow of Peterborough & m1877 Mary Currier Richardson of Pelham; NH-0002-647

George W; b1844 s/o Nathan & Sallie J Chapman of Greenland NH; m Annie M L S De Rochemont; ch Alice M, Martha C, Albert L, Edward A, Percy D; NH-0002-311

Isaiah; b1761 s/o Thomas & Abigail of Greenland NH; m Bethsheba Shaw; ch Levi b1792 m Patience Marsden, 9 others; NH-0003-311

James; m Lorana Fellows d/o Peter & Lydia Ladd; liv Alexandria NH; ch Gilbert H, Caroline M, Olive A; NH-0007-120

John C; b1845 s/o Otis & Esther of Campton; m1868 D Jennie Garland d/o William P & Louisa Avery; liv Plymouth NH; ch Albert L, Hubert E, Arthur G, Ethel L; NH-0007-598

Levi; s/o Nathaniel of Strafford NH; m Sarah Page of Epsom NH; ch 8 sons, 3 dau; NH-0007-120

Levi; b1792 s/o Isaiah & Bethsheba Shaw; mc1815 Patience Marsden of Portsmouth; liv Greenland NH; ch Abigail, Martha, Olive, Francis A; NH-0003-311

Nathan; b1818; m1841 Sallie J Chapman b1818 d/o Nathaniel of Greenland; liv Greenland NH; ch George W b1844 m Annie M L S De Rochemont; NH-0003-311

S P; m1856 Mary J Hoyt d/o Horace F & Caroline E Hardy; liv Lebanon; ch Ida m Albert F Brown, Walter; NH-0007-325

Thomas; s/o John; liv Strafford Corner; ch Tamson m Dea Thomas Berry; NH-0003-703

Thomas; b1731; m Abigail --- b1734; liv Greenland NH; ch Isaiah b1761 m Bethsheba Shaw, 3 sons, 6 others; NH-0003-311

Washington; m Maria Dale of Salem MA; liv Middleton MA, Henniker; ch Rev Augustus b1824 m Dora Richardson Snow & m Mary Currier Richardson;

BERRY, (continued)
NH-0002-647

BETTON;
Silas; s/o James of Windham; m --- Thornton d/o Hon Matthew; liv Salem; NH-0003-38

Thornton; b1800 s/o Hon Silas of Salem; liv Salem, Derry; NH-0003-28

BICKFORD,
Alfred Porter; s/o Nathan & Eliza W Dickey; m1870 Elizabeth (Lizzie) J Goss d/o William & Maryett Abbott of Epsom; liv Epsom NH; ch William P b1871, Nathan A b1872, Alfred G b1875, Harry M b1883; NH-0004-471 & 475

Capt Charles; m Betsey Durgin; liv Barnstead, Dummer; ch John, Nathan, Rebecca, Betsey, Polly, Sophia, Esther, Tempie; NH-0005-855

George Coburn; b1847 s/o Hezekiah Cook MD & Pauline A Coburn; m1877 Florence Stetson of Charlestown MA; liv New London NH; ch Alice Florence b1878, Horace Stetson b1880, George Owen b1881 dy, Walter Howard b1884 dy; NH-0004-441

Hezekiah Cook MD; b1817 s/o Daniel & Martha Adams of New London NH; m1846 Paulina A Coburn of Dracut MA & m1869 Maria Richardson d/o Wm Gray of Billerica; liv Boston & Billerica & Woburn MA, Newport RI, New London NH; ch/o Pauline - George Coburn b1847 m Florence Stetson, John Truman b1849 dy, Harriet Augusta b1853 m Rev Frank Houghton Allen; ch/o Maria - Gertrude Maria b1870, Lucy Gray b1873 dy; NH-0004-441

Isaac; s/o John; liv Northwood, Piermont, Orford NH; ch John; NH-0007-567

John M; b1818; m1839 Catharine Furbush d/o Daniel & Nancy; liv Dummer NH; NH-0005-857

Morrill D; b1836 s/o Nathan & Eliza W Dickey; m1862 Eliza J Hoyt of Epsom; liv Epsom NH; ch Susie A, Addie E; NH-0004-475

Nathan; b1797 s/o Thomas & Olive Haynes; m1823 Eliza W Dickey d/o Robert & Hannah

BICKFORD (continued)

Osgood of Epsom; liv Boston, Epsom; ch Susan G b1824 m Rev Jonathan A Knowles, Salina O b1829 m Capt Arthur C Locke, Eliza A b1833, Morrill D b1836 m Eliza J Hoyt, Alfred P m Lizzie J Goss; NH-0004-475

Nathaniel; b1774 s/o Jonathan & Sarah Wilmot of Dover; m Mary Bean b1780 d/o Benjamin of Moultonborough; liv Tuftonborough NH; ch Isaac C b1821 m Deborah C Bean d/o James; NH-0006-441

Thomas; m Olive Haynes; liv Epsom; ch John, Mehitable, Samuel, Nathan b1797, Daniel, Olive, Dearborn; NH-0004-475

BINGHAM,

Asa; s/o Jeremiah & Lydia Gilbert; m Lucy Cutting d/o Col Zebedee; liv Lyme NH; ch Wallace A, 2 dau; NH-0007-539

Elisha; liv Enfield NH, CT, Jay NY; Elias b1772, Phebe b1778; NH-0007-251

George Azro; b1826; m twice; liv Concord & Lyndon VT, Littleton; ch 5; NH-0007-109

Jeremiah; m Lydia Gilbert d/o Col Thomas; liv Bridgewater MA, Lyme NH, NY; ch Asa m Lucy Cutting, 8 sons, 1 dau; NH-0007-539

BISHOP,

John; m Abigail Parker; liv Hanover; ch James M MD b1821; NH-0007-187

BIXBY,

Samuel; b1754; m Elizabeth Strong & m Sarah Nelson, & m Martha Ketchum; liv Tolland CT, Lyme NH; ch/o Elizabeth - Alfred, 3 others; ch/o Sarah - Lewis, Samuel, 3 others; ch/o Martha - Zophar, Alpheus, Persis m Capt Thomas R Ames, 3 others; NH-0007-529

BLACKMER,

John MD; m Ellen S Dearborn d/o John S of Effingham; liv Plymouth & Springfield MA, Effingham NH, Centre Sandwich; NH-0006-554

Orlando C; m Ellen E Dowe d/o Ulysses & Esther Owen of Hanover; liv Pomfret VT, IL; ch Norbourn H; NH-0007-323

BLAIR,

BLAIR (continued)

---; d1836; m Lois Baker of Candia; liv Campton; ch Hanna Palmer b1830 dy, Moses Baker b1832 d1857, Hon Henry William b1834, Lois Esther bc1836; NH-0001-285

Hon Henry William; b1834 s/o --- & Lois Baker; m Eliza Nelson; liv Campton & Plymouth NH; ch Henry Patterson; NH-0001-285

Joseph C; b1809 s/o Peter; m Dolly P Noyes; ch Joseph C m Christine S Burleigh, 3 others; NH-0007-214

Joseph C; s/o Joseph C & Dolly P Noyes; m Christine S Burleigh d/o Daniel R & Eunice K Coffin; liv Campton NH; ch Joseph C, Laura A, Agnes B; NH-0007-214

Walter; s/o Samuel L; liv Holderness, Plymouth; ch Arthur W b1848; NH-0007-569

BLAISDELL,

Elijah; b1782 s/o Hon Daniel & Sally Spinger of Canaan; mc1802 Mary Fogg of Hampton & m Mrs Mary Kingsbury of Plainfield NH; liv Pittsfield, Canaan, Lebanon; ch/o Fogg - Daniel b1806, 10 others; NH-0007-72 & 83

John M; s/o Pelatiah C & Lois Cook of Campton; m Julia Hall d/o Alpheus & Rosilla Avery of Sandwich; ch Edith M; NH-0007-210

Pelatiah C; m Lois Cook; liv Campton NH; ch John M m Julia Hall, George F, 7 others; NH-0007-210

Pettingill; b1824 s/o Sanborn & Mehitable Sanborn of Dorchester; m Lorette Lillis of Dorchester; ch Henri G, Ella Mable, Pettengill S; NH-0007-239

Samuel; liv Gilford NH; ch William, John, Daniel, Enoch, Aaron, Philip, Samuel; NH-0004-739

BLAKE,

Rev Charles E; b1818; liv Exeter, Newmarket, Madison, Gardner City & Farmington ME; ch Sadie, Lizzie m Rev E S Stackpole, Edwin; NH-0006-813

Charles H; b1832 s/o W H of Rochester; m Mary C Webster &

BLAKE (continued)
m1872 Hattie Dearborn of Centre Harbor; liv Moultonborough NH; ch/o Mary - E E, Emma F, Lizzie S, Mary C, 1 other; NH-0006-415

Dalton; m Deborah ---; liv Dalton NH; ch Nahum b1811, Sarah b1813; NH-0005-520

Dalton; bc1792 (1798) s/o Moses & Lucy Goodrich; liv Dalton & Peterborough NH; ch Nahum, Paschal, Julia m --- Cook, Deborah m --- Hunt, Mary m --- White, 5 others; NH-0005-509 & 519

Ira S; s/o Simon; m Lucy D Jackson; ch Harry B; NH-0006-775

James; liv Sanbornton & Haverhill NH; ch Nathan m Mary Tirell of Bridgewater, Paine, Chase, Joseph, W Henry; NH-0007-363

Jeremiah Esq; s/o Enoch of Pittsfield NH; m Louisa A Tilton d/o William Jr & Abigail Brown; ch Mary, Ellen, Warren, Alvah; NH-0004-504

Moses; bc1744; m Lucy Goodrich of Lunnenburg MA; liv Milton MA, Dalton NH; ch Sally m John Blakeslee, Lucy m Jared Barker, Bathsheba b1785 m John Blakeslee, Ruth b1787 m William Ewen Jr s/o William, Dalton bc1792; NH-0005-509 & 519

BLAKESLEE,
H F; m Caroline H Kingsbury d/o George & Sally Everett; liv IL; ch George m Mary R Holt, Mary E m John L Holmes, Frank A, Willie Everett; NH-0002-302

John; m Sally Blake d/o Moses & m Bathsheba sis/o Sally; liv N Haven CT, Dalton NH; ch John; NH-0005-525

BLANCHARD,
Augustine; b1793 s/o Augustus; m Mrs Betsey Ambrose Purington of Sandwich & m Rebecca F Currier; ch/o ? - Caroline, Harriet, John Augustus, Elizabeth, Charles m Mary J Donovan; NH-0006-673

Augustus; m1792 Esther Crosby; liv Hopkinton, Sandwich; ch Augustine b1793 m Mrs Betsey

BLANCHARD (continued)
Ambrose Purington & m Rebecca F Currier; NH-0006-673

Benjamin; s/o Bridget; m Tuba Keizer; liv Hampstead & Canterbury & Northfield NH; ch Edward, 8 others; NH-0004-519

Benjamin; m1744 Kezia Hastings; liv Dunstable NH; NH-0002-437

David; b1788 s/o Joseph & Relief Osgood; m Betsey Gregg d/o John & Lydia Melvin of Acworth; liv Acworth NH; ch Hiram b1816 m Polly E Gove, 6 others; NH-0004-215

Capt Ebenezer; s/o Capt Edward & Isabella Wasson of Northfield; liv Sanbornton Bridge & Franklin NH; ch 1 dau m --- West, 1 dau m --- Kenrick; NH-0004-533

Capt Edward; s/o Benjamin; m Isabella Wasson of SCO; liv Northfield NH; ch John, Elizabeth m Thomas Chase Sr of Northfield, Richard, Daniel, Capt Ebenezer, 5 sons; NH-0004-531

Hiram; b1816 s/o David & Betsey Gregg of Acworth NH; m1843 Polly E Gove d/o Hon Jonathan & Polly Fisher of Acworth; liv Bradford NH; ch George H b1848; NH-0004-215

Joseph; b1755 s/o Nathaniel; m Relief Osgood d/o Aaron; ch David b1788 m Betsey Gregg, 1 son; NH-0004-215

Nathaniel; ch Joseph b1755 m Relief Osgood, Aaron, Lemuel; NH-0004-215

BLISS,
Jonathan; b1799; m Lucretia Leverett d/o Hon William of Windsor VT & m Mary Kidder d/o Dr Samuel of Charlestown MA & m Mrs Maria Kidder of Medford MA; liv Haverhill, Plymouth, Gainesville AL; NH-0007-83

Reuben; m1809 Nancy Williams; liv Rehobath MA, Lyme NH; ch George R m Dolly P Goodell d/o John, John W m Nancy B Goodell d/o John, 8 others; NH-0007-544

BLODGETT,
Asahel; liv Plymouth, Orford NH; ch Webster P, Mary m --- Hickok, Martha m --- Simpson,

BLODGETT (continued)
Hattie m --- Sherburne, Nellie m --- Pebbles; NH-0007-570

Darius; m twice; liv CT, Lyman & Monroe NH; ch Rufus C, Darius F, 15 others; NH-0007-554

Elbridge G; b1832 s/o Noah & Esther Packard of Plymouth MA; m1862 Sarah G Johnson d/o Samuel & Eliza of Campton; liv Plymouth NH; ch Effie E; NH-0007-592

Dr George A; b1855 s/o Asahel & Sally Clough; m1883 Ellen D Hazelton d/o Rufus B & Martha; liv S Groton NH; NH-0007-294

Hon Isaac Newton AM; b1838 s/o Hon Caleb & Charlotte B of Canaan; mc1860 Sarah A Gerould (Gould) d/o Rev Moses & Cynthia S; liv Franklin; ch 1 dau; NH-0004-39, NH-0007-75

Joseph; s/o Jonathan; m Mary L Wight d/o Nathaniel; liv Gilead ME, Berlin NH; ch 10 or 11; NH-0005-790

Rev Julius Caesar; b1806; m1837 Abigail C Shaw d/o Rev Elijah; liv Salisbury, Sanbornton NH; NH-0004-616

Elder Julius L; b1806 s/o Edward of Franklin NH; liv Kensington; NH-0003-356

W D; b1810 s/o Abial & Margaret Davis; m Lovina Melvin d/o Walter & Dorothy Phillips; liv Plymouth NH; ch Fred R, Nellie E m John L Potts of MI, 1 son dy; NH-0007-591

BLOOD,
Aretas; b1816 s/o Nathaniel & Roxellana Proctor; m1845 M L K Kendall; liv Windsor VT, Evansville IN, Lowell, Lawrence, Manchester NH; ch Nora m Frank P Carpenter, Emma; NH-0002-75

Frank; b1797 s/o Samuel & Sally Bartlett; m Sally Cummings d/o Henry & Jane Merrill; ch Parker b1826 m1876 Mahala Phelps d/o Henry & Sarah Wheet, Samuel b1830, Cyrus b1838; NH-0007-292

Henry T I; m Sarah Longa d/o Nelson & Ann Barnes of Merrimack; liv Merrimack; ch Clinton, Charley, Annie,

BLOOD (continued)
Bertha, Mary, & 1; NH-0002-542

Josiah; liv W Dunstable; ch Josiah Jr; NH-0002-437

Nathan; b1747 s/o Nathan; m1772 Elizabeth Noyes d/o Dea Enoch; liv Hollis; NH-0002-450

Nathaniel; liv W Dunstable, Groton MA?; ch Nathaniel, Francis, Daniel, Timothy, Nathan; NH-0002-437

BOARDMAN,
Benjamin; b1798; m Anne Stickney of Concord; liv S Reading & Lawrence MA, Sanbornton & Meredith Bridge NH; NH-0004-702

BOODEY,
Azariah; s/o Zachariah; liv Cocheco (Madbury); ch Robert, Rev Joseph, 1 dau m John Caverly; NH-0003-716

BOULTER,
Nathaniel; m Grace; liv Exeter NH; ch Mary b1648 m James Prescott; NH-0001-281

BOUTWELL,
William T; b1803 s/o Nehemiah & Elizabeth Jones; m1834 Hester Crooks; NH-0002-509

BOWEN,
Freeman G; b1786; m Hannah P Perkins of Haverhill; liv Boscawen; ch 8; NH-0007-575

BOWERS,
James; m Nancy Symonds d/o Capt Joseph & Hannah Dodge; ch Hon S L; NH-0002-355

BOWLES,
Amasa; m Jerusha Parker; ch 1 dau m Kimball W Noyes, Willis, Leonard m Lizzie M Atwood of Littleton, Simon m Marcia E Gove, Alden, Phebe, 5 others; NH-0007-445

Jonathan; b1776; m Phebe Parker of Richmond; liv Rochester MA, Richmond & Lisbon NH; ch Sally, John b1812 m1836 Abigail D Blake & m1868 Electa J Harris d/o Daniel of Lisbon, George P, Esther; NH-0007-273

BOYD,
---; m Charlotte Odell d/o James; ch Charles A; NH-0003-550

BOYDEN,
Dr Joseph; liv Worcester MA,

BOYDEN (continued)
Tamworth NH; ch Wyatt B, Ebenezer; NH-0006-777

BOYNTON,
Dr Charles Hart; b1826 s/o Ebenezer & Betsey Hart of Meredith NH; m1854 Mary H Cummings d/o Joseph & Mary Huse of Lisbon; liv Alexandria & Lisbon NH; ch Alice; NH-0007-457

David; s/o Ebenezer & Sally Davis of Meredith NH gs/o David; m Mary C Cox Sawyer; ch Frank N m Emma A Shaw, 3 others; NH-0007-395

Dea John; m1745 Ruth Jewett of Rowley; liv W Dunstable, Newbury MA?; ch John, Jacob; NH-0002-437

John Jr; m1745 Lydia Jewett of Rowley; liv Newbury MA?, W Dunstable; ch Isaac, Joel; NH-0002-437

Joshua; liv W Dunstable; ch Joshua Jr, Benjamin, Elias; NH-0002-437

Moses; liv Ware NH, Thornton; ch Hazen, William, Betsy, Moses, Samuel, Nancy, Nathaniel, Clarissa, Eleazer, Newton; NH-0007-643

Stephen; s/o Thomas; liv Orford; ch Daniel T, 1 dau m John Whitcher, Joseph P; NH-0007-634

BRACEWELL,
Col John AM; b1837 s/o Miles of Clitheroe ENG; m1864 Mary Harriet Hope of Lowell MA; liv Eng, Dover NH, Lowell & N Adams MA; ch 1 son, 3 dau; NH-0001-199, NH-0003-875

BRACKETT,
Adino Nye; b1777 s/o Lt Joseph & Mary Weeks of Lee NH; m1807 Mary W Weeks; liv Lancaster NH; ch Adino Nye, James Spaulding, 4 others; NH-0005-361

Ambrose S; m Nancy Brown d/o John & Sarah Gregg; liv Bradford NH; ch J Q A b1842 m Angeline M Peck; NH-0004-219

Benning; liv Wolfeborough NH; ch John b1768 m Betsey Folsom, 16 others; NH-0006-308

John; b1768 s/o Benning; m Betsey Folsom; liv Wolfeborough NH; ch John M b1807;

BRACKETT (continued)
NH-0006-308

John L; b1811 s/o Thomas & gs/o George; m1836 Ellen A Smith d/o S P of Portsmouth NH; liv Greenland; ch Anna D m Rev J W Garland of CND, Simeon S m Abby Barrell d/o Charles C of York ME; NH-0003-306

J Q A; b1842 s/o Ambrose S & Nancy Brown; m1878 Angeline M Peck of Arlington MA; liv Boston; ch John Gaylord b1879; NH-0004-219

William; liv Sudbury MA, Charlestown & Littleton NH; ch William C, Charles W; NH-0007-487

BRADFORD,
Dr Austin; s/o John Jr gs/o John of Kingston MA ggs/o William gggs/o John ggggs/o William Jr gggggs/o Gov William; m Aurelia Bissell; liv Vergennes VT; ch Lucy A m Jason Henry Dudley; NH-0005-254

Rev Ephraim; b1776 s/o Capt John B of Milford; m1806 m Mary Manning Barker d/o Dea Ephraim of Amherst NH; liv New Boston NH; ch 2 sons, 4 dau; NH-0002-606

BRADLEY,
Rev Denis M; b1846; liv Castle Island IRE, Manchester NH, Portland ME; NH-0002-104

Moses H; b1782 s/o John & Hannah Ayer of Concord; liv Bridgewater, Bristol, Sanbornton; NH-0007-68

BRAINARD,
Barzilla; m1811 Sally Dunning of Canaan VT; NH-0005-664

Daniel; liv Stewartstown; ch Barzilla, Rachel (Locke), Daniel Jr; NH-0005-664

BREDLEY (BURLEY),
Gyles; m Elizabeth ---; liv Ipswich; ch Andrew, James b1659 m Rebecca Stacy & m Elizabeth ---, Giles, John; NH-0003-237

BREWSTER,
Charles Warren; b1802 s/o Samuel & Mary Ham of Portsmouth; m1828 Mary Gilman d/o Ward & Hannah; liv Portsmouth; ch Lewis W, Charles G, Mary G, Helen A G, 5 others; NH-0003-114

BREWSTER (continued)
Daniel; s/o George; liv Wolfe-
borough NH; ch Nathaniel T,
John L, Jonathan M; NH-0006-
306
George; bro/o Daniel; liv
Wolfeborough NH; ch Daniel,
John; NH-0006-306
BRIDGEMAN,
John L; b1817 s/o Abel of
Hanover gs/o Rev Abel; m1844
Hortensia A Wood; liv Hanover
NH; ch Don S, Adna A, Emma H;
NH-0007-318
BRIGGS,
James F; b1827 s/o John & Nancy
Franklin of Bury ENG; m
Roxana Smith d/o Obadiah &
Eliza of New Hampton; liv
Manchester, Holderness,
Fisherville, Hillsborough; ch
1 son, 2 dau; NH-0001-294,
NH-0002-29
John R; liv Paris & Woodstock
ME, Milan & Dummer NH; ch
Alfred H, Luther; NH-0005-858
BRONSON,
David; s/o Jonathan; liv
Landaff NH, Southington CT;
ch Huldah m --- Noyes,
Stephen, Isaac, David; NH-
0007-401
Joel; b1802; m Ruth Hall of
Bethlehem & m --- Batchellor
wid/o Stillman; liv Landaff,
Lyndon VT, Littleton NH; ch/o
Ruth - 1 dau m Hollis M
Parker of Littleton; NH-0007-
502
BROOKS,
Capt Benjamin; liv Dalton NH;
ch Benjamin; NH-0005-527
Isaac Esq; b1757 s/o Isaac &
Joanna Holden of Woburn MA;
m1807 Abigail Kendrick d/o
Benjamin Esq of Amherst; liv
Wilton NH; ch Isaac dy,
Luther Dana d1829, Abigail m
Ninian C Dodge; NH-0002-249
Lt William; m1759 Abigail Kemp;
liv Hollis; NH-0002-450
BROUGHTON,
Charles A; s/o John & Sally
Merrill of Conway NH; m
Hannah Quint; ch Clara M m
Ora S Hiscock, 3 others; NH-
0006-848
John; s/o Mark & --- Knox of
Conway; m Sally Merrill; liv
Conway NH; ch Charles A m
Hannah Quint, 3 others; NH-

BROUGHTON (continued)
0006-848
Mark; m --- Knox; liv Conway
NH; ch Hannah m Jedediah
Stone, John m Sally Merrill,
Julia m John Twombly,
Octavus, Harriet m Mark
Merrill, Mary m Elijah
Stuart; NH-0006-848
BROWN,
Aaron; m Harriet E Rowe d/o
Robert & Sally T Sinclair;
liv Fremont; ch Nellie; NH-
0003-135
Abraham; b1649 s/o Henry &
Abigail --- of Salisbury;
m1674 Elizabeth Shepard; liv
Salisbury; ch Abraham b1690 m
Hannah Morrill; NH-0003-201
Abraham; b1690 s/o Abraham &
Elizabeth Shepard of Salis-
bury; m Hannah Morrill; liv S
Hampton; ch Samuel b1716, 2
sons, 5 dau; NH-0003-201
Abraham; b1745 s/o Samuel;
m1770 Mary Emmons; ch Abraham
b1773 m Betsey Ring, Samuel,
Abel, 2 dau; NH-0003-201
Abraham; b1773 s/o Abraham &
Mary Emmons; m1798 Betsey
Ring b1774 d/o Page Esq; liv
E Kingston; ch Rev Samuel E
b1806 m Elvira L Small,
Abraham R b1810, Rufus b1812
m Harriet S Bacheldor & m Ann
E Roberts & m Affa E Floyd;
NH-0003-201
Adam; b1793 s/o Capt Moses &
Lydia Kimball; m Susan
Plummer & m1839 Sarah A
Pickering b1799 d/o Richard &
Polly Thompson of Newington;
liv Wolfeborough NH; ch/o
Susan - Adam Plummer dy; ch/o
Sarah - Susan P m Francis
Page Adams; nh-0006-383
Albert A; s/o David & Margaret
S Plaisted; m Elizabeth C
Innis d/o Asa F & Sally
Stephens; liv Holderness NH;
ch Drucilla m --- Perkins;
NH-0007-395
Alson L; b1827 s/o Joseph &
Relief Ordway; m1849 Mary A
Currier d/o William & Sophia;
liv Campton, Whitefield; ch
William Wallace, Oscar A,
Alice S m Edward Ray, Joseph
W, Etta C m E A Sanborn; NH-
0005-492
Rev Amos LLD; b1804 s/o Stephen

BROWN (continued)
& Susan Bagley; liv Machias
ME, Havanna NY; NH-0003-358
Chad; m Elizabeth ---; liv MA,
Providence RI; ch John m Mary
Holmes, 4 others; NH-0003-880
Colville Dana; b1814 s/o John &
Elizabeth Daggett; m1840 Mary
Eliza Rhodes d/o Capt Elisha
H; liv Washington DC; NH-
0003-880
Dana Jacob; b1859 s/o Jacob F &
Betsey Emeline Willey; m1879
Nellie Allen d/o Elisha P &
Eunice Beacham; liv Ossipee
NH; ch Fred H; NH-0006-623
David; liv Hampton NH; ch Levi
b1777 m Lydia Lovering,
Samuel, Simon, John, Mary m
Jacob Dearborn; NH-0003-424
David; s/o Jonathan of Meredith
NH; m Margaret S Plaisted d/o
William & Nancy of Center
Harbor NH; liv Holderness NH;
ch Albert A m Elizabeth C
Innis; NH-0007-395
Capt David; b1777 s/o Jacob &
Hannah Lamprey; m Ruth
Lamprey d/o Reuben & m ---
Mardon of Rye; liv N Hampton;
ch/o Ruth - Reuben, Reuben L,
Capt Simon b1809 m Harriet A
Leavitt, Nancy, David, Jacob
L, Adna, Albert D, Sarah dy,
2 dy; NH-0003-420
Edwin F; b1837 s/o Lyman & Lucy
of Moultonborough; m1862
Susie V Choate; liv Moulton-
borough NH; NH-0006-415
Elisha; b1717 s/o James & Mary
Harris of Providence RI; m
Martha Smith; liv RI; ch
Elisha b1749 m Elizabeth
Brown, 3 sons; NH-0003-880
Elisha; b1749 s/o Elisha &
Martha Smith; m Elizabeth
Brown of Rehoboth; ch Elisha
b1784, John b1784 m Elizabeth
Daggett; NH-0003-880
Elisha Rhodes; b1847; m1870
Fannie Bickford d/o Dr
Alphonzo; liv Providence RI,
Dover NH; ch Alphonzo Bick-
ford b1872, Harold Winthrop
b1875; NH-0003-880
Garland; m Olive A Smith d/o
Dea Ebenezer & Mary Smith of
Strafford; ch Sarah C, Zephyr
H, Fred L, Henry E; NH-0003-
716
George; d1879; m Rosetta C

BROWN (continued)
Currier d/o John & Mary
Morgan; ch Henry C, Carrie M,
2 others; NH-0004-414e
George A; b1844 s/o Abram of
Bristol; m1869 Augusta S
Shute d/o Thomas & Mary
Emerson; liv Plymouth NH; ch
Dora E, Flora E, Milanzo; NH-
0007-597
George O; s/o Nicholas & Eliza
Ann Page of Campton; m Alice
J Roberts; liv Campton NH; ch
Irving H, Amy M; NH-0007-209
Henry; m Abigail ---; liv
Salisbury; ch Abraham b1649 m
Elizabeth Shepard; NH-0003-
201
Jacob; s/o Nathan; m Abigail
Berry of Greenland; liv
Hampton Falls; ch Thomas,
Nathan W, Joseph C, John B;
NH-0003-344
Jacob; b1740; m Hannah Lamprey
d/o Morris; liv N Hampton; ch
Elizabeth, Jacob, Abigail,
Capt David b1777 m Ruth
Lamprey & m --- Mardon,
Nancy, Sally; NH-0003-420
Jacob F; b1821 s/o John & Sally
S Goodwin of Ossipee; m1844
Betsey Emeline Willey of
Wakefield; ch Eugene F, Dana
Jacob b1859 m Nellie Allen,
Herbert H, Ida m L M Chad-
wick; NH-0006-623
James; m Elizabeth W Langford
d/o Dea Anthony & Nancy
Walton; liv Chester; ch Dr
James F MD b1838 m Abbie
Scribner; NH-0003-159
James; s/o John & Mary Holmes;
m Mary Harris d/o William;
liv Providence RI; ch Elisha
b1717 m Martha Smith, 9
others; NH-0003-880
Dr James F MD; b1838 s/o James
& Elizabeth W Langford of
Chester; m Abbie Scribner d/o
Daniel & Ann Langford of
Raymond; liv Chester; ch
James, Annie; NH-0003-159 &
148
John; m Sarah Walker; liv ENG,
Salem, Lynn MA; ch Sarah,
John, Benjamin, Thomas,
Elizabeth, Jacob, Mary,
Thomas, Stephen, Sarah Abial
S; NH-0003-344
John; s/o Chad & Elizabeth; m
Mary Holmes d/o Rev Obadiah;

BROWN (continued)
ch James m Mary Harris, 4 others; NH-0003-880

John b1688; m --- Drew & m --- Nevins; liv ENG, Portsmouth & Dover & Madbury NH; ch/o Drew - Josiah; ch/o Nevins - Joseph, Edward, John, Nicholas b1743 m Betsey Tibbets, Samuel, Mary m Garland Smith; NH-0003-716

John; b1777; m Sarah Gregg of New Boston NH; liv Henniker & Bradford NH; ch Hannah m Erastus F Brockway, Jerusha, Livonia m Francis T Simpson, Joel H m Sarah R P Richmond of Boston, Jeremiah m Mary H Talbot, Nancy m Ambrose S Brackett; NH-0004-219

John; b1784 s/o Elisha & Elizabeth Brown; m Elizabeth Daggett of Seekonk RI; ch Colville Dam b1814 m Mary Eliza Rhodes, 1 other; NH-0003-880

John; b1785 s/o Jacob; mc1806 Sally S Goodwin of Milton; liv Ossipee NH; ch Capt John b1811 m Lydia Quint of Ossipee, Jacob F b1821 m Betsey Emeline Willey, Jeremiah Quincy, 5 sons, 2 dau; NH-0006-623

John B; b1799 s/o Jacob & Abigail Berry; m1834 Sarah M Leavitt b1808 d/o Thomas of Hampton Falls; liv Hampton Falls NH; ch Hon Warren b1836 m Sarah G Norris; NH-0003-344

Dea John S R; b1819 s/o Gen Richard; m Achsa A Mills; liv Loudon; ch Anna E, Clara J, Abby M P, Richard H P, Hamlin D, John P M, Mary A; NH-0004-502

Dr Jonathan; b1805 s/o Abel & Sarah Page of Kensington; liv VA; NH-0003-357

Rev Joseph; ch Betsey m Hon Samuel Livermore of Holderness NH; NH-0001-229

Joseph; s/o Jonathan gs/o Benjamin ggs/o John; m Ann Brown; liv Kensington; ch Moses, Jonathan, Joseph, Sewell, Nehemiah, Nathan, Stephen m Susan Bagley, William, John, 4 dau; NH-0003-366

Joseph; b1796 s/o Stephen &

BROWN (continued)
Anna Davis; m Relief Ordway d/o Stephen & --- Brown of Salisbury MA; liv Bristol, Campton, Thornton; ch Alson L b1827 m Mary A Currier, Stephen, Mary A m H S Chase, Amos, Warren G b1834 m Ruth B Avery & m Charlotte Elliott, Relief m Elijah Averill, Joseph, Augusta m George W Merrill; NH-0005-492

Capt Joseph; b1802 s/o Stephen & Susan Bagley; m1825 Mary Ann Weare b1807 d/o Joseph H & Betsy Mitchell of Seabrook NH; ch Joseph W b1826 m Sarah B Hilliard, Stephen A b1839; NH-0003-366

Rev Joseph H; b1833 s/o James & Judith B Harran of New Hampton NH; m1863 Hattie N Huse of Danville VT; liv Strafford, Hill; NH-0007-381

Joseph W; b1826 s/o Capt Joseph & Mary Ann Weare; m Sarah B Hilliard d/o Joseph C; ch Susan L, Sarah A, Mary L; NH-0003-366

Langdon; m Augusta M Marston d/o David & Sarah Dearborn; liv Rye; George H; NH-0003-331

Levi; b1777 s/o David of Hampton NH; m1803 Lydia Lovering d/o Thomas; liv N Hampton; ch Hannah L b1807 m John P Grouard, Lydia b1811 m Pepperell Frost of N Hampton, Thomas L; NH-0003-424

Capt Moses; b1759; m Lydia Kimball; liv Wenham MA, Wolfeborough NH; ch Sally, m Taft Brown, Oliver, Adam b1793 m Susan Plummer & m Sarah A Pickering, Irena m Nathaniel Ambrose Esq of Moultonborough, Moses P, Polly m William Smith; NH-0006-383

Nicholas; s/o Daniel gs/o Nicholas; m Eliza Ann Page d/o Daniel & Sabrina Clement; liv Campton NH; ch George O m Alice J Roberts; NH-0007-209

Nicholas; b1743 s/o John & --- Nevins; m Betsey Tibbetts b1753; liv Strafford; ch Reuben, Miriam, Patience b1776, Judith, Nicholas, Mary, Daniel, Betsey, Nancy;

BROWN (continued)
NH-0003-716
Philip;    m1775    Elizabeth
Bachelder;  ch Thomas  b1775,
William  b1778,  David b1779,
Joanna  b1782,  Levi  b1784,
Philip  Jr  b1787  m  Abigail
True,  Timothy  b1789,  Asa
b1793,  Eliphalet b1796;  NH-
0004-505 & 508
Philip Jr;  b1787 s/o Philip &
Elizabeth   Bachelder;    m
Abigail True; ch True m Eliza
C Kelly, 1 dau m David Putnam
of Penacook NH; NH-0004-505
Gen  Richard;  b1787 s/o Job of
Gilmanton;  m 3;  ch Sara  A,
Dea  John S R b1819 m Achsa A
Mills,  Jane S R,  Mehitable,
Elvira W,  Adeliza, Huldah M;
NH-0004-502
Rufus;   b1812 s/o Abraham  &
Betsey  Ring of  E  Kingston;
m1843 Harriet S Bacheldor d/o
Amos  of E Kingston & m1851
Ann E Roberts d/o Watkins of
Shanballymore   IRE  &  m1878
Affa  E Floyd d/o Joseph S  &
Betsey A Tenney; liv Lawrence
MA, Concord NH; NH-0003-201
Samuel;  m  Susanna Dolloff d/o
Abraham & Rachel; liv Bridge-
water;  ch Horace m Mary  A
Fletcher d/o Jesse & Patience
Hobert, 3 sons; NH-0007-129
Dea Samuel; m Clarissa Hoit d/o
Thomas of Tuftonborough;  liv
Milwaukee  WI;  ch Thomas  H;
NH-0006-441
Samuel;  b1716 s/o Abraham  &
Hannah Morrill of S Hampton;
ch  Abraham b1745 m  Mary
Emmons,  Moses,  5 dau;  NH-
0003-201
Samuel;  d1835  s/o William  of
ENG;   liv  Orford NH;   ch
William,   Sabrina  m   ---
Lovejoy,  Cyrus, Irene;  NH-
0007-564
Rev Samuel; b1806 s/o Abraham &
Betsy Ring; m Elvira L Small
of   Portland   ME;     liv
Kensington  NH,  Portland ME,
Hampton Falls,  S Hampton; ch
Rev  S  Emmons  b1847,  Rev
Charles Rufus b1849,  William
Edwin b1853,   Frank Warren
b1857,  Gilman Abraham b1861,
1 other; NH-0003-201
Capt  Simon;   b1809 s/o  Capt
David & Ruth Lamprey  of  N

BROWN (continued)
Hampton; m1836 m Harriet  A
Leavitt b1815 d/o Moses  &
Sarah  of Hampton;  liv  N
Hampton; ch Edwin L, Freeman
A m Meribah A Lane wid/o
Jonathan Dow of Hampton, Otis
S  m  Emma F  Johnson  d/o
Joseph,  Ella M m John P Hoyt
of Hampton, 2 dy; NH-0003-420
Stephen;   s/o  Joseph  &  Ann
Brown;   m Susan Bagley of
Salisbury MA;  ch Capt Joseph
b1802 m Mary Ann Weare, Amos,
Polly,  Nancy, John, Stephen,
Moses,  Jonathan,  Susan; NH-
0003-366
Stephen T;  m  Anna  Davis  of
Goffstown;    liv   Plymouth,
Bristol;   ch  John m  Sarah
Ingalls of Bristol,  Samuel m
Susan  Dolloff of  Bristol,
Joseph b1796 m Relief Ordway,
Enos F m Lovina Heath, Martha
J m Daniel Simonds,  Sarah m
Jacob  Colby  of S  Weare,
Hannah m William Colby,  Mary
m   J B  Warner  of  Boston,
Stephen dy,  Asenath m Calvin
Fuller; NH-0005-492, NH-0007-
181
Titus   Olcott;   b1764;   liv
Tolland CT,   Lancaster NH,
Norway ME;  ch J B;  NH-0005-
361
True;  s/o  Philip Jr & Abigail
True;  m  Eliza C Kelly;  ch
Charles K, Nellie S, Mabel T;
NH-0004-505
Hon Warren;  b1836 s/o John B &
Sarah  M Leavitt of Hampton
Falls  NH;  m1867  Sarah  G
Norris  b1841 d/o Daniel L  &
Sophia  Osgood of Dover;  liv
Hampton Falls NH; ch Harry B,
Arthur W,  Gertrude N, Mildred
L; NH-0003-344
Warren G;  b1834 s/o Joseph  &
Relief  Ordway;  m1861  Ruth
Avery  &  m1865  Charlotte
Elliott  b1848 d/o Ephraim  &
Eliza Broat of Brownfield ME;
liv WA Terr,   Thornton  &
Whitefield NH; ch/o Charlotte
- Josie R,  Dasie A,  Carl E,
Kenneth W; NH-0005-492
William; m Lucretia B Gray d/o
Capt James; liv Epsom NH; ch
1  son,  1 dau,  Susan m ---
Forbes; NH-0004-911
William;  s/o  William of SCO;

BROWN (continued)
liv Chester NH; ch Anna m Col John Head, Hon Hiram; NH-0001-224
Dr William W; b1804 s/o Ebenezer & Mary Whitter of VT; liv Poplin, Chester, Manchester; ch William C, Charles L; NH-0003-148

BRUNSON,
David; m Azubah Judd d/o Nathan & Azubah Eastman of Landaff; ch Rebecca W m George F Eastman of N Haverhill; NH-0007-137

BRYANT,
Matthew; bc1800; liv Enfield NH; ch George H, James F, Betsey H, Amos M, Matthew Jr; NH-0007-262
Hon Napoleon B; b1825; mc1849 Susan M Brown of Northfield NH; liv E Andover NH; 3 ch; NH-0001-187

BRYER,
Charles A; b1862 s/o Jonathan K & Maria Annis; m1882 Nellie M Putney; liv Groton NH; ch Ernest K, Merton M; NH-0007-293
Clarence L; s/o Jonathan K & Maria Annis; m1865 Abbie M Goss & m Nancy E Griffin; liv Groton NH; ch/o Abbie - Clarence M b1866, Nellie M dy; ch/o Nancy - Nancy M, Herbert G, Nellie R, Joseph P, Satie N; NH-0007-293
Clark; m Mary Hall; liv Groton NH; ch Horatio N b1853 m1876 Mary E Cummings; NH-0007-294
Jonathan K; s/o David & Betsey; m1844 Maria Annis d/o J B & m Lydia Fellows d/o Prescott & Betsey; liv Gilmanton, Groton; ch/o Maria - Clarence L m Abbie M Goss & m Nancy E Griffin, John A, D Parker, Herbert K, Charles A b1862 m Nellie M Putney; ch/o Lydia - Anna, George B, Leon B; NH-0007-293

BUCK,
Louis; m Polly ---; liv Dalton NH; ch Louis b1807, Mary Ann b1809; NH-0005-520
Lyman Jr; s/o Lyman; m1758 Lucia W Kasson of Newbury VT; liv Waterford VT, Haverhill NH; ch 5; NH-0007-369
William D MD; b1812; m Grace

BUCK (continued)
Low & m1860 Mary W Nichols of Manchester; liv Williamstown VT, Lebanon & Concord & Manchester NH; NH-0002-126

BUCKFORD,
Alphonso MD; b1817 s/o Thomas of Dover; liv Dover; NH-0003-849

BUCKLEY,
Dana E; s/o Dennis & Julia Kern; m Mary Adams d/o Calvin S & Huldah Sabins; liv Grafton NH; ch Nellie A, Meta A, Charles D; NH-0007-284

BUCKLIN,
Albert M; s/o James & Lydia Tucker; m Polly Rollins d/o Sewell & Martha Dean; liv Grafton NH; ch Ebenezer P, George A, Alpheus S, Sewall A; NH-0007-281
Alonzo; m Calista Goss d/o Reuben & Susan Lathrop of Canaan; ch Anna B, Emma; NH-0007-281
Charles; s/o Jesse; m Choice Cole; ch Charles W, James, Milo m Mrs Calista Bucklin; NH-0007-281
Jesse; liv Grafton NH, RI; ch James m Lydia Tucker, Charles m Choice Cole, 6 others; NH-0007-281

BUCKNAM,
Gen Edward; b1741; m Susannah Page d/o David; liv Lancaster NH, Athol MA; ch Edward, George, Mary b1769 m Coffin Moore, Eunice, 3 dau; NH-0003-241, NH-0005-359

BUEL,
Capt Benjamin; b1767; m Violetta Sessions b1778 of VT; liv VT, CT, Colebrook NH; ch Minerva b1801 m1822 Johnson Jordan, Sharlie Maria m Sidney Allen, Abigail m Daniel Egery; NH-0005-233 & 616

BUFFUM,
Hon David Hanson; b1820 s/o Timothy & Anna Austin of N Berwick ME; m1853 Charlotte E Stickney d/o Alexander H of Great Falls; liv N Berwick ME & Great Falls NH; Charlotte A d1877 ch Edgar Stickney, Harry Austin, David Hanson Jr; NH-0001-271, NH-0003-699
Jedediah; b1806 s/o John; liv

BUFFUM (continued)
Grafton, Monroe NH; ch Sophia m --- Jones, Merritt S, John A, Frank M, Charles L; NH-0007-554
John; liv Grafton, Monroe NH; ch Lucinda m --- Turner, Jedediah b1806, 6 others; NH-0007-554
Joseph; s/o Jonathan & Ruth Joslin; m Mary Corliss of Alexandria; liv Grafton NH; ch William C m Mary Spooner, 7 others; NH-0007-282
Timothy; m Ann Austin of Dover; liv N Berwick ME; ch Hon David Hanson b1820 m Charlotte E Stickney, dau wid/o Hon John H Burleigh of S Berwick ME, dau m Isaac P Evans of Richmond IN; NH-0001-276
William C; s/o Joseph & Mary Corliss of Grafton; m Mary Spooner d/o James & Hannah Snow; liv Grafton NH; ch Joseph, Edwin, Seth, Lizzie m Daniel Floyd; NH-0007-282

BUGBEE,
Frank; b1836 s/o Ralph & Irena Goss of Waterford VT; m1863 Maria P Towne d/o Barton G of Lancaster sis/o Dr Frank; liv Lancaster NH; ch Hattie b1864 dy; NH-0005-397
Ralph; b1796 s/o Amos Bugby of Ashford CT; m1820 Irena Goss of Waterford VT; liv Waterford VT; ch Frank b1836 m Maria P Towne, 5 others; NH-0005-397

BUGBY,
Amos; b1749 s/o Josiah b1708 of Woodstock CT; liv Ashford CT; ch Ralph Bugbee b1796 m Irena Goss; NH-0005-397
Edward; bc1594; m Rebecca ---; liv ENG, Roxbury MA; ch Sarah, Joseph b1640 m Experience Pitcher; NH-0005-397
Joseph; b1640 s/o Edward & Rebecca; m Experience Pitcher d/o Andrew of Dorchester MA; liv Roxbury MA, Woodstock CT; ch Josiah b1684, 4 sons, 4 others; NH-0005-397

BULLARD,
Benjamin; m Ruth Woodice; liv Oakham MA, Deering NH; ch Benjamin dy, Cynthia m John

BULLARD (continued)
Parker, Ruth m Amos Whitamore, Polly m Samuel Abbott, Sally m John Whitamore, Eliza m Elbridge Wilson & m James Wilson, Calvin m Mary Dunlap & m Jane Dresser & m Laura A Wilson, Martha m George Eaton, Benjamin m Rosanna Whitcomb, Joel m Clara Alcock; NH-0002-387

BULLOCK,
Arial K; s/o Hezekiah & Mary Martin of Grafton; m Orpha Simonds of Alexandria; liv Alexandria NH; ch Kendrick S, Mary E, Gilbert A m Clara A Gale, 2 others; NH-0007-116
Benjamin; m Sybil Drake d/o Capt Daniel; liv Grafton NH; ch Dolly m Joseph W Page, 6 others; NH-0007-278
Bradford; s/o Elisha & Maria Leeds; m Lovina Gale of Alexandria; ch Elisha H m Abbie C Allen & m Sarah M French, 8 others; NH-0007-116
Elisha H; s/o Bradford & Lovina Gale; m Abbie C Allen of Lyme NH & m Sarah M French d/o John & Maria J Flanders; liv Alexandria NH; ch/o ? - Abbie M, Georgia A; NH-0007-116
Gilbert A; s/o Arial K & Orpha Simonds of Alexandria; m Clara A Gale d/o Luke & Louisa A Perkins; liv Alexandria NH; ch Eva L; NH-0007-116
Hezekiah; m Mary Martin; liv Grafton; ch Pluma, Sabra, Gilbert, Arial K m Orpha Simons, 3 others; NH-0007-116
James; s/o Benjamin & Sybil Drake; m Sarah Page; liv Grafton NH; ch James B m Rhoda Hoyt, 5 others; NH-0007-282
James B; s/o James & Sarah Page of Grafton; m Rhoda Hoyt d/o Thomas C & Rhoda H Wheelock; liv Grafton NH; ch Belle J, Alberto J, Rosa E, Sarah A, Sybil A; NH-0007-282

BUMP,
James E; s/o James; m Nancy J Hutchins d/o Stephen & Mary Avery of Rumney; liv Campton NH; ch Ada M, Curtis G, Waldo J; NH-0007-215

BUNKER,
 Charles S; b1811; m1833 Sarah P
  Conover d/o William & Harriet
  Morris; liv Barnstable,
  Groton Hollow, Plymouth,
  Rumney NH; ch Charles E,
  George H, Henrietta F,
  Harriet E, Sarah M m Henry
  Alexander, Albert C, Lewis F;
  NH-0007-612
BURBANK,
 Abraham; b1781 s/o David gs/o
  Capt Moses of Boscawen; liv
  Webster NH; NH-0004-687
 Barker; s/o Capt Eliphalet; m
  Polly Ingalls d/o Fletcher;
  ch Judge R I; NH-0005-884
 Gen James; liv ME; ch Prof
  Adino Jr, Daniel, Catherine m
  William P Scribner; NH-0005-
  827
BURGE,
 Ephraim; liv Chelmsford MA,
  Hollis NH; ch Ephraim B Jr;
  NH-0002-437
 Ephraim B Jr; s/o Ephraim; ch
  Rev Josiah B, Dr Benjamin B;
  NH-0002-437
BURLEIGH,
 Alvin; b1842; m1873 Elvira Page
  of Haverhill; liv Plymouth;
  ch 2 sons; NH-0007-112.15
 George William; b1830 s/o John
  Adams of S Berwick; m1854
  Louise H Bryant d/o Col J S
  of Haverhill; liv Great
  Falls; ch 1 son, 2 dau; NH-
  0003-604
 John; liv Deerfield; ch John
  Adams b1800; Hon William; NH-
  0003-604
 John Adams; b1800 s/o John of
  Deerfield; liv S Berwick,
  Somersworth; ch George
  William b1830; NH-0003-604
 Micajah Currier; b1818 s/o
  William & Deborah Currier;
  m1847 Mary Frances Russell of
  Somersworth; liv Somersworth;
  ch William Russell b1851,
  Mary Elizabeth m Charles W
  Wright of Great Falls, Edward
  Stark, Charlotte Russell; NH-
  0003-695
 William; m Deborah Currier; liv
  Gilmanton NH, S Berwick ME;
  ch Micajah Currier b1818 m
  Mary Frances Russell, John
  Holmes, William, Mary
  Currier, Elizabeth; NH-0003-
  695

BURLEY,
 Capt Benjamin; b1803 s/o Thomas
  & Nancy Hoit; m1826 Elizabeth
  Ann Cilley d/o Greenleaf &
  Jane Nealy of Nottingham NH;
  liv Epping; ch Joseph C b1830
  m Sarah E Haley, Nannie Jane
  b1832; NH-0003-237
 Giles (Gyles); m Elizabeth ---;
  liv Ipswich MA; ch Andrew,
  James b1659 m Rebecca Stacy &
  m Elizabeth ---, Giles,
  John?; NH-0003-402
 Harrison G; b1834 s/o Jonathan
  & Sarah C Neal; of Newmarket;
  m1877 Fannie E Connor b1848
  d/o Jewett & Lydia Norris;
  liv Newmarket; ch Walter D,
  Lillian M; NH-0003-402
 James; b1659 s/o Giles & Eliza-
  beth of Ipswich MA; m1685
  Rebecca Stacy d/o Thomas &
  Susannah Worcester & m Eliza-
  beth ---; ch/o Elizabeth -
  William, Joseph, Thomas,
  James, Josiah b1701 m Hannah
  Wiggin, Giles; NH-0003-402
 Jonathan; b1804 s/o Josiah &
  Susan Edgerley of Newmarket;
  m1831 Sarah C Neal d/o John &
  Betsey Sawyer; liv Newmarket;
  ch A Augusta m Charles E
  Smith of S Newmarket,
  Harrison G b1834 m Fannie E
  Connor, Lavina J m Horace B
  Doe of Durham; NH-0003-402
 Joseph C; b1830 s/o Capt
  Benjamin & Elizabeth Ann
  Cilley; m1855 Sarah E Haley
  d/o Samuel of Epping; liv
  Epping & New Market NH; ch
  Nannie b1857 m Harry W
  Burleigh of Franklin, Harry
  Benjamin b1867, Alice b1870,
  Jenny Cilley b1872, Benjamin
  Thomas b1874; NH-0003-237
 Josiah; b1701 s/o James &
  Elizabeth; m Hannah Wiggin
  d/o Hon Andrew & --- Chase;
  liv Newmarket; ch Josiah m
  --- Tuttle, Thomas, Samuel;
  NH-0003-402
 Josiah; s/o Josiah & Hannah
  Wiggin; m --- Tuttle; ch
  Sarah, Josiah b1760 m Susan
  Edgerley, Judith, Hannah,
  Betsey (Deborah), Mary; NH-
  0003-402
 Josiah; b1760 s/o Josiah & ---
  Tuttle; m Susan Edgerley
  b1767; liv Newmarket; ch

BURLEY (continued)
Josiah, Susan, Mark, Clarissa, Deborah, Betsey, Jonathan b1804 m Sarah C Neal, Jeremiah, Lavina; NH-0003-402

Thomas; b1697 s/o James & ?; ch Thomas b1723 m Sarah Haley; NH-0003-237

Thomas; b1723 s/o Thomas; m Sarah Haley d/o Thomas & Sarah Gordon; liv Epping NH; ch Thomas b1766 m Nancy Hoit & m Mary Lawrence Brown; NH-0003-237

Thomas; b1766 s/o Thomas & Sarah Haley of Epping NH; m1798 Nancy Hoit d/o Capt Benjamin & m1818 Mary Lawrence Brown wid/o Ezekiel Brown & d/o Gordon & Mary Prescott Lawrence; ch/o Nancy - Capt Benjamin b1803 m Elizabeth Ann Cilley; NH-0003-237

BURLEY (BREDLEY),
James; b1659 s/o Gyles Bredley & Elizabeth of Ipswich; m Rebecca Stacy & m Elizabeth ---; liv Exeter NH; ch Thomas b1697, 2 sons; NH-0003-237

BURNHAM,
Dr Abel C; b1812 s/o Thomas & Rachel Conant; m1849 Caroline M Dascomb b1823 d/o George & Mary Steele of Hillsborough NH; liv Amherst & Hillsborough NH; NH-0002-426

Hon Henry Eben; b1844 s/o Henry L & Maria A Bailey of Dunbarton NH; m1874 Lizzie H Patterson d/o John D Esq of Manchester; liv Manchester NH; ch Gertrude E, Alice M, Edith D; NH-0002-32, NH-0004-301

Henry Larcom; b1814 s/o Bradford & Hannah Dane Whipple of Dunbarton NH; m1842 Maria A Bailey d/o Josiah of Dunbarton; liv Dunbarton & Manchester NH; ch Henry Eben b1844 m Lizzie H Patterson; NH-0004-301

John; b1648 s/o Thomas & Mary Tuttle; m Elizabeth Wells; ch Thomas b1673, 8 others; NH-0002-426

Jonathan; s/o Abraham & Susan Perkins of Hampton Falls; m Susan Hall d/o Jonathan; liv

BURNHAM (continued)
Rumney NH; ch Charlotte, Lucy, Mary, Betsey, Nancy, Jabez W, Susan P, Jonathan P b1808 m Hortense Burnham, Lydia, Sarah H; NH-0007-606

Jonathan P; b1808 s/o Jonathan & Susan Hall of Rumney; m1834 Hortense Burnham; liv Rumney NH; ch Joseph W, Samuel P, Willie J, 2 dau dy; NH-0007-606

Joshua; b1754 s/o Stephen & Mary Andrews; liv Gloucester MA; ch Thomas b1783, 9 others; NH-0002-426

Miles; b1793 s/o Jacob gs/o Paul of Durham NH; m Salome Hall d/o David; liv Chester; ch Hosea Ballou MD b1829, 5 others; NH-0003-239

Noah; liv Gilmanton & Bethlehem NH; ch Benjamin, 8 others; NH-0007-166

Robert; b1581; m1608 Mary Andrews; liv Norwich ENG; ch John, Robert, Thomas b1623 m Mary Tuttle, 4 others; NH-0002-426

Samuel; liv Gilmanton & Bethlehem NH; ch Joanna m --- Phillips, Elizabeth m --- Richardson; NH-0007-166

Stephen; s/o Thomas; m Mary Andrews; liv Gloucester MA; ch Joshua b1754, 12 others; NH-0002-426

Thomas; b1623 s/o Robert & Mary Andrews of Norwich ENG; m1645 Mary Tuttle; liv Chebacco MA; ch John b1648 m Elizabeth Wells, 11 others; NH-0002-426

Thomas; b1673 s/o John & Elizabeth Wells; ch Stephen m Mary Andrews, 5 others; NH-0002-426

Thomas; b1783 s/o Joshua; m1807 Rachel Conant; liv Milford & Antrim & Hillsborough NH; ch Dr Abel C b1812 m Caroline M Dascomb, 1 son; NH-0002-426

BURNS,
Charles A; b1809 s/o Samuel & Abigail Jones of Milford NH; m1833 Elizabeth Hutchinson d/o Abel & Betsey Bartlett of Milford; liv Milford; ch Charles Henry b1835 m Sarah N Mills & 8 others; NH-0002-40

Charles Henry; b1835 s/o Charles A & Elizabeth

BURNS (continued)
Hutchinson of Milford; m1856 Sarah N Mills of Milford; liv Milford, Wilton, Nashua NH; ch Charles A, Bessie m Mr Gregg; Blanche, Ben E, Arthur d1877, 3 dy; NH-0002-39
Capt David; b1782 s/o Maj John b1755; m1807 Susannah Knight d/o Artemas of Bethlehem; liv Francestown, Whitefield; ch John b1808, Calvin W b1811; NH-0005-463
John; b1700; liv Ireland, Milford NH; ch Thomas, 2 sons, 4 others; NH-0002-40
Samuel; b1779 s/o Thomas & Elizabeth Hartness of Milford NH; m1801 Abigail Jones; liv Milford NH; ch Charles A b1809 m Elizabeth Hutchinson; NH-0002-40
Thomas; s/o John; m Elizabeth Hartness of Lunenburg MA; liv Milford NH; ch Samuel b1779 m Abigail Jones, 2 sons, 3 others; NH-0002-40
Hon William; b1821 s/o Robert of Hebron NH; m1844 Clementine E Hayes of Orford; liv Littleton & Lancaster NH; NH-0005-218, NH-0007-103
BURNSIDE,
Thomas; m Susan McGregor d/o Rev James; liv Londonderry & Stonington NH; ch James, Samuel, Alexander, 1 dau m Chauncey Curtis; NH-0005-542
BURRALL,
John; m Lydia Hoyt d/o Joseph & Mary Patterson; liv Strafford; ch John, Elizabeth m Dana White of Strafford; NH-0007-325
BURT,
Charles W; b1820 s/o Willard & Martha Wood of Westmoreland NH; m1854 Julia Loomis d/o Horace of Colebrook; liv Colebrook NH, Detroit MI; NH-0005-247
BUSWELL,
Elisha; b1757; m1799 Abigail Perkins b1762; ch William, Moses m Betsey Jones, John, Nancy; NH-0004-504
John L; s/o Moses & Betsey Jones; m Mary E Sanborn d/o Capt Daniel L; ch Frank J, Abby J; NH-0004-504
Moses; s/o Elisha & Abigail

BUSWELL (continued)
Perkins; m Betsey Jones; ch John L m Mary E Sanborn, 2 dy; NH-0004-504
BUTLER,
Josiah; b1779 s/o Nehemiah of Pelham; liv VA, Deerfield; NH-0003-27
Luther; b1803 s/o Samuel & Clarissa Buck of Pelham NH; m Abigail Chamberlain of Bath; liv Boston, Haverhill NH; ch Mira, George C, Clara; NH-0007-368
BUTMAN,
Paul; s/o Amos; liv Kingston, Enfield; ch Frank, John K, Laura A m Ashley Goss of Franklin MA, Henry R, Dexter D, Mary m D H Butman of W Lebanon, Charles M, Ella F; NH-0007-423
BUTRICK,
Charles; m Betsy Blake & m Achisa Waugh; liv Concord MA, Deering NH; ch/o Betsy - Charles m Lucinda Whitcomb, Olvin m Loisa Sweetser, Elias B dy, Samuel m --- Sweetser & m --- Fuller, Otis m Julia A Blood, Edward m Lenora J Bryant, John B m Maria Bixby & m --- Barker & m Martha Barker; ch/o Achsa - Betsy, Robert W, Uriah H dy, Danbridge m Martha Bumford; NH-0002-386
BUTTERFIELD,
Ebenezer; m1811 Lucy Hobard; liv Groton NH; ch Lucy m J T Reed, Clarissa A m S Fish, Lydia H m D Estey, Fanny O m Noah L Jewell, Ebenezer B b1821 m Aurilla E Kendall, Sarah m Rensellaer Kendall; NH-0007-294
Ebenezer B; b1821 s/o Ebenezer & Lucy Hobard of Groton; m1847 Aurilla E Kendall d/o Lemuel & Philinda Hastings; liv Groton NH; ch Lucia E b1848 dy, Eva A b1849 dy, Edward b1850 dy, Eva E m Alvin Goodhue, Addie T m G H Bailey, Ida A m Albert Hobart, Frank b1857 m Anna M Jewell; NH-0007-294
Frank; b1857 s/o Ebenezer B & Aurilla E Kendall of Groton; m1884 Anna M Jewell d/o Benjamin & Mary L Wheeler; ch

BUTTERFIELD (continued)
Hubert F; NH-0007-294

BUTTERICK,
Charles W; s/o Nathan & Mary Clifford; m Mary A Dickinson d/o Jonathan & Lucy H Dean; liv Alexandria NH; ch Mary L; NH-0007-119
Nathan; s/o Eli; m Mary Clifford of Alexandria; liv Concord MA, Alexandria NH; ch Nathan B, John A, George F, Charles W m Mary A Dickinson; NH-0007-119

BUXTON,
Rev Edward; b1803 s/o Capt Benjamin & Hannah Flint of New Boston; m1838 Elizabeth McFarland of Concord & m1843 Lois Jewett of Gilford & m1871 Mrs Louisa F Pillsbury of Londonderry; liv Greenland & Rochester & Webster NH; NH-0004-687

BUZZELL,
Andrew James Hale MD; b1831 s/o Dr Aaron of New York City; liv Dover; NH-0003-849

BYTHROW,
Horace A; s/o Lewis; m Sarah S Wheeler of Pomfret VT; liv Lebanon NH; ch Horace Herbert, Ella m Frank Hutchinson, Jennie m Ed Curtis of Cornish NH, Charles M; NH-0007-421

-C-

CALEF,
Joseph; m Miriam Bartlett d/o Hon Josiah; ch Miriam m Dr Joseph Eastman; NH-0003-316

CALFE (CALEF),
Col John; b1731; m1754 Judith Chellis; ch Joseph b1756 m Miriam Bartlett & m ? & m S Batchelder, Mary b1758 m1786 Rev Zaccheus Colby of Pembroke, Hannah b1760 m1780 Rev Elihu Thayer DD of Kingston, John b1763 m Abigail Bartlett of Pembroke, Samuel b1764, Amos, b1769, Robert b1772 m Polly Sleeper; NH-0003-376
Joseph; b1756 s/o Col John & Judith Chellis; m1781 Miriam Bartlett d/o Gov Josiah & m ?

CALFE (CALEF) (continued)
& m 1792 S Batchelder; ch/o Miriam - Josiah B b1782; ch/o S - Moses Hook b1798, John P B b1801; NH-0003-376

CALLEY,
Chase W; b1823 s/o David & Martha Masten of Holderness; m1856 Mary E Keyes d/o Lewis; liv Plymouth NH; ch 1 dau m Charles A Jewell, Frank C, Epes J; NH-0007-596
Jeremiah M; s/o David of Holderness; m Mary Shepard of Holderness; ch Willis H m Harriet Smith, 4 others; NH-0007-128

CAMP,
Amos; b1814 s/o David & Theoda Bridgman of Hanover; m Abigail M Graves; ch Malvina M, Emily, Frank B, Eunice T; NH-0007-320
Asa; s/o David & Theoda Bridgman of Hanover; m Mary A Woodward; ch Carlton N, Fred O, Frank P, Ardell I m L C Flanders, Ada L, Emma E m Oren H Waterman, Milton D, Willie A; NH-0007-320
Cyrus; s/o David & Theoda Bridgman of Hanover; m Nancy Knapp; ch George W, Hattie M, Hattie I m B F Bartlett of Lyme, Lewis P; NH-0007-320
David; b1782 s/o Israel & Bettie Hurlbutt; m1808 Theoda Bridgman d/o Elder Isaac; liv Hanover NH; ch Rufus b1809 m Betsey Hurlbutt, Isaac b1810 m Oliver P Wright(?), David b1812 m Elvira E Smith & m Adaline F Shedd, Amos b1814 m Abigail M Graves, Esther b1819 m Abel D Johnson, Cyrus m Nancy Knapp, Asa m Mary A Woodward, Franklin b1824 m Eliza Dowe; NH-0007-320
David b1812 s/o David & Theoda Bridgman of Hanover; m1834 Elvira E Smith & m1858 Adaline F Shedd; ch/o ? - Charles H, John S, Susanette, Laura Ann, Sarah F m Chandler P Smith, Abbie L, Esther T, Albert D, Julius W, Leonard W; NH-0007-320
Isaac; b1810 s/o David & Theoda Bridgman of Hanover; m1833 Oliver P Woodward(?); ch Carlos D, Julia S m Austin

CAMP (continued)

Wright of Sparta WI, Joanna W m Asa W Fellows, Ellen M, Aurora O m Charles R Woodward of Lebanon, Delia M m David J Hurlbutt, Edna P m David J Hurlbutt, Isaac B, Millard C, Clarence H, Esther T m B B Holmes; NH-0007-320

Israel; b1756; m Bettie Hurlbutt; liv Milford & Washington CT, Hanover NH; ch Abial b1781 m Sally Camp, David b1782 m Theoda Bridgman, Betsey b1783 m1805 Buel Barnes, Israel m Anna Barnes, Jonah b1792 m Elvira Smith of Chelsea VT, Esther b1800 m Col Ashbel Smith, 7 others; NH-0007-320

Rufus; b1809 s/o David & Theoda Bridgman of Hanover; m Betsey Hurlbutt; liv Hanover NH; ch Elizabeth m William L Barnes, David H, Mary T m Jackson Spaulding, Laura A; NH-0007-320

CAMPBELL,

Hon Charles H; b1827 s/o Capt Daniel & Susan Story of Amherst; liv Nashua; ch Col George Hylands, 3 others; NH-0002-250

Daniel; b1660; liv Argyleshire SCO; ch Henry; NH-0002-250

Daniel; b1739 s/o Henry & Martha Black; m1760 Jane Hylands of Londonderry; liv Londonderry, Amherst; ch Capt Daniel Jr b1778; NH-0002-250

Capt Daniel; s/o Thomas & gs/o Robert; m1834 Sabrina Moor d/o John & gd/o Rev Solomon & m1847 Matilda Moor; ch/o Sabrina - Clark b1836 m Ann Perkins of Mont Vernon, Alfred M b1838 m Mary Abbie Cochran of New Boston, John b1840 dy, John b1846, Sabrina b1846; ch/o Matilda - Hamilton M b1848 m Hattie Andrews of New Boston, Mary Ann b1851 m Charles Bales of Wilton; NH-0002-601

Rev Gabriel; b1838 s/o Robert of Dalrymple Parish Ayrshire SCO; m Louise T McMahon of Manchester MI; liv Ypsilanti MI, Minneapolis MN; NH-0007-334

Henry; s/o Daniel of Argyle-

CAMPBELL (continued)

shire SCO; m Martha Black; liv Londonderry; ch Daniel b1739; NH-0002-250

CANNEY,

Burritt; s/o John of Ossipee NH; m --- Thompson d/o Theodore; NH-0006-626

Dr Hanson; b1841 s/o Paul & Eliza Hanson of Strafford; liv Auburn; NH-0003-148

Isaac; m Hannah Thompson; ch Moses B b1809 m Mary Abbott, Zalmon, Benjamin, Eliza, William, Priscilla, Isaac, Sylvester G m Maria Briard; NH-0006-527

Moses B; b1809 s/o Isaac & Hannah Thompson; m Mary Abbott d/o Hull & Mercy Twombly of Berwick ME; liv Salem MA; ch Mary Frances b1830 m George A Beacham, Eliza A b1836 dy; NH-0006-527

Sylvester G; s/o Isaac & Hannah Thompson; m Maria Briard of Kittery ME; liv Salem MA; ch Ida M, Flora M, 3 others; NH-0006-527

William; m Rose Allen; liv Somersworth, Tuftonborough; ch Edmond, Joseph, Benjamin, Ebenezer, John, William, James, Abigail m Joseph Peavey, 1 son, 3 dau; NH-0006-440

CANNEY (KENNY),

Thomas; m Jane ---; ch Thomas, Joseph m1670 Mary Clements, 1 dau m Henry Hobbs, Mary m Jeremy Tebbets; NH-0003-769

CARBEE,

John H; b1791 bro/o Moses & William; liv Newbury VT, Bath; ch Samuel Powers MD b1836 m1885 N Della Buck of Haverhill, 9 others; NH-0007-377

CARLETON,

Dr Charles; m1872 Kate Elizabeth Carr d/o Daniel & Caroline L Tappan; liv Bradford NH, Salem MA; ch Frank Carr b1879; NH-0004-199

Edmund; b1797; m1836 Mary Kilburn Coffin of Boscawen NH; liv Haverhill, Scytheville, Littleton NH, ch Edmund, Thomas m Carrie M Allen of Manchester & m Addie Stone of Watertown MA,

CARLETON (continued)
Alfred; NH-0007-102 & 490
John L; s/o Ebenezer of Bath
NH; m Lucretia Goodall d/o
Ira Esq; liv Bath NH; NH-
0007-63
CARLISLE,
Jacob; s/o James & Sally
Dushong of Waterborough ME;
m1843 Mary O Colcord d/o
William & Olivia Steele of
Exeter; liv Exeter NH; ch
James W, Josephine m Woodbury
Berry, George E, Cora m
Dudley Burpee, Walter S, Eva,
Etta, Jacob; NH-0003-293
CARLTON,
Francis; s/o Timothy & Rebecca
Fields; liv New Orleans LA,
Merrimack; ch 2 dau; NH-0002-
543
Isaac; s/o Jesse & Nancy
Harriman; m Abigail Merrill;
liv Newbury VT; ch Chester M
b1831 m1865 Martha M Bacon, 9
others; NH-0007-378
Jesse; m Nancy Harriman; liv
Boxford MA, Bath; ch John,
Isaac m Abigail Merrill, 3
sons, 5 dau; NH-0007-378
Peter; s/o Timothy & Rebecca
Fields; liv Merrimack; ch
Sarah, Hannah; NH-0002-543
Timothy; m Rebecca Fields d/o
Henry; ch Rebecca, John,
Sophia m --- Ritterbush,
Eliza m Joseph Wilson, Henry,
Francis, Peter, Susan, Isaac
dy & Isaac; NH-0002-543
CARPENTER,
Alba H; b1854 s/o Horace H &
Elizabeth; m1880 Isabel
Barrett d/o Luther wid/o
Elisha B Ferrin; liv Bridge-
water NH; ch Ethel May b1883;
NH-0007-175
Alonzo P; b1829 s/o Isaah of
Waterford VT; m1853 Julia R
Goodall; liv Bath & Concord
NH; ch Lillian m Frank S
Streeter Esq of Concord NH,
Philip, Arthur, Edith, Helen;
NH-0007-66
Charles H; b1818 s/o David
Morrill & Mary Perkins; m1841
Joanna Maxfield; liv Chi-
chester NH; ch John T, Mary
J, Electa A, Sally P, Clara
A; NH-0004-253
David Morrill; b1793 s/o Josiah
& Hannah Morrill; m1818 Mary

CARPENTER (continued)
Perkins d/o Jonathan Chesley
& Hannah Dennett of Loudon;
liv Chichester & Concord &
Epsom NH; ch Charles H b1818
m Joanna Maxfield, Josiah
b1829 m Georgianna Butters
Drake, Clara A m Samuel C
Merrill, Sarah L m Prof James
W Webster, Frank P, 2 dau dy;
NH-0001-43, NH-0004-253
Joseph; s/o William; ch Josiah
b1762 m Hannah Morrill, 3
sons; NH-0004-253
Josiah; b1762 s/o Joseph; m1790
Hannah Morrill of Canterbury;
liv Stratford CT, Canterbury
NH; ch David Morrill b1793 m
Mary Perkins, Clarissa m
David P Shaw, 4 others; NH-
0004-253 & 254
Josiah Esq; b1829 s/o David
Morrill & Mary Perkins; m1858
Georgianna Butters Drake d/o
Col James; liv Chichester &
Pittsfield NH, KY; ch Georgia
Ella b1859; NH-0001-43
Josiah; b1762 s/o John; m1790
Hannah Morrill of Canterbury;
liv Strafford CT, Chichester
NH; ch Nancy, Daniel Morrill
b1793 m Mary Perkins, John
Thurston, Clarissa, Hannah,
Oliver; NH-0001-43
Philip; b1856 s/o Judge A P of
Bath NH; m1880 Fannie H Rouse
of Winstead CT; liv Bath &
Lancaster NH, New York City;
NH-0005-237, NH-0007-67
William; bc1605 s/o William; m
Abigail ---; liv ENG, Wey-
mouth MA; ch Joseph; NH-0001-
43
CARR,
Challes D; b1813 s/o Nathan &
Elizabeth Chase; m Hannah B
Prescott; ch Georgiana F,
Challes F, Samuel M; NH-0004-
503
Capt Daniel; bro/o Dea John; m
Elizabeth Worth; liv W New-
bury MA, Haverhill NH; ch
Melinda b1796, Daniel b1798 m
Rhoda Bagley & m Hannah
Sawyer, 2 dy, 2 sons, 2 dau;
NH-0007-351
Daniel; b1798 s/o Capt Daniel &
Elizabeth Worth; m Rhoda
Bagley & m Hannah Sawyer; liv
Haverhill NH; ch/o Rhoda -
Nathan, Charles F, Frank B, 6

CARR (continued)
others; ch/o Hannah - Samuel
E, Daniel E, 2 others; NH-
0007-351
Daniel; b1801 s/o Moses of
Newbury MA; m1827 Rhoda Bart-
lett d/o Joseph & m1839
Caroline L Tappan d/o Weare
of Bradford; liv Bradford NH;
ch/o Rhoda - William A b1828
m Harriet Martin; ch/o
Caroline - Frank Tappan b1844
m1872 Helen Frances Collins
d/o John H & Ester Pierce of
Bradford, Kate Elizabeth
b1846 m Dr Charles Carleton;
NH-0004-199
Elliott; s/o Robert of Salis-
bury MA; m Hannah Dow; liv
Salisbury MA, Loudon NH; ch
Capt John m Sally Brown,
Nathan b1781 m Elizabeth
Chase, Hannah, Betty, Nancy,
Rhoda, Sally; NH-0004-503
Henry T; s/o Capt John & Sally
Brown; m Jemima Osborn; ch
Ann Genette, John, Mary,
Jane, Sarah; NH-0004-503
Jacob; s/o David of Holderness;
m Harriet Beede d/o Thomas &
Mary Hackett; ch John B m Ann
F Fogg & m Jane H Huckins;
NH-0007-126
Dea John; bro/o Capt Daniel; m
Hannah Worth of W Newbury MA;
liv W Newbury MA, Haverhill
NH; ch Joshua m Mary Cary, 11
others; NH-0007-351
Capt John; s/o Elliott & Hannah
Dow; m1800 Sally Brown; ch
Edmund, Elliott, Jemima,
Clarissa, John, Abraham,
Isaac, Jacob, Henry T m
Jemima Osborn, Hannah, Mary;
NH-0004-503
John B; s/o Jacob & Harriet
Beede; m Ann F Fogg of
Franklin NH & m Jane H
Huckins d/o Ira & Grace
Beede; liv Ashland NH; ch/o
Jane - Cora m --- Jackson;
NH-0007-126
Joshua; s/o Dea John & Hannah
Worth; m Mary Cary d/o George
of Rochester VT; liv Haver-
hill NH; ch 1 dau m --- Gale,
1 other; NH-0007-351
Nathan; b1781 s/o Elliott &
Hannah Dow; m1812 Elizabeth
Chase; liv Salisbury MA,
Loudon NH; ch Challes D b1813

CARR (continued)
m Hannah Prescott, Elizabeth,
Nancy, Martha J T, Sarah M;
NH-0004-503
Robert; liv Salisbury MA; ch
John, Sylvanus, Joseph,
Benjamin, Nathan, Joanna,
Abigail, Martha, Elliott m
Hannah Dow, Susanna, Nancy,
Betty, Mary; NH-0004-503
Robert; liv Gilford NH; ch
John, Richard; NH-0004-740
William A; b1828 s/o Daniel &
Rhoda Bartlett; m1856 Harriet
Maria Martin & m1876 Mary E
Proctor of E Washington NH;
ch/o Harriet - William M
b1857 m1882 Mary L Hart-
shorne, Mabel M b1859 m1884
Henry C Barlett, Charles B
b1860 dy, Frank M b1862 dy;
NH-0004-199
CARRIGAIN,
Philip; b1772 s/o Dr Philip of
Concord; liv Concord; NH-
0004-5
CARTER,
Ephraim; b1800 s/o John; m
Charlotte Otis d/o Joshua of
Strafford gd/o Micajah; ch
Joshua O, Martha J m Israel P
Ham of Dover, Joseph L,
Andrew J, Martin Van Buren,
Abigail S dy, David Y m Flora
E Hunton of Farmington,
George F m Almira Meader of
Rochester NH; NH-0003-615
Dr Ezra; liv Concord; ch Dr
William G; NH-0004-97
Dr Ezra; m1742 Ruth Eastman d/o
Capt Ebenezer; liv Concord;
NH-0004-97
James; b1768 s/o Josiah &
Tabitha Howe; ch James G,
Solon b1801 m Lucretia
Joslin; NH-0004-44
John; liv Barrington; ch Sally,
Betsey, Mollie, Susan, John m
Susan Holmes & m wid ---
Grover & m Mary Leighton; NH-
0003-615
John; s/o John of Barrington; m
Susan Holmes & m wid ---
Grover & m Mary Leighton of
Dover; ch/o Susan - Joseph,
Joel, Ephraim b1800 m
Charlotte Otis, Susan, John,
Betsey, Joshua, Cyrus, Isaac;
ch/o Grover - Hiram H; NH-
0003-615
Josiah; bc1726 s/o Samuel

CARTER (continued)
bc1677 gs/o Rev Samuel; m
Tabitha Howe; liv Leominster
MA; ch James b1768; NH-0004-
44
Sanborn B; b1819; ch Buel
Clinton b1840; NH-0006-263
Solon; b1801 s/o James; m
Lucretia Joslin; liv Leo-
minster MA; ch Col Solon
Augustus b1837 m Emily A
Conant; NH-0004-44
Col Solon Augustus; b1837 s/o
Solon & Lucretia Joslin of
Leominster MA; m1860 Emily A
Conant of Leomister MA; liv
Keene NH; NH-0004-44
Rev Thomas; b1610; liv ENG,
Dedham & Watertown & Woburn
MA; ch Rev Samuel b1640; NH-
0004-44
CARY,
Samuel; b1734; m1755
Deliverance Grant of Bolton
CT; liv Lyme NH; NH-0007-521
CASS,
Chandler; b1813 s/o Jacob; m
Diana Glover; liv Haverhill
NH; ch Hosea B, George C,
Ovett A m A W Newcomb of
Orford, Carrie D m Rexford
Pierce of Haverhill; NH-0007-
379
CASWELL,
Daniel; s/o Daniel; m Delia
Davis of Andover NH; ch Delia
Severance, John m Alice
Tucker; NH-0007-282
John; s/o Daniel & Delia Davis;
m Alice Tucker d/o Ezra &
Judith Burbank; liv Grafton
NH; ch Albert B, Willie G;
NH-0007-282
CATE,
Asa Piper; b1813 s/o Simeon &
Lydia Durgin; m1840 Clara
Proctor; liv Northfield NH;
ch Clara Moulton, Abbie
Josephine, 1 other; NH-0004-
530 & 702 & 885
Benjamin; b1814 s/o John; m
Eliza A Wells d/o Stephen of
Loudon; liv Loudon NH; ch
William W, Carter E b1852 m
Electa Dunavan; NH-0004-506
John; b1783 s/o Stephen & Anna;
ch 1 dy, Nancy, Miles,
Benjamin b1814 m Eliza A
Wells; NH-0004-506
Shadrach; b1779 s/o Stephen &
Anna; m Rebecca Chamberlin;

CATE (continued)
ch Hiram, Hannah, Rebecca,
Eliza, Sally, Judith,
Shadrach, Moses, 3 others;
NH-0004-506
Stephen; m Anna ---; liv Deer-
field & Loudon NH; ch
Shadrach b1779 m Rebecca
Chamberlin, Charles b1781,
John b1783, Stephen b1785,
Jonathan b1785, Sally b1787,
Meshach b1789; NH-0004-506
CAVERLY,
Moses; m1714 Margaret Cotton;
liv ENG, Portsmouth NH; ch
several sons; NH-0003-716
Rovert Boodey; b1806 s/o John &
--- Boodey of Strafford; liv
Strafford, Limerick ME,
Lowell MA, Washington DC; NH-
0003-716
CAVERNO,
Horace F; m Rebecca B Daniels
d/o Albert H & Elizabeth T
Sherman; liv Strafford; ch
John L b1851, Albert D,
Bernice E; NH-0003-616
Jeremiah; s/o John; m Margaret
Brewster; ch John, Sarah,
Lydia, Jeremiah, Polly,
Arthur, George W, Margaret,
Sullivan, David B; NH-0003-
704
John; b1742 s/o Arthur; m Sarah
Tibbetts of Barrington; ch
Molly, Jeremiah m Margaret
Brewster; NH-0003-704
CAVIS,
Solomon; b1800; m Almira Minot;
liv Bristol & Bow NH; ch
George M, Harriet M m ---
Abbott; NH-0007-192
CHADBOURNE,
Dr Thomas; s/o Dr William of
Conway; m --- Green d/o Dr
Peter; liv Concord; NH-0004-
97
CHAMBERLAIN,
Edmund; b1776; m Polly Simonds;
liv Rockingham VT, Lancaster
& Colebrook NH; ch Susan m
Frederick G Messer, Mary m
Ethean Colby; NH-0005-616
James L; b1824 s/o Hon Loammi &
gs/o Capt Isaac of Chelmsford
MA; m1854 Mary A Prescott of
Mason; liv Mason; ch Ida F,
Nettie F dy; NH-0002-526
Capt John; liv Groton MA,
Merrimack; ch Nabby, Rachel,
Susie, Josiah, Rebecca,

CHAMBERLAIN (continued)
Silas, Joseph; NH-0002-542
Joseph; s/o Capt John; ch Joseph, Samuel, Reuben, Moody, James, Roxy, Milly, Augustus; NH-0002-542
Samuel; s/o Joseph; liv Merrimack; ch Frank A, Samuel G; NH-0002-542
Samuel G; s/o Samuel of Merrimack; liv Merrimack; ch Ellen dy, Charlotte dy, Elvord G, Harriet dy; NH-0002-542
CHAMBERLIN,
Isaac H; s/o Phineas; m Jane Lang; ch Charles P m Sarah M Parker of Haverhill; NH-0007-139
James; m Elizabeth Whiting of Willington CT; ch Julia A E m Samuel Smith, 2 others; NH-0007-140
John; m1774 Mary Jackson & m1794 Joanna Banfield; liv Brookfield, Wolfebough; ch Ira, David; NH-0006-305
Phineas; liv Newbury VT, Bath NH; ch Abial, Isaac H m Jane Lang, George, 4 dau; NH-0007-139
Robert Nelson; b1856 s/o Antoine & Electa B Sears of Bangor NY gs/o Francois of Frances; m1882 Maria H Mason d/o Ira & Ann J Howard of Berlin; liv Berlin NH; ch Lafayette Ray; NH-0005-237
William H; s/o Lewis of Chazy NY gs/o Ira; m Jane Aldrich of Chazy NY; liv Alexandria NH; ch Jennie L, Nettie M, Carrie B; NH-0007-120
CHAMPNEY,
Ebenezer; b1743; m1764 d/o Rev Caleb Trowbridge of Groton, m1778 Abigail Parker, & m1796 Susan Wyman; liv Cambridge MA; NH-0002-9
CHANDLER,
Adam; m Sally McAllister; liv Bedford NH; ch Henry of Manchester, John M of Manchester, Hon George Bryon m Flora A Daniels & m --- Martin; NH-0001-185
Hon George Bryon; s/o Adam & Sally McAllister; m1862 Flora A Daniels d/o Hon Darwin J & m1870 --- Martin d/o Col B F; liv Bedford & Manchester NH; ch/o Martin - Benjamin

CHANDLER (continued)
Martin, Alexander Rice dy, Byron; NH-0001-185
Hazen; bro/o John; liv Berlin NH; ch Daphne m Reuben H Wheeler, 5 or 6 others; NH-0005-790
Henry; bro/o William; m Martha Brown; liv Pomfret CT, Hanover NH; ch Jeremiah m Lucy Egerton, 8 others; NH-0007-315
Capt Isaac; b1811; m1837 Elizabeth Downing Furber d/o William & Alice C & m1876 Charlotte M Cochrane d/o Levi & Alice Coleman of Fayette ME; liv Windsor CT, Ludlow MA, Great Falls NH; ch/o Elizabeth - Mary Eliza b1839 dy, Charles Furber b1841, Arabella m James Emery Randall Esq, Albert F b1844; NH-0003-699
Jeremiah; s/o Henry & Martha Brown; m Lucy Egerton; liv Hanover NH; ch Henry m Martha S Clark, 10 others; NH-0007-315
John; bro/o Hazen; liv Shelburne, Milan, Berlin NH; ch Elizabeth L m Merrill C Forist; NH-0005-790
John; b1837; m Helen Leavitt d/o Ware & Mahala of Campton; liv Campton, Plymouth NH; ch Minnie F, Nellie G, Charles E, 5 sons, 1 dau; NH-0007-594
Nathan S; d1862; m Mary A ---; liv Concord NH; ch William b1835, John K, George H; NH-0001-255
Nathaniel L; m1860 Laura A Goodale d/o Thomas Newton & Caroline G Calkins of Hillsborough; ch Christabel b1861 m Charles S George; NH-0002-429
Seth; liv Piermont; ch Theron, Stevens b1802, 6 others; NH-0007-569
Stevens; b1802 s/o Seth of Piermont; liv Lebanon, Piermont, Orford NH; ch Worthen D, 2 dau; NH-0007-569
Uri Jr; b1806 s/o Uri gs/o Abner; liv Piermont NH; ch Gilman, Frank, Hiram, 1 dau, 3 others; NH-0007-574
William; bro/o Henry; m Mary Grosvenor & m Patty Hill & m

CHANDLER (continued)

Eunice Tenney d/o John of Hanover; liv Pomfret CT, Hanover NH; ch 4 sons, 7 dau; NH-0007-315

William E; b1835 s/o Nathan & Mary A; m1859 --- Gilmore d/o Gov Joseph A & m1874 --- Hale d/o Hon John P; liv Concord NH, Washington DC; ch Joseph b1860, William Dwight b1863, Lloyd Horowitz b1869; NH-0001-255

CHAPMAN,

George Willey; b1830; m Eleanor H Towle of Haverhill; liv New Chester, Hill, Haverhill; NH-0007-85

Rev John Alfred Metcalf DD; b1829 s/o Nathaniel & Martha Meserve of Greenland; m1853 Emma J G Knox d/o Nehemiah Esq of Pembroke NH; liv Greenland NH, Boston MA, NY; ch Mattie Ethol b1866, Alfred Knight b1868; NH-0003-307

Nathaniel; m Martha Meserve; liv Greenland NH; ch Sally (Sarah) J m Nathan Berry, Joseph W, Nathaniel, Martha J m Eli Waterhouse, Lucy R, Rev John Alfred Metcalf DD b1829, George W dy; NH-0003-311 & 307

CHASE,

Amos; m Elizabeth Kimball of Hopkinton; liv Seabrook, Deering; ch John m Sarah Hanson, Mary m Nathaniel Whitcher of ME, Edward m Mary Patten, Rhoda m Samuel Straw of Hopkinton, Dolly m Abram Dow of Seabrook, Rachel m Enoch Gove of Weare, Lizzie m Elisha Frye of Sandwich; NH-0002-380

Amos; b1801 s/o Charles & Mary Calef; m1827 Hannah P Hook d/o Josiah & Sarah Whittier; liv Kingston NH; ch William H, Josiah H, Amos Charles b1833, Sarah E m Stephen F Nichols, Isaac H, Mary S m James M Philbrick; NH-0003-381

Amos Charles; b1833 s/o Amos & Hannah P Hook; m1858 Hattie E Draper d/o Rev L & m1866 Emily A Belden d/o Haynes W Esq of E Havens VT; liv Kingston; ch/o Hattie - Alma

CHASE (continued)

F, Clara N m J N Sanborn of E Kingston; ch/o Emily - Charles Q, Hattie E, Harry B, Howard; NH-0003-381

Baruch; m Ellen Wiggin d/o Benjamin of Hopkinton; liv Hopkinton NH; ch Samuel, Benjamin Wiggin; NH-0004-407

Carlton; b1794 s/o Charles & Sarah Currier of Hopkinton; m1820 Harriet Cutter of Bellows Falls; liv Bellows Falls VT, Claremont; ch 8; NH-0004-409

Charles; m Sarah Currier d/o John & Sarah Clarke; liv Hopkinton NH; ch Carlton, Cyrus, Sarah; NH-0004-414d

Charles; b1755; m1787 Mary Calef d/o William; liv Seabrook, Kingston NH; ch Nathaniel, Charles, Samuel, Amos b1801 m Hannah P Hook, Merriam, Sarah m Aaron Patten, Nancy m Moody Colby; NH-0003-381

Charles A; b1857 s/o Samuel R of Campton; m1881 Ida M Abbott; liv Rumney NH; ch Charles J; NH-0007-620

Charles K; b1830 s/o Simon & Sarah Wingate of Rochester NH; m1855 Ellen M Burleigh of Sandwich NH & m1876 Abbie McD Whitehouse d/o John McDuffee; liv Rochester; ch/o Ellen - Charles S, Grace M J, Nellie, Jessie dy, Harry W; ch/o Abbie - Sarah McD, Maud H; NH-0003-755

Ebenezer S; s/o Robert; m Lomira Cora; liv Bath; ch Ebenezer S, Jonathan, 8 others; NH-0007-423

Edward; s/o Amos & Elizabeth Kimball; m Mary Patten; liv Deering; ch Eliza m Daniel G Dow & m William B Walker, Edward dy, Ann B m Samuel H Jones, David P m Phila Patten, Mary; NH-0002-381

Ezra; s/o Samuel & Esther Manahan; m Mary Eastman; ch Ezra Allen; NH-0002-379

Francis Russell; b1818 s/o Jonathan; m1843 Huldah Perley Fessenden of Fryeburg ME; liv Gilmanton & Conway & Northfield NH; NH-0004-702 & 885, NH-0006-268

CHASE (continued)

Horace; b1788; m Betsey Blanchard of Hopkinton & m Lucy Blanchard sis/o Betsey & m Mrs Ruhama Clarke of Manchester; liv Unity, Hopkinton NH; ch/o Betsey - Mary Elizabeth d1843, Samuel B, Charles C, Horace G; NH-0004-408

Ira A; b1854 s/o Ira S & Cordelia P Simonds of Bristol; liv Bristol NH; NH-0007-71

Ira M; s/o Samuel & Esther Manahan; m Josephine Leland; ch Frederick, Edwin, Roscoe, Harry, Laura; NH-0002-379

Dr Ira S; b1816 s/o David of Gilmanton gs/o Stephen; m Cordelia P Simonds; liv Alexandria, Bristol; NH-0007-196

Rev John; liv Kittery ME; ch Josiah, John m Harriet Dennett, Thomas, Bradstreet; NH-0003-755

John; s/o Rev John of Kittery ME; m Harriet Dennett of Kittery; liv Berwick ME; ch Sally, Betsey, Thomas, John, Josiah, Simon b1786 m Sarah Wingate, Mark, Abraham; NH-0003-755

John; s/o Amos & Elizabeth Kimball; m Sarah Hanson of Weare; ch Otis m Phebe Willard, Amos m Mary Hanson of Weare, Edward m Sarah Chase, Winslow m Hannah Dow, James m Maria Thomson, Moses m Martha Blood, Charles m Eunice Thompson, David m Lydia A Chase, David dy, Rodney dy; NH-0002-381

Jonathan; s/o Samuel & Esther Manahan; m Clarissa Kimball; ch Charles M m Charlotte Turner, Sarah F m William Wilson, Cleora J m Henry Wallace, Stephen K m Martha ---, Clara Anna m John Barnard, Minnie Bell; NH-0002-379

Jonathan; liv Wolfeborough NH; ch Nancy m --- Edgerly, Thomas; NH-0006-306

Moody; m Susan Locke; ch Stephen m Nancy Kelley & m Mehitable Goodale, Rhoda m Samuel Palmer, Herod m Hannah Gove & m Mrs Caroline Gove & m Mrs Hannah E Varney, Hiram

CHASE (continued)

m Hannah Wood, Cyrus m Delia Wood, Sarah m George Day, Louisa m --- Nelson & m --- Dunham, Lovinia m --- Nelson, Judith m Moses Harrington David m --- Call of Weare, Dexter m --- Smith, 2 dy; NH-0002-381

Samuel; m Esther Manahan of Francestown; ch Mary m David Bailey, Jonathan m Clarissa Kimball, Ezra m Mary Eastman, Samuel m Lydia Holbrook, Wells m Maria Bailey, Sarah m Erastus H Bartlett, Ira M m Josephine Leland, Betsy Jane m Theophilus H Kimball; NH-0002-379

Samuel; s/o Samuel & Esther Manahan; m Lydia Holbrook; ch Samuel David; NH-0002-379

Simon; b1786 s/o John & Harriet Dennett of Berwick ME; m1813 Sarah Wingate d/o Enoch of Milton; liv Rochester; ch Betsey, E· Wingate, George W, John D, Mary Y, Harriet L, Charles K b1830 m Ellen M Burleigh & m Abbie McD Whitehouse, Sarah F, Maria Josephine, 1 dy; NH-0003-755

Stephen; s/o Benjamin Pike of Chester NH; m1838 Sarah T Goodwin of S Berwick ME; liv Hanover NH; ch Frederick m1871 Mary F Pomeroy of Detroit MI; NH-0007-327

Wells; s/o Samuel & Esther Manahan; m Maria Bailey; ch Samuel Warren m Virginia Hulth, Charles; NH-0002-379

Willard D MD; b1836; m1769 Josephine L Clark of Wilton; liv Claremont, Greenfield, Peterborough; NH-0002-665

William; m Lydia ---; liv Seabrook NH; ch Mary m James Whitaker, Sally m John Downing, Lydia m John Whitaker, Nancy m Isaac Wilkins, Abigail m James Wilkins, Betsy; NH-0002-378

William Little; liv Bristol & Lyme NH; ch Hannible b1832; NH-0007-545

CHEEVER,

Dr Nathaniel F; m --- Spear d/o W T of Nashua; liv Greenfield & Nashua NH; NH-0002-339

CHENEY,

43

CHENEY (continued)
David; d1855; m Anna Worth of
Newbury; liv Newbury MA,
Bristol; ch Leonard m Rebecca
B Haynes d/o David & Rebecca
Bailey of Alexandria; NH-
0007-121
Dea Elias; b1741; liv Thornton
NH, Old Newbury; Dea Elias;
NH-0002-83
Dea Elias; s/o Dea Elias of
Thornton NH; liv Thornton; ch
Dea Moses m Abigail Morrison;
NH-0002-83
Gilman; b1822 s/o Jesse of
Antrim NH; m Ann Lincoln
Riddle of Merrimack; liv
Antrim NH, MA, CA, Montreal
CAN; ch William G b1859; NH-
0001-215
Jesse; s/o Dea Tristram of
Antrim NH; m --- Blanchard of
Deering NH & Deborah
Winchester of Hillsborough
NH; liv Antrim NH; ch
Benjamin P, James S, Gilman
b1822 m Ann Lincoln Riddle, 6
others; NH-0001-215
Jonathan; liv Londonderry,
Bradford NH; ch Daniel;
Stephen, Lydia, Jonathan,
Eben, Hannah, Calvin Lyman,
Simon; NH-0004-199
Dea Moses; s/o Dea Elias; m
Abigail Morrison; liv Holder-
ness & Peterborough NH; ch
Hon Person Colby b1828 m S
Anna Moore & m Mrs Sarah
White Keith, Sarah B m Rev S
G Abbott, Abby M m George
Washburn; Ruth E m Joseph W
Lord; Marcia A m J P F Smith,
Hattie O m Dr C F Bonney; Rev
Oren B DD, Elias H, Moses,
Charles G d1862, 1 dau; NH-
0001-162, NH-0002-83
Hon Person Colby b1828 s/o Dea
Moses & Abigail Morrison;
m1850 S Anna Moore & m1859
Mrs Sarah White Keith d/o
Jonathan White of Lowell MA;
liv Holderness, Peterborough
& Manchester NH; ch Agnes
Annie b1869; NH-0001-162, NH-
0002-83
Stephen; s/o Jonathan; ch
Frederick; NH-0004-199
Tristram; m Polly ---; liv
Dalton NH; ch Calvin b1806,
Clarissa b1809, Curtis b1811;
NH-0005-520

CHESLEY,
Andrew; liv Jackson NH; ch
Nathaniel, Esther m Daniel
Pinkham, Susan; NH-0006-952
Charles; b1827; m1859 m Mrs
Sarah E Swasey Twitchell of
Wakefield; liv Wakefield,
Washington DC; ch John H; NH-
0006-259
Nathaniel; s/o Andrew; ch Ann m
Solomon Burnham, Joanna m
Joseph Trickey, John m Olive
Gray, Andrew m Abigail
Meserve, Charlotte m Alfred
Hatch, Nathaniel m Catharine
Young; NH-0006-952
CHICK,
John; m Sarah Hidden Clark; liv
Limington ME; ch Delia P m
Martin L Schenck; NH-0006-776
CHILD,
Bradley G; b1818 s/o John; m
Hannah Child of Exeter; liv
Bath NH; ch Charles, Myra m
Dr H H Hollister, Flora m S W
Plimpton, Alice m H H Jones,
4 others; NH-0007-142
Dudley; b1819 s/o Dudley; m
Hannah E Hibbard; liv Bath
NH; ch Lizzie J m SW Belden
of St Johnsbury VT, Franklin
L, Edwin W; NH-0007-141
Dwight P; b1810 s/o John; m
Nancy Child of Exeter; liv
Bath NH; ch William, Henry L,
Parker M, John D m Julia Dow,
Adaline H, Jennie M, Juliette
m William H Thom of Westboro
MA; NH-0007-141
John; liv Woodstock CT, Bath
NH; ch Dwight P b1810 m Nancy
Child, Bradley G b1818 m
Hannah Child; NH-0007-141
CHILDS,
John; s/o William of Watertown
MA; m ? & m1668 Mary Warren
b1651 gd/o John; liv Water-
town; ch/o Mary - John b1669
m Hannah French; NH-0004-359
John; b1669 s/o John & Mary
Warren of Watertown MA; m
Hannah French d/o Capt
William; liv Watertown; ch
Jonathan b1696 m Abigail
Parker; NH-0004-359
Jonathan; b1696 s/o John &
Hannah French of Watertown
MA; m1729 Abigail Parker; liv
Grafton MA; ch Josiah m Ruth
---; NH-0004-359
Richard L; m Kate M Gutterson

CHILDS (continued)
d/o John & S Frances Stearns; liv Henniker NH; ch Anna L, Emily F, Francis L; NH-0004-358

Solomon; b1743 s/o Josiah & Ruth of Grafton MA; m1767 Martha Rice d/o Elijah of Westborough MA & m Mrs Sarah Goodwell Ward; liv Henniker; ch/o Martha - Solomon b1781 m Mary Long & m Lucinda Child; NH-0004-359

Solomon; b1781 s/o Solomon & Martha Rice of Henniker; m1806 Mary Long of Hopkinton NH & m Lucinda Child d/o William & Mary Heaton; liv Henniker NH; ch/o Mary - Horace b1807 m1837 Matilda R Taylor d/o John & Sally Jones of Lempster; NH-0004-359

William; bro/o Ephraim; liv Watertown MA; ch John m ? & m Mary Warren; NH-0004-359

CHRISTIE,
Daniel M LLD; b1790; m Mrs Dorothy Dix Woodman d/o John Wheeler Esq wid/o Hon Charles Woodman of Dover; liv Antrim & Dover NH; ch Mary Spalding m Col John W Kingman, Sarah Jane m Col Samuel C Fisher of Dover NH, Helen Marr, Lizzie Wheeler m Hon Robert I Burbank of Boston, Rebecca Harris, Emma Josephine m Frank Hobbs Esq of Dover; NH-0003-590

Jesse; m Mary; liv Londonderry; ch Mary b1728, Capt George b1731; NH-0002-262

Dea Jesse; m Mary Gregg d/o Samuel & Mary Moor gd/o Capt James & Janet Cargil; liv New Boston; ch Jeane, Peter, Samuel b1764 m Zibiah Warren, John, Mary, Elizabeth, James, Mary Ann, Jesse, Robert, Anna, William; NH-0002-262

Josiah W Esq; m Mary Bell; liv Antrim; ch Dr Morris b1832 m Susan S Hill; NH-0002-262

Dr Morris; b1832 s/o Josiah Esq & Mary Bell of Antrim; m1863 Susan Hill d/o George W & Sabrina Woodbury of Johnson VT; liv Antrim; ch George W b1868; NH-0002-262

Samuel; b1764 s/o Dea Jesse & Mary Gregg of New Boston; m

CHRISTIE (continued)
Zibiah Warren d/o Josiah & Jane Livingston of New Boston; liv Antrim; ch Hon Daniel M LLD, Josiah W Esq m Mary Bell, Mary Christie m Rev Levi Spalding, & 5 others; NH-0002-262

CHUBBUCK,
Levi; liv Bartlett NH; ch Levi m Ann Davis, Barnet, Hannah m John Thompson of Conway, Sally m John Carlton, Betsey m --- Walker, Jane m David Carlton; NH-0006-915

Levi; s/o Levi of Bartlett; m Ann Davis; liv Bartlett NH; ch Edwin, George, Mary A, Emeline m Hon G W M Pitman, Rhoda m Tobias Dinsmore; NH-0006-915

CHURCHILL,
David C; b1790; m1816 Patty Franklin; liv Fairlee VT, Lyme NH; ch David C Jr m Lydia A Perry d/o Rev Baxter, Charles H, Lewis F, Jonathan F, 4 others; NH-0007-544

Joseph; liv Newmarket, Brookfield; ch John T, Joseph T d1874, 1 dau m Henry H Gilman of Wakefield; NH-0006-460

CILLEY,
Bartlett G; b1835; m1862 Martha Jane Ames d/o Dr Jason H & Clara George; liv Andover NH; ch George Ames b1863, Winfred Bartlett b1865; NH-0004-198 & 212

Benjamin; m Betsey Edmunds; liv Seabrook & Weare NH; ch Benjamin Jr m Polly Emerson; NH-0004-418

Benjamin Jr; s/o Benjamin & Betsey Edmunds; m Polly Emerson; liv Newbury NH; ch Stephen, Ezra, Moses, Benjamin, James M b1808 m1835 Sarah B Richardson d/o Henry & Charlotte Batchelder of Corinth VT, Sally; NH-0004-418

Ezra; m Laura L Morse d/o Joseph & Sarah Sargent; ch Joseph E, Wesley E, Sarah C B, Almon B; NH-0004-420

Greenleaf; m Jane Nealy; liv Nottingham NH; ch Elizabeth Ann b1804 m Capt Benjamin Burley, Hon Jonathan; NH-0003-237

CILLEY (continued)
Horatio Gates; b1805 s/o Hon
Horatio G of Deerfield; liv
Deerfield, Lewiston ME; NH-
0003-27
CLAFLIN,
Preston; bro/o Rufus & Aller-
ton; m Lydia B Williams of
Attleboro; liv Lyme NH; ch
Preston Williams b1800,
Eliza, Artemas, Julia,
Lemuel, Jeduthan, John W m
Maria H Culver d/o James of
Hanover, Celinda m Andrew
English, Marinda; NH-0007-542
Preston Williams; b1800 s/o
Preston & Lydia B Williams;
liv Lyme NH; ch Preston m
Mary E Southard d/o Rev
Marshall & m Martha M Hoag of
Ryegate VT & m Hattie I
Loomis of Colebrook NH, Julia
A m Daniel R Prescott, John N
m Ellen Houghton & m Melissa
Skinner; NH-0007-542
CLAGGETT,
Hon Clifton; liv Litchfield NH;
NH-0002-10
William; b1790 s/o Hon Clifton
& gs/o Wyseman; m Sarah F
Plumer d/o George & m Mary
Thompson d/o Col E; liv
Portsmouth; ch/o ? - William
C; NH-0003-21
Wyseman; b1721; m1859 Lettice
Mitchell of Portsmouth; liv
Bristol ENG, Litchfield NH;
ch Clifton Clagett; NH-0002-
495
Wyseman; b1721 s/o Wyseman of
Bristol ENG; m1759 ---
Warner; liv Portsmouth; NH-
0003-19
CLAPP,
Allen; b1794 s/o Asa gs/o
Joshua; m1819 Hannah Newcomb
b1793 d/o John, gd/o
Benjamin; liv Walpole & Marl-
borough NH; ch Allen N b1837
m Josie M Mason & 6 others;
NH-0002-132
Allen N; b1837 s/o Allen &
Hanna Newcomb of Marlborough
NH; m1863 Josie M Mason of
Sullivan NH; liv Manchester;
ch Annie M, Freddie dy; NH-
0002-132
CLARK,
Abner; liv Stark NH; ch Olive
b1796, Jared b1800; NH-0005-
570

CLARK (continued)
Benjamin; b1791; m Polly
Thornton of Lyman; liv
Landaff NH; ch 11; NH-0007-
401
Benjamin; m Elizabeth Wiggin;
liv Stratham NH; ch Daniel
b1809 m Hannah W Robbins & m
Anne W Salter, 2 others; NH-
0002-17
Daniel; s/o Eben; liv Landaff;
ch Benjamin M, Mary m ---
Eastman, Ellen m --- Haywood,
Arthur M, 4 others; NH-0007-
555
Daniel; liv Piermont; ch Enoch,
Daniel, Smith, John; NH-0007-
635
Daniel; b1809 s/o Benjamin &
Elizabeth of Stratham; m1840
Hannah W Robbins & m1846 Anne
W Salter; liv Epping, Man-
chester NH, Washington DC;
ch/o Anne - 3 sons 1 dy, 1
dau dy; NH-0002-17
Dr David Weld; b1779; m1802
Mary Snow of Greenwich MA;
liv Sturbridge MA, Effingham
NH, Parsonsfield ME; NH-0006-
554
Eben; s/o John; liv Landaff; ch
Moses, Daniel, 4 others; NH-
0007-555
Harry S; s/o Hon Daniel of Man-
chester NH; m Mary Anna Dear-
born d/o John & Lydia
Batchelder of Hampton NH; ch
Frank, Daniel, Harry, Gracia
Lydia; NH-0003-328
James B; b1825 s/o Jonathan of
Bath NH; m Drusilla M Bisbee
of Haverhill NH; liv Haver-
hill NH; NH-0007-376
John; s/o William & Annie
Wallace of New Boston; m
Rebecca Wallis; liv Hancock
NH; ch Rev Dr William, 3
sons, 5 dau; NH-0003-581
John; s/o Daniel of Piermont;
liv Warren NH; ch Joseph,
John L, Stevens K, 2 others;
NH-0007-635
John; b1806; m Harriet Whitney;
liv Lisbon NH; ch Leonard W,
7 others; NH-0007-453
Joseph; liv Greenland, Wolfe-
borough; ch Mary m Samuel
Avery, Enoch, 6 others; NH-
0006-312
Joseph; b1759 s/o Simeon of
Columbia CT; liv Rochester;

CLARK (continued)
NH-0003-602
Hon Joseph Bond; b1823 s/o Samuel & Betsey Clement; m1862 Mrs Jane Smith d/o James H Peabody & Roxanna of Manchester NH; liv Gilford, Wolfeborough & Manchester NH; ch Mary P, Joseph M; NH-0001-179

Lewis N; b1847; m Persis Georgianna Green d/o Daniel & Polly Wheeler; liv CAN; ch Saidee F b1872, Lewis E b1874 dy, Leon S b1876 dy, Maude H b1877; NH-0004-821

Lewis Whitemore; b1828 s/o Jeremiah & Hannah Whitemore of Barnstead NH; m1852 Helen M Knowlton d/o Capt William; liv Pittsfield & Manchester; ch Mary Helen & John Lewis; NH-0002-26

Dr Nathaniel T; m Clara L Bond; liv Loudon & New London & Bradford & Manchester NH; ch C Blanche; NH-0004-505

Ninian; s/o William & Annie Wallace of New Boston; m Nancy Cochran & m Sally Warner; liv Hancock NH; ch/o ? - Peter C, Nancy m Oliver Whitcomb, Warner, Hon Reed Page b1807 m --- Perkins, Avery Monroe, Augustus N, Edwin Robert, Sarah Almira dy, Mary Ann; NH-0003-582

Hon Reed Page; b1807 s/o Ninian & ?; m --- Perkins d/o Dea James of Londonderry; liv Londonderry; ch Joseph R, Marianna m Prof W H Seaman of Washington DC, William, Sarah Elizabeth; NH-0003-581

Richard B; b1830 s/o Rev John of Groton; m1855 Sarah S Gault d/o William; liv Rumney; ch Charles F b1856, Jennie H, Willie R b1863, Georgie P M b1872; NH-0007-612

Robert; m Letitia Cochran; liv Londonderry IRE, Londonderry NH; ch William m Annie Wallace, Ninian, 2 sons, 2 dau; NH-0003-581

Samuel; m Betsey Clement; liv Gilford NH; ch Hon Joseph Bond b1823 m Mrs Mary Jane Smith & m Roxanna ---, Samuel C, Hannah B m William G Hoyt,

CLARK (continued)
6 others; NH-0001-179
Samuel C Esq; b1832; m Clara E Hale d/o Capt Josiah of Dover; liv Lake Village; ch Samuel C Jr, Clara Belle; NH-0004-704

Samuel Otis; b1828 s/o Robert & Mary Dearborn of Effingham; m1857 Eliza Ann Moore; liv Newfield & Limerick ME; NH-0006-555

Thomas; b1791 s/o Thomas & Jean Alexander of Acworth NH; m Sally Meloon & m Margaret Currier; liv Plymouth NH; ch/o Sally - 1 son, 4 dau; ch/o Margaret - Thomas dy, Thomas F, George, John C, Robert F, Helen M, Martha M, Clara W dy; NH-0007-593

William; s/o Robert & Letitia Cochran; m Annie Wallace; liv New Boston; ch Robert, John m Rebecca Wallis, Ninian m Nancy Cochran & m Sally Warner, 3 dau; NH-0003-581

William F; m Frances E Colburn d/o Josiah of Haverhill; liv New Hampton & Haverhill NH; ch 1 dau m W A Fellow of Lyme; NH-0007-369

CLARKE,
Greenleaf; m1810 Julia Cogswell d/o Dr William & Judith Badger of Atkinson; liv Atkinson NH & Haverhill MA; ch William Cogswell b1810, John Badger b1820 m Susan Greeley Moulton & 3 sons & 1 dau; NH-0001-177 & 262 & 311

Hon Greenleaf; s/o Greenleaf gs/o Dr William; liv Atkinson; NH-0003-124

Col John Badger; b1820 s/o Greenleaf & Julia Cogswell; m1852 Susan Greeley Moulton of Gilmanton; liv Atkinson & Manchester & CA; ch Arthur Eastman b1854, William Cogswell b1856; NH-0001-311, NH-0002-55

Joseph B; b1823; liv Gilford, Manchester NH; NH-0002-33

Nathaniel; b1644; m1663 Elizabeth Somerly b1646 d/o Henry & Judith; liv Newbury MA; ch Nathaniel b1666 m Elizabeth Toppan; NH-0002-27

Nathaniel; b1666 s/o Nathaniel & Elizabeth Somerly of

CLARKE (continued)
Newbury MA; m Elizabeth Toppan b1665 d/o Dr Peter & Jane; live Newbury MA; ch Nathaniel b1689 m Sarah Greenleaf; NH-0002-27
Nathaniel; b1728 s/o Nathaniel & Sarah Greenleaf; m1753 Mary Hardy of Bradford MA b1733; liv Haverhill MA & Plaistow NH; ch Nathaniel b1766 m Abigail Woodman; NH-0002-27
Nathaniel; b1766 s/o Nathaniel & Mary Hardy; m Abigail Woodman; liv Plaistow NH; ch Mary b1800 m Isaac Smith; NH-0002-27
Hon William Cogswell; b1810 s/o Greenleaf & Julia Cogswell; of Atkinson NH m1834 Anna Maria Greeley d/o Stephen Esq of Gilmanton NH; liv Atkinson, Laconia, & Meredith Bridge Manchester NH; ch Stephen Greeley, Anna Norton, Julia Cogswell, Greenleaf; NH-0001-261, NH-0002-20
CLAY,
Charles L; b1845; m Stella L Reddington d/o Henry; liv Andover, Littleton NH; NH-0007-496
James; b1789 s/o Jonathan of Buxton ME; m1818 Olive Elwell gd/o Benjamin sis/o Ithiel; liv Chatham NH; ch Ithiel Elwell b1819 m1862 Caroline C Eastman d/o Jonathan K & Phoebe Clements, John C b1821 m Mary Bonzie, Mehitable b1823 m Alfred Eaton, Mason H b1826 m Maria Carlton, Abby A b1828 m Francis Smith, Merritt E b1831 m Maria Abbott; NH-0006-985
CLEMENT,
Carleton; bro/o Samuel & Richard; m Kesiah Dow; liv Deering; ch Jonathan D m Charlotte L Merrill & m Cynthia J Hanson, Squiers S m Hannah Gage, Richard m Nancy Hutchin & m Belinda Colby, Kesiah D m Adam Dickey; NH-0002-386
David B; b1812 s/o Simeon of Thornton NH; m1837 Mary Rollins d/o Joshua & Lydia; liv Bridgewater NH; ch Lydia R, David B Jr b1842 m Ellen M Hickins, Mary S R m Joseph A

CLEMENT (continued)
Barlett; NH-0007-173
David B Jr; b1842 s/o David B & Mary Rollins of Bridgewater; m1871 Ellen M Hickins d/o Joseph & Almira Prescott; liv Bridgewater NH; ch Willie D, Josie H, Harry B, Myra, Ellen, Rose, Jane, Mary; NH-0007-173
John; m Molly ---; liv Haverhill MA, Hopkinton NH; ch John, Timothy, Phineas, Benjamin, James, Ruth, Polly, Sally, Betsey; NH-0004-406
Jonathan D; s/o Carleton & Kesiah Dow; m Charlotte L Merrill & m Cynthia J Hanson; ch/o Charlotte - Charlotte m Horace Gould, Jonathan m Vienna Dickey; ch/o Cynthia - Moses H m Ora Dow & m Eliza Dow; NH-0002-386
Joshua; b1764; m1790 Abbie Head d/o Gen Nathaniel of Pembroke; liv Goshen & Pembroke NH; ch Dolly b1794 m Jesse Gault; NH-0004-390
Richard; bro/o Carleton & Samuel; m Mrs Carleton Clement; NH-0002-386
Samuel; bro/o Carleton & Richard; m Sarah Buntin; NH-0002-386
Squiers S; s/o Carleton & Kesiah Dow; m Hannah Gage; ch Carleton m Mary G Comstock, Charles H m Anna Preston; NH-0002-386
CLIFFORD,
Lemuel; s/o Ithiel; m Betsey Fullerton d/o William; liv Wolfeborough NH; NH-0006-302
CLINE,
Benjamin; s/o Peter & --- Richardson; m Caroline Farwell; liv Lyme NH; ch Benjamin, Bernice m ---, Cutting, Charlotte m ---, Gordon, Laura m --- Perkins, Mary m --- Webb, 4 sons; NH-0007-541
Peter (Klein); m --- Richardson; liv GER, Plymouth & Lyme NH; ch Benjamin m Caroline Farwell, Winthrop dy; NH-0007-541
CLISBY,
Joseph; mc1827 Sally Hill; liv Northfield NH; ch Mandana F, Maria D, Sarah C, Clara A;

CLISBY (continued)
NH-0004-531
CLOUGH,
Lt Abner; m Sally Clough d/o Leavitt of Canterbury; liv Epping & Canterbury NH; ch Leavitt m Hannah Sargent, Abner m Sarah Haselton, Jeremiah m Polly Hook & m ?; NH-0004-502
Abner; s/o Lt Abner & Sally Clough; m Sarah Haselton; ch Lucy, Abial H, Jeremiah A; NH-0004-502
Charles C; s/o Rev Jeremiah & Sabrina Clough; m Mary E Osgood d/o Ira Esq of Loudon; ch Charla E; NH-0004-509
Charles Newell; b1849 s/o Col David M & Almira Batchelder; m Emma T Morrill; ch David Morrill Jr; NH-0004-233
Cyrus; s/o William; ch Frederick, Timothy, Julia m Reuben Moulton, Cyrus; NH-0007-376
Dan; b1814 s/o Abner & Nancy of Lyman; m Betsey Hutchins of Bath; liv Bath NH; ch Solon H m Lizzie Week of Bath; NH-0007-141
Col David M; b1805 s/o Leavitt Jr & Abigail Morrill; m1828 Almira Batchelder b1805 d/o Ebenezer of Canterbury & m1856 Mrs Caroline Gibson Tallent; liv Gilmanton & Canterbury NH; ch/o Almira - Ann Maria b1830 dy, Henry Leavitt b1834, Mary S b1836 dy, Edwin Davis b1843 m Eliza Couch of Concord, Charles Newell b1849 m Emma T Morrill; NH-0004-233
Jeremiah; liv Canterbury NH; ch Jeremiah, Henry, Thomas, Abner, Joseph m --- Lawrence of Epping, Leavitt m Hannah Fletcher & m Peggy Mason, 1 dau m --- Gerrish of Boscawen; NH-0004-233
Jeremiah; s/o Lt Abner & Sally Clough; m Polly Hook & m ?; ch/o Polly - Adaline; NH-0004-502
Rev Jeremiah; b1792 s/o Jonathan Jr & Betsy Clough of Loudon NH; m1813 Sabrina Clough d/o Leavitt of Canterbury & m1840 Deliverance Hodgdon of Northfield NH; liv

CLOUGH (continued)
Canterbury & Loudon NH; ch/o Sabrina - 6 dy, Jeremiah L m Clara Clough, Charles C m Mary E Osgood; ch/o Deliverance - Christiana; NH-0004-509
Jeremiah L; s/o Rev Jeremiah & Sabrina Clough; m Clara Clough d/o Hon Joseph of Loudon; ch Lucy S, Jeremiah J; NH-0004-509
John; s/o Theophilus Jr of Enfield NH; liv Enfield NH; ch Emeline; NH-0007-253
Jonathan Sr; b1724; m1756 Elizabeth Thompson & m 2; liv Salisbury MA, Loudon NH; ch/o Elizabeth - Joseph, Nathan, Sarah, Jonathan Jr m Betsy Clough, Love; NH-0004-509
Jonathan Jr; s/o Jonathan Sr & Elizabeth Thompson; m Betsy Clough of Epping NH; liv Loudon NH; ch Rev Jeremiah b1792 m Sabrina Clough & m Deliverance Hodgdon, Joseph, Benjamin, Jonathan, Sally; NH-0004-509
Joseph; b1795 gs/o Thomas; m1817 Mehitable Ambrose Chase d/o Stephen of Northfield; liv Canterbury NH; NH-0004-915
Leavitt; s/o Lt Abner & Sally Clough; m Hannah Sargent; ch Leavitt Jr, David S, Sally; NH-0004-502
Leavitt; s/o Jeremiah of Canterbury NH; m Hannah Fletcher of Loudon & m Peggy Mason of Chichester; ch/o ? - Sally m Abner Clough of Loudon Hill, Hannah m Josiah Haines of Canterbury, Susan m Jeremiah Clough, Leavitt Jr b1778 m Abigail Morrill; NH-0004-233
Leavitt Jr; b1778 s/o Leavitt & ?; m1800 Abigail Morrill b1779 d/o Dea David; ch Henry b1801, William Patrick b1802, Mary Ann b1804 m1825 Dea Jonathan Brown of Gilmanton, Col David M b1805 m Almira Batchelder & m Mrs Caroline Gibson Tallent, Merinda b1808 m Jonathan Prescott of Gilmanton, Leavitt Morrill b1809, Thomas Carmel b1812 m Martha Emery of Concord,

CLOUGH (continued)
Daniel Webster b1814; NH-0004-233
Lucien B; liv Albany NY, Manchester NH; NH-0002-32
Nathan C; m Mary E Sanborn d/o Gould & Sally Rollins, ch Minnie E, Alice; NH-0004-504
Theophilus; liv Enfield NH; ch Theophilus Jr, Henry; NH-0007-253
Theophilus Jr; s/o Theophilus of Enfield; liv Enfield NH; ch Theophilus, Wingate, John; NH-0007-253
William; liv New Salem & Lyman NH; ch Zacheus, Enoch, Bailey, Cyrus, Abner, Jeremiah; NH-0007-514
William Patrick; b1802 s/o Leavitt Jr & Abigail Morrill; liv Canterbury, Andover; ch Cornelia m Rev Howard Moody; NH-0004-233
Wingate; s/o Theophilus Jr of Enfield NH; ch Bartlett W, 2 sons, 2 dau; NH-0007-253

CLOUTMAN,
Eliphalet; m Hannah Bean; liv Wakefield, Conway; ch Joseph A; NH-0006-853
John; liv Wakefield NH; ch Mary, John F m Patience T Edgerly, Ann, Gilman, Alfred, Hersey, Jeremiah A; NH-0003-629
John F; s/o John of Wakefield NH; m Patience T Edgerly d/o Andrew; ch Erastus F (name changed to Ralph Carlton), Martha m James Davis, John F b1831 m Amanda M Davis & m Ellen E Kimball, Horatio G, James A, Ellen F m Edward D Seymour; NH-0003-629
John F Jr; b1831 s/o John F; m1854 Amanda M Davis d/o Eleazer of Alton NH & m1869 Ellen E Kimball d/o Samuel A; liv Boston, Farmington; ch/o Ellen - Nellie A, John F; NH-0003-629

COBURN,
Asa; m Hannah Carleton of Colebrook; liv Wheelock VT, New London, Littleton NH; ch George C, Charles R, John, Sarah m Wilber Clark, Abby m --- Cribbs of WI, Clara m Sabatha Lovejoy of WI, Ida m W P Davis of White River Jct

COBURN (continued)
VT, 2 others; NH-0007-498
F W; m Susan Willey d/o Alfred S of New Durham & m Mary J Willey sis/o Susan; liv Pelham & New Durham NH; ch/o Susan - Charles, Frank W Jr m Leona Smith of Rochester, Alonzo G m Annie Adams of New Durham; ch/o Mary - Alma J, Susan M; NH-0003-659
John H; m Elizabeth Fields d/o John; ch Catherine m John H Upham of Amherst; NH-0002-543

COCHRANE,
John; b1704 s/o John & Elizabeth Arwin; m Jennie McKeen; liv Londonderry IRE, Londonderry NH; ch James; NH-0002-602
John; s/o James of Windham; m Jemima Davis d/o Benjamin; liv New Boston; ch Hon Robert B b1794 m Elizabeth Warren, Hon Gerry W, Hon Clark B AM; NH-0002-602
Hon Robert B; b1794 s/o John & Jemima Davis of New Boston; m Elizabeth Warren d/o Capt Robert of New Boston; liv New Boston; ch Prudence b1824, Annis C C b1825 m John O Parker, Sophia P b1830, Rev Warren R b1835 m1864 Leila C Cochrane d/o William C & Harriet Crombie, Elizabeth D b1837 m1870 W W Story of Antrim, Clark B b1843 m Mary E Andrews of New London NH; NH-0002-602
Rev Sylvester; m Hannah Symonds d/o Capt Joseph & Hannah Dodge; liv MI & Antrim; ch Judge Lyman; NH-0002-355

CODMAN,
Moses; m Jennie Wallace & m Betsy Bennett & m Jane Ross; liv W Deering; ch/o Jennie - William W m Dorcas Millen, John m Hannah Codman; ch/o Betsy - Lucy m Horace Ferson, Nathan m Hannah Crees; NH-0002-384
William; m Mary ---; liv Deering; ch Henry m Sophronia Patten, Peter, Charles m Mahala Atwood, Abbie; NH-0002-382

COE,
John; b1797 s/o Rev Curtis & Annie Thompson; m Lavinia T

COE (continued)
Senter d/o Samuel M; liv Centre Harbor & Durham & Dover NH; ch Curtis S, Annie L m Charles P Towle, John L, Ellen L m Dr S J Quimby, Rufus L, Daniel W; NH-0004-728
Robert; b1596; m Anna ---; liv Epswich ENG, Watertown MA, Wethersfield & Stamford CT, Hampstead & Middlebury & Jamaica LI; ch 3 sons; NH-0004-728
COFFIN,
Charles Carleton; b1823 s/o Thomas & Hannah Kilburn of Boscawen; m1846 Sallie R Farmer sis/o Prof M G; liv Boscawen & Webster NH, Malden, Boston MA; NH-0004-176 & 688
Judge Peter; m Abigail Starbuck d/o Edward & Katherine of Nantucket; liv Dover; ch Tristram b1665; NH-0003-773
Tristram; bro/o Mary & Eunice s/o Joanna Thember; m Dionis ---; liv Brixton ENG, Salisbury & Newbury MA; ch 2 sons; NH-0004-176
Tristram; bc1691 s/o Tristram; ch Deborah b1738; NH-0003-773
COGSWELL,
Francis; b1800 s/o Dr William & Judith Badger of Atkinson; m1829 Mary S Marland d/o Abraham of Andover MA; liv Atkinson, Tuftonborough, Ossipee & Dover NH & Andover MA; ch John F of Andover MA, Thomas M of Lawrence MA; Mary M m William Hobbs Esq, 5 others; NH-0001-177, NH-0003-598
Dr George; s/o Dr William; ch Gen William; NH-0003-121
Hon George AM MD; b1808 s/o Dr William & Judith Badger; m1831 Abigail Parker d/o Peter Esq of Groveland MA & m1846 Elizabeth Doane d/o Hon Elisha of Yarmouth MA; liv Atkinson NH, Boston & Bradford MA; ch Abby Parker b1832 m Hon George F Choate, George Badger b1834 m Catherine Babson Brown, William Wilberforce b1837 dy, William b1838 m Emma Thorndike Proctor & m Eva M Davis, Sarah Parker

COGSWELL (continued)
b1843, Elisha Doane b1847 dy, Susan Doane b1847 dy, Doane b1851, Caroline Doane b1852; NH-0001-204
James; d1878 s/o Joseph & Hannah Burnham; liv Enfield NH; ch John R, Emily A m Eben R Dustin, Frank S; NH-0007-253
Lt John; s/o William & Susannah of Ipswich MA; m Hannah Goodhue; ch Nathaniel m Judith Badger; NH-0001-137
Joseph; m Hannah Burnham; liv Ipswich MA, Enfield NH; ch 5 dau, Joseph, James; NH-0007-253
Dr Joseph; m1788 Judith Colby; liv Warner, Durham, Tamworth; ch Ebenezer m Betsey Wiggin, Ruth m Eben Allen, Mary Sargeant b1805 m Jacob C Wiggin, Joseph m Amanda F Page; NH-0006-767
Joseph; s/o Dr Joseph & Judith Colby; m Amanda F Page; liv Tamworth NH; ch Susan, Nathaniel Winslow, Emma J m Charles Robertson, Rev Elliott Colby b1814 m Sophia Ann Adams d/o Dea Thomas of Gilmanton; NH-0006-767
Joseph; b1793 s/o Dr William; m1817 Judith Peaslee; ch William of Medford MA, Francis of Cambridge MA, Thomas of Boston MA; NH-0001-177
Nathaniel; s/o Lt John & Hannah Goodhue of Ipswich MA; m Judith Badger; ch Dr William m Judith Badger; NH-0001-137
Rev Nathaniel; b1796 s/o Dr William & Judith Badger; m1825 Susan Doane; liv Yarmouth MA; ch John B D of MA; NH-00010177
Parsons Brainard; b1828 s/o David & Hannah Haskell; liv Henniker NH; NH-0004-89
Thomas; b1746; m Ruth Badger; liv Haverhill MA, Gilmanton NH; NH-0004-703
Hon Thomas; b1798 s/o William & Judith Badger of Atkinson gs/o Hon Joseph; m Mary Noyes; liv Atkinson & Gilmanton NH; ch Mary C m Dr Burgess, Martha B m Dr Batchelder, James W, Thomas;

COGSWELL (continued)
NH-0001-160, NH-0004-703 &
793
Thomas; b1841 s/o Hon Thomas &
Polly Noyes of Gilmanton; m
Florence Mooers d/o R D of
Manchester; liv Gilmanton NH;
ch 1 dau, 2 sons; NH-0004-807
William; s/o John & Elizabeth
Thompson of ENG, Ipswich MA;
m Susannah ---; ch Lt John m
Hannah Goodhue; NH-0001-137
Dr William; s/o Nathaniel &
Judith Badger of Haverhill
MA; m Judith Badger d/o Gen
Joseph & m Hannah Perason of
Gilmanton NH; ch/o Judith -
Rev William DD b1787 m Joanna
Strong; NH-0001-137
Dr William; b1760 s/o Nathaniel
of Atkinson; m1786 Judith
Badger d/o Hon Joseph Sr of
Gilmanton; ch William b1787,
Julia b1789 m Greenleaf
Clarke, Hannah Pearson b1791
m Gov William Badger, Joseph
Badger b1793 m Judith
Peaslee, Rev Nathaniel b1796
m Susan Doane, Thomas b1798,
Francis b1800 m Mary S
Marland, George b1808, John
B1810 dy; NH-0001-177, NH-
0003-123
Dr William; m Judith Badger d/o
Gen Joseph Sr of Gilmanton
NH; liv Atkinson NH; ch Hon
George b1808 m Abigail Parker
& Elizabeth Doane, 8 others;
NH-0001-204
Rev William DD; b1787 s/o Dr
William & Judith Badger of
Atkinson NH; m1818 Joanna
Strong d/o Rev Jonathan of
Randolph MA; liv Atkinson,
Hanover & Gilmanton NH, S
Deedham & Boston MA; ch 1 dau
dy, Wiliam Stong b1828, Mary
Joanna b1832 m Rev E O
Jameson, Caroline Strong
b1840; NH-0001-137
COLBURN,
Abel; m Betsey Bailey d/o
Richard & Hannah; liv Hebron,
Groton; ch Lucinda, Zila,
Abel, Betsey, Ezekiel b1800 m
Johanna Bartlet; NH-0007-293
Ezekiel; b1800 s/o Abel &
Betsey Bailey; m1828 Johanna
Bartlett d/o Joseph & Abiah
Cheeney; ch Alzina m Cyrus
Moore, George E b1831 m1869

COLBURN (continued)
Josie Temple d/o Charles &
Roxana Divol, Henry H; NH-
0007-293
J D; b1833 s/o Uriah of Went-
worth; m Adaline Downing; liv
Rumney NH; ch Nettie A m
Frank P White of Woodsville,
Fred A b1858, David A b1863,
Linda J b1869; NH-0007-614
James F; s/o Uriah; ch James M,
Joseph A; NH-0007-639
Lt Robert; m1747 Elizabeth
Smith; liv Billerica MA,
Monson (Hollis) NH; ch
Robert, Benjamin, Nathan; NH-
0002-437
Robert; s/o William; m1745
Elizabeth Leeman d/o Samuel &
m Elizabeth Smith d/o Elias;
liv Hollis; NH-0002-440
Thomas; m Mary ---; liv Dun-
stable; ch Thomas b1761,
Isaac b1763, Zaccheus b1765;
NH-0002-461
Uriah; liv MA, Wentworth NH; ch
Joseph, Uriah, Mehitable,
Joshua, James F; NH-0007-639
William; liv Billerica MA,
Hollis NH; ch Robert,
William; NH-0002-440
COLBY,
Anthony; b1795 s/o Joseph &
Anne Heath; m Mary Everett &
m Eliza Messenge Richardson
of Boston MA; liv New London;
ch/o Mary - Daniel E m
Martha Greenwood, Robert m
Mary Colgate, 1 dau m1851
James Colgate of NY; NH-0001-
251
Daniel; bro/o Nathaniel; m ---
Emery & m Lucy Cowen; ch/o
Emery - Belinda m Richard
Clement, Pamelia, Charles,
Squiers, Samuel, Diana, 2 dau
dy; NH-0002-384
Dr Elijah; b1798 s/o Isaac of
Hopkinton NH; liv Concord NH,
New Bedford MA; NH-0004-97
Ethan; b1810; m1843 Mary
Chamberlain d/o Edmund; liv
Sanbornton, Littleton, St
Johnsbury VT, Colebrook NH;
ch Edward, Charles, Sarah m
Melrose V Knight; NH-0005-618
George H; b1841 s/o Leonard &
Sarah B Rand of Pembroke NH;
m1860 Helen M Hadley of
Milford NH; liv Plymouth NH;
ch Leonard T P, Sadie G,

COLBY (continued)
Clarence G; NH-0007-596
Ichabod; liv Ossipee NH; ch Moses, Benjamin, John T G, Mary m Isaac Stillings; NH-0006-629
Joseph; b1762; m Anne Heath; liv Hopkinton, Newlondon; ch Sara m Jonathan Herrick, Judith m Perley Burpee, Joseph, Anthony b1795 m Mary Everett; NH-0001-251
Nathaniel; bro/o Daniel; m Patty Muzzey & m Mary McKeen; liv Hopkinton, Deering; ch/o Patty - John, Elizabeth m Frank Russell, Nancy m Elbridge McKeen; ch/o Mary - Eben m Ella Gove, Elbridge, Lucy; NH-0002-384
Prescott; m1853 Helen Maria Hawkes d/o Colburn & Clarissa Brown of Bradford; liv Bradford NH; ch 1 dau dy, Belle m J Currier of Bradford, Jesse Prescott m Clara Gillingham d/o Moody, Flora; NH-0004-203
COLCORD,
Edward; m Anne ---; liv Dover NH; ch Jonathan, Mary b1649 m1670 Benjamin Fields, Edward bc1651, Samuel, Hannah m1665 Thomas Dearborn, Sarah m1668 John Hobbs, Shua b1660, Deborah b1664 m Tristram Coffin, Abigail b1667, Mehitable m1697 Nathaniel Stevens of Dover; NH-0003-769
Lt Samuel Jr; s/o Lt Samuel b1656; m1704 Elis Folsom d/o Lt Peter of Exeter; ch Peter b1705, Elizabeth b1708, Samuel b1710 m Mehitable Lad, Mary b1715 m1736 Col Eben Stevens; NH-0003-376
Samuel; b1710 s/o Lt Samuel Jr & Elis Folsom; m1732 Mehitable Lad b1713; ch Elizabeth b1739, Mary b1744, Daniel b1747, Mehitable b1751 m Wm Patten; NH-0003-377
COLE,
Hon Benjamin James; b1814 s/o Isaac & Hannah Atwood; m1838 Mehitable A Batchelder d/o Nathan & Peace Clifford of Lake Village; liv Gilford & Lake Village NH; ch Ellen A, Octavia M m Col Henry B Quimby; NH-0004-773
Clifford; liv Stark NH; ch

COLE (continued)
Weedon b1800; NH-0005-571
Emerson; liv Stark NH; ch Nancy b1799, Eleanor b1802; NH-0005-571
Emerson; m Helen Elizabeth Green d/o Daniel & Polly Wheeler; liv Milan & Berlin NH; ch Helen Alzinella b1862; NH-0005-821
Isaac; s/o Solomon & --- Barker; m Hannah Atwood of Atkinson NH; liv Chester & Landaff & Franconia & Salisbury NH; ch Hon Benjamin James b1814 m Mehitable A Batchelder, Isaac, John A; NH-0004-773
Richard; s/o Luther; m Sylvia Dwinells of Harvard MA; ch Jane, Ann M, Victoria, George H m Katie A Almond; NH-0007-281
Solomon; b1742; m --- Barker; liv Rowley & Methuen MA, Landaff & Lisbon NH; ch Timothy, John, Isaac m Hannah Atwood, Benjamin, Solomon, Kimball, Samuel, Asa; NH-0004-773
COLEMAN,
Jabez; m1699 Mary Prescott d/o James Sr & Mary Boulter; ch Joseph; NH-0003-375
COLLINS,
John Harriman; s/o Enos of Warner; m Esther Pierce Marshall d/o Nathan Richardson & Abigail Hawks of Bradford NH; liv Warner & Bradford NH; ch Abigail m --- Blaisdell, Helen Frances m Frank Carr of Bradford; NH-0004-205
Col Samuel; ch Lydia H m Joseph Bean; NH-0003-168
COLMAN,
Charles; s/o Col Dudley; ch Hon Dudley C, Charles; NH-0006-458
Col Dudley; liv Newburyport MA, Brookfield NH; ch 1 dau m Leon Chappotin, John, Dudley, Charles, Henry; NH-0006-458
CONANT,
---; m Sally Gage d/o Dea Aaron; liv Merrimack; ch Hannah m Freeman Hill; NH-0002-543
Dea Abel; b1755 s/o Josiah; m1781 Pegga Jewett; liv

CONANT (continued)
Hollis; NH-0002-450
Josiah; m1745 Catharine Emerson; liv Salem MA, W Dunstable; ch Josiah Jr, Abel; NH-0002-437
CONN,
Granville P AM MD; b1832 s/o William & Sarah Priest of Hillsborough; m1858 Helen M Sprague of E Randolph VT; liv E Randolph & Richmond VT, Concord NH; ch 2; NH-0004-162
CONNER,
Jedediah; s/o Jonathan & Mary Jewett of Exeter; m Elizabeth Jenkins & m Abigail Gilman; liv Exeter; ch/o Elizabeth - Elizabeth W m Hon Parker Sheldron of Gardiner ME, Daniel, Susan F m Rev Joel Terry of Kane IL, Jewett m Lydia Norris; ch/o Abigail - Mary dy; NH-0003-292
Jeremiah; liv Exeter; ch Jonathan, Philip, Samuel, Benjamin, Hannah m --- Rawlins, Ann m --- Lyford; NH-0003-292
Jewett; s/o Jedediah & Elizabeth Jenkins of Exeter; m1838 Lydia Norris d/o Josiah R & Betsey of Exeter; liv Exeter; ch William N m Emma W Hart, Fannie E m1877 Harrison G Burley of Newmarket NH, Ellen A m1870 Orin F Hart of Chelsea MA, Mary E m1881 Freeman Sanborn of Newmarket NH; NH-0003-292
Jonathan; s/o Jeremiah of Exeter; liv Exeter; ch Jonathan m Mary Jewett, Jeremiah, John, Mehetable m --- Think, Anne m --- Giddings; NH-0003-292
Jonathan; s/o Jonathan of Exeter; m Mary Jewett of Exeter; liv Exeter; ch Jesse, Daniel, Nathaniel, Jedediah m Elizabeth Jenkins & m Abigail Gilman, Mary m Ezekiel Barstow of Exeter, Eunice; NH-0003-292
William N; s/o Jewett & Lydia Norris of Exeter; m1866 Emma W Hart of Boston MA; ch Arthur J b1868; NH-0003-292
CONNOR,
Abel; b1782 s/o John Thing & Susanna Kimball; m1808 Hannah

CONNOR (continued)
Whitney d/o Alexander & Lois of Henniker & m1830 Martha Greeley of Hopkinton & m1833 Mary L Nichols of Hopkinton; liv Henniker NH; ch/o Hannah - Hannah b1809 dy, John Thing b1809 dy, Liva b1811 m Solomon Heath of Bow, Liza b1813 dy, Alexander W b1815 m Harriet Spofford of Barre VT, Alvira b1817 m J G M Foss of Hopkinton, Eunice C b1818 m E P Leach of Dunbarton, John K b1820 m Mary J Darling of Henniker, Hannah C b1822 m P M Flanders of Hopkinton, Abel De La Fayette b1824 m Louisa Bacon of Henniker & m Lucy S Goodell of Hillsborough; NH-0004-355
Cornelius; s/o William (Coner); m Sarah ---; liv Exeter, Salisbury MA; ch Sarah b1656, John b1660, Samuel b1662, Mary b1663, Elizabeth b1665, Rebecca b1668, Ruth b1669, Jeremiah b1672 m Ann Gove, 1 dau (Ursula); NH-0004-355
Jeremiah; b1672 s/o Cornelius & Sarah; m1696 Ann Gove d/o Edmund; liv Exeter; ch Jeremiah, Jonathan b1699 m Mehitable Thing, Philip, Samuel, Benjamin, Hannah, Ann; NH-0004-355
John Thing; b1745 s/o Jonathan & Mehitable Thing of Exeter, m Susanna Kimball of Exeter; liv Hopkinton & Henniker NH; ch Mehitable b1770, George b1773, Anna b1775, John b1779, Abel b1782 m Hannah Whitney & m Martha Greeley & m Mary L Nichols, Susan b1789; NH-0004-355
Jonathan; b1699 s/o Jeremiah & Ann Gove; m Mehitable Thing b1706 d/o John & Mehitable; liv Exeter; ch Anne b1724, Mehitable b1726 dy, Jeremiah bc1730, Jonathan b1737, Anne b1739 m --- Giddings, Mehitable b1742 m --- Thing, John Thing b1745 m Susanna Kimball; NH-0004-355
CONVERSE,
Benjamin P; s/o Theron & Mary Porter; m Miranda H Walker; ch Sarah, Louisa, Alma, Herbert, Sidney A, Etta; NH-

CONVERSE (continued)
0007-537
Erastus; b1809 s/o Lyman &
Polly Kent of Lyme; m Rebecca
Handley of Acton MA; liv Lyme
NH; ch Henry E, George E,
Ella C; NH-0007-537
Joel; b1750 s/o Thomas of
Thompson CT; m Demaris --- of
CT & mc1785 Betsey Bixby; liv
Lyme NH; ch/o Demaris - Lyman
m Polly Kent, Otis m
Clarrissa Porter, Demaris m
Asa Taintor of Orford; ch/o
Betsey - Joel m Abigail
Coult, Theron m Mary Porter &
m Miriam Carpenter, Marquis m
Electa White, Betsey m Asa
Taintor of Orford, Amasa,
Sally m Joshua Thornton of
Lyman, John Kendrick; NH-
0007-537
Joel; s/o Joel & Betsey Bixby
of Lyme; m Abigail Coult; liv
Lyme NH; ch William A C; NH-
0007-537
Joshua; b1813 s/o Joshua &
Polly Piper of Rindge NH;
m1835 Jane B Damon d/o Galen
& Jane Barker & m1869 H
Jennie Dearborn d/o Joseph &
Harriet Drew; liv Salmon
Falls NH, Lowell, Rollins-
ford; ch/o Jane - Mary Jane m
James A Place of S Berwick
ME, William, Henry,
Josephine; NH-0003-679
Lyman; s/o Joel & Demaris of
Lyme; m Polly Kent; liv Lyme
NH; ch Asenath, Eliza,
Erastus b1809 m Rebecca
Handley, Mary A, Demaris W,
Fanny L; NH-0007-537
Marquis; s/o Joel & Betsey
Bixby of Lyme; m Electa
White; liv Lyme NH; ch Peter
M, Alonzo T; NH-0007-537
Theron; s/o Joel & Betsey Bixby
of Lyme; m Mary Porter & m
Miriam Carpenter; ch/o Mary -
Alpheus - Mary P m Moses Wood
of Boston, Louisa, Benjamin P
m Miranda H Walker, 1 other;
ch/o Miriam - Theron B dy,
Eleazer C, Miriam E m Frank J
Smith of Ypsilanti MI; NH-
0007-537
COOK,
Arthur B; s/o Moody Jr & Lucy
Eaton; m Dora B Foss d/o
George & Deborah; liv Campton

COOK (continued)
NH; ch Nelson B, Fannie G;
NH-0007-207
Asa S; b1823 s/o John & Sarah
Sinclair of Sandwich NH;
m1850 Mary J Cole d/o John &
Harriet Coburn of Lowell MA;
liv Gloucester Point NJ,
Hartford CT, Petrolea CANADA
West; ch Millard Fillmore
b1851, John Franklin b1854
m1874 Josephine Emma
Garrison, Harriet Elizabeth
b1857 m1880 Philemon Wads-
worth Robbins, Albert
Sinclair b1864, Mary Sinclair
b1871 dy; NH-0006-711
Charles P; b1820 s/o Timothy &
Mary Price; m Susan B Staples
d/o Nicholas W of Tamworth;
liv Tamworth NH; ch Clinton
S; NH-0006-772
Coffin; s/o Ephrain gs/o
Samuel; m Rebecca Baker d/o
Col Moses & Molly Wyatt; ch
Corydon W m Sarah J Garman
d/o James & Deborah Waldey of
Laconia, 2 others; NH-0007-
207
Cornelius; liv ENG, Moulton-
borough, Sandwich; ch Joel,
Dr Lot; NH-0006-709
George P; b1845 s/o William G &
Judith Merrill; m1871 Eliza-
beth Paige d/o Moody & Emily
Hobart; liv Plymouth NH; ch
Emily E, Hettie E, William G,
Jason O; NH-0007-598
James; b1760; m1783 Clarrissa
Gilbert d/o Col Thomas; liv
CT, Lyme NH; ch Gilbert, Mary
m Dr W W Amsden, Nancy m ---
Irwin, James, Lewis m Rhoda
Conant, Thomas m Betsey
Flint, 8 others; NH-0007-533
Joel; s/o Cornelius; liv Sand-
wich NH; ch John b1795, 7
others; NH-0006-709
John; b1795 s/o Joel of Sand-
wich; liv Lowell, IL, Sand-
wich NH; ch John Otis, Hon
Asa S; NH-0006-709
Joseph; s/o Moody Jr & Lucy
Eaton; m Sarah P Cook & m
Eliza A Kenrick d/o Alex-
andria & Eliza Barker of
Plymouth NH; liv Campton NH;
ch/o Sarah - 1; ch/o Eliza -
Sarah m --- Adams; NH-0007-
207
Moody; liv Newburyport MA,

COOK (continued)

Campton NH; ch Amanda, Moody Jr m Lucy Eaton, 6 others; NH-0007-207

Moody Jr; s/o Moody; m Lucy Eaton d/o David of Plymouth; ch Joseph m Sarah P Cook & m Eliza A Kenrick, Arthur B m Dora B Foss, Daniel E, 2 others; NH-0007-207

Thomas; s/o James & Clarissa Gilbert; m Betsey Flint; liv Lyme NH; ch Nancy E m William Thomas, Harriet F, Elizabeth m A P Colby, Matilda P m E G Parker, Hannah F m Sylvester Stockwell; NH-0007-533

Timothy; m1815 Mary Price; liv Albany, Tamworth; ch Stephen S m Orpheia Yates of OH, Charles P b1820 m Susan B Staples, William P m Rebecca Guptill of Parsonsfield, George D, Jonathan, Harriet m --- Durgin & m Fletcher Merriam, Mary m Stephen Ellis, Susan F m Stephen Ellis; NH-0006-772

COOLEY,

Alonzo; b1815 s/o Ephraim & Hannah Hall; m1840 Emeline Wallace of Franconia; liv Lisbon NH; ch Laura J, John F, Dennis W, Sarah E, Persis E, Hiram K, Edwin W, Orisa M, Alice M, Elra M; NH-0007-456

Ephraim; b1785; m1807 Hannah Hall & m1818 Electa Young of Landaff; liv Boston, Lisbon NH; ch/o Hannah - Ephraim, Alonzo b1815 m Emeline Wallace; ch/o Electa - Alden; NH-0007-456

Newton S; b1819; m1856 Catherine York of Boston; liv Chelsea VT, Boston MA, Littleton NH; ch 1 son, 1 dau; NH-0007-501

COOPER,

James; m1863 Margaret Shirley d/o John & Margaret Houston; ch Thomas Shirley b1865, John Maxwell b1867, Ella Margaret b1869, Robert James b1871, Mary Emma b1874; NH-0002-329

COPELAND,

William J; b1841 s/o Rev William H of Lebanon ME; liv Presque Isle, Berwick; NH-0003-605

COPP,

Charles H; s/o Moses; liv Tuftonborough NH; ch George W b1854; NH-0006-442

Capt David; b1738 s/o Jonathan & Esther; liv Rochester, Wakefield; NH-0006-471

David Jr; bc1770 s/o David of Wakefield; liv Dover; NH-0003-588

John; m Ruama Rollins; ch Eveline, John G; NH-0004-53

COREY,

Day P; b1807; m Eliza Corey of Lyman; liv Bath, Lisbon NH; ch James K, Benjamin F; NH-0007-457

John Y; b1821; m Sarah J Corey; liv Colebrook, Lisbon NH; ch 1 dy, 7 others; NH-0007-454

CORLISS,

Alexander; s/o Elihu; liv Orford NH; ch Abigail m --- Bowles, John S, 3 others; NH-0007-566

Gen Cyrus; b1811 s/o Isaac & Dorothy Heath of Alexandria; m1832 Alma Reed d/o Samuel & Anna Sayles; liv Plymouth NH; ch Cyrus, Almira m Charles McQuesten, Frank R, Clara A m J H Morrison, George H b1846 m Eva Harvey, Emily m Martin Merrill; NH-0007-592

George H; b1846 s/o Gen Cyrus & Alma Reed of Plymouth; m Eva Harvey; ch Fred G, Cyrus L; NH-0007-592

James; s/o Willard & Catharine Spiller; m Deborah H Spiller d/o William W & Judith Cross; ch 1 dau m --- Fadden, 1 other; NH-0007-126

Willard; s/o William of Haverhill MA; m Catharine Spiller d/o John & Mary Fullsifer of Bridgewater; ch James m Deborah H Spiller, 5 others; NH-0007-126

COTTON,

Joel F; b1839; m1864 Lavinia F Gilman d/o Benjamin; liv Moultonborough NH, Charlestown MA; ch Curtis B, Fannie; NH-0006-415

William H; b1846 s/o Oliver & Sarah Furber of New Market; m1876 Persis A Wood of Lebanon; liv Lebanon; ch 1 son; NH-0007-96

COUCH,
Enoch; b1793; m Nancy Eastman &
m Jane O Stickney of Brown-
field ME; liv Boscawen NH;
ch/o Jane - Nancy E b1835,
Joseph b1837, Mary S b1844 m
Orlando Whitney; NH-0004-694
Hiram Morrill MD; b1818; m
Mahala Tilton; liv Georgetown
MA; NH-0004-617
Elder John; b1814; m1855 Almeda
Greeley & m Maria G Picker-
ing; NH-0004-617

COVELL,
Ebenezer; s/o Isaac Covil; m
Mary Fellows; ch Orin m Julia
A Kidder, Otis E, Loring G m
Mrs Burnside, Ezra S,
Eleanor, Freeman P m Rebecca
Hicks; NH-0005-586

COVIL,
Isaac; b1749; liv Enfield &
Colebrook NH; ch Content m
Asa Terry, Ruth m Danforth
Wallace, Sally m Ephraim
Benedict, Judah m Charlotte
Luther, Ebenezer Covell m
Mary Fellows, Nathaniel,
Daniel; NH-0005-586
Judah; s/o Isaac; m Mary
Fellows; ch James m Clarissa
Mills, William m Hannah
Corbett, Timothy m Abiah
Cogswell, John W m Phebe
Pulsifer, Joseph Y m Jane
Mills, Elmira m Mack
Springer, Mary P, Phebe A m
Samuel E Day; NH-0005-586

COWAN,
James Wellington MD; b1814 s/o
James & Harriet Fiske of
Pleasant Valley NY; liv
Dover; NH-0003-848

COX,
Daniel; s/o Capt Thomas &
Miriam Dearborn; m Charlotte
Smith d/o David & Charlotte
Haynes (Mary Haines) of N
Hampton NH; ch Thomas H m Ida
F Cummings d/o George F &
Angeline Baker; NH-0007-125 &
394
Edwin; m Arzelia Jane Pease d/o
Simeon D & Betsey Batchelder
of Meredith; liv Meredith NH;
ch Clarence; NH-0004-867
George L; s/o John; m Paulina
Moore of Ellsworth; liv
Amherst ME; ch Charles F m
Ella L Boynton d/o James W &
Louisa; NH-0007-394

COX (continued)
Moses M; s/o William & Eliza-
beth Folsom; m Louisa
Cummings; liv Holderness NH;
ch Willie H, Nathan B m Fanny
C Batchelder d/o Simeon & Ann
Banks; NH-0007-394
Robert; b1771 s/o Charles; m
Hannah Stanton d/o Isaac W of
Preston CT; ch Capt Russell,
Louisa m N S Calley; NH-0007-
394
Capt Thomas H; s/o Charles &
Mary Elliot; m Miriam Dear-
born d/o Samuel & Abigail
Ward of Plymouth NH; liv
Holderness NH; ch Daniel m
Charlotte Smith; NH-0007-125
& 394
William; s/o William & Fanny
Batey of Holderness; m Eliza-
beth Folsom d/o Benjamin &
Agnes; ch Moses M m Louisa
Cummings; NH-0007-394

CRAFTS,
Samuel; m --- Sturtevant of
Hebron; liv Hebron ME, Milan
NH; ch Rev F A, Col Welcome
A; NH-0005-833

CRAGIN,
Aaron H; b1821 s/o Aaron of
Weston VT gs/o Benjamin;
m1848 Isabelle Fuller; ch
Harry W; NH-0007-94
Augustus; b1802 s/o Francis
(Cragon) & Sarah Cummings;
m1830 Almira Boynton; ch
Daniel b1836 m Jane L
Dolliver, 9 others; NH-0002-
725
Daniel; b1836 s/o Augustus &
Almira Boynton; m1859 Jane L
Dolliver d/o John & Lucette
of Lyndeborough; liv
Merrimack NH, Wilton; NH-
0002-725

CRAGON (CRAGIN)
Francis, s/o John & Judith
Barker; m Elizabeth Law; liv
Temple; ch Francis b1773 m
Sarah Cummings, 2 others; NH-
0002-725
Francis; b1773 s/o Francis &
Elizabeth Law; m Sarah
Cummings; ch Augustus
(Cragin) b1802 m Almira
Boyton; NH-0002-725
John; m Sarah Dawes; liv SCO,
Woburn MA; ch John b1677 m
Deborah Skelton, 7 others;
NH-0002-725

CRAGON (CRAGIN) (continued)
John; b1677 s/o John & Sarah
Dawes; m Deborah Skelton; ch
John b1701 m Judith Barker, 2
others; NH-0002-725
John; b1701 s/o John & Deborah
Skelton; m Judith Barker of
Concord; liv Acton & Temple
NH; ch Francis m Elizabeth
Law, 8 others; NH-0002-725

CRAIG,
Charles C; b1849 s/o Amos of
Campton; m Mary A Merrill d/o
Reuben & Mary Blood; liv
Rumney NH, Quincy; ch Charles
J, Harry N, Hattie F m R R
Swett of Plymouth, Alice M,
Louise A; NH-0007-619

CRAIN,
Nahum; m Lydia ---; liv Dalton
NH; ch Ona b1806, Willard H
b1808; NH-0005-520

CRANDAL,
Joel; m Hannah ---; liv Dalton
NH; ch Nahum b1801; NH-0005-
519
Joel; m Susanna ---; liv Dalton
NH; ch Eliza b1808, Robert B
b1809; NH-0005-519

CRANE,
Alvin; m Betsey Streeter; liv
Dalton, Lisbon NH; ch Frank,
1 dau m Miles Bowles, Joel m
Nancy Daly, 1 dy; NH-0007-445
Ebenezer; m1822 Rebecca G
Russel of Dublin NH; liv
Dalton NH; ch M E; NH-0005-
526
Joel; s/o Alvin & Betsey
Streeter; m Nancy Daly; ch
Levi, Hosea, Adams m Polly
Daly, Joel, David m Betsey
Spooner, 3 sons, 8 dau; NH-
0007-445
John Summerfield; b1834 s/o
Luther & Rebecca Manter of
Springfield MA; m1856 Clara J
Smith of Nashua; liv Gilford
NH; ch Mazellah L; NH-0004-
780
Robert; m Polly ---; liv Dalton
NH; ch Juliana b1804, Maryan
b1806, Edward L b1808, Robert
Jr b1810; NH-0005-520
William; m Rhoda ---; liv
Dalton NH; ch Moses b1803,
Patty b1805, Otis b1807,
Viana b1809; NH-0005-520

CRAWFORD,
Abel; bc1765; m --- Rosebrook
d/o Eleazer; ch Ethan Allen

CRAWFORD (continued)
b1792 m Lucy Howe; NH-0005-
439
George; m Mary Y Glidden d/o
Charles Mills & Alice G
Smith; liv Portsmouth OH; ch
George W, John G, Minnie
Alice; NH-0004-545

CRESSY,
Cyrus; b1786 s/o Richard &
Susan Evans; m Hannah Sawyer;
liv Bradford; ch Hannah
b1812, William Sawyer b1813,
Jabez Woodbury b1815, Greeley
Miller b1819, Cyrus Miller
b1822, Addison Searl b1825,
Antoinette b1834; NH-0004-
199
Edward; m Eliza Jones d/o
Samuel & Elizabeth Andrews of
Bradford NH; liv Bradford; ch
James m ? & m Antoinette
Cheney d/o Savory, Mariette m
George Denny, Elizabeth m
Edward Richardson; NH-0004-
205
Richard; b1737; m Susan Evans
b1741 of Methuen; liv Beverly
MA, Hopkinton, Bradford NH;
ch Jabez b1762 dy, Hannah
b1764 dy, Susannah b1767 dy,
Mary b1770, Ebenezer b1773
dy, Richard b1775, Hannah
b1778, William b1781, Cyrus
b1786 m Hannah Sawyer; NH-
0004-199

CRIPPEN,
J J; m Helen F G Durrell d/o
David & Polly P Colby of
Bradford; liv Salina KS; ch
Henry D, J J Jr, Helen E; NH-
0004-217

CROCKETT,
---; m S Rebecca Randall; ch
Annie R m James Yeaton; NH-
0004-471
Samuel; b1780 s/o Capt Joshua
of Newburyport MA; m Sarah
Wilcomb; liv Meredith NH; ch
Col Seldon b1804 m Lucy
Eliott, 3 sons, 1 dau; NH-
0004-827
Col Seldon; b1804 s/o Samuel &
Sarah Wilcomb of Meredith NH;
m1831 Lucy Eliott d/o Thomas
& Susan Learned of Watertown
MA; liv Boston MA; ch Seldon
Frank, Sarah W m William W
Hague, Susan E m S Stillman
Blanchard, Grace H m J L
Grandin, Lucy E m S A

CROCKETT (continued)
Shannon; NH-0004-827
CROMBIE,
James; s/o John & Joan Rankin;
m Jane Clark d/o Robert of
Londonderry; liv Londonderry,
New Boston NH; ch John b1770
m Lydia Clark; NH-0002-609
John; m1721 Joan Rankin; liv
IRE, Londonderry NH; ch James
m Jane Clark; NH-0002-609
John; b1770 s/o James & Jane
Clark; m Lydia Clark d/o
Ninian Esq; liv New Boston
NH; ch Ninian Clark; NH-0002-
609
John Clark; s/o Ninian Clark &
Rebecca Patten; m Maria E Lee
of Toronto CAN; liv Elko NV;
ch Rebecca Patten; NH-0002-
609
Ninian Clark; s/o John & Lydia;
m1829 Rebecca Patten d/o Capt
Samuel of Derry NH; liv New
Boston; ch Nannie Moor m
Henry Hall, John Clark m
Maria Elea, Moses Colvard m
Carrie E Bell of Francestown
NH, Samuel Patten, Mary
Eliza, Samuel Patten, Hattie
Rebecca, James Patten; NH-
0002-609
William A; m Sarah L Murray d/o
Orlando Dana & Mary J
Wetherbee; liv Burlington VT;
ch William Murray, Arthur
Choate, Maud Elizabeth; NH-
0002-205
CROOKER,
Israel; s/o Stephen & Sally
Gage; liv Merrimack; ch Frank
W, Sarah, Mary m George Bean
of Merrimack, Ida m Charles
Wilson of Merrimack; NH-0002-
543
Stephen; m Sally Gage d/o Dea
Aaron; liv Merrimack; ch
Stephen D, Abner C, Simeon W,
Israel, James P; NH-0002-543
CROSBEE,
Dr Jonathan; m Hannah --- & m
Mary ---; liv Dover; NH-0003-
845
CROSBY,
Abel L; b1816 s/o William &
Sally Noyes of Groton; m1838
Pauline Phelps d/o Henry &
Sarah Wheet; liv Groton NH;
ch Artemas B b1839 m Annette
Hall & m1877 Mrs Lizzie
Carleton Sanderson, Mary P

CROSBY (continued)
b1844 m H L Ingalls; NH-0007-
293
Prof Alpheus; b1810 s/o Asa &
Betsey Hoit; m1834 Abigail
Grant Jones Cutler d/o Joseph
& Abi C Grant of Newburyport
MA & Martha Kingman d/o
Joseph Esq of W Bridgewater
MA; liv Sandwich NH, Salem
MA; NH-0001-247
Dr Asa; b1765 s/o Josiah & Sara
Fitch; m Betsey Hoit (Hoyt)
d/o Judge Nathan; liv Amherst
& Hanover & Strafford & Sand-
wich NH; ch Josiah MD b1794 m
Olive Light Avery, Judge
Nathan b1798 m Rebecca
Marquand Moody & Matilda;
Dixi b1800 m Mary Jane Moody
d/o Stephen of Gilmanton;
Alpheus, John, Thomas & 3
others; NH-0001-243, NH-0002-
125, NH-0006-730
Dixi MD; b1800 s/o Asa & Betsey
Hoit; m1827 Mary Jane Moody
d/o Stephen of Gilmanton NH;
liv Gilmanton, Laconia, Dart-
mouth, Sandwich & Hanover NH;
ch Prof Alpheus B d1877; NH-
0001-246
James J; b1823 s/o Samuel &
Elizabeth Bartlett gs/o Evan
Bartlett; m1848 Emeline E
Buel d/o Asahel & Lois Hardy;
ch Lois, Abial F, Minnie E;
NH-0007-388
Josiah; b1730; m Sara Fitch of
Bedford MA; liv Amherst NH &
Billerica MA; ch Dr Asa; NH-
0001-243
Josiah MD; b1794 s/o Asa &
Betsey Hoit; m1829 Olive
Light Avery d/o Daniel of
Gilford NH; liv Sandwich &
Manchester NH; ch Dr George A
& 2 sons & 2 dau; NH-0001-
244, NH-0002-125
Judge Nathan; b1798 s/o Asa &
Betsey Hoit; m Rebecca
Marquand Moody d/o Stephen
Esq of Gilmanton NH & m1870
Matilda Fearing d/o James
Pickens of Boston wid/o Dr J
W of Providence RI; liv Sand-
wich, Gilmanton NH, Amesbury,
Lowell, & Newburyport MA; ch
Frances Coffin m Dr Henry A
Martin of Boston, Hon Stephen
Moody, Maria Stocker m Maj
Alexander McD Lyon of Erie

CROSBY (continued)
PA, Ellen Grant m N G Norcross Esq of Lowell MA, Susan Coffin m Charles Francis s/o James of Lowell MA, Rebecca Marquand m Z B Caverly, and 3 others; NH-0001-245, NH-0007-87

Oliver; b1769 s/o Oliver of Bellerica MA; liv Dover NH, Atkinson ME; NH-0003-589

Thomas R MD; b1816 s/o Dr Asa & Betsey Hoit of Gilmanton NH; m Louisa Partridge Burton d/o Col Oliver; liv Gilmanton, Hanover, Meriden, Manchester, Dartmouth NH, Washington DC; NH-0001-248, NH-0007-334

William; b1784 s/o Jaazaniah; m1806 Sally Noyes of Hebron; liv Groton NH; ch David b1807, Elizabeth b1810 m Elam Ross, Abel L b1816 m Pauline Phelps; NH-0007-293

CROSS,
Bethuel; liv Wentworth, Orford NH; ch Hannah m Jonathan Clark s/o Benjamin, 6 others; NH-0007-565

David; b1772 s/o Abial of Salem NH; m Olive Kimball b1782 d/o Thomas & Olive Lovejoy of Pembroke; liv Weare, Salem NH; ch David b1817 m Anna Quackenbush Eastman; NH-0002-31

David; b1817 s/o David & Olive Kimball of Weare NH; m1856 Anna Quackenbush Eastman d/o Hon Ira Allen; liv Manchester NH; ch Clarence Eastman d1881, Allen Eastman d1864, Edward Winslow b1875, 2 dy; NH-0002-31

Ephraim; liv Salisbury MA, Haverhill, Piermont NH; ch Charlotte m William Gannet; NH-0007-575

Isaiah; bc1790; liv Landaff, Bath, Lyman, Monroe NH; ch Freeman H, 6 others; NH-0007-554

Nathan; m Sarah --- & m Mary ---; ch/o Sarah - Peter b1729, Sarah b1731; ch/o Mary - John b1735; NH-0002-461

Steven; m Peggy Bowen; ch Abraham m Ruth Sawyer of Canterbury; NH-0004-523

William; m Abigail Ladd; liv Methuen & Haverhill MA,

CROSS (continued)
Haverhill NH; ch David, Eliza, Lydia m Jacob Woodward s/o Judge James, 4 others; NH-0007-351

CULVER,
John; b1760; m1782 Dinah Post; liv Lyme NH; ch David b1797 m Mary Miller, 9 others; NH-0007-537

CUMINGS,
Jerahmael; b1711 bro/o Samuel Esq; m1736 Hannah Farwell; liv Groton MA, W Dunstable; ch Rev Henry DD, Capt Jotham; NH-0002-437

Capt Jotham; b1741 s/o Jerahmael; m1763 Anna Brown; liv Hollis; NH-0002-450

Samuel Esq; b1709 bro/o Jerahmael; m1732 Prudence Lawrence of Groton; liv Groton MA, W Dunstable, Hollis; ch Samuel, Thomas, Benjamin; NH-0002-437

Dea William; liv Groton?, W Dunstable, Hollis; ch Ebenezer, William, Philip; NH-0002-438

CUMMINGS,
Alvah; b1799 s/o Rev David of Swanzey NH; m1825 Polly Grout d/o Col Ebenezer; liv Acworth & Sullivan NH; ch Dr A R, Dr E G, Oscar, George A m Mary Lizzie Smith, Mary J m --- Young of Concord, Sally Ann m --- Young of Acworth, Laura m --- Smith of Acworth, Milon D; NH-0004-155

Archelaus; b1809; m Mary Fletcher sis/o Hiram A; liv Temple, Colebrook, Canaan VT; ch Edward N m Lucretia Merrill, Augusta P m Charles Parsons, Anna m John Buckingham of Boston MA; NH-0005-624

Daniel; b1796 s/o Henry of Plymouth NH; m Lois Kidder of Groton; liv Groton; ch Alice m Elbridge Tilton, Lois A m Alden Judkins, Daniel K, Henry, Adaline C m Romanzo J Hunkins, Frank E, James A; NH-0007-189

Daniel K; s/o Daniel & Lois Kidder of Groton; liv Bridgewater; ch Orville D, Emma M, Mary; NH-0007-189

Daniel M; b1810 s/o Warren of Cornish NH; m Emily M

CUMMINGS (continued)

Hamilton of Sharon VT; liv Woodstock VT, E Lebanon, Enfield; ch 10; NH-0007-264

Edwin N; m Lucretia F Merrill d/o Sherburn Rowell & Sarah B Merrill; ch Edward, Jane, John; NH-0005-643

Eleazer; b1701 s/o Nathaniel & Elizabeth; m1734 Mary Varnum of Dracut & m1764 Phebe Richardson of Litchfield; ch/o Phebe - Eleazer b1765, Phebe b1768; NH-0002-462

Eleazer; b1704 s/o Abraham; m Rachel Proctor; ch Eleazer b1730, Abraham b1734; NH-0002-461

Enoch P; m Dolly W Pillsbury d/o John & Susan Wadleigh of Sutton NH; ch Charles P; NH-0004-149

Ephraim; b1706 s/o Thomas; m Elizabeth Butler; ch Peter b1733, Sarah b1736, David b1738, Elizabeth b1740, Ephraim b1743, Hannah b1745, Priscilla b1747; NH-0002-461

Frank; m Hannah A Pease d/o Simeon D & Betsey Batchelder of Meredith; liv Holderness; ch Hannah I; NH-0004-867

Frank E; s/o Daniel & Lois Kidder of Groton; liv Natick MA; ch Etta Louise, Helen Augusta; NH-0007-189

George A; b1833 s/o Alvah & Polly Grout; m1854 Mary Lizzie Smith d/o Frederick P of Manchester NH; liv Franklin & Concord & Acworth NH; ch Frank G, Ida E dy; NH-0004-155

Henry; b1833 s/o Daniel & Lois Kidder of Groton; m1857 Hannah Bailey d/o Abel & Alfreda Foster; liv Plymouth NH; NH-0007-597

James A; s/o Daniel & Lois Kidder of Groton; liv W Plymouth; ch Mary Lois; NH-0007-189

John Sr; s/o Isaac of SCO; m Sarah Howlet; liv Topsfield MA, Dunstable; ch John Jr, Nathaniel, Sarah, Thomas b1659, Abraham, Isaac, Ebenezer; NH-0002-461

Jonathan; s/o Nathaniel of New Hampton NH; m Nancy Brown d/o Daniel of Bridgewater; ch

CUMMINGS (continued)

Joshua F m Lettice T Hannaford & m Jane Wilkinson; NH-0007-127

Joshua F; s/o Jonathan & Nancy Brown; m Lettice T Hannahford & m Jane Wilkinson of Guilford NH; ch S B, Jonathan; NH-0007-127

Noah; b1810 s/o Adams & Leah Hubbard of Lyndon VT; m1837 Almira J Kidder b1813 of Bristol NH; liv Colebrook NH; ch Daniel E m1874 Lucy A Eceleston of Rocks Brook RI, Elvira Cummings m1882 Milton Harriman; NH-0005-622

Stephen H; b1822 s/o Joseph; m1846 Maria T Newcomb of Orford & m1870 --- Mitchell wid/o David of Temple ME; liv New Hampton, Lisbon, Haverhill NH; ch/o Maria - Ada m --- Worthen, 3 others; NH-0007-369

William; b1702 s/o John Jr; m Sarah Harwood d/o William; ch Sarah b1728, Ebenezer b1730, John Harwood b1733, Dorcas b1737; NH-0002-461

William; b1741; m1768 Mehitabel Eastman of Hollis; liv Groton MA, Hollis & Hebron NH; NH-0002-450

Hon William Huse; b1817 s/o Joseph & Mary Huse of New Hampton NH; m1843 Harriet Sprague Rand d/o Hamlin & Harriet Sprague; liv New Chester, Haverhill, Lisbon NH; ch Harriet Sprague m O P Newcomb, William E, Mary Rand; NH-0007-455

CUMNER,

John; b1788 s/o Robert Francis & Sylvia Sturtevant; m1813 Hannah Thomas Bartlett of Bridgewater MA; liv Wayne ME & Bridgewater; ch Maryetta d1871, Francis d1881, James d1881, Cathamander, William B, John T, Nathaniel Wentworth b1829 m Harriet Elizabeth Wadley, Charles W, Benjamin G, & 2 dy; NH-0001-298, NH-0002-129

Nanthaniel Wentworth; b1829 s/o John & Hannah Thomas Bartlett of Wayne ME; m1856 Harriet Elizabeth Wadley d/o Moses D of Bradford NH; liv Wayne &

CUMNER (continued)

Wilton ME, Waltham & Lowell MA, Manchester NH, Washington DC; ch Harry Wadley VT b1860 m1884 Nellie B Pope d/o Edwin Esq of Boston, Arthur Bartlett b1871; NH-0001-299, NH-0002-129

Robert Francis; d1825; m1785 Sylvia Sturtevant; liv ENG, Wareham & Sandwich MA, Wayne ME; ch John b1788, Polly; NH-0001-297, NH-0002-129

CURRIER,

Aaron; s/o Samuel; liv Wentworth NH, Corinth VT; ch 1 dau m --- Haines, Sally m --- Currier, Ezra B, David D, Samuel, 7 others; NH-0007-640

Aaron; s/o Aaron & Abigail Huse; m Anna Hoag of Grand Isle VT; liv Plymouth NH; ch Phebe C, Daniel H, Mary A, James, Solon, Henry C, Eliza A, Armina J, Emily; NH-0007-590

Amos; b1768 s/o John & Sarah Clarke; m Mary Sargent d/o Dea Nathan; liv Hopkinton NH; ch Sarah b1797 m Benjamin Piper & m Jonathan Jones, Seth Franklin b1799, John b1802 m Mary Morgan, Charles Chase b1805, Hannah Sargent b1812 m1866 Dr J G Brown; NH-0004-414d

Daniel; s/o William; liv Plymouth NH; ch William m Sophia R Dow of Pembroke NH, Edwin m Mary A Smith d/o Crosley & Louisa B Smith, Jessie M m Edwin B Evens of Plymouth NH; NH-0007-127

Eben F; b1805 s/o Joshua & Mary Farrington; m1832 Sophia Noyes; liv Canaan NH; ch Moses E m Arabella Hadley, Amos N, Elizabeth R, Mary A; NH-0007-228

Frank D; b1813 s/o Horace S & Emma P of Canaan; liv E Canaan; NH-0007-75

Isaac; m Elizabeth Hadlock; liv Amesbury MA, Deering NH; ch Polly, John, Isaac m Lydia J Head, James m Mary A Howlet, Sarah m Daniel Cram; NH-0002-387

Isaac; s/o Isaac & Elizabeth Hadlock; m Lydia J Head; liv Manchester NH; ch John N m

CURRIER (continued)

Nancy Patten; NH-0002-387

James; s/o Richard; liv Enfield NH; ch L W; NH-0007-259

James A; b1819 s/o Chellis of Enfield gs/o Richard; m1847 Fanny Perkins of Lyme; liv Haverhill NH; ch John Rix, Leuella m Eben Heath of Danville VT; NH-0007-373

John; b1737 s/o Nathan & Mehitable Silver of Amesbury; m1761 Sarah Clarke; liv Amesbury MA, Hopkinton NH; ch John d1826, Clark d1813, Seth d1842, Anna m Moses Flanders, Hannah d1793, Sarah m Charles Chase, Stephen m Lucy Story, Priscilla m1804 Abram Davis of Hopkinton, James m Betsey Filman, Amos b1768 m Mary Sargent; NH-0004-414d

John; b1802 s/o Amos & Mary Sargent of Hopkinton NH; m1823 Mary Morgan; ch Celestia E m R T Crowell, Rosetta C m George Brown, Mary L m William E Greene & m1876 Alfred Poor, John F m Nellie H Putney; NH-0004-414d

John F; s/o John & Mary Morgan; m Nellie H Putney; liv Hopkinton NH; ch Mary M, Charles C, John, True P; NH-0004-414d

Joseph; s/o Thomas & Mary Osgood of Amesbury; m1708 Sarah Brown; liv Amesbury; ch Nathan b1710 m Mehitable Silver, 3 sons, 5 dau; NH-0004-414d

Hon Moody LLD; m 3 times; liv Manchester, Lowell MA; NH-0002-66

Nathan; b1710 s/o Joseph & Sarah Brown of Amesbury; m1736 Mehitable Silver; liv Amesbury; ch John b1737 m Sarah Clarke, 4 sons, 3 dau; NH-0004-414d

Capt Nathaniel; liv Eaton NH; ch Roderick E; NH-0006-791

R W; m Lucinda W Willis of E Lebanon; liv Enfield NH; ch David W dy, Mary L m Albert Merrill, Kate W m John H Hayes; NH-0007-263

Reuben W; m1820 Lois Sanborn Stevens d/o Benjamin & Lois Judkins of Brentwood; ch 10; NH-0003-190

CURRIER (continued)
Richard; b1617; m Ann ---; liv Salisbury & Amesbury MA; ch Thomas b1646 m Mary Osgood, Hannah; NH-0004-414d
Richard; liv Enfield, Salisbury; ch Jonathan G b1809, Mehitable, 8 others; NH-0007-326
Samuel; liv Hampsted & Wentworth NH; ch Aaron, David, Samuel, Daniel; NH-0007-640
Thomas; b1646 s/o Richard & Ann; m1668 Mary Osgood d/o William; liv Amesbury; ch Joseph m Sarah Brown, 8 sons, 3 dau; NH-0004-414d
CUSHING,
Daniel; m1786 Tamsen Hayes d/o Jonathan & Mary Wingate; ch Dea Peter; NH-0003-634
James R; b1800; m Hannah Lawrence & m Charity M Daniels; liv Salisbury NH, Haverhill MA; ch/o Hannah - 4; NH-0004-617
CUSHMAN,
Hartwell C; s/o Stephen; liv Orford NH; ch Peleg E, William A, Henry I, 1 dau m --- Wilson; NH-0007-568
Horace; b1802 s/o Parker b1773 of Charlestown NH; m Abigail Oakes & m Phebe Williams; liv Littleton & Lancaster & Dalton NH; ch/o ? - Edward F, Eliza A m --- Brooks, Charles M, Mary M m James D Harriman MD of Hudson MA, Cornelius J; NH-0005-527
Samuel; b1783 s/o Job of Hebron ME; m1812 Maria J Salter d/o John of Portsmouth; liv ME, Portsmouth NH; ch Elizabeth S m Hon Samuel Tither of Sanburton, 11 others; NH-0003-24
Stephen; liv Landaff, Orford NH; ch John J, Hartwell C, Rebecca m --- Blood, Ephraim, Asa; NH-0007-568
CUTLER,
Amos; b1762 s/o Capt Solomon & Rebecca Page; m1785 Elizabeth Carlton d/o James & Elizabeth Sherwin; liv Rindge; ch Charles b1796 m Melinda Wright, 4 sons, 4 others; NH-0002-666
Charles; b1796 s/o Amos & Elizabeth Carlton; m1831 Melinda Wright b1805 d/o Abel

CUTLER (continued)
& Zilpha Rice of Ashby MA & m1848 Esther Whitcomb of Saxton's River VT; liv Rindge; ch/o Melinda - John Harrison MD b1834 m Martha Louise Ryan; ch/o Esther - Virgil M; NH-0002-666
David; b1705 s/o Thomas & Sarah Stone; m Mary Tidd d/o Joseph & Mary; ch David, Joseph, Solomon b1740 m Rebecca Page & m Hepsebeth Bush, Thomas, Abigail Hodgman, Mary Page, 2 others; NH-0002-666
James; bc1606; m Anna & m1645 Mary King wid/o Thomas of Watertown & mc1662 Phebe Page d/o John; ch/o Anna - James b1635 m Mrs Lydia Wright; NH-0002-665
James; b1635 s/o James & Anna; m1665 Mrs Lydia Wright of Sudbury; liv Cambridge Farms; ch Thomas b1677 m Sarah Stone, 6 others; NH-0002-665
John Harrison MD; b1834 s/o Charles & Melinda Wright of Rindge; m1865 Martha Louise Ryan b1845 d/o Samuel & Hannah Shedd of Jaffrey; liv Greenville & Peterborough NH; ch Samuel Ryan b1866, Charles Henry b1867, Castella Melinda b1869, Martha Evangeline b1875, Anne Louise b1877; NH-0002-666
Capt Solomon; b1740 s/o David & Mary Tidd; m1761 Rebecca Page of Bedford & m Hepsebeth Bush of Stirling MA; liv Rindge NH; ch/o Rebecca - Amos b1762 m Elizabeth Carlton, 7 others; ch/o Hepsebeth - 2; NH-0002-666
Thomas; b1677 s/o James & Mrs Lydia Wright; m Sarah Stone d/o Samuel & Dorcas; ch David b1705 m Mary Tidd, 7 others; NH-0002-665
Zara; bc1785; m Mary Waldo d/o Mary gd/o Gen Israel Putnam; liv Conway, Lunenburg VT; NH-0006-265
CUTTER,
Calvin MD; b1807; liv Nashua & Dover & Jaffrey NH; ch Dr John Clarence; NH-0003-848
Charles W; s/o Jacob, liv Portsmouth; NH-0003-22
Daniel B MD; b1808; m

CUTTER (continued)
Clementine Parker of Jaffrey
& m Mrs Tryphena T Richardson
of Peterborough; liv Jaffrey,
Peterborough; NH-0002-664
Edward J MD; b1855; liv Peter-
borough NH, Boston MA; NH-
0002-668
John; m Abigail DeMary of
Rindge; liv Woburn MA,
Jaffrey NH; ch John m Betsey
Crosby of Jaffrey, 11 others;
NH-0007-212
CUTTING,
Ezra F; s/o Horace & Sophronia
Dimick of Lyme; m Fannie P
Mead; liv Lyme NH; ch Henry
P, Frank, Ada M, Annie B, Edd
M; NH-0007-536
Horace; s/o Col Zebedee & Phebe
Strong; m Sophronia Dimick;
liv Lyme NH; ch Adolphus D,
Ezra F m Fannie P Mead, Henry
P, Alfred, Clark T, 5 dau;
NH-0007-536
Isaac; s/o Isaac; m Acksah
Allen; liv Lyme NH, VT, CAN;
ch David, Hollis A, Eliza m
--- Townsend, Rachel m ---
Dimick, 1 son; NH-0007-536
James; s/o Zebulon of Hanover;
liv Haverhill NH; ch Joseph
B, John W b1818 m Eliza S
Woodbury, James L, Jerusha m
Benjamin Hatch, Julia m
Charles Bridgman, Laura m
Joseph McGreggor; NH-0007-364
John W; b1818 s/o James; m1844
Eliza S Woodbury of Haver-
hill; liv Haverhill NH; ch F
P, Helen A m J A Davis, John
H; NH-0007-364
Col Zebedee; bro/o Isaac &
Lathrop; m Phebe Strong; liv
Lyme NH; ch Dudley b1796 m
Mary Bixby, Horace m
Sophronia Dimick; NH-0007-536
Zebulon; liv Hanover; ch James,
Abijah; NH-0007-364
CUTTS,
Edward; s/o Edward of Kelley
ME; m Mary Hurke Sheafe d/o
Jacob of Portsmouth; liv
Portsmouth; NH-0003-21

-D-

DALEY,

DALEY (continued)
Daniel James; b1859; liv
Berlin; NH-0005-240
DALTON,
Samuel; s/o James & Elizabeth
Whitton of New Hampton NH; m
Mahaley Robinson; ch John M,
Alvin B, Ida, Charles L m
Harriet E Ingals d/o Josiah &
Lucy Ladd of Alexandria; NH-
0007-121
DAM,
John; m Elizabeth ---; liv
Dover; ch John m --- Hall d/o
Sergt John & m1664 Elizabeth
Furber d/o William, Elizabeth
b1649, Mary b1651, William
b1653 m Martha Pomfret d/o
William, Susanna b1661,
Judith b1666 m1684 Capt
Thomas Tebbets; NH-0003-770
William; m Martha Pomfrett d/o
William; ch Pomfrett; NH-
0003-772
DAMON,
Warren; s/o Daniel of Redding
MA; m Nancy Pierson d/o
Samuel & Abbey Hartshorn; ch
Warren m Adeline F Blaisdell,
2 sons, 3 dau; NH-0007-212
Warren, s/o Warren & Nancy
Pierson; m Adeline F
Blaisdell d/o Moses & Abra
Holmes of Campton; liv Lowell
MA, Campton NH; ch Charles H;
NH-0007-212
DANA,
Hon Samuel; b1739; liv Brighton
MA & Amherst NH; NH-0002-10
DANFORTH,
Dr Isaac; b1835 s/o Hon Albert
H of Barnard NY; m1868 Eliza-
beth Skelton d/o Rev John of
Chicago; liv Greenfield NH;
NH-0002-339
Nathaniel; liv Eaton NH; ch
Lucian, Lorinda m Jonathan
Kennison, Eliza m William
Lary; NH-0006-791
DANIELL,
J F; ch Hon Warren F, Frank H,
Susan K m Alvah Woodbury
Sulloway; NH-0004-324
Jeremiah F; m Sarah Reed of
Harvard MA & mc1838 Annette
Eastman of Concord; liv
Franklin NH, Pepperell & Dor-
chester & Methuen MA; ch/o
Sarah - Warren F b1826 m
Elizabeth D Rundlett & m
Abbie A Sanger, Mary dy; NH-

DANIELL (continued)
0001-235, NH-0004-324
Hon Warren F; b1826 s/o Jeremiah F & Sarah Reed; m1850 Elizabeth D Rundlett of Stratham NH & m1860 Abbie A Sanger of Concord; liv Franklin NH, Pepperell & Boston MA; ch/o Elizabeth - Harry W; ch/o Abbie - Eugene S, Otis, Warren F Jr, Jerie R; NH-0001-235, NH-0004-324

DANIELS,
Albert H; b1816 s/o Isaac & Rebecca Chapman; m1842 Elizabeth T Sherman d/o John of Smithfield RI; ch John S, Rebecca B m Horace F Caverno, Elizabeth D m Charles F Berry of New Durham; NH-0003-615
Isaac; b1782 s/o Peletiah; m1809 Rebecca Chapman; ch Enoch, Albert H b1816 m Elizabeth T Sherman, Rebecca; NH-0003-615
Peletiah; b1734; ch Ruth, Bridget, Peletiah, Sarah, Mehitable, Lydia, Andrew, Isaac b1782 m Rebecca Chapman; NH-0003-615

DARLING,
Daniel MD; b1816 s/o Daniel & Elizabeth Leavitt of Plymouth NH gs/o Daniel of Sanbornton; m1839 Sarah C Pillsbury d/o Tristram & Sally Buck; liv Concord & Wells River VT, Rumney NH; ch Elizabeth m Elisha A Webster, Lydia m David B Mears, Susan m Henry W Herbert of Rumney, Sarah, Daniel m Cynthia Southworth; NH-0007-608
Daniel; s/o Daniel MD & Sarah C Pillsbury; m Cynthia Southworth of Hill; liv Wells Rivert VT, Rumney NH; ch Daniel; NH-0007-608

DAVID,
Col James B; m Abigail Frances Shirley d/o Robert & Sophia McCutchins; liv Amherst, Somerville MA; ch James Quincy b1874; NH-0002-329

DAVIDSON,
Loammi Esq; m --- Tarleton d/o Col Ames of Piermont NH; liv Wentworth NH; NH-0007-112.19

DAVIS,
Ames; b1761; m Olive Veasey d/o Simeon of Stratham NH; liv

DAVIS (continued)
Amesbury MA, Stratham & Greenland NH; ch 2 dy, George W b1806 m Catherine M Henry, 6 others; NH-0003-309
Aquila; b1760 s/o Capt Francis & Elizabeth Ferrin; m Abigail Stevens d/o Theodore & Abigail Watts of Concord; liv Warner NH; ch Paine b1786, Sarah A b1788 m --- Virgin, Abigail b1790 m --- Davis, Theodore S b1792, Nathaniel A b1794 m Mary Clough, Persis H b1796 m --- Currier, Nathan b1799, 1 dau b1801 dy, Charles b1803, Aquila b1806, James b1809; NH-0004-413
Benjamin F; s/o George W & Sally Martin of Grafton; m Julia A Robinson; liv Grafton NH; ch Estella M; NH-0007-279
Charles; b1824 s/o Samuel of Plainfield; m Caroline T Miner d/o Elisha gd/o Thomas of Canaan; liv Canaan NH; NH-0007-231
Charles E; s/o Martin & Lydia Aldrich; m Ella George d/o Charles & Jane Bennett; ch Edwin A; NH-0007-122
Charles Frederick; b1837 s/o Eliphalet; m1860 Frances Sawyer b1838 d/o William & Jeannette McKeith Wilson George of Topsham VT; liv Cambridge MA, Bradford NH; ch Clara Jeannette Allen b1861 dy, Florence Bartell b1863, Lewis Warner b1865, Arthur Wilson b1867, Ida Carleton b1869, Marian Frances b1871, Sarah Wentworth b1878, Marhsall Graham b1882; NH-0004-200
Curtis; b1814 s/o Daniel & Mary Brown of Bradford NH; m1835 Martha Kemp b1818 of Pomfret VT; liv Cambridgeport MA; ch Christine Van Ness b1840 m James Mellen Jr, Ermina Frances bc1842, Curtis Rockwell, Mary Lizzie b1846 m Samuel Noyes Jr, Edwin Alberto dy; NH-0004-219
Dr Dana D; m Lavinia K Barlett d/o Levi & Hannah Kelly; ch William D m Louise Harding of VA; NH-0004-677
Daniel; b1766 s/o Isaac & Katuria Woodward; m Mary

DAVIS (continued)

Brown b1771; liv Bradford NH; ch Samuel b1790, Enoch b1791 dy, Enoch b1793, Dorcas b1795, Eliphalet b1796, Lydia b1799, Dimond b1802, Hiram b1807 m Marietta Ferrin, Lyman b1809 m Mary Eliza Palmer, Isaac b1811, Curtis b1814 m Martha Kemp; NH-0004-200 & 219

Darius K; bro/o Abel S & C B; m1854 Susanna E Howe; liv Northfield & E Haverhill NH; ch Addie D m Dr O D Eastman of Woodsville; NH-0007-370

David L; b1822 s/o David L & Alma Smith of Hanover; m1857 Lizzie R Peabody of Lebanon; liv Enfield NH; NH-0007-260

Dudley; s/o Samuel & Ruth Stevens; m Achsah Ballou & m Hannah Homans; liv Grafton NH; ch/o George W m Sally Martin, 9 others; NH-0007-279

Dr Ebenezer Harriman; s/o Samuel of Bradford; m 2; liv Manchester NH; ch 1 son; NH-0004-193

Capt Francis; b1723 s/o Francis & Joanna Davis of Amesbury MA gs/o Francis ggs/o Philip of ENG; m Elizabeth Ferrin b1724 d/o Jonathan & Sarah; liv Amesbury MA, Warner NH; ch Gertrude b1746, Zebulon b1748, Jeremiah b1751, Wells b1753, Ichabod b1755, Francis b1757, Elizabeth b1759, Aquila b1760 m Abigail Stevens, Paine b1762, Nathan b1764; NH-0004-413

George W; s/o Dudley & ? of Grafton NH; m Sally Martin of Grafton; liv Grafton NH; ch Mary Ann, Benjamin F m Julia A Robinson; NH-0007-279

George W; b1806 s/o Amos; m1850 Catherine M Henry b1814 d/o William & Julia English of Balston NH; liv Greenland NH, FL; ch George H dy; NH-0003-309

Hiram; b1807 s/o Daniel & Mary Brown; m1832 Marietta Ferrin b1809; ch Caroline Salome b1833 m1858 Frederick Martin, James Warren b1834 dy, Mary Jane b1836 m Jacob Jones, Harriet Newell b1839 m1858 Ira Sargent of Bradford; NH-

DAVIS (continued)
0004-201

Isaac; m Katuria Woodward; liv Plaistow, Bradford; ch Betsey b1760 m Stephen Ward, Molly b1762 m Abner Ward of Bradford, James b1764 m --- Brown, Daniel b1766 m Mary Brown, John b1768 dy, Susan b1770 m Moses Bailey, Sally b1772, John (Washington) b1774 m Sally Ward; NH-0004-200 & 219

James; liv Plaistow & Warren NH; ch Jonathan M b1809, 7 others; NH-0007-634

James; b1764 s/o Isaac & Katuria Woodward; m --- Brown; ch Daniel m Betsy Davis of Charlestown NH, Polly m Samuel Jackman of Enfield, Catharine m Isaac Ward s/o Abner, Betsy, Sally m John Ward, Dolly m Heman Burpee of Enfield NH, James m Lucy Davis d/o Joshua of Charlestown, Stephen, Sophronia m Benjamin Davis s/o Joshua of Charlestown; NH-0004-200

John (Washington); b1774 s/o Isaac & Katuria Woodward; m Sally Ward sis/o Stephen & Abner of Bradford; ch John S, Gardner, Harrison, Calvin, Hannah, Julia, Fanny, Preston; NH-0004-200

Joseph; b1813 s/o Oliver Jr & Relief Heath; m1840 Mrs Eliza Burns Wallace wid/o Dr John of Milford NH; liv Hancock; ch Charles J m Sarah Tubbs, Emma C dy; NH-0002-364

Joseph A; m Priscilla Merrill of Lyman; liv Bath Upper Village NH; ch Samuel M, Phebe M m Henry Chandler, Charlotte E m Henry M Peters of Manteno IL, Joseph A m Parthena E Haywood of Haverhill, 1 dy; NH-0007-145

Lyman; b1809 s/o Daniel & Mary Brown; m1841 Mary Eliza Palmer b1826; ch Curtis b1842, Homer Eliphalet b1845, Dorcas Jane b1848, Walter Farsons b1850, Caroline Elizabeth b1852, Samuel Dimond b1854, Joseph Hiram b1857, Lydia Frances b1859; NH-0004-201

DAVIS (continued)

Mard N; s/o Timothy & Mary Coffin; m Lucy Greenwood d/o Gilman & Bellona Reed; ch Timothy; NH-0007-214

Martin; s/o Samuel; m Lydia Aldrich of Grafton; ch Charles E m Ella George; NH-0007-122

Nathaniel A; b1794 s/o Aquila & Abigail Stevens of Warner NH; m Mary Clough of Boscawen; liv Warner; ch Stephen C b1830, Lucretia A b1830 dy, Walter Scott b1834, Gilman b1836, Lucretia A b1842, Mary E b1844, Stillman C b1846, Henry C b1850; NH-0004-413

Oliver; s/o Eleazer; ch Oliver Jr b1767 m Sally Pollard & m Relief Heath, David, Jonas; NH-0002-364

Oliver Jr; b1767 s/o Oliver; m Sally Pollard & m Relief Heath; liv Hancock, Acworth; ch/o Sally 6 dau & 1 son; ch/o Relief - Joseph b1813 m Mrs Eliza Burns Wallace, & 4 sons & 2 dau; NH-0002-364

Samuel; b1692 s/o James of Madbury; liv Madbury; ch Betsey b1753 m Elihu Hayes; NH-0003-643

Samuel; b1790 s/o Daniel & Mary Brown; liv Bradford; ch Ebenezer Harriman, Gilbert, Lydia, Elizabeth, Franklin; NH-0004-200

Stephen; bro/o Ezekiel & Francis; liv Wentworth; ch Irene m --- Lewis, John T, 2 others; NH-0007-569

Walter Scott; b1834 s/o Nathaniel & Mary Clough of Warner; m1857 Dollie Jones d/o Daniel Sr; liv Davisville; ch W S Bertine b1860 dy, Horace J b1862, Chassie H b1865 dy, Nattie A b1868 dy, Mamie A b1870, Charles b1874 dy; NH-0004-413

William H; b1832 s/o Eleazer of New Durham; m1857 Elizabeth Caverly d/o Dea Samuel of Tuftonborough NH & m Mrs Nancy L Smith Caverly; liv Tuftonborough NH; ch/o ? - Charles A, Willie E; NH-0006-445

DAY,

Charles H; m1867 Harriet Emmons

DAY (continued)

of Bristol; liv Rochester & Haverhill NH; ch 3; NH-0007-369

Timothy; m Judith Webster of Chester NH; liv Cape Ann MA, Enfield NH; ch David; NH-0007-258

DAYTON,

James; b1769; liv Hartford CT, Orford NH; ch Daniel, Capt Henry, Maria m --- Hodge, Eliza, 5 others; NH-0007-564

DEAN,

Isaac D; s/o Isaac & Theodora Robinson; m Elizabeth Wood of Lebanon; ch Watson m Mary Jones, 6 others; NH-0007-281

Josiah R; s/o Watson & Mary Jones; m Edna Prescott d/o John H & Mary Russell; ch Herman E; NH-0007-281

Watson; s/o Isaac D & Elizabeth Wood; m Mary Jones; ch David B, Sarah E, Charles H, Josiah R m Edna Prescott; NH-0007-281

DEANE,

Barnabas; s/o Robert & Eliza Webb; m Grace Dean; liv Ashland NH; ch Benjamin; NH-0007-128

John; s/o Robert & Eliza Webb; m Elizabeth Splain; liv Ashland NH; ch Robert, Lizzie, 1 other; NH-0007-128

Robert; s/o Benjamin of IRE; m Eliza Webb; ch Barnabas m Grace Deane, John m Elizabeth Splain; NH-0007-128

DEARBORN,

Asa; b1771 s/o Jeremiah of Kensington; m Ruhamah Choate; liv Portsmouth; ch Ruhamah m John Kent; NH-0003-111

Asahel MD; b1798 s/o Asahel & Elizabeth Drake of Effingham NH; m Louisa Dalton of Parsonsfield; liv Effingham, Hampton; NH-0006-555

Cornelius Van Ness; b1832 s/o Samuel & Fanny Brown; m1857 Louie Frances Eaton d/o Moses W & Louisa S of Francestown & gd/o Dr Thomas; liv Corinth VT, Francestown, Manchester, Peterborough & Nashua NH; ch John Eaton b1862, George Van Ness b1869; NH-0001-195, NH-0002-207

Edmund; b1789; ch Samuel G,

DEARBORN (continued)

Henry G, Thomas H B; NH-0004-523

Godfrey; m ? & m1662 Dorothy Dalton wid/o Philemon; liv Exeter ENG, Exeter NH; ch/o ? - Henry m Elizabeth Marrian, Thomas m Hannah Colcord & m Huldah Smith, John b1642 m Mary Ward, Sarah, 2 dau; NH-0003-328

Henry; s/o Godfrey & ?; m1665 Elizabeth Marrian; liv Exeter & Hampton NH; ch John, Abigail, Samuel, Elizabeth, Sarah, Elizabeth, Henry; NH-0003-328

Henry C; s/o Washington & Abigail Cook; m Frances M Shepard d/o Darwin & Laura of Ashland; ch Adelle C, George H, Alice M; NH-0007-130

Isaac; s/o Edward; m Olive Davis; liv Jackson NH; ch William, Mary, John L, Sally, James, Beckey, Eliza, Olive, George; NH-0006-952

J L; b1804 s/o John & Abigail Nelson of Sandwich; m1833 Huldah Avery of Franklin; liv Groton, Rumney NH; ch Ellen B dy, Abigail N m Lyman Merrill; NH-0007-611

Jeremiah; s/o Nathaniel gs/o Samuel ggs/o Henry gggs/o Godfrey; liv Kensington; ch Asa b1771 m Ruhamah Choate; NH-0003-111

Jeremiah W; b1832 s/o John & Sally Wadleigh of Parsonsfield ME; m1853 Mary G Smart; liv E Parsonfield ME, Effingham NH; NH-0006-554

John; b1642 s/o Godrey & ?; m1672 Mary Ward d/o Thomas; liv Exeter; ch John, Thomas, Mary; NH-0003-328

John; b1810 s/o Simon N & Hannah Towle of Hampton NH; m1838 Lydia Batchelder b1811 d/o Sandborn & Mary Elkins; liv Hampton NH; ch Orion M b1841, Mary Anna m Harry S Clark; NH-0003-328

Joseph Freese; b1710 ggs/o Godfrey; m1735 Sarah Sherborn (Sherburne) b1710; liv Hampton NH; ch Josiah b1738 m Sarah Freese; NH-0003-328

Joseph Freese; b1761 s/o Josiah & Sarah Freese; ch Simon N m

DEARBORN (continued)

Hannah Towle; NH-0003-328

Hon Joseph J; b1818 s/o Sewall & Sarah Dow gs/o Edward; liv Deerfield NH, Bangor ME; ch Joseph Henry; NH-0003-167

Josiah; b1738 s/o Joseph Freese & Sarah Sherborn (Sherburne); m Sarah Freese b1737; ch John, Joseph Freese b1761, Josiah, Sarah, Samuel, Anna, Samuel, Molley, Freese, Anna; NH-0003-328

Josiah; b1751 s/o Peter of Chester NH b1710; m Susannah Emerson d/o Samuel Esq of Chester NH; liv Chester & Weare NH, Corinth VT; ch Samuel b1792 m Fanny Brown, 10 others (9 sons); NH-0001-195, NH-0002-207

Nathaniel; s/o Dea John of Chester; liv Northwood, Deerfield; NH-0003-38

Samuel; b1792 s/o Josiah & Susannah Emerson; m Fanny Brown of Vershire VT; liv Corinth VT; ch Cornelius Van Ness b1832 m Louie Frances Eaton, & 6 others; NH-0001-196, NH-0002-207

Samuel Gerrish MD; b1827 s/o Edmund & Sarah of Northfield; m1853 Henrietta M Starrete of Mont Vernon; liv Mont Vernon, Milford, Nashua; ch Frank A b1857, Samuel G; NH-0002-201

Dea Simon; m Anne Gookins & m Martha Haven sis/o Rev Dr Samuel of Portsmouth & John; liv Greenland, Wakefield; ch 6 sons 5 dau; NH-0006-471

Simon N; s/o Joseph Freese; m Hannah Towle; liv Hampton NH; ch Sarah Ann m David Marston of Hampton, John b1810 m Lydia Batchelder, Simon, Dolly m Emery Batchelder of Hampton Falls, Lavinia m Joseph Leavitt of N Hampton, Abigail m Adna Lane of Hampton; NH-0003-328

Thomas; s/o Godfrey & ?; m1665 Hannah Colcord d/o Edward & m1701 Huldah Smith d/o John; liv Exeter; ch/o Hannah - Samuel, Ebenezer, Thomas, Jonathan; NH-0003-328

Washington; s/o Edwin & --- Rogers of Lincoln NH; m Abigail Cook of Campton NH;

DEARBORN (continued)
ch Henry C m Frances M Shepard, 3 others; NH-0007-130

DEERING,
Isaac; s/o Isaac; m Sarah Sawyer; ch Maj Arthur b1820, 3 dau, 7 sons; NH-0004-260

DEMERITT,
Jacob D; s/o Eli; m Martha V Barron; liv Madbury, Woodstock NH; ch James Y, Elizabeth L, Hiram B, Alaric B; NH-0007-643
John; b1813 s/o John & Betsey Leavitt; m Huldah L Davis b1811 d/o Dearborn & Sarah Leavitt; liv Effingham NH; ch Abronia L b1837, John L b1840, Sarah A b1842, Mary E b1847, Lucy C b1851; NH-0006-557
Mark; b1762 s/o Paul & Betsey Davis; m1816 Abigail E Leighton b1799 d/o Joseph of Farmington; liv Farmington NH; ch Charles M, Hannah m John Bickford of Rochester, John F, Martha E m William Wentworth of Farmington, Joseph L b1831, Paul L, Lois S m William Henderson of Rochester, Emma B m E P Hodsdon of St Louis; NH-0003-637
Paul; b1757; m1780 Betsey Davis; liv Madbury & Farmington NH; ch Susan m Benjamin Libbey, Hannah b1784, Lois m Joseph Hayes, Mark b1762 m Abigail E Leighton; NH-0003-637

DEMING,
Harvey; b1833; m Mary Elliott d/o Ira E; liv Bath NH; ch 3 son, 1 dau; NH-0007-144

DERBY,
Jedediah; liv Lyons, CT, VT; ch William H b1802 m Hannah Avery, Leander m Amanda Strong; NH-0007-543
William H; b1802 s/o Jedediah; m Hannah Avery of Orford VT; liv Troy VT, Lyme NH; ch John H b1832 m 1866 Ruhama E Gordon, Lewis S b1836 m Miriam S Pushee Miller wid/o Prosper; NH-0007-543

DEWEY,
George; b1805 s/o Luke of Hanover; m Laura A Chedel of Pomfret VT; ch Edward G, Henry G, Laura A, Mary J, Ellen M; NH-0007-314

DEXTER,
Clark; b1799; m Ruth Caswell; liv Lisbon NH; ch Francelia, 4 dau, 5 sons; NH-0007-449
Joseph; s/o Ephraim; m Mercy Streeter d/o Joel; liv Lisbon NH; ch Joseph m Lucy Ann Carlton, 1 dau m Henry Buzzell of N Lisbon; NH-0007-446

DICKEY,
Adam; m Betsy Furgurson; liv Londonderry, Deering; ch William m Mary Wilson, Jennie m David Wilson; NH-0002-385
William; s/o Adam & Betsy Furgurson; ch Betsy Jane dy, Alexander m Sarah McKeen, Angeline m Leonard McKeen, Mary m James S Allen, Eliza Jane, Caroline dy, Clara W m Gawn W Mills, Adam m Esther Smith, Caroline dy, William m Theresa Smith, Mandana, Perkins, 3 dy; NH-0002-385

DICKINSON,
Amos; b1815; m Huldah Bartlett d/o Daniel & Ruth; liv New Chester; ch Nellie F m O E Eastman, Sarah E m Roswell Blake, Watson A m Ella Sargent d/o B F of Lowell MA, Charles H m1876 Ida May Gordon d/o John B; NH-0007-186
Elijah; s/o Elijah; m twice; liv Amherst MA, Monroe NH; ch Andrew J, 13 others; NH-0007-553

DIMICK,
Alfred; s/o Dea Adolphus Dimock & Betsy Gilbert; m Lydia H Davison; ch William, Lucinda D m G P Amsden, Marie E; NH-0007-534
James P; b1804 s/o John Dimock & Abigail Gilbert of Lyme NH; m1830 Pamelia A Blanchard of Vershire VT; liv Lyme NH; ch Abbie A, Paulina D m A G Washburn, John G, Mary E dy, Charles H, James A; NH-0007-534
Shubael; s/o John Dimock & Abigail Gilbert of Lyme NH; m --- Gardner d/o William; ch 1 dau m L H Horton; NH-0007-534

DIMOCK,
Dea Adolphus; b1775 s/o Shubael
& Lydia Stearns; m1800 Betsey
Gilbert; liv Lyme NH; ch
Alfred Dimick m Lydia H
Davison, 11 others; NH-0007-
534
John; s/o Shubael; m Abigail
Gilbert; liv Lyme; ch Shubael
Dimick m --- Gardner, Daniel
Dimick, James P Dimick b1804
m Pamelia A Blanchard; NH-
0007-534
Shubael; m Lydia Stearns & m
Lydia Polk; liv Tolland CT,
Lyme NH; ch/o Stearns -
Shubael, John m Abigail
Gilbert, Capt David m Sally
Perkins & m Rachel Allen, Dea
Adolphus b1775 m Betsey
Gilbert, Samuel, 6 others;
NH-0007-534
DIMOND,
Furber G; s/o Reuben & Judith S
Goodwin; m Mary Currier d/o
David & Rhoda Morse; liv
Orange NH; ch Francis, Edward
C, Nellie M, Lillian M, David
A, Rhoda D, Willie L, Susie
M; NH-0007-558
Gould; s/o Isaac & Sally Shaw;
m Sally Rollins d/o Jonathan
of Loudon; ch Isaac P, Lucy M
m John B Moore of Gilmanton
NH, Mary E m Nathan C Clough,
Jonathan M m Maria Peaslee;
NH-0004-504
Isaac; b1767; m Sally Shaw; ch
Isaac, Betsy, Isaac, Sally,
Polly, John, Abigail, Andrew,
Gould m Sally Rollins, Ruth;
NH-0004-504 & 508
Jonathan M; s/o Gould & Sally
Rollins; m Maria Peaslee; ch
Ardena M, Saddie B, Inez P;
NH-0004-504
Reuben; s/o Gould & Dolly
Marden; m Judith S Goodwin of
Northfield NH; ch Furber G m
Mary Currier, 10 others; NH-
0007-557
DINSMORE,
Dr Daniel; bc1800; m ---
Mudgett d/o Elisha; liv
Conway, Dundee; ch Elisha M;
NH-0006-955
Elijah; s/o Samuel of Lee; liv
Conway; ch Elijah Jr, Stephen
m Mehitable Fry, Solomon,
John, Thomas, Lydia m
Ebenezer Hall of Bartlett;

DINSMORE (continued)
NH-0006-848
Elijah Jr; s/o Elijah of Conway
NH; liv Conway NH; ch Samuel,
Elijah, Daniel, Foxwell; NH-
0006-848
John; s/o Elijah of Conway NH;
ch Dean, John, Solomon,
Harriet m Jefferson Tufts,
Almira m Rev James McMillan
of Bartlett; NH-0006-848
John; b1781 s/o Robert & Sarah
Dinsmore; m Betsey Talbot of
Francestown; ch Horace Fuller
b1814; NH-0002-287
John; b1803 s/o John; m ---
McMillan & m --- Knox; ch/o ?
- Henry K, Abby m Moses
Davis, Almira m Joseph A
Cloutman; NH-0006-848
Joseph; s/o Stephen & Mehitable
Fry; m Lydia Hart; ch Martha
m Charles Whitaker, Andrew,
Eveline, Aurilla m Joseph
Nute, Honora m Lemuel Potter;
NH-0006-848
Robert; b1751; m Sarah Dickey;
ch John b1781 m Betsey
Talbot, Betsey b1796 m John
Dodge; NH-0002-287
Stephen; s/o Elijah of Conway
NH; m Mehitable Fry; ch
Joseph m Lydia Hart, John,
William, Stephen, Sarah m ---
Gilman, Polly, Nancy m Jacob
Webster; NH-0006-848
DIX,
Gov John Adams; b1798 s/o Col
Timothy Jr gs/o Timothy ggs/o
Jonathan; liv Boscawen NH;
NH-0004-178
DODGE,
Charles E; s/o William F; m Ida
Bray d/o Samuel L of White-
field; liv Manchester NH; NH-
0005-483
Charles William; b1842 s/o
Perley & Harriet Woodbury;
m1869 Rebecca C Christy &
m1878 Leila J Small; ch/o
Lelia Martha Belle b1882,
Maurice Whipple b1881 dy; NH-
0002-36
George Dudley; b1836 s/o George
Hubbard & Mary Keely; m1864
Marianna Laighton d/o Dr Wm
of Portsmouth; ch 4 sons, 2
dau; NH-0003-348
George Hubbard; b1807 s/o
Dudley gs/o Nathaniel
Hubbard; m1835 Mary Keely d/o

DODGE (continued)
Rev George of Haverhill MA; ch 4 sons, 3 dau, George Dudley b1836 m Marianna Laighton; NH-0003-348
Gideon; s/o James of New Boston; m1785 Charity Cole of Beverly MA; liv Bennington; ch John & 3 others; NH-0002-286
Hazen G; m Anna L Fisher d/o Levi & Fanny Wilkins; liv Merrimack; ch Elwin H; NH-0002-543
John; s/o John; m Polly Dodge & m Mary T Lovett; liv New Boston; ch/o Polly - Joseph A b1818 m Mary A Tewksbury, 2 others; NH-0007-591
John F; b1833 s/o Solomon & Susan Felch; liv Bennington; NH-0002-287
John W; b1815 s/o Daniel & Sally Wright of Hanover gs/o Dea John Wright; m1855 Mrs Clemantine Whipple d/o Henry H Chandler of Hanover; liv Enfield NH; ch Fannie L b1859; NH-0007-261
Joseph A; b1818 s/o John & Polly Dodge of New Boston; m Mary A Tewksbury; liv Plymouth NH; ch John, Lizzie m William R Park Jr of Plymouth; NH-0007-591
Levi MD; b1819; liv Francestown, Peterborough, Fall River MA; NH-0002-655
Levi B; b1822; m Hannah Cobleigh, Littleton NH, Lyndon VT; ch 1 dau m Carlos P Day, Marshall C m Martha A King of Landaff; NH-0007-488
Perley, b1799 s/o William & Rachel Poland of New Boston NH; m1831 Harriet Woodbury d/o Hon Peter of Francestown & sis/o Hon Levi; liv New Boston, Francestown, Amherst NH; ch Peter Woodbury b1839 m Sophia Phelps, Charles William b1842 m Rebecca C Christy, Martha W b1846 m1877 James B Whipple; NH-0002-35
Peter Woodbury; b1839 s/o Perley & Harriet Woodbury; m1863 Sophia Phelps; liv Amherst; ch Charles Perley b1864; NH-0002-36
William; b1795 s/o Simeon; m Eunice Newell; liv Frances-

DODGE (continued)
town & Whitefield NH; ch Eunice N, William Franklin, Levi W, Henry C; NH-0005-466
DOE,
Charles Currier; b1823 s/o James & Patience Langley; m1845 Mehitable P Davis d/o Amos & Nancy Libby of Epsom NH; liv Epsom NH; ch Walter C b1846 m Elva Cass of Epsom, Amos b1849 m Mellie Hobnan of Dixfield ME, James A b1852 m Augusta Ladd of Deerfield NH, Sarah A b1854 m Calvin D Clark of Barnstead NH, George W b1857; NH-0004-474
Eugene G; b1849 s/o Oliver & Lovina P Colton of Rumney; m1876 Hattie M Swain; liv Rumney NH; ch Harry E, Frank J b1879, Harold O; NH-0007-613
James; s/o John; m Patience Langley; liv Durham & Lee & Barrington NH, Grafton, Pittsfield; ch John m Abby Davis, Nancy m John Garland of Nottingham, Drucilla m L Kimball & m Moses Brown of Andover, Abigail m John T Gilman, Charles Currier b1823 m Mehitable P Davis, Gilman L m Nancy Ellenwood, Mary J m David Garland of Nottingham, Hezekiah H m --- Sleeper; NH-0004-474
Oliver; b1821 s/o Jacob & Sarah Jones; m1846 Lovina P Colton; liv Rumney NH; ch Warren W, Eugene G b1849 m Hattie M Swain, Ellen M, Belle M; NH-0007-613
DOLE,
Charles Augustus; b1834 s/o Stephen & Martha of Lunenburg MA; m1863 Caroline L McQuesten of Plymouth & m1866 Helen M Stevens of Haverhill; liv Haverhill, Wentworth, Lebanon; ch/o Helen - 2 dau; NH-0007-112.25
Erastus; s/o Henry & Sarah Butler; m Samantha Cook d/o Moody & Lucy Eaton & m Flora E Hoyt d/o Dr Peter L & Elizabeth A Davis; liv Limerick ME, Campton NH; ch/o ? - Moody C, Herbert E; NH-0006-211
Henry; s/o Henry & Anna Poore;

DOLE (continued)
m Sarah Butler d/o John & Sarah of Newbury MA; ch Erastus m Samantha Cook & m Flora E Hoyt, Moses C m Lucy Cook d/o Moody & Lucy Eaton & m Sarah E Blair d/o Judge Walter & Eliza Farnum; NH-0007-211

DOLLOFF,
Abraham; mc1793 Rachel Locke sis/o Benjamin; liv Bristol NH; ch Levi m Roxy Locke d/o Benjamin, 2 sons, 6 dau; NH-0007-183

Orrin L; b1833 s/o Levi & Roxia Locke; m1859 Clarinda Elliot d/o Daniel & Dorcas Baker; liv Bridgewater NH; ch Alba O m Nellie Vose d/o John & Emily Haywood of Alexandria, 1 dau m Frank H Elliot of Concord, Mabel M b1868, Maud M b1868; NH-0007-175

DOLPHIN,
Matthew; m Sarah Shirley d/o John & Margaret Houston; ch George Alfred b1867, Carrie Shirley b1869; NH-0002-329

DORE,
Ezekiel; liv Wakefield, Ossipee; ch Hermon R, Jacob C; NH-0006-627

DORR,
Charles; b1789; m Phebe Hobbs of Newfield ME & m Mary Shackford d/o Nathaniel C; liv Newington, Wakefield; ch George S b1851 m Fannie H Twombly; NH-0006-529

George S; b1851 s/o Charles & Mary Shackford of Wakefield; m1884 Fannie H Twombly d/o Daniel & Frozilla of Wolfeborough; NH-0006-529

DOW,
Daniel G; m Eliza Chase d/o Edward & Mary Patten; ch Harriet m Lawrence Keiley, Amos C m Sarah S Nichols, Daniel G m Jennie Raymond, Edward C m Roanna Chase & m Emily A Webber, Ann C m Gilbert P Hill; NH-0002-381

Ernest W; s/o Lt Samuel H & Catharine L Munson; m Blanche Hinman of Munnsville NY; ch Helen K; NH-0007-215

Dr Jabez; b1776 s/o Nathan & Elizabeth Bachelder of Kensington NH; liv Dover NH; NH-

DOW (continued)
0003-357 & 846
Jeremiah; m Mary Hall of Strafford & m Mrs Mary Wentworth d/o Gee & Phebe Littlefield Nason of Dorchester; liv Newmarket & Barnsted NH; ch/o ? - Lt Samuel H m Catharine L Munson, 10 others; NH-0007-215

Joseph Emerson; s/o Gen Moses of Haverhill; m Abigail Arnold d/o Hon Jonathan of RI & m Nancy Bagley of Thornton; liv Littleton & Franconia NH; ch/o Abigail - Catherine dy, James Barber, Moses Arnold b1810 m Elizabeth T Houghton, George Burrill, Charles Marsh; NH-0007-99 & 271

Gen Moses; s/o John of Atkinson; m Phebe Emerson; liv Haverhill, ch 2 sons, 2 dau; NH-0007-80

Moses Arnold; b1810 s/o Joseph E & Abigail Arnold; m1835 Elizabeth T Houghton of Andover MA; liv Littleton & Franconia NH; ch Mary m Rev G R W Scott, Emma m Leonard F Cutter; NH-0007-271

Dr Samuel; b1802 s/o Dr Jabez of Dover; liv Dover; NH-0003-847

Lt Samuel H; s/o Jeremiah & ?; m Catharine L Munson; ch Walter H m Clara A Osgood, Ernest W m Blanche Hinman, Mary C m Dea William Chase of N Tisbury Martha's Vineyard; NH-0007-215

Walter H; s/o Lt Samuel H & Catharine L Munson; m Clara A Osgood d/o Luther & Eliza Sanburn; liv Campton NH; ch Luther O; NH-0007-215

DOWE,
Charles Byron; b1828 s/o Ulysses & Esther Owen of Hanover; m1833 Vina H Ross d/o Isaac & m Ellen Smith wid/o E B Foster; liv Hanover NH; ch/o Vina - Lemuel A; NH-0007-322

Lemuel; s/o Ephraim b1701 gs/o Thomas & Susanna of Ipswich MA; m Annie Millington; liv Coventry CT, Hanover NH; ch Susanna, Abigail, Anna, Lydia, Solomon, Leumuel Jr m Triphena Dodge; NH-0007-322

DOWE (continued)
Lemuel Jr; s/o Lemuel & Annie Millington; m Triphena Dodge; liv Hanover NH; ch Francis b1791 m Mary L Church, Minerva, Tryphena, Ulysses b1808 m Esther Owen, 2 dy; NH-0007-322
Solomon; s/o Lemuel & Annie Millington; ch Solomon Jr, Agrippa; NH-0007-322
Ulysses; b1808 s/o Lemuel Jr & Triphena Dodge of Hanover; m Esther Owen; liv Hanover NH; ch Charles Byron b1828 m Vina H Ross & m Ellen Smith, Ellen E m Orlando C Blackmer; NH-0007-322
DOWLIN,
Timothy; b1799 s/o Timothy Leavitt & Elizabeth Collins; m1824 Catharine Hawks d/o Farrington; ch Elizabeth Collins b1826 m Moses E Gould, Timothy Leavitt b1828 m1868 Sarah Jane Ingraham, John Hawks b1829 m1853 Ella Frances Colby of Warner, Sarah Jane b1831 m1851 Alfred Colburn Smith, Mary Ann b1832 m --- Flanders of Manchester NH, Abby Hawks b1834 m1854 Ezra Dow Cilley of Manchester, George Washington b1836, Marshall Richardson b1839 m Sophia Ann Magoon, Louisa Catharine b1841 m --- Bradstreet; NH-0004-201
Timothy Leavitt; b1762 s/o William & Sarah Norris; m1790 Elizabeth Collins; ch --- b1791 dy, --- b1793 dy, Samuel b1794, Deborah b1796, Dolly b1798 dy, Timothy b1799 m Catharine Hawks, --- b1803, William Jr b1805, --- b1807, Polly b1809 dy, Caroline b1811 m Cummings Pierce, Irene b1813 m Patrick Scully; NH-0004-201
William; b1720; m Sarah Norris of Epping NH; ch Anne b1755, Timothy Leavitt b1762 m Elizabeth Collins, Elizabeth b1764 dy; NH-0004-201
DOWNING,
Joshua; m Patience Chase of Weare; liv Henniker; ch John m Sally Chase, Joshua Jr m Sarah Loveren, Lydia m William Forsaith, David dy,

DOWNING (continued)
Judith dy, Mary m Samuel Dunlap, Stephen m Mrs Eliza P White, Daniel dy, Nathan m Martha Clark, Abial m David Gregg, Peter m Mary A Gutterson; NH-0002-380
Lewis; b1792 s/o Samuel & Susanna Brown; m1815 Lucy Wheelock d/o Jonathan & Lucy Beaman; liv Lexington MA, Concord NH; ch Lucy Maria b1818, Lewis Jr b1820, Alonzo b1822, Mary Ann b1826, Emily b1828, Ellen b1828; NH-0004-140
Samuel; b1757; m Susanna Brown d/o Benjamin & Sarah Reed of Lexington & m Eunice Bridge of Lexington; liv Lexington MA, Newbury NY; ch/o Susanna - Polly b1783, Oliver b1785, Samuel b1787, Susanna b1788, Sally b1790, Lewis b1792 m Lucy Wheelock, William b1796; ch/o Eunice - Emily b1801, Charles b1802, George W b1804, Andrew J b1815, Fanny dy; NH-0004-140
DRAKE,
Abraham; s/o Robert; m Jane ---; ch Susannah, Abraham b1654 m Sarah ---, Sarah b1656, Mary b1658, Elizabeth b1660, Hannah b1662, Robert b1664; NH-0003-425
Abraham; b1654 s/o Abraham & Jane; m Sarah ---; ch Sarah b1686, Abraham b1689 m Theodate Roby, Jane b1691 m John Shurborne, Mary b1692 m Shubar Sanborn, Nathaniel b1695 m Jane Lunt; NH-0003-425
Abraham; b1689 s/o Abraham & Sarah; m Theodate Roby; ch Elizabeth b1712 m Jeremiah Page, Theodate b1713 m Josiah Sanborn, Abraham b1715 m Abigail Weare, Samuel b1717 m Esther Hobbs, Sarah b1720 m Samuel Batchelder, Mary b1722 m Elisha Marston, Abigial b1724 m John Taylor, John b1728 dy, Simon b1730 m Judith Perkins, Thomas b1733 m Patience Towle; NH-0003-425
Carr L MD; b1798 s/o John & Mary Leavitt of Effingham; m1821 Margaret Titcomb of Effingham; liv Effingham NH,

DRAKE (continued)
Tamworth, Ossipee; NH-0006-555
Cyrus K; m Lucinda Morse; liv Effingham NH; ch Olin M MD b1847 m Mary Whiting of Ellsworth ME, Thomas N MD b1858 m Florence E Thomson of Pittsfield ME; NH-0006-556
Capt Daniel; liv Taunton MA; ch Sybil m Benjamin Bullock, 10 others; NH-0007-278
Dr Darvis; m --- Quigg d/o Abel G; liv Chester NH, Westford MA; NH-0003-148
Evan; s/o Capt Reuben of Hollis; m Sarah Philbrook of Weare NH; ch Sarah m Nathan Cram, Reuben, Hannah m Jonathan Cram, Lydia m Loiel Cram, Evan Jr m Nancy Balch of New Boston NH; NH-0002-384
Col James; liv Pittsfield NH; ch Frank J, Georgianna Butters b1836 m Josiah Carpenter, Nathaniel S; NH-0001-46
John; liv ENG; ch John, Robert b1580; NH-0004-256
Joseph; m Mary Wells; liv Goffstown, Deering; ch Joseph dy, Benjamin, Daniel dy, Roxanna dy, David m Lucretia Alcock, Sarah m James Ross, Freeman m Mary Alcock, Lyman m Eliza Wood & m Esther Hadley, Hiram; NH-0002-385
Oliver; b1830 s/o Thomas & Mehitable of Chichester; m1862 Sallie S Knowlton d/o Hosea C Esq of Chichester; liv Chichester NH, Boston & Lynn MA, Greenville CA; ch Alma K, 1 son 2 dau; NH-0004-256
Capt Reuben; liv Salem, Hollis; ch Daniel, Stephen m Abigail Jewett, Evan m Sarah Philbrook; NH-0002-384 & 451
Robert; b1580 s/o John of ENG; liv Devon Co ENG, Exeter & Hampton NH; ch Nathaniel, Susannah, Abraham m Jane ---; NH-0003-425, NH-0004-256
Samuel; b1717 s/o Abraham & Theodate Roby; m1743 Esther Hobbs; ch Theodate b1744 m Samuel Page, Elizabeth b1745 m John Fogg, Mary b1747 m Stephen Coffin, Esther b1749 dy, Samuel b1751 m Mary

DRAKE (continued)
Jenness, John b1753 m Huldah Lane, Esther b1756 m Benjamin Dearborn, Sarah b1759 m James Hobbs, Abigail b1761 m John Jenness; NH-0003-425
Samuel; b1751 s/o Samuel & Esther Hobbs; m Mary Jenness; ch Abraham b1783, Abigail b1784 m Moses Batchelder, Theodate b1786 m Joseph Jenness, Mary b1788, Samuel b1790 m Elizabeth Berry, Ebenezer T b1792 m Abigail Berry, Elizabeth b1795 m Thomas Brown, Sarah b1798; NH-0003-425
Stephen; s/o Capt Reuben of Hollis; m Abigail Jewett of Hollis; liv Deering; ch Lois m Christie Duncan of Hancock NH, Stephen m --- Hall of Groton MA, Hannah m --- Spaulding, Nathaniel m --- Aimes, Jeremiah m Sally Eastman, Abigail m Timothy Wyman Jr of Hillsborough NH; NH-0002-384
Thomas; s/o Abraham gs/o Abraham; liv Epping & Chichester NH; ch Josiah; NH-0004-256
Thomas; b1796 s/o Josiah of Chichester; m Mehitable Seavey d/o Daniel of Chichester; liv Chichester NH; ch Oliver b1830 m Sallie S Knowlton, Simon S, Francis, Samantha T, Sallie, Joanna M; NH-0004-256
DREW,
Amos W; b1808 s/o Benjamin & Sally Harriman; m1835 Julia Esther Lovering d/o Hubbard & Abigail Bumford; liv Stewartstown NH; ch 6 son dy, Lucy Abigail b1843, Irving W, Benjamin F, Warren E, Ellen J, Holman A, Edward Everett; NH-0005-678
Benjamin; b1785 s/o Samuel & Betsey Webber; m Sally Harriman d/o John & Sally Heath of Hampstead; liv Bridgewater, Stewartstown; ch Amos W b1808 m Julia Esther Lovering, Edwin W b1827 m Marietta Hall, Benjamin, 1 son, 3 dau; NH-0005-678
Edwin W; b1827 s/o Benjamin & Sally Harriman; m1852

DREW (continued)

Marietta Hall d/o Luther F & Mary Piper of Stewartstown; liv Stewartstown NH; ch John W, Walter, Carrie m F H Noyes, Byron, Alice, Hattie H; NH-0005-682

Hon Irving Webster; b1845 s/o Amos W of Colebrook; m1869 Caroline (Carrie) H Merrill d/o Sherburn Rowell & Sarah B Merrill of Colebrook; liv Lancaster NH; ch Niel, Pitt, Sara M; NH-0005-231 & 643

Joseph; s/o Levi & Mary Baker; m Elizabeth Wallace d/o Nathaniel of Moltonboro NH; ch Asa m Nancy Chase d/o Parker & Polly of Campton NH, 8 others; NH-0007-127

Levi; m Mary Baker; liv New Hampton & Madbury NH; ch Joseph m Elizabeth Wallace, Benjamin m Elizabeth Greeney, 3 others; NH-0007-127

Samuel; liv Loudon NH; ch Hitty, Joseph, Judith, John, Stephen, Samuel, Sally, Nathan, Altazera; NH-0004-508

Samuel; m Betsey Webber; liv Shapleigh ME, Plymouth, Bridgewater; ch Benjamin b1785 m Sally Harriman; NH-0005-678

William; s/o Sir Edward; liv ENG; ch John b1642; NH-0005-678

DUDLEY,

A T; m Polly Hoyt d/o Joseph & Mary Patterson; ch Dorr m Lydia Gould d/o John, Horace, Betsey m Solon Wright; NH-0007-324

Jason Henry; b1842 s/o Jonathan & Minerva Armstrong; m1869 Lucy A Bradford d/o Dr Austin & Aurelia Bissell of Vergennes VT; liv Colebrook NH; ch Allen B b1871, William H b1873 dy; NH-0005-252

Jonathan; d1872 s/o Jacob gs/o Samuel P ggs/o Stephen gggs/o Stephen gggg-s/o Samuel; m Minerva Armstrong; liv Andover & Hanover NH; ch Jason Henry b1842 m Lucy A Bradford; NH-0005-252

Gov Thomas; d1653 s/o Capt Roger of ENG; liv MA; ch Joseph, Samuel; NH-0005-252

DUNCAN,

Christy; s/o James & Jane Christie; m Lois Dow; ch Lydia A m Rev --- Stone of Cabot VT, Sarah m Rev Daniel Rice, James, Stephen D, John m Mrs Almira P Wilkins, Nathaniel, Elizabeth; NH-0002-354

George; s/o George; m Margaret Cross & m 1 other; liv IRE, Londonderry NH; ch George; NH-0002-354

George; s/o George; m Letitia Bell; liv IRE, Londonderry NH; ch Robert m Sarah Todd, Hon John, & 5 others; NH-0002-354

Hiram; bc1805 s/o Samuel & Sarah Miller; liv Jaffrey; ch Sarah Miller m Hon Peter Upton; NH-0002-354

James; m Jane Christie; liv Hancock; ch Sarah m Samuel Fox, Letitia m Martin Fuller, George, Susan m John Brooks, James, Christy m Lois Dow, Rebecca m Hon T P Fuller of Hardwick VT, Isaac; NH-0002-354

John; s/o Christy & Lois Dow; m Mrs Almira P Wilkins; liv Hancock; ch George C, Christy H; NH-0002-354

Robert; s/o George & Letitia Bell; m Sarah Todd d/o Col Andrew of Londonderry; liv Hancock; ch Dea Josiah; NH-0002-354

Samuel; m Sarah Miller of Peterborough; ch Hiram bc1805; NH-0002-354

DUNLAP,

Archibald; m Martha Neal d/o Joseph of Chester; liv IRE, Chester NH; ch Maj John Dunlap b1746 m Martha Gilmore, & m 2 others; NH-0001-264, NH-0002-211

Hon Archibald Harris; b1817 s/o John & Jennie Nesmith of Antrim; m1841 Lucy Jane Fogg of Exeter d/o Josiah Raymond gd/o Maj Josiah of Hampton & Chester; liv Antrim & Nashua NH; ch James H, Georgia A, John F(P), Abbie J, Charles H; NH-0001-264, NH-0002-211

Maj John; b1746 s/o Archibald & Martha Neal of Chester; m Martha Gilmore; liv Chester

DUNLAP (continued)
  NH, Bedford; ch John m Jennie
  Nesmith, Robert N, Hon
  Archibald Harris; NH-0001-
  264, NH-0002-211
John; s/o Maj John & Martha
  Gilmore; m1807 Jennie Nesmith
  d/o Dea Jonathan of Antrim;
  liv Chester, Antrim; ch Hon
  Archibald H b1817, Robert;
  NH-0002-211
DUNN,
  Ellery D; b1822; m Susan Dow of
  Littleton; liv Wilton ME,
  Littleton NH; ch 1 dau; NH-
  0007-492
  Leonard E; m Ellen Chandler d/o
  John; liv Dummer NH; NH-0005-
  858
DURELL,
  Daniel Meserve; b1769 s/o
  Nicholas of Lee; liv Dover;
  NH-0003-589
DURRELL,
  David; b1807 s/o Nicholas of
  Bradford NH; m1836 Polly P
  Colby d/o Samuel & Sally
  Patch; liv Bradford; ch
  Lizzie S m Walter S Leach,
  Mary Elvira, Helen F G m J J
  Crippen; NH-0004-217
  Joseph; s/o Eliphalet; m Olive
  Garmon; liv Gilford & Gilman-
  ton NH; ch Nicholas, Thomas
  b1798 m Sarah Hutchinson,
  Polly m Jerry Hutchinson; NH-
  0004-806
  Nicholas; m Polly Batchelder of
  Northwood; liv Bradford NH;
  ch Samuel, David b1807 m
  Polly P Colby, Levi, Mary m
  Levi O Colby; NH-0004-217
  Thomas; b1798 s/o Joseph &
  Olive Garmon; m1819 Sarah
  Hutchinson d/o Levi & Esther
  Melcher & m1862 Mrs Francis A
  Burns; liv Gilmanton &
  Laconia NH; ch/o Sarah -
  Joseph B, Ann M m John
  Wallace of Sanbornton, Martha
  C dy, Sarah A m George
  Folsom, Thomas F, Eliza J m
  Hiram Richardson of Concord,
  Lewis E, Charles W; NH-0004-
  806
DUSTIN,
  Ira; s/o Samuel of Haverhill
  MA; m Nancy Hall of Thornton;
  ch Ezekiel m Elsie B
  Parmenter of Sterling; NH-
  0007-129

DUSTIN (continued)
  Moses; liv Stark NH; ch Sarah
  b1790, Lois b1791, Marcy
  b1793, Rachel b1795, Olive
  b1797, Alice b1798, Almira
  b1800; NH-0005-570
  Nehemiah; m Betsey Ann Smith
  d/o John Jr & Betsey Burnham;
  ch David G, Ziba H, Eben R;
  NH-0007-263
DUSTON,
  David; s/o Obadiah gs/o Thomas
  of N Salem NH; m Abiah
  Duston; ch Ruth, Abial,
  Thomas, David, Obadiah b1806
  m Anne Whittaker & m Fidelia
  Cook, Mary, Ebenezer; NH-
  0003-482
  Obadiah; b1806 s/o David &
  Abiah Duston; m1831 Anne
  Whittaker of Haverhill MA & m
  Fidelia Cook wid/o Edward; ch
  Hannah m John Hallowell of
  CA, Ruth, Harriet m John N
  Hunt of Bradford MA, Thomas m
  Augusta Griffin of Hampstead
  NH, Elizabeth, Lorin; NH-
  0003-482
  Thomas; m Hannah ---; liv N
  Salem NH; ch Thomas, Obadiah,
  Caleb; NH-0003-482
DYER,
  Elisha; m ? & m Lucy Curtis;
  liv Stewartstown NH; ch/o ? -
  Marshall, Betsey, Orville,
  Jerub b1806, Joseph b1809;
  ch/o Lucy - George Nelson
  b1811, Fannie b1813, Mary Ann
  b1815, William C b1818, John
  b1824; NH-0005-664

-E-

EAMES,
  Jeremiah; m Anna ---; liv
  Northumberland & Stewartstown
  NH; ch Jeremiah, Anna,
  William, Lois b1799, Persis
  b1801, Cyrus b1804, Hiram
  b1806, Emily b1808, Susan
  b1809, Adeline b1812; NH-
  0005-664
EASTBROOK,
  Hobart; s/o Joseph gs/o Dea
  Nehemiah; m twice; liv
  Lebanon NH; ch Anna m ---
  Hurlburt, 1 dau, 2 sons; NH-
  0007-420

EASTMAN,

---; m Martha Peaslee d/o Maj Jacob & Martha Chellis of Kingston; ch Jacob P; NH-0003-382

Dea Abiathar; s/o Richard & Molly Lovejoy; m1775 Phebe Merrill d/o Thomas; ch Samuel, Lydia m Frye Holt, Abiathar b1781 m Susan Durgin, Henry m Esther Eastman, Thomas m Eunice Hill, Caleb dy, Caleb m Adeline Yolpy; NH-0006-844

Abiathar; b1781 s/o Dea Abiathar & Phebe Merrill; m Susan Durgin; ch Rev Benjamin Durgin b1802 m Lois F Averill & m Nancy Fisher Whitney; NH-0006-844

Lt Amos; b1751 s/o Amos Sr of Pennacook NH; m1774 Ruth Flagg; liv Hollis NH; NH-0002-451

Arza; b1812; m Maria Winch of Bethlehem; liv Littleton NH; ch Charles B, Maria m George Bowman, Willard, Lewis m Mary Moore, Ina A m Orissa Clough; NH-0007-487

Asa; b1770 s/o Jonathan & Molly Chandler of Concord ggs/o Capt Ebenezer of Pennacook; m Molly Kimball; liv Chatham NH; ch Jonathan Kimball b1796 m Phoebe W Clements, Hon Philip b1799, Susan, Mary C, Eliza, Robert K, Asa P, Esther J; NH-0006-984

Rev Benjamin Durgin; b1802 s/o Abiathar & Susan Durgin; m Lois F Averill & m Nancy Fisher Whitney; liv ME, N Conway NH; ch/o ? - Charles W, George Vernon; NH-0006-844

Benjamin H; m Julia A Merrill d/o David & Sarah Lee; liv Holderness NH; ch Daniel W m Emma P Ray d/o Benjamin F & Ann L of Nantucket MA, Charles W; NH-0007-395

Col Cyrus; b1814 s/o Jonathan & Sally Heath of Danville VT; m1838 Susan French Tilton of Danville VT & m1868 Mrs Julia Ross Brackett; liv Littleton NH; ch/o Susan - Lucia W m H P Ross, Charles F, Martha A m Lorenzo C Kenney, Laura B; NH-0007-492

Maj Daniel; b1792 s/o Noah &

EASTMAN (continued)

Hannah Holt of N Conway; m Martha Chadbourne d/o Dr William; ch William C; NH-0006-844

Hubert; s/o Moses & Sally Smith; m Louisa Rice; liv Haverhill; ch Wilbur F, 1 dau m John Chamberlin of Bath; NH-0007-137

Hon Ira Allen; b1809 s/o Capt Stephen & Hannah of Gilmanton NH gs/o Lt Ebenezer; m1833 Jane Quackenbush d/o John N Esq of Albany liv Troy NY, Gilmanton NH; NH-0004-39 & 796

Dr J C; b1811 s/o Dr Joseph & Miriam Calef; m Ann A Wilson d/o Capt Leonard & Elizabeth Gregg & m Mary Helen Harris d/o Dr Jerome & Mary Tewksbury of Amesbury MA; liv Hampstead NH; ch/o Ann - Mary Bartlett m Mrs Lavosier Hill of New York City, Ella; ch/o Mary - Josiah Bartlett, Susie A; NH-0003-316

James; s/o Stephen & Miriam Quimby; m Polly French; ch Larnard L, Richard B, Mary F m George Smith of Plainfield, Stephen, James Jr m Susan L Williams; NH-0007-332

James Jr; s/o James & Polly French; m Susan L Williams; liv Hanover NH; ch Stephen, Martha J m C A Manning MD, James F; NH-0007-332

James; b1753 s/o William & Rebecca Jewett of Bath NH; m Mary Searles; liv Bath NH; ch James, Moses m Sally Smith, Amos dy, Searle m Rebecca Bailey & m Sally Moulton, Mary, William, Joel m Lucretia Rix, Eber; NH-0007-137

Joel; s/o James & Mary Searles of Bath NH; m Lucretia Rix; ch Alfred W; NH-0007-137

Joel; b1760 s/o Edward gs/o Thomas ggs/o Samuel Esq; m Betsey Pettengill b1762 of Sandown; ch Joel b1798 m Ruth Gerrish Odell; NH-0006-266

Hon Joel; b1798 s/o Joel & Betsey Pettengill; m1832 Ruth G Odell of Conway; liv Conway NH; NH-0004-617

Jonathan; s/o William & Rebecca

EASTMAN (continued)
Jewett of Bath NH; liv Littleton; ch Jonathan, Simeon, Lwis, Arza; NH-0007-137
Jonathan Kimball; b1796 s/o Asa & Molly Kimball of Chatham; m Phoebe W Clements b1803 d/o Jacob & Phoebe Coffin of Gorham ME; ch Asa b1825, Jacob C b1827, Jonathan b1830, Caroline C b1833 m Ithiel E Clay, Mary A C b1835, Kimball b1839; NH-0006-984
Dr Joseph; s/o Timothy & Abigail Gale; m Miriam Calef d/o Joseph & Miriam Bartlett; liv E Kingston, Meredith NH; ch Dr J C b1811 m Ann A Wilson & m Mary Helen Harris, Susan m Lorenzo Bachelder of Derry, Joseph; NH-0003-316
Moses; s/o James & Mary Searles of Bath; m Sally Smith of Bath; ch Melissa m Solon S Southard, Hubert m Louisa Rice, Wilber F, Calista, Susan, Lucia m Moses Abbott, Henry, Ruth, Abbie; NH-0007-137
Hon Moses; b1770; m Sukey Bartlett & m Eliza Sweetser; ch/o Sukey - Joseph Bartlett AM b1804 m Mary Huse d/o John of Hill; ch/o ? - Elbridge G; NH-0004-617
Nehemiah; b1782 s/o Ebenezer of Gilmanton; liv Farmington; NH-0003-601
Noah; b1753 s/o Richard & Molly Lovejoy; m1775 Hannah Holt; liv N Conway NH; ch Benjamin, Noah, Noah, Esther, Maj Daniel b1792 m Martha Chadbourne, Hannah H, Polly C, Richard, Job, Susan, Frye H, John, Phebe B; NH-0006-844
Obadiah; s/o William & Rebecca Jewett of Bath NH; m Elizabeth Searles of Temple NH; ch Betsey, Hannah, Rebecca, William, Jonathan, Seaborn, Peter, Stephen R; NH-0007-137
Richard; m Molly Lovejoy; liv Pembroke, Conway, Fryeburg; ch Squire Richard Jr m Abiah Holt, Noah b1753 m Hannah Holt, Dea Abiathar m Phebe Merrill, Jonathan; NH-0006-844

EASTMAN (continued)
Squire Richard Jr; m Abiah Holt sis/o Hannah; liv N Conway NH; ch Sally m Abiel Lovejoy, Jonathan m Phebe Lovejoy, Polly m Amos Barnes, Phebe m Humphrey Cram, Hannah m Isaac Merrill, Richard m Elmira Morrill & m Louisa Morrill, Abia m William C Ford, William m Nancy Lovejoy & m Ruth Trickey, Dorcas m Samuel Merrill, Patty m Jonathan Stickney, Kezia m Henry Tucker, Betsey m John Hill, Amos m Betsey E Merrill, Clarissa m Rev Stephen Merrill, Harriot m Gen George P Meserve, John L m Margaret Douglass, Irena m Jonathan E Chase; NH-0006-844
Richard H; m Mary Nye Weeks b1813 d/o James Brackett & Elizabeth Stanley; ch Mary m1886 James Weeks Jr; NH-0005-382
Royal; b1816 s/o Richard of Falmouth ME; liv Somersworth; NH-0003-604
Rufus H; b1831 s/o Benjamin H of Holderness; m1855 Martha H Belcher of Stoneham MA; ch 2; NH-0007-396
Searle; s/o James & Mary Searles of Bath NH; m Rebecca Bailey & m Sally Moulton; ch/o ? - Priscilla M m Ebenezer C Stevens, Orrin, Joel m Ellen Moulton of Lyman; NH-0007-137
Stephen; s/o William & Ruth Chase of Bath NH; m Lydia Ford; liv Lyman; ch Pamelia, Clarinda, Eber, Stephen A, Abbie S, Dan, Solenda; NH-0007-137
Thomas; m Lydia Holmes; liv Hopkinton & Holderness NH; ch Thomas m Sarah Howe d/o Ebenezer, 5 others; NH-0007-395
Thomas; liv Hopkinton, Bridgewater NH; ch Aquilla, John, Thomas, Stephen b1784 m Sally Emmons & m1834 Sally Piper wid/o Reuben, Benjamin, Hannah m Jonathan Fellows; NH-0007-172
Timothy; m Abigail Gale d/o Col of E Kingston; liv Raymond, E Kingston; ch Dr Joseph m

## EASTMAN (continued)

Miriam Calef; NH-0003-316

William; bc1814 s/o Jonat & Hannah of Haverhill MA; m1838 Ruth Chase & m Rebecca Jewett; liv Bath NH; ch/o Ruth - Ruth, Stephen m Lydia Ford, William Jr; ch/o Rebecca - Obadiah m Elizabeth Searles, Hannah m Dea John Ladd of Haverhill, Azubah m Nathan Judd, James b1753 m Mary Searles, Moses m Azubah Snow & m Lois Martin, Jonathan, Peter, Amos; NH-0007-137

William Jr; s/o William & Ruth Chase of Bath NH; ch Stephen m Lydia Ford, Miriam m Capt John Barber; NH-0007-137

William W; b1850 s/o Sylvester & Louisa Whitcher of Joy NY; m1879 Georgia A Aldrich; liv Benton; NH-0007-152

## EATON,

---; ch Ebenezer b1757 m Hannah French, Nathaniel b1767, John b1765 m Phebe Brockway, Joshua b1768 m Sarah Hoyt & m Anna Blaisdell Hill; NH-0004-208

Albert; b1830 s/o Joshua & Anna Blaisdell Hill; m1851 Augusta Colby of Sunapee b1832; ch Joshua A b1854 dy, Mary J b1856, Ardell b1862 dy; NH-0004-208

Ebenezer; b1757; m1780 Hannah French b1759; ch Abigail b1783, Samuel b1785, Elisha b1788, Hannah b1792; NH-0004-208

Elisha; b1788 s/o Ebenezer & Hannah French; m1811; ch E H b1816 m1840 Roena F Ayer b1818; NH-0004-208

Frederick; b1835 s/o John & Janet Cole Andrews; m1861 Mary Helen Shirley d/o Robert M & Sophia McCutchins of Goffstown; liv Bradford, Manchester, Toledo OH; ch Helen b1866 dy; NH-0002-329, NH-0004-651

George Roscoe; b1837 s/o Stephen W & Marianda B Knox of Portland ME; m1860 Sarah J Parker; liv Berlin & N Stratford & Lancaster NH; ch Minnie P, Georgie May, Sadie Jane; NH-0005-388

## EATON (continued)

Harrison MD; b1813 s/o Moses & Judith Merrill; m1838 Charlotte M Eaton of Hopkinton & m1868 Harriet N Lane of Candia; liv S Weare, Merrimack; ch Henry Harrison b1839; NH-0002-547

James; m --- McClure & m ?; liv Deering; ch/o McClure - John, David, Samuel, James, Isaac, William, Polly m David Bass, Roxanna m Isaac Wilkins, 1 son; NH-0002-386

Job; b1671 s/o Thomas & Eunice Sangletery; m1698 Mary Simons; ch Thomas b1701 m Mehitable ---, 3 others; NH-0004-211

John; m Anna ---; liv ENG, Salisbury & Haverhill MA; ch Thomas John; NH-0005-388

John; s/o John & Anna; liv Salisbury MA; ch John; NH-0005-388

John; s/o Nathaniel & Mary Dodge; m Mary Kimball d/o Caleb & Sarah Sawyer; ch Frederick, Ruth m Robert Sherburn of Concord, Rebecca, John m Janet Cole Andrews, Sarah m Samuel Dresser, Hiram, Lucretia K, Jacobs MD, Charles, Lucien B, Rev Horace DD m Anna R; NH-0004-651

John; s/o Wyman & Ruth Merrill of Hampton NH; m Jemima Green; liv Buxton ME; ch Tristram b1781, 8 others; NH-0005-388

John; b1733 s/o Thomas & Mehitable; m Abigail Peasley b1734 & m Sarah Clarke; ch/o Abigail - Ebenezer, Mehitable m Daniel Cressey, Nathaniel, Daniel, John, Joshua b1768 m Sarah Hoyt & m Mrs Anna Blaisdell Hill; ch/o Sarah - Thomas, Abigail m Benjamin Colby, Elizabeth m Nathaniel Gould; NH-0004-211

John; s/o John & Mary Kimball; m Janet Cole Andrews; ch John b1829, Caroline b1831, Nathan Andrew b1833, Frederick b1835 m Mary H Shirley, Lucien Bonaparte b1837, Christina Landon b1839, James Andrew b1841, Charles b1843; NH-0004-651

Gen John; m Alice Shirley d/o

EATON (continued)

James & Adeline Quincy; ch James Shirley b1868, Elsie b1871, John Quincy b1873; NH-0002-329

John Hill; b1819 s/o Joshua & Anna Blaisdell Hill; m1841 Hannah T Twiss of Newbury b1823 & m1852 Mary J Lawrence b1823 of Alstead; ch/o Hannah - Roxana B b1846 dy, Ellen M b1848 m1880 Charles E Palmer, Hannah M b1850 m1879 Frederick A Messer; ch/o Mary - Martha J b1853 m1879 Lawrence E Davis, Louisa L b1854 m1881 Dolman C Hoyt; NH-0004-208

Joseph; s/o John; ch John; NH-0005-388

Joshua; b1768 s/o John & Abigail Peasley; m Sarah Hoyt & m1817 Mrs Anna Blaisdell Hill b1788 of Amesbury MA; liv Haverhill MA, Bradford NH; ch/o Sarah - Moses b1793 m Polly Presbury b1796, Mary b1795 m1815 John Brockway b1793, William A b1800 m Hannah Morse, Sarah b1805 m Simeon Shattuck, Martha b1808 m1833 Osman Bailey b1806; ch/o Anna - Joshua b1817 m Alzina E Gillingham & m Mrs Louisa A Niel Plumer, John Hill b1819 m Hannah T Twiss & m Mary J Lawrence, Roxana B b1823 dy, Daniel b1827, Albert b1830 m Augusta Colby; NH-0004-208 & 211

Joshua; b1817 s/o Joshua & Anna Blaisdell Hill; m1840 Alzina E Gillingham b1823 d/o James & Elizabeth of Newbury & m1852 Mrs Louisa A Niel Plumer b1823 d/o Samuel & Lois Clark McNeil of Weare NH; liv Bradford NH; ch/o Alzina - Alzada b1841 m1866 Benjamin F Hoyt, Alzira b1841 dy, Alverton b1843 dy, Alzina b1848; ch/o Louisa - Joshua Willis b1856 m Nettie E Boyce; NH-0004-208 & 211

Joshua Willis; b1856 s/o Joshua & Mrs Louisa A Plumer of Bradford; m1877 Nettie E Boyce b1858; ch Ethel E b1878; NH-0004-208 & 211

Moses; s/o Maj Nathaniel; m Judith Merrill d/o Dea David;

EATON (continued)

liv Hopkinton; ch Harrison MD b1813 m Charlotte M Eaton, David; NH-0002-547

Nathaniel; m Mary Dodge of Lunenburg MA; ch John m Mary Kimball, Elijah, Nathaniel; NH-0004-651

Samuel; m Susanna Noyes; liv Atkinson & Landaff NH; ch Timothy b1790 m Martha Northy, Ebenezer b1792, Phebe, Lydia, Samuel, 7 others; NH-0007-398

Stephen W; s/o Tristram of Buxton ME; m Miranda B Knox of Portland; liv Portland ME; ch Stephen M, Samuel K, George Roscoe b1837 m Sarah J Parker, Minnie m Myron Hovey of Boston, Charles P, Woodman S, Howard B, Edward; NH-0005-388

Thomas; m ? & m1658 Eunice Sangletery of Salisbury MA; liv Haverhill; ch/o Eunice - Job b1671 m Mary Simons, 8 others; NH-0004-211

Thomas; b1701 s/o Job & Mary Simons; m Mehitable ---; ch John b1733 m Abigail Peasley & m Sarah Clarke, Timothy, Mehitable; NH-0004-211

Timothy; b1790 s/o Samuel & Susanna Noyes; m Martha Northy of Lisbon; liv Landaff NH; ch John, Betsey, James, Samuel A; NH-0007-398

Wyman; b1725 s/o John of Salisbury MA; m1745 Ruth Merrill; liv Hampton NH; ch John m Jemima Green; NH-0005-388

EDES,

Hiram J MD; b1815; liv Peterborough NH, MO, Cedar Rapids IA; NH-0002-667

EDWARDS,

Capt Ebenezer; b1757; m Lucy Wheeler of Lincoln MA & m Mary Flint of Lincoln MA; liv Acton MA, Sharon & Temple NH; ch/o Lucy - Nathaniel b1785 m Sarah Wilson, 10 others; ch/o Mary - 4; NH-0002-676

Nathaniel; b1785 s/o Capt Edwards & Lucy Wheeler; m1808 Sarah Wilson of New Ipswich; ch Sarah, Mary, Abby, Susan W, Maj Supply W b1817 m Elizabeth Winn, Elizabeth, Nathaniel P, Charles W; NH-

EDWARDS (continued)
0002-676
Maj Supply W; b1817 s/o
Nathaniel & Sarah Wilson;
m1840 Elizabeth Winn b1820;
liv Temple NH; ch John
Wheeler b1844, Charles Warren
b1847, George Walter b1849,
Edwin Brooks b1851, Emma
Josephine b1853, Alma Jane
b1856; NH-0002-676
ELA,
George W; b1807 s/o Joseph &
Sarah Emerson of Portsmouth
NH; m Mary Adelaide Lane of
Sutton; liv Dover & Concord
NH, Allenstown; ch 1 dau dy,
Maj Robert Lane b1838, Capt
Richard b1840; NH-0004-162b
Israel; d1700; m Abigail Bos-
worth; liv Haverhill MA; ch
John b1683 m Rachel Page, 1
son, 3 dau; NH-0004-865
Jacob; bc1711 s/o John & Rachel
Page; m ? & m Mrs Edna Little
Gale; liv Haverhill MA; ch
John bc1740 m Ruth Whitter, 7
others; NH-0004-865
John; b1683 s/o Israel &
Abigail Bosworth of Haverhill
MA; m Rachel Page; ch Jacob
bc1711 m ? & m Mrs Edna
Little Gale, 4 others; NH-
0004-865
John; bc1740 s/o Jacob & Mrs
Edna Little Gale of Haverhill
MA; m Ruth Whittier; ch
Nathaniel W b1766, John
Whittier b1766 m Mehitable
Dame; NH-0004-865
John Whittier; b1766 s/o John &
Ruth Whittier; m1793
Mehitable Dame of Durham NH;
liv Durham & Lee & Barnstead
NH; ch Ednah, Joseph b1797 m
Sally Miller Moulton, John;
NH-0004-865
Joseph; b1797 s/o John Whittier
& Mehitable Dame; m1832 Sally
Miller Moulton d/o Jonathan
of Meredith; liv Norway
Plains, Meredith NH; ch Laura
E m Daniel S Bedee & m Alvin
Peavey, John W, Charles H,
Ednah m George E Gilman,
Luella C dy; NH-0004-865
William S; b1807 s/o Benjamin &
Abigail Emerson of Lebanon;
m1832 Louisa R Greenough of
Lebanon & m1871 Elizabeth
Kendrick; liv Lebanon NH;

ELA (continued)
ch/o Louisa - Richard E, 1
son dy; NH-0007-424
ELDREDGE,
Rev Erasmus Darwin; b1804 s/o
Dr Micah & Sally Buttrick of
Dunstable MA; m Isabella Hill
of Portsmouth NH; liv Hampton
& Salisbury & Kensington NH;
ch Mary m Rev Dr Lane of GA,
Rev Henry E, Frederick E; NH-
0003-355
Marcellus; b1838 s/o Heman of
Chatham MA; liv Portsmouth;
NH-0003-113
ELKINS,
Elder Daniel; m ? & m --- Gray
sis/o Daniel; liv Jackson NH;
ch/o ? - Polly m David Gould;
ch/o Gray - Daniel, Joseph,
Granville, Rebecca m Asa
Davis, Joanna m John T Lucy,
Eunice m James C Trickey,
Ruth m James C Trickey; NH-
0006-954
David H; b1831 s/o David B &
Mary Batchelder of Hampton
NH; m1856 Mary E White b1836
d/o Nejmain & Mary Green of
Phillipston MA; liv Woburn &
Milton MA, Hampton NH; ch
Mary A dy, Benjamin W, David
H, Lizzie E, Albert W, Mattie
L, John W, Herbert G; NH-
0003-351
Gershom; s/o Henry & Mary;
m1667 Mary Sleeper d/o
Thomas; liv Hampton; ch
Jonathan b1668, Moses b1670,
Mary b1674, Joanna b1677,
Henry, Samuel m Mary Tilton,
Thomas b1682; NH-0003-351
Granville; s/o Elder Daniel &
--- Gray of Jackson NH; ch W
E, 1 dau m --- Davis, Albert;
NH-0006-954
Henry; m Mary ---; liv Boston,
Exeter, Hampton; ch Gershom m
Mary Sleeper, Eliezer (Eliza)
m1673 Deborah Blake d/o
Jasper; NH-0003-351
Henry; s/o Jeremiah; m Susannah
Clough & m Mary Sweatt; liv
Kingston, Danville; ch/o
Susannah - John m Luella B
Philbrick, Abel, Thomas,
Eleanor, Susanah; NH-0003-164
Jeremiah; liv Kingston, Dan-
ville; ch Henry m Susanna
Clough & m Mary Sweatt, 2
others; NH-0003-164

ELKINS (continued)
Jeremiah; b1795; m Sarah G Emerson & m Mary A Bunker; liv Andover & Meredith NH; NH-0004-703
John; s/o Henry & Susannah Clough; m1843 Luella B Philbrick d/o Josiah & Sarah Quimby; liv Danville; ch Sarah Frances m George M Cook of Exeter, Charles Henry, Mary Ellen m Alden E Spoffard, Susan Emily, Herman Foster; NH-0003-164
Jonathan; m Sally Philbrick; liv Haverhill NH; ch Rev Moses b1801; NH-0007-363
Moses; m1701 Amiah Shaw; liv Hampton, Kingston; ch Obadiah b1708 m Abi French, 6 sons, 4 dau; NH-0003-376
Obadiah; b1708 s/o Moses & Amiah Shaw; m1731 Abi French; ch Jacob b1734, Obadiah Jr b1741, Peter b1746, Joseph b1751; NH-0003-376
ELLINGWOOD,
John; m Rachel Barrows of Bethel ME; liv Milan NH; ch Hester Ann, Isaac H, John W, Freeman, 2 others; NH-0005-831
ELLINWOOD,
James S; s/o John & Ruth Baker; m Rachel G Turner; ch Frank P m Maria P Bartlett, Mary S, Flora J, Clara E m Myron E Johnson, Sarah Lyzzie, Clark S, Scott L; NH-0002-385
John; s/o Rolandson & Abigail Hildreth; m Ruth Baker, ch John B m Lenora Alcock & m Evatine Page, James S m Rachel G Turner, Mary dy, Abigail dy, Ruth S m Luther Cheney; NH-0002-385
Joseph; s/o Rolandson & Abigail Hildreth; ch Nancy m --- Long, Hattie m John Burbank, Joseph, Phineas, Eunice, Abbie m --- Walker, Horace, Mary Ann m Charles Joy; NH-0002-385
Rolandson; m Abigail Hildreth & m Eunice Nichols; liv Amherst, Deering NH; ch/o Abigail - David m Alice Aiken, John m Ruth Baker, Abigail m Phineas Wilkins, Joseph; ch/o Eunice - Charles, Mary Jane m Benjamin

ELLINWOOD (continued)
Nickerson, Eliza m Joseph Nickerson, David m --- Stetson, Harriet L m Rodney Wilkins; NH-0002-385
ELLIOT,
Albert J; s/o Jason & Mary Colby; m Armena H Russell & m Mary B Stonecliffe d/o David & Anable Gifford of Hager MI; liv Campton Village NH; ch Lela M; NH-0007-208
Jason; s/o Thomas & Ruth A Burbank; m Mary Colby d/o Nathan; ch Albert J m Armena H Russell & m Mary B Stonecliffe; NH-0007-208
ELLIOTT,
Amos C; m Rosanna H Bedell of Bath; liv Landaff, Lisbon NH; ch Lyman A, Thomas N, William B, James G F m Ella F Brand of Boston; NH-0007-449
Daniel; b1806; m1828 Dorcas Baker & m Sarah Buzzell; liv Rumney NH; ch/o ? - Selestie m Dr A Stephen Russell, Edmund H m Ellen Cheever, 7 sons, 7 dau; NH-0007-610
Edmund H; s/o Daniel of Rumney NH; m1860 Ellen Cheever d/o Ezekiel & Orissa Blanchard of MA; liv Rumney NH; ch Willie H b1861, Lizzie D b1863 dy, Henry A b1867, Freddie b1876, 1 son dy; NH-0007-610
Noah; s/o Winthrop; m Lucretia Austin; ch Wintrop m Mary C Page, Roswell m Polly Blake, Roxana m Silvester Jeffers; NH-0007-376
ELLIS,
B F; b1832 s/o Ichabod & Nancy Richford of Campton; m1854 Dorothy A Sargent of Bridgewater; liv Plymouth NH; ch Gilman F; NH-0007-592
ELWYN,
John Langdon; b1801 s/o Thomas & Eliza Langdon of Clifton ENG; liv Boston, Portsmouth; NH-0003-103
EMERSON,
Benjamin; b1792 s/o Joseph & Lydia Durrell of Alfred ME; m1845 Mrs Rebecca Story Porter d/o Rev Isaac & Rebecca Bradstreet Story of Marblehead MA wid/o Emerson Porter; & m1847 Frances Leighton d/o Gen Samuel &

EMERSON (continued)
Frances of Eliot ME; liv Alfred ME, Gilmanton, Pittsfield; NH-0004-600 & 702

Charles; b1840 s/o Joseph & Julia A George of Farmington; m1866 Frances V Dolby; ch Ralph G; NH-0003-638

Rev Daniel; liv Hollis NH; ch Capt Daniel b1746 m Anna Fletcher, Dr Peter b1749, Lt Ralph b1761 m1784 Alice Ames; NH-0002-451

Capt Daniel; b1746 s/o Rev Daniel of Hollis; m1768 Anna Fletcher; liv Hollis; ch Rev Daniel Jr, Rev Joseph, Rev Ralph DD, William; NH-0002-451

David; b1787 s/o Judge Samuel & Elizabeth Parker of Plymouth; m1810 Lucy Blake of Hebron; liv Plymouth NH; ch Roswell, David G, Deborah I, Ruth C, Ira S m Eunice Nutting; NH-0007-590

Ira S; s/o David & Lucy Blake of Plymouth; m Eunice Nutting d/o Thomas & Eunice Jewett; liv Plymouth NH; ch Mary Lizzie, Thomas I; NH-0007-590

John; ch Samuel b1792 m Mary Moulton, Rev John; NH-0006-243

Joseph; m Lydia Durrell b1748 d/o Benjamin & Judith; liv Alfred ME; ch Benjamin b1792 m Mrs Rebecca Story Porter & m Frances Leighton; NH-0004-600

Joseph; b1763 s/o Timothy & Abigail Thompson of Durham; m1791 Marcia Hayes b1770 d/o Joseph; liv Farmington NH; ch Timothy, Wentworth, Abigail, Joseph b1808 m Julia A George, Margaret; NH-0003-638

Joseph; b1807 s/o Joseph of Norwich VT; m Anna P Shurtleff & m1883 Alice Cameron of Ryegate VT; liv Hanover NH; ch/o Anna - Roswell S; NH-0007-332

Joseph; b1808 s/o Joseph & Marcia Hayes of Farmington; m1836 Julia A George b1810 d/o Rev Enos of Barnstead; liv Farmington; ch Frank b1837, Charles b1840 m Frances V Dolby; NH-0003-638

Luther MD; b1785 s/o Dea Owen

EMERSON (continued)
of Chelmsford MA; m1811 Patience Wood of Dracut MA; ch Luther, Julia A m O T Emerson Esq of Haverhill MA, Joseph W, Rufus, John, Charles B, 7 others; NH-0003-483

Judge Samuel; m Elizabeth Parker wid/o Zachariah; liv Plymouth NH; ch David b1787 m Lucy Blake, 9 others; NH-0007-590

Timothy; m Abigail Thompson of Durham; liv Durham; ch Joseph b1763 m Marcia Hayes, Sally, Andrew, Polly, Abigail; NH-0003-638

William P; m Mary Ann Manter d/o Samuel & Isabella Reid; liv Londonderry; ch William, John, Mary Ann, Sarah, Clarissa, Ida; NH-0003-586

EMERY,
Caleb; liv Lyman & Monroe NH; ch Solomon H, 2 dau, Edward, 5 others; NH-0007-553

Noah; b1725 s/o Daniel of Kittery ME; m Joanna Perryman d/o Nicholas; liv Exeter; NH-0003-30

Smith; m Susan Huntington Moulton d/o Col John & Susan Sargent; ch Caroline Porter, Alice Huntington; NH-0004-728

ENGLISH,
Andrew; m Celinda Claflin d/o Preston & Lydia B Williams; ch D Frye, Chester; NH-0007-542

Andrew; s/o James; m Mary Goodell d/o Dea Jonathan; liv Lyme NH; ch Asenath m Daniel French & m Benjamin Trussell, Eunice m Moses Emery, Lois m Isaac W Hall, Mary m George Pierson, David, John, Andrew, Lewis, Rebekah m James P Webster; NH-0007-527

John W; b1824; m Melissa Hubbard of Littleton; liv Waitsfield, Hartland & S Woodstock VT, Littleton NH; ch Fred H, Eugene G; NH-0007-498

EUDY,
William; b1801; m Nancy Swett of Bethlehem; liv Leyden MA, Bethlehem, N Littleton NH; ch Sarah m Benjamin Bean, Alonzo, William D m Maria

EUDY (continued)
Brown of Bethlehem, 5 others;
NH-0007-503

EVANS,
Alfred R; b1849 s/o Otis &
Martha Pinkham of Shelburne
gs/o Daniel Pinkham; m1881
Mrs Dora J Briggs d/o Charles
W Bean of Gorham; liv Gorham
NH; NH-0005-233

Benjamin; b1772 s/o Tappan of
Newburyport; m --- Wadleigh;
liv Warner & Sutton NH; ch
Abigail m Reuben Porter,
Susan dy, Susan m Dr Eaton,
Lucinda m Nathan S Colby,
Sophronia m Stephen C Badger,
Sarah m H D Robertson, Hannah
M m Abner Woodman, Benjamin
dy; NH-0004-675

Daniel; s/o Jonathan; m Phila
Clemens; ch Otis m Martha
Pinkham; NH-0005-874

Edward; d1818; m Sarah Flagg;
liv IRE, Chester NH; NH-0004-
617

James; liv Moultonborough NH;
ch James, Smith B, Alvah C,
Daniel B, 1 son, Emma F m Dr
George L Mason, 1 dau m ---
Grant, 5 dau; NH-0006-404

John C; b1829 s/o Miles & Sally
Chase; m1867 Jane N Frost d/o
Newell & Judith Bayley of
Seabrook NH; liv S Hampton;
ch Sally G, Gideon W, John N,
Harry W; NH-0003-524

Jonathan; m Mary Lary; ch
Hazen, Jabez, Augustus; NH-
0005-874

Lemuel; m --- Willie; liv Rye &
Strafford NH; ch Miles m
Sally Chase & m Susan
Clifford, 12 others; NH-0003-
524

Miles; s/o Lemuel & --- Willie;
m Sally Chase d/o Abram of
Seabrook & m Susan Clifford
of Gilmanton NH; liv
Strafford & Seabrook NH; ch/o
Sally - Arthur L, John C
b1829 m Jane N Frost, Charles
A, 3 dy; NH-0003-524

P G; m Helen Mar Twitchell d/o
Adams & Lusylvia Bartlett; ch
Helen C; NH-0005-850

Robert; m Mary C Tucker of
Vershire; liv Vershire VT,
Piermont NH; ch 1 dau m ---
Risley, Joseph O; NH-0007-575

Simeon Adams MD; b1837 s/o Dea

EVANS (continued)
John & Mary Adams of Fryeburg; m1866 Louisa H Illsley
of Fryeburg & m1871 Susan
Hill of Conway; liv Hopkinton, Conway; ch/o Louisa - 2;
ch/o Susan - 3; NH-0006-857

Simon; bro/o Jonathan; ch
Ezekiel, Elijah, Lydia, John;
NH-0005-874

EVERETT,
George W; b1819; m Ellen T Lane
of Gloucester MA; liv New
London; NH-0004-441

Richard Clair; b1764; m1793
Persis Wilder d/o Maj Jonas;
liv Lancaster; ch Drusilla S
m Dr Benjamin Hunkins, Persis
F m Maj John W Weeks, Almira
J m Thomas Peverly Esq,
Abigail C m Ephraim Cross,
Elizabeth A, 2 dy; NH-0005-
210

EWEN,
William; m Ruth ---; liv Dalton
NH; ch Mary Ann b1808; Edward
b1810; NH-0005-520


-F-


FAIRBANKS,
Charles Albert MD; b1849 s/o
Albert A of Dover; liv Dover;
NH-0003-850

FALES,
William W Jr; b1853; m1871 Anna
N Sherburne d/o Joseph; liv
Rumney NH; ch Alice Belle,
Cora May, Eva Delle, Daisy
Maude; NH-0007-613

FALL,
Samuel; liv Bartlett NH; ch
Rebecca m Samuel Parker,
Judith m --- Allard; NH-0006-
916

FARLEY,
Benjamin M; b1783 s/o Benjamin
& Lucy Fletcher gs/o Lt
Samuel of Hollis; liv Hollis,
Boston MA; NH-0002-39

Capt Caleb; b1730; m1754 Elizabeth; liv Billerica MA,
Hollis NH; NH-0002-451

Lt Samuel; m1744 Hannah Brown;
liv Bedford MA, W Dunstable;
ch Benjamin; NH-0002-438

FARMER,
Minot; b1750 s/o Benjamin;

FARMER (continued)
m1775 Abigail Barron; liv Hollis NH; NH-0002-451
Moses Gerrish; b1820 s/o Col John & Sally Gerrish of Boscawen; m1844 Hannah T Shapleigh of Berwick ME; liv Salem, Newport RI; NH-0004-689

FARNSWORTH,
Hiram M; b1822; m1845 Mira J Phelps d/o Mason; liv Haverhill, Wentworth, Rumney NH; ch Belle C, Clarence A dy, Emma L m Velorus Thurston of IN, Eva M m Freeman Collins, Clarence L; NH-0007-613

FARR,
Evarts Worcester; b1840 s/o John & Tryphena Morse of Littleton; m1861 Ellen F Burpee of New Hampton NH; liv Littleton; ch 3; NH-0007-111
George A; b1836 s/o John & Tryphena Morse of Littleton; m Eliza C Boynton of Hallowell ME; liv Littleton NH; ch 3; NH-0007-491
John; m1833 Tryphena Morse & m1852 Mrs E M Bowman & m1862 Mrs Emma M Woolson; liv Littleton; ch/o Tryphena - Caroline E, George, Mary Ellen, John Jr, Evarts W, Caroline m Dr B F Page, Charles A; ch/o Woolson - Stella B; NH-0007-108
Noah; s/o Ebenezer b1779; m1803 Lydia Cobleigh of Chesterfield; liv Littleton NH; ch John, 1 dau m M D Cobleigh, Noah; NH-0007-486
Noah; s/o Noah; ch Noah, Theron A, Lydia m Martin Hatch, Philander, Deborah M b1814 dy, Elizabeth m Noah Gile; NH-0007-486
Theron A; b1839 s/o Gilman & Philena Allen of Littleton; m Alice Goold d/o Marcus L; liv Littleton NH; ch Walter H, Harry M; NH-0007-495

FARRAR,
Timothy Jr; b1778 s/o Hon Timothy of New Ipswich; liv Portsmouth, Hanover, Exeter, Boston; NH-0003-33
Dea Samuel; liv Lincoln; ch Samuel Esq, Prof John, Dea James, Rebecca m Rev Jonathan French; NH-0003-416

FARRAR (continued)
William; m1812 Margaret Kibbee d/o Gaius of Minehead VT; liv Lancaster; NH-0005-245

FARRIMAN,
Joseph B; b1797; liv Plymouth, Warren NH; ch 1 dau m J S Jewett, 2 dau; NH-0007-634

FARRINGTON,
Elijah; b1784 s/o Jeremiah & Molly Swan of Conway; m1814 Lois L --- b1793; liv Conway NH; ch Albert E, Mary H m Capt Samuel Haselton of Conway, James MD b1822 m Harriet L Chase; NH-0006-853, NH-0006-853
James MD; b1822 s/o Elijah & Lois L of Conway; m1851 Harriet L Chase; liv Rochester; ch Nellie F b1854 m1879 George McDuffee, Josephine C b1859 m Arthur V Sanborn; NH-0003-747
Jeremiah; s/o Stephen & Apphia Bradley of Concord; m Molly Swan; liv Conway NH; ch Hannah, Polly, Stephen, Elijah b1784 m Lois L ---, James MD, Nancy, Jeremiah; NH-0003-747, NH-0006-853
Jeremiah; m Mary Ellen Morton d/o Leander S & Martha L Hawkes of Conway NH; ch Martha, Mabel E, Leander Morton, Ethel, J Arthur; NH-0006-902
Stephen; bc1706-10; m Aphhia Bradley; liv Concord NH; ch Stephen, John, Jeremiah, Samuel, 4 dau; NH-0003-747

FAVOR,
Amon M; b1832 s/o William & Betsey Worthley of Ware NH; m1860 Mary Bedee d/o Taylor & Irene Smith; liv Hebron NH; ch John A b1862, Oreste G b1864, Anson L b1874, Lucy M, Sylvia A; NH-0007-390

FELCH,
Horace C; b1824 s/o John & Sally Clark; m1856 Helen H White of Stanstead P Q; liv Bradford NH; ch Fred R b1860 m1884 Jennie L Lund, Emma B b1870; NH-0004-201
John; b1794; m1818 Sally Clark of Hopkinton b1789; liv Weare & Bradford NH; ch Horace C b1824 m Helen H White; NH-0004-201

FELLOWS,
  Benjamin; b1799 s/o Josiah &
  Jemima Quimby of Bristol; m
  Miriam C Hoyt d/o Samuel &
  Judith; liv Bristol NH; ch
  Milo m Susan D Lock, Belinda
  m Franklin Robinson; NH-0007-
  182
  Col Enoch Quimby; b1825 s/o
  John & Mary J Quimby of
  Sandwich NH; m1847 Mary E
  Quimby d/o Col Joseph L &
  m1887 Lydia Dunning of
  Brunswick ME; liv Sandwich
  NH; ch/o Mary - William B,
  Mary Lizzie b1861, Sarah
  Frances b1868, 2 others; NH-
  0006-723
  Isaac; b1764; m Jane Burnham &
  m1804 Rebecca Hurlbutt; liv
  Kensington & Hopkinton &
  Hanover NH; ch/o ? - Jane,
  Isaac, Asa W, Ira, Lyman,
  Rebecca, Elijah, Fanny, Mary
  C, Alvin; NH-0007-320
  John; b1791 s/o Stephen b1749
  of Poplin NH; m Mary J Quimby
  d/o Enoch; liv Sandwich NH;
  ch Christopher C b1820, Col
  Enoch Quimby b1825 m Mary E
  Quimby & m Lydia Downing; NH-
  0006-723
  Joseph W; b1835 s/o John &
  Polly Hilton of Andover NH; m
  Frances Moore & m1878 Mrs
  Lizzie B Davis; liv Man-
  chester NH; NH-0002-39
  Josiah; s/o John; m Jemima
  Quimby; liv Bristol NH; ch
  Abner b1781, Jeremiah b1782,
  Josiah Jr b1784 m Susan
  Sanborn, Jonathan b1786,
  Elizabeth b1788, Molly b1790,
  Peter b1791, Ruth b1795,
  Jemima b1796, Benjamin b1799
  m Miriam C Hoyt; NH-0007-182
  Josiah Jr; b1784 s/o Josiah &
  Jemima Quimby of Bristol; m
  Susan Sanborn; liv Bristol
  NH; ch Louisa m Jesse F
  Kendall, Calvin P m Mary J
  Worthen, Samuel S m Mary S
  Rollins, Rufus m Elizabeth
  Nelson; NH-0007-182
  Milo; s/o Benjamin & Miriam C
  Hoyt of Bristol; m Susan D
  Lock d/o Benjamin & Nancy
  Gurdy of Bristol; ch Albert
  R, Smith D, Oscar F, Milo A,
  Leslie H, Susie M, Alice A;
  NH-0007-182

FELLOWS (continued)
  Samuel S; s/o Josiah Jr & Susan
  Sanborn of Bristol; m Mary S
  Rollins d/o Joseph; ch Mary F
  m J D Prescott, Scott; NH-
  0007-182
  William Bainbridge Esq; b1858
  s/o Col Enoch Q & Mary E
  Quimby of Sandwich NH; m1881
  Ida G Scribner d/o Franklin
  Esq of Ashland NH; liv Ash-
  land & Tilton NH; ch 2; NH-
  0004-886, NH-0006-253, NH-
  0007-92
FENNER,
  Albert Gallatin; b1813 s/o
  Elhanan W of Taynton MA; liv
  Dover; NN-0003-848
FERGUSON,
  David; liv Rathkeale So IRE; ch
  David m --- Fitzgerald, 4
  sons, 2 dau; NH-0002-128
  David; s/o David; m --- Fitz-
  gerald d/o Councilor of Lime-
  rick IRE; liv Rathkeale So
  IRE; ch John b1829 m Eleanor
  Hughes, 7 others; NH-0002-
  128
  Fitzgerald; m Eleanor Hughes
  b1838 d/o Michael & Elenor of
  New York City; liv Rathkeale
  So IRE, New York City, Man-
  chester NH; ch Eleanor, Mary
  C, John D, Alfred W; NH-0002-
  128
FERNALD,
  James E Esq; m Laura Ann White-
  house d/o George L & Liberty
  N Dame; liv Farmington; ch
  George W; NH-0003-629
  John; s/o Seth & Celia Huntoon;
  m Betsey B French of Orange &
  m Mary E Patten d/o Jonathan
  & Margaret Clark; liv Orange
  NH; ch/o Betsey - Clara A;
  NH-0007-557
  Seth; d1881 s/o Thomas of
  Loudon NH; m Celia Huntoon of
  Unity NH; liv Orange & Loudon
  NH; ch John m Betsey B French
  & m Mary E Patten, 6 others;
  NH-0007-557
FERRIN,
  Jonathan; s/o Enos of
  Alexandria; m Harriet Webster
  d/o Bailey; liv Bridgewater,
  Alexandria; ch Bailey W,
  Augustus J m Sarah Robie,
  Francis L, Vienna V, Morris
  T, Enos B, Melissa J,
  Benjamin F, Hiram W, Levi E,

FERRIN (continued)
Harriet A, Mary E m Oren
Rowe, Abigail D, Moses A,
Laura J m --- Rockwell, Ira
K; NH-0007-188
Levi; s/o Phillip & Nancy Mc-
Murphy; m Sarah M Clough d/o
Amos & Elsie Flanders of
Lowell MA; ch Emma J m Rev
Alexander McGregor of Ames-
bury MA, Frank C; NH-0007-122
Phillip; s/o Ebenezer of Bristol
VT; m Nancy McMurphy of Alex-
andria; ch Levi m Sarah M
Clough, 8 others; NH-0007-122
FIELD,
S L; m1860 Imogene Thomas d/o L
B & Amanda Cross of Pulaski
NY; liv Plymouth NH; ch
Florence E m George D
Spaulding of Rumney; NH-0007-
597
FIELDS,
Henry; bro/o Marsten; liv
Merrimack, Andover MA; ch
John dy, Henry, Rebecca m
Timothy Carlton, Susan; NH-
0002-543
John; bro/o Joshua & Marston;
liv Andover MA, Merrimack; ch
Henry, Elizabeth m John H
Coburn; NH-0002-543
Joshua; bro/o Marsten & Henry;
liv Andover MA, Merrimack; ch
Joshua, Jonas, James, John,
Sally; NH-0002-543
Joshua; s/o Joshua; liv Merri-
mack; ch Hannah, Smith, Sally
m Peter Carlton, Joshua,
Jonas; NH-0002-543
Marsten; bro/o Henry; liv
Andover MA, Merrimack; ch
Isaac, Marsten, Betsy,
Hannah, Priscilla; NH-0002-
543
Smith; s/o Joshua; liv Merri-
mack; ch Sally, Joshua,
Charles, Mary, Hermon S; NH-
0002-543
FIFE,
Jeremiah; b1779 s/o William &
Phebe White; m1803 Abigail
Holt b1777; liv Pembroke NH;
ch Thursay b1805 m Benjamin
Hagget, Nathan H b1807 m
Addie Brooks, Sarah b1809 m
Samuel Worth, Abigail b1811 m
John Hagget, Jeremiah b1813,
James b1816 dy, Capt William
b1821 m Mary D Gault,
Rhuhamah b1824, Noah b1827 m

FIFE (continued)
Mary Wilson, Elcy b1830 m
John Spurlin; NH-0004-583
Seth Wyman; b1846 s/o Moses &
Eliza of Chatham; liv Frye-
burg; NH-0006-271
William; b1746; m1772 Phebe
White b1745; liv SCO, N Pem-
broke NH; ch Jeremiah b1779 m
Abigail Holt; NH-0004-583
Capt William; b1821 s/o
Jeremiah & Abigail Holt of
Pembroke NH; m1843 Mary D
Gault b1820 d/o Andrew &
Sarah Dudley; liv Pembroke
NH; ch Helen A b1843 m Joseph
J Rand, William W b1848 m
Louisa H Blake, Edwin H b1851
m1885 Lizzie Alden, Sarah F
b1853; NH-0004-583
William W; b1848 s/o Capt
William & Mary D Gault of
Pembroke NH; m1871 Louisa H
Blake b1840; liv N Pembroke;
ch Henry W b1871, Frank D
b1874, Horace E b1880, Sarah
A b1882; NH-0004-583
FIFIELD,
Ebenezer O; s/o Jonathan &
Dorcas Pearson of Salisbury
NH; m Anna G Gough of Boston;
liv ME, Lowell; NH-0004-618
James MD; m Lucinda Talmer of
Claremont; liv Claremont; NH-
0004-618
Jesse MD; m Sarah Burnham; liv
Waterloo NY; NH-0004-618
John E S; b1842 s/o Samuel &
Elmira Martin; m1866 Eliza E
Fifield d/o David & Sarah
Abbott of W Concord; ch Rose
Elmira, Addie Grace, Sarah
Abbott, Edith May, Elwin
Augustus; NH-0007-173
Samuel; b1806 s/o Moses; m1826
Elmira Martin d/o Daniel &
Betsey Cass; ch Daniel M
b1828, Edwin A dy, John E S
b1842 m Eliza E Fifield; NH-
0007-173
Rev Winthrop; m Sophia Garland
& m Sarah A O Piper; liv
Epsom; NH-0004-618
FISHER,
Ezra; m --- Bixby of Frances-
town; liv Deering; ch Giles m
--- Campbell, William dy,
Ezra; NH-0002-386
Jonathan; m Rebecca ---; liv
Dalton NH; ch Lyman R b1808,
Christopher b1809; NH-0005-

FISHER (continued)
520
Jonathan; liv Dalton NH; ch
Thomas, Jonathan; NH-0005-527
Levi; m Fanny Wilkins d/o
Alexander & Lydia Gage; liv
Merrimack; ch Levi W, Sarah
W, George W, Anna L m Hazen G
Dodge, Cynthia M; NH-0002-543
Levi W; s/o Levi & Fanny
Wilkins; liv Merrimack; ch
Maria, Fanny W; NH-0002-543
Thomas; m Eunice ---; liv
Dalton NH; ch Aaron b1804,
Lorenzo Dow b1806, Olivet
b1807; NH-0005-520
FISK,
Franklin W; b1820 s/o Ebenezer
& Hannah Proctor of Hopkin-
ton; m1854 Mrs Amelia Allen
Austin of Woodstock CT; liv
WI; ch 3; NH-0004-409
Ralph; s/o Nathan of Nashua; m
Nancy Roby d/o James & Lucy
Cutter of Amherst; liv
Boston, Providence; ch
William F, Anna A, Lucy W m
Alonzo Fisk, Emily m Rev Geo
P Wilson; NH-0002-217
FITCH,
Charles Darwin; b1815 s/o Dr
Samuel & Eunice Perry; m1857
Lizzie D Peavey d/o Dea Peter
& Dorcas Holt; liv St
Francesville LA, Greenfield
NH; ch Frances Louisa,
Orianna P; NH-0002-348
Dr Samuel; s/o Samuel of MA; m
Eunice Perry of Sherborn MA;
liv Acton MA, Greenfield NH;
ch Louisa m Jeremiah Peavey,
Phebe dy, Francis P, Charles
Darwin b1815 m Lizzie D
Peavey; NH-0002-348, 338
FITTS,
John M; b1843 s/o Thankful
Moore; m Emma M Carr of
Orford; liv Dorchester NH; ch
John B; NH-0007-238
FITZ,
John M MD; b1820; m Nancy Chase
of Warner; liv Bradford; NH-
0004-618
FLAGG,
Eleazor; liv Concord MA, W
Dunstable; ch John; NH-0002-
438
FLANDERS,
Ezekiel; b1815; m Sarah Eaton;
liv Alton, Moultonborough NH;
ch Henry b1843; NH-0006-414

FLANDERS (continued)
George M; s/o Sylvester & Sarah
Morse; m Maria C Aldrich d/o
George & Alsea Reed; liv
Grafton NH; ch Bertha M,
Sarah E, Georgia; NH-0007-286
Israel; m Polly Wells d/o
Ephraim; liv Bradford VT,
Benton NH; ch John R m Eliza
J Brown, 3 others; NH-0007-
152
Nathaniel; b1818; m1846 Mary
Ann McMurphy of Wentworth;
liv Dorchester, Canaan,
Littleton NH; ch Walter P m
Ella Remick, Emma C, George m
Alice J Allen of Littleton;
NH-0007-497
Onisephorus; m Elizabeth Dan-
forth sis/o Timothy; liv
Hampton, Eaton; ch Stephen,
Samuel, Shepherd, Anna m
Richard Lary; NH-0006-803
Peter; s/o John of Bradford VT;
liv Haverhill NH; ch Charles
F; NH-0007-370
Sylvester; s/o Joshua &
Margaret Pollard; m Sarah
Morse of Canaan; ch Julia T m
William Hall, William A,
George M m Maria C Aldrich;
NH-0007-286
Walter P; m Susan E Greeley d/o
Jonathan Esq of New London;
liv Warner & New London NH,
Milwaukee WI; NH-0004-441
William A; s/o Sylvester of
Canaan; m Angie L Clark of
Canaan; liv Wentworth NH; ch
5; NH-0007-112.26
FLETCHER,
Abel; m Betsey Gillman; liv MA,
Bridgewater NH; ch Samuel G
b1804 m Lydia Prescott & m
Dorothy S Prescott & m Mary C
Sleeper & m Sally Prime,
Rhoda m Samuel Mead, Jane H m
Samuel Currier, Betsey m
William Wheeler, Mary m Moses
Farnham, Franklin dy, Eliza
Ann m J Lyford, Sarah m Asaph
Dearborn; NH-0007-172
Arthur F; b1836 s/o Cyrus &
Mary L Sleeper; m1859 Betsey
Jane Wheeler & m1864 Ellen S
Brown d/o Edmun & Sarah
Hogsdon; liv Bridgewater NH;
ch/o Betsey - Cyrus W b1860;
ch/o Ellen - Blanch Jane,
Mary Ellen; NH-0007-173
Rev Elijah; m Rebecca ---; liv

FLETCHER (continued)
Westford MA, Hopkinton NH; ch Grace b1782 m1808 Daniel Webster, Rebecca m Judge Israel Kelly; NH-0004-408

Judge Everett; b1848 s/o Hiram A & Persis Hunking of Colebrook; liv Lancaster NH; NH-0005-231

Hiram Adams; b1806 s/o Ebenezer & Peddy Smith of Springfield VT; m1834 Persis E Hunking d/o Dr Benjamin of Lancaster; liv Colebrook & Lancaster NH; ch 1 dy, Emily dy, Almira m W S Ladd, Richard, Everett, Nelly m William A Holman of Pittsburg PA; NH-0005-215 & 247

Nathan; s/o Joshua & Sarah Brown; m Nancy Pillsbury of Bridgewater; ch Cyrus b1810 m Mary L Sleeper d/o Moses W, Arthur F b1811, Samuel W, Julia Ann b1816, Arvilla m Charles Barnard; NH-0007-173

Philip; s/o Simeon & Mary Davis; m Mary Harper; liv Greenfield NH; ch Philip Jr; NH-0002-343

Samuel G; b1804 s/o Abel & Betsey Gillman; m Lydia Prescott & m Dorothy S Prescott & m Mary L Sleeper wid/o Cyrus & m Sally Prime wid/o Noble of Manchester; liv Bridgewater & Plymouth NH; ch/o Lydia - S G; ch/o Dorothy - Emeline L m Randall J Pillsbury, Ruth A dy, George F, Henry G; NH-0007-172

Simeon; b1722; m Mary Davis; liv Chelmsford MA, Greenfield NH; ch Persis m --- Beasom, Annie m --- Ordway, Mary m --- Balch, John, Olive, Philip m Mary Harper, Simeon m Mary Huston; NH-0002-342

FLINT,
John W; b1803 s/o Samuel; m Clarissa Goodell d/o Luther; liv Lyme NH, Bath; ch Francis L m A H Warden of Hanover, John Perry; NH-0007-540

Lyman Thomas; b1817; m1844 Hannah W Willard of Lyndon VT; liv Williamstown VT, Colebrook & Concord NH; NH-0005-247

Capt Moses; bro/o Samuel; m

FLINT (continued)
Elizabeth Spaulding of Fitzwilliam; liv Lyme NH; ch George, Oliver S b1808 m Persis Goodell, 6 sons, 4 dau; NH-0007-540

Oliver S; b1808 s/o Capt Moses & Elizabeth Spaulding; m Persis Goodell d/o John; liv Lyme NH, Bath, Hanover; ch Harlan P, Julia M m James Esden of Peacham VT, Lucy A m Alexander Warden; NH-0007-540

Samuel; bro/o Capt Moses; liv Lyme NH; ch Samuel b1801 m Fanny Goodell, John W b1803 m Clarissa Goodell; NH-0007-540

Samuel; b1801 s/o Samuel; m Fanny Goodell d/o Luther; liv Lyme NH; ch Martha J, Mary E, John M, 5 others; NH-0007-540

FLOOD,
John; liv Eaton NH; ch Joseph, James, Solomon; NH-0006-791

FOGG,
Abraham; b1797 s/o John & Abigail Blake; m1821 Mary Robinson; liv Hampton NH; ch Jeremiah R, Mary A m Robert C Thomson of Exeter, John H b1828, Rebecca F m J Warren Sanborn of Kingston NH, Susan E, Sarah J; NH-0003-329

Daniel; b1743 s/o Daniel & Anna Elkins of Rye; m Deborah Brinley; liv Kensington, ENG; NH-0003-358

David; b1759 s/o Col Seth & --- Philbrick; m Catharine Barber & m Ruth Dustin; liv Epping Corner, Enfield; ch Jesse J b1785 m Lucy Pierce; NH-0003-240

David; b1809 s/o Jesse J & Lucy Pierce; m Ruth Fogg d/o Sherburne & Mehitable Maloon of Epping & m Irene Burnham b1809 d/o Jacob of Nottingham; liv Enfield, Epping; ch/o Ruth - Lucy Maria b1830 m Davenport Morrison of Fairlee VT, Andrew Jackson b1831 m Mary Emma Willis of Exeter, Martin Van Buren b1834 m Ruth Jane Rollings & m Annie Martha Swain; ch/o Irene - Lewis Everett b1843 m1872 Ellen Pitkin Newhall d/o Rev Matthew of Greenland, Mary Adelaide b1852 m1874 Harold W Windram of Lynn MA; NH-0003-

FOGG (continued)
240
George Gilman; b1813 s/o David
& Hannah Gilman Vickery; liv
Meredith Centre & Concord NH;
NH-0004-869
James; b1668 s/o Samuel & Mary
Page of Hampton NH; m1695
Mary ---; ch Mary, James,
John, Sarah, Enoch, Hannah;
NH-0003-329
Rev Jeremiah; b1712 s/o Seth &
Sarah Shaw of Hampton; liv
Kensington; NH-0003-354
Jeremiah; m Elizabeth Parsons;
ch Maj Jeremiah b1749, Joseph
b1753, Dr Daniel b1759, Dr
John b1764; NH-0003-359 & 361
Maj Jeremiah; b1749 s/o Rev
Jeremiah & Elizabeth Parsons;
m1738? Lydia Hill of Cam-
bridge; NH-0003-358 & 361
Jesse J; b1785 s/o David & ?; m
Lucy Pierce; liv Enfield; ch
David b1809 m Ruth Fogg & m
Irene Burnham; NH-0003-240
Dea John; b1702 s/o John gs/o
James ggs/o Samuel; m Eliza-
beth Drake; ch John m Abigail
Blake, 10 dau; NH-0003-329
John; s/o Dea John & Elizabeth
Drake; m Abigail Blake; ch
Susannah C, Abraham b1797 m
Mary Robinson, Elizabeth,
Betsey dy, Abigail B, Mary,
Meribah; NH-0003-329
John H; b1828 s/o Abraham &
Mary Robinson; m1852 Mary E
Drake b1832 d/o Samuel &
Mehitable Pickering of N
Hampton NH; liv Hampton NH;
NH-0003-329
Joseph; b1753 s/o Rev Jeremiah
& Elizabeth Parsons; m Mary
Sherburne & m Abigail
Westwork; liv Remington,
Ossipee; NH-0003-361
Josiah; s/o Maj Josiah; liv
Exeter, Chester NH; ch
William Perry, Lucy Jane m
Hon Archibald Dunlap; NH-
0002-212
Martin Van Buren; b1834 s/o
David & Ruth Fogg; m1855 Ruth
Jane Rollings d/o Sherburne &
Nancy Sanborn of Epping & m
Annie Martha Swain b1839 d/o
Richard & Sarah Sherburne
Swain of Barrington; ch/o
Ruth - Edson b1856 m
Georgianna Sanborn d/o Dr ---

FOGG (continued)
of Kingston, Emma Jane b1860;
NH-0003-240
Samuel; m1652 Anne Shaw d/o
Roger & m Mary Page d/o Robat
(Robert); liv Hampton NH;
ch/o Anne - Samuel b1653 m
Hannah Marston, Joseph, John,
Daniel, Mary; ch/o Mary -
Seth b1666 m Sarah ---, James
b1668 m Mary ---, Hannah; NH-
0003-329
Samuel; b1653 s/o Samuel & Anne
Shaw of Hampton NH; m1676 m
Hannah Marston d/o William &
gd/o Robert; ch Samuel,
Joseph, Daniel?; NH-0003-329
Seth; b1666 s/o Samuel & Mary
Page of Hampton NH; m Sarah
---; ch Benoni, Hannah, Seth,
Sarah, Esther, Samuel, Simon,
Abner, Abigail, Daniel,
Jeremiah, Ebenezer; NH-0003-
329
Col Seth; m --- Philbrick & m
Mrs Smith; liv Hampton,
Epping; ch/o Philbrick -
Sally b1758, David b1759 m
Catharine Barber & m Ruth
Dustin, Caleb b1761, Jonathan
b1764, Sherburne b1768 m
Mehitable Maloon & m Mrs
Hannah Hubbard Sargent, Polly
b1770, Seth b1771, ch/o Smith
- Eleanor b1777 m Dr George
Kittredge; NH-0003-240 & 241
Sherburne; b1768 s/o Col Seth &
--- Philbrick; m1792
Mehitable Maloon b1769 of
Epping & m1839 Mrs Hannah
Hubbard Sargent of Brentwood;
liv Epping; ch/o Mehitable -
1 son b1793 dy, Seth b1793,
Maria b1796, Jonathan b1798,
Franklin b1801, Jesse b1805,
Ruth b1808 m David Fogg; NH-
0003-240
FOLLETT,
Nicholas; m Hannah ---; ch
Sarah, Mary, Nicholas b1677
m1700 Mary Hall, Sarah; NH-
0003-770
William; mc1671 Elizabeth Drew
wid/o William; liv Dover; ch
1 son; NH-0003-770
FOLLANSBEE,
Edward E; s/o John & Susan
Pattie of Grafton; m Eliza A
Potter d/o George & Nancy A;
liv Grafton NH; ch William B,
John E, Daniel; NH-0007-283

FOLLANSBEE (continued)
John; s/o Moses & Priscilla Heath; m Susan Pattie of Goffstown; liv Grafton NH; ch Edward E m Eliza A Potter, 10 others; NH-0007-283

John H; s/o Sam; ch 1 son, Abbie m A D Caswell, Sam; NH-0007-185

Moses E; b1819 s/o John of Ware NH; m1842 Jane Luflin d/o Edward & Phebe Burnham; liv Hebron NH, Salem, Lawrence; ch George E b1843, Eddie B b1861 dy; NH-0007-389

FOLLINSBEE,
Dr William; b1800; m Hannah J Follinsbee & m Rachel P Moore; liv Francestown, Peterborough; NH-0002-664

FOLSOM,
Benjamin; b1757 s/o Joshua & Abigail Mead; m1782 Abigail Peaslee b1760 d/o John of Newton NH; ch John b1784 (b1783) m Mehitable Morrill; Mead b1785, Sarah b1787 m Israel Norris of Epping, Abigail M b1797 m --- Jones of Gilmanton & m Timothy Hanson of Farmington, Hannah F b1799 m David Sawyer of Newbury MA, Thomas b1802; NH-0003-235 & 236

David E; b1838 s/o Thomas & Sophia Morrill of W Epping NH; m1878 Lucy T Jones d/o Benjamin H; liv MT; ch George B dy, David M; NH-0003-235

George; b1825 s/o Thomas & Sophia Morrill of W Epping NH; liv CA; ch Mary A, George F, Edwin, Charles A; NH-0003-235

Henry Asa; bc1845 s/o Jesse & Elizabeth Varney of Sandwich; liv Hanover; NH-0006-251

Ira L; s/o Peter & Abigail Sanburn; m Hannah M Hale d/o Royal & Susanna Elliot of Boscawen; liv Grafton NH, Alexandria; ch Charles L, Elvirus F; NH-0007-286

John; b1783 (b1784) s/o Benjamin & Abigail Peaslee; m Mehitable Morrill b1790; liv Epping NH; ch Ann E, Mary P, John Lewis m Mary Ann Beede, Benjamin M; NH-0003-236

John Lewis; s/o John Mehitable Morrill of Epping NH; m1842

FOLSOM (continued)
Mary Ann Beede b1816 d/o Moses of Fremont NH; liv W Epping; ch Charles E b1845, Abby B b1848 dy, Evelyn A b1852; NH-0003-236

Joshua; m Mary Brackenbury; liv Epping & Deering NH; ch Betty dy, John m Patience Richardson, Anna S m John Johnson, Joshua m Catherine Hoffman, Samuel m Nancy Loveren, Abigail m Moses Brown, Sarah m William Wallace of Henniker NH, Mary m Thomas Whittle of Weare NH, Lydia m Samuel Tutherly, Hannah m Rufus Tutherly, David dy, Rachel m Daniel Alley; NH-0002-381

Joshua; b1716; m Abigail Mead; liv Exeter & Epping NH; ch Abigail b1744, Thomas b1746, Bettie b1748, Joshua b1750, John b1753, Mary b1755 m Fry of Kittery ME, Benjamin b1757 m Abigail Peaslee, Samuel, Abigail b1763 m Daniel B Alley; NH-0003-235

Levi; bc1850 bro/o John T D; liv Tamworth; NH-0006-251

Thomas; b1802 s/o Benjamin & Abigail Peaslee; m1823 Sophia Morrill d/o Ephraim & Mary Page of Berwick ME; liv W Epping NH; ch Maria b1824 m Eben Merrill of Amesbury, George b1825, Alvira M b1827 dy, Charles N b1829 dy, Abby P b1831, Mary E b1833 m Levi W Hoag, Thomas Charles b1836 m Mary Bickford, David E b1838 m Lucy T Jones; NH-0003-235

FOOTE,
James L Esq; b1856 s/o Thomas & Lydia Taber; liv Manchester; NH-0004-617

FORBUSH,
Daniel; b1826; m Lydia Lovjoy d/o William; liv Dummer NH; NH-0005-857

FORD,
Abel; s/o Richard & --- Kimball of Grafton; m Clarissa Greeley d/o Wilder & m Mrs Judith Ladd d/o Moses Atwood of Bristol; liv Orange NH; ch/o ? - John m Sophia Pierce; NH-0007-557

Alden; b1803; liv Orford, Piermont NH; ch Absolom, Alden,

FORD (continued)
Abram D, Edward; NH-0007-576
John; s/o Abel of Orange NH; m
Sophia Pierce d/o Oliver of
Moriah NY; ch Olin J, Jennie
I, Wallace A, Clara E; NH-
0007-557
FORREST,
Andrew J; s/o Isaiah; m Arvilla
R Kenerson d/o John; ch
Irving M, Newall K, Isaiah A,
Hattie E, Frannie E, Emma M;
NH-0006-803
Charles G; s/o William; m Mrs
Sally T Mead; liv Northfield
& New London & Tilton NH; ch
Almeda M, Honoria A, Martha
J, George F D; NH-0004-522
Isaiah; liv Bridgewater MA,
Eaton NH; ch Eunice, Lucy,
Isaiah; NH-0006-803
John; liv IRE, Canterbury NH;
ch Robert, John, William,
James, 1 dau m --- Gibson, 1
dau m --- Gibson, 1 dau m ---
Clough; NH-0004-522
Samuel Esq; d1867; m Agnes
Randall b1800 of N Conway;
liv Northfield NH; ch James
N; NH-0004-522
FORSAITH,
Samuel Caldwell; b1827 s/o
Robert & Elizabeth Caldwell
of Goffstown NH; m1848 Nancy
W Pierce; & m1875 Clara J
Smith d/o Col J C & Clara J;
Liv Manchester & Goffstown &
Milford NH, Biddeford ME;
ch/o Nancy - Frank P, George
B, William; ch/o Clara J -
Samuel C Jr b1876, Clarence S
b1878, Darwin J b1880; NH-
0002-84
FORSYTH,
Dea Matthew; m Esther Graham
d/o Robert; liv Edinburgh
SCO, IRE, Chester NH; ch Lt
Robert; NH-0002-203
FOSS,
Aaron Waldron; b1824 s/o James
B & Sarah Waldron of Straf-
ford; m1849 Elizabeth O
Caverly d/o Rev John & Nancy
French; liv Strafford; ch
Clara C m Calvin Rea, Albert
C b1851 m Lillie E Tasker,
Sarah A b1853 m George W
Brock, John James b1855,
Aaron H b1857; NH-0003-714
Charles A; b1814 s/o Jacob D;
m1841 Abiah W Foss; liv

FOSS (continued)
Barrington; ch Ada Sarah
b1852, 4 dy; NH-0003-614
Ebenezer; liv Concord &
Thornton NH; ch Carter m1822
Mary Whitney, 12 others; NH-
0007-629
Ephraim; s/o Joshua; liv
Charlestown MA, Norfolk VA;
ch Jacob D b1784 m Sally
Garland, Ephraim, Sallie m
Ephraim Locke of Boston,
Mollie m James Bodge of
Barrington, Lydia m Isaac
Daniels of Barrington,
Abigail m Clement Daniels of
Barrington & m Jacob Hale of
Barrington; NH-0003-614
George; b1721; m Mary Martin
b1726; liv Rye, Strafford
Ridge; ch Rachel b1747 m ---
Berry, Judith b1748 m ---
Berry, John b1752, Abigail
b1754 m --- Perkins, George
b1757, William b1760, Richard
b1760, James b1762, Mary
b1764 m William Foss, Samuel
b1766, Nathan b1766 m Alice
Babb; NH-0003-714
Jacob D; b1784 s/o Ephraim;
mc1809 Sally Garland of
Northwood NH; ch Eliza G
b1811, Charles A b1814 m
Abiah W Foss, Nathaniel G dy,
Lydia S b1823, Sally L b1826;
NH-0003-614
James B; b1795 s/o Nathan &
Alice Babb; m1824 Sarah
Waldron d/o Aaron; liv Straf-
ford; ch Aaron Waldron b1824
m Elizabeth O Caverly, Hannah
W m Joseph Stiles, Richard W,
Adeline W m Charles A Hill,
Mary A m Gilbert Shaw; NH-
0003-714
John H; s/o Ebenezer & ---
Hoyt; m Elizabeth Chase d/o
Moses; ch John R m Nancy M
Richards & m Mary Wilkins & m
Mrs Laura A Thompson, 12
others; NH-0007-213
John R; s/o John H & Elizabeth
Chase; m Nancy M Richards & m
Mary Wilkins & m Mrs Laura A
Thompson d/o Samuel & Eliza-
beth Davis Emerson; liv
Campton Village NH; ch/o ? -
Emma M, Lucia M, Edwin B,
Laura E; NH-0007-213
Joshua; liv Strafford Corners &
Barrington NH; ch Thomas,

FOSS (continued)

Joshua, John, Moses, Ephraim, Abigail m Micajah Otis of Strafford, Lydia m Simon Locke of Hollis ME; NH-0003-614

Nathan; b1766 s/o George & Mary Martin; m Alice Babb d/o William & Jemima; ch James B b1795 m Sarah Waldron, George B, Richard, Sally m William Foss, Eliza m Joshua Foss, Harriet m Cotton H Foss; NH-0003-714

FOSTER,

Abiel; b1735; m1761 Hannah Badger d/o Gen Joseph of Gilmanton & m Hannah Rogers of Ipswich MA; liv Andover MA, Canterbury NH; NH-0004-229

Rev Amos AM; b1797; m1825 Harriet A White; liv Canaan, Putney VT; NH-0004-618

Rev Benjamin F; b1803; m1832 Ruth H Kimball & m Mary C Perry; NH-0004-618

Caleb; bro/o Richard; liv Hanover NH; ch Horace, Celina m Alden Kendrick, Caleb Converse m Laura Houston & m Emily E Jones & m Sarah J Dewey; NH-0007-323

Caleb Converse; s/o Caleb of Hanover; m Laura Houston & m Emily E Jones & m Sarah J Dewey; liv Hanover NH; ch/o Emily - John Henry m Laura Storrs, Emily m F W Davison; ch/o Sarah - Charles A, 1 dau; NH-0007-323

Edmund; b1754 s/o Abraham; m1783 Phoebe Lawrence d/o Col William of Littleton; liv Groton & Littleton MA; ch John m Sophia Willard, 2 sons, 6 others; NH-0004-27

Ezra; liv Littleton; ch Henry, Nancy m --- Parker, George b1806; NH-0007-515

Hon Herman; b1800; m1826 Harriet M A Whittemore of W Cambridge MA; liv Andover, Boston MA, Hudson, Warner, Manchester NH; NH-0002-26

Isaac; m Mary Dodge of Lyman; liv Jefferson, Littleton NH; ch Allen m Angeline Carter; NH-0007-490

John; s/o Edmund & Phoebe Lawrence; m Sophia Willard;

FOSTER (continued)

liv Groton MA, Westminster VT, Fitzwilliam & Keene NH; ch William Lawrence b1823 m Harriet Morton; NH-0004-27

John; b1815; m Lovina Briggs of Littleton; liv Jefferson, Littleton NH; ch Fred m Mary Liddell of St Johnsbury VT, 5 others; NH-0007-490

Gen John Gray; b1823 (1822) s/o Capt Perley of Whitefield; liv Nashua, Boston; NH-0002-218, NH-0005-484

John L; b1837 s/o George & Phila Hoskins of Lyman; m1875 Augustia L Stevens d/o Grove S of Haverhill; liv Manchester, Boston, Littleton, Lisbon; ch 4; NH-0007-98

Dr Samuel; mc1750 Mehitabel Ingalls; liv Chester; NH-0003-147

William Lawrence; b1823 s/o John & Sophia Willard; m1853 Harriet Morton d/o Hon Hamilton E of Hopkinton; liv Westminster VT, Keene & Concord NH; NH-0004-27

FOWLER,

Andrew J; s/o Robert; m Julia A Wilkins d/o Joseph C & Mary Barber; liv Grafton NH; ch Mary L, Lizzie A, Clarence A, George A; NH-0007-288

Asa; b1811 s/o Benjamin & Mehitable Ladd; m1837 Mary Dole Cilley Knox d/o Robert & Polly Dole Cilley of Epsom NH gd/o Gen Joseph Cilley; liv Pembroke & Concord NH; ch 4 sons, 1 dau; NH-0004-15

Benjamin(e); b1769 s/o Symonds & Hannah Weeks; m1795 Mehitable Ladd b1776 d/o John & Jerusha Lovejoy of Pembroke NH gd/o Capt Trueworthy & Mehitable Harriman Ladd of Kingston NH; liv Newmarket & Epsom & Pembroke NH; ch Asa b1811 m Mary Dole Cilley Knox, Trueworthy Ladd b1816 m Catharine L Sargent, 9 others; NH-0004-15 & 581

Blake; s/o David gs/o Abner; liv Bridgewater NH; ch Dr Hadley b1825; NH-0007-195

Henry; b1785; m Phebe Field b1784; liv Yanktown NY; ch Moses Field b1819 m Ellen Lizette Gilbert; NH-0002-434

FOWLER (continued)

Joseph; s/o Philip Sr; m Martha Kimball d/o Richard & Ursula Scott; liv ENG, Ipswich MA; ch Philip b1648 m Elizabeth Herrick; NH-0004-15

Moses Field; b1819 s/o Henry & Phebe Field of Yanktown NY; m1869 Ellen Lizzette Gilbert d/o John & Mrs Ann Burrows Attwill; NH-0002-434

Philip Sr; bc1590; m Mary --- & m Mary Norton wid/o George; liv Marlborough ENG, Ipswich; ch Margaret m Christopher Osgood, Joseph m Martha Kimball; NH-0004-15

Philip; b1648 s/o Joseph & Martha Kimball; m1674 Elizabeth Herrick d/o Henry & Editha Laskin; liv Ipswich MA; ch Philip b1691 m Susanna Jacob, 8 others; NH-0004-15

Philip; b1691 s/o Philip & Elizabeth Herrick of Ipswich MA; m1716Susanna Jacob d/o Joseph & Susanna Symonds ggd/o Dep Gov Samuel Symonds; liv Ipswich MA, New Market NH; ch Philip, Jacob, Symonds b1734 m Hannah Weeks, 11 others; NH-0004-15

Robert; ch Robert m Anna Bean & m 2 others; Andrew J m Julia A Wilkins, 14 others; NH-0007-288

Symonds; b1734 s/o Philip & Susanna Jacob; m1756 Hannah Weeks b1738; liv Ipswich MA, Newmarket & Epsom NH; ch Benjamin(e) b1769 m Mehitable Ladd, Winthrop b1788 m Abigail Davis, 9 others; NH-0004-15 & 581

Winthrop; b1788 s/o Symonds; m1810 Abigail Davis b1790 d/o Samuel & Abigail Brown of Epsom; liv Epsom NH; ch Hannah b1810 dy, Abigail b1812 dy, Abigail b1815, Betsey b1818, Samuel b1821, Symonds b1823 dy, Winthrop b1825 dy, Winthrop Jr b1827 m Ann L Locke, Nancy b1830; NH-0004-582

Winthrop Jr; b1827 s/o Winthrop & Abigail Davis of Epsom NH; m1860 Ann L Locke d/o Ephraim & Sarah Dyer of Epsom; liv Pembroke NH; ch Minot Locke b1863, George Winthrop b1864,

FOWLER (continued)

Edward Martin b1868; NH-0004-583

FREEMAN,

Col Edmund; liv Norwich CT, Lebanon NH; ch Nathaniel; NH-0007-419

Hon Jonathan; liv Hanover; ch Asa b1788, Peyton R Esq; NH-0003-590

Peyton Randolph; b1775 s/o Hon Jonathan of Hanover; liv Portsmouth; NH-0003-21

FRENCH,

Abram; m1796 Hannah Lane of Stratham NH; liv Stratham & Pittsfield NH; ch Enoch m Eliza Cate, 4 others; NH-0001-157

Amos; m1837 Susan Matilda Johnson d/o Moses & Lovinia Hardy of Enfield; liv Lebanon, Enfield, Hartford VT; ch John J, William W, George B, Charles F; NH-0007-255

Bernard; m Betsey Morrill d/o Benjamin & Sarah Currier of E Kingston; liv S Hampton; ch George, Fred; NH-0003-203

Charles H; m1863 Mary H Howard d/o Ezra P & Mary Trow; ch Mary H; NH-0002-214

Charles N; b1829 s/o Josiah & Judith Marston of Rumney NH; m1857 Hannah M Ellis d/o William B & Louisa Dickinson of Thetford VT; liv Rumney NH; ch John C b1860, Henry E b1865, Walter b1879; NH-0007-607

Clinton; b1809 s/o Josiah & Judith Marston of Rumney; m1834 Mary Ann Wilbur; liv Rumney NH; ch Lorenzo H, Nancy G, Hattie A; NH-0007-607

Daniel; b1769 s/o Gould of Epping; liv Deerfield, Chester; NH-0003-25

Daniel; s/o Offin; m Abigail Cressy d/o John of Bradford; ch Mary Jane m Joshua P Marshall, Ira m Hester Goewey, Sabrina A m Frederick Cheney s/o Stephen, Christine P m Thomas Little, John m Emma Day d/o Ward; NH-0004-202

David C; liv Warren NH; ch David A, 6 others; NH-0007-

FRENCH (continued)
633
David J; b1805 s/o Joshua & ggs/o Timothy; liv Loudon NH; ch Dr Isaac S d1878 m Augusta French; NH-0004-512
Enoch; s/o Abram & Hannah French; m1823 Eliza Cate of Epsom; liv Pittsfield NH; ch John C b1832 m Annie M Philbrick, 4 others; NH-0001-157, NH-0002-133
Ezekiel; b1754 s/o Nathaniel of Poplin NH; m1778 Phebe Ward b1758 d/o Bagley of Poplin NH; liv Epping & Sandwich NH; ch Nathaniel b1781 m Grace Beede Crosby, Susanna b1783 m James O Freeman Esq & m Dr Lot Cook, Rebecca b1784 m Josiah Smith s/o Eliphalet, Phoebe b1792 m Nathaniel Burley Jr & m Elder Scarriott & m John Crosby, Sarah (Sally) b1795 (b1797) m Dr Charles White, James b1799; NH-0006-670 & 706
George Barstow; b1846 s/o James of Tuftonborough; liv Nashua; NH-0006-265
George P; b1840 s/o Amos & Abiah Wells of Rumney; m Ellen W Fletcher d/o George W; liv Rumney NH; ch Alice E b1878, Joseph Garfield b1881; NH-0007-607
Ira; s/o Daniel & Abigail Cressy; m Hester Goewey of Lansingburg NY, liv Bradford NH, Lansingburg NY; ch Hattie; NH-0004-202
Jacob; s/o Henry & --- Jones of S Hampton; m Abigail Shaw of Kensington & m 2 others; liv Kensington, PA; ch John b1801, Abigail dy, Irena m Moses Stokes; NH-0003-365
James; b1811; m1842 Eveline A Moulton d/o of Simon of Moultonborough; liv Moultonborough NH; ch James E, George B, Lydia, John Q A dy; NH-0006-413
James E; b1845 s/o James of Tuftonborough; m1867 Martha E Hill d/o William of Great Falls; liv Moultonborough NH; NH-0006-415
John; s/o Oliver of Sutton NH; m Polly Brown & m Maria J Flanders; ch John H m Hannah

FRENCH (continued)
M Dow d/o Lorenzo & Margaret French of Warren, 8 others; NH-0007-557
John; b1801 s/o Jacob & Abigail Shaw; m1826 Harriet Brown b1807 d/o John & Lucy Rowe & m1864 Irena Brown b1815 sis/o Harriet; liv Kensington NH; ch/o Harriet - John C, Lucy A, Irena S, Harriet A; NH-0003-365
John C; b1832 s/o Enoch & Eliza Cate of Pittsfield NH; m1858 Annie M Philbrick d/o L B Esq of Deerfield NH; liv Pittsfield & Manchester NH, Boston MA; ch Lizzie A, Susie P, George Abram; NH-0002-133
John F; b1818 s/o Rev Jonathan & Rebecca of N Hampton; m1843 Lemira Leavitt b1823 d/o Simon & Dolly; liv N Hampton; ch Nellie L m Newell W Healey of Hampton Falls, John L, Oliver S m Clara B Drake of N Hampton, Annie D m John F Hobbs of N Hampton; NH-0003-421
Jonathan; m1736 Johanna Elkins; liv Salisbury MA, Danville; ch Johanna dy, Henry, Elizabeth, Jonathan dy, Jonathan, Joseph, Mary, Mehitable, Lt Jonathan b1757 m --- Batchelder, 3 others; NH-0003-163
Jonathan; b1740 s/o Moses & Esther Thayer of Braintree; m1773 Abigail Richards d/o Benjamin of Weymouth; liv Andover; ch Rev Jonathan b1778 m Rebecca Farrar, 4 dau; NH-0003-415
Lt Jonathan; b1757 s/o Jonathan & Johanna Elkins; m --- Batchelder d/o Dea Elisha & Theodate; liv Danville; ch Mary m Nathaniel Clark, Jonathan, Phineas b1791 m Jane Eaton & m Eliza Worthen, Lucy m Osmond Spoffard, Robert; NH-0003-163
Jonathan MD; b1778 s/o Lt Joseph of Salisbury; m --- Shaw; liv Hampton NH, Amesbury MA; NH-0004-618
Rev Jonathan; b1778 s/o Jonathan & Abigail Richards of Andover; m Rebecca Farrar

FRENCH (continued)
d/o Dea Samuel of Lincoln; liv N Hampton; ch 5 sons, 6 dau; NH-0003-415

Joseph; liv Warren & Epping NH; ch John, David C, 10 others; NH-0007-633

Joshua; liv Loudon NH; ch Sally, John, David, Timothy, Sally, Daniel, Charles; NH-0004-508

Josiah; m Judith Marston; liv Rumney NH; ch Betsey m Daniel Hardy, Amos, Clinton b1809 m Mary Ann Wilbur, Pamelia m Israel Hardy, Samuel b1813 m Hannah P Stevens, Emeline m George Merrill, John b1820 m1845 Lucy Ann Glover d/o Seth, Charles N b1829 m Hannah M Ellis; NH-0007-607

Moses; b1700 s/o Thomas gs/o John; m1730 Esther Thayer d/o Ephraim & Sarah; liv Braintree; ch Jonathan b1740 m Abigail Richards, 6 others; NH-0003-415

Nathaniel; b1725 s/o Samuel b1699 gs/o Joseph b1676 ggs/o Samuel gggs/o Edward; liv Poplin NH; ch Ezekiel b1754 m Phebe Ward; NH-0006-706

Capt Nathaniel; bro/o Ezekiel; m1780 Martha Jewell d/o Rev Jacob; liv Sandwich NH; ch Sargeant, Nathaniel, Anna, Martha, Dorothy m John Severance; NH-0006-671

Nathaniel; b1781 s/o Ezekiel & Phoebe Weed; m Grace Beede Crosby; ch Dr Otis, Ezekiel; NH-0006-670

Offin; liv Bradford; ch Offin m Phebe Eaton, Ruana m Jonathan Muzzy of Weare, Paskey, Soeera m James Gilman of Hillsborough, Daniel m Abigail Cressy, Phebe m Jonathan Muzzy of Weare, Susan m Jonathan Peaslee of Weare, James m Hannah Eaton, Judith, Aaron, 2 dy; NH-0004-202

Peter; b1788 s/o Henry & Anna Shepard of Kingston NH; m Mary Stevens of Danville & m Elizabeth Kimball d/o Benjamin & Abiah; liv Kingston; ch/o Mary - Henry; NH-0003-374

Phineas; b1791 s/o Lt Jonathan

FRENCH (continued)
& --- Batchelder of Danville; m Jane Eaton b1793 & m Eliza Worthen d/o Ezekiel of Bridgewater MA; liv Danville; ch/o Jane - Susan E m Moses B Gove & m1861 Timothy Tilton & m1863 Horatio Beede, Jonathan b1818, Joseph, Jabez; ch/o Eliza - James M, Sophronia A; NH-0003-163

Robert S; b1801 s/o Jonathan of Danville NH; m1835 Sarah Kimball b1805 d/o Abel & Abigail Wood of Fremont; liv Chester & Fremont NH; ch Sarah E; NH-0003-297

Samuel; b1813 s/o Josiah & Judith Marston of Rumney; m1848 Hannah P Stevens d/o William L; liv Rumney NH; ch Orlando B b1850 m1879 Eva L Wyatt, Ella M, Martha dy, William L, Charles F, Anna dy; NH-0007-607

Timothy; liv Loudon NH; ch Betty, Joshua, Betty, Mary, Timothy, Rachel, Joanna; NH-0004-508

FRETTS,
Henry; m Joanna Barnes d/o Lt Reuben; ch Harriet, Lorena, George, Catherine dy, Richard, Henry, Emmeline; NH-0002-542

Richard; s/o Henry & Joanna Barnes; liv Merrimack; ch Emma, Henry, Laura; NH-0002-542

FROST,
George E; b1856 s/o Pepperell & Lydia Brown; m1878 Maria G Hall d/o Ephraim of Lawrence MA; ch Levi W; NH-0003-424

Henry; b1832 s/o Washington & Samantha Laurence of Granby CAN; m1860 Elizabeth Burrows Gilbert d/o John & Mrs Ann Burrows Attwill; ch Henry Gilbert b1864, William Lawrence b1868; NH-0002-434

Pepperell; b1815 d/o William & Sally Johnson of Parsonfield ME; m1843 Lydia Brown b1811 d/o Levi & Lydia Lovering & m1880 Hannah Libbey White d/o James Libbey wid/o P White; liv ME, MA, N Hampton NH; ch/o Lydia - Thomas B, Lydia A m William J Breed of Lynn MA, Levi W dy, George E b1856

FROST (continued)
m Maria G Hall; NH-0003-424
William;  b1788 s/o Simon &
Eunice of ME; m Sally Johnson
b1791 d/o David & m Mrs
Oliver Murfey; liv Parson-
field ME; ch/o Sally - David,
Lydia, Pepperell b1815 m
Lydia Brown & m Hannah Libbey
White, Jonathan J, Simon,
Sarah J, Mary A, Anna; ch/o
Murfey - Betsey F, Olive T,
Ann M; NH-0003-424
FULLER,
Calvin;  m Asenath Brown d/o
Stephen T & Anna Davis; liv
New Boston; ch George; NH-
0007-182
Capt David; s/o Joshua & Joanna
Taylor; m1782 Elsea Gleason &
m1792 Jerusha Adams b1774 d/o
Jonathan & Hannah Yemmons &
m1793 Orinda Bingham b1772;
ch/o Elsea - David b1783 m
Keziah Kimball, Elsea b1786 m
Lemuel Bingham of Gilsum;
ch/o Orinda - Levi b1794 dy,
Jerusha b1796, Lyman b1798,
Levi b1801 dy, Orinda b1803 m
Samuel Isham Jr, George W
b1805 d7, Bradford b1807,
Alvira b1809; NH-0002-425
David;  b1783 s/o Capt David &
Elsea Gleason; m1806 Keziah
Kimball d/o Benjamin & Hannah
Parker of Hillsborough; liv
Gilsum & Hillsborough &
Francestown NH; ch David
Gardner b1806 m Jane
Converse, Mark W b1808 m
Sarah Conn, John Gibson b1810
m Ann Jones, William F b1812;
NH-0002-425
David Gardner;  b1806 s/o David
& Keziah Kimball; m1830 Jane
Converse d/o Josiah & Sally
Dean of Amherst NH; liv Utica
& Rome NY, Washington DC,
Richmond VA, Concord NH; ch
Sarah Jane b1836 m Joseph
Harlow of Plymouth MA, Henry
W b1838 m Elizabeth Beecher,
George C b1840 m1861 Josie
French d/o Joseph & ---
Shackford of Concord NH;
Ethelinda G b1849 dy; NH-
0002-425
Henry W;  b1838 s/o David
Gardner & Jane Converse;
m1863 Elizabeth Beecher d/o
Laban & Frances Lewis of

FULLER (continued)
Boston MA; liv Boston MA; ch
Fred b1872; NH-0002-425
John Gibson;  b1810 s/o David &
Keziah Kimball; m Ann Jones
d/o Nathaniel & Betsy Robbins
of Hillsborough; liv Hills-
borough; ch Abbie A b1834 m
Stephen Westcott, Helen Marr
b1836 dy, Wirt Ximeo b1850 m
Addie A Russell; NH-0002-425
Joshua;  b1728; m Joanna Taylor;
liv CT, Surry; ch Joshua,
Levi, Capt David m Elsea
Gleason & m Jerusha Adams & m
Orinda Bingham; NH-0002-425
Mark W;  b1808 s/o Daniel &
Keziah Kimball; m1831 Sarah
Conn d/o William & Sally
Priest of Hillsborough; ch
Susan b1840; NH-0002-425
Martin;  m Letitia Duncan d/o
James & Jane Christie; ch
Thomas James Duncan, Lydia J
m Rev L H Stone of Cabot VT,
Mary m Stearns Foster of
Keene, Hiram; NH-0002-354
Wirt Ximeo;  b1850 s/o John
Gibson & Ann Jones of Hills-
borough;  m1870 Addie A
Russell d/o George E &
Caroline Carter Grant of
Boston MA; liv Boston MA; ch
Wirt R b1871, Addie May
b1874; NH-0002-426
FULTON,
Charles J;  s/o Joseph W & Lucy
A Sargent; m Mary A Wilson;
ch John W, Charles Warren;
NH-0002-390
James;  b1777 s/o Robert & Sarah
Brown; m1803 Hannah Faulkner
b1779; liv Deering; ch Betsy
b1803, James b1806 m Eunice
Gregg, Lyman b1807, Jennie
b1810 m John Gillis, Robert
b1812 m Mary Richardson,
Curtis b1814 m Elizabeth
Glover, Abiel b1816 dy, Mary
b1818, Charles b1821, Hannah
b1823 m John Reed of Nashua
NH; NH-0002-377 & 389
James;  b1806 s/o James & Hannah
Faulkner of Deering NH; m1835
Eunice Gregg d/o Capt Samuel
& Lydia Dodge of Deering; liv
Andover & Methuen MA, Deering
NH; ch Lydia A b1836, Joseph
W b1839 m Laura A Harndon & m
Lucy A Sargent, Hannah J
b1842 m Henry Gove, Charles J

FULTON (continued)
  b1848 m Mary A Wilson, Mary E
  b1853 m Urvin G Rowell; NH-
  0002-377 & 389
Joseph W; b1839 s/o James &
  Eunice Gregg of Deering; m
  Laura A Harnden & m Lucy A
  Sargent; ch/o Laura - James
  Arthur, Warren Gregg; ch/o
  Lucy - Charles J m Mary A
  Wilson, Mary E m Irving G
  Rowell; NH-0002-390
Robert; b1752; m Sarah Brown
  b1750; liv Francestown; ch
  Alexander b1773, Samuel
  b1775, James b1777 m Hannah
  Faulkner, John b1780,
  Jonathan b1782, Robert b1785
  m Sally Wilkins; NH-0002-377
  & 389
FURBER,
William; bc 1614; m Elizabeth
  ---; ch William b1646 m ? &
  m1694 Elizabeth Heard d/o
  Capt John wid/o James Nute,
  Jethro, Susanna m1664 John
  Bickford, Elizabeth m1664
  John Dam, Bridgett m Thomas
  Bickford; NH-0003-770
FURBISH,
Henry Hart; b1835 s/o
  Dependence H & Persis H Brown
  of Gray ME; m1856 Harriet A
  Ordway d/o Reuben of Portland
  ME & m1883 Susan A Emery d/o
  George F of Portland ME; liv
  Portland ME, Berlin NH; ch/o
  Harriet - Willard H b1862, 2
  others; ch/o Susan - Persis E
  b1884; NH-0005-825
FURBUSH,
Daniel; b1791; m Nancy Grapes &
  m Betsey Leighton d/o William
  & Mary; liv Dummer NH,
  Chelsea MA; ch 8 sons, 4 dau;
  NH-0005-857
FURNALD,
Dimond; liv Loudon NH; ch
  Sarah, Polly, Nabby, Thomas,
  David, Robert, Josiah,
  Comfort, Rachel, Eunice,
  Susa, John, Dimond, Chase,
  Charlotte; NH-0004-508

-G-

GAGE,
Aaron; liv Methuen MA, Merri-

GAGE (continued)
  mack; ch Isaac, Dea Aaron,
  Phineas, Moses, Mehitabel m
  Thomas Underwood, 1 dau m
  Josiah Tinker of Bedford; NH-
  0002-543
Dea Aaron; s/o Aaron; liv
  Merrimack; ch Hannah, Aaron,
  Naomi m Daniel Muzzy, Sally m
  --- Conant & m Stephen
  Crooker, Benjamin, Isaac,
  Solomon, Mary, Martha, Fanny;
  NH-0002-543
Calvin; s/o Phineas; liv
  Enfield NH; ch Hiram, Lucy m
  John H Morse, Julius; NH-
  0007-258
Converse; b1817 s/o Phineas &
  Phebe Eaton; m1844 Cerlania
  Carroll d/o John P & Rachel
  Powers of Croyden NH; liv
  Enfield & Sutton NH; ch Susan
  E b1847 m Charles W Purmort,
  George dy, George W b1853;
  NH-0004-649
Enoch; s/o Phineas; liv Merri-
  mack, Bradford; ch Foster,
  Walter, Joseph, Ann E; NH-
  0002-543
Ezekiel; m Alice A Woodbury d/o
  John & Betsy A Hobbs; ch
  Frank P; NH-0002-648
Hiram; s/o Phineas & Phebe
  Eaton; m Mary Goss & m Susan
  Fuller; liv Royalton VT; ch
  Henry; NH-0004-649
Horace MD; b1811; m Louise
  Putney of Dunbarton; liv
  Hopkinton & Wilmot & E Weare
  NH; ch Horace P; NH-0004-374
Jesse E; s/o Phineas & Phebe
  Eaton; m Hannah T Sweatland
  of E Lebanon NH; ch Lura,
  Phebe, Roswell m Sarah F
  Little, 2 others; NH-0007-285
Moses; s/o Aaron; liv Merri-
  mack; ch Betsy, Moses, Sally,
  Ruth, John, David, Joseph N,
  Mehitabel, Susan, Charles;
  NH-0002-543
Phineas; s/o Aaron; liv Merri-
  mack; ch Lydia m Alexander
  Wilkins, Sally, Anna, Isaac,
  Benjamin, Polly dy, Mary,
  Enoch, Stephen, Parker dy,
  George; NH-0002-543
Phineas; m Phebe Eaton; liv
  Haverhill MA, Enfield NH; ch
  Jesse m Hannah Swetland,
  William m Eliza Sanborn,
  Samuel m Rosamond Alden & m

GAGE (continued)
Nancy Little, George m Mary Whitford, Calvin m Abigail Prescott, Hiram m Mary Goss & m Susan Fuller, Converse b1817 m Cerlania Carroll, Eliza m Benjamin Collins & m Benjamin Perley, Amelia, Abigail m Francis Robbins, Nancy m Aaron Wells; NH-0004-649

Roswell; s/o Jesse E & Hannah T Sweatland; m Sarah F Little d/o Elbridge G & Nancy Mc-Kinney; liv Grafton NH; ch Ella R, Eva M, Emma J, Fred; NH-0007-285

Stephen; s/o Phineas; liv Merrimack, Amherst; ch Parmelia, Sophronia, Mary A, Parker, John, Orlando; NH-0002-543

GALE,
Dr Amos G; b1807 s/o Dr Amos of Kingston gs/o Dr Josiah Bartlett; m Mary Greene Ayer d/o Hon Richard H; liv Hooksett, Manchester; NH-0004-374

Benjamin; b1771; m Sally Noyes; liv Kingston & Landaff NH; ch John F, 4 others; NH-0007-402

Charles A; b1818; m1850 Laura G Wetherbee; liv Gilmanton & Haverhill NH; ch Charles A, 3 sons; NH-0007-378

Daniel; b1775 s/o Stephen & Susannah Flanders; m Abigail Page d/o Dea Benjamin & Hannah Sanborn of Epping; liv Gilmanton NH; ch Hazen, Daniel M, Napoleon Bonaparte b1815, Benjamin P; NH-0004-830

Daniel B; b1816 bro/o Hon Jacob; m Charlotte E Pettengill of Salisbury; liv St Louis; NH-0004-618

Hon Jacob; b1814 bro/o Daniel B; m Charlotte Bartlett d/o Dr Peter; liv Peoria IL; NH-0004-618

Rev Jonathan; b1820; m Caroline Persis Staples of Londonderry & m1848 Mrs Catharine C Johnson Pinkham; liv Jamaica VT, Jackson NH; ch/o Caroline - Francis Asbury, Caroline P m C C Pendexter; ch/o Catharine - Cyrus E, Kate J m David Wakefield, Fred H, George E, J Hubert; NH-0006-

GALE (continued)
955
Luke; s/o Stephen & Margaret Sanburn; m Louisa A Perkins d/o Elias & Rebecca Simonds; ch Sarah L, Clara A, Orrin S m Emma R Bailey; NH-0007-116

Orrin S; s/o Luke & Louisa A Perkins; m Emma R Bailey; ch Shirley L, Angie L; NH-0007-116

Stephen; s/o Eliphalet; m Margaret Sanburn of Bristol NH; ch Luke m Louisa A Perkins, 12 others; NH-0007-116

Stephen; b1739; m Susannah Flanders; liv Exeter & Raymond & Gilmanton NH; ch Daniel b1775 m Abigail Page; NH-0004-830

GALLINGER,
Jacob H; b1837; m1860 Mary Anna Bailey d/o Maj Isaac of Salisbury NH; liv Cornwall Ontario, Cincinnati OH, Keene & Concord NH; ch Alice M, Kate C, William H, Ralph E, 2 others; NH-0004-159

GAMBLE,
William; b1708; m ---; liv Eng & Boston MA; NH-0002-41

GANNET,
William; liv Springfield VT, Haverhill; ch William H, J M, John P, C T; NH-0007-576

GANNETT,
Matthew; s/o Seth; m --- Latham & m Priscilla Hayford; ch/o ? - Consider, Seth, Hitty, Matthew, Allen, Faxon, Consider, Maria; NH-0006-767

Nathaniel Brett; s/o Seth; m Sally Mason; liv Tamworth NH; ch Consider, Susan m Seth Hayford, Nancy m --- Wentworth, Louisa m --- Wentworth, Jane m --- Johnson, Miranda m --- Gray, Lewis, Warren; NH-0006-767

Seth; liv Bridgewater, Tamworth NH; ch Matthew m --- Latham & m Priscilla Hayford, Nathaniel Brett m Sally Mason, Seth, Thomas m Hannah Hart, Philena m Nathaniel Hayford, Phebe m Isaac Glines, Hannah m Oliver Washburn, Hitty m Jacob Hardin, Susan m Jacob Snow; NH-0006-767

**GARLAND,**

Alexis; s/o Eben & Lydia Hayes of Bartlett NH; ch Benjamin C, Eben O, Richard A, Fred E; NH-0006-913

Daniel; s/o Daniel & Sally Kennard; m Charlotte Caswell d/o Abraham & Polly Brown; ch Sally, Calista, 7 others; NH-0007-284

Eben; s/o Richard & Sarah Watson; m Lydia Hayes of Rochester; liv Bartlett NH; ch Alexis, Richard dy, Otis dy, 4 dau; NH-0006-913

George W; b1832 s/o Jonathan & Deborah of Holderness; m1863 Eliza A Batchelder d/o Increase & Susan Hart; ch Willie R b1865; NH-0007-597

Jacob; s/o John of Newbury & Hampton; m1682 Rebecca Sedy; liv Chester, Hampton; ch Jacob b1682, 11 others; NH-0003-377

Richard; d1853; m Sarah Watson of Rochester; liv Bartlett, Dover; ch Eben m Lydia Hayes; NH-0006-913

True; m Lydia N Scruton d/o David & Lydia C Reed of Holderness NH; liv Pittsfield NH; ch Monroe T; NH-0007-396

**GARNSEY,**

Cyril; m Saloma Garfield b1769 of Warwick MA; liv Richmond, Whitefield; ch Dr Darius; NH-0005-482

**GARVIN,**

Ebenezer; b1773 s/o Capt James & Dorothy Wentworth; m Lydia Wentworth; liv Wakefield NH; ch Col James b1794 m Nancy Philbrook & m Mary Guptil, Wentworth m1823 Sarah Wentworth, John, Capt Ebenezer b1815 m Almira Lang, Betsy, Sarah, Lois, Mary m1832 Peter Young of Acton; NH-0006-524

Capt Ebenezer; b1815 s/o Ebenezer & Lydia Wentworth of Wakefield NH; m1848 Almira Lang b1824 d/o Samuel & Lydia Thurber; liv Wakefield NH, Wolfboro Jct; ch James Wentworth b1849 m Charlotte J Maleham, Mary Eliza b1852, Samuel Francis b1858, Lydia Maria b1861, John Howard; NH-0006-524

James; m Sarah Hobbs; liv IRE,

**GARVIN** (continued)

Rollinsford, Somersworth; ch James, Sarah, Elizabeth, Rachel, John, Thomas, Capt Paul; NH-0006-524

Capt James; b1747 s/o Capt Paul; m1770 Dorothy Wentworth; ch Ebenezer James b1773 m Lydia Wentworth; NH-0006-524

Col James; b1794 s/o Ebenezer & Lydia Wentworth of Wakefield NH; m1818 Nancy Philbrook d/o Eliphalet & m1827 Mary Guptil; liv Wakefield NH; ch John W; NH-0006-524

James Wentworth; b1849 s/o Capt Ebenezer & Elmira Lang; m1872 Charlotte J Maleham d/o William A & Nancy Pike; ch Bertha Maud b1873, Clara Maleham b1875, James Philip b1880, Samuel Francis b1885; NH-0006-524

John W; s/o Col James; ch Charles Parker, Florence Jones, Hattie Caroline; NH-0006-524

William R; b1830 s/o Samuel & Susan Roberts of Rollinsford; m1862 Frances H Yeaton of Rollinsford; liv Rollinsford; ch Annie Bertha, Clara W, William R, Susie, Homer, Gertrude, Samuel R; NH-0003-680

**GATES,**

Bazeleel; m Sarah Evans d/o Jonathan; liv Shelburne NH; ch Caleb m Bathsheba Porter, Jefferson m Maria Porter; NH-0005-874

Caleb; s/o Bazeleel & Sarah Evans; m Bathsheba Porter; liv Shelburne NH; ch Woodbury m --- Evans d/o Hazen, Cass, Matilda, Frank; NH-0005-874

**GATHERCOLE,**

John; m Maria C Keysar d/o John & Sarah Clark Wiswall; ch James C, Sarah E, Phebe E; NH-0005-695

**GAULT,**

Jesse; b1790 s/o Matthew & Elizabeth Bunton; m Dolly Clement d/o Joshua & Abigail Head; liv Springfield & Hooksett NH; ch Matthew b1817, Almira C b1819 m Harlan P Gerrish, Hon Jesse b1823 m Martha A Otterson, Martha H

GAULT (continued)
b1828; NH-0004-389
Hon Jesse; b1823 s/o Jesse & Dolly Clement; m1846 Martha A Otterson d/o Isaac C & Margaret Head of Hooksett; liv Hooksett; ch --- m Frank C Towle of Suncook, 2 sons, 2 dau; NH-0004-389
Matthew; b1755; m Elizabeth Bunton; liv Chester; ch Jesse b1790 m Dolly Clement, 11 others; NH-0004-389
GAYER,
William; m Dorcas Starbuck d/o Edward & Katherine of Nantucket; ch Demaris m Nathaniel Coffin; NH-0003-773
GEORGE,
Austin; b1803 s/o Moses & Susannah Nevins; m Sarah Morrison of Plymouth; ch Henry S b1838 m Mary J Farnham; NH-0007-585
Charles S; m1881 Christabel Chandler d/o Nathaniel L & Laura A Goodale; ch Charles A b1882, Allison S b1882 dy; NH-0002-429
Edmond W; b1834 s/o Samuel & Ruth Walker; m1860 Rachel P Clement; liv Hebron NH; ch Lewis C, Charles E m1885 Sadie L Wise d/o Willard W & Susan Duston; NH-0007-388
Henry S; b1838 s/o Austin & Sarah Morrison; m1859 Mary J Farnham; liv Plymouth NH; ch Fred N b1860; NH-0007-585
John Esq; b1780; m Ruth Bradley & m Mary Hatch d/o Samuel of Greenland NH; liv Hopkinton & Concord NH; ch/o Ruth - Capt Paul Rolfe b1807, Clarissa Bartlett m Hon Hamilton E Perkins, Susan Emery dy; ch/o Mary - John Hatch b1824 m Susan Ann Brigham & Salvadora Meade Graham; NH-0001-98, NH-0004-410
John Hatch; b1824 s/o John & Mary Hatch gs/o Samuel Hatch; m1849 Susan Ann Brigham d/o Capt Levi of Boston MA & m1864 Salvadora Meade Graham d/o Col James D; liv Concord NH; ch/o Susan - John Paul, Charles Peaslee, Benjamin Pierce, Jane Appleton m Henry E Bacon, Anne Brigham; ch/o Salvadora - Charlotte Graham;

GEORGE (continued)
NH-0001-98, NH-0004-28
Moses; b1774 s/o William; m1800 Susannah Nevins; ch Matilda, Austin b1803 m Sarah Morrison, Amanda m Samuel Noyes, Elmira m Noah Cummings, Washington b1804 m Louisa Abbott; NH-0007-585
Capt Paul Rolfe; b1807 s/o John Esq & Ruth Bradley; m1855 Caroline Livingston d/o William of Lowell MA; liv Concord & Hopkinton NH, Lowell MA; NH-0004-410
Samuel; b1803 s/o James b1773; m1822 Ruth Walker d/o Daniel & Hannah Hazelton; liv Hebron NH; ch Edmond W b1834 m Rachel P Clement, Edwin W b1834 m1882 M Ellen McDermid d/o William & Abigail French; NH-0007-388
Stephen; s/o Asa & Sally Worthley; m Susanna Allen of VT; ch Stephen m Lucina P Hill, 11 others; NH-0007-287
Stephen; s/o Stephen & Susanna Allen; m Lucina P Hill of Grafton; ch Mary m --- Ford, 6 others; NH-0007-287
Washington; b1804 s/o Moses & Susannah Nevins; m1838 Louisa Abbott d/o John & Phebe Wells; liv Plymouth NH; ch Ellen A m James Peabody, Harriet A, Martha C, Louisa V, Wilber O, Charles W; NH-0007-585
William W; b1807; m Lucy B Whipple of Croydon; liv Sunapee & Canaan NH; ch 1 dy, Isabell m Dr Asa Wheat of Canaan, Harriet S m James H Kelly, Frances K, Charles Day, Allen H m Jane E Wheat of Canaan; NH-0007-229
GERRISH,
Maj Enoch; b1750 s/o Capt Stephen; liv Boscawen; ch Isaac b1782 m Caroline Lawrence; NH-0004-157
Col Enoch; b1882? s/o Isaac & Caroline Lawrence of Boscawen; m1854 Miranda O Lawrence d/o Joseph S & Harriet N; liv Boscawen & Concord NH; ch Frank Lawrence b1866, Lizzie Miranda b1860; NH-0004-157
Isaac; b1782 s/o Maj Enoch of

GERRISH (continued)

Boscawen; m Caroline Lawrence; liv Boscawen; ch Col Enoch b1882? m Miranda O Lawrence; NH-0004-157

Capt Stephen; liv Boscawen; ch Col Henry, Maj Enoch b1750, 1 son; NH-0004-157

GIFFORD,

Ezra L; s/o Ezra T & Almira Kimball of Alexandria; m Helen L Braley d/o John W & Harriet M; ch Leon C, Ada L, Minnie S, Harry L; NH-0007-120

Ezra T; s/o Peleg & Phebe Brownell; m Almira Kimball d/o John & Kesiah; liv Alexandria & Grafton NH; ch Phebe A, Adelaide, Ellen, Ezra L m Helen L Braley, Walter, Thomas W, Lorenzo N, Mary; NH-0007-120 & 287

John; s/o Benjamin; m Ruth Luther; liv Westport MA; ch Peleg m Phebe Brownell of Westport MA, 11 others; NH-0007-287

GILBERT,

Ahimaaz; s/o Zadok & Rhoda Allen; liv Lyme NH; ch Phineas, 8 others; NH-0007-538

Hammond Barnes; b1834 s/o Joseph & Alvira Moore; m1869 Julia Etta Beverly d/o John Randolph of Paris IL; ch Joseph Beverly b1870, Mary Florence b1873 dy, Clifford Hammond b1875, Julia Gertrude b1878 dy; NH-0002-434

Sir Humphrey; bro/o Sir John, Sir Adrien, Sir Walter; liv ENG; ch Raleigh; NH-0002-433

Humphrey; m Elizabeth Kilham d/o Daniel; liv Ipswich MA, Wenham; ch John m Martha Dodge & 3 dau; NH-0002-433

John; s/o Humphrey & Elizabeth Kilham; m Martha Dodge; liv Glouchester; ch William, Jonathan; NH-0002-433

John; b1773 s/o Joseph & Sarah Robbins; mc1797 Susan Pollard b1773 d/o Benjamin; liv Hillsborough & Greenfield NH; ch Joseph b1799 m Alvira Moore, Benjamin b1801, John b1804 m Mrs Ann Burrows Attwill, Nancy Dutton b1807, Sarah Tarbell b1816; NH-0002-

GILBERT (continued)

431 & 434

John; b1804 s/o John & Susan Pollard; m1833 Mrs Ann Burrows Attwill of Woodbridge ENG b1802; liv Boston MA; ch Elizabeth Burrows b1834 m Henry Frost, Ellen Lizette b1845 m Moses Field Fowler; NH-0002-431 & 434

John; b1832 s/o Joseph & Alivra Moore; m1855 Abby Jane Keay b1832 & m1861 Lizzie Lake Keay b1834; ch Susan Alice b1858, John Clark b1860 dy, Mary Abby b1862, James Porter b1867, Carrie Louise b1870, Bessie b1872; NH-0002-434

Jonathan; s/o John & Martha Dodge; ch Daniel m Elizabeth Porter, Benjamin m Estha Perkins, Joseph m Mary Coggswell & m Elizabeth Whipple; NH-0002-433

Joseph; bro/o Capt Samuel; liv Littleton MA; ch John, 1 dau; NH-0002-431

Joseph; s/o Jonathan; m Mary Coggswell & m Elizabeth Whipple; liv Littleton MA; ch/o ? - John m Sarah Cummings, Samuel, Mary, Elizabeth m Aaron Stratton, Daniel, Joseph b1751 m Sarah Robbins, Abigail Haynes; NH-0002-434

Joseph; b1751 s/o Joseph & ?; m Sarah Robbins b1751; liv Littleton MA, Hillsborough NH; ch John b1773 m Susan Pollard, Paggee b1776 m Joseph Harwood & m William Willard; NH-0002-434

Joseph; b1799 s/o John & Susan Pollard; m Alvira Moore of Marlborough b1800; ch Almira b1828 dy, Susan Page b1830 m Rodney S Lakin, John Clark b1832 m Abby Jane Keay & m Lizzie Lake Keay, Hammond Barnes b1834 m Julia Etta Beverley; NH-0002-434

Raleigh; s/o Sir Humphrey; liv Compton Castle; ch Humphrey bc1615; NH-0002-433

Col Thomas; s/o Col Samuel of Lyme; m Lydia Lathrop; liv Hebron CT, Lyme NH; ch Clarissa m Maj James Cook, Anna m James Pearson, Abigail m John Dimick, Thomas Lathrop

GILBERT (continued)
m Sally Dimick & m Deborah
Waite, Lydia m Jeremiah
Bingham, Sally m Joseph
Porter, Betsey m Dea Adolphus
Dimick, Polly m Ezra Conant;
NH-0007-526

GILE,
Johnson; liv Enfield NH; ch
Thomas, Daniel, Samuel,
Ebenezer, 2 dau; NH-0007-252

GILL,
John H; b1809 s/o William &
Ruth Hazelton; m1831 Atassa
Blodgett d/o Rev Ebenezer & m
--- Clark wid/o Nathan; liv
Plymouth NH; ch/o ? - 3 sons,
3 dau; NH-0007-592

GILLINGHAM,
Albert L; b1846 s/o Moody &
Julia Twiss; m1876 Elizabeth
Robertson d/o Robert; ch Lena
M; NH-0004-419

Charles H; b1843 s/o Moody &
Julia Twiss; m Elinda Maud
d/o John & Mary Marriott; ch
Maud C, Annie E, Mary A,
Moody, Ralph B; NH-0004-419

James; m1692 Rebecca Bly d/o
John of Salem; liv Salem MA;
ch Rebecca b1693, Hannah
b1694, James b1696, Benjamin
b1697, Martha b1699, Deborah
b1700, John b1704, Mary
b1705, William b1706,
Jonathan b1709, David b1711;
NH-0004-419

James; s/o James; m Polly
Little of Sutton & m Betsey
Lane of Newbury; liv Newbury
NH; ch/o Polly - James,
Daniel, Ruth; ch/o Betsey -
John, Huldah, Joseph L,
Sally, Madison, Moody b1811 m
Julia Twiss, Sally, Ruth,
Soranus, Triphena C, Triphosa
J, Alzina E, Oliver P, Bain-
bridge; NH-0004-419

Moody; b1811 s/o James & Betsey
Lane; m Julia Twiss b1815 d/o
Jeremiah & Marion Peaslee of
Newbury; liv Newbury NH,
Warrensburg NY; ch Charles H
b1843 m Elinda Maud, Albert L
b1846 m Elizabeth Robertson,
Freeman H b1850 m1877 Annie
Peirce d/o Cumming & Caroline
Dowlin, Clara I b1853 m1883
Jesse P Colby s/o Prescott &
Helen M Hanks; NH-0004-419

GILLIS,
John; m Hannah Aiken d/o
William; liv Deering NH; ch
William Aiken, Thomas,
Worcester, John, David,
Horace, Hannah m Reuben Bout-
well; NH-0002-375

GILMAN,
Benjamin R; b1834; m1858 R A
Pitkin; liv Columbia, Cole-
brook; ch Annie; NH-0005-623

David; b1785 s/o James &
Deborah Goodhue; m1812 Sally
Clark d/o Moses of Sanborn-
ton; liv Newmarket & Meredith
NH; ch James b1813 m Susan
Mead, Martha, David; NH-0004-
867

Emerson; bc1795 s/o Stephen &
Dorothy Cough; m Delia Way;
liv Lowell MA, Unity NH; ch
Virgil Chase b1827 m Sarah
Louise Newcomb, & 7 others;
NH-0001-146, NH-0002-210

Horace Way; b1833 bro/o Virgil
C Gilman; m1854 Adaline W
Marsh d/o Fitch P of Hudson;
liv Unity & Lowell & Nashua
NH; ch William V b1856,
Edward M b1862; NH-0002-209

Capt Israel; b1758; m1778
Abigail Folsom; liv New-
market, Tamworth; ch Israel
b1779, Sally b1787; NH-0006-
765

James; (name changed from
Graves) s/o Phineas Graves of
Tuftonborough NH; ch Charles
W, James M, William H, John
W, Edward V, Lyford J, George
F, Phineas G; NH-0006-440

James; b1750 s/o Timothy of New
Market NH gs/o James ggs/o
Moses; m Deborah Goodhue; liv
Meredith NH; ch James,
Samuel, Uriah, Deborah, David
b1785 m Sally Clark, Josiah;
NH-0004-867

James; b1813 s/o David & Sally
Clark; m1836 Susan Mead b1810
d/o William & Eunice Roberts;
liv Meredith NH; ch Granville
B b1837 m Carrie Fletcher,
Martha Jane b1839, James
Marshall b1842 m Mattie
Smith, Mary Susan b1843,
David Frank b1846, Sarah
Frances b1849 dy, Ellen
(Lill) b1851 m Fred S Pres-
cott, Fanny M dy; NH-0004-867

James Marshall; b1842 s/o James

GILMAN (continued)
  & Susan Mead of Meredith NH;
  m Mattie Smith; liv CA, ch
  Marshall F, Herbert M, Carrie
  A, James G, Arthur F, 1
  other; NH-0004-867
  Capt Jeremiah; b1719; m Sarah
  ---; liv Exeter & Wakefield
  NH; ch 9; NH-0006-470
  Lt Jonathan; s/o Benjamin &
  Elizabeth; m1746 Mehitable
  Kimball b1724 d/o Caleb; liv
  Wakefield NH; NH-0006-470
  Joseph; b1807 s/o Andrew &
  Hannah Huckins of Effingham
  gs/o Dudley; m1831 Jane R
  Beede d/o Elijah & Anna Felch
  & m1851 Maria B Cushing d/o
  William & Mary Page; liv
  Tamworth NH; ch/o Jane - Mary
  J, Lydia B m Charles R
  Jackson, Andrew, Albert,
  George E; ch/o Maria - Anna
  M, Sarah F m Samuel O
  Kimball; NH-0006-769
  Samuel F; bro/o David; liv
  Gilmanton & Bethlehem NH; ch
  1 dau m George C Cheeney,
  Albert; NH-0007-166
  Samuel Taylor; s/o Hon
  Nathaniel of Exeter; liv
  Exeter; NH-0003-32
  Stephen; m Anna Huntoon & m1793
  Dorothy Clough; liv Kingston
  NH, Lowell MA; ch/o Dorothy -
  Emerson bc1795 m Delia Way, &
  11 others; NH-0001-146, NH-
  0002-210
  Virgil Chase; b1827 s/o Emerson
  & Delia Way; m1850 Sarah
  Louisa Newcomb d/o Gideon Esq
  of Roxbury NH; liv Unity &
  Nashua NH, Lowell MA; ch
  Hariet Louise m Charles W
  Hoitt of Nashua, Alfred
  Emerson dy; NH-0001-146, NH-
  0002-210
GLEASON,
  Timothy; liv Loudon NH; ch
  John, Edmund, Polly, Timothy,
  Sophia, Moses, Nancy,
  Charlotte, Jeremiah, Warren;
  NH-0004-508
GLIDDEN,
  Charles Mills; m Alice G Smith
  d/o Jeremiah & Betsy Glidden
  of Northfield; liv OH; ch
  Mary Y m George Crawford,
  Steven S m Susan Gannet; NH-
  0004-545
  Squire Charles Sr; d1811; liv

GLIDDEN (continued)
  Northfield NH; ch 1 dau m
  Judge Wadleigh, 1 dau m
  Jeremiah Smith; NH-0004-532
  Steven S; s/o Charles Mills &
  Alice G Smith; m Susan Gannet
  of Ironton OH; ch Aingia A,
  Jesse, 2 sons, Susan G; NH-
  0004-545
GLINES,
  Jabez; b1811; m1840 Merriam
  Alexander d/o Enoch & Merriam
  Colby; ch Erastus O b1841
  m1862 Rebecca J Bunker,
  Alonzo W b1848 m1867 Hattie E
  Corey; NH-0004-286
GLOVER,
  Everett F; s/o Frederick & Lucy
  A Fifield of Rumney NH; m
  Laura Hutchins; ch Louie R
  b1878; NH-0007-612
  Franklin H; b1825; m Phebe
  Streeter of Bethlehem & m
  Alma C Whippleof Lisbon; liv
  Woodstock, Littleton NH; ch/o
  ? - Charles H m Anna Remick
  of Littleton, Joseph, 1 dau;
  NH-0007-498
  Frederick; b1832 s/o Robert; m
  Lucy A Fifield; liv Rumney
  NH; ch Nellie F m W E Walker,
  Everett F m Laura Hutchins,
  Charles E; NH-0007-612
GODFREY,
  Capt James; ch Jonathan,
  Adeline b1812 m Josiah H
  Barker; NH-0003-330
  Joseph; m Sarah Dearborn; liv S
  Hampton NH; ch Reuben b1816 m
  Mary A Davis, 5 others; NH-
  0002-214
  Reuben; b1816 s/o Joseph &
  Sarah Dearborn; m1846 Mary A
  Davis d/o Benjamin A & Sarah
  W Gilson; liv Meredith,
  Nashua; ch Ellen E dy, Mary
  Frances, Charles J; NH-0002-
  214
GOFFE,
  Maj John; s/o Col John of Deer-
  field; liv Bedford; ch 2
  sons; NH-0002-47
GOOCH,
  Arthur W; m Mary A York d/o
  Daniel G & Betsey P Nudd; liv
  Exeter, Kingston; ch Mary
  Alice; NH-0003-364
GOODALE,
  Chandler d/o Thomas Newton &
  Caroline G Calkins Goodale &
  wid/o Nathaniel L Chandler;

GOODALE (continued)
ch Grace L b1868, Carl Z b1870, Myrtle b1876, Alice b1881 dy, 1 son b1885; NH-0002-429

John Harrison; b1816 s/o Jonathan & Sarah Hadlock (Goodell) of Deering; m1848 Celestia S Mooney of North-field NH & m1871 Josephine B Atkinson of Tilton NH; liv Nashua; ch/o Josephine - Charlotte A b1875; NH-0002-379 & 429

Jonathan; s/o Robert & Mary Fowler; m Sarah Hadlock; liv Deering; ch Levi m Mary Howlett, Isaac, Lydia m Jabez Morrill, Clara m Robert Carr, Betsy m Mark Sterrett, John Harrison b1816 m Celestia S Mooney & m Josephine B Atkinson; NH-0002-379

Jonathan; s/o Stephen & Mary Greenleaf of Deering; m Lucy Locke; liv Deering; ch Louisa m John D Muzzy, George W m Martha L Newton, Elbert m Celestia T Smith & m Laura A Chandler, Hilliard m Sarah E Tead, Levi W m Frances E Kidney, James L, Elizabeth H m Robert D Carr; NH-0002-379

Levi; b1797 s/o Jonathan & Sarah Hadlock (Goodell); m1817 Mary Howlett b1799 d/o Thomas & Mary Newton; liv Hillsborough NH; ch Thomas Newton b1819 m Caroline G Calkins & m Mrs Addie L Mather Smith, Mary H b1824 m Daniel B Smith & m George Jones, Sarah A b1826 m John Severence & m Charles P Pike; NH-0002-429

Robert; m ? & m Mary Fowler; liv Salem MA, Weare NH; ch/o Mary - Jonathan m Sarah Hadlock, Stephen m Mary Greenleaf, Mehitable m --- Young & m --- Corlis of Weare NH, Esther; NH-0002-379

Robert; s/o Stephen & Mary Greenleaf of Deering; m Elizabeth Loveren; liv Deering; ch Fanny m Peter Y Frye, Lewis m Emma J Whittle, Eliza Ann m Albert Hadlock, Harriet dy, Frank P; NH-0002-379

Stephen; s/o Robert & Mary Fowler; m Mary Greenleaf; liv Deering; ch Polly m Jonathan Gove, Jonathan m Lucy Locke, Robert m Elizabeth Loveren, Stephen m Judith Rowell, Mehitable m Stephen Chase, Nancy m John Corlis, Hannah m Hilliard Loveren, Clarisy; NH-0002-379

Stephen; s/o Stephen & Mary Greenleaf of Deering; m Judith Rowell; liv VT; ch Mary m Calvin Metcalf, David m Ella E Batchelder, Stephen m Abbie L Myreck, Mercy H m A E Austin, Clara m P F Stowell, Caroline dy, Justin M m Ellen Herbert, Walter F dy; NH-0002-379

Thomas Newton; b1819 s/o Levi & Mary Howlett; m1840 Caroline G Calkins & m Mrs Addie L Mather Smith of Newport NH; liv Hillsborough NH; ch/o Caroline - Laura A b1842 m Nathaniel ' L Chandler & m Elbert Goodale, Mary C b1846 m Capt George A Robbins, Addie J b1853 m O H Warner; ch/o Addie - Emilie E b1884; NH-0002-429

GOODALL,
Ira; bc1789 s/o Rev David of Littleton NH; liv Bath; ch 5 sons, 5 dau; NH-0007-61

GOODELL,
David; s/o David; m Elizabeth Hutchinson; liv Amherst; ch David b1774 m Mary Raymond; NH-0002-260

David; b1774 s/o David & Eliza-beth Hutchinson of Amherst; m Mary Raymond of Mont Vernon; liv Hillsborough, Antrim; ch Dea Jesse R b1807 m Olive Atwood Wright & m Mrs Ruth Wilkins Bennett; NH-0002-260

Hon David H; b1834 s/o Dea Jesse R & Olive Atwood Wright; m1857 Hannah Jane Plumer d/o Jesse T of Goffs-town NH; liv Hillsborough, New London & Antrim NH, Boston MA; ch Dura Dana b1858, Richard C b1868; NH-0001-233, NH-0002-260

Isaac; bc1634 s/o Robert & Katherine; m Patience Cook; ch Isaac Jr b1670 m Mary ---; NH-0002-428

GOODELL (continued)

Isaac Jr; b1670 s/o Isaac & Patience Cook; m1692 Mary ---; ch Samuel b1694 m Anna Fowler, 11 others; NH-0002-428

Dea Jesse R; b1807 s/o David & Mary Raymond of Hillsborough; m Olive Atwood Wright b1807 of Sullivan NH & m Mrs Ruth Wilkins Bennett; liv Hillsborough & Antrim NH; ch/o Olive - Hon David H b1834 m Hannah Jane Plumer; NH-0001-233; NH-0002-260

John; s/o Dea Jonathan; m Lucy Storrs d/o Augustus of Hanover; liv Lyme NH; ch Lora, Persis m O S FLint, Mary m David Hurlburt, Emeline L m Elihu Hurlburt, Nancy B m John W Bliss of Lyme, John S m Maria H Cowell & m Anna L Case, Maria, Marinda, Dolly P m George W Bliss of Lyme, Augusta m John Stump of KS, Harriet N m John McClave of CO; NH-0007-528

Dea Jonathan; liv Lyme NH; ch John m Lucy Storrs, David, Luther m Patty Waterman; NH-0007-528

Jonathan; b1769 s/o Robert & Mary Fowler; m1795 Sarah Hadlock; liv Deering NH; ch Levi b1797 m Mary Howlett, Isaac b1799, Lydia b1802 m Jabez Morrell, Clara b1806 m Robert Carr of Hillsborough NH, Betsy b1808 m Mark Starrett, John H b1816 m Celesta S Mooney & m Josephine B Atkinson; NH-0002-429

Luther; s/o Dean Jonathan; m Patty Waterman; ch Luther, Patty m Nathaniel Kendrick, Fanny m Samuel Flint, Clarissa m John W Flint, Dolly m E W Bradbury; NH-0007-528

Luther; s/o Luther & Patty Waterman; ch Alvin, Levi O, Louisa; NH-0007-528

Robert; b1604 gggs/o Robert; m Katherine ---; liv Ipswich ENG, Salem MA, Danvers; ch Mary bc1630, Abraham bc1632, Isaac bc1634 m Patience Cook; NH-0002-428

Robert; s/o Samuel & Anna

GOODELL (continued)

Fowler; m1742 Lydia Wallace & m1764 Mary Fowler; liv Salem MA, Weare NH; ch/o Lydia - Robert Jr, Samuel; ch/o Mary - Stephen b1766 m Mary Greenleaf, Jonathan b1769 m Sarah Hadlock, Mehitable m --- Young & m --- Corles of Weare NH, Esther; NH-0002-428

Samuel; b1694 s/o Isaac Jr & Mary ---; m1717 Anna Fowler of Saulsbury; ch Robert m Lydia Wallace, Enoch m Mary Fowler, Bartholomew, Esther (Collins), Hannah (McIntire), Mary m Jude Hacket, Anna m Enoch Fowler, 1 dau m Moses Day; NH-0002-428

GOODNO,

Henry; m Nancy Jackson d/o Joseph; liv Canterbury, Shelburne, Gilead; ch Moses, 7 others; NH-0005-892

GOODNOW,

Asa; m Orril Burnap; liv Sudbury MA, Deering NH; ch Ansa m Elizabeth Eaton, Persis m Daniel W Carpenter & m Dr Josiah R Parington & m Samuel Wilson, Dexter dy, Orril dy, Fidelia m George W Colby; NH-0002-387

GOODRICH,

Charles B; b1812; m1827 Harriet N Shattuck of Portsmouth; liv Hanover & Portsmouth NH; NH-0003-22

GOODWIN,

Daniel; b1789; m Sarah Heath; liv Newton, Kingston; ch John B m Dorothy Marden, Samuel, Hannah, Mary, Henry, Frank, Thomas, William, Abby, Elizabeth; NH-0003-386

Daniel Lewis; b1839 s/o John B & Dorothy Marden of Kingston; m Sarah F Brown d/o Thomas M & Martha McKinley; liv Plaistow, Haverhill MA, Kingston NH; ch John D, Lewis M, Lydia A, Mattie E, Susie F, Helen G; NH-0003-387

George; s/o William & Betsy Chadbourne; m Julia Moulton; liv Tamworth NH; ch Charles W b1849 m Abbie M Walker, Jeremiah C b1851 m Emma Bean, Luella b1855 m William Corson; NH-0006-774

Ichabod; s/o Samuel & Nancy

GOODWIN (continued)
Thompson Gerrish of Berwick ME; m1827 Sarah Parker Rice d/o William of Portsmouth; liv Portsmouth; ch 1 son, 2 dau, 4 others; NH-0003-101
Jeremiah C; b1851 s/o George & Julia Moulton of Tamworth NH; m Emma Bean of Penacook; liv Tamworth NH; ch Flossie, Aggie; NH-0006-774
John B; s/o Daniel & Sarah Heath; m1836 Dorothy Marden d/o Thomas & Hannah Hunt; liv Kingston; ch Daniel dy, Daniel Lewis b1839 m Sarah F Brown, John T, Hiram F, Samuel, Rhoda C m Henry G Starrett of N Andover MA, Harriet N dy, William W, Hannah D, Sarah m William Badger of Newton; NH-0003-386
Samuel; m1817 Martha Nurs of Littleton; liv Landaff & Littleton NH; ch Chester M, Martha A m George E Bartlett, Samuel G, Charles S, Olive m Charles King of Whitefield; NH-0007-487
William; m Betsy Chadbourne; ch Nathan m Sally Williams of Ossipee, William m --- Folsom of Tamworth, Jeremiah, Samuel m --- Frost of Newfield, George m Julia Moulton, 3 dau; NH-0006-774
GOOKIN,
Rev Daniel; s/o Daniel; m Hannah Savage; ch Rev Nathaniel m Dorothy Cotton; NH-0003-312
Rev Nathaniel; s/o Rev Daniel & Hannah Savage; m Dorothy Cotton ggd/o Rev John Cotton of ENG; liv Hampton NH; ch Rev Nathaniel b1713 m Ann Fitch; NH-0003-312
Rev Nathaniel; b1713 s/o Rev Nathaniel & Dorothy Cotton; m Ann Fitch; liv N Hampton NH; ch Nathaniel m Mary Shackford; NH-0003-312
Nathaniel; s/o Rev Nathaniel & Ann Fitch; m Mary Shackford; liv Portsmouth NH; ch Mary Shackford m Stephen Weeks; NH-0003-312
GORDON,
Alexander; m1663 Mary Lysson d/o Nicholas; liv Watertown MA, Exeter NH; ch Thomas

GORDON (continued)
b1678 m Elizabeth Harriman, 7 others; NH-0003-291
Amos; s/o Jesse & Susan Bartlett; m Hannah E Pattee; ch Isaac, Charles Henry m Dorcas D Calley; NH-0007-118
Charles Henry; s/o Amos & Hannah E Pattee; m Dorcas D Calley d/o David & Mary M Smith of Bristol; liv Alexandria NH; ch Carl A, Helen M; NH-0007-118
Cyrus; b1810 s/o David of Henniker gs/o Jonathan; m1836 Olive Jesseman; liv Dorchester, Lyme NH; ch Laura A m S F Ball, Ruhama E m J H Derby, Asa F, Sarah A dy; NH-0007-546
Francis A; m Martha Dickinson McGaw d/o Isaac; liv Henniker, Merrimack; ch Robert McGaw, Arthur G; NH-0002-544
George H; s/o Jeremiah H & gs/o Peaslee; m Maria D Pierce of Thetford VT; liv Landaff, Lyme NH; ch 3 sons, 1 dau; NH-0007-546
Hiram L; s/o Moses & Jane Pattee; m Catharine Coburn d/o James & Sybil Chamberlain; liv Alexandria NH; ch Sybil J, Sarah E Caton, Elmer H, Robert B, Lendal A, James C, Mary A; NH-0007-118
Isaac B; m Louise Wells d/o Dr D E & Mary E Wells; ch Roy W, Ross S; NH-0007-118
Jesse; s/o George; m Susan Bartlett of Kingston NH; liv New Hampton & Alexandria NH; ch Moses m Jane Pattee, Amos m Hannah E Pattee, 8 others; NH-0007-118
John S; s/o Nathaniel gs/o Nathaniel ggs/o Timothy; m1814 Frances Gordon d/o Nathaniel & gd/o Nathaniel & ggd/o Thomas; liv Exeter NH; ch Hon Nathaniel b1820 m Alcina Eveline Sanborn & m George Anne Lowe, Mary D m Edwin Gordon of Hyde Park MA; NH-0003-291
Moses; s/o Isaac & Susan Bartlett; m Jane Pattee d/o William & Judith Worthin; ch Moses W, Hiram L m Catharine Coburn; NH-0007-118

GORDON (continued)
Hon Nathaniel; b1820 s/o John S & Frances Gordon of Exeter; m1853 Alcina Eveline Sanborn d/o Moses of Kingston NH & m1868 George Anne Lowe d/o John Jr of Exeter; liv MD, Exeter NH; ch/o Alcina - Moses Sanborn, John Thomas dy, Nathaniel, Frances Eveline, Mary Alcina Elizabeth; NH-0003-291
Thomas; b1678 s/o Alexander & Mary Lysson of Exeter NH; m Elizabeth Harriman of Haverhill; ch Timothy, Nathaniel, 9 others; NH-0003-291

GOSS,
Dr Ebenezer Hander; m --- Walker d/o Rev Timothy; liv Bolton MA, Concord NH, Brunswick ME; NH-0004-97
Herbert Irvin; b1857 s/o Abel B & Lucy G Ross of Waterford VT; liv Minneapolis MN, Lancaster NH; NH-0005-239
Jethro; mc1804 Susanna Cate; liv Canaan, Portsmouth; ch Levi M m Almira Cole, 2 sons, 2 dau; NH-0007-325
Capt John; b1739; m1774 Catherine Conant of Hollis; liv Salisbury MA, Hollis NH, Hardwick VT; NH-0002-452
John Abbott; b1847 s/o William & Maryette of Epsom; m Electa Ann Carpenter d/o Charles H of Chichester; liv Pittsfield NH; ch Charles C b1871, Clara N M b1874; NH-0004-470
John W; b1831 s/o Daniel & Malinda Weeks of Gilmanton; m1852 Olive A Henderson wid/o Charles; liv Sandwich, Bridgewater; ch John H b1862; NH-0007-174
Jonathan; s/o Samuel; m Sally Yeaton; liv Epsom NH; ch Noah dy, William b1820 m Maryett Abbott & m Mrs S Robecca Crockett, Hannah Y m Nathaniel Edmunds of Chichester, Nancy L m Edward Edmunds & m Jeremiah Mack & m Jonathan Marden, Sally m Jefferson Edmunds, Mary C m George Morse of Loudon, Andrew J; NH-0004-470
Levi M; s/o Jethro & Susanna Cate; m Almira Cole; liv Plainfield; ch Susan m

GOSS (continued)
William Tilton, Mary m Philip Bullock, Ransom L, Parker J, Almira m George Barnard, 2 dy; NH-0007-325
William; b1820 s/o Jonathan & Sally Yeaton; m1846 Maryett Abbott d/o William & Esther Fowler of Pembroke NH & m1873 Mrs S Rebecca Crockett d/o --- Randall; liv Epsom; ch/o Maryett - John Abbott b1847 m Electa Ann Carpenter, Elizabeth J b1849 m Alfred Porter Bickford, Noah William b1861, Nathan Jonathan b1863; NH-0004-470

GOULD,
Dea Aaron; b1808 s/o Amos; liv Canaan & Piermont NH; ch Luella m --- Malder, Harriet m --- Ford; NH-0007-576
Edwin B; b1839 s/o Jonathan S & Sabra Ruth of Hillsborough NH; m1869 Jennie E Kelsey of Nottingham NH; liv Suncook, Lebanon, Nashua; NH-0007-96

GOVE,
Abram; m Mary Nudd of Kensington; ch Sarah m Nathaniel Chase, Nanna m --- Jones, Jonathan m Polly Goodale, Abram Jr m Nancy Jones, Samuel m Abigail Newman, Mary, Betty m Moody Lakin, Polly m Jesse Patten, Lydia, Ebenezer m Nancy Rowell, Benjamin m Mary Wallace, Jemima m Gardne Brooks; NH-0002-376
Benjamin; s/o Abram & Mary Nudd; m Mary Wallace; ch Mary Ann m Enoch Hadley, Caroline m Thomas Butterfield, Maria m --- Page, Benjamin F m Melissa Patten, Hannah Jane, Elizabeth, Charles F m Aurelia Wordsworth, 1dy; NH-0002-376
Hon Charles Frederick AM; b1793 s/o Dr Jonathan & Polly Dow of Goffstown; m1844 Mary Kennedy d/o Ziba Gray of Nashua; liv Goffstown & Nashua NH; NH-0002-12
Cyrus A; b1846 s/o Moses B & Susan E French; m Augusta C Cass of Stanstead CAN & m1881 Minnie D Smith of Chester; ch Susie E; NH-0003-163
Eben; s/o Page P & Eliza

GOVE (continued)

Collins; m Hannah E Pierce d/o Hiram & Hannah March of Moria NY; ch Hattie M, Lizzie L, Alpheus P; NH-0007-286

Ebenezer; m twice; liv Hampton & Wentworth NH; ch Enoch, Winthrop, Edward, William, 3 others; NH-0007-639

Edward; b1792 s/o Stephen & Huldah Bassett; m1817 Elizabeth Morrell b1797; ch Stephen M b1821 m Lydia M Locke, Edward L b1826 m Mary D Thorndyke & m Anna Maxfield; NH-0003-514

Edward L; b1826 s/o Edward & Elizabeth Morrell; m1851 Mary D Thorndyke d/o Thomas W of Weare & m1867 Anna Maxfield; ch/o Mary - Lucy T m George C Herbert of Lynn MA, William H; ch/o Ann - Mary A, Charles E; NH-0003-514

George Sullivan MD; b1828 s/o John Mills & Anna Montgomery; m1855 Maria Pierce Clark d/o Morris & Lucy Fisher of Whitefield gd/o Judge Ambrose Cossitt of Claremont; liv Whitefield NH, Burlington WI; ch Della Emily b1864 dy, Anna Maria b1867; NH-0005-503

Hezekiah; m --- Fogg of Seabrook; liv Weare NH; ch Hezekiah m Lucy Lock, Judith m James Gregg; NH-0002-380

Hezekiah; s/o Hezekiah & --- Fogg; m Lucy Lock; ch Hannah m Solomon Bartlett, Belinda m David Rowell, Phebe m Jonathan Peaslee of Weare NH, Lucy J, Judith Ann m David Wilkins, Albert m Eliza Ann Goodale, Dana B; NH-0002-380

John; s/o John; m Hannah Chase d/o John; liv Weare NH, Lynn MA; ch Abigail, Squire, Rhoda B, John H b1813; NH-0003-347

John H; b1813 s/o John & Hannah Chase; m1850 Martha J Kenyon of N Providence RI & m1856 Sarah P Wells b1819 d/o Moses & Hannah Dow; liv VT, Lynn MA, Hampton Falls NH; ch/o Sarah - Sarah A b1857; NH-0003-347

John Mills; b1787 s/o Elijah of Weare; m Anna Montgomery b1790 of Francestown; liv Acworth & Whitefield NH; ch

GOVE (continued)

Jehiel dy, Vienna m Leonard Bowles, Laura m Joseph L Taylor, John T, Elijah B, Ira S M, Hannah P m Joel McGregory, George Sullivan MD b1828 m Maria Pierce Clark, Charles P dy; NH-0005-503

Jonathan; s/o Abram & Mary Nudd; m Polly Goodale; ch Polly m Richard Manahan, Almira m Thompson Manahan, Jemima m Joseph Gerry, Horace m Sarah Forsaith, Jennie m Giles Alcock; NH-0002-376

Levi; m --- Currier; liv Amesbury MA; ch Lydia m William McKeen, Sarah m Jonathan Goodale, Eunice m Ebenezer Loveren, Polly m Ephraim Codman of Hillsborough NH, Hannah m Peter Codman, Levi Jr, Nathan m Ann Call; NH-0002-380

Moses B; m Susan E French d/o Phineas & Jane Eaton of Danville; liv Grand River NH; ch Eliza J b1839, Cyrus A b1846; NH-0003-163

Nathaniel; bro/o Abram; m Elizabeth ---; liv Deering, VT; ch Daniel, Nathaniel Jr, Peter, Enos; NH-0002-387

Page P; s/o Ebenezer & Hannah Philbrick of Sanbornton NH; m Eliza Collins of Corinth VT; ch Lydia M, Putnam, Eben m Hannah E Pierce; NH-0007-286

Robert; m Sarah Huntington; liv Weare, Deering; ch Hannah m Herod Chase, John m Sarah Dunsack & m Mrs Relief Dickey, Huldah B m James B Estes, Annie m Amos Breed; NH-0002-380

Samuel; s/o Abram & Mary Nudd; m Abigail Newman; ch Rodney m Nancy Smith, John m Caroline Alcock, Joseph m Aurilla Cram, Samuel m Harriet Newman, Eliza m William Whittle & m Stephen Downing, Sarah m Greely Bartlett & m John Hoyet, Benjamin, 2 dy; NH-0002-376

Stephen; b1754; m1777 Huldah Basset d/o Daniel of Lynn MA & m Miriam Jones; ch/o Huldah - Patience, Lydia, Judith, Anna, Stephen, Edward b1792 m Elizabeth Morrell; NH-0003-

GOVE (continued)
514
Stephen M; b1821 s/o Edward & Elizabeth Morrell; m1843 Lydia M Locke; ch Henry M, Melvin L, Horace N, Otis M; NH-0003-514
Winthrop; s/o Ebenezer; liv Wentworth NH; ch Dolly m --- Marden, David, Ebenezer, 2 others; NH-0007-639

GRAHAM,
Francis; liv Boston MA, Hillsborough NH; ch Anne b1743 m Dea William McKean, Francis Jr (Grimes) b1747 m Elizabeth Wilson; NH-0002-423

GRANT,
Addison M; b1854 s/o Charles & Francis M Anderson; m Mary E Hall of PA; liv Lawrence MA; ch Herbert A, Carrie L, Blanche M; NH-0003-128
Lt Benjamin; s/o Benjamin; m Sarah Sloan d/o Capt John; ch Abdon dy, Alanson; NH-0007-525
Charles; b1783 s/o John of Greenfield; m1809 Mary Ballard b1788; liv Greenfield, Andover MA, Londonderry NH; ch Mary b1810 m David Abbott of Andover MA, Eliza b1812, Hannah B b1815 m Nathan C Abbott of Andover MA, Margaret b1818 m Aaron N Luscomb of Andover MA, Charles C b1820 dy, Charles Cummings b1822 m Salome V Center & m Frances M Anderson & m Vernelia S Brown & m Hattie S Coffin, William B dy, Phoebe C b1826 m Daniel Troy of Andover MA, Josiah A b1829; NH-0003-128
Charles Cumming; b1822 s/o Charles; m1843 Salome V Center d/o Thomas & Lucy Sawyer of Hudson NH & m1849 Frances M Anderson d/o Alexander of Londonderry NH & m(1856?) Vernelia S Brown d/o Jonas of Cambridge VT & m1872 Hattie S Coffin b1839 d/o Thomas & Betsey Hall of Auburn; liv Auburn; ch/o Salome - Louisa C b1843 m1862 John Y Demeritt & m James M Preston, Charles H b1845, Warren S b1848; ch/o Frances - Josiah A b1850 dy, Luther A

GRANT (continued)
b1853 dy, Addison M b1854 m Mary E Hall, Irving F b1856 m Belle Leavitt; ch/o Vernelia - Ella V b1866 (adopted); ch/o Hattie - Charles H b1873, Hattie F b1875, Perley C b1876, Mary B b1879, George E b1880; NH-0003-128
Edward; b1775 s/o Joseph; m Elizabeth Leavitt d/o Jeremiah & Elizabeth Linscott; liv Ossipee NH, Lebanon ME; ch Dr Nathaniel b1804 m Charlotte S Hobbs; NH-0006-640
John; liv Greenfield; ch Charles b1783 m Mary Ballard, John, James, Philip, Joseph, Polly, 1 dau m --- Alcock; NH-0003-128
Lewis P; b1859 s/o Willard of Groton; m Marian Smith d/o Benjamin H & Sally M Smith; liv Plymouth NH; NH-0007-598
Dr Nathaniel; b1804 s/o Edward & Elizabeth Leavitt; m Charlotte S Hobbs d/o William & Catherine Weatherby of Norway ME; liv Norway ME, Wakefield & Ossipee NH; ch William Henry b1834 m Louisa A Ambrose & m Fanny Magoon, John Gasper Spurzheim b1836, Charles Whitman b1838, Mary Ellen b1840 dy, Mary Ellen b1842 m Charles B Gafney Esq, Charlotte M b1844 m Arthur L Hodsdon; NH-0006-640
William Henry; b1834 s/o Dr Nathaniel & Charlotte S Hobbs; m1859 Louisa A Ambrose sis/o Chaplain T A & m1866 Fanny Magoon d/o Henry C & Mehitable Clement; liv Wakefield & Tamworth & Ossipee NH; ch/o Fanny - Willie Clinton b1867 dy; NH-0006-640

GRAVES,
Abram; s/o Phineas of Tuftonborough NH; m --- Dennett; liv Canaan; ch Frances, Hannah B, Eunice D, Belinda A, Mark M m Mary A Bowers, Oliver N, Phineas H, Joanna S, Angeline P, Phebe J m George W Abbott, Lydia P; NH-0006-439
Josiah Griswold MD; b1811; m1846 Mary Webster Boardman d/o Col William of Nashua NH;

GRAVES (continued)
liv Walpole & Nashua NH & Scituate MA; NH-0001-235, NH-0002-199
Phineas; m twice; liv Tuftonborough NH; ch Abram m --- Dennett, James (name changed to Gilman), Samuel, John, Phylenia, Lois, Cynthia, Polly, Hannah, Sally, Joanna, Olive; NH-0006-439
Samuel; s/o Phineas of Tuftonborough NH; ch Sarah m Jesse Drew, Laura m James M Gilman, Janvrin, Calvin, Lyford, Carrie, Herbert; NH-0006-440
GRAY,
Augustus W; b1843 s/o Charles & Olive Stiles; m1866 E Abbie Wilkins; ch George A, Charles H; NH-0002-288
Calvin; s/o Joseph & Chloe Abbott; m Clarissa King; ch Henry Newton b1826 m Mary Ann Heath, Harriet N m Henry K French of Peterborough NH, Charles D m Kate Spaulding of Mason, Calvin b1800; NH-0002-726
Charles; b1800; m1820 Edna Wilson & m Olive Stiles; liv Hancock; ch/o Edna 7; ch/o Olive - Augustus W b1843 m E Abbie Wilkins; NH-0002-288
Daniel; liv Jackson, Nottingham; ch James, Stephen, Daniel, Samuel H m Sally Perkins & m Eliza Nute, John, Lewis; NH-0006-952
Henry Newton; b1826 s/o Calvin & Clarissa King; m1853 Mary Ann Heath of Barre MA; liv Wilton; ch Ella H m William H Putnam of Wilton, Charles N m Mina O Jones of Wilton, William H m Minnie Follansbee of Wilton; NH-0002-726
Hosea; b1818 s/o James & Sarah Elkins of Jackson NH; m1858 Mary A Sampson d/o William & Mary Perkins; liv Lancaster NH, ch Janett; NH-0005-385
Capt James; b1749; m1769 Jane Wallace & m Susannah Parsons d/o Rev Moses of Newbury MA; liv Newburyport MA, Epsom NH; ch/o ? - Susan m --- Perkins, Moses Parsons b1779, Theodore Parsons b1781, Katharine L b1783 m Dr John Proctor, Lucretia B b1785 m William

GRAY (continued)
Brown, James H b1787, Judith Parsons b1789 m John Rand of Epsom; NH-0004-911
John; m Miranda Gannett; ch Warren G; NH-0006-953
Joseph; m Chloe Abbott, ch Calvin m Clarissa King; NH-0002-726
Paul; liv Standish ME, Eaton NH; ch John, James, Paul; NH-0006-790
Samuel H; s/o Daniel; m Sally Perkins & m Eliza Nute d/o Col John; ch/o Sally - Albert, Mary m J L Wilson, Lorinda m George Meserve, Adelaide m Joseph Mead, Sarah m George Everett, Emily J m Horace Whiting; ch/o Eliza - Abbie m Cyrus F Perkins, Alvah H, Charles W, Almira, Almeda; NH-0006-952
GREELEY,
Andrew L; b1835 bro/o Luther J b1840; m Mrs Mary A Osborne; liv NV; NH-0004-618
Carlos S; b1811; m1841 Emily R Robbins of Hartford CT; ch 1; NH-0004-618
Horace; b1811; liv Amherst, W Haven & Pultney VT, Eire PA, New York City; NH-0002-250a
Jonathan; m Mary Bartlett d/o Gov Josiah; liv E Kingston NH; ch Dr Jonathan B b1785; NH-0003-846
Col Joseph; m Hannah Thornton d/o James & Mary Parker; liv Nashua; ch Charles A, Edward P, James B MD; NH-0002-546
Col Samuel; m1773 Mary Leavitt of Brentwood; liv Brentwood & Gilmanton NH; ch Stephen Leavitt Esq b1788 m Nancy Norton, 8 others; NH-0004-794
Stephen Leavitt Esq; b1788 s/o Col Samuel & Mary Leavitt; m1810 Nancy Norton b1786 d/o Dr Bishop of Newburyport; liv Gilmanton Centre; ch Anna Maria m Hon William C Clarke, Stephen Sewall Norton; NH-0004-794
GREEN,
Daniel; b1808 s/o Thomas & Lydia Fairbanks Evans; m1831 Polly Wheeler b1812 d/o Thomas & Sally Blodgett of Gilead ME; liv Shelburne & Berlin NH; ch Sullivan Dexter

GREEN (continued)

b1832 m Catherine E Carbary, Lucinda Angelina b1834 m Moses Hodgdon Jr, Francis Daniel b1837 m Roancy F Blodgett, Nancy Berden b1839, Charles Volney b1841, Helen Elizabeth b1843 m Emerson Cole, Persis Georgianna b1847 m Lewis N Clark, John Woodman b1850 m Fannie E C Mason; NH-0005-817

Edward; s/o Thomas; m Nancy Birdin; ch Lyman, Darius, Manson; NH-0005-873

Capt Ephraim; b1784 s/o Isaac & Abigail Chamberlain; m1807 Sarah French of Rockingham VT; liv VT, Plymouth NH; ch Hannah, Henry C, Harriet, Sarah P m Jacob Kimball of Hebron, Charles, Samuel W, Elizabeth A H, Frederick E A; NH-0007-592

Dr Ezra; b1746; m1778 Susanna Hayes d/o Reuben of Dover; liv Malden MA, Dover NH; NH-0003-846

Francis Daniel; b1837 s/o Daniel & Polly Wheeler; m1858 Roancy F Blodgett b1837 of Berlin NH; ch Willie Alfred b1859?, Francis Herman b1861; NH-0005-817

John Woodman; b1850 s/o Daniel & Polly Wheeler; m Fannie E C Mason; liv Berlin NH; ch Earl S b1882; NH-0005-817

Jonas; s/o Thomas; m Mercy Lary & m Susannah Lary sis/o Mercy; ch Oliver; NH-0005-873

Peter; b1746 s/o Nathaniel of Worcester MA; liv Concord; NH-0004-2

Samuel; b1770 s/o Nathaniel; liv Concord, Washington; NH-0004-5

Sullivan Dexter; b1832 s/o Daniel & Polly Wheeler; m1866 Catherine E Carbary b1841 of MI; liv Berlin NH, Detroit MI; ch Fred Dexter b1867, Carrie Carbary b1870 dy, Mary Helen b1871, Gracie b1874 dy, Harry Daniel b1876, 1 dy, Theodore Albert b1884; NH-0005-817

Thomas; ch Edward m Nancy Birdin, George m Hannah Lary, Jonas m Mercy Lary & m Susannah Lary; NH-0005-873

GREEN (continued)

Thomas; b1783 s/o Thomas; m Lydia Fairbanks Evans d/o Simeon & Eunice Hayden & m Cynthia Stanley; liv Reading MA, Shelburne NH, Guildhall VT; ch/o Lydia - Alpha m Clovis Lowe, Amos, Daniel b1808 m Polly Wheeler, Edmund, Aaron, Lydia m Paul Perkins; NH-0005-817

GREENE,

Herman H; b1802 s/o Samuel & ?; m1837 Ellen C Wiggin of Hopkinton; liv Hopkinton NH, Bangor ME; ch Herman W; NH-0004-408

Capt James; mc1802 Mercy Nelson d/o Moses of Croydon NH; liv Claremont NH, Waterbury VT; ch Hannah b1809, 3 others; NH-0005-222

Samuel; b1770 s/o Nathaniel of Concord; m Ann N & m 2 others; liv Hopkinton NH, Washington DC; ch/o ? - Herman H b1802 m Ellen C Wiggin; NH-0004-408

GREENFIELD,

Charles; b1826 s/o John & Phebe of Rochester NH; m1846 Areline B Downs b1826 d/o Gershom & Sally P of Rochester; liv Rochester; ch Millie A m Horace L Worcester of Rochester, John, Ella S m Justin M Leavitt of Baxton ME, Sarah E, Hattie A, Frank; NH-0003-756

John; b1781 s/o Simon Torr & Sarah Ham Torr of Rochester; m Phebe ---; liv Portsmouth; ch Charles b1826 m Areline B Downs, Sarah E m E G Wallace of Rochester, Ella G m Daniel J Parsons, George m Mary F Parsley d/o John of Strafford; NH-0003-756

GREENOUGH,

Charles F; b1849 s/o Elbridge R & Elizabeth R Eastman; liv Warren OH; NH-0004-618

William S; m1869 Elizabeth McFarland Noyes d/o Hon John W & Clara D McFarland; liv Wakefield MA; ch Chester Noyes, William Weare; NH-0003-159

GREGG,

Alexander; b1746 s/o Hugh of IRE (SCO); m Mary Christie of

GREGG (continued)
IRE b1749; ch Jane b1774, Hugh b1776, Peter C m Mary Mills, Alexander b1780, James b1784 m Judith Hadlock, Samuel b1786 m Lydia Dodge & m Mary Currier, Anna b1789 m Enos Merrill, Reuben b1793; NH-0002-376 & 389

James; s/o Alexander & Mary Christie; m Judith Hadlock; ch Christie m Mary Merrill, Lydia m --- Stone; NH-0002-376

Joseph A; s/o Hon David A of Derry; liv Derry; NH-0003-28

Peter C; s/o Alexander & Mary Christie; m Mary Mills; ch David, Nancy, Mary Ann, Jane, Reuben m Catherine Gregg of Deering, Robert, Samuel, Emily, Christie; NH-0002-377

Reuben; bro/o Alexander; m --- Wilson sis/o Alexander & m --- Houston; ch/o Wilson - Hugh m Margaret Dodge, Thomas m Mary Currier, Mary m --- Page, Sally, Betsy; ch/o Houston - Nancy m Jonathan Nesmith, Alexander m Rebecca Wilkins, Harriet, Houston, James m Hannah Whitaker, John m Betsy Dodge, Milton m --- Peasley; NH-0002-377

Samuel; b1786 s/o Alexander & Mary Christie; m Lydia Dodge b1784 & m Mary Currier; liv Deering; ch/o Lydia - Eunice b1812 m James Fulton of Deering, James b1814, Asenith b1816 m Josiah Loveren, Samuel b1819 m Abby Wyman, Lydia Ann b1822 m Almos Fairfield, Rebecca b1825; NH-0002-376 & 389

GRIDLEY,
Dr G; m --- George d/o David Esq; liv Concord; NH-0004-97

GRIFFIN,
Ebenezer; s/o James & Phebe Abbott of Wilmington MA; m1792 Betsey Carter of Leominster MA; liv Chelmsford MA; ch George m Clarissa White, 11 others; NH-0002-496

George; s/o Ebenezer & Betsey Carter; m Clarissa White d/o John & Susannah of Litchfield; liv Litchfield; ch Josephine, Mary White, Susan Grace, George Byron, John

GRIFFIN (continued)
White, Norris Clement, Orville Carter dy, Arthur George; NH-0002-496

Nathan; s/o Samuel & --- Foster; m Sally Wright; liv Nelson NH; ch Gen Simon G b1824 m Ursula J Harris; NH-0001-58

Samuel Esq; m --- Foster d/o Rev Jacob; liv Methuen MA, Nelson NH; ch Nathan m Sally Wright, Gen Samuel; NH-0001-58

Gen Samuel G; b1824 s/o Nathan & Sally Wright; m1850 Ursula J Harris d/o Jason Esq of Nelson NH & m Margaret R Lamson of Keene NH; liv Nelson NH; NH-0001-58

Sgt Theophilus; liv Derryfield; NH-0002-48

GRIMES,
Francis (Graham); m Sarah Cochran, liv Londonderry, Deering; ch John m Betsy Wilson, James m Jane Giffin; NH-0002-385

Francis Jr (Graham); b1747 s/o Francis Graham; m Elizabeth Wilson of Deering & Londonderry NH; liv Deering & Londonderry NH; ch John b1772 m Elizabeth Wilson; NH-0002-423

Francis; b1805 s/o John & Betsy Wilson of Deering NH; m Mary Chase d/o Judge Henry B & Dorothy Bean of Warner NH & m1853 Mrs Lucinda Egleston; liv Windsor, Hillsborough; ch/o Mary - Sarah F b1838 m Alfred Johnson, John Henry b1840, Mary Chase b1842, Helen D b1844 m George R Whittemore, Lissa A b1851; ch/o Lucinda - Frank C b1857 m Abbie J Davis; NH-0002-422

Frank C; b1857 s/o Francis & Mrs Lucinda Egleston; m1880 Abbie J Davis of Hillsborough; ch Francis Grimes b1881; NH-0002-423

Hiram; b1798 s/o John & Elizabeth Wilson; m1832 Clarissa Forsaith d/o James & Nancy of Deering; liv Deering & Hillsborough NH; ch John b1828, Nancy Jane b1830, Elvira Elizabeth b1833, James Forsaith b1835 m Sarah Ann Jones, Clarissa A b1838; NH-

GRIMES (continued)
0002-423

James Forsaith; b1835 s/o Hiram & Clarissa Forsaith; m1864 Sarah Ann Jones d/o Eben & Mary Carr of Hillsborough NH; liv Hillsborough; ch James Wilson b1865, John Harvey b1867, Warren Parker b1868, Marry Carr b1871, Henry Clitz b1872, Clara Forsaith b1875, Cecil P b1878; NH-0002-423

John; b1772 s/o Francis Jr (Graham) & Elizabeth Wilson; m Elizabeth Wilson of Deering; liv Deering & Hillsborough NH; ch Wilson b1816, Hiram b1798 m Clarissa Forsaith, Jane, Susan m Alden Walker, Francis, David W, Sarah C, James; NH-0002-423

John; s/o Francis (Graham); m Betsy Wilson; ch Hiram m Clarissa Forsaith, Jane m James Butler, Susan m Alden Walker, Francis m Mary Chase & m Lucinda Egleston, David m Harriet Tuttle & m Elizabeth Jones, Sarah C, James W m Elizabeth Neally; NH-0002-385

John; liv Hancock & Londonderry NH; ch William; NH-0002-353

GRISWOLD,

Charles B; b1832 s/o Alvira & Frances White of Lebanon NH; m1858 Alzina M Sawyer of Malone NY; liv Haverhill & Lebanon NH; ch Charles S; NH-0007-374

GROUT,

Col Ebenezer; bro/o William; liv Watertown MA, Acworth; ch Polly m Alvah Cummings, Benjamin; NH-0004-155

GUPPEY,

John; s/o Capt James of Beverly MA; liv Dover; Joshua J, Jeremy B; NH-0003-885

GUTTERSON,

John; b1832 s/o Nathan & Sarah Atwood; m1854 S Frances Stearns d/o Dr Isaac & Eunice P Marshall of Dunbarton; liv Lynn MA, Goffstown, Dunbarton, Henniker; ch Kate M m Richard L Childs, Clara C, Alice M, Sarah B; NH-0004-358

Josiah; m Rachel Sawyer of Dracut MA; liv Pelham & Weare NH, Francestown; ch Nathan b1796 m Sarah Atwood; NH-

GUTTERSON (continued)
0004-358

Nathan; b1796 s/o Josiah & Rachel Sawyer; m1821 Sarah Atwood d/o Jacob & Sarah Cross of Atkinson NH; liv Weare & Dunbarton & Henniker NH, Francestown; ch William W, Sarah J m Alfred L Boynton of Weare & m Otis Hanson of Henniker, Maria L m David S Carr of Goffstown, John b1832 m S Frances Stearns; NH-0004-358


-H-


HACKETT,

William Henry Young; b1800 bro/o Charles A; m1826 Olive Pickering d/o Joseph W of Portsmouth; liv Gilmanton & Belmont & Portsmouth NH; ch Frank W; NH-0003-23, NH-0004-719

HADDOCK,

Charles B AM DD; b1796 bro/o William T AM & Lorenzo MD; m Susan Saunders d/o Richard Lang of Hanover & m Mrs Caroline Kimball Young; liv Dartmouth, W Lebanon; NH-0004-619

HADLOCK,

Stephen O; s/o James & Mary J Fifield; m Mary E Straw d/o Daniel of Grafton; liv Grafton NH; ch Arthur J; NH-0007-286

HAINES,

Joshua; b1723; liv Greenland, Wolfeborough; ch Jacob, Matthias, Joseph; NH-0006-309

HALE,

Aaron; s/o John of Hollis NY; m Mary Kent; ch John, Aaron, Thomas, Edwin, Sarah m --- Hanks, Daniel T, 2 others; NH-0007-566

Abner; s/o Thomas; m Rebecca Williams; ch Hiram S m Roene Little, 9 others; NH-0007-283

Hiram S; s/o Abner & Rebecca Williams; m Roene Little d/o Elbridge G & Nancy McKinney; liv Grafton NH; ch Harry; NH-0007-283

Col John; b1731; liv Sutton MA,

HALE (continued)
Hollis NH; ch John Jr, David, Dr William b1762; NH-0002-452

John Parker; b1775 s/o Samuel of Portsmouth; liv Portsmouth, Barrington, Rochester; NH-0003-602

John Parker; b1806 s/o John P; liv Dover; NH-0003-592

Joseph W; liv Barrington, Conway; ch Lorenzo T; NH-0006-853

Sewall; s/o Simeon B & Jane Williams; m Sarah A Cole d/o Jesse & Sally Whitney; liv Grafton NH; ch George C; NH-0007-283

Simeon B; s/o Thomas; m Jane Williams; ch Sewall m Sarah A Cole; NH-0007-283

HALEY,
Abel; liv Rochester, Tuftonborough, Wolfeborough; ch Abel S, Levi T; NH-0006-311

Thomas; b1692 s/o Sgt ---; m Sarah Gordon; ch Sarah m Thomas Burley; NH-0003-237

HALL,
Abram; liv Lunenburg VT, Lyman NH; ch Abram, Lydia m Reuben Smith; NH-0007-515

Aruna; s/o Nathaniel & Mehitable Storrs; m Rebecca Demary; liv Lebanon NH; ch Edward O, George N, Henry S, Mary O m --- Eastbrook, Alfred A, 7 others; NH-0007-419

Benjamin; b1790; m1810 Mary Brown b1795; liv Candia & Bristol NH; ch Rufus, Lyman, Oliver S m Isabel Morrison, Albon; NH-0007-183

Burgess A; b1838 s/o Joshua H & Mary Mills of Rumney; m1867 Annette M Hardey d/o David & Sarah; liv Rumney NH; ch Lurlyn H dy, Gertrude E b1870, Marinette b1872, Alice E b1879; NH-0007-606

D Fletcher; b1820 s/o John & Ruth Fletcher of Rumney; m1842 Betsey Doe d/o Jefferson; liv Rumney NH; ch Charles D b1843, Chester W b1844, Mary G b1846 dy, Betsey J m F W Fellows, George J, Fayette A; NH-0007-605

Daniel; m Patience Taylor of Sanbornton; liv Wakefield NH;

HALL (continued)
ch Hannah m John Sanborn; NH-0006-475

Hon Daniel; b1832 s/o Gilman & Eliza Tuttle of Barrington; m1877 Sophia Dodge d/o Jonathan T & Sarah Hanson of Rochester NH; liv Barrington & Dover NH; ch Arthur Wellesley b1878; NH-0001-229, NH-0003-873

Ebenezer; b1721 s/o Joseph b1728; m1746 Dorcas Abbott d/o Edward of Concord gd/o Thomas ggd/o George; liv Concord NH; ch Obadiah b1748 m Mary Perham, 11 others; NH-0004-542

Lt Edward; b1727 s/o Edward; m1727 Lydia Brown; liv Wrentham & Uxbridge MA, Croydon NH; ch Hannah b1749 m Ezekiel Powers; NH-0001-51

Frank H; s/o Rufus; m Josephine Elliot of Barnstead; ch John b1739; NH-0003-704

Gilman; s/o Daniel of Barrington NH; m Eliza Tuttle; liv Dover & Barrington NH; ch Daniel b1832 m Sophia Dodge, 8 others; NH-0001-229, NH-0003-873

Henry; m Nannie Moor Crombie d/o Ninia Clark & Rebecca Patten; liv Manchester; ch Hattie James, Rebecca Clark; NH-0002-609

Henry; b1740 s/o Henry & Joanna Sargent; m Betsey Bradley of Haverhill MA; liv Rumney & Chester NH; ch John b1762 m Ruth Prescott; NH-0007-614

Isaac W; m Lois English; liv Francistown NH, Landaff; ch Damon B, John E, 2 sons, 1 dau; NH-0007-368

J Cummings; m1854 Caroline B Wheet d/o Joshua R & Huldah Kidder of Groton; ch Alpha C, Carrie A, Ida A, Ira S Wheet, Anna; NH-0007-292

Jacob G; b1797 s/o Jonathan & Desire Butterfield; m1818 Hannah Randlett; liv Rumney NH; ch Dr A C, Ruth A dy, O S; NH-0007-605

James H; m Maria K Whitford d/o Elliot & Elizabeth Bowman; ch Susibell W, Webb E, James E, Annie May dy; NH-0002-216

James; b1810 s/o William Jr of

HALL (continued)

Brookline NH; m1835 Mary A Boutwell d/o Maj Nehemiah of Lyndeborough, & m1853 Mary J Fisher d/o Matthew A & Jane W Christie of Francestown NH; liv Lyndeborough, Francestown, Brookline; ch/o Mary A - Edward T, Mary F m Dea George W Peabody, & 3 others; NH-0002-296

James; b1842 s/o Joshua Jr & Sarah F Whitney of Pepperell MA; m1876 Anna M Whitford; liv N Chelmsford MA, Milford & Nashua NH; NH-0002-216

Jeremiah; b1777 s/o Obadiah & Mary Perham; m1801 Hannah Haines of Northfield NH; liv Northfield; ch Dr Adino Brackett b1819 m Mary Cowles, Eliza B, 4 others; NH-0004-529 & 542

Dea John; bro/o Ralph of Charlestown MA; liv Dover NH 1649; ch Ralph; NH-0001-229

John; liv Londonderry, Chester, Derryfield; NH-0002-41

Capt John; s/o Thomas; liv Ellington CT, Lyme NH; ch Mary m Alvah Jeffers, Thomas m Emily Breck, Annie m William P Morey, Sarah m Robert Spear, Lucy F m Samuel Johnson, David C, Rudolph, 3 others; NH-0007-539

John; b1673 s/o Richard; m1706 Mary Kimball of Bradford MA; liv Bradford MA; ch Henry b1712 m1734 Joanna Sargent; NH-0007-614

John; b1762 s/o Henry & Betsey Bradley; m1783 Ruth Prescott d/o Jedediah of Deerfield NH; liv Chester & Rumney NH; ch Josiah b1784 m Sarah White; NH-0007-614

John; b1763 s/o Henry; m Ruth Prescott & m1818 Ruth Fletcher; liv Rumney NH; ch/o Fletcher - D Fletcher b1820 m Betsey Doe, 2 sons; NH-0007-605

Jonathan; m Desire Butterfield; liv Chester & Rumney NH; ch Sara m Ebenezer Bradley, Jacob G b1797 m Hannah Randlett, 4 sons, 6 dau; NH-0007-605

Joseph; b1680 s/o Richard of Bradford gs/o Richard of Dor-

HALL (continued)

chester; liv Bradford; ch Ebenezer b1721 m Dorcas Abbott, 8 others; NH-0004-542

Joshua Jr; m Sarah F Whitney; liv Pepperell MA; ch James Horace b1842 m Anna M Whitford, Charles T; NH-0002-216

Joshua H; b1792 s/o Henry of Andover; m1822 Mary Mills d/o David & Betsey; liv Rumney NH; ch David b1823, Sarah dy, Hannah m William C Morse, Caroline M m B W Clough, Burgess A b1838 m Annette M Hardy; NH-0007-606

Josiah; b1784 s/o John & Ruth Prescott; m Sarah White; liv Groton & Rumney NH; ch Rev King Solomon b1819 m Ann Elizabeth Buswell; NH-0007-614

Rev King Solomon; b1819 s/o Josiah & Sarah White of Groton NH; m1847 Ann Elizabeth Buswell d/o Dr Caleb & Eliza Follansbee; liv Warner & Lake Village NH, Metheun MA; NH-0004-777

Obadiah; b1748 s/o Ebenezer & Dorcas Abbott of Concord NH; m1770 Mary Perham of New Ipswich NH; ch Jeremiah b1777 m Hannah Haines, 6 others; NH-0004-542

Hon Obed; liv Madbury, Upper Bartlett; ch Obed, Elijah, Abigail, Hannah m Benjamin Gould of Conway Centre, Maria, Mary, Martha, Caroline; NH-0006-914

Oliver S; s/o Benjamin & Nancy Brown; m Isabel Morrison of W Rumney; liv Bristol NH; ch Nancy J m Uriah H Kidder, Adna, Oliver P, Carrie B m Otis S Damon; NH-0007-183

Ralph; s/o Dea John of Dover NH; liv Dover NH; ch Ralph Jr of Barrington NH; NH-0001-229

Ralph Jr; s/o Ralph of Dover NH; liv Barrington NH; ch Solomon of Barrington NH; NH-0001-229

Ralph; liv Jackson NH; ch Ralph, Lydia m Thomas Rogers, Betsey m William Johnson, Hannah m John Perkins, 1 dau m Joseph Thompson of Bartlett; NH-0006-952

HALL (continued)
Rufus; s/o Israel gs/o John; m Mary Ann Young of Barrington; ch David O, Frank H m Josephine Elliot; NH-0003-704
Samuel; b1747; m Bridget Gilman d/o Jeremiah; liv Dover, Wakefield; ch Joshua Gilman; NH-0006-475
Solomon; s/o Ralph Jr of Barrington NH; liv Barrington NH; ch Daniel of Barrington NH; NH-0001-229
Thomas; s/o Capt John; m Emily Breck; liv Lyme NH; ch Jane B m W P Eastman; NH-0007-539
Walter R; b1796; m1826 Lucinda Cummins of Groton; liv Dorchester NH; ch J C, Mary Ann m Stillman Merrill; NH-0007-238
William; b1789 s/o Webster; m1823 Mrs Charlotte Chase Hall of Concord NH; liv Hanover NH; ch William b1825 m1848 Almeda E Waterhouse of Orford; NH-0007-321
HAM,
Abner; b1821 s/o Benjamin of Farmington NH; liv Rochester & Dover NH, Cambridge MA; NH-0003-849
Dodavah; s/o Dodavah; m Abigail Hill d/o Benjamin & Betsey Spokesfield of Thornton; ch Joseph H, 4 others; NH-0007-213
John; b1774; m Wealthy C Brigham; liv Dover & Lower Gilmanton NH; NH-0004-702
John Randolph MD; b1842 s/o Charles gs/o Ephraim of Dover; liv Dover; NH-0003-850
Levi B; m Martha A Goodhue of Epsom & m Livona Gilman of Bethlehem; liv Gilmanton & Haverhill NH; ch/o ? - John F, Hattie I; NH-0007-373
Nicholas; b1787; m Hannah Chase & m1838 Sally Washburn d/o Alden & Sally Allen; liv Albany; ch/o Hannah - Belinda m Oliver Chase, John, Lowell; NH-0006-766
HAMBLET,
Eli; s/o Thomas & Tamar Gilson; m1839 Lucy Frost of Tyngsborough & m1844 Rebecca Butler b1819 d/o Enoch & Susan Marsh of Pelham; liv Hudson; ch/o Rebecca - R

HAMBLET (continued)
Souvina, Arvilla; NH-0002-485
Joseph; s/o Joseph Hamlet; ch Thomas b1775 m Tamar Gilson; NH-0002-484
Thomas; b1775 s/o Joseph; m1806 Tamar Gilson d/o Solomon & Tamar Lawrence; liv Hudson, Chelmsford MA; ch Eli m Lucy Frost & m Rebecca Butler, Drusilla m Joseph Phelps, Dorcas S m Reuben Frost & m Joseph Skinner, Alvan, Joseph, Gilbert; NH-0002-484
HAMILTON,
Dr Cyrus; b1765; m Lovina Bush; liv Brookfield MA, Norwich VT, Lyme NH, Hanover; NH-0007-521
HAMLET (HAMBLET),
Jacob; m1668 Hannah Parker & m Mary Dutton & m Mary Colburn; ch/o ? - Joseph, William, Jacob, Henry; NH-0002-484
Joseph; s/o Jacob & ?; liv Dracut MA; ch Joseph Hamblet; NH-0002-484
William; b1614; m Sarah Hubbard; liv Cambridge & Billerica MA; ch Jacob m Hannah Parker & m Mary Dutton & m Mary Colburn; NH-0002-484
HAMMOND,
Rodney; b1810 s/o Nathan; ch Ann A m David S Batchelder, Esther D m Henry W Tilton, Mary N m D S Johnson & m1876 Rev Thomas Wyatt; NH-0007-174
Thomas; b1814 s/o Thomas & Hannah Burnham of Dunbarton, m1839 Esther D Hammond & m1845 Sarah N Hammond d/o Nathan & Mary L Noyes; liv Bridgewater NH; ch/o Esther - Melissa W, Nathan D m Isabel Smith & m Mary L Noyes; NH-0007-174
HANAFORD,
John S; m Lydia Clark d/o John gd/o John; liv Holderness, Campton; NH-0007-214
HANNAFORD,
Samuel Gray; b1822 s/o Amos C & Hannah Lyford of Northfield NH; m1842 Lucy M Hannaford d/o Jabez R & Ruth Noyes of Boscawen; liv Sanbornton, W Stewartstown; ch Russell, Fordyce A; NH-0005-686
HANSON,
Dominicus; b1813 s/o Joseph &

HANSON (continued)
Charity Dame; m1839 Betsey S Chase b1814 d/o Simon of Rochester; liv Rochester; ch Charles A C b1844, George W b1854 dy; NH-0003-745
Joseph; b1764; m1798 Charity Dame b1775 of Rochester; liv Dover, Rochester; ch Humphrey, Mary D m Dr James Farrington of Rochester, Hannah dy, Joseph S, Meribah m Dr Joseph H Smith of Lowell MA, Joanna m John McDuffee of Rochester, 1dy, Hester Ann m Daniel M Mooney, Dominicus b1813 m Betsey S Chase, Asa P; NH-0003-745
Timothy; b1787; m1844 Abigail Peasley Folsom b1797 wid/o Nicholas Jones of Gilmanton; liv Farmington, Dover; NH-0003-638
HARDY,
Aaron P; b1815 s/o Daniel & Sarah Conner; m1842 Adelia W Brickett d/o Jonathan & Lydia Kent; liv Londonderry; ch George H b1851, Hattie E b1854, John P b1855, Frank A b1865; NH-0003-584
Baxter P; b1841 s/o Israel & Pamelia French; m Mattie L Wyatt d/o Thomas & Sarah Clark; ch Hattie May b1873, Ernest B b1876; NH-0007-613
Daniel; m Sarah Conner d/o Joseph of Pembroke NH; liv Bradford MA, Londonderry NH; ch Aaron P b1815 m Adelia W Brickett; NH-0003-584
David P; s/o Ichabod & Emeline M Webster of Hebron; m1859 Sarah Fox d/o David P & Sally Powers; liv Hebron MA; ch Nettie A, Edward D, Ellen E, Mary Addie, Lucy May, Lizzie W; NH-0007-388
Dudley; m Hannah Johnson; liv Wakefield, N Wolfeborough; ch Loammi b1805 m Mary Bean Haines, Ezra; NH-0006-631
Ichabod; b1808 s/o Daniel; m1836 Emeline M Webster; liv Hebron NH; ch David P b1838, Lucy E m George J Cummings, Ellen S, Emily, David P .m Sarah Fox; NH-0007-388
Israel; b1809 s/o David of Groton; m1835 Pamelia French d/o Josiah; ch Baxter P b1841

HARDY (continued)
m Mattie L Wyatt, Harriet b1849; NH-0007-613
Loammi; b1805 s/o Dudley & Hannah Johnson; m Mary Bean Haines d/o Capt John; ch Arvilla m Angevine Pitman of Bartlett & m Albert H Thompson of Raymond; NH-0006-632
Phineas; liv Bradford MA, Hollis; ch Phineas, Thomas, Noah, Jesse; NH-0002-438
Walter D; b1857 s/o Anthony C & Eliza Martin of Lebanon; liv Franklin Falls, Tilton NH; NH-0004-886
HARMON,
Dr Melvin A; b1857 s/o Bion E & Caroline Huckins of Danvers MA; m Nellie Towle d/o Ransellear & Caroline Gilman of Freedom; liv Ossipee NH; ch C Retta; NH-0006-630
Silas; bro/o Abner; liv Scarborough ME, Eaton NH; ch Jotham, Roswell, 9 others; NH-0006-792
HARPER,
John A; b1779 s/o William & Mary Lane of Sanbornton; liv Deerfield & Sanbornton NH; NH-0004-701
HARRIMAN,
Samuel; b1814; m1843 Eunice Gould d/o Augustine; liv Bridgewater & Colebrook NH, Stewartstown; NH-0005-623
Gen Walter; b1817 s/o Benjamin E of Warner NH; m1841 Apphia K Hoyt d/o Capt Stephen of Warner NH & m1844 Almira R Andrews of Warner; liv Warner & Concord NH, Harvard MA; ch Georgia m Joseph R Leeson of Boston, Walter Channing m Mabel Perkins, Benjamin E m Jessie B Farmer d/o Col Isaac W of Manchester; NH-0001-74, NH-0004-672
William; m Lucy H Thayers of Waitsfield VT; liv Barnet VT, Dalton, Littleton NH; ch Henry D; NH-0007-498
William; s/o John of Bridgewater; m1855 Caroline S Penniman d/o Caleb D & Clarissa; liv Plymouth NH; ch Harriet G m George A Clark, Alma m H H Whittemore, Emily m O B Davis, George D, Lizzie

HARRIMAN (continued)
M; NH-0007-593
HARRIS,
Dr Augustus; b1811; m1840 Louisa A Cox of Norway ME; liv Paris ME, Colebrook NH; ch 2 dau; NH-0005-599
John; b1769 s/o Richard & Lydia Atherton of Harvard MA; m Mary Poor d/o Eliphalet & Elizabeth Little of Hampstead; liv Hopkinton NH; ch George, Catharine m Timothy Wiggin Little of Hopkinton, Eliza Poor, Ann; NH-0004-407
Rufus; s/o Simon & Susanna Crawford of Bridgewater; m Violet S Sanborn & m Alvira Webber; liv Ashland NH; ch/o ? - William F m Electa T Emmons of New Hampton; NH-0007-125
Stimpson; s/o Joshua of Lisbon; m Pamelia Bailey of Lyman; liv Lisbon NH; ch Philemon, Elery, 1 dau m Stephen Huntoon, 2 sons, 3 dau; NH-0007-444
HART,
Edson P; s/o Abel; m Mary J Morrison & m Mary S Stinson; ch/o ? - 5; NH-0007-215
Edwin A; b1849 s/o George & Louisa Bailey; m Eugenia C Delaplaine; liv Boston MA, Minneapolis MN; ch Bertha (adopted); NH-0004-216
George; b1811 s/o George & --- Lawrence gs/o Nicholas Lawrence of Weston VT; m1835 Louisa Bailey d/o Cyrus & Martha Millet of Salem NH; liv Boston MA, Tabor VT, Bradford NH; ch Louisa A b1838 m Arthur T Morse, Almendo b1840 dy, George A b1841 dy, George Herman b1844 dy, Edwin A b1849 m Eugenia C Delaphaine, William S b1851; NH-0004-216
Rev Harrison N MD; b1830 s/o John & Mary C Gilman of Sandwich; liv Hinsdale, Manchester, Centre Sandwich NH; ch Elmer B; NH-0006-649
Capt John; m Polly Willey; liv Portsmouth, Conway; ch Lydia m Joseph Dinsmore, Honor m James Willey s/o Samuel Esq; NH-0006-849

HARTSHORN,
George W; b1827 s/o Colburn & Elizabeth Fay of Lunenburgh VT; liv Canaan VT; NH-0005-257
HARTSHORNE,
David Henry; b1823 s/o Joseph & Mary Ellsworth; m1853 Amanda Forsaith; ch George Henry b1853, Joseph Albert b1855, Sarah Maria b1859 dy, Mary Lizzie b1861; NH-0004-209
Joseph; b1791 s/o John & Hannah Prince of Amherst NH; m1817 Mary Ellsworth b1791 of Deering; liv Hillsborough & Bradford NH; ch David Henry b1823 m Amanda Forsaith, Mary Antoinette b1826 dy, Ann Maria b1827 m1854 Henry Canfield & m1856 Hiram Farrington, Sarah Dutton b1829, Elizabeth Adaline Gibson (Adopted) b1820 m1841 Caleb Knight & m Emery Bailey; NH-0004-209
HARTWELL,
Rev Henry H; b1819 s/o William & Betsy Wilkins of Hillsborough NH; m1842 Flora Ann Sweatt of Webster NH & m1861 Mrs Sally Hirsch d/o Maj Sterling Sargent of Allenstown; liv Allenstown; ch/o Flora - 3 sons, 1 dau m Charles T Daniels of Lawrence; ch/o Sally - 1 dau m Pork Mitchell of Manchester; NH-0004-166
HARVEY,
Dudley Ladd, b1811 s/o James & Lois Folsom Ladd of Epping; m1835 Mary Swain d/o Jonathan & Sarah Dearborn of Epping; liv Epping NH; ch Mary A, Jonathan Swain; NH-0003-236
Isaiah; liv Loudon NH; ch Molly, Judith, David, Hannah, Sally, Jonathan, Susannah, Patty, Chase; NH-0004-508
Jacob S; m Almira M Putney d/o Hazen & Susan Page; ch Walter, Fred P, Albert; NH-0004-646
James; b1780 s/o Jonathan & Susan Hadlock of Nottingham; m1809 Lois Folsom Ladd of Epping; liv Epping; ch Dudley Ladd b1811 m Mary Swain, 2 others; NH-0003-236
Dea Matthew; b1750 s/o Jonathan

HARVEY (continued)
of Amesbury MA; m1779 Hannah
Sargent of Weare; liv Sutton
NH; ch Hon Jonathan b1780,
Hon Matthew b1781, Philip S,
John, Benjamin, Susan m
Joseph Emerson of Hopkinton,
Hannah m Dr Dinsmore of
Henniker; NH-0004-641
Matthew; b1781 s/o Matthew of
Sutton; m Margaret Rowe of
Newburyport MA; liv Hopkinton
& Concord NH; ch Margaret
Elizabeth, Frederick; NH-
0004-408
HARWOOD,
Joseph; m1801 Pattee Gilbert
d/o Joseph & Sarah Robbins;
ch Mary Wilder b1802 m
Steadman Willard, Joseph
Gilbert b1804 m --- Fletcher
of Westford, John Alfred
b1807 dy, Nancy Elvira b1810
dy; NH-0002-434
HASELTON,
Nathaniel; liv Westmoreland &
Orford NH; ch Col John b1805
m Mercy D Phelps; NH-0007-567
Sewell; b1798; m1828 Sarah S
Alexander d/o Enoch & Merriam
Colby; ch Rufus R b1831 m
Lydia S Farnham, Sarah M
b1835 m1855 David Roberts;
NH-0004-286
HASKINS,
Eli; b1759; m Rhoda Drake; liv
Taunton MA, Grafton NH; ch
Asa L m Lucy A Collins & m
Betsey Lattimer, 7 others;
NH-0007-280
HASSEL,
Elias; m Mary ---; liv Deering,
Hillsborough; ch Hannah m
Samuel Morrill; NH-0002-384
HASTINGS,
Asa; b1752; m1775 Molly Lowell
b1752; liv Alexandria,
Bristol; ch Jonas b1779 m
Polly Ordway & m Nancy
Atwood, 9 others; NH-0007-193
John; m Mary C Hibbard d/o
Timothy; ch 1 dau m Henry
Haddock; NH-0007-139
Jonas; b1779 s/o Asa & Molly
Lowell; m1805 Polly Ordway &
m1812 Nancy Atwood; liv
Bristol NH; ch John b1806
m1833 Dorothy Emmons d/o
Benjamin Jr, 11 others; NH-
0007-193
Moses A; b1848; liv Bethel ME,

HASTINGS (continued)
Gorham NH; NH-0005-230
HATCH,
Hon Albert Ruyter; b1817; liv
Greenland, Portsmouth; NH-
0003-23
Alfred; s/o Gamaliel &
Priscilla Sampson of Tamworth
NH; m Charlotte Chesley; ch
Susie C m Joseph F Granville
of Effingham; NH-0006-774
Charles W; b1820; m1848 Mary
Christiner Hall d/o Rev Ralph
of Strafford; liv Greenland;
ch Marianna, Ruth Allen; NH-
0003-305
Charles W; b1849 s/o George &
Julia Moulton of Tamworth NH;
m Abbie M Walker of New Fane
VT; liv Tamworth NH; ch
George, Percy; NH-0006-774
David; liv Halifax MA, Tamworth
NH; ch Gamaliel m Priscilla
Sampson, Jabez; NH-0006-774
Gamaliel; s/o David; m
Priscilla Sampson; liv Tam-
worth NH; ch Newland S m
Hannah Howard, Melden, Alfred
m Charlotte Chesley, Phoebe;
NH-0006-774
Jonathan; s/o Joseph; m Olive
Truscott; liv Lyme, Hanover
NH; ch William b1812 m Sarah
Chandler & m Annette A Ross;
NH-0007-319
Newland S; s/o Gamaliel &
Priscilla Sampson of Tamworth
NH; m Hannah M Howard; ch
Otis G b1827 m Ann M Marston,
Hannah Remick, 4 others; NH-
0006-774
Hon Otis G; b1827 s/o Newland S
& Hannah Howard; m Ann M
Marston of Parsonsfield ME;
ch Lettie A m W H Lary, Mabel
E; NH-0006-773
Samuel; bc1790 s/o Samuel; m
Nancy Wiggin; liv Greenland;
ch Elizabeth, Charles W,
Sarah A, Samuel A b1826 m
Lucy H Adams & m Mrs Harriet
B Little, Harriet J; NH-0003-
306
Samuel A; b1826 s/o Samuel &
Nancy Wiggin; m1856 Lucy H
Adams d/o Rev John F & m1877
Mrs Harriet B Little wid/o
Silas Little of Newbury MA &
d/o Nathan Moulton of Hampton
Falls NH; liv Greenland; ch/o
Lucy - Ida M, John William,

HATCH (continued)
Charlotte A, George A; NH-0003-306
William; b1812 s/o Jonathan & Olive Truscott; m Sarah Chandler & m Annette A Ross; liv Hanover NH; ch/o Sarah - Augusta B m Clarence E Delano; ch/o Annette - Isaac R, Ollie T; NH-0007-319
HAVEN,
Alfred Woodward; b1801 s/o John & gs/o Rev Samuel DD; m1827 Louisa Sheafe d/o James Esq & m1832 Margaret Houston d/o John of Exeter; liv Portsmouth; ch/o Louisa 1, ch/o Margaret 6; NH-0003-114
Nathaniel A Jr; b1790 s/o Hon Nathaniel A & gs/o Rev Samuel DD; liv Portsmouth; NH-0003-21
HAWES,
David C; m Mary H Sanborn d/o Caleb T & Polly M Melcher; liv New Bedford MA; ch Levi M, David E, Frank S, Samuel C, Henry W, Mary A; NH-0003-352
HAWKES,
Colburn; b1794 s/o Farrington & Sarah Knowlton; m1826 Clarissa Brown d/o Dudley of Wilmot; liv Bradford NH; ch John Milton b1826 m1854 Esther Hill of Brentwood NH; Bartlett b1828 dy, Robert Bartlett b1829, Helen Marie b1832 m Prescott Colby, Sarah Knowlton b1835, Miner b1845 m Georgia Bailey & m Medora George; NH-0004-203
David Knowlton; b1804 s/o Farrington & Sarah Knowlton; mc1825 Susan Straw; ch Emeline bc1826 m Orlando Bailey, John, Hartwell, William, Frederick, Esther, Helen m Burke Belknap; NH-0004-203
Farrington; b1770 s/o David & Sarah Colburn of Dunstable MA; m Sarah Knowlton sis/o David of Newburyport MA & m1831 Mrs Sarah Young of Pelham NH; liv Hudson & Warner & Bradford NH; ch/o Sarah Knowlton - Abigail b1792 m Nathan R Marshall, Colburn b1794 m Clarissa Brown, Farrington b1796,

HAWKES (continued)
Catharine b1798 m1825 Timothy L Dowlin, John b1801, David Knowlton b1804 m Susan Straw, Daniel b1806, Moody b1809; NH-0004-202
Farrington; b1796 s/o Farrington & Sarah Knowlton; liv Cambridgeport MA; ch Henry; NH-0004-202
John; b1801 s/o Farrington & Sarah Knowlton; liv NY, OH; ch Abigail b1834, Elhanan Winchester b1836; NH-0004-202
Miner; b1845 s/o Colburn & Clarissa Brown of Bradford NH; m Georgia Bailey d/o Edwin of Bradford & m Medora George d/o Willman; ch/o Georgia - Ralph b1869; ch/o Medora - Mertie; NH-0004-203
Moody; b1809 s/o Farrington & Sarah Knowlton; liv W Cambridge MA, Kirtland NY; ch Frederick Henry, Abigail Lamira, Albert Winn, Sarah Hall; NH-0004-203
HAYES,
Dr Albert Hamilton; b1836 s/o Joseph & Betsey Brewster; m1877 Jessie B Benjamin d/o E M Esq of San Francisco CA; liv Alton NH, Boston MA & CA; ch Lloyd Benjamin b1880; NH-0001-202
Benjamin; b1700 s/o John & Mary Horne; m Jane Snell wid/o Tristram Heard; liv Rochester; ch Benjamin b1726, Abigail bapt1728, George bapt1730, Elisabeth bapt1732, Hannah bapt1733; NH-0003-632
Benjamin; b1726 s/o Benjamin & Jane Snell of Rochester; liv Rochester; ch George Snell b1760; NH-0003-634
Charles Woodman; b1836 s/o Samuel Davis & Comfort Chesley of Madbury; m1866 Ellen Marie Weeks b1843 d/o William & Marie of Strafford Corner; liv Madbury; ch Nellie Marie b1870, Anne Lillian b1873, Cora Enniette b1877 dy; NH-0003-643
David M; b1787 s/o David; m Hannah March & m Almira Morris & m Philda Edgerton; liv Hanover NH; NH-0007-318
Elihu; s/o Hezekiah & Margaret Cate of Barrington; ch Sarah

HAYES (continued)

A m Nicholas Pike, Elisabeth m Dea Solomon Hayes, Reuben, Jonathan; NH-0003-633

Elihu; b1751; m1772 Betsey Davis d/o Samuel; liv Barrington; ch Jonathan b1774 m Mary Ham; NH-0003-643

Hezekiah; bc1719 s/o John & Tamsen Wentworth Chesley; m Margaret Cate; liv Barrington; ch William, Elihu, Hezekiah; NH-0003-633

Hezekiah; s/o Hezekiah & Margaret Cate of Barrington; m Sophia Cate; liv Barrington; ch Dea Solomon m Elizabeth Hayes; NH-0003-633

Ichabod; bc1691 s/o John & Mary Horne; m Abigail ---; liv Littleworth; ch Sarah b1716 m Nathaniel Horne of Dover, Ichabod b1718 m Elizabeth Hayes, Ezekiel b1720 dy, Daniel b1723 m Sarah Plummer d/o Richard of Modbury, Moses bc1725, Aaron bc1727, Abigail b1730, Hannah b1734 m William Wentworth of Milton; NH-0003-632

Ichabod; b1718 s/o Ichabod & Abigail; m Elizabeth Hayes d/o John & Tamsen Wentworth Chesley, ch Abigail b1742 m Ichabod Hansom of Windham ME, Ichabod b1744, Ezekiel b1746, Daniel b1748, Moses b1750, Aaron b1752, James C, Tamsen b1755 dy, Abra b1757, Betty b1762 m Maj Joseph Mooney of Alton, John b1764; NH-0003-634

Ichabod; b1775; m1796 Deborah French b1779 & m Sarah Plumer; liv Farmington NH; ch/o Deborah - Martin L b1812 m Eliza Pearl, 13 others; ch/o Sarah - 2; NH-0003-634

James; s/o Paul of Barrington; liv Barrington; ch Paul m --- Horne; NH-0003-633

Joel M; b1828; m1852 Susan Waterman; ch Charles W, Roswell M, David M, Samuel; NH-0007-318

John; m1686 Mary Horne; liv SCO, Dover; ch John b1686 m Tamsen Wentworth Chesley & m Mary Roberts, Peter m Sarah Wingate, Robert, Ichabod bc1691 m Abigail ---, Samuel

HAYES (continued)

bc1694 m Leah Dam, William b1698 m Hannah Sanborn, Benjamin b1700, 1 dau m --- Phipps of Salisbury, 1 dau m --- Ambrose of Salisbury, 1 dau m --- Amrose of Chester; NH-0003-632 & 703

John; b1686 s/o John & Mary Horne; m Tamsen Wentworth Chesley d/o Dea Gershom Wentworth of Somersworth wid/o James Chesley & m Mary Roberts wid/o Samuel Wingate; liv Tole-end; ch/o Tamsen - John b1711, Paul b1713, Thomas b1715 m Hannah ---, Elihu, Hezekiah bc1719 m Margaret Cate, Elizabeth b1722 m Ichabod Hayes, Abra bc1723 m John Montgomery, Robert bc1725, Wentworth bc1727 m Mary Main & m Susan Burnham Roberts, Samuel bc1729, Jonathan b1732 m Mary Wingate; NH-0003-632

John; s/o John & Mary Horne; m Tamson Wentworth Chesley; liv Dover; ch Joseph b1746 m Peggy Brewster & m Elizabeth Wingate, 10 others; NH-0003-703

Jonathan; b1732 s/o John & Tamsen Wentworth Chesley; m Mary Wingate d/o Mary Roberts; liv Tole-end; ch Mary, Robert, Jonathan, Tamsen m Daniel Cushing, Nancy m William Cushing, Sarah m Samuel Jackson of Rochester NH, Robert, Betsey m Stephen Jackson of Rochester NH; NH-0003-634

Jonathan; b1774 s/o Elihu & Betsey Davis; m1794 Mary Hamm b1773 of Barrington; liv New Durham, Madbury; ch Samuel Davis b1796 m Comfort Chesley, 1 other; NH-0003-643

Joseph; b1746 s/o John & Tamson Wentworth Chesley; m Peggy Brewster & m Elizabeth Wingate; liv Strafford NH; ch/o Peggy - Joseph, 7 others; NH-0003-703

Joseph; s/o David of Strafford & Alton NH; m Betsey Brewster d/o George of Wolfeborough; liv Alton NH; ch Dr Albert Hamilton b1836; NH-0001-202

Martin L; b1812 s/o Ichabod &

HAYES (continued)
Deborah French of Farmington;
m Eliza Pearl d/o Joseph; liv
Natick, Farmington; ch 1 dau
m George E Davis of Lawrence
MA; NH-0003-634
Moses; bc1725 s/o Ichabod &
Abigail; liv Rochester; ch
Sarah b1750, Anna b1753,
Peter b1755, Enoch b1757,
Abigail b1760, Moses b1763,
Joshua b1765, Jacob b1769,
Hannah b1771, Mary b1774; NH-
0003-634
Paul; s/o James of Barrington;
m --- Horne; ch Elizabeth,
James; NH-0003-633
Paul; b1713 s/o John & Tamsen
Wentworth Chesley; liv
Barrington; ch Paul, James;
NH-0003-633
Peter; s/o John & Mary Horne; m
Sarah Wingate d/o John gd/o
John; liv Tole-end; ch Ann
b1718, Reuben b1720 m Abigail
Shackford, Joseph b1722,
Benjamin b1723, Mehitable
b1725, John, Elijah, Ichabod;
NH-0003-632
Reuben; b1720 s/o Peter & Sarah
Wingate; m Abigail Shackford;
ch Susanna m Dr Ezra Green;
NH-0003-633
Robert; bc1725 s/o John &
Tamsen Wentworth Chesley; liv
Barrington; ch Joshua m ---
Locke; NH-0003-633
Samuel; s/o Samuel gs/o John &
Tamsen Wentworth Chesley; ch
Capt John, Dea Samuel; NH-
0003-633
Samuel bc1694 s/o John & Mary
Horne; m1720 Leah Dam b1695
d/o William & Martha Pomfret;
liv Back River; ch Mary b1728
m Jotham Nute of Dover,
Abigail m Tristram Pinkham of
Dover; NH-0003-632
Samuel Davis; b1796 s/o
Jonathan & Mary Ham; m1827
Comfort Chesley b1806 d/o
Samuel & Nancy of Madbury;
liv Madbury; ch Ann Sophia
b1829 m John S F Ham, Samuel
Chesley b1834 m Elizabeth
Hoitt, Charles Woodman b1836
m Ellen Marie Weeks; NH-0003-
643
Thomas; b1715 s/o John & Tamsen
Wentworth Chesley; m Hannah
---; liv Tole-end; ch Ezekiel

HAYES (continued)
b1742, Susan b1745, Abigail
bc1748, Thomas; NH-0003-633
Wentworth; bc1727 s/o John &
Tamsen Wentworth Chesley;
m1753 Mary Main b1732 d/o Rev
Amos of Rochester & m1777
Susan Burnham Roberts b1741
wid/o --- Roberts; liv
Rochester; ch/o Mary - Amos
b1754, Betty b1757 m Timothy
Roberts of Milton, John b1760
dy, Elihu b1763, Theodore
b1766, Molly b1768 dy, Tamsen
b1772 m Samuel Locke; ch/o
Susan - John b1780; NH-0003-
633
William; b1698 s/o John & Mary
Horne; m1720 Hannah Sanborn;
ch Mary b1721, Hanna b1723,
William, Patience m --- Hall;
NH-0003-632
HAYFORD,
Nathaniel; m Philena Gannett;
liv Bridgewater, Tamworth NH;
ch Daniel, Seth m Susan
Gannett, Nathaniel, Polly m
--- Flanders, Warren m Sophia
Gannett; NH-0006-766
Warren; s/o Nathaniel & Philena
Gannett; m Sophia Gannett;
liv Tamworth NH; ch Sarah m
Isaiah Forrest, William, 4
others; NH-0006-767
HAYNES,
Martin Alonzo; b1842 s/o
Elbridge G of Springfield NH;
m1863 Cornelia T Lane of
Manchester; liv Gilford NH;
ch 2 dau; NH-0004-779
HAYWOOD,
Capt Alvah E; s/o Nathaniel; m
Lucretia Jeffers d/o James;
ch Chastina L m S H Baker, 3
sons, 2 dau; NH-0007-360
Nathaniel; liv Springfield VT,
Haverhill NH; ch Benjamin,
Capt Alvah E m Lucretia
Jeffers; NH-0007-360
HAZELTON,
Charles; b1813 s/o David & Mary
Ward of Plymouth; m1843
Hannah Sargent of Hopkinton;
liv Plymouth NH; ch Martha,
Charles W, Henry W, Arthur S;
NH-0007-590
David; m1800 Mary Ward d/o
Enoch; liv Plymouth NH;
ch Ruth, Mary Ann, Charles
b1813 m Hannah Sargent; NH-
0007-590

HAZEN,
Asa; liv CT, Hartford VT; ch Allen, Thomas, Austin, Asa, Lucius m Hannah Downer, Tracy; NH-0005-498

Austin; s/o Asa; liv Berlin VT; ch Allen, Austin, William, Asahel, Sophia m Rev David Stoddard; NH-0005-498

Louis Tracy; b1836 s/o Lucius & Hannah Downer of Hartford VT; m1863 Ellen Frances Johnson d/o Frank & Eleanor Stevens of Newbury VT; liv Newbury & Barnet VT, Whitefield NH; ch Frank J, Maria F, John D, Grace S; NH-0005-498

Lucius; s/o Asa; m Hannah Downer d/o John & Hannah; liv Hartford VT; ch Lucius D, Louis Tracy b1836 m Ellen Frances Johnson, Hannah M m Dr H C Newell; NH-0005-498

HEAD,
Col John; b1791 s/o Nathaniel Jr & Anna Knox of Bradford MA; m Anna Brown d/o William of Pembroke NH; liv Pembroke & Hooksett NH; ch Hannah A m Col Josiah Stevens Jr, Sallie B; Gen Natt b1828 m Abbie M Sanford, John A, William F b1832 m Mary H Sargent; NH-0001-224, NH-0004-385 & 388

Col Nathaniel Jr; b1754 s/o Gen Nathaniel of Pembroke NH (s/o Col James); m Anna Knox d/o Timothy of Pembroke NH; liv Bradford MA, Chester NH; Col John b1791 m Anna Brown, 6 sons; NH-0001-224, NH-0004-385 & 388

Gov Natt; b1828 s/o Col John & Anna Brown; m1863 Abbie M Sanford of Lowell MA; liv Hooksett NH; ch Lewis Fisher dy, Alice Perley dy, Annie Sanford; NH-0001-223, NH-0004-385

William F; b1832 s/o Col John & Anna Brown of Hooksett NH; m1858 Mary H Sargent of Allenstown d/o Maj Sterling; liv Hooksett; ch Eugene S, Sallie; NH-0004-388

HEALD,
Amos; b1765 s/o Oliver & Lydia Spaulding; m1789 Sybil Brown of Temple; liv Nelson; ch Oliver b1790 m Patty --- & m Relief Little; 1 son, 5

HEALD (continued)
others; NH-0002-580

David; s/o Oliver & Patty ---; m1856 Mary Susan Frost d/o Ebenezer of Ashburnham MA & m1862 Mary E Stone d/o Calvin & Elvira Wallingford of Marlborough; liv Milford; ch/o Mary S - Ella F b1858 dy; ch/o Mary E - Edward S, Frank H, Florence M, Clara M, Mary S, Hattie L; NH-0002-580

Ephraim; m Mary Shirley d/o Daniel M & Jane Moore; ch George b1849, Hattie b1852; NH-0002-328

John; liv Berwick ENG, Concord MA; ch John m Sarah Dean, 7 sons; NH-0002-580

John; s/o John; m1661 Sarah Dean; ch John m --- Hale, 5 sons; NH-0002-580

John s/o John & Sarah Dean; m --- Hale; liv Acton MA; ch Oliver m Lydia Spaulding, 2 sons; NH-0002-580

Oliver; s/o John & --- Hale; m Lydia Spaulding d/o Dea Isaac of Townsend MA; liv Temple; ch Amos b1765 m Sybil Brown, 1 son, 9 others; NH-0002-580

Oliver; b1790 s/o Amos & Sybil Brown; m1816 Patty --- b1794 & m1857 Relief Little of Peterborough NH; liv Milford; ch/o Patty - Addison, Albert, Sarah D m William Crosby, Emily m J Q A Ware, Henry, Lydia m M W Harris, William dy, David m Mary Susan Frost & m Mary E Stone, Almira m Alonzo French, Edwin; NH-0002-580

HEALY,
Joseph S; s/o Elliot & Judith Heath of Northfield NH; m Mary Garlin & m Elizabeth Hammond of Bristol NH; ch Albert, Eller, Joseph H, Fred N m Hannah Stevens d/o Jonathan Ackerman; NH-0007-119

HEARD,
David; b1758 s/o Richard & Sarah Fiske; m1784 Eunice Baldwin of Wayland & m1789 Sibyl Sherman of Wayland; liv Wayland MA; ch/o Sibyl - William b1795 m Susan Mann; NH-0006-720

James; m Susannah (Shuah); ch

HEARD (continued)

Mary, Elizabeth, Katherine, Abigail, Ann, John; NH-0003-771

John; m Isabel ---; liv Kittery; ch James m Susannah (Shuah); NH-0003-771

John; m Elizabeth Hull d/o Rev Joseph; ch Benjamin bc1643 m Elizabeth Roberts d/o Thomas, William, Mary bc1649 m John Ham, Abigail b1651 m Jenkin Jones, Elizabeth b1653 m James Nute & m William Furbur, Hannah b1655, John bc1658, Joseph bc1660, Samuel b1663 m Experience Otis d/o Richard, Tristram bc1666, Nathaniel b1668 m Sarah ---, Dorcas; NH-0003-771

Richard; b1720 s/o Zachariah & Silence Brown; m Sarah Fiske of Wayland; ch David b1758 m Eunice Baldwin & m Sibyl Sherman, Richard; NH-0006-720

William; b1794 s/o David & Sibyl Sherman of Wayland MA; m1825 Susan Mann of Orford NH; liv Wayland NH; ch Samuel H M, Hon William Andrew b1827 m Anne Elizabeth Marston & m Emily Maria Marston, Jared M, Susan E; NH-0006-720

Hon William Andrew; b1827 s/o William & Susan Mann of Wayland MA; m1850 Anne Elizabeth Marston d/o Hon Moulton H & m1855 Emily Maria Marston sis/o Anne; liv Sandwich NH; ch/o Anne - Edwin M; ch/o Emily - William, Arthur M; NH-0006-723

Zachariah; b1675; m1707 Silence Brown of Wayland; liv Cambridge & Wayland MA; ch Richard b1720 m Sarah Fiske, 4 others; NH-0006-720

HEATH,

Andrew S; s/o Reuben & Alice Nichols; m Sarah A Baldwin d/o Edward F & Sarah Bowen; ch Gilbert E, Mace C, Warren A, George A m Emma L Braley d/o Lorenzo B & Elizabeth Briggs; NH-0007-283

Daniel; m Sarah March of Newburyport NH; liv Enfield NH; ch Jonathan, Daniel, Eben, David, Holland, Ichabod, Lydia, Sarah, Dorset; NH-0007-259

HEATH (continued)

John C; s/o Samuel P & Mary A Dunlap of Salisbury NH; m Jennie Morrell d/o Samuel & Harriet of Andover NH; ch Mary, Willie, Ernest; NH-0007-120

Richard W; s/o Sargent & Eliza Stevens; m Nancy M Gibson d/o George W & Mary A Stevens of Springfield NH; ch Aurilla, Ida M, Amber A, Henry S, Warren C, Lura; NH-0007-283

Samuel P; m Mary A Dunlap; liv Salisbury NH; ch Eliza, John C m Jennie Morrell; NH-0007-120

Sargent; s/o Richard; m Eliza Stevens; ch Richard W m Nancy M Gibson; NH-0007-283

HEBARD,

Moses; liv CT, Canaan NH; ch Aaron b1771; NH-0007-420

HERBERT,

Samuel; b1813 s/o John gs/o James; m1831 Maria L Darling d/o Benjamin; liv Rumney NH, Wentworth; ch Ellen M, Charles W, Caroline, Henry, H W, Mary, John; NH-0007-112.19 & 606

HERRICK,

Henry; b1604 s/o Sir William of Bean Manor; m Editha Laskin; liv ENG, Salem MA; ch Elizabeth m Philip Fowler; NH-0004-16

HERSEY,

James; liv Newmarket; ch Jonathan b1746, Jemima b1750 m John Piper; NH-0006-305

Peter; s/o Peter; m Mary Folsom; ch Mary, Jeremiah, Nancy, Peter, Jacob b1803; NH-0003-540

HEWES,

Cyrus; b1790; m Margaret Pelton & m ?; liv Lyme NH; ch/o Margaret - Sewell m Mary E Drake & m Sarah M Webb, 7 others; NH-0007-525

John Freeman; b1784 s/o Nathaniel & Sarah Freeman; ch John R m --- Stark; NH-0007-525

John R; s/o John Freeman; m --- Stark d/o Albert; ch Kate V m John F Elliott, 9 others; NH-0007-525

Nathaniel; m Sarah Freeman; ch John Freeman b1784, Sylvanus

HEWES (continued)
b1789 m Miriam Wright, 8 others; NH-0007-525

Sewell; s/o Cyrus & Margaret Pelton of Lyme; m Mary E Drake & m Sarah M Webb; ch/o ? - Fred L, Alice S; NH-0007-525

Sylvanus; b1789 s/o Nathaniel & Sarah Freeman; m Miriam Wright d/o Nathan; liv Lyme NH; ch Eunice M m Joseph W Gerrish of Lebanon, Sarah F m F W Baker, Caroline M, Nathan Wright; NH-0007-525

HEWITT,
Elbert; b1843 s/o Lucian of Pomfret VT; m Augusta Merrill d/o Alvin I of Hanover; liv Hanover NH; NH-0007-336

HEYWOOD,
Henry; b1835; m1866 Catherine R Hubbard of Springfield VT; liv Guidhall VT, Lancaster NH, WI; NH-0005-229

Hon William; b1804; m Susan Hibbard d/o Hon David of Concord VT; liv Lunenburgh & Guildhall VT, Lancaster NH; ch 1 son, Edward dy, 1 son, Isabel; NH-0005-215

HIBBARD,
Charles F; m Susan M Keysar d/o John & Sarah Clark Wiswall; ch Harry; NH-0005-695

Elisha; s/o Thomas; m Sally Barnett d/o Nehemiah & Sally; ch Elisha B m Julia Brown & m Salome C Sullaway, 4 others; NH-0007-284

Elisha B; s/o Elisha & Sally Barnett; m Julia Brown & m Salome C Sullaway d/o Joseph & Lucinda Clifford; ch/o Julia - Harry L; ch/o Salome - 1 dau m Emerson; NH-0007-284

George; b1794 s/o Aaron; m Myra Runnells of Piermont; liv Dath, Piermont NH; ch Benjamin, 5 others; NH-0007-575

Harry; b1816 s/o Hon David of Concord VT; m1848 Mrs Sarah Hale Bellows d/o Hon Salma Hale of Keene NH; liv Bath NH; NH-0007-64

Thomas; m Lucy Sylvester; liv ENG, Haverhill NH; ch Samuel, Elisha, Simson, 1 dau m --- Wood, 1 dau m --- Ryder, 1

HIBBARD (continued)
dau m --- Bliss; NH-0007-353

Timothy; liv CT, Bath NH; ch John C, David, Aaron m Lydia Morse, Mary C m John Hastings; NH-0007-139

HICKS,
David; b1796 s/o Benjamin of Lee; m1824 Eliza Garland d/o John & Betsey Hight; liv Jefferson NH; ch Horace D, Elizabeth m N R Perkins, Alice J m James Tate, John A, Harriet J, Joseph G; NH-0005-419

Levi O; b1808; m Betsey Jordon d/o Benjamin; liv Dalton & Colebrook NH; ch 11; NH-0005-624

HIDDEN,
John Deering; b1829 s/o Dea William Price & Eunice Purington of Tamworth NH; m1861 Angelina P Robinson; ch Samuel A; NH-0006-771

Rev Samuel; s/o Price & Eunice Hodgskin; m Betsey Price; liv Tamworth NH; ch Dea William Price b1799 m Eunice Purington, Elizabeth m Dr Ebenezer Moore, Sophia m Jonathan C Gilman, Sarah, George; NH-0006-771

Dea William Price; b1799 s/o Rev Samuel & Betsey Price of Tamworth; m1822 Eunice Purington d/o James & Hannah Wilson of Sandwich; liv Tamworth NH; ch Sarah m Edward Moulton, Eliza A m Samuel Woodman, Sophia, John Deering b1829 m Angelina P Robinson, Samuel, William B, Julia P, Harriet A; NH-0006-771

HIGHT,
James; liv Portsmouth, Jefferson; ch Mehetable m John Garland; NH-0005-407

HILDRETH,
Brigham; d1872 s/o Jonathan; liv Lisbon NH; ch Phebe m --- Howland, Olivia m --- Young, Betsey m --- Cox, David B, Chester C, Timothy T, 1 other; NH-0007-453

David; m Levina Bowles & m Mrs Almina Bowles, liv Lisbon NH; NH-0007-454

Elkanah; m Sally Whipple; liv Chesterfield, Lisbon NH; ch Asa m Celia Quimby; NH-0007-

HILDRETH (continued)
454
Jotham Sr; m Abigail Sargent d/o Joshua; liv Amherst, Lyndeborough NH; ch Jotham b1807, Abigail m Jacob Crosby; NH-0002-512

HILL,
Charles F; m --- Parker sis/o Charles H & Benjamin F; liv Limerick ME, Searsport, Wolfeborough, NJ; ch C E; NH-0006-255

Daniel; m --- Emery; liv Salisbury MA; ch John, Timothy m Betsey Lapham, 2 sons, 2 dau; NH-0004-524

Judge David Hammonds; b1833 s/o Oliver & Lucinda Hammonds of Berwick ME; m1865 Mary Moulton d/o William E of Parsonfield ME; liv Sandwich NH; ch Walter D H, Bertha Mary; NH-0006-249

Freeman; m Hannah Conant d/o --- & Sally Gage; liv Merrimack; ch George, Sarah, 1 dy; NH-0002-543

James R; b1821; m ? & m1854 Sophia L Pickering; liv Stratham & Concord NH; ch/o ? - 1 dau m Josiah E Dwight; ch/o Sophia - Edson J, Solon P, Joseph C, Cora; NH-0004-103

Col John; s/o Leavitt & Sarah Russell; m Sally Freeman & m Elizabeth Eastman; ch/o Sally - Otis F, Amos A, John; ch/o Elizabeth - Mary F m David Richardson, Elizabeth m Rev Lyman Cutler of Pepperell MA & m Rev A C Thompson of Roxbury, George F, Thomas, Summer C, Susan A m Dr A S Evans; NH-0006-851

Joseph B; b1796 s/o Rev Ebenezer of Mason NH; m Harriet Brown of Antrim; liv TN, Mason & Colebrook NH, W Stewartstown; NH-0005-612

Leavitt; bro/o Dr Thomas P; m Sarah Russell; liv Conway NH; ch Col John m Sally Freeman & m Elizabeth Eastman, Sally m Col Asa Adams of Sandwich, Eunice m Thomas Eastman, Thomas, Abigail m Ambrose Merrill, Charles, Mary m Dr Jonathan R Thompson, Leavitt, Amos; NH-0006-851

HILLIARD,
Abraham; b1778 s/o Joseph & Anna Lovering; liv Kensington; NH-0003-358

Francis; b1825 s/o Jonathan & Mary Hodgdon; m1867 A Maria Blodgett b1838 d/o Rev Julius C & Abigail C of Kensington; liv Kensington; ch Marion, Nellie, Wendell P, Mary A; NH-0003-363

Jonathan; b1783 s/o Joseph & Anna Lovering; m1810 Mary Hodgdon b1792 d/o Hanson & Mary Caldwell of Dover; ch Rufus K, Joseph, William, Francis b1825 m A Maria Blodgett, 6 dy; NH-0003-363

HINMAN,
William; b1771 s/o John; liv Glasgow SCO, Bath, Monroe; ch 1 dau m William Shaw, William, Alexander H, Robert S; NH-0007-552

HITCHCOCK,
Charles Henry AM PhD; b1836 s/o Edward of Amherst MA; m --- Barrows d/o E P of Andover; ch 5; NH-0007-336

John Raymond; b1821 s/o John & Sarah Webster of Claremont NH; m1875 Dawn Lary d/o Andrew G & Levee Chandler; liv Gorham & Shelburne NH; NH-0005-927

HOAG,
Levi W; m Mary E Folsom d/o Thomas & Sophia Morrill of W Epping; ch George E, Clement H, David F, Albert B, Mahlon, Walter; NH-0003-235

HOBART,
Abel; m Betsey Wallace; liv Holland MA, Columbia NH; ch Horace, Anson L, Roswell, Harvey, 1 son, 5 dau; NH-0005-726

Peter; s/o Gershom; liv Groton MA; ch Col David b1722 m 2, Col Samuel b1734 m Anna --- & m ?; NH-0002-452

HOBBS,
Col David L; s/o Capt David of N Hampton & gs/o Dea Benjamin; m Judith Jenness d/o Samuel; liv Freedom NH; ch Dr Moses L b1800 m Fannie Marston & m Caroline Dodge, Victory, John, Alvah, Mary m Dr Moses Marston & m Dr Stephen Adams; NH-0003-417

HOBBS (continued)

Ezra T; s/o Joseph & Dorothy Cooley of Ossipee NH; liv W Ossipee NH; ch Frank P; NH-0006-627

Frank; s/o Josiah of Wakefield; m Emma Josephine Christie; NH-0006-260

John F; b1859 s/o John W F & Mary Folsom Nightingale; m1879 Annie D French d/o John F & Lemira Leavitt; NH-0003-419

John O; m Anna Maria Moore d/o Stephen & Mary L Greeley of Loudon NH; liv Deerfield & Newport NH; ch Kate; NH-0004-514

John W F; b1815 s/o Jonathan & Fanny Dearborn; m Elizabeth J Drake d/o Dea Francis & m Mary Folsom Nightingale d/o James Folsom of Exeter & wid/o James Nightingale & m Olive A Drake Hobbs b1828 d/o Samuel J Drake of N Hampton & wid/o Thomas Hobbs; liv Boston MA, N Hampton NH; ch/o Elizabeth - 4; ch/o Mary - John F b1859 m Annie D French, Lizzie M; NH-0003-417

Jonathan; b1774 s/o Thomas & --- Sherburne of Hampton; mc1798 Fanny Dearborn d/o John; liv N Hampton; ch Mary F, Fanny, Leocady D, Sarah, Fanny, Horatio D, W J C, John W F b1815 m Elizabeth J Drake & m Mary Folsom Nightingale & m Olive A Drake Hobbs, Harriet N; NH-0003-417

Joseph; s/o Nathaniel & --- Leavitt; m Dorothy Cooley; liv Ossipee NH; ch Samuel, Lavina m Joseph Doe of Tamworth, Dorothy m Mark F Jewell, Joseph T m Nancy Pinner, Larkin D m Dorothy C Hobbs, Anna m Benjamin F Fellows of Tamworth, Olive F m Deborah Jenness, Wentworth H m --- Hall, Ezra T; NH-0006-627

Joseph T; s/o Joseph & Dorothy Cooley of Ossipee NH; m Nancy Pinner; ch Joseph Pinner; NH-0006-627

Josiah H; b1834 s/o Dr Daniel S & Judith G of Madison; m1878 Mary E Erwin; liv Albany NY, Madison; ch Josiah Irving

HOBBS (continued)

b1880; NH-0006-263

Larkin D; s/o Joseph & Dorothy Cooley of Ossipee NH; m Dorothy C Hobbs d/o John; liv W Ossipee NH; ch Warren J, Wentworth B; NH-0006-627

Dr Moses L; b1800 s/o Col David L & Judith Jenness of Freedom NH; m1829 Fannie Marston d/o Simeon & Abihail Leavit & m1858 Caroline Dodge d/o John of Newburyport MA; liv N Hampton; ch David, Joseph B, Victory, Ann Jennette m John Smith of Saybrook NH, Leavitt M; NH-0003-417

Nathaniel; m Nancy Kent d/o John & Temperance Lapish of Rochester; liv N Berwick ME; ch Nathaniel; NH-0003-111

Nathaniel; m --- Leavitt; liv Hampton, Effingham; ch Benjamin, Nathaniel, Jonathan, Joseph m Dorothy Cooley, Reuben; NH-0006-627

Oliver F; s/o Joseph & Dorothy Cooley of Ossipee NH; m Deborah Jenness; ch Frank K m Sarah Atwood, Orodon P, Elizabeth m Edward Hersey, Lucinda m Jeremiah Conner; NH-0006-627

Samuel; s/o Joseph & Dorothy Cooley of Ossipee NH; liv Ossipee NH; ch Joseph W, Christopher C, 9 others; NH-0006-627

Thomas; m --- Sherburne; liv Hampton; ch Jonathan b1774 m Fanny Dearborn; NH-0003-417

Wentworth H; s/o Joseph & Dorothy Cooley of Ossipee NH; m --- Hall d/o Daniel; liv Ossipee NH; ch Ora A m Ernest Hall, Frank O, Charles E; NH-0006-627

HODGDON,

Moses; liv Milan NH; ch Samuel F, Moses, Charles N, Elizabeth m Dexter Wheeler, Emily m J H Chandler, Ruth m Capt L P Adley; NH-0005-832

Moses; m1853 Lucinda Angelina Green d/o Daniel & Polly Wheeler; liv Milan NH; ch Melvin Elmer b1854, Mary Ella b1855 m W Eugene Richards, Charles Dexter b1856 dy, Daniel G b1858, John Albert b1860, Helen Georgianna

HODGDON (continued)
b1862, Minnie E b1864, Walter
F b1866, Moses A b1868,
Charles Dexter b1870, Lewis C
b1872; NH-0005-820
HODGE,
James; liv Newmarket, Jackson;
ch John, 1 dau m Jonathan
Pitman of Bartlett, 1 dau m
Frank Guptill of Chatham; NH-
0006-955
John; s/o Alexander of SCO; liv
Landaff, Lebanon; ch West B,
Damon F, John P, Ida A, 3
others; NH-0007-569
HODGSON,
Samuel; b1842 s/o Ellis & Sarah
Lassey of Halifx ENG; m
Elizabeth A Dow of Ashland;
liv ENG, Lowell, Lake
Village, Meredith NH; NH-
0004-860
HODSDON,
Arthur L; m Charlotte M Grant
d/o Dr Nathaniel & Charlotte
S Hobbs; ch Walter Grant,
Herbert Arthur, Mary Ellen;
NH-0006-643
Cyrus R; liv Kennebunk ME,
Piermont NH; ch Aaron G; NH-
0007-575
Ebenezer; s/o Elder Thomas of
Berwick ME; mc1797 Sally
Wentworth d/o Lt Timothy &
Amy Hodsdon; liv Ossipee NH;
ch Betsey m Rev Henry Smith &
m Rev Sydney Turner of
Bingham ME, Olive H m Dea
Jonathan Ambrose, Thomas,
Sally m Andrew Folsom & m
John Burley of Sandwich,
Belinda m Hollis Burleigh of
Ossipee, Amy W m Calvin
Sanborn, Ebenezer b1811 m
Catherine Tuttle, 3 others;
NH-0006-625
Ebenezer; b1811 s/o Ebenezer &
Sally Wentworth of Ossipee
NH; m1834 Catherine Tuttle
d/o Lt George & Sarah Giles
of Effingham NH;· ch John W,
Edward P m Emma B Demeritt
d/o Mark of Effingham NH,
Sarah E m Alphonzo A Spear;
NH-0006-625
HOGG,
Alexander; ch William m Anna
Follansbee, Samuel, & 1 dau m
--- Pettingill; NH-0002-382
Thomas; bro/o Alexander; liv
Deering; ch Samuel Dana & 1

HOGG (continued)
dau; NH-0002-382
William; m Anna Follansbee; ch
Jonathan m Rebecca Hogg,
Priscilla m Benjamin Colby,
William, Mary m Jonathan
Kelley, Sarah, Benjamin m
Catherine Blood, Follansbee m
Susan McCoy, Lucy m Moses
Chase, John, NH-0002-382
HOITT,
Gen Alfred; b1806; m1828 Susan
Demeritt of Northwood & m1877
Mrs Mary A Smart of Boston
MA; liv Northwood, Lee,
Dover; ch/o Susan - 13; NH-
0003-859
Benjamin; b1790 s/o Thomas; m
Mehitable Babson d/o Isaac of
Dunbarton; liv Hampstead &
Barnstead NH; ch Thomas Lewis
b1827 m Martha Seavey, 4
sons, 7 dau; NH-0004-715
Philip; s/o Samuel; liv
Piermont, Littleton; ch Wells
P; NH-0007-166
Thomas; bc1750; liv Chester NH;
ch Benjamin b1790 m Mehitable
Babson, James S, 1 dau m J B
Merrill Esq; NH-0004-715
Thomas Lewis; b1827 s/o
Benjamin & Mehitable Babson;
m Martha Seavey; liv Barn-
stead & Pembroke NH; ch
Henrietta Babson b1876; NH-
0004-715
HOLBROOK,
Dr Guy; b1845 s/o Thomas of
Lemington VT; liv St Johns-
bury VT, W Stewartstown,
Colebrook & Manchester NH;
NH-0005-600
HOLDEN,
Charles A; s/o Milton & Jane
Walker; m1864 Lucy A
Greenough d/o William &
Mehitable Hills; liv Rumney
NH; ch Georgiana, Sarah A,
Carrie dy, William M dy; NH-
0007-611
Daniel; b1809 s/o Asa & Nancy
Wyman of Billerica MA; m1834
Sarah Haynes d/o Reuben of
Sudbury MA & m1844 Roxanna
Haynes sis/o Sarah; liv
Belvidere, Dracut, W Concord
NH, Framingham MA; ch/o Sarah
- 4; ch/o Roxanna - 7; NH-
0004-153
Milton; b1804 s/o David &
Bridget Atwell of Groton;

HOLDEN (continued)
m1828 Jane Walker; liv Boston, Rumney NH; ch Annette m George C Spaulding, Charles A m Lucy A Greenough; NH-0007-611

HOLMAN,
Hon Charles; b1833 s/o Porter & Persis Reed of Sterling MA; m1863 Mary S Osgood d/o George W & Susan Marston of Amesbury MA; liv Boylston MA, Nahsua NH; ch Charles Francis b1866; NH-0002-201

HOLMES,
Edward A; m Areanna Evelyn Sanborn d/o James Monroe & Julia A Currier of E Kingston; liv Boston; ch Lois M; NH-0003-200

Rev Hiram; b1806 s/o Joshua & Polly Cater of Rochester NH; m1837 Susanna Brown d/o Josiah & Lydia of Weare; liv Wolfborough, Bradford; NH-0004-218

HOLT,
Rev Edwin; b1805; m1828 Emily Titcomb of Newburyport MA; liv New London CT, New York City, Portsmouth NH, IN; NH-0003-308

Henry H; s/o Franklin b1818 gs/o Jedediah; m1866 Martha A Warren d/o Asa; liv Lyme NH; ch Alice M, 2 others; NH-0007-546

Joseph; b1738; m Elizabeth Widdrington b1739; liv ENG, NH; ch Nathan b1762 m Sarah Black b1762; NH-0004-583

Dea Joshua; liv Andover MA, Greenfield NH; ch Rev Peter, Dea Solomon, Dea Joshua, Dea John, Dea Timothy, Dea Stephen, Mary m Isaac Foster, Phebe m Dea Joseph Batchelder, Chloe m Capt Francis Bowers, Hannah m Capt Ephraim Holt, Bethia m Dea Daniel Kimball of Hancok; NH-0002-344

Lester; s/o Lemuel; ch John N, Parker, Freeman J; NH-0007-543

HOOK,
Daniel; s/o Jesse G & Clarissa Fowler; m Mrs Charlotte Clifford d/o Calvin & Huldah Sabin Adams; liv Grafton NH; ch Elmer D, Dana E; NH-0007-

HOOK (continued)
284
Jesse G; s/o Daniel & Priscilla Travis; m Clarissa Fowler; ch Jesse G, Priscilla E, Daniel m Mrs Charlotte Clifford; NH-0007-284

HORN,
James H; liv Farmington, Dummer; ch William, Ezra; NH-0005-855

HORNE,
Daniel; m Relief Roberts d/o --- & Susanna Barnham; liv Farmington; ch Timothy; NH-0003-634

Jacob; m --- Twombly; liv Somersworth, Wolfeborough; ch 10; NH-0006-304

Jeremiah MD; b1816 s/o Jeremiah of Rochester gs/o Isaac of Dover; liv Lowell MA, Dover NH; NH-0003-849

HOSKINS,
Luther; s/o Elkanah; liv Littleton & Lyman NH; ch Luther B; NH-0007-516

HOSLEY,
James (Horsley); m Martha Parker b1649 d/o John of Cambridge; ch James m Maria ---; NH-0002-355

James; b1649; m Martha Parker; ch James b1675; NH-0002-135

James; b1675 s/o James & Martha Parker; ch James b1702 m Ennie Jervett; NH-0002-136

James; s/o James & Martha Parker; m Maria ---; liv Billerica MA; ch James b1704 m Exercise ---; NH-0002-355

James; b1702 s/o James; m Ennie Jervett; ch James b1734; NH-0002-136

James; b1704 s/o James & Maria ---; m Exercise ---; ch Dea James b1734; NH-0002-355

Dea James; b1734 s/o James & Exercise ---; liv Townsend, New Ipswich; NH-0002-355

James; b1734 s/o James & Ennie Jevett; liv Townsend MA, Hancock NH; ch Samuel b1767 m Polly Dodge; NH-0002-136

Jewett D; b1820 s/o Luke G & Polly Niles of Hillsborough NH; m Mary S Moore of Hillsboro; liv W Lebanon NH; ch Anna A m A J Grover, Jennie, Harry H, 2 others; NH-0007-426

HOSLEY (continued)

Hon John; b1826 s/o Samuel & Sophia Wilson of Hancock; m1854 Dorotha H Jones of Weare NH; liv Manchester; ch Marion J m William Parsons MD; NH-0002-135

Samuel; b1767 s/o James; m Polly Dodge; liv Hancock NH; ch Samuel b1802 m Sophia Wilson; NH-0002-136

Samuel; b1802 s/o Samuel & Polly Dodge; m Sophia Wilson; liv Hancock NH; ch Hon John b1826 m Dorotha H Jones, Martha E m George G Wadsworth of Chelsea MA, Lucretia J m Oliver Dearborn of Denver CO; NH-0002-135

HOUGH,

Clement; adopted s/o Wetherell & Mehitable Slapp; m1823 Aseneth D Ferris & m1825 Theody Wells; liv CT, Lebanon NH; ch/o Aseneth - 1 dy; ch/o Theody - Thomas Wells, Ruth m --- True, Henry B, 5 others; NH-0007-420

HOUSTON,

Gilmore; b1807 s/o David & Esther Willy of Thornton; m Sarah Griffin of Thornton & m Lydia Snow; liv Plymouth NH; ch/o ? - Annette C m C A French of Henniker, 3 sons, 2 dau; NH-0007-593

HOVEY,

Dr Daniel; b1792 s/o Daniel & Beulah Hovey of Lyme; m1817 Hannah H Harris d/o Joshua Esq of Canaan; liv Guildhall VT, Canaan & Lyme NH, Greenfield MA; NH-0007-522

HOWARD,

David; b1753; m Molly Kingman & m ?; liv Bridgewater, Tamworth NH; ch/o Molly - Polly m Henry Remick, Keziah m Consider Gannett, Hannah b1789 m Newlon S Hatch, Azubah m Ford Whitman, Huldah m Joseph Chapman, David; ch/o ? - Algernon S & Amasa; NH-0006-766

Ezra P; b1818 s/o Joseph & Phebe Pettengill; m1844 Mary Trow b1818 d/o Levi & Betsy Averill of Mont Vernon; liv Wilton, Lowell, Nashua, Cambridge MA, Temple & Washington NH, Rochester NY; ch

HOWARD (continued)

Joseph Woodbury b1844 m Nancy J Hasselton, Mary H b1844 m Charles H French, Martha J b1847; NH-0002-213

Joseph; b1792 s/o Silas & Sybil Reed; m Phebe Pettengill b1796 d/o William of Milton & m Abiah Parker; liv Wilton; ch/o Phebe - Ezra P b1818 m Mary Trow, John S G b1821, Joseph A b1823; ch/o Abiah - Adeline P b1834, Hannah G b1836; NH-0002-213

Joseph Woodbury; b1844 s/o Ezra P & Mary Trow; m1868 Nancy J Hasselton of Wilton; liv Nashua; ch Charles W, Frank B, Mary H; NH-0002-213

Nathaniel; liv Suffolk ENG, Dorchester MA; ch William, Nathaniel; NH-0002-213, NH-0005-865

Nathaniel; liv Chelmsford; ch Nathaniel, Jacob; NH-0002-213

Phineas; b1765 s/o William of Temple NH; m Leonia Powers; ch Joseph b1809 m Zerviah Roberts b1812; NH-0005-865

Silas; m Sybil Reed d/o Capt Wm of Westford; liv Lyndeborough NH; ch Silas, Samuel, Joseph b1792 m Phebe Pettengill, Jacob, John, Benjamin, Martha m --- Hutchinson of Milford, Abigail m --- Blanchard of Albany NY, Rachel m --- Emerson & m --- Dodge, Sybil dy; NH-0002-213

William; liv Temple NH; ch Phineas b1765 m Leonia Powers, Asa, James, Nathaniel, William; NH-0005-865

William; b1775 s/o William & Martha of New London CT; m Betsey Pierce b1775 of Chester & m1820 Abigail Stratton of Fairlee VT; liv Norwich CT, Orford NH; ch/o Betsey - William b1803 m Sarah E Page, Henry, Elizabeth, Mary P, James P, John, Nancy; ch/o Abigail - Louisa, Thomas, Sarah, George, Jane; NH-0007-557

William; b1803 s/o William & Betsey Pierce; m Sarah E Page of Sharon VT; liv Orford NH, Sharon VT; ch Elizabeth m --- Avery, Martha m --- Pierce,

HOWARD (continued)
Kate; NH-0007-565
William H; m Charlotte Webster Straw d/o Ezekiel Albert & Charlotte Smith; liv Somerville MA, Manchester; ch William H, Sarah Cheney; NH-0002-80

HOWE,
Calvin; b1806; m1836 Eliza H Judkins of Gilmanton & m1850 Mrs Clara N Evans d/o William Fisk of Concord; liv Enfield & Concord NH, Kingston, N Barnstead, Lower Gilmanton; ch/o Eliza - 1 son; NH-0004-152

Daniel; s/o Peter; liv Benton NH; ch Samuel m Merab Royce d/o Samuel of Haverhill, Daniel M m Susan J Clough, Susanne m D K Davis, Lydia m J A Clark, Timothy E, Julia A m J G Drew, 2 sons; NH-0007-152

Daniel M; s/o Daniel of Benton; m Susan J Clough of Lisbon; ch Kendrick L, Paul M, Sam, Kate S; NH-0007-152

Micah C; m1859 Harriet C Smith; liv Newbury & Hanover NH; ch Angie F m George W Lambert, Etta S, Alberton; NH-0007-333

Nathaniel; s/o Nathaniel & Elizabeth Fite; m Mary Jane Choate & m1851 Susan E Sargent; liv Enfield NH; ch/o Mary - Eliza J m David Noyes, Sarah B m B C Leach; NH-0007-262

Phineas; s/o Dea Jotham; liv Hopkinton, Deerfield, Weare; NH-0003-27

HOWLAND,
Jeremy; m Martha Jillson of Richmond; liv RI, Lisbon NH; ch Silas m Eliza Oakes of Lisbon, Hosea, Washington W, Simon B, Charles W, 2 dau, 6 sons; NH-0007-447

Stephen; s/o George; ch Samuel, 1 dau m Nathan Grimes, Isaac, Jeremiah, 7 others; NH-0007-570

HOWLET,
John; m Phebe Johnson of Henniker; liv Henniker; ch Mary, Betsy m Nehemiah Knight, Enoch m ? & m Hannah Metcalf, Sally m Benjamin Flint, Thomas m Eunice

HOWLET (continued)
Collins, John b1795 m Phebe Cressy, Alice m Israel Andrews, Stephen, George m Marinda Cram, Perley dy, James m Dorcas Stevens, David dy, Benjamin dy, Caleb dy, Phebe dy; NH-0004-204

Thomas; s/o John & Phebe Johnson of Henniker; m Eunice Collins d/o Enos of Warner; ch John, Perley, Enos, Elizabeth, Sarah; NH-0004-204

HOYT,
Aaron Beede; b1802 s/o Dr Moses & Anna Beede of Ossipee NH; m Catharine H Blanchard d/o Augustus of Sandwich & m1873 Sarah A Doeg d/o Augustus & Huldah Cousins of Alfred ME; liv Boston, Baltimore, Sandwich NH; ch/o Catharine - Moses C, Augustus B, Esther A m William R Smith, Catharine, Elizabeth Grace; NH-0006-715

Benjamin F; m Alzada Eaton d/o Joshua & Alzina Gillingham; ch Frederick G b1867, Warren A b1868, Nettie A b1870, Carrie A b1873, Chester F b1879; NH-0004-211

Ebenezer; s/o Capt Joseph; m twice; liv Grafton NH; ch Ebenezer S m Lucretia R Cawell; NH-0007-278

Ebenezer S; s/o Ebenezer; m Lucretia R Cawell; ch Thomas J m Ellen F Barney, Augustus F m Ann M Cole, 9 others; NH-0007-278

Horace F; b1811 s/o Joseph & Mary Patterson; m1833 Caroline E Hardy d/o Daniel of Lebanon; ch Mary J b1837 m S P Berry, Dea Horace F Jr b1842 m1868 Minnie R Coates, Eliza b1848 m Simon Ward Jr; NH-0007-324

James; s/o William & Charlotte Pickering of Newington NH; m1833 Lydia Smith d/o Israel O of York ME; liv Portsmouth, Newington; ch Israel S, Corinne, James A, Joseph S, Florence, Benjamin S, Mary H, William A; NH-0003-394

John; liv Newington NH; ch Hanson, William m Charlotte Pickering, 1 dau m James Pickering, 1 dau m Ebenezer Adams; NH-0003-394

HOYT (continued)
Joseph; s/o Moses & Lydia Gould
of Newport; m1802 Mary
Patterson; liv Hanover NH; ch
Polly b1805 m A T Dudley,
Betsey b1810, Horace F b1811
m Caroline E Hardy, Joseph
b1813, Lydia b1817 m John
Burrall; NH-0007-324
Moses; b1738; m Lydia Gould;
liv Newport NH; ch Joseph
b1778 m Mary Patterson; NH-
0007-324
Dr Moses; m Anna Beede d/o
Aaron & Anna Winslow; liv
Ossipee NH; ch Aaron Beede
b1802 m Catharine H Blanchard
& m Sarah A Doeg; NH-0006-715
Stephen; b1769; m Phebe
Presbury b1772 d/o Dea
William; liv Hopkinton &
Bradford NH; ch William P
b1794, Stephen Jr b1795, John
b1797, Hiram b1800, George W
b1803, Olive P b1806, Elisha
E b1808, John Raymond b1811,
Elbridge Gerry b1814 m1843
Mary Anne Spaulding b1814 of
Warner; NH-0004-204
William; s/o John of Newington
NH; m Charlotte Pickering d/o
Winthrop; liv Newington NH;
ch Phebe, Winthrop, Hanson,
Charlotte, William, Hannah,
Dennis, Thomas, James; NH-
0003-394
HUBBARD,
Dr George H; b1825; m Sally
Martin Jones d/o Samuel &
Elizabeth Andrews of Bradford
NH; liv Bradford Centre; ch
George; NH-0004-205
John; liv Hampton, E Sandwich;
ch Nathaniel b1777 m ---
Ambrose & m Mehitable Morse,
Sarah m --- White, Mary m ---
Plummer, Susan m --- Badger,
Catherine m Dr Sanborn, Lucy
m --- Moulton, Martha m Rev
Joshua Dodge; NH-0006-769
Nathaniel; b1777 s/o John; m
--- Ambrose & Mehitable Morse
d/o Caleb of Moultonborough;
liv Sandwich & Tamworth NH;
ch/o Ambrose - Oliver A; ch/o
Morse - Betsey m Joshua
Smith, Martha m Zenas
Blaisdell, Mary, Susan, Lucy
Nathaniel b1820 m1868 Sarah
Remick d/o Capt Enoch, Judith
m Henry Brown, Lucy, Sarah m

HUBBARD (continued)
Charles Sanborn; NH-0006-769
Thomas; m Betsey Messer d/o
Stephen; liv Andover & Dracut
& Bradford MA, Shelburne NH;
ch Erastus m --- Wilson d/o
Abraham, Rufus m --- Wilson
d/o Abraham, Enoch m ---
Peabody d/o Amos, Leonard m
--- Peabody d/o Amos, Jeffer-
son m --- Green d/o George,
Maria m Joshua Kendall; NH-
0005-873
HUCKINS,
Dr Enos; b1845 s/o Enos &
Betsey Ingalls of Warren;
m1868 Martha G Merrill; liv
Ashland, Plymouth NH; NH-
0007-596
James; s/o Robert; m Louisa
Plaisted; liv Ashland NH; ch
James F m Mary S Smith,
Cordelia m --- Cheany; NH-
0007-124
Robert; s/o James of New
Hampton NH; m Deborah Gordon
& m Rebecca McGoon & m
Abigail Muddgett; ch/o ? -
James m Louisa Plaisted, 11
others; NH-0007-124
HUGGINS,
John; b1753; m Anna Mordough
b1757 of Wakefield NH; liv
Greenland & Wolfeborough NH;
ch Samuel b1788 m Sally L
Wyatt; NH-0006-386
Nathaniel; b1820 s/o Samuel &
Sally L Wyatt; m1849 Ruth P
Nudd; liv Wolfeborough NH; ch
George L, Everett N b1855;
NH-0006-386
Samuel; b1788 s/o John & Anna
Mordough; m1817 Sally L Wyatt
b1795 of Wenham; liv Wenham
MA, Wolfeborough NH; ch
Elizabeth Gardner b1818 m1839
Charles Remick, Nathaniel
b1820 m Ruth P Nudd, John
b1823 dy, John P b1826 m1857
Lydia S Moore, Samuel J
b1828, Mehitable b1830, Sally
Ann b1834 m1859 Alvin S
Cotton & m Abiel C Eaton,
Almon Wyatt b1837 dy, Everett
Newell b1837 dy, Mary R b1839
m1867 James H Martin; NH-
0006-386
HUGHES,
Barnett; s/o John & Mehitable
Buzzel; m Jane Wilson of
Windham; ch Barnett Jr m

HUGHES (continued)
Martha L Clark & m Esther J Baker, 6 sons, 4 dau; NH-0007-129

Barnett Jr; s/o Barnett & Jane Wilson; m Martha L Clark of Franklin NH & m Esther J Baker d/o Samuel S & Adis Drew; liv Ashland NH; ch/o Martha - 7; ch/o Esther - Lucy Ashland; NH-0007-129

Frank L; s/o Thomas N of Holderness; m Elizabeth A Shepard d/o John C & Elmira of Ashland; liv Ashland NH; ch Elmer C; NH-0007-125

Thomas N; s/o Barnett & Jane Grimes; liv Holderness; ch Frank L m Elizabeth A Shepard, 2 others; NH-0007-125

HULL,
Nathaniel; s/o Jonathan; liv Plymouth NH; ch Luther C b1833 m Lucy M Wood; NH-0007-591

William G; b1826 s/o Moses & Zilpha Ward of Plymouth; m1854 Elizabeth Crockett; liv Plymouth NH; ch Arthur C, Herbert W; NH-0007-590

HUMPHREY,
Hon Moses; b1807 s/o Moses Leavitt & Sarah Lincoln of Hingham MA; m1831 Lydia Humphrey; liv Concord; ch 1 dau; NH-0004-101

HUNKING,
Dr Benjamin; m Drusilla Everett d/o Hon Richard C; liv Newbury VT, Lancaster NH; NH-0005-348

HUNKINS,
Romanzo J; m Adaline C Cummings d/o Daniel & Lois Kidder of Groton; liv Groton; ch Willie H; NH-0007-190

HUNT,
Anthony; s/o Philip Jr gs/o Philip Sr of Sanbornton; m Mary Chase of Deerfield NH; liv Gilmanton NH, Woodbury VT; ch Sarah, Lucian dy, Lucian m Caroline Higgins; NH-0004-540

Enoch; liv Gilford NH; ch William, Samuel, Joseph, Ebenezer S, John S, Enoch; NH-0004-742

Joshua W; m Eliza Ann Lund d/o Charles & Eliza Stevens; ch

HUNT (continued)
Alma F, William E, Charles L; NH-0002-217

Nathan; b1800 s/o Zebulon; m Harriet Ricker; ch David S; NH-0007-379

HUNTINGTON,
Elias; bc1756; m Mrs Mary Eaton of Hanover; liv Lebanon; ch Elias Jr, Mary m Daniel Richardson of Lebanon; NH-0007-316

Elias Jr; s/o Elias & Mrs Mary Eaton of Lebanon; m1818 ?; liv Lebanon; ch Newton S b1822, 1 dau; NH-0007-316

HUNTLEY,
William G; s/o Newman A & Caroline Gaylord; m Susan E Fletcher d/o Jotham H & Lucinda Clark of Plattsburg NY; NH-0007-284

HUNTON,
Palmetus Esq; b1809 s/o Dr Arial & Polly Pingry; m Louisa Parsons; NH-0004-619

Sylvanus; b1811 s/o Dr Arial & Polly Pingry; m Clarissa M Baily; NH-0004-619

HUNTOON,
Rev Benjamin; b1792; m Susannah Pettengill & m Lydia Bowman & m Mrs Ann Payson; liv Canton MA; NH-0004-619

HUNTRESS,
Hamlin; b1861 s/o Joseph L of Sandwich; m1885 Amy L Rollins d/o John A; liv Moulton-borough NH; NH-0006-414

HURLBUTT,
David; s/o Nathaniel & Bettie Taylor; m Gratia Taylor; liv Hanover NH; ch Nathaniel m Marinda Spencer, John, Elihu m Emeline L Goodell, 10 others; NH-0007-323

Elihu; s/o David & Gratia Taylor; m1842 Emeline L Goodell of Lyme; liv Hanover NH; ch C O, Lucy R m --- Sherman, Fannie G m George Medbury, Willard G, Harriet A m J V Hazen, Ida; NH-0007-323

Nathaniel; b1736 s/o Gideon; m Bettie Taylor; liv Washington CT, Hanover NH; ch David m Gratia Taylor, 7 others; NH-0007-323

Nathaniel; s/o David & Gratia Taylor of Hanover; m Marinda Spencer; liv Hanover NH; ch

HURLBUTT (continued)
David J, Ruth m Lucius
Stearns, Ellen m Frank
Biathrow, 1 other; NH-0007-
323
Sylvester M; s/o Chester of
Dalton; m Rhoda Hildreth of
Victory VT & m Ormacinda
Edmands of Dalton; liv
Littleton NH; ch 2 dau; NH-
0007-501
HUTCHINGS,
George H MD; b1840; m Emily M
Lathrope; liv Charlestown &
Woburn MA, Salisbury NH; ch
2; NH-0004-619
HUTCHINS,
Charles R; b1854 s/o Unite K &
Emeline Blake of Rumney; m P
M Brown; ch Lesta C b1881;
NH-0007-610
Erastus T; s/o Thomas of Alex-
andria; m Annie H Robie d/o
Caleb T & Hannah Kineston;
liv Alexandria NH; ch Mabel
A, Josie L, Bert C, Earl L;
NH-0007-119
Frank D; b1850; liv Putney VT,
Lancaster NH; NH-0005-237
Hamilton AM; b1805 s/o Abel;
liv Concord; NH-0004-6
Jeremiah; liv Haverhill MA,
Bath NH; ch Samuel James,
Samuel, 3 sons, 7 dau; NH-
0007-136
Stilson; m Clara Eaton; liv
Whitefield NH; ch Hon Stilson
b1838; NH-0005-485
Thomas; s/o Thomas gs/o Thomas;
m Hannah Dedman & m Sarah
Dadman; liv Alexandria NH;
ch/o ? - Horatio E, Francis
S, Erastus T m Annie H Robie;
NH-0007-119
Unite K; b1820 s/o Benjamin C &
Philena Heith of Bradford VT;
m Emeline Blake d/o Gideon &
Johanna Sanborn; liv Rumney
NH; ch Benjamin F, Joseph,
Unite S, Charles R b1854 m P
M Brown, Pascal dy, Flora M
m1884 Joseph O Sanborn b1863
s/o Samuel & Caroline of
Ellsworth; NH-0007-610
William V; m Martha Newell of
Windsor VT; liv Bath NH; ch
Zebina N, James R, Martha A,
2 others; NH-0007-140
HUTCHINSON,
Aaron; bc1755; liv Lebanon NH;
ch Henry b1785, James b1786 m

HUTCHINSON (continued)
Eunice Kimball; NH-0007-92 &
93
Abel; b1795 s/o Nathan &
Rebecca Peabody; m1816 Betsey
Bartlett b1796 d/o Isaac &
Elizabeth; liv Milford; ch
Elizabeth b1816 m Charles
Burns; NH-0002-40
Benjamin; d1733; m Jane
Phillips d/o Walter &
Margaret & m1714 Abigail
Foster; liv Salem; ch/o Jane
Benjamin b1693 m Sarah
Tarbell & 10 others; NH-0002-
40
Benjamin; b1693 s/o Benjamin &
Jane Phillips of Salem; m1715
Sarah Tarbell d/o John & Mary
Nurse; liv Salem, Bedford MA;
ch Nathan bp1717 m Rachel
Stearns & 6 others; NH-0002-
40
Daniel G; m Nancy Capen of
Stewartstown & m Eliza
Blodgett d/o Marcena; liv
Lyndeborough, Colebrook; ch/o
? - Erasmus D b1823; NH-0005-
623
Elisha; s/o Joseph gs/o Joseph
ggs/o Joseph; liv Amherst NH;
ch Jesse m Mary Leavitt,
Andrew, Sarah; NH-0002-581
James; b1786 s/o Aaron of
Lebanon NH; m1815 Eunice
Kimball of Plainfield; liv
Lebanon; NH-0007-93
Jesse; s/o Elisha; m Mary
Leavitt d/o Andrew of Mont
Vernon; liv Milford; ch
Jesse, David, Noah, Mary,
Andrew, Zephaniah, Caleb,
Jesse, Joshua, Benjamin,
Judson, Rhoda, John W b1821 m
Fannie B Patch, Elizabeth,
Abby m Ludlow Patten; NH-
0002-581
John; b1821 s/o Jesse & Mary
Leavitt; m1843 Fannie B Patch
of Lowell MA; ch Henry J m
Lillie Phillips, Viola m
Lewis A Campbell s/o Judge
William, Judson Whittier; NH-
0002-581
Joseph; b1633 s/o Richard &
Alice Bosworth; liv Eng,
Salem MA; ch Benjamin m Jane
Phillips; NH-0002-40
Jotham Patten; b1824; m1851
Abigail Elizabeth Hadley of
Rumney; liv Sidney ME,

HUTCHINSON (continued)
Laconia & Nashua NH; NH-0004-703

Hon Liberty Haven; b1844 s/o Edwin F & Elizabeth Flint of Milan; liv Milan NH; NH-0005-853

Nathan; bp1717 s/o Benjamin & Jane Phillips; m Rachel Stearns; liv Bedford MA, Amherst; ch Nathan b1752 m Rebecca Peabody, 5 others; NH-0002-40

Nathan; b1752 s/o Nathan & Rachel Stearns; m1778 Rebecca Peabody b1752 d/o William & Rebecca Smith; liv Amherst; ch Abel b1795 m Betsey Bartlett, 6 others; NH-0002-40

Richard; dc1662; m1627 Alice Bosworth; liv N Markham Eng, Salem MA; ch Joseph b1633; NH-0002-40

Richard; b1602 s/o Thomas gs/o Thomas ggs/o Lawrence; m Alice; liv Arnold ENG, Salem MA; ch Joseph, 3 others; NH-0002-581

Timothy Harden; b1810 s/o Timothy & Nizaulla Rawson of Sangerville ME; m1856 Eliza A Hazelton d/o James & Betsey of Orford NH; liv Shelburne & Gorham NH; NH-0005-931

-I-

INGALLS,
Dea Daniel; liv Andover MA, Merrimack NH; ch Polly, Sally, Rebecca, Elizabeth dy, Daniel T, Henry P, Putnam; NH-0002-544

Daniel T; s/o Dea Deaniel; liv Merrimack; ch Horace P, Mary, George C, Lucian, Nancy; NH-0002-544

George C; s/o Daniel T; liv Merrimack; ch Helen L, Daniel T Jr; NH-0002-544

George H MD; b1805; liv Peterborough NH, Proctorsville VT; NH-0002-668

H L; m Mary P Crosby d/o Abel L & Pauline Phelps of Groton; liv Concord NH; ch Linna A, Della L; NH-0007-293

INGALLS (continued)
Moses; s/o Daniel; m Susan Heath; ch Daniel, Frederick, Robert m Rowena Hills, Fletcher m Mercy Lary; NH-0005-872

Robert; s/o Moses; m Rowena Hills; ch Caroline, Rufus m Emeline Lary ggd/o Capt Joseph of Gilead; NH-0005-872

INNIS,
Asa F; s/o Archiles & Betsy Cotton; m Sally Stevens d/o David & Sally of Grafton; liv Holderness NH; ch Nancy S m R Bruce Piper, 3 dau; NH-0007-395

-J-

JACKMAN,
Samuel; m Ruth Woodrage; liv MA, Enfield NH; ch Samuel Jr, William; NH-0007-258

William; s/o Samuel & Ruth Woodrage; liv Enfield NH; ch William C, James G m Lorietta A Child of Pomfret VT, Lucy A m --- Fifield, Samuel H; NH-0007-258

JACKSON,
Charles A; s/o Joseph & Elizabeth Adams; m Elizabeth S Dean of Gilmanton; ch Samuel, Charles R, Elizabeth m --- Tilton; NH-0006-775

Joseph; m Elizabeth Adams of York ME; liv Tamworth, Madbury; ch Charles A m Elizabeth S Dean; NH-0006-775

Robert; s/o Samuel; m Mary Ann Braidon d/o Robert; liv Peterboro NH, Lunenburg VT, Coventry; ch Marcus B b1809, Dan Y, William W, Elizabeth W m Samuel Bixby of Warren, Fletcher, Thomas B, John W; NH-0007-368

JACLARD,
Sebastian; b1800 bro/o Daniel; liv Metz FRA, New York City, Moultonborough NH; ch Augustus P b1834 m Harriette S Lee d/o Nathan M of Moultonborough; NH-0006-416

JACOBS,
Fernando C; b1813 s/o Justin & Polly Sargent of Warren VT; m

JACOBS (continued)
Julia A Cooper & m 2 others; liv NY, Colebrook NH, Stanstead PQ, Canaan VT; ch/o Julia - Alma P m Capt H S Hilliard, Sarah C m David O Rowell, Henry F, Charles J, J Anna; NH-0005-687
JAMES,
Maj Jabez; liv Gilford NH; ch John, Jonathan; NH-0004-742
JAMESON,
Rev Ephraim O; b1832; m1858 Mary Cogswell d/o Rev William DD of Gilmanton NH; liv Concord NH, Salisbury & Medway & Millis MA; NH-0004-300
JANVRIN,
George; b1762 s/o John & Elizabeth Stickney; m Dolly Lovering of Kensington; liv Seabrook; ch Sally, Dolly, George, Lorany, Ruth, Fanny, Jefferson b1803 m Mary Wadleigh, Miranda, Eliza; NH-0003-346
Jean; s/o Jean & Elizabeth LeConsteur of Isle of Jersey; m1706 Elizabeth Knight of Portsmouth; liv Portsmouth NH; ch John b1707 m Elizabeth Stickney, George m Abigail Pickering, Molly m Thomas Pickering of Newington, Betsey dy; NH-0003-346
Jefferson; b1803 s/o George & Dolly Lovering of Seabrook; m1840 Mary Wadleigh of Meredith; liv Seabrook, Hampton Falls; ch Miranda m Henry McDevitt, Eliza m Joseph T Sanborn, George Albert; NH-0003-346
John; b1707 s/o Jean & Elizabeth Knight; m1751 Elizabeth Stickney d/o Capt Moses of Newbury MA, liv Newington, Seabrook; ch John, James, William, George b1762 m Dolly Lovering, Elizabeth; NH-0003-346
Joshua N; m Mary French; liv Seabrook NH, Newburyport; ch Susan, Joshua b1802, Matilda, John, Mary J, Sally; NH-0003-514
JEFFERS,
Alvah; m Mary Hall d/o Capt John; liv Enfield & Lyme NH; ch Mary m H C Davison of Hartford CT, Ellen m H F

JEFFERS (continued)
Carr, Marinda m Hannibal Chase, Sarah F m Albert J Pushee; NH-0007-545
Josiah; m Lydia Goodwin of Hampstead; liv Haverhill NH; ch James M, Silvester b1817 m Roxana Elliot, 6 others; NH-0007-364
Silvester; b1817 s/o Josiah & Lydia Goodwin of Haverhill NH; m Roxana Elliot; liv Haverhill NH; ch 1 dau m --- Blake; NH-0007-364
Stephen; bro/o James, Josiah & John; m Phebe Whitaker d/o Ebenezer; liv Benton, Hampstead; ch Stephen m Louisa K Knight, 2 sons, 2 dau; NH-0007-364
Stephen; s/o Stephen & Phebe Whitaker; m Louisa K Knight d/o Allen of Benton; liv Haverhill NH; ch Ernest W, Milan E; NH-0007-364
JENNESS,
Hon Benning Wentworth; b1806; m1827 Nancy Walker Shackford d/o Samuel Esq of Strafford NH; liv Deerfield & Strafford NH; ch Ellen m Hon H B Wiggin of Orange NJ, Annie m Dr H L Ambler of Cleveland OH; NH-0003-712
Cornelius; liv Rochester, Ossippe, Wolfeborough; ch John, Joseph; NH-0006-308
Joseph; m Anna Knox & m 3 others; liv Rye; ch Joseph Disco b1818 m Mary E Foye, Sheridan, Elizabeth m William Rand; NH-0003-469
Joseph Disco; b1818 s/o Joseph & Anna Knox; m1841 Mary E Foye d/o Nathaniel G & Martha E Dow of Rye NH; liv Rye; ch Susan L dy, Emma J dy; NH-0003-469
JEPPERSON,
Daniel; b1790 gs/o Wilber; m1812 Betsey Ash d/o David; liv Douglas MA, Lisbon NH; ch Nathaniel; NH-0007-452
JESSEMAN,
George; liv RI, Lisbon NH; ch Sally m Smith Wetherby; NH-0007-446
JEWELL,
Bradbury; s/o Eld Mark Jr & Ruth Vittum; m1806 Mary Chapman; ch Bradbury m

137

JEWELL (continued)
Lucinda Chapman, David; NH-0001-63, NH-0004-576
Bradbury; s/o Bradbury & Mary Chapman; m Lucinda Chapman; liv Tamworth & Newmarket NH, Newton Upper Falls MA; ch Col David Lyman b1837 m Mary A Grover & m Ella Louise Sumner; NH-0001-63, NH-0004-576
Col David Lyman; b1837 s/o Bradbury & Lucinda Chapman; m1862(1860) Mary A Grover d/o Ephraim of Newton MA, m1865 Ella Louise Sumner d/o Lewis of Needham MA; liv Tamworth & Suncook NH; NH-0001-63, NH-0004-576
Erastus P; b1836 s/o Mark F of Sandwich; NH-0006-250
James; m1802 Sally Hobart; liv Groton; ch James M, Sally m Gillman Wheeler, William A b1808, Andrew B b1811, John E b1815, David b1817, Noah L b1819, Mark b1821 m Mary A Woodbury & m Johanna B Noyes, Dustin B b1825, Benjamin G b1826; NH-0007-390
John; b1813; m Lydia L Currier; liv Sandwich & Holderness NH; ch 8; NH-0007-396
John Woodman; b1831 s/o Milton & Nancy Colley of Strafford; m1853 Sarah Folsom Gale d/o Bartholomew of Upper Gilmanton; liv Strafford; ch Sarah A b1856 m Rev W W Browne of Evansville WI, John Herbert b1859, Mertie Folsom b1859; NH-0003-713
Levi; m Hannah Marston d/o Thomas & Hannah Knowles of N Hampton; liv Stratham NH; ch Emiline, John L, Mary E, Hannah M, Sarah F, DeWitt C, Orinda A; NH-0003-425
Mark; liv Devonshire ENG, Durham & Sandwich NH; ch Mark Jr m Ruth Vittum, Bradbury, John; NH-0001-63, NH-0004-576
Eld Mark Jr; s/o Mark; m1776 Ruth Vittum of Sandwich NH; liv Tamworth NH; ch Bradbury m Mary Chapman, 15 others; NH-0001-63, NH-0004-576
Mark; b1821 s/o James & Sally Hobart; m1845 Mary A Woodbury d/o Nathaniel & Mary Gale & m1850 Johanna B Noyes d/o

JEWELL (continued)
Elijah & Johanna Bartlett; liv Hebron NH; ch Mary A, Celia A, Edward M b1871; NH-0007-390
Mark F; m Dorothy Hobbs d/o Joseph & Dorothy Cooley of Ossipee NH; liv Sandwich; ch E P, Jefferson H; NH-0006-627
Milton; b1803 s/o Simeon & Jane French; m1830 Nancy Colley b1808 d/o Richard & Sarah of Madbury; liv Strafford; ch John Woodman b1831 m Sarah Folsom Gale, Hannah E dy, Mary J m Wingate T Preston of Barrington, Asa W, Charles M, Cyrena T, Enoch T, Betsey A, Samuel F; NH-0003-713
Simeon; b1776; m1796 Jane French b1766 of Salisbury MA; liv Brentwood & Northfield & Sanbornton NH; ch John, Milton b1803 m Nancy Colley, Betsey, Samuel F; NH-0003-713
JEWETT,
Lt Ebenezer; b1743 s/o Dea Nathaniel; m1793 Mary Rideout; NH-0002-452
Pearson; s/o Aaron; liv Wentworth; ch Samuel C; NH-0007-576
Dea Stephen; m1752 Hannah Farwell Cumings wid/o Ens Jerahmael; liv Rowley MA?, Hollis NH; ch Stephen Jr, Noah, Jonathan; NH-0002-438
Dea Stephen Jr; b1753 s/o Dean Stephen of Hollis; m1778 Elizabeth Pool; NH-0002-452
Sylvanus; m Harriette N Kingsbury d/o George & Sally Everett; ch Hattie Newell dy; NH-0002-301
JOHNSON,
Abel D; m Esther Camp d/o David & Theoda Bridgman of Hanover; liv Hanover NH; ch Susan T, Charles F, Fayette B; NH-0007-321
Alfred; m1860 Sarah F Grimes d/o Francis & Mary Chase; ch Edwin Francis b1861, Alfred Grimes b1867; NH-0002-422
D S; m1861 Mary N Hammond d/o Rodney; ch Ora P, Herman F; NH-0007-174
Daniel; m Alma Averill d/o Ebenezer & Anna Johnson; ch Isaac U; NH-0002-579
Henry C; s/o Philanthropy &

JOHNSON (continued)

Sarah Reed gs/o Robert; m Hannah D Carter d/o John Jr & Margaret Dow of Concord; liv Grafton NH; ch George H; NH-0007-287

Hon James Willis; b1826 s/o Moses & Lovinia Hardy of Enfield; m1846 Susan Smith d/o Rev Uriah of Barnard VT; liv Enfield NH; ch Ella H m William W Hill, Carrie E m Dr Otis Marrion, Belle F m Otis Fellows, Helen S; NH-0007-254

Joseph; d1848; m Polly ---; liv Enfield NH; ch Sally m Oliver Hardy of Bradford VT, Moses b1789 m Lovinia Hardy, John, Mary m Johnson Hardy of Lebanon, Betsey m Ziba Hamilton of Lebanon, Martha C m --- Brock of Newbury VT, Jesse, James R, David F; NH-0007-254

Moses; b1789 s/o Joseph & Polly of Enfield NH; m1812 Lovinia Hardy of Lebanon; liv Enfield NH; ch Susan Matilda b1816 m Amos French, Hon James Willis b1826 m Susan Smith; NH-0007-254

Sylvanus D; m Harriet Shirley d/o Daniel M & Abigail McCutchins; ch Cora Bell b1859 dy, Horace Shirley b1867 dy, Shirley Moore b1869, Helen Inette b1871; NH-0002-328

Thomas Franklin; b1848; m1877 Abbie Loverin d/o Alfred of Colebrook; liv Pittsburg & Colebrook NH, Postville IA; NH-0005-255

Dr Willis; b1786; liv Sturbridge MA, Peterborough NH, Mason; NH-0002-644

JONES,

Benjamin; s/o Jesse & Hannah Kidder; m Betsey Powell of Litchfield NH; ch William R m Frances H Senter & m Georgiana V Senter; NH-0007-285

Caleb; liv Merrimack; ch Eliza B, Caleb G, Amos, George, Charlotte H, Harriet, Mary; NH-0002-544

David; liv Merrimack; ch Amos, David T, Daniel, Sarah E, George H, Rosa E, Louisa M; NH-0002-544

JONES (continued)

David R; s/o David T; ch Nellie L; NH-0002-544

David T; s/o David; liv Merrimack; ch David R; NH-0002-544

Ebenezer; b1792 s/o James & Anna Cooledge; m1816 Mary Turner Carr d/o Nathan & Elizabeth Smith; liv Unity NH, Hillsborough; ch Charlotte b1818 m Alonzo Tuttle of Hillsborough, Nathan P b1820 dy, Parker b1821 m Julia C Andrews of Pawlet VT, James b1823, George b1826 m Mrs Merri Goodale Smith of Hillsborough, Mary E b1828 m David Grimes of Hillsborough, Harvey b1830, Ebenezer b1832 m Malvina Shedd, Sarah A b1836 m Col James F Grimes; NH-0002-427

Ebenezer; b1832 s/o Ebenezer & Mary Turner Carr; m Malvina Shedd of Hillsborough; liv Hillsborough; ch James H b1860, Parker b1864; NH-0002-428

Frank; b1832 s/o Thomas of Barrington; m1861 Martha Sophia Leavitt wid/o Hiram Jones; liv Portsmouth NH; NH-0003-108

Hiram; s/o Thomas of Barrington; m Martha Sophia Leavitt; ch Emma I m Col Charles A Sinclair; NH-0003-110

James; s/o William; m Anna Cooledge d/o Nathaniel & Sarah Parker; ch Jonathan b1778, Anna b1780 m Alexander McClintock & m Asa Goodell, James b1782 m Sarah Smith, Silas b1784 m Catherine Rolf, Cooledge b1786 m Pierce Stone, Sarah b1788 dy, Nathaniel b1789 m Betsy Robbins, Ebenezer b1792 m Mary Turner Carr, Parker b1794 m Judith Clapp, Solomon b1796, Warren b1798 m Thankful Dyer, Sarah P b1801 m Charles Baldwin; NH-0002-427

James; b1782 s/o James & Anna Cooledge; m Sarah Smith; ch George; NH-0002-427

James T; ch Ernest J, Leslie E, Idella M, Grace M; NH-0002-544

JONES (continued)

Jeremiah; b1791 s/o Samuel & Salome Crane of Farmington; m1827 Tamson Roberts; ch 1 son dy, 1 dau; NH-0003-639

Jonathan; m Sarah Currier d/o Amos & Mary Sargent of Hopkinton NH wid/o Benjamin Piper; ch John F m Maria H Barnard, 3 others; NH-0004-414e

Jonathan; liv Merrimack; ch Laura; NH-0002-544

Elder Nathan; b1818; m Polly C Bailey of Newbury & m Mary A Gile of Canaan; liv Wilmot, Canaan; ch 6; NH-0007-229

Samuel; b1786 s/o John of Hopkinton; m1810 Elizabeth Andrews of Sutton & m1851 Amanda Eaton; liv Bradford NH; ch/o Elizabeth - George b1811, Timothy Peaslee b1813 m Mary Watson, Fanny b1815 m --- Francis, Eliza b1817 m Edward Cressy, Seth Straw b1819, Samuel Woodbury b1821, Sally Martin b1825 m Dr George H Hubbard; NH-0004-204

Dr Samuel Woodbury; s/o Samuel; m Harriet Wadleigh of Bradford; liv Manchester NH, Washington DC, Boston MA, FL; ch 1 son; NH-0004-193

Smith E; b1819; m Sarah Kelso b1820 of Bethlehem; liv Gilmanton, Bethlehem, Littleton NH; ch 3 dy, 1 dau m Frank I Parker, Ella Z m Amos H Mills, Frank H m Bertha Kittredge of Walden VT; NH-0007-490

Stephen; m1663 Elizabeth Field; ch Capt Stephen; NH-0003-772

Timothy Peaslee; b1813 s/o Samuel & Elizabeth Andrews of Bradford NH; m1839 Mary Watson d/o Nicodemus of Warner; liv Bradford; ch Wilbur Fisk b1840 dy, Prudence Elizabeth b1842, Mary Augusta b1842? m1876 George Harvey Steele s/o Elder Eleazer of Bradford, Samuel Nicodemus b1850 dy, Frank Woodbury b1854; NH-0004-204

Thomas; liv Barrington; ch Frank b1832, Hiram, 4 sons, 1 dau; NH-0003-108

William; liv Wilmington MA,

JONES (continued)

Hillsborough NH; ch James m Anna Cooledge, 3 sons, 5 dau; NH-0002-427

William R; s/o Benjamin & Betsey Powell; m Frances H Senter of Hudson NH & m Georgiana V Senter of Hudson NH; liv Grafton NH; ch/o Frances - Flora J, Charles L, Mary F, Carl L; NH-0007-285

JONSON,

Hon Jesse; b1765 s/o Jesse; liv Hampstead, Enfield; ch George W; NH-0007-251

JORDAN,

Benjamin; bro/o Philip; m1780 Mary Walker of Coventry RI; liv Rehobath MA, RI, Plainfield & Columbia NH; ch 14; NH-0005-728

Hon Chester Bradley; b1839 s/o Johnson & Minerva Buel of Colebrook NH; m1879 Ida R Nutter d/o Oliver & Roxannah C Wentworth; ch Roxannah Minerva b1882, Hugo b1884 dy; NH-0005-233

Ichabod Goodwin; b1806 s/o Capt Ichabod of Saco ME; liv Somersworth, Berwick ME; NH-0003-604

Johnson; b1798 s/o Benjamin of Plainfield NH; m1822 Minerva Buel d/o Capt Benjamin & Violetta Sessions; liv Colebrook NH; ch Hon Chester Bradley b1839 m Ida R Nutter, 9 others; NH-0005-233

Philip; b1748 bro/o Benjamin; m Martha Hill; liv Rehobath MA, RI, Plainfield & Columbia NH; ch John, Cynthia J, William, Benajah, Asa, Huldah, Nancy m --- Frizzell of Colebrook, Caleb; NH-0005-728

JUDD,

Nathan; m Azubah Eastman d/o William & Rebecca Jewett of Bath NH; liv Landaff; ch Azubah m David Brunson; NH-0007-137

JUDKINS,

Alden; m Lois A Cummings d/o Daniel & Lois Kidder of Groton; ch Emma F; NH-0007-189

Enoch B; b1850 s/o Joseph & Hannah E Blake; m1873 Nellie A True; ch Etta M b1878; NH-0003-384

JUDKINS (continued)
Dr Frank L; b1850 s/o Daniel of Freedom; liv Moulton-borough NH, Lynn MA; NH-0006-411
Henry; s/o Joel & Mehitable Calkins; m1776 Mary French & m1780 Mary Barnet; ch/o Mary B - Henry Jr b1783, 8 others; NH-0003-376
Henry; b1750 s/o Joel & Mehitabel Calkins; m Mary Barnard; ch Hannah, Mary, Abigail, Esther, Henry m Lydia Brown, Joel, Mahitable; NH-0003-384
Henry; s/o Henry & Mary Barnard; m1811 Lydia Brown; ch S B b1812, Louisa S b1814 dy, Joseph b1817 m Hannah E Blake & m Abbie S Thyng; NH-0003-384
Joel; b1712 s/o Samuel; m1735 Mehitabel Calkins; ch Samuel b1736, Moses b1738, Aner b1739, Leonard b1741, Joseph b1743, Abi b1745, Mehitable b1747, Benjamin b1749, Henry b1750 m Mary French & m Mary Barnard (Barnet), Caleb b1753; NH-0003-376 & 384
John; b1719 s/o Samuel; m1750 Esther Sweat; ch John b1753, Stephen b1756, Elisha b1758, Samuel b1760; NH-0003-384
Joseph; b1817 s/o Henry & Lydia Brown; m1846 Hannah E Blake & m1865 Abbie S Thyng; liv Kingston; ch/o Hannah - Henry E b1847, Enoch B b1850 m Nellie A True, Arthur R b1859; NH-0003-384
Samuel; bro/o Benjamin; m1710 Abigail ---;liv Kingston; ch Joel b1712 m Mehitabel Calkins, John b1719 m Esther Sweat; NH-0003-376 & 384

-K-

KELLEY,
Amasa; b1765; liv Amesbury MA, Pittsfield, Chichester; ch Daniel R Esq; NH-0004-247
John; b1796 s/o Simeon & Elizabeth Knight of Plaistow; NH-0003-148
Joseph; m Susan Crawford; liv

KELLEY (continued)
Newburg VT, Plymouth NH; ch Joseph D, Lovina, William C m Cora T Page; NH-0007-121
Rev William; b1744; m Lavinia Bayley d/o Rev Abner of Salem NH; liv Newbury MA, Warner NH; NH-0004-662
William C; s/o Joseph & Susan Crawford; m Cora T Page d/o Daniel & Abigail; ch Lillian W; NH-0007-121
KELLY,
Albert L; b1802 s/o Hon Israel W & Rebecca Fletcher; m Caroline Pierce; liv Frank-fort & Wintersport ME; NH-0004-619
Israel W; b1804 s/o Hon Israel W & Rebecca Fletcher; m Luella S Pierce of Frankfort ME; liv Boston MA, ME; NH-0004-619
John; b1796 s/o Dea Simeon of Plaistow; liv Plaistow, Derry, Chester, Atkinson; NH-0003-25
John; b1786 s/o Rev William of Warner; liv Northwood, Con-cord, Exeter; NH-0003-32
Nathaniel K; b1800; m1836 Anna Dow d/o John Esq of Atkinson NH; m1868 Mary S Peaslee; liv Plaistow; NH-0003-442
KEMP,
Lyman; m Electa Brown of Lyme; liv Pomfret & Stockbridge VT, Lyme NH, Burr Oak KS; ch Harriet L, Minerva J, Joseph A, Alvah J, George V, Melissa L; NH-0007-545
William; liv Pomfret VT, Lyme NH, Dorchester; ch Jasper H, Wallace W, 1 son, 4 dau; NH-0007-545
KENDALL,
Henry C; s/o Asa & Sarah Emmons; m Francelia Hoyt d/o Enos; liv Grafton NH; ch Clinton W, Raymond H; NH-0007-287
KENDRICK,
Capt Daniel; b1736 s/o Daniel; m1782 Mary Pool; liv Hollis NH; ch Daniel, William P; NH-0002-453
KENESON,
John; b1784; m1804 Polly Jackson d/o Phillip & Mary Place; liv Eaton NH; ch Randall Seavey b1811 m Almira

KENESON (continued)
Morse & m Miranda S Forest, 1 son, 7 dau; NH-0004-729, NH-0006-804
Randall Seavey; b1811 s/o John & Polly Jackson of Eaton NH; m1838 Almira Morse d/o Moses of Centre Harbor & m Miranda S Forest b1816 d/o Isaiah & Deborah Mason of Eaton; liv Eaton & Centre Harbor NH; ch/o Almira - Elvira m George B Blake, Newell; ch/o Miranda - Adelaide H m Lewis R Veasey; NH-0004-729
KENISTON,
Charles S; b1856 s/o David Dustan & Sarah Cone of Rumney; m1879 Elvira Williamson; ch David, Edna Blanche; NH-0007-614
Cyrus; b1823 s/o John & Mary Baker; m1856 Pamelia Hutchinson of Reading MA; liv Plymouth NH; ch Kathleen dy, John b1859 m Elizabeth P Freeman, W H dy; NH-0007-588
David Dustan; b1801 s/o William & Sarah Morrison of Sanbornton; m Sarah Cone d/o Jonathan of Thornton & m1853 ?; liv Rumney NH; ch/o Sarah - Marinda m William Currier, Sarah m Chase Leavitt, David dy, Mary m Dexter Merrill, Hannah m --- Dorthey, Maloma m --- Addison, John dy, Ellen m Marcus M Emerson, George D b1831 m Carrie Melligan; ch/o ? - Edward, Hattie, Julia, Carrie, Susie, Elvia, Charles S b1856 m Elvira Williamson; NH-0007-614
Davis Baker; b1850 s/o George Washington & Deborah Davis; m1876 Ada Elizabeth Howe d/o Lucius M & Elizabeth Cutter of Plymouth; liv Campton, Plymouth; ch Elizabeth Howe b1876, Davis Baker Jr b1880, Sarah Thorndike b1881; NH-0007-205
George D; b1831 s/o David Duston & Sarah Cone of Rumney; m1875 Carrie Melligan; liv Rumney NH; ch George E, Earl V; NH-0007-614
George Washington; b1810 s/o William & Sally Morrison of Sanbornton; m1837 Deborah Davis Baker d/o Col Davis &

KENISTON (continued)
Hannah Church of Campton; liv Thornton, Campton; ch Emma Elizabeth b1839 m William Thornton, George Hancock b1840, Ann b1847 dy, Davis Baker b1850 m Ada Elizabeth Howe; NH-0007-205
John; s/o William Jr of Sanbornton; m1820 Mary Baker d/o Maj Benjamin of Campton; liv Plymouth NH, Campton; ch Cyrus b1823 m Pamelia Hutchinson, Mary m W D Blaisdel, Martha J m Thomas F Glynn, Deborah m Dr Silas W Davis; NH-0007-588
John; b1859 s/o Cyrus & Pamelia Hutchinson of Plymouth; m1884 Elizabeth P Freeman d/o Asa; ch Carl Winthrop; NH-0007-588
William; m Sally Morrison; liv Sanbornton NH; ch George Washington b1810 m Deborah Davis, Samuel; NH-0007-205
KENNEY,
Gen Edward Oakes; b1816; m1839 Nancy S Smith of Brownington VT & m Livonia Hale d/o Maj Ezra; liv Bethlehem & Littleton NH; ch/o Nancy - Lorenzo C; ch/o Livonia - Edward S, Nellie S m W H Whiting; NH-0007-499
KENNISTON,
Jeremiah; bro/o James R; liv Eaton NH; ch Jonathan, Uzziel, Nicholas, Thomas, Isaac, Ivory; NH-0006-791
KENRICK,
John; b1764; m Sarah Colby b1771; liv Haverhill & Amesbury MA; ch Stephen Esq b1806 m Clarissa A Blanchard, Timothy, 7 others; NH-0004-321
Stephen Esq; b1806 s/o John & Sarah Colby of Haverhill MA; m1833 Clarissa A Blanchard d/o Capt Ebenezer of Franklin; liv McIndoes Falls VT, Franklin NH; ch 4 dy, Dr Timothy G b1849, Stephen, Charles; NH-0004-321
KENT,
Abel; liv Newburyport MA, Lyme NH; ch Abel m Joanna Shaw d/o Col Dan, Stephen, Moses m Mary Stark d/o Phineas, Polly m Lyman Converse, Sally m Isaac Porter; NH-0007-538

KENT (continued)

Charles; s/o Stephen gs/o Abel; m1837 Elvira Converse & m Mary Pushee; liv Lyme NH; ch/o Elvira - George C, Ellen M m J K Carr, Julia L m J T Hosford; NH-0007-538

Col Henry Oakes; b1834 s/o Richard Peabody & Emily Mann Oakes; m1859 Berenice A Rowell d/o Samuel of Lancaster; Liv Lancaster NH; ch Berenice Emily b1866, Henry Percy b1870; NH-0001-21, NH-0005-372

Jacob; b1726 s/o John; liv Essex & Newbury MA, Plaistow NH; ch Jacob, John m Tabitha Peabody, Joseph; NH-0001-21

James Maraner; b1804 s/o Maraner; m Fanny Brown of Hookset NH; liv Derry, Chester, Boston; ch James B b1823, William b1824 dy, Lucien b1828, Sarah F b1829 m John Little of Atkinson, Charles H b1835 m1869 Mrs Cora M Curtis d/o Josiah Lite of Lynn MA, Margaret F b1846; NH-0003-160

John; liv ENG, Durham; ch Nancy m Maj William Cutts, John m Temperance Lapish; NH-0003-110

John; s/o John; m Temperance Lapish d/o Capt Robert of Durham; liv Rochester; ch Mehitable, Temperance, Nancy m Nathaniel Hobbs & m Dr Daniel Hodsdon, John b1799 m Ruhamah Dearborn, Kinsman; NH-0003-110

John; b1799 s/o John & Temperance Lapish of Rochester; m1827 Ruhamah Dearborn d/o Asa & Ruhamah Dearborn of Portsmouth; liv Barnstead, Portsmouth; ch John Horace b1828 m Adeline Penniman; NH-0003-110

John; s/o Jacob of Newbury VT; m Tabitha Peabody d/o Lt Richard of Woodstock CT; liv Newbury VT, Lyman NH; ch Richard Peabody b1805 m Emily Mann Oakes; NH-0001-21, NH-0005-366

John; bc1700; liv Cape Ann & Essex MA; ch Jacob b1726; NH-0001-21

John Horace; b1828 s/o John &

KENT (continued)

Ruhamah Dearborn; m1852 Adeline Penniman d/o Bethuel & Sophia of New Bedford MA; liv New York City, San Francisco CA, PANAMA, Portsmouth NH; ch John Horace Jr, Horace Penniman; NH-0003-110

Maraner; liv Newburyport MA, Derry; ch James Maraner b1804 m Fanny Brown, 5 sons, 1 dau; NH-0003-160

Moody; b1779 s/o Joseph of Newbury MA; liv Deerfield, Concord; NH-0004-5

Richard Peabody; b1805 s/o John & Tabitha Peabody of Newbury VT; m1832 Emily Mann Oakes d/o Henry & Emily Mann of Waterford & Fairlee VT; liv Lancaster NH; ch Col Henry Oakes b1834 m Berenice A Rowell, Edward Richard, Charles Nelson; NH-0001-21, NH-0005-366

KETCHAM,

Silas; b1835 s/o Silas & Cynthia Doty of Barre VT; m1860 Georgia C Hardy d/o Elbridge of Amherst NH; liv Brattleborough & Wardsborough VT; ch George C, Edmund; NH-0004-410

KEYES,

Jonathan F; bc1811; m Mary W Woods; liv Hancock NH, Bennington VT, Holderness; ch Mary E m Thomas P Cheney, Lucy A m R R Dearborn, Alice J m E G Clapp, Fanny M, Josephine W m --- Blakslee, Capt O W, Henry F; NH-0007-131

Joseph C; b1826 s/o Lewis & Henrietta Ramsey of Rumney; m Sarah H George & m1865 Almira E Willoughby d/o S K & Dorothy; liv Rumney NH; ch/o Sarah - Frank b1852, Fred C b1854, Ellen M dy; ch/o Almira - Grace b1872; NH-0007-610

KEYSAR,

Edmund; m Betsey Young; liv Northfield, Stewartstown, Canterbury, Clarksville; ch John b1816 m Sarah Clark Wiswall, Betsey m J P Wiswall, Miles H, 12 others; NH-0005-694

John; b1816 s/o Edmund & Betsey

KEYSAR (continued)
Young; m Sarah Clark Wiswall b1817 of Clarksville; liv Stewartstown, Clarksville; ch Maria C m John Gathercole, Sarah, Phebe Y m E S Parker, Wiswall, Clark dy, Susan M m Charles F Hibbard, Berkley m Eliza L Moses; NH-0005-694

KEYSER,
James H; s/o William; m Eliza A Poor; liv Benton NH; ch Bion C, 3 dau; NH-0007-153

KIDDER,
Amos; m Hannah ---; liv Dalton NH; ch Hannah Bailey b1803; NH-0005-519

Amos; m Susannah ---; liv Dalton NH; ch Adeline b1806, Amos Jr b1808; NH-0005-519

Benjamin; liv Bristol NH; ch John b1793 m Ruth Fellows, Joseph; NH-0007-181

Charles G; b1844 s/o Jonathan & Mary Dimond of Dorchester; m1867 Lucinda B Davis d/o Benjamin & Sarah A Kimball; ch George Davis b1881; NH-0007-295

Daniel; b1838 s/o John & Betsey; m1862 Emeline F Hardy; liv N Groton NH; ch Fred, Ada; NH-0007-295

Frederick; s/o John & Ruth Fellows of Bristol; m Samantha S Chandler d/o Timothy & Lois; liv Bristol NH; ch Ellen G, Cora A m O J Muzzey, H Dana, 1 other; NH-0007-181

James M; m Lucy L Houghton of Bradford VT; liv Weathersfield VT, Bethlehem NH; ch William H, Cynthia A, Josie F; NH-0007-167

John; b1793 s/o Benjamin of Bristol; m Ruth Fellows; liv Bristol NH; ch Frederick m Samantha S Chandler, John W, Charles m Susan Johnson, Arianna m Richard Sawyer; NH-0007-181

Thomas; liv Alstead, Enfield; ch Jason b1781; NH-0007-252

KILBURN,
Elijah; s/o John gs/o John of Walpole NH; m Rebecca Genison; liv Walpole NH; ch Josiah b1801 m Emily Bonney & m Mrs Lydia A Wilder Colby; NH-0007-488

KILBURN (continued)
Josiah; b1801 s/o Elijah & Rebecca Genison of Walpole; m1827 Emily Bonney & m1861 Mrs Lydia A Wilder Colby; liv Littleton NH; ch/o Emily - Benjamin W b1827, Edward b1830, Emily B b1833; NH-0007-488

KILTON,
Marcus M; s/o James M & Sally Ford; m Eva M Gage d/o Roswell & Sarah Little; ch Fanny M, Ray, Madge E; NH-0007-283

KIMBALL,
Aaron R; s/o Aaron b1788; m Hannah R Kimball d/o Stephen & Hannah; ch Almira J, Selden, Perley, Persus R, Arthur m Lamar Ford; NH-0007-286

Amos; m Abigail Corliss of Haverhill MA; liv Haverhill MA, Barnet VT, Haverhill NH; ch John b1775 m Mehitable Carleton; NH-0007-354

Andrew; m Maria Shirley d/o John & Margaret Houston; ch Lauron H b1850, Emma J b1852, Ella F b1854, Clara M b1857, George A b1859, John S b1855 dy; NH-0002-329

Arthur; s/o Aaron R & Hannah R Kimball; m Lamar Ford d/o George N & Amanda M Davis of Danbury NH; liv Grafton NH; ch Archie E; NH-0007-286

Benjamin; b1784 s/o Capt Peter; liv Boscawen NH; NH-0004-178

Benjamin; b1794 s/o John & Sarah Moulton; m1820 Ruth Ames d/o David & Phebe Hoyt of Canterbury; liv Canterbury & Boscawen & Fisherville NH; ch John b1821 m Maria H Phillips, Elizabeth, Benjamin A, 2 dy; NH-0001-90, NH-0004-144

Caleb; m Sarah Sawyer; liv Hamstead; ch Mary m John Eaton, Jacob, 1 dau m --- Moore, 1 dau m John Adams of Sutton, 1 dau m --- Haddock, 1 dau m --- Pinkerton of Boscawen, 1 dau m --- McCrillis; NH-0004-651

Caleb; b1665 s/o Richard & Mary Gott of Wenham; m Sarah ---; liv Exeter NH, Wenham MA; ch John b1699 m Abigail Lyford &

KIMBALL (continued)
m Sarah Wilson, 7 others; NH-0001-89, NH-0004-144

Caleb Jewett; b1817 s/o Isaac & Lucinda Tenney; m1841 Ruth Burge Felt d/o David & Susan Pollard of Temple; liv Milford, Wilton, Bennington; ch George E; NH-002-286

David; b1799; m1828 Caroline R Swett of Newburyport; liv Topsfield MA, Portsmouth NH; ch 3 dau, 1 son; NH-0003-107

Ebenezer; m Polly Aiken d/o Dea James; liv Wenham MA, Antrim NH; ch Dr Gilman b1804 m Mary Dewar & m Isabella Defries; NH-0002-263

George; b1787 s/o Benjamin & Nancy Wilder of Harvard MA; liv Union & Warren ME, BERMUDA, Canaan NH; NH-0007-72

Dr Gilman; b1804 s/o Ebenezer & Polly Aiken; m Mary Dewar d/o Henry of Edinburgh SCO & m Isabella Defries d/o Henry of Nantucket MA; liv New Chester NH, Chicopee, Lowell MA; NH-0002-263

Isaiah P; b1819 s/o Isaac & Betsey Fellows of Peacham VT; m1844 Lydia B Page of Landaff; ch Anette m Pliny E Crafts of Bradford VT, Elizabeth m George W Forbes of Greenfield MA, Ella F, Kate J; NH-0007-143

John; b1699 s/o Caleb & Sarah; m1722 Abigail Lyford & m1740 Sarah Wilson of Exeter; liv Exeter NH; ch/o Abigail - Joseph b1730 m --- & m Sarah Smith; ch/o Sarah 9; NH-0001-90, NH-0004-144

John; b1767 s/o Joseph & Sarah Smith; m1793 Sarah Moulton d/o Benjamin of Kensington NH; liv Exeter & Canterbury NH; ch Benjamin b1794 m Ruth Ames, 8 others; NH-0001-90, NH-0004-144

Hon John; b1821 s/o Benjamin & Ruth Ames; m1846 Maria H Phillips of Rupert VT; liv Concord & Boscawen & Suncook & Manchester NH, Lowell & Lawrence MA; ch Clara Maria b1848 m Augustine R Ayers; NH-0001-89, NH-0004-144

John Peverley; b1827 s/o

KIMBALL (continued)
Richard & Sally Sanborn of Boscawen; m1852 Mary Eliza Hill d/o Samuel of Canterbury & m Mrs Mary A Kilton; liv Canterbury NH; ch/o Mary Eliza - George Edwin dy, Frank Edwin b1859, Ida Grace b1859, Georgianna Eliza b1867; NH-0004-233

Joseph; b1730 s/o John & Abigail Lyford; m --- & m Sarah Smith; liv Exeter & Canterbury NH; ch/o Sarah - John b1767 m Sarah Moulton, 8 others; NH-0001-90, NH-0004-144

Joseph; m Betsy Wilkins; liv Weare, Deering; ch Eliza m Francis Mitchell; NH-0002-384

Peabody W; s/o Russel & Louisa Bean; m1865 Jane Pearson d/o George of Lyme; liv Haverhill NH; ch George R, Ellen L; NH-0007-354

Richard; m Ursula ---; liv Ipswich ENG, Watertown & Ipswich MA; ch Richard b1623 m Mary Gott, 10 others; NH-0001-89, NH-0004-144

Richard; b1623 s/o Richard & Ursula; m Mary Gott; liv ENG, Wenham MA; ch Caleb b1665 m Sarah ---, 7 others; NH-0001-89, NH-0004-144

Richard; b1798 bro/o Benjamin of Canterbury; m1826 Sally Sanborn d/o John Peverly of Canterbury; liv Boscawen; ch John Peverley b1827 m Mary Eliza Hill & m Mrs Mary A Kilton; NH-0004-233

Richard; b1798 s/o Nathaniel of N Berwick; liv Dover, Somersworth, Rochester; NH-0003-592

Robert; b1786 s/o Joseph; m1817 Fanny Willis of Wolcott VT; liv Morristown VT, Plainfield & Lebanon NH; ch Mary Elizabeth, Robert Byron b1827; NH-0007-428

Russell; b1798; m Louisa Bean of Lyman; liv Kingston & Haverhill NH; ch 3 dy, Peabody W m Jane Pearson; NH-0007-354

KING,
Asa; b1779 s/o James of Sutton; m Polly Cheney of Sutton & m1814 Sarah Burns d/o Maj John & Sarah Smith; liv

KING (continued)
Whitefield NH; ch/o Polly - Nathaniel Cheney b1801, Sally m Col Joseph Colby, Polly m Stephen Nichols, Eliza m1825 Ashael Aldrich, James A; ch/o Sarah - Hannah m Richard Lane, John m --- Stalbird, Jane m Stillman Jenney, George b1834; NH-0005-465

James; m Hannah Young of Landaff; liv Sutton & Haverhill NH; ch 9; NH-0007-351

KINGSBURY,
Dr Charles Franklin; b1824; m1857 Sarah A Pierce of Cavendish VT; liv Gilsum & Lyme NH, Stoddard; ch Ella S b1858 m Dr J Walter Bean b1855; NH-0007-523

George; b1795 s/o Joseph & Silence Richards of Francestown; m1822 Sally Everett d/o Eleazer & Lucy Battelle of Francestown; ch Harriette N m Sylvanus Jewett, George m Betsey A Hyde, Sarah E, Hanna F dy, Caroline m H F Blakeslee, Mark Justin; NH-0002-301

George; s/o George & Sally Everett; m Betsey A Hyde of Francestown; ch George Albert m Sadie Heald, Warren m Ella A Wagner, Henry L m Nellie H Stevenson; NH-0002-301

John Langdon; s/o Joseph & Silence Richards of Francestown; m Abigail Hyde; ch 6; NH-0002-301

Joseph; s/o Joseph of Dedham MA; m Silence Richards; liv Francestown; ch George b1795 m Sally Everett, Leonard, Hannah m Stephen Whipple, Joseph m Betsey Everett, Julitta m Rev Almon Benson of Centre Harbor NH, John Langdon m Abigail Hyde, 3 dy; NH-0002-300

Joseph; s/o Joseph & Silence Richards of Francestown; m Betsey Everett; ch 4, 2 dy; NH-0002-301

KINNE,
Elisha P; s/o Amos; m Chloe Waterman of Canaan & m Susan C Waterman sis/o Chloe; ch Truman T, Esther m Alvin I Merrill, Chastina m D A Poland, Ansel, Otis C,

KINNE (continued)
Elisha; NH-0007-424

Nathan; m Betsey Farrington; liv Old Pomfret CT, Waterford VT; ch Vine m Roxana Gould, Nathan Jr m Charlotte Hayward of Berlin VT, 7 others; NH-0007-497

KINSMAN,
Stephen D; s/o Dr John & Susan Lumber gs/o Isaac; m Belinda Rowe d/o Alexander & Sally Bean; ch Alanson W Barney (adopted); NH-0007-212

KITTREDGE,
Dr George; m Eleanor Fogg d/o Col Seth & Mrs Smith; liv Newmarket; ch Dr George; NH-0003-240

George Washington MD; b1800 s/o Dr Jacob of Dover; liv Dover; NH-0003-847

Jacob MD; b1794 s/o Dr Jacob of Dover; liv Dover; NH-0003-847

Jerry; m Mary Ann Ritterbush d/o --- & Sophia; liv Merrimack; ch Mary J m Scott W Lane of Manchester, Emma E m George P Butterfield, Jerry C; NH-0002-543

Jonathan LLD; b1793 s/o Dr Jonathan & Apphia Woodman of Canterbury; m1829 Julia Balch; liv New York City NY, Canaan, Lyme, Concord; ch 8; NH-0007-73

Sumner; m Mary Marshall d/o Nathan Richardson & Abigail Hawks of Bradford NH; liv MA, Warner & Bradford Corner NH; ch Everett; NH-0004-205

KNAPP,
Abial; d1832 bro/o Jonathan; liv Norton MA, Lyman NH; ch Betsey, Mehitable, Elijah m Sally Elliott; NH-0007-514

James; liv Haverhill; ch Susan m --- Woodbury, Arthur, 1 son; NH-0007-635

KNIGHT,
Capt Artemas; m Tabitha Saunders of Worcester MA; liv Franconia & Westmoreland NH; ch Thomas b1783, 2 sons, 4 dau; NH-0007-269

Elijah; b1813 s/o Benjamin & Lucy Baker of Hancock NH; m1842 Mary Jane Griffin d/o James & Jerusha Palmer of Manchester NH; liv Concord & Manchester & New Market NH;

KNIGHT (continued)
ch 2; NH-0004-153

Moses; s/o Moses; liv Landaff; ch Caroline m --- Bartlett, Fanny m --- Morse, Ezra C; NH-0007-640

Thomas; s/o Capt Artemas & Tabitha Saunders; liv Franconia NH; ch Oliver, James, Horace, Dr Luther M, Thomas, George R, 1 dau m John Wilson, 1 dau m --- Hoit, 4 others; NH-0007-269

KNOWLES,

Hiram S; s/o Simeon & Abigail Rollins; m Mary F Cram d/o Levi; liv Campton Village NH; ch William N, Edwin G; NH-0007-212

Joseph; b1758; m Sarah Locke b1761 of Chester NH; liv Wilmot & Northfield NH; ch William b1781 m Zilpha Thorn, Joseph Jr b1783, Christian b1786, Sarah b1786, Sally b1789 m Josiah Bachelder, Hannah b1792 m --- Haines, John b1794, Polly b1797 m Josiah A Woodbury, 1 son, 1 dau; NH-0004-546

Dea Levi; b1797 s/o Simeon gs/o David ggs/o Ezekiel gggs/o John; m1822 Mary Colcord d/o Samuel of Nottingham; liv Northwood; ch Christiana Colcord m Samuel W Morse of Boston MA; NH-0003-433

Wesley; b1806 s/o William & Zilpha Thorn; m1832 Jane W Gilman b1805 & m1860 Sophronia Clement Johnson b1817; ch/o Jane - Charles W b1835, George C b1838 dy, Lucian E b1842, Laura J C b1843 m1866 Marcus A Hardy; NH-0004-546

William; b1781 s/o Joseph & Sarah Locke; m1805 Zilpha Thorn b1782; ch Wesley b1806 m Jane W Gilman & m Sophronia Clement Johnson, Betsey C b1808, Cyrene b1813 dy, Joseph b1817, William F b1822 m Sarah Pratt Robinson; NH-0004-546

William F; b1822 s/o William & Zilpha Thorn; m1850 Sarah Pratt Robinson b1827 of Boston MA; liv Boston & Cambridge MA; ch Addie Viola b1854, Carrie Way b1857,

KNOWLES (continued)
William Fletcher Jr b1861; NH-0004-546

KNOWLTON,

Ebenezer; m Elizabeth Rawlins of VT; liv Northwood; ch Hosea Chase b1799 m Betsey Seavey, 8 others; NH-0004-255

Hosea Chase; b1799 s/o Ebenezer & Elizabeth Rawlins; m1825 Betsey Seavey d/o Moses Esq of Chichester & m1863 Adaline B Sherburne; liv Northwood & Kensington & Concord & Chichester NH, Boston MA; ch/o Betsey - Eben, Melissa, Alonzo, Sallie S; NH-0004-255

KNOX,

Charles O; s/o Edward of W Ossipee; ch Orrin, Monroe, Albert, Hiram; NH-0006-628

Edward; b1780 s/o John gs/o Jonathan of Berwick ME; liv W Ossipee; ch Alvah, Daniel, Edward, Ephraim, Charles O, Joseph, Maria, Elizabeth J, Sarah, Almira, Mary; NH-0006-628

Edward; s/o Edward of W Ossipee; ch Orrin, Monroe, Albert, Hiram; NH-0006-628

Ephraim; s/o Edward of W Ossipee; liv W Ossipee NH; ch Charles E, Alvah W, Herbert E, Manville E, William O; NH-0006-628

-L-

LADD,

---; m Elisha Sanborn d/o Capt John & Ruth Rand; liv Epping NH; ch James, John, Nathaniel m Nancy Lougee, Eliza, Sally, Mary, Ruth; NH-0004-503

Babson S; b1848 s/o John S & Mary A Butler of Cambridge MA; m Ella Cora Brooks d/o Hon John W of Milton MA; liv Boston; ch Paul Dean; NH-0003-231

Daniel; m Ann ---; liv ENG, Ipswich MA, Salisbury, Haverhill; NH-0003-231, NH-0004-858

Daniel; b1742; mc1765 Judith Lyford of Raymond; liv Epping & Lee & Loudon NH; ch Gideon

LADD (continued)
m Polly Osgood, 8 others; NH-0004-858

Daniel W; s/o Rev Nathaniel & Mary Gordon Folsom; m Lucy Ann Dustin; ch Eliza Ann, Nathaniel W, Joseph F G, John S; NH-0003-231

Daniel Watson; b1798 s/o Nathaniel & Dorothy Smith; m1820 Rebecca Plumer b1799 d/o Samuel & Betsey Cilley gd/o Gen Joseph Cilley; liv Concord & Epping NH; ch Daniel Watson b1821, Sarah P b1822, Samuel P dy, Lydia Watson b1827, S Plumer b1829 m Sarah P Dodge; NH-0003-231

Daniel Watson; b1821 s/o Daniel Watson & Rebecca Plumer; m Dorothy E Thyng b1828 d/o Jonathan Esq of Epping; ch Silvina W dy, Bina W, Charles W dy, Lizzie W dy, Jenny W, Sylvia W m F R Hazelton of Concord NH, Daniel W, Alva W b1862; NH-0003-231

Dudley F; liv Gilmanton & Bethlehem NH; ch Lorenzo S, Plummer B, 1 dau m Daniel Crane, Josiah M, 1 dau m --- Morrison; NH-0007-166

Eliphalet; b1755 s/o Timothy gs/o John ggs/o Samuel gggs/o Daniel; m1778 Mary Park of Windham; ch Alice m John B Swasey; NH-0004-865

Gideon; s/o Daniel & Judith Lyford; m Polly Osgood of Loudon; liv Loudon NH; ch Seneca Augustus b1819 m Susan Tilton & m Catherine S Wallace, 3 sons, 8 others; NH-0004-858

Hiram; b1800 s/o John of Unity NH; m1827 Aurelia Palmer b1804 of Castleton VT; liv Dalton NH; ch Hannibal E, William S, Mary m George N Abbott of Newbury VT, Lucy m George W Stratton, Kate G m William Barry Smith of Erie PA; NH-0005-528

James; s/o Nathaniel & Mary Ames of Epping; m Elizabeth Gould of Hamlin; liv Hereford CAN; ch Mary A, James G, Betsey G, Nathaniel Gould MD m Abigail V Mead, Zoroaster, Seneca, Endocia, Ira W, Sophronia, William, Susan

LADD (continued)
Laurett; NH-0003-231

John; b1782 s/o Nathaniel & Mary Ames of Epping; m1806 Profinda Robinson of New Market; liv Epping; ch Caroline P, John S b1809 m Adelia Babson & m Mary A Butler, Mary A b1816; NH-0003-231

John S; b1809 s/o John & Profinda Robinson of Epping; m Adelia Babson of Rockport & m1847 Mary A Butler of Bedford; liv Cambridge MA; ch/o Mary - Babson S b1848, Mary Adelia dy, Mary Butler b1851, Allston Channing b1854, John Franklin b1856; NH-0003-231

Nathaniel; s/o --- & Elisha Sanborn of Epping NH; m Nancy Lougee; liv Loudon; ch Charles E; NH-0004-503

Nathaniel; m Mary Ames of Canterbury; liv Epping; ch James m Elizabeth Gould, Nathaniel m Dorothy Smith, Daniel m Elizabeth Goodwin, Mary m Elisha Sanborn of Loudon, John b1782 m Profinda Robinson; NH-0003-231

Nathaniel Gould MD; s/o James & Elizabeth Gould of Hereford CAN; m Abigail V Mead; liv Malden; ch William S m Caroline Elliot, Helen, Smith M, Wesley, Mary F, Marshall, Abie Josephine; NH-0003-231

Nathaniel; s/o Nathaniel & Mary Ames of Epping; m1793 Dorothy Smith of Epping; ch Rev Nathaniel m Mary Gordon Folsom, Dorothy m Winthrop Hilton of New Market, Daniel Watson b1798 m Rebecca Plumer; NH-0003-231

Rev Nathaniel; s/o Nathaniel & Dorothy Smith; m Mary Gordon Folsom; ch Louisa, Mary J A, Daniel W, Olivia E V; NH-0003-231

S Plumer; b1829 s/o Daniel Watson & Rebecca Plumer; m1853 Sarah P Dodge; ch Sarah P, Peter, Paul, Rebecca, Silas B dy, Lydia W, Evelyn L dy, Ellen L, Clara M, Louis P, Laura J, Dexter, Harry, Samuel Y, Cora B; NH-0003-231

Ruel W; s/o William & Mary

LADD (continued)
Sturdevant; m Elizabeth Wright d/o Dr Samuel & Mary Ann Webster; liv Ashland NH; ch Maria F, Adele C; NH-0007-127

Seneca Augustus; b1819 s/o Gideon & Polly Osgood of Loudon NH; m1840 Susan Tilton of Meredith & m1852 Catherine S Wallace d/o William Esq of Henniker; liv Meredith NH; ch/o Susan - Fannie C A m D W Coe, Charles F A; ch/o Catherine - Virginia B; NH-0004-858

Story Butler; m Eliza Brigham Paine d/o Maj Gen Holbert E of Washington DC; NH-0003-231

William; s/o Elias; m Mary Sturdevant d/o John & Charlotte of Moultonboro NH; ch Hale M, Ruel W m Elizabeth Wright, 2 others; NH-0007-127

William S; s/o Nathaniel Gould MD & Abigail V Mead of Malden; m Caroline Elliott; liv Portland OR; ch William M, Charles E; NH-0003-231

William Spencer LLD; b1830 s/o Hiram & Aurelia Palmer of Dalton; m1860 Almira B Fletcher d/o Hiram A & Persis Hunking; liv Lancaster NH; ch Fletcher, William P, Mary E; NH-0005-227

LAKIN,
Rodney S; m1846 Susan Page Gilbert d/o Joseph & Alvira Moore; ch Willis Gilbert b1847, Clara Frances b1850 dy, John Clark b1852; NH-0002-434

LAMPREY,
John; liv Gilford NH; ch John, Richard, Samuel, Reuben; NH-0004-743

LAMSON,
George; s/o Gideon of Exeter; liv Exeter, NY; NH-0003-32

LANCASTER,
Rev Daniel; b1796; m1827 Annie E Lemist d/o John of Dorchester MA & m1831 Eliza Gibbs Greeley d/o Daniel Esq of Foxcroft ME; liv Gilmanton & Concord NH, Middletown NY & New York City; ch 5; NH-0004-795

LANE,
Edmond J; m Elizabeth Barker

LANE (continued)
d/o Levi & Mary Wiggin; ch Edmond B; NH-0003-548

Capt George; m Mary Barker d/o Levi & Mary Wiggin of Stratham; liv Stratham; ch Amanda, Henry; NH-0003-548

Isaac; b1760 s/o John & ? of Chester; m1780 Abigail Garland; liv Chester; ch Sally, Abigail, Molly, Anna, John, Betsey, Isaac b1799 m Caroline Marshall, Peter; NH-0003-160

Isaac; b1799 s/o Isaac & Abigail Garland of Chester; m1837 Caroline Marshall b1808 d/o Henry & Hannah Whittier of Brentwood NH; liv Chester; ch Mary Ellen dy, William H dy, Henry Harrison b1845 m1878 Emma Tenney b1847 d/o Dea William & Emeline Murray, Martha Brown; NH-0003-160

Jeremiah; s/o Dea Joshua & Batsheba Robie; m Mary Sanborn d/o Lt Joseph; ch Mary m Thomas Berry of Greenland, Joshua, Jeremiah, Simeon, Levi b1774 m Anna Batcheldor; NH-0003-347

Jesse; b1746 s/o Robert & Mary Thatcher; m1770 Hester Wright b1750 of Killingworth CT; liv Lebanon CT, Newport NH; ch Dr Robert b1786 m Mary Kelsey; NH-0004-647

John; s/o William & Sarah Webster; m Mary Libbey of Rye; ch John b1709 m Hannah Lamprey & m Mary Knowles; NH-0003-160

John; b1709 s/o John & Mary Libbey; m Hannah Lamprey & m Mary Knowles; liv Chester; ch/o ? - John, Daniel, Ezekiel, David, Mary, Hannah, Nathan, Isaac dy, Sarah, Isaac b1760 m Abigail Garland, Jonathan; NH-0003-160

Joshua; m Bathsheba Robie; liv Hampton; ch Dea Jeremiah m Mary Sanborn, 15 others; NH-0003-347

Dr Josiah; b1778 s/o Joshua of Stratham NH; m ? 7 m Sarah Pearson; liv Dover & Gilmanton NH, NY, OH, PA; NH-0003-846

Levi; b1774 s/o Dea Jeremiah &

LANE (continued)

Mary Sanborn; m1798 Anna Batchelder b1775 d/o Dea David of Hampton Falls; liv Hampton Falls; ch Jeremiah, Mary A, Sarah, Emery, Nancy, Rhoda, David E, Abigail B, George G, Levi E b1819 m Cynthia S Lane & m Ann Elizabeth Carhen; NH-0003-347

Levi E; b1819 s/o Levi & Anna Batchelder; m1849 Cynthia S Lane b1817 d/o Dearborn & Hannah Merrill of Hampton Falls & m1785? (1885) Ann Elizabeth Carhen b1839; liv Hampton Falls; ch/o Cynthia - Annie S b1855 m Charles F Wadleigh; NH-0003-347

Richard; m Hannah King; liv Whitefield; ch Charles Irwin b1854, Edward Austin b1854; NH-0005-483

Dr Robert; liv Sutton, Concord; ch 1 dau m George W Ela Esq; NH-0004-98

Robert; b1713; m1744 Mary Thatcher of Lebanon CT; liv Killingworth CT, Newport NH; NH-0004-647

Stephen; liv Gilmanton & Stewartstown NH; ch Sarah, Charles, Eliza, Hannah, Mary b1807; NH-0005-664

William; m Mary --- & m Mary d/o Thomas Brewer of Roxbury; liv Boston; ch/o ? - Samuel, John, Mary, Sarah, William b1659 m Sarah Webster, Elizabeth, Ebenezer; NH-0003-160

William; b1659 s/o William & Mary of Boston; m Sarah Webster of Hampton NH b1659; ch John m Mary Libbey, Sarah, Elizabeth, Abigail, Joshua, Samuel, Thomas; NH-0003-160

LANG,

Andrew; m Eliza Scott of Richmond; liv Barnet VT, Dalton NH; ch J M, 1 dau m ---Britton; NH-0005-526

Daniel; s/o William H; m Hannah Page of Bath; ch 2 sons, 2 dau; NH-0007-138

Hon David R; b1830 s/o Sherburn of Bath; m1859 Josephine R Smith; liv Orford; ch Paul b1860, Kittie R, Edward J, David R, Mary J; NH-0007-112.7 & 112.8

Henry S; b1825 s/o Sherburne &

LANG (continued)

Mehitable Ricker of Bath NH; m Martha Lang d/o Henry H & m Martha Jane Hibbard d/o John of Bath; ch/o ? - 2 sons, 2 dau; NH-0007-138

Joseph W; b1798 s/o Josiah & Sarah Widden; m1824 Mehitable Clark Young d/o Benjamin Esq & m1866 Mrs Julia A Taylor d/o Capt John B & Comfort Sanborn of Sanbornton; liv Tuftonborough & Meredith NH; NH-0004-862

Josiah; s/o Josiah of Greenland NH; m Sarah Widden; liv Tuftonborough & Meredith & Portsmouth NH; ch Joseph W b1798 m Mehitable Clark Young, Thomas E, Josiah dy; NH-0004-862

Moses; b1816 s/o Daniel of Bath; m Calista Clough of Landaff & m Jane H Kimball of Bath; liv Bath NH; ch/o Calista - 2 sons, 1 dau (adopted) m William Clough of Somerville MA; NH-0007-141

William; bro/o Samuel; liv Portsmouth NH, Bath, Irasburg VT; ch David; NH-0007-555

LANGDON,

James Fogg; b1804 s/o Woodbury & Mary Woodlock of Durham NH; m1827 Rhoda Hill; liv Plymouth NH, Concord; ch Mary Elizabeth dy, Woodbury Fogg m Annie Merrill, Mary Elizabeth m Hiram Hill of St Johnsbury VT, John G m Helen M Parker, Josephine m Orlando Leach; NH-0007-587

John; s/o Capt Tobias; m Mary Hall d/o Kinsley of Exeter; ch Woodbury, John b1739 m Elizabeth Sherburne; NH-0003-100

John; b1739 s/o John & Mary Hall; m Elizabeth Sherburne; liv Portsmouth; ch 1 dau m Thomas Elwyn Esq of Canterbury ENG; NH-0003-100

John G; s/o James Fogg & Rhoda Hill; m Helen M Parker; ch Fanny, John G; NH-0007-587

Tobias; m Elizabeth Sherburne d/o Henry; liv Keverel ENG, Piscataqua; ch Capt Tobias m Mary Hubbard; NH-0003-100

Capt Tobias; s/o Tobias & Elizabeth Sherburne; m Mary

LANGDON (continued)
Hubbard of Salisbury; ch John
m Mary Hall, 6 sons; NH-0003-
100
Woodbury Fogg; s/o James Fogg &
Rhoda Hill; m Annie Merrill
of Stratham; ch Frank; NH-
0007-587
LANGFORD,
Dea Anthony; liv Wallingford
ENG, Portsmouth; m Nancy
Walton; ch Elizabeth W m
James Brown; NH-0003-159
LARABEE,
Horace; m Wealthy Howard; liv
VT; ch Stephen C b1813 m
Cynthia Sawyer; NH-0004-580
Stephen C; b1813 s/o Horace &
Wealthy Howard of VT; m
Cynthia Sawyer of Orford NH;
liv Bradford VT; ch George H
MD b1840, Edward E; NH-0004-
580
LARGE,
John H; b1818; m1856 Emma Keyes
d/o Luther H; liv ENG, Haver-
hill NH; ch 3 sons, 4 dau;
NH-0007-364
LARNARD,
Abel; m Mary Ann Webb; liv
Windham CT, Columbia NH; ch 2
sons; NH-0005-725
LARY,
Andrew G; b1799 s/o Capt Joseph
& Hannah Blake; m1827 Levee
Chandler d/o Amos & Ruth Head
of Pembroke; liv Gilead ME,
Shelburne & Gorham NH; ch 1
dau m --- Hitchcock, 1 dau;
NH-0005-926
Daniel; liv Wolfeborough,
Madison; ch Tilly, Richard,
Daniel, James; NH-0006-804
LATHAM,
Arthur; m1782 Mary Post d/o
Peter; liv Lyme NH; ch Robert
b1783, William Harris b1788,
Mary b1790 m Thomas Kendrick,
Allen b1792, Bella b1794,
Nehemiah b1796, Arthur b1802
m Caroline Hinckley, Bezer;
NH-0007-531
Arthur; b1802 s/o Arthur & Mary
Post; m Caroline Hinckley d/o
Col Oramel; liv Lyme NH,
White River Jct VT, MO; ch
Arthur, W C, Caroline H m
Noah B Safford Esq, Mary L m
James M Wilson, 6 others; NH-
0007-531

LAWRENCE,
David; m Annie Gordon; liv
Exeter (Stratham) Epping; ch
David m Lydia Sias, Edward,
Gordon, Samuel?, Annie m ---
Morrill & m --- Johnson; NH-
0003-243
David; s/o David & Annie
Gordon; m1765 Lydia Sias
b1745 d/o Joseph & Ruth
Mathes of Durham; liv Epping;
ch Sarah m Joseph Clough of
Canterbury, Joseph Sias, Ruth
m --- Clough & m Enoch
Gerrish of Boscawen, David,
Jotham, Samuel b1779 m Betsey
Thyng; NH-0003-243
Fred; m Marion Bachelder d/o
Henry F & Lydia S Rogers; ch
Henry B; NH-0004-501
Jotham; s/o David of Epping;
liv Exeter; NH-0003-31
Jotham; s/o David & Lydia Sias;
ch Alex H; NH-0004-243
Rufus King; b1815 s/o Samuel &
Betsey Thyng of Epping; m1864
Laura P Davis d/o Jacob &
Anna of Nottingham; liv
Epping Corners; ch Samuel L
b1865 dy, Annie E b1868; NH-
0003-243
Samuel; b1779 s/o David & Lydia
Sias of Epping; m Betsey
Thyng d/o Dudley & Aphia; liv
Epping; ch Elizabeth b1810
m1830 Dr Edward B Moore,
Rufus King b1815 m Laura P
Davis; NH-0003-243
LAYTON,
Thomas; m Joanna ---; ch Thomas
m Elizabeth Nutter d/o Elder
Hatevil, Mary m Thomas
Roberts, Elizabeth m Capt
Philip Cromwell, Sarah; NH-
0003-772
LEAVITT,
James M MD; b1852 s/o James B &
Mary Lamper; m1881 E E
Leavitt of S Boston MA; liv
Effingham NH; NH-0006-555
Jonathan; m Charlotte Odell d/o
James wid/o --- Boyd; ch
Joseph H; NH-0003-550
Peter; m Mehitable Marden; liv
Dummer NH; ch 4 son, 7 dau;
NH-0005-856
LeBARON,
Robinson; b1822 s/o Ira of
Hardwick VT; m Julia Barrett
& m Jane G Shepard wid/o
William H; ch/o Jane - Sarah

LeBARON (continued)
B m James A Baker; NH-0007-598

LEE,
David; liv Moultonborough NH; ch Nathan M, Edward S; NH-0006-403

Edward S; s/o David; liv Moultonborough NH; ch George F; NH-0006-403

Nathan M; s/o David; liv Moultonborough NH; ch David G, Frank S, Edward M, 1 dau m --- Jaclard, 1 dau m James M Smith, Annetta m Hayes Lougee Esq; NH-0006-403

LEIGHTON,
Andrew J; b1831; m Helen Bedell d/o William of Bath; liv Newbury VT, Bath NH; ch 5; NH-0007-145

Charles; b1815 s/o Jacob & Sarah Wentworth of Ossipee NH; m Sally Wentworth; liv Ossipee NH; ch Elizabeth m I L Sanders, Jacob, Leonard, Charles; NH-0006-621

Charles; s/o Charles & Sally Wentworth; ch Olive J, Albert W, George H, Charles B; NH-0006-621

Ephraim; liv Rochester, Ossipee; ch Susan m --- Drake & m Rev Joshua Roberts, Abigail m --- Beaman, Mehitable m --- Drew & m --- Sanborn, Nancy m --- Killham, Olive, Sally m Oliver Scates, Jacob b1787 m Sarah Wentworth; NH-0006-621

Jacob; b1787 s/o Ephraim; m Sarah Wentworth of Dover; liv Ossipee NH; ch Ephraim, Charles b1815 m Sally Wentworth, Elizabeth m Israel L Sanders, Jacob, Leonard, Elivra m Benjamin B Smith, 5 others; NH-0006-621

Joseph; liv Barrington & Farmington NH; ch Levi W bc1794 m Tamson A Chamberlin, John, Abigail b1799 m Mark Demeritt of Farmington NH; NH-0003-637

Levi W; bc1794 s/o Joseph; m Tamson A Chamberlin; liv Farmington NH; ch Hannah m John K Colbath & m John Killroy, Mary C, John W, Levi W m1855 Sophia Averill b1832 d/o Bernard & Harriet

LEIGHTON (continued)
Richardson of Mount Vernon, Tamson A m E P Mooney of Farmington, Emily m Stephen W Bennett of Farmington; NH-0003-637

Stephen D; b1806; m1828 Sarah Carbee of Newbury VT; liv Sheffield & Newbury VT, Bath; ch Andrew, Albert H, 9 others; NH-0007-367

William; m Mary ---; liv Farmington, Dummer; ch Sarah, Phebe, Mercy, Betsey, Joseph, Thomas, William, 1 other; NH-0005-855

LELINGHAM,
Jacob; m Hannah Torry; liv Thornton NH; ch William, Jacob m Mary K Edgerly, Henry, Daniel, Walter, Pinkham, Samuel, Catharine, Hannah; NH-0007-629

LERNED,
Ebenezer; b1762 s/o Thomas & Hannah Brooks of Medford MA; m1802 Mary Hall of Londonderry & m1814 Catharine Perkins d/o Timothy & Hannah Trowbridge; liv Hopkinton NH, Leominster MA; ch/o Mary - Louisa, Mary Eliza m --- Flanders, Margaret, Brooks Holyoke; ch/o Catharine - Catharine Crosby Perkins, Edward Augustus, Hannah Brooks, Lucy Ann, Elizabeth Trowbridge; NH-0004-407

LEVERETT,
William; b1813; m Catharine R Spaulding of Rumney; liv Plymouth; NH-0007-112.11

LIBBEY,
George; liv Landaff, Warren; ch Walter, John A, 3 others; NH-0007-576

Nathaniel; b1795 s/o Luke of Landaff; liv Warren NH; ch Ezra; NH-0007-634

LINCOLN,
Leavitt; b1797 s/o William & Jael Cushing of Marlborough NH; m1821 Sibyl Heald d/o Capt Thomas of New Ipswich NH & m Mary Heald Shattuck sis/o Sibyl wid/o Francis Shattuck & m1876 Delia McDonough; liv Townsend MA, Ashby, Winchendon; ch/o Sibyl - William L, Maria, Henry Martin, Cyrus Stone, 4 others; NH-0002-630

LINCOLN (continued)

William; m Jael Cushing; liv Marlborough NH; ch Leavitt b1797 m Sibyl Heald & m Mary Heald Shattuck & m Delia McDonough; NH-0002-630

LISCOMB,

Elisha P; b1802 s/o John & Hannah Waters of Pomfret CT; m1833 Ethalinda Loomer of Lebanon & m1844 Mrs Mary J Wilkins of Exeter NH; liv Lebanon NH; ch/o Ethalinda - Emily, Edward A, Charles F; ch/o Mary - Mary M, William P; NH-0007-421

LITTLE,

Maj Alfred; b1823 s/o Henry & Susan of Webster NH; liv Concord NH; NH-0004-690

Amos; liv Plaistow & Warren NH; ch Judith m --- Merrill, Jonathan, 11 others; NH-0007-634

Arthur DD; b1837 s/o Simeon B & Harriet Boyd of Webster NH; m1863 Laura E Frost of Thetford VT; liv Bradford NH, Fond Du Lac WI, Chicago; NH-0004-690

Rev Ebenezer L AB; b1837; m Susan C Lamson; liv Clifton NY, Lapeer & Alpena MI; NH-0004-620

Dea Enoch; s/o Dean Enoch & gs/o Enoh; liv Webster NH; NH-0004-690

Ephraim; b1820 s/o Richard & Priscilla Plumer of Webster; m1847 Jane G Farmer sis/o Prof M G; liv Webster NH; NH-0004-690

George Peabody; b1834 s/o Elbridge Gerry & Sophronia Phelps Peabody; m1854 Elizabeth A Knox d/o Daniel M of Pembroke NH; liv Pembroke NH, Palmyra NY; ch George William dy, Clarence Belden, Mary Georgianna, Lizzie Ellen m Lester Thurber of Nashua, Nettie Knox, Lucy Bowman, Clara Frances; NH-0004-580

Henry DD; b1800 s/o Jesse & Martha Gerrish of Webster; m1831 Susan Morton Smith of Hatfield MA; liv Oxford OH, Madison IN; ch 4 sons, 4 dau; NH-0004-691

Jacob DD; b1795 s/o Jesse & Martha Gerrish of Webster NH;

LITTLE (continued)

m1826 Lucy Gerrish of Canterbury & m1836 Ann Dorothy Thompson; liv Granville OH, Warsaw IN; ch Rev Charles, 2 sons; NH-0004-691

Jesse; m Martha Gerrish; liv Webster NH; ch Jacob DD b1795 m Lucy Gerrish & m Ann Dorothy Thompson, Henry DD b1800 m Susan Morton Smith; NH-0004-691

John Webster MD DDS; b1818 bro/o Rev Valentine AB; m Sarah P White & m Elizabeth J Goodwin; liv Concord; NH-0004-619

Simeon Bartlett; b1797 s/o Benjamin Esq; m1824 Harriet Boyd of Antrim NH & m1851 Phebe Kilburn of Webster; NH-0004-692

Thomas Dearborn; b1823 s/o Thomas Rowell & Nancy Webster; m1851 Susan E Smith b1828 d/o Robert MD of Amesbury MA & m Lucy L Davis b1844 d/o Andrew of Rutland VT; liv Salisbury NH; ch/o Susan - Thomas Rowell b1853 m1876 Carrie B Hawkins d/o Lewis A, Charles Webster b1855 dy, Susan Paulina b1858 m1882 Rev Samuel H Barnum s/o Rev S W of New Haven CT, John Webster b1861 m1884 Hannah M Moors d/o H C W, Alice Maria b1866, Robert Smith b1870, William Dearborn b1874 dy; ch/o Lucy - Edwin Dearborn b1778; NH-0004-623

Thomas Rowell; bro/o Rev Valentine AB; m Nancy Webster d/o John of Salisbury; liv Newburyport MA, Salisbury NH; ch Thomas Dearborn b1823 m Susan E Smith & m Lucy L Davis; NH-0004-623

Rev Valentine AB; b1790 bro/o John Webster MD DDS; m Mary Clark of ME & m Miranda C Church; liv Lowell ME, Salisbury NH; NH-0004-619

William MD; b1753; liv Shirley MA, Peterborough, Hillsborough Bridge; NH-0002-667

LIVERMORE,

Arthur; bc1766 s/o Judge Samuel of Londonderry; liv Chester; NH-0003-25

Edward St Loe; b1761 s/o Hon

LIVERMORE (continued)
Samuel of Londonderry; liv
Concord; ch Harriet b1788;
NH-0004-5
Matthew; b1703 s/o Samuel;
Watertown MA; NH-0003-19
Hon Samuel; b1832 bro/o Hon
Israel; m1759 Jane Browne d/o
Rev Arthur of Portsmouth; liv
Waltham MA, Portsmouth NH,
New Holderness, Londonderry;
ch Edward St Loe b1761,
Arthur b1766 m Louise Bliss
of Haverhill NH; NH-0004-5,
NH-0007-89
Solomon Kidder; b1779 s/o Rev
Jonathan of Wilton; m Abigail
Adkins Jarvis of Cambridge
MA; ch 6; NH-0002-573
LOCK,
Benjamin; b1765 s/o Ebenezer &
Lucy Wood; m Anna Eastman of
Weare; liv Deering; ch
Ebenezer m Sarah Bartlett,
Benjamin dy, Jonathan dy,
Benjamin m Betsy Bartlett of
Weare, Luther m Lydia Johnson
of Weare, Anna dy, Roswell,
Anna m Col John Bartlett,
Lucy m Solomon Bartlett; NH-
0002-377
Ebenezer; b1734 s/o Ebenezer &
Elizabeth of Woburn MA; m
Lucy Wood; ch Ebenezer m
Mollie Eastman, Jonathan m
Lucy Brooks, Benjamin b1765 m
Anna Eastman; NH-0002-377
Ebenezer; s/o Ebenezer & Lucy
Wood; m Mollie Eastman of
Weare; liv Deering; ch
Frederic dy, Reuben, Charles;
NH-0002-377
Ebenezer; s/o Benjamin & Anna
Eastman of Deering, m Sarah
Bartlett, liv Lempster; ch
Eleanor m Jonathan Page of
Weare, Marvin m Abigail
Wilkins; NH-0002-377
Jonathan; s/o Ebenezer & Lucy
Wood; m Lucy Brooks of Woburn
MA; liv Deering; ch Lucy m
Hezekiah Hadlock; NH-0002-377
Marvin; s/o Ebenezer & Sarah
Bartlett; m Abigail Wilkins;
ch James F m Martha E Chase;
NH-0002-377
LOCKE,
Alfred; s/o James & Keziah D
Peaslee; m Mary E Muzzey; ch
Fred E, Arthur W; NH-0002-378
Andrew J; s/o James & Keziah D

LOCKE (continued)
Peaslee; m Lizzie H George;
ch Harry D, Hattie B; NH-
0002-378
Benjamin; b1770; m Hannah Favor
& m1826 Nancy Gurdy; liv
Sandown & Bristol NH; ch -
Favor b1797 m Sally Dolloff,
Roxy m Levi Dolloff, Sherburn
b1801 m Sally Hill, Levina m
Henry Wells, Joanna m Jacob
Webster, Philena m Timothy
Wiggins, Benjamin Jr m
Harriet Mason, Hannah m Kiah
Wells, Sally m Winthrop R
Fellows, Levi m Susan Gilman
& m Mrs Sarah Robinson,
Dorothy m M H Page, Harriet m
Phillip S Drake, Susan D m
Milo Fellows; NH-0007-180
David; liv Rye & Lyman NH; ch
Simeon; NH-0007-516
George S; m Belle Marshall d/o
Anderson J & Frances Perkins;
liv Concord; ch George S; NH-
0005-395
James; s/o Stephen & Sally Hop-
kins; m Keziah D Peaslee; ch
Levi J, Oliver m Mary E
Porter, Andrew J m Lizzie H
George, Lucinda dy, Lucina m
James F Hinkley, Elbridge G H
dy, Alfred m Mary E Muzzey,
Irene R dy, Keziah M dy; NH-
0002-378
Stephen; m Sally Hopkins of
Charlestown MA; ch Sarah,
Stephen dy, Susan m Moody
Chase, Nancy m Christopher
Simons of Weare NH, Lucy m
Jonathan Goodale of Deering,
Stephen m Sarah Peaslee,
James m Keziah D Peaslee; NH-
0002-377
Stephen; s/o Stephen & Sally
Hopkins; m Sarah Peaslee; ch
Stephen dy, Irena m James
Priest of Weare NH, Sabra m
Gilbert Small of Weare, Lewis
N m Harriet C Kendall, Ira D
m Asceneth Moshier, Nancy E m
Gillman Clough, Lorinda dy,
Lavina dy; NH-0002-378
LOMBARD,
Erasmus Darwin; b1835 s/o Dr
Lyman & Betsey Loomis of
Colebrook NH; m1865 Minnie
Dudley of Hanover NH; liv
Colebrook; ch Bessie; NH-
0005-599
J E; m Ellen L Merrill d/o

LOMBARD (continued)
Sherburn Rowell & Sarah B Merrill; ch Darwin, Lyman; NH-0005-643
Joseph; s/o Joseph gs/o Joseph ggs/o John gggs/o David ggggs/o John of Springfield MA; m Mary Faulkner, Liv Brimfield MA, ch Dr Lyman b1788 m Betsey Loomis; NH-0005-635
Dr Lyman; b1788 s/o Joseph & Mary Faulkner of Brimfield MA; m1820 Betsey Loomis d/o Joseph & Anna Bissell of Hebron CT; liv Colebrook NH; ch Ann Smith m Hazen Bedel, Mary F, Isabel A m Corydon Farr, Emma E m S S Merrill, Erasmus D, Joseph Erastus; NH-0005-635

LONG,
Commodore John Collings; b1795 s/o Capt George & Marcy Hart gs/o Pierce; m1829 Mary O Gilman d/o Nathaniel of Exeter; liv Exeter; NH-0003-286

LONGA,
Charles; s/o Nelson & Ann Barnes of Merrimack; liv Nashua, Merrimack; ch Mary E; NH-0002-542
Nelson; m Ann Barnes d/o Reuben; liv Merrimack; ch Washington, Charles, John, Sarah m Henry T I Blood; NH-0002-542

LOOMIS,
Joseph; b1766; m1789 Anna Bissell b1763; liv Hebron CT, Colebrook NH; ch Abial Anson b1791, Lewis b1793, Anna m Heman Beach, Horace, Betsey m Dr Lyman Lombard, William m Harriet Thompson; NH-0005-620
Lewis; b1793 s/o Joseph & Anna Bissell; ch Rollin, Eliza m Alger Baldwin, Martha m Cornelius Adams, Marion m Dr Lyman W Alger, James Lewis m Martha Hall; NH-0005-620
William; s/o Joseph & Anna Bissell; m Harriet Thompson; ch Maria E m John L Harvey, Helen M m Sumner Cummings, Edwin m Ellen Folsom, Anson m Sarah Garfield, Harriet Isabel m Preston Claflin; NH-0005-620

LORD,
Oliver Hubbard; b1811 s/o Ephraim & Sally Goodwin of Berwick ME; m1838 Mary W G Stevens d/o Dr Whiting of Shapleigh ME; liv Salmon Falls, Great Falls; ch George Bordman m Lizzie C Mott, Mary A m James P Dixon, Annie A m Charles E Marston, Edward Oliver m Mary B Horne, 3 others; NH-0003-698
Robert; liv Ossipee NH; ch Robert, 1 dau m --- Mason of Tamworth; NH-0006-628
Samuel; m Nancy Dearborn Mc-Clary d/o Gen Michael & Sally Dearborn of Epsom; liv Portsmouth; ch Augustus; NH-0004-467

LOTHROP,
James Eldridge MD; b1826 s/o Daniel of Rochester NH; liv Dover; NH-0003-849

LOUGEE,
Dr Isaac William; b1818 s/o John F of Gilmanton NH; m Julia A Ross d/o Thomas of Gilmanton & m1866 Ellen Wheeler d/o Hazen of Barn-stead NH; liv New Durham & Rochester NH, Alton; ch/o Julia - Mary A; ch/o Ellen - William W, Arthur J; NH-0003-748
John; m --- Gilman of Exeter; liv ENG, Exeter NH; ch John; NH-0003-748
John F; s/o Joseph gs/o John of Exeter; liv Gilmanton NH; ch Joseph S, Dr Isaac William b1818, William S, Elizabeth M m L S Nute of Alton NH; NH-0003-748
Sylvester T; m Ruhamah Burleigh; liv Effingham NH; ch George W MD b1859 m1886 Edith Merrow d/o Dr A D, Frank T MD b1862 m1889 Elva N Staples d/o Rev L T of Parsonsfield; NH-0006-556

LOVEJOY,
Dea Abiel; s/o Henry; m Anna Stickney; liv Concord & Conway NH; ch Abiel, William, Jeremiah, Phoebe m Dea Jonathan Eastman, Betsey m William Randall, Nancy m William Eastman; NH-0006-849
Clark; b1807 s/o Samuel & Nancy Clark; m Sally Chandler of

LOVEJOY (continued)
Piermont & m Sabrina Brown;
liv Orford NH; ch/o Sally - 1
dau m William Chandler; ch/o
Sabrina - S Josiah, Albert G;
NH-0007-566
Enos; b1806; m Mary S Hale; liv
Orford NH; ch Samuel W, John
H, Frank J, Lewis P, Nancy C
m Alonzo Stark, Nelson H dy;
NH-0007-567
Isaac; s/o Jacob; liv Hebron,
Hanover, Enfield; ch Augustus
C b1810; NH-0007-264
Jeremiah; s/o Dea Abiel & Anna
Stickney; liv Conway NH; ch
Henry, Jedediah, Abiel C,
Polly m Samuel Willey, Phoebe
m --- Fairfield of Saco ME,
Betsey m Thomas Abbott, Nancy
m Nathaniel S Abbott; NH-
0006-849
Jonathan F; m Laura Hubbard of
Littleton; liv Littleton NH;
ch Charles W, Amos H, Warren
W, Ira W, Angie m Willard
Hurlburt of CA, George E, 1
dy; NH-0007-502
Samuel; b1773; m1798 Nancy
Clark of Framingham MA; liv
Rindge & Orford NH; ch Clark
b1807 m Sally Chandler & m
Sabrina Brown, 9 others; NH-
0007-566
William; b1796; m1822 Rebeckah
Bickford Hodgdon wid/o
Russel; liv Dummer NH; NH-
0005-856
LOVELL,
Hon Warren; b1802; m1831 Susan
Badger of Meredith; liv
Rockingham VT, Wentworth,
Meredith Village; ch 2 dau;
NH-0007-112.20
LOVEREN,
Ebenezer; s/o Reuben & Sarah
Hilliard of Deering; m Annie
Rowell; ch Gilbert m Celenda
Cram of Weare, Alvah m
Matilda Smith, Reuben m Rhene
Codman of Hillsborough,
David, Nancy m ---
Richardson; NH-0002-376
Ebenezer; bro/o Reuben; m
Eunice Hadlock; ch Ebenezer
Jr b1792 dy, John m Clarissa
Richardson, Betty dy, Sarah m
Joshua Downing, Benjamin m
Esther Bartlett; NH-0002-376
John; s/o Ebenezer & Eunice
Hadlock; m Clarissa Richard-

LOVEREN (continued)
son; ch Josiah m Asanath
Gregg & m Nancy Peabody,
Eunice m Jacob Gordon of
Henniker, Hannah m Humphry
Nichols, Clarissa m Hiram G
Patten, Ebenezer m Susan
Crowe, Emeline dy; NH-0002-
376
Reuben; s/o Ebenezer of
Kensington; m Sarah Hilliard;
liv Deering; ch Dolly m David
Rowell of Deering, Sally m
Daniel Gove of Weare,
Ebenezer m Annie Rowell,
Elizabeth m Robert Goodale,
Mary m Joab Patterson of
Hopkington NH, Reuben m
Abigail Bartlett, Anna m
Daniel Bartlett Jr, Hilliard
m Hannah Goodale, Huldah m
Daniel Simons, Nancy m Samuel
Folsom; NH-0002-375
Reuben; s/o Reuben & Sarah
Hilliard of Deering; m
Abigail Loveren; ch Daniel m
Elsie Eastman of Weare & Mrs
Nancy Dodge, Reuben m Martha
Whittle of Deering, Joseph H
m Elizabeth Whittle; NH-0002-
375
LOVERIN,
Alfred; b1813; m1838 Lucy Drew
sis/o Hon Amos W & Edwin W &
m Susan Fletcher; liv Loudon
& Colebrook NH; NH-0005-619
Benjamin MD; b1786; m Abigail
Greeley; liv Sutton; NH-0004-
619
LOVERING,
Dr Frank S; b1861 s/o John N of
Freedom; liv Sandwich,
Moultonborough; NH-0006-413
Hubbard; b1791; m Abigail
Bumfod b1791 of Wakefield;
liv Loudon, Colebrook; ch
Julia Esther b1815 m Amos W
Drew; NH-0005-680
Moses; m Nellie Taylor of
Exeter; liv Exeter & Loudon
NH; ch Willabee, Nellie,
Osgood, Taylor, Nancy, Moses,
Jesse, Mary, Zebulon b1777 m
Abigail Buswell, John,
Daniel, William, Sarah; NH-
0004-501 & 511
Samuel B; s/o Zebulon & Abigail
Buswell of Loudon; m1834 Mary
S Rogers b1811 of Northfield
& m1859 Lucy Grace of Hills-
borough NH & m1880 Lavina

LOVERING (continued)
Hoyt b1832 d/o Dea Benjamin & Hannah Eastman of Fisherville NH; liv Loudon NH ch/o Mary - Nancy A b1836 m Josiah Young, James B b1838 m Jennie Hamilton, Harlan P b1843 m Eliza Wentworth of Boston, Abigail M b1845 m Augustus A Arling of Canterbury & m George Simmons of Boston MA, Clara A b1848 dy, Frank O b1856 dy; ch/o Lucy - Clara A b1860 m Herman W Mudgett MD, Frank O b1863, Edward (Edwin) E b1865; NH-0004-501 & 511

Zebulon; b1777 s/o Moses & Nelly Taylor; m1807 Abigail Buswell b1787 of Kingston NH; ch Samuel B b1806 m Mary S Rogers & m Lucy Grace & m Lavina Hoyt, True, Almira b1811 m Kinsley Mason, Annis J b1814 m George W Neal, Sarah B b1816 m James Mc-Austin, Louisa b1819 m Aaron B Young, Laura L b1822 m Rev Stephen Eastman, Abigail b1824 m Osni P Hamblet, Alonzo B b1827 m Sarah Davis, 2 others; NH-0004-501 & 511

LOW,
Nathaniel MD; b1792 s/o Dr Nathaniel of S Berwick ME; liv Portland ME, Dover NH; NH-0003-847

LOWE,
Prof Thaddeus S C; b1832 s/o Clovis & Alpha Greene of Jefferson NH gs/o Thomas Greene of Berlin Falls NH; m1855 Leontine Augustine Gachon of NY; liv NY, Norristown PA; ch Louisa F, Ida Alpha, Leon Percival, Ava Eugenie, Augustine Margaret, Blanche, Thaddeus, Edna Zoe, Sobieski; NH-0005-425

LOWELL,
Isaac; s/o Daniel of VT; m Mehitable Orsborn of Loudon NH; liv Orange NH; ch Elijah O m Sarah Batchelder d/o Jonathan & Sally Tucker; NH-0007-557

LUFKIN,
George W; b1835 s/o Edward; m1854 Elmira Lowd & m1866 Louisa Dow d/o J B of Goffstown; liv Hebron NH; NH-0007-

LUFKIN (continued)
390

LUND,
Charles; b1821 s/o Oliver & Orpah Danforth; m1846 Eliza Stevens d/o Samuel G & Betsey Davis; ch Eliza Ann m Joshua W Hunt, Charles H, Alma L, Marcus O; NH-0002-216

Henry Willard; b1854 s/o Hezekiah & Mary Shores of Granby CT; liv Canaan VT; NH-0005-257

Oliver; b1779 s/o Thomas & Sarah Whitney; m1814 Orpah Danforth b1788 d/o William; liv Nashua; ch George, Orpah, Laura m John A Foster, Charles b 1821 m Eliza Stevens, Sabra m E P Parker, Handel; NH-0002-216

Thomas; bc1660; liv Dunstable; ch Thomas b1682 m Mary ---, Elizabeth b1684, William b1686; NH-0002-216

Thomas; b1682 s/o Thomas; ch Dea Thomas b1712 m Mary ---, Elizabeth b1715, William b1717, Ephraim b1720, Phinehas b1723; NH-0002-216

Dea Thomas; b1712 s/o Thomas; m Mary ---; liv Nashua; ch Thomas b1739 m Sarah Whitney; NH-0002-216

Thomas; b1739 s/o Dea Thomas & Mary; m Sarah Whitney; ch Hannah, John, Thomas, Isaac, Oliver b1779 m Orpah Danforth, Sarah Huldah, Noah; NH-0002-216

LYFORD,
Dr Byley; b1822 s/o Jeremiah & Naomi Dickey; m1851 Vashti P Shattuck d/o Hon Zebadiah & Vashti; liv Hillsborough & Nashue & Tilton NH; ch 1 dau m George G Trowbridge; NH-0004-885

Rev Francis H; b1820; m1843 Eunice T Pickering of Barnstead & m Catherine S Cox of Holderness; liv Pittsfield, Barnstead, Manchester, MO, Littleton NH; ch/o Eunice - 1 dy, Ardenia m George E Gay of Malden MA; ch/o Catherine - 2 dy, Kate Idell; NH-0007-506

James Otis Esq; b1853 s/o James of Boston MA; m1882 Susan A Hill; liv Tilton NH, Washington DC; NH-0004-885

LYFORD (continued)
Stephen; liv Newmarket, Brook-
field; ch Stephen, Levi,
Theophilus W; NH-0006-459
LYNDE,
Simon; b1625 s/o Enoch of
London; liv HOLLAND, Boston;
ch Benjamin b1666; NH-0002-
504

-M-

MacCARRIGAIN,
Dr Philip; m Clough d/o Thomas
Esq of Canterbury; liv New
York City, Concord; NH-0004-
97
McCLARY,
---; liv IRE, Epsom NH; ch John
b1719 m Elizabeth Harvey, Maj
Andrew m Elizabeth McCrillis,
Margaret m Dea Samuel
Wallace, Jane m John McGaffy,
Ann m Richard Tripp; NH-0004-
465
Maj Andrew; m Elizabeth Mc-
Crillis; ch James Harvey
b1762 m Betsey Dearborn,
Andrew b1765, John b1767 m
Abigail Pearson, William
b1795 Isabel Dickey, Eliza-
beth m Capt Simon Heath,
Margaret m Rev Haseltine of
Epsom, Nancy m John Stevens;
NH-0004-464
John; b1719; m Elizabeth Harvey
of Nottingham; liv Epsom; ch
John Jr, Gen Michael b1753 m
Sally Dearborn, Andrew dy,
Mollie m Daniel Page of Deer-
field; NH-0004-465
John; b1767 s/o Maj Andrew &
Elizabeth McCrillis; m1791
Abigail Pearson of Epsom; ch
Charles; NH-0004-464
Gen Michael; b1753 s/o John &
Elizabeth Harvey of Epsom;
m1779 Sally Dearborn of
Northampton; liv Epsom; ch
John b1785, Andrew b1787
m1813 Mehitable Duncan, Nancy
Dearborn b1789 m Samuel Lord,
Elizabeth Harvey b1791 m
Jonathan Steele, Mary b1794 m
Robert Parker; NH-0004-466
McCLINTOCK,
Michael; liv Eng & Londonderry;
ch William; NH-0002-41

McCLURE,
David; b1802 s/o Samuel; m
Emeline Kidder d/o Jonathan &
Susan Hagar; liv Hebron NH;
ch George W b1832 m Mary Ann
Merrill; NH-0007-390
George W; b1832 s/o David &
Emeline Kidder; m1854 Mary
Ann Merrill d/o Uriah & Mary
Dickey; liv Hebron NH; ch 1
son, Emma m George S Smith;
NH-0007-390
Samuel; m Mehitable Wilkins d/o
Andrew; liv Merrimack; ch
Sarah, Samuel; NH-0002-546
Samuel; liv Groton, Deerfield
MA; ch Robert, David b1802 m
Emeline Kidder, Annie m ---
Jewell, Fannie; NH-0007-390
McCRILLIS,
--- MD; m --- Kimball d/o Caleb
& Sarah Sawyer; liv Sandwich;
ch Hon H W, 1 dau m ---
Griswold of Bangor ME; NH-
0004-651
Henry; m Margaret ---; liv
Epsom & Sandwich NH; ch Jane,
John, Henry b1781, David
b1783, William b1785,
Margaret b1787, James b1790,
Neal b1792, Mary b1794, Nancy
b1796, Elizabeth b1799,
Andrew b1801; NH-0006-673
McDEVITT,
Henry; m Miranda Janvrin d/o
Jefferson & Mary Wadleigh; ch
William Henry; NH-0003-347
McDUFFEE,
Daniel; s/o John & Martha of
Rochester NH, adopted by Col
John; ch John m Abigail Torr;
NH-0001-153
Franklin; b1832 s/o John &
Joanna Hanson of Dover; m1861
Mary Fannie Hayes d/o John of
Farmington; liv Rochester ch
John, Edgar, Willis; NH-0001-
153, NH-0003-741
George; s/o John & Joanna
Hanson; m Lizzie Hanson 1
son, m Nellie Farrington d/o
Dr James of Rochester; NH-
0001-153
John; m Martha ---; liv London-
derry ENG, Rochester NH; ch
Mansfield, Archibald, Col
John, Daniel; NH-0001-153,
NH-0003-743
John; s/o Daniel; m Abigail
Torr d/o Simon & Sarah Ham;
liv Rochester NH; ch John

McDUFFEE (continued)
b1803 m Joanna Hanson; NH-0001-153, NH-0003-743
John; b1803 s/o John & Abigail Torr of Rochester NH; m1829 Joanna Hanson d/o Joseph & Charity Dame of Rochester NH; liv Rochester & Dover NH; ch Joseph, Franklin m Mary Fannie Hayes, John Randolph, Anna M m Frank S Brown of Hartfort CT, Mary Abbie m Charles K Chase, Sarah, George m Lizzie Hanson & Nellie Farrington d/o Dr James of Rochester, Oliver dy; NH-0001-153, NH-0003-743

McFERSON,
Robert; bro/o William; m Mary Christie of Londonderry; ch Sarah, Katherine m Thomas Murdough of Acworth NH, Robert dy, Thomas, Nancy m David McKeen, James Christie m Mary Bennett, William; NH-0002-378
William; bro/o Robert; m Mary Blair; liv Cork; ch Anna m Robert Mills, Hannah, Mary, Hugh m Hannah Butterfield, Robert m Sally Wilkins & m Sally Gregg, Sally, Rosanna, William m Jane Forsaith; NH-0002-378

McGAFFEY,
John; b1833; m1855 Louisa A Pratt d/o F W Esq; liv Sandwich NH, OH; ch Ernest, 1 son, 2 dau; NH-0006-248
Samuel; s/o John of N Sandwich; ch Neal; Eliphalet, Josiah; NH-0006-247

McGAW,
Isaac; liv Windham, Merrimack; ch Margaret Jane m Edward P Parker, John Armour, Sarah Elizabeth, Martha Dickinson m Francis A Gordon, Anna Eliza m Carmi Parker; NH-0002-544
Isaac; b1785 s/o Jacob of Merrimack; liv Bedford, Merrimack; NH-0003-38
Jacob; b1737; liv Lineygloss IRE, Merrimack NH; ch John, Margaret, Jacob, Robert, Rebecca, Isaac, Martha; NH-0002-544

McGILVERAY,
John; liv SCO, Merrimack; ch John, Robert, William, Alexander, David, Jacob,

McGILVERAY (continued)
Martha m Alexander Anderson of Derry, Margaret, Simon; NH-0002-544
John; s/o Simon; liv Merrimack; ch Franlkin D, John C, D Albertie, Clarie F m Everett E Parker of Merrimack, Annis B, Harriett M; NH-0002-544
Simon; s/o John; liv Merrimack; ch John, Eliza J m James Hale, William, Harriet, George Newel; NH-0002-544

McGREGOR,
Dr George W; b1853; m Augusta Eaton d/o Stephen of Franconia; liv Bethlehem, Lunenburg VT, Littleton NH; NH-0007-505

McGREGORY,
Rev James; liv IRE, Londonderry NH; ch David b1710; NH-0005-502
Joel; b1820 s/o Loma & Fanny White of Whitefield; m1846 Hannah Philbrick Gove; liv Whitefield NH; ch Anna E m Joel M Sartwell, George G, Charles I, John L, Joel W, Stella F; NH-0005-502

McINTOSH,
Frederick; b1840; m1872 Mary J Barrett d/o Hamilton & Mary Shute of Plymouth; liv Rumney NH, W Plymouth, Boston; ch Martha Grace b1873, Florence Maria b1878; NH-0007-613

McKEEN,
Albert; s/o William Jr & Lydia Hadlock; m Vienna Paine of Candia NH; ch Frank A m Clara Bowers, Susie A m George H Andrews, Mary E m J N Andrews; NH-0002-375
James; liv IRE; ch James, John, William; NH-0002-374
John; s/o James; m Janet ---; ch James, Robert, Samuel m Agnes ---, Mary; NH-0002-374
Robert; s/o William & Ann Grimes; m Sally Barnes of Deering NH; ch Leonard m Angeline Dickey of Deering, Elbridge m Jane Colby & m --- Colby, Adaline m Galusha Smith of Boston MA; NH-0002-375
Samuel; s/o John & Janet ---; m Agnes ---; liv Amherst NH; ch William m Ann Graham (Grimes), 5 sons; NH-0002-

McKEEN (continued)
375
William; s/o Samuel & Agnes ---
; m Ann Grimes sis/o Francis
of Deering; liv Deering NH;
ch John m Ann Ramsey of
Greenfield NH, David m Nancy
Ferson of Deering, Robert m
Sally Barnes, William Jr m
Lydia Hadlock, Moses, Samuel,
Rose m --- Clough of White-
field NH, Mary m --- With-
ington, Betsy m William
McNeil of Rockingham VT,
Jane, Agnes; NH-0002-375
William Jr; s/o William & Ann
Grimes; m Lydia Hadlock; ch
Walter m Leonora Gould of
Hillsborough NH, Albert m
Vienna Paine, Levi m Carrie
Massey of Nashua NH, J C
Dodge dy, Sarah m A W Dickey
of Deering NH; NH-0002-375
McKINNEY,
William; m Jane Shirley d/o
James & Abigail McCutchins;
liv Newberg IN; ch Margaret
b1806, Mary b1808, John
b1810, James b1810, William
b1814, Thomas 1817, Joshua
b1819, Nancy b1822, Harriet
b1825, Martha b1828, Cornelia
b1830, Cordelia b1830; NH-
0002-328
McMASTER,
John; b1775 s/o William of
Francestown; m Lydia Whittier
(Whicher); liv Whitefield NH;
ch Sally b1798 m Nathaniel
Hutchins, Janet b1801 m
Benjamin Brown, Lydia b1803 m
George Quimby, Mary B b1813 m
David Lang, 1 son; NH-0005-
465
McMILLAN,
Col Andrew; liv IRE, N Conway
NH; ch Lewis, James, John,
Gilbert, Martha m Dr Chad-
bourne, Betsey m --- Webster
of Bartlett; NH-0006-843
McMURPHY,
Alexander; m Mary Palmer of
Sutton NH; liv Londonderry &
Alexandria NH; ch Daniel m
Betsey Huntington of Bristol
NH; NH-0007-116
Daniel Jr; s/o Daniel & Betsey
Huntington; m Sarah E Roades
d/o Silas & Rebecca Haywood;
liv Alexandria NH; ch
Albertus N, Silas A m Emma

McMURPHY (continued)
Tilton; NH-0007-116
Silas A; s/o Daniel J & Sarah E
Roades of Alexandria NH; m
Emma Tilton of Bristol; ch
Lizzie I; NH-0007-116
McNEIL,
John; m Christiana; liv IRE &
Londonderry; NH-0002-41
Capt John; s/o Daniel gs/o
John; m Lucy Andrews d/o
Isaac Esq; liv Hillsborough;
ch Mary b1779, Gen Solomon
b1782, Gen John b1784, Lucy
dy; NH-0002-402
Gen John; s/o Capt John & Lucy
Andrews; m --- Pierce d/o
Gov; ch Frances m Hon Charles
E Potter, John W S; NH-0002-
402
McQUESTEN,
Peter; liv Plymouth NH; ch O S,
Dea Alvah; NH-0007-587
McQUESTIN,
Capt Isaac; b1811 s/o Robert H
& Lydia Barrett; m1842
Margaret A Chase d/o Maj
Francis & Dorothy Bixby; liv
Litchfield; ch Eugene F,
Francis H, Jennie F m
Frederick L Center; NH-0002-
496
Capt James F; b1835 s/o Henry &
Eliza Chase of Litchfield;
m1863 Marcia V McQuesten d/o
Edward & Harriet Colby; NH-
0002-494
William; m --- Arbuckle; liv
IRE, Litchfield; ch William,
John, Simon, 5 dau; NH-0002-
495
MACK,
Andrew; s/o John & Isabella
Brown; m Elizabeth Clark d/o
Robert of Londonderry NH; ch
Dea Andrew m Maria L Burns, 7
others; NH-0004-795
Dea Andrew; s/o Andrew & Eliza-
beth Clark; m1824 Maria L
Burns d/o Thomas Esq; liv
Gilmanton, Haverhill; ch 4;
NH-0004-795
John; m Isabella Brown; liv
Londonderry NH; ch Andrew m
Elizabeth Clark, 7 others;
NH-0004-795
Robert Clark; b1818 s/o Robert
& Ann Clark of Londonderry
gs/o Andrew & Elizabeth Clark
of Londonderry ggs/o John
Isabella Brown of IRE; m1856

MACK (continued)
Jane Duncan Patterson d/o Capt Thomas & Hannah Duncan of Londonderry; liv Londonderry NH; NH-0003-583
William Barker MD; b1852 s/o William F of Bellows Falls VT; liv Dover; NH-0003-850

MAGOUN,
Simon; m Betsey Barstow; ch Calvin B MD b1798 m1835 Mary E Harbour, Cyrus S MD b1815 m 2; NH-0003-189

MAHURIN,
Capt Ephraim; b1780; m Rebecca Bundy of Walpole; liv Westmoreland, Stratford NH; NH-0005-775

MANAHAN,
Adam; m ?1 & m ?2; ch/o ?1 John, Richard m Polly Gove, William m Mary Bowers, Joseph; ch/o ?2 Mary m --- Bailey, Elvira m Solomon Bailey, Stephen m Nancy Bailey, Thompson m Almira Gove, Mark Valentine; NH-0002-382

MANN,
George W; b1821 s/o Samuel & Mary Howe; m1843 Susan M Witcher & m1855 Sarah T Bisbee; liv Benton NH, Landfaff; ch/o ? - Ezra B, Edward F, Geo H, Orman L, Osman C dy, Melvin J, Hosea B, Susan M, Minnie S, Moses B; NH-0007-153
Jared; b1770 s/o John & Lydia Porter of Orford NH; m Mindwell Hale d/o Dr Samuel of Pepperell MA; liv Orford NH; ch Susan m William Heard; NH-0006-722
John; s/o Nathaniel & Elizabeth George of Mansfield CT; m Margaret Peters d/o John of Hebron CT; ch John m Lydia Porter; NH-0006-722
John; s/o John & Margaret Peters; m Lydia Porter of Hebron CT; liv Orford NH; ch Jared b1770 m Mindwell Hale; NH-0006-722
Nathaniel; s/o Samuel & Esther Ware; m1704 Elizabeth George; liv Mansfield CT; ch John m Margaret Peters; NH-0006-722
Samuel; b1647 s/o William & Mary Jared; m Esther Ware of Dedham MA; liv Wrentham MA;

MANN (continued)
ch Nathaniel m Elizabeth George; NH-0006-721
Solomon; s/o John of Orford NH b1743; ch Emily m Henry Oakes; NH-0001-24
William; m Mary Jared; liv Kent Co ENG, Cambridge MA; ch Samuel b1647 m Esther Ware; NH-0006-721

MANSON,
Alexander; s/o Capt Joseph of Kittery ME; m Mary N Martin & m Mrs H A Bigelow; liv Haverhill NH; ch/o Mary - Mary m Moses P Boswell, Alexander, Elizabeth T m George Kimball, Phebe m W F Carmon, Lucy F m James Boswell, Charles; ch/o H A - Adella m E E Shepherdson; NH-0007-363
Jacob; s/o Dea John gs/o George; m twice; liv Eaton; ch 10, Jacob b1828; NH-0006-625
John; liv Effingham, Eaton; ch Benjamin, Mark, Jacob; NH-0006-793

MANTER,
Francis; b1797 s/o George & Mary Senter; m1820 Harriet Crowningshield of Salem MA; liv Londonderry; ch George b1824, Harriet b1829 m James Platts, Mary F b1837 m George Platts; NH-0003-585
George; b1767; m Mary Senter b1765 d/o Samuel; liv Plymouth MA, Londonderry NH; ch Francis b1797 m Harriet Crowningshield, Samuel b1799 m Isabella Reid, Alden, David, Mary, Parnell; NH-0003-585
Dr George; b1824 s/o Francis & Harriet Revall (Crowningshield) of Londonderry; liv Auburn, Manchester; ch George F, Corey, Olivia; NH-0003-148 & 585
Samuel; b1799 s/o George & Mary Senter; m1823 Isabella Reid b1798 d/o David of Londonderry; ch Mary Ann b1824 m William P Emerson, Samuel b1825, Isabella b1828, David b1828 dy, James b1828, Clarissa b1841; NH-0003-585

MARBLE,
William C; m Sarah Barker d/o Gilman & Emeline Smith of

MARBLE (continued)
Exeter; liv Methuen; ch Maud, Charles, Ernest; NH-0003-296
MARSH,
Charles; bro/o Benjamin L; liv Chester NH & Boston MA; NH-0001-184
David; m Sarah Colby wid/o John Kenrick; liv Haverhill; ch Nathaniel, Mary m Rev G W Kelley of Haverhill MA; NH-0004-321
Newton; s/o Edmond & Emma Cook; m Lydia Butler d/o John & Mary Poor; ch Christopher H m Mrs Mary A Heath d/o Henry Plummer, 5 others; NH-0007-207
MARSHALL,
Anderson J; b1819 s/o Antipas P & Nancy A Lucas of Northumberland; m1840 Frances Perkins d/o George & Mary Waite of Lancaster; liv Lancaster NH, Lawrence MA, St Louis MO; ch Antipas P, Emma F m George L Williams, Belle m George S Locke; NH-0005-394
Anson Southard; b1822; m1861 Mary Jane Corning; liv Lyme & Concord NH, Fitchburg MA; ch Anson Southard Jr b1863; NH-0004-34
Antipas P; s/o Anderson J & Frances Perkins; ch Fred A, Frank P, Winnie A; NH-0005-394
Farrington Hawks; b1829 s/o Nathan Richardson & Abigail Hawks of Bradford NH; m --- Farrington; liv Boston; ch Walter, Minnie, Fred; NH-0004-206
John Webster; b1835 s/o John & Judith Jackman of Salisbury NH; m1864 Martha J Wadleigh d/o Benjamin E & Oliver Chandler of Bradford NH; liv Boston MA; ch Elmer Wadleigh, John Edgar; NH-0004-213
Joshua; s/o Antipas of Gloucester MA; m Betsey Day d/o Eliphalet & Tirzah French; liv Stratford NH; NH-0005-775
Joshua Pierce; b1818 s/o Nathan Richardson & Abigail Hawks of Bradford NH; m Mary Jane French; liv MA, Bradford Corner NH; ch Daniel Richardson m Vilona L Simonds of

MARSHALL (continued)
Washington DC, William, Addison Joseph, Mary; NH-0004-205
Micajah; s/o Abel; m1811 Charlotte P Kimball & m1817 Martha P Southworth d/o Nathaniel & m Eliza Russ; liv Lyme NH; ch/o Martha P m Parker I Morrison, Mary F m S C Dimick, Anson Southard, G Clark, 12 others; NH-0007-541
Nathan Richardson; b1792 s/o Richard & Esther Pierce; m Abigail Hawks of Bradford; liv Bradford NH; ch Sarah Knowlton b1812 m1849 John Furnald, Catharine b1814, Mary b1815 m Sumner Kittredge, Joshua Pierce b1818 m Mary Jane French, Betsey B b1818 dy, Esther b1820 dy, Esther Pierce b1821 m John Harriman Collins, Joseph Addison b1826 m Marietta C Page & m Sarah M Chapman, Luella b1828 m Edwin M Bailey, Farrington Hawks b1829 m --- Farrington; NH-0004-205
Richard; m Esther Pierce; liv Bradford NH; ch Richard, Esther m Josiah Melvin, Sarah m Asa Sargent of Warner, Nathan Richardson b1792 m Abigail Hawks; NH-0004-205
MARSTEN,
Caleb; liv Gilford NH; ch Capt Caleb O; NH-0004-744
MARSTON,
Benjamin; b1807 s/o Thomas & Hannah Knowles of N Hampton; m Sarah D Nutter; liv N Hampton; ch Thomas E m Margaret Dow, 1 other; NH-0003-424
Benjamin S; s/o Jeremiah of Bridgewater; m Laura A Boardman d/o John & Mary Melvin; ch Charles H b1848; NH-0007-390
Caleb G; b1835 s/o David & Sarah Dearborn; m Vianna Palmer; ch Annie May; NH-0003-331
David; s/o Thomas & Hannah Knowles of N Hampton; m Mary Tasker; ch Mary E, David T, Almira, Charles, Lucy A, Cyrus L; NH-0003-424
Capt David; b1781 s/o Samuel of

MARSTON (continued)
Chichester NH; m Susanna Brunson; liv N Benton; ch William C m Lucy Frary, 2 dau; NH-0007-353

David; b1797 s/o Elisha Smith & Judith Morrill; m1832 Sarah Dearborn b1807 d/o Simon N; liv Hampton NH; ch Augusta M m Langdon Brown, Caleb G b1835 m Vianna Palmer, Lovinia M m Ambrose Swasey of Cleveland OH, Melborn b1845; NH-0003-331

Elisha Smith; b1750 s/o Elisha; m Judith Morrill; ch David b1797 m Sarah Dearborn, 6 sons, 1 dau; NH-0003-331

John; s/o Elisha gs/o Jonathan ggs/o John gggs/o Thomas; m Nancy Moulton d/o Gen Jonathan; liv Moultonborough; ch Elisha, Caleb M, Hon Moulton Hoyt b1806 m Anne M Ambrose; NH-0006-719

Jonathan; s/o Samuel of Coventry; m Phebe Howe of Landaff; liv Coventry, Canton NY; ch Orrin, Jonathan H, Bartlett m Anna S Brown, 5 others; NH-0007-353

Josiah; b1794 s/o Josiah; m Hannah Drew & m1852 Mary Ann Dearborn b1800 d/o Joseph Freese; liv Hampton, Portsmouth NH; ch/o Hannah - Mary A m Capt Joseph Marden of Portsmouth, Hannah m Samuel P Garland of Rye, 1 other; NH-0003-331

Hon Moulton Hoyt; b1806 s/o John & Nancy Moulton of Moultonborough; m1830 Anne M Ambrose d/o Col Jonathan of Moultonborough; liv Sandwich NH; ch Anne Elizabeth m Hon William A Heard, Emily Maria m William A Heard, Elvira B m Samuel G Lane of Concord, Carrie B m Samuel C Tozzer of Lynn MA, Alfred A; NH-0006-719

Thomas; b1728; m Elizabeth Page; ch Jeremiah, Thomas b1756 m Hannah Knowles, Abraham, Deborah, Elizabeth; NH-0003-424

Thomas; b1756 s/o Thomas & Elizabeth Page; m1783 Hannah Knowles d/o David; liv N Hampton; ch Elizabeth m Levi

MARSTON (continued)
Jewell, Hannah m Levi Jewell, Mary, Thomas m Mary Leavitt, David K m Mary Tasker, Deborah m Edward Lang, Sally b1799, Fanny b1802, Almira, Benjamin b1807 m Sarah D Nutter; NH-0003-424

Thomas; m Mary Easton d/o William; liv Salem MA, Hampton NH; ch Isaac, Bertha, Ephraim, James, Caleb, Mary, Sarah; NH-0003-331

Thomas; s/o Thomas & Hannah Knowles of N Hampton; m Mary Leavitt; ch Sophia; NH-0003-424

William; m Sabina ---; liv Salem, Hampton; ch Thomas, William, John, Frifenia; NH-0003-331

William; liv ENG, Hampton; ch Thomas; NH-0006-719

MARTIN,
Asa W; s/o Sylvester & Elizabeth Ford; m Amy Flagg d/o Joseph & Hannah Wheeler; liv Grafton NH; ch Charles Henry m Elida Clark, 5 sons, 2 dau; NH-0007-279

Col Benjamin Franklin; b1813 s/o Truman & Mary Noyes of Peacham VT; m1836 Mary Ann Rice of Boston sis/o Hon Alexander H & Willard Rice; liv Peacham VT, Millbury, Meredith Bridge, Newton Lower Falls MA, Middleton, Manchester NH; ch Fanny R m Hon George B Chandler, 2 dau; NH-0001-269

Carlos S; s/o Samuel R & Mercy French; m Emma J Kyser d/o Hiram & Patience of Wilmot; liv Grafton NH; ch Ned D, Ethel M, Minnie F, Bert A, Charles T; NH-0007-279

Charles Henry; s/o Asa W & Amy Flagg of Grafton NH; m Elida Clark of Contoocook NH; liv Concord; ch Charles Henry, Amy; NH-0007-279

James; b1799 s/o Samuel & Sally Cochrane; m Elsie Bailey; liv Epsom NH; ch Sally b1822 m --- Sleeper, Samuel b1828, James b1830, Thomas b1832; NH-0004-469

James M; s/o James & Janet Ford; m Martha Richards d/o David & Hannah Story; ch

MARTIN (continued)
Frances H m Martin Pierce; NH-0007-279

Joseph; liv Lebanon NH; ch Jonathan, John, Sylvanus, Joseph, Elizabeth m Oliver Smith of Chelsea VT, Susannah, Jemima; NH-0007-421

Joseph P; m Louisa B Francis d/o Joseph G & Fanny Bowen; ch Charles J; NH-0007-122

Levi; s/o Levi & Annie Kilton; m Eunice Reed of Grafton NH; ch Samuel R m Mercy French, 6 others; NH-0007-279

Levi; m Annie Kilton; liv Rehoboth RI, Grafton NH; ch Levi m Eunice Reed, James m Janet Ford; NH-0007-279

Rev McDonald; m Johanna Weber of Plymouth NH; liv Pembroke NH; ch Charles L m Orpha Ferrin d/o Zebulon & Abigail Blake, 3 others; NH-0007-122

Nathaniel; liv Portsmouth, Dorchester; ch Simeon, Nathaniel, 1 dau; NH-0007-530

Nathaniel Esq; m 2; liv Loudon; ch Rue, Jane, Elizabeth, Hannah, Mary, Abigail, Nancy, Sally, Theophilus B Esq m Sally L Rowell; NH-0004-506 & 508

Nathaniel; m Margaret Mitchell; liv Londonderry NH; ch William b1712 m Hannah Cochrane; NH-0003-858, NH-0004-268

Noah MD; b1801 s/o Samuel & Sally Cochrane; m1825 Mary Jane Woodbury d/o Dr Robert of Barrington; liv Great Falls & Dover NH; ch Elizabeth A, Caroline M; NH-0003-858, NH-0004-468

Oliver S; s/o John gs/o Joseph; m Mary Martin & m1863 Amanda A Moore of Chelsea VT; liv Chelsea VT, Lebanon NH; ch/o Mary - Dr Joseph H; NH-0007-421

Elder Richard; liv Gilford NH; ch Richard Jr, John L, 1 dau m George Saunders; NH-0004-743

Robert A; m Aramintha Barney of Grafton; liv SCO, Grafton NH; ch Harriet, Edson H m Mrs Anna S Caswell d/o Horace B & Eveline Williams; NH-0007-284

Samuel; b1762 s/o William &

MARTIN (continued)
Hannah Cochrane; liv Pembroke; ch Polly, Thomas, James b1799 m Elsie Bailey, Noah MD b1801 m Mary Jane Woodbury, Nancy; NH-0004-468 &469

Samuel R; s/o Levi & Eunice Reed; m Mercy French of Sutton NH; ch Carlos S m Emma J Kyser, 3 others; NH-0007-279

Simeon; s/o Nathaniel; ch Rev Nathaniel, Ezekiel, 2 sons, 2 dau; NH-0007-530

Theophilus B Esq; s/o Nathaniel Esq; m Sally L Rowell; liv Loudon & Concord NH; ch Nathaniel dy, Mary E, Abby, Nathaniel E; NH-0004-506

William; b1712 s/o Nathaniel & Margaret Mitchell; m Hannah Cochrane; ch Mary, James, Nathaniel, William, Robert, Samuel b1762 m Sally Cochrane, Hannah; NH-0004-468

MASON,
Benjamin M; b1811 s/o Capt Lemuel B & Mary Chamberlain; m1838 Anne E Brown d/o John G & Joanna; liv Moultonborough NH; ch William NH, M Ella, George L dy; NH-0006-417

Daniel S; b1809; m1835 Angeline W Webster & m1849 Anna C Taylor; liv Bristol NH; ch/o Angeline - John, 1 dau m Albert Blake Jr, 2 others; NH-0007-191

Eliphalet; liv Greenland & Lyman NH, Bath; ch Joshua d1873, Shubael S, John; NH-0007-516

Joseph; m Polly Randall; liv Kearsarge Village; ch William, Nathaniel R b1814 m Ruth Hutchins; NH-0006-895

Hon Larkin D; b1810 s/o Tufton & Sarah Gilman of Tamworth; m Joanna W Folsom d/o Col Levi & m Catharine Staples d/o Nicholas W; liv Tamworth NH; ch/o Catharine - Clinton S, Joanna F, Charles T T, Nicholas W, John L, Justin E, Henry M, Sadie O, Mamie E; NH-0006-772

Capt Lemuel; b1759; m Sarah Nutter & m Mary Chamberlain d/o Ephraim; liv Durham, Newington, New Durham, Alton,

MASON (continued)
Gilford, Moultonborough; ch/o Mary - Benjamin M b1811 m Ann E Brown, Dr W H H; NH-0006-417

Hon Nathaniel; b1796 s/o Abner of Bath ME gs/o John; m1821 Ruth Smith of Bath NH & m1849 Louisa Farley; liv Lisbon, Bath, Bristol; NH-0007-194

Nathaniel R; b1814 s/o Joseph & Polly Randall; m1839 Ruth Hutchins d/o Dearborn & --- Eaton of Fryeburg ME gd/o Capt Nathaniel; liv N Conway NH; ch Freeman H m Martha Nutter, Frank L m Katharine Dame, Mahlon L, Mangum E dy; NH-0006-895

Capt Peter G; s/o Tufton & Sarah Gilman of Tamworth; m Mary Bradbury; liv S Tamworth NH; ch Francis J dy, Thomas B; NH-0006-772

Samuel K; b1832; m1858 Helen M Smith of Bristol; liv New Hampton, Bristol; NH-0007-70

Stephen; liv Hampton, Moulton-borough, Tamworth; ch Tufton b1767 m Sarah Gilman, Tristram, Jeremiah, John, Samuel, Mary, Abigail; NH-0006-772

Tufton; b1767 s/o Stephen; m1793 Sarah Gilman d/o Col Jeremiah of Burton; liv Tamworth NH; ch Capt Peter G m Mary Bradbury, Elizabeth D, John, Sarah, Hon Larkin D b1810 m Joanna W Folsom & m Catharine Staples, Harriet m Ebenezer Dow, Samuel W, 7 others; NH-0006-772

Dr William H H; b1817 s/o Lemuel B of Gilford; m1844 Mehitable S Moulton d/o Simon & m1853 Sarah J Brown d/o John G; liv Moulton-borough NH; ch/o Sarah - 1 day, Dr George L b1854 m1878 Emma Evans, Charles; NH-0006-411

MASSUERE,
James; liv Stark NH; ch John b1795, Marcy b1797, James b1799; NH-0005-570

MAXFIELD,
Nathaniel; liv Loudon NH; ch Betsey, Stephen, Eliphalet, Mehetable, Ruth, Nathaniel, James, Joseph, Nathan, Elle,

MAXFIELD (continued)
Hannah, Samuel; NH-0004-508

Rufus A; b1835 s/o Stephen C & Clarissa Staples; m1856 Mary A Spaulding d/o Joshua of Pepperell MA; liv Nashua NH, Lowell & Salem MA; NH-0001-289

Stephen C; d1862; m Clarissa Staples of Chichester NH; liv Newbury VT, Nashua NH, Lowell MA; ch Rufus A b1835 m Mary Spaulding, James G MD, J P, Stephen W, Susan T, Helen A, 4 dy; NH-0001-289

MAYNARD,
John H; b1805 s/o Asa & Mary Linfield; m1832 Jane Kimball of E Concord NH & mc1871 Apha Kimball of Hopkinton NH; liv Concord MA, Loudon, E Concord & Manchester NH; NH-0002-135

MAYO,
Hiram; m Betsey Whipple d/o Joel; liv Vershire VT, Lyme NH; ch George S, Joel W, Wesley N, Julia A, H Burt; NH-0007-545

John H MD; b1857; m1883 Alice M Gould of Northfield; liv Mooretown VT, Peterborough NH; NH-0002-665

MEAD,
William; s/o William of Meredith; m Eunice Roberts b1789; ch Susan; NH-0004-867

MEADER,
Elisha; s/o Paul; m Susan Smith & m Abigail Foss; ch/o Susan - Samuel K, Joseph S, Paul N, Elisha, Betsey, Mahala, Deborah; ch/o Abigail - Daniel W m Lydia Swartz, Moses B, Elisha K; NH-0007-352

Paul; liv Durham NH, Warren; ch Elisha m Susan Smith & m Abigail Foss, George, Joseph, Moses, 4 dau; NH-0007-352

MEANS,
David McGregor; s/o Col Robert of Amherst NH; m Catherine Atherton d/o Hon Joshua; ch Wiliam Gordon b1815 m Martha Allen, James Edward, Alfred Spaulding; NH-0001-103

Col Robert; m --- McGregor d/o Rev David of Londonderry NH; liv IRE, Merrimack & Amherst NH; ch Robert, David McGregor m Catherine Atherton; NH-

MEANS (continued)
0001-103
William Gordon; b1815 s/o David McGregor & Catherine Atherton; m1840 Martha Allen d/o Bethuel & Martha Bent of Newton MA; liv Amherst & Manchester NH, Boston MA; eight ch; NH-0001-103

MEARS,
Ira; m Hannah Barnes d/o Reuben; liv Merrimack; ch Jane, Mattie, George, Stella; NH-0002-542

MELCHER,
Joseph; m Mary Rowell; liv Hampton Falls; ch Polly M b1798 m Caleb T Sanborn, Samuel b1810; NH-0003-352

MELLEN,
Henry; b1757 s/o Rev John of Stirling MA; liv Dover; NH-0003-588

MELVIN,
Benjamin Franklin; b1824 s/o Richard & Betsy Straw; m1856 Hannah D Colby b1827 of Warner; liv Warner; ch Frank Otis b1857, Celia Addie b1860 dy, Maud Muller b1866; NH-0004-206

Josiah; m Esther Marshall d/o Richard; liv Bradford; ch Esther b1795, Richard b1797 m Betsy Straw, Mary M b1799, Sarah P b1802, Hartwell b1805, Nathan R b1807, Susan M b1808, Lucy M b1811, Ruth b1815, Jonah Galusha b1817, Weare Tappan b1820; NH-0004-206

Proctor Darling; b1817 s/o Richard & Betsy Straw; m1845 Harriet Bagley d/o David; ch Margaret F b1846 m --- Holmes, Richard Edson b1849, Betsy A b1854 dy, Walter b1856; NH-0004-206

Richard; b1797 s/o Josiah & Esther Marshall of Bradford; m Betsy Straw; liv Bradford NH; ch Proctor Darling b1817 m Harriet Bagley, Grosvenor Stickney b1819, Harriet Maria b1821 m Clark Whitcomb, Benjamin Franklin b1824 m Hannah D Colby, Elizabeth b1827 m1853 Eben Wright, 1 son b1829 dy, Mary Ann b1831 dy, Esther Maria b1835 m Baxter Codman of Hills-

MELVIN (continued)
borough, Henrietta b1838 m George W Page, Josiah b1841; NH-0004-206

MERRILL,
Abel; b1646 s/o Nathaniel & Susanna Jourdaine; m1671 Priscilla Chase; liv Newbury; ch Abel b1671 m Abigail Stevens; NH-0002-483

Abel; b1671 s/o Abel & Priscilla Chase of Newbury; m1694 Abigail Stevens; liv W Newbury; ch Samuel, Abel, Thomas, John, Nathaniel m Elizabeth Sarjeant, Abigail m John Kent, Martha m Joshua Marsh, Priscilla m Ezekiel Clark; NH-0002-483

Dea Abel; b1809 s/o Capt Benjamin & Sarah Haines; ch Rev John L, Rev Benjamin, Rev Charles H; NH-0007-355

Abner; b1791; m Sarah W Leavitt; liv Newbury MA, Exeter NH; ch Mary E, Jeremiah L b1819 m Mary E Moses, Joseph W, Charles A, Benjamin L, Abner L, Henry R, David W; NH-0003-298

Albert H; b1831 s/o Nathaniel & Rachel Morse; m Delia Miller d/o Benjamin; ch Delia A m William Walker, E Minnie m H A Praddex, Etta F m Frank Emerson, George O, Ben E, Abbie D; NH-0007-324

Benjamin; b1768 s/o Nathaniel & Olive Lund; m1820 Mrs Sarah Plummer Caton; liv Hudson; ch Benjamin A, Ebenezer B, James B b1824 m Persis A Winn, William T; NH-0002-484

Capt Benjamin; b1784 s/o Abel; m Sarah Haines of Rumney; liv Warren, Haverhill NH; ch Dea Abel b1809, Henry b1820 m Mary J Weeks & m Helen C Currier, 7 others; NH-0007-355

Blaisdel H; s/o Seth & Elmira Maynard; m1858 Sarah Woodman d/o James & Lucy; liv Rumney NH; ch Georgiana, Lucy dy, Carrie, Lucia M, Agnes K; NH-0007-612

Clark; s/o John & Betsey Darling; m Elizabeth Crowell of Hill; ch Hannah m Benjamin Southmayd, Moses, Elizabeth m Merrill Greely, George S,

MERRILL (continued)
Rose m Eben Blodgett, Edwin C, Albert L, Ruth A m William Kelly, Clarence N; NH-0007-180

David; b1771; liv Haverhill NH, Haverhill MA; ch Schuyler, 1 dau m Harry M Patridge, John H, David C, Samuel, 2 sons, 1 dau; NH-0007-355

Ebenezer; s/o John; liv Lisbon; ch Edson E, Nathaniel M; NH-0007-402

Edgar; b1841 s/o Winthrop & Martha Noyes of Campton; m1871 Abbie Sanborn & m1882 Dora A Brown; liv Plymouth NH; ch/o Abbie - Herbert M, Martha E; NH-0007-595

Enos; s/o Thomas & Lydia Abbot; m1810 Anna Gregg d/o Alexander & Mary Christie; liv Deering; ch Anna A b1811, Charlotte Lucretia b1813, Hannah b1815, Thomas A b1817 m Lucinda Wilkins, Mary Jane C b1819, Lydia A b1825, Eliza Judith b1827; NH-0002-380 & 389

Ezekiel; b1782 s/o Jacob; m Jane Bradley & m Mary Pervert; liv Plymouth NH; ch/o ? - Joseph W, 1 dau m Horace Eaton, Benjamin P, Ezra W, Mary A, 6 sons, 3 dau; NH-0007-589

Ezekiel E; b1819 s/o Giles & Mehitable Elliot of Rumney; m1848 Mary Cook of Campton; liv Plymouth NH; ch John E; NH-0007-595

Henry; b1820 s/o Capt Benjamin & Sarah Haines; m Mary J Weeks & m Helen C Currier; liv Haverhill NH; ch/o Mary - William H, Harriet L, Charlotte J, John W, 1 other; ch/o Helen - Arthur K; NH-0007-355

Hiram W; b1821 s/o Samuel of Gilmanton NH; m1855 Mary E Foster d/o Samuel & Mary Sawyer; liv Plymouth NH; ch Mary E, Carrie, James A, Arabella M; NH-0007-592

Jacob; b1790; m1814 Nancy Dearborn of Rumney NH; liv Plymouth NH; ch 9; NH-0007-396

James B; b1824 s/o Benjamin & Mrs Sarah Plummer Caton;

MERRILL (continued)
m1857 Persis A Winn d/o William & Persis G of Hudson; liv Hudson; ch A Gertrude, J Everett, George A; NH-0002-484

Jeremiah L; b1819 s/o Abner & Sarah W Leavitt; m Mary E Moses d/o Theodore & sis/o Dea John F of Exeter; liv Exeter; ch Joseph W m Louis Clement Lane; NH-0003-289

John; b1768 s/o Jonathan & --- Farnum; m Betsey Darling of Sanbornton; liv Bristol & Concord NH; ch John, Clark m Elizabeth Crowell, 4 others; NH-0007-180

John; b1808; m Hannah D Allen of Haverhill; liv Pembroke, Littleton NH; ch Henry m Carrie A Brackett, Richard B, Elizabeth m Edmund D Lucas of Littleton, Eleanor m William R Terrett, Abbie m R E Rockwell of E Orange NJ, Isabella m Charles F Dean of Roselle NJ, Hannah F; NH-0007-491

John; b1810 s/o Daniel of Warren NH; m1831 Mary C S Wells of Plymouth; liv Boston; ch Ann Eliza m George P Preston, Charles H, Fannie M m George P Preston, John Motley; NH-0007-355

Jonathan; m --- Farnum of Concord; liv Concord & Bristol NH, Alexandria; ch John b1768 m Betsey Darling, 4 sons, 4 dau; NH-0007-180

Jonathan; b1750; liv Newbury NH; ch Jonathan, Abraham, Mehitable, Sally, Samuel m Fanny Bancroft, Jane; NH-0005-640

Joseph W; s/o Jeremiah L & Mary E Moses of Exeter; m1866 Louise Clement Lane d/o Joshua J & Susan Bryant of Stratham; liv Exeter; ch William Edward b1867, Mary Louise b1871, Jeremiah Herbert b1875, Susan Emma b1881; NH-0003-289

Lyman; m1856 Abigail N Dearborn d/o J L & Huldah Avery; ch Nellie b1863; NH-0007-611

Mark; m Harriet Broughton d/o Mark & --- Knox of Conway NH; ch Ormond W; NH-0006-848

Martin; m1859 Emily Corliss d/o

MERRILL (continued)

Gen Cyrus & Alma Reed of Plymouth NH; ch Rena A; NH-0007-592

Nathaniel; m Susanna Jourdaine; liv ENG, Newbury MA; ch Nathaniel, John, Abraham, Susanna, Daniel, Abel b1646 m Priscilla Chase; NH-0002-483, NH-0005-640

Nathaniel; s/o Thomas & Lydia Abbott; m Anna Wilkins; ch Thomas Azro, Lydia m Levi H Sleeper of Manchester, John W m Maria A Holt, William D m Lavinia Wilson, Martha m Eben Sumner, Mary m Cristy Gregg; NH-0002-380

Rev Nathaniel; s/o Abel & Abigail Stevens of W Newbury; m Elizabeth Sarjeant; liv Nottingham West; ch Nathaniel b1739 m Olive Lund, Betty B (Betsey) b1741, Mary b1743 dy, John b1745, Abel b1747, Dorothy b1749, Olive b1751 m1779 Isaac Merrill, Sarah b1753, Benjamin b1756, Ruth, Molly, Theodore; NH-0002-483 & 462

Nathaniel; b1739 s/o Nathaniel & Elizabeth Sarjeant of Nottingham West; m1767 Olive Lund of Dunstable; ch Benjamin b1768 m Mrs Sarah Plummer Caton, Oliver, Asa; NH-0002-483

Nathaniel; liv Warren NH; ch Moses, Nathaniel bc 1794; NH-0007-634

Nathaniel; bc1794 s/o Nathaniel; liv Warren NH; ch Nathaniel, George B, Asa B, Laura m --- Wicks, 3 others; NH-0007-634

Nathaniel; bro/o Ebenezer; m Rachel Morse d/o Daniel; liv Newbury, Hanover NH; ch Louisa m John Stevens of Canaan, Nathaniel P m Lucy Chandler, Horatio N, Albert H b1831 m Delia Miller, 3 dau, 2 sons; NH-0007-324

Nathaniel P; s/o Nathaniel & Rachel Morse; m Lucy Chandler; ch Edwin P, Annie m N W Emerson; NH-0007-324

Samuel; s/o Jonathan of Newbury NH; m Fanny Bancroft b1789 of Dunbarton; liv Newbury NH, Croydon; ch Sherburn Rowell

MERRILL (continued)

b1810 m Sarah B Merrill & m Mrs Sarah N Butler McDole, Joshua B, Frances m William Leavitt, Mary J m Morrill Barnard, Seneca Sargent b1826 m Emma Lombard & m Arvilla Piper; NH-0005-640

Samuel; L; b1796 s/o Abel; liv Warren NH; ch Ira b1820; NH-0007-633

Seneca Sargent; b1826 s/o Samuel & Fanny Bancroft; m1871 Emma Lombard d/o Dr Lyman & Betsey Loomis & m1876 Arvilla Piper d/o Thomas & Esther Beecher wid/o Samuel P Pitkin; liv Colebrook NH; ch/o ? - Seneca Sherburn; NH-0005-646

Seth; m Elmira Maynard; liv Concord & Rumney NH; ch Blaisdel H m Sarah Woodman, Robert B b1835 m Eliza A Merrill d/o David & Phebe Rowan; NH-0007-612

Sherburn Rowell; b1810 s/o Samuel & Fanny Bancroft; m1836 Sarah B Merrill of Noblesborough ME & m1879 Mrs Sarah N Butler McDole; liv Woodstock, Colebrook; ch/o Merrill - Lucretia F m Edward N Cummings, Sarah L m Ira A Ramsay, Ellen L m J E Lombard, Caroline H m I W Drew, Mary J m W H Shurtleff; NH-0005-640

Thomas; m Lydia Abbott of Andover MA; ch Thomas A DD m Eliza Allen, Nathaniel m Anna Wilkins, Enos m Anna Gregg, John m Nancy Barnard, Charlotte Lucretia m Jonathan Clement; NH-0002-380

Thomas Esq; s/o Dea John of Concord; liv Conway NH; ch Thomas m Hannah Ambrose, William, Enoch, Amos m Lois Willey, Phebe m Abiathar Eastman, Stephen m Elizabeth Bayley, Mehetable m Roland Crocker, Jonathan A m Lydia Merrill, John m --- Boyd of Portland, Benjamin; NH-0006-847

MESERVE,

Clement; bro/o Jonathan; liv Marlburg, Jackson, Bartlett; ch Silas; NH-0006-914

Clement; s/o Clement of Dover;

MESERVE (continued)
m Lydia Tuttle; liv Jackson NH; ch Judge Silas m Betsey Meserve, Isaac, Ephraim b1773 m Sally Gray; NH-0006-976

Daniel; b1778 s/o Jonathan & Mary Davis; m1804 Betsey Pendexter d/o Hon John & Martha Jackson; liv Jackson, Bartlett; ch Eliza Pendexter b1805 m1825 Joseph O Emery, Jonathan b1808, Col Samuel Pendexter b1811 m1845 Lucia J Rowell, Mary D b1814 m1838 Solomon D Pendexter, George Washington b1818, Martha P b1821 m1844 Merrill Wyman, David Webster b1824 m1873 Sarah Frances Hobbs of Fryeburg ME, John Langdon b1828 dy; NH-0006-936 & 973

Ephraim; b1773 s/o Clement & Lydia Tuttle; m Sally Gray; ch Israel, Sophia m Robert McCarter, Abigail m Andrew Chesley, Charlotte, Sally, Florinda m William Emery, Ira D, Silas m Hannah Cogswell, Melissa, Stephen D, Oliver P m Nancy L Eastman, Clement, Winfield S, Horace B; NH-0006-976

George P; b1798 s/o Col Jonathan & Alice Pendexter; m Harriot Eastman d/o Richard; ch George W, 8 dau; NH-0006-973

Isaac; s/o Silas of Bartlett; liv Bartlett NH; ch Emily A, 5 dau; NH-0006-914

James M; s/o Nathaniel & Sally Trickey; m Martha Meserve d/o Gen George P; ch 1 dau m Frank Black, J E, W A; NH-0006-973

John; s/o Jonathan & Mary Davis; m Dorcas Hardy of Fryeburg ME; ch Nathaniel P m Adeline Chesley, James, Silas, John, Chandler, Joanna m Daniel Meserve, Abbie m George Starbird, Phebe; NH-0006-973

Jonathan; m Mary Davis; liv Madbury, Jackson; ch Col Jonathan b1772 m Alice Pendexter, Daniel m Betsey Pendexter, John m Dorcas Hardy, Nathaniel m Sally Trickey, Betsey m Judge Silas Meserve, Mary m Hubbard Harriman & m

MESERVE (continued)
Elijah Seavey, Joanna m Joseph Pitman; NH-0006-973

Col Jonathan; b1772 s/o Jonathan & Mary Davis; m1797 Alice Pendexter d/o Hon John & Martha Jackson; ch Gen George P b1798 m Harriot Eastman d/o Richard, Capt Daniel b1801, Martha P b1804 m Capt Joshua Trickey, John P b1812, Maj Andrew J b1815, Alice P dy; NH-0006-936 & 973

Nathaniel; s/o Jonathan & Mary Davis; m Sally Trickey d/o James; liv ME; ch James M m Martha Meserve; NH-0006-973

Nathaniel P; s/o John & Dorcas Hardy; m Adeline Chesley d/o John; ch 1 dau m Ephraim Gould, 1 son; NH-0006-973

Oliver P; s/o Ephraim & Sally Gray; m Nancy L Eastman d/o William; liv Jackson NH; ch 1 dau m Charles Stilphen; NH-0006-976

Judge Silas; s/o Clement & Lydia Tuttle; m Betsey Meserve d/o Capt Jonathan; liv Bartlett NH; ch Stephen, Ezra, John Langdon, Isaac, Lydia, Mary, Alice, Harriet; NH-0006-914 & 976

Silas; s/o Ephraim & Sally Gray; m Hannah Cogswell; ch Silas D, Sarah m --- Charles; NH-0006-976

MESERVEY,
Rev Atwood Bond; b1831 s/o William & Elvina Bond of Appleton ME; m1861 Lizzie Bean of Candia & m1869 Loanna Sherburne Mead of Northwood & m1883 Clara Bell Fall of Great Falls; liv Meredith & New Hampton & Northwood NH; ch/o Lizzie - Lizzie; ch/o Loanna - John Edwin dy; ch/o Clara - Arthur Bond; NH-0004-874

MESSER,
Frederick Gould; b1799; m1828 Susan Chamberlain b1804 d/o Edmund; liv Jericho VT, Colebrook NH, Portland ME; NH-0005-618

Stephen; m Anna Barker; liv Methuen & Andover MA, Shelburne NH; ch John, Stephen, Samuel, Enoch, Hannah m David Blake, Susannah m Oliver Pea-

MESSER (continued)
body of Shelburne, Nancy m
Amos Peabody of Shelburne,
Esther m Joseph Ordway & m
Aaron Rowell, Betsey m Thomas
Hubbard, Sarah m Isaac
Carlton, Mehitable m Simon
Evans; NH-0005-891
METCALF,
John W; b1803 s/o Burgess; liv
Piermont NH; ch Burgess C, 4
others; NH-0007-574
MILLEN,
David; b1806; m Jane Aldrich of
Lisbon; liv Littleton NH; ch
Hollon H, 1 dau m George
Corey, Charles W; NH-0007-487
MILLER,
Benjamin D; b1810 s/o Elijah of
Hanover; m Marinda Tenney & m
Anna Wright d/o David; liv
Hanover NH; ch/o Marinda -
Henry T, Delia A m Albert
Merrill, Eliza m J Steven;
ch/o Anna - Otis W; NH-0007-
324
Dr Frederick; b1789; liv Peter-
borough; NH-0002-667
Gen James; b1776 m Patty
Ferguson; liv Greensfield &
Peterborough & Temple NH, ch
James b1804 dy; NH-0002-339
Luke MD; b1815; liv Peter-
borough & Troy NH; Winchendon
MA, Chatfield & Lanesboro MN;
NH-0002-668
MILLS,
Adam; s/o Robert & Margaret
Dinsmore; m Lydia; ch Gawn W
m Clara Dickey, Robert m
Fanny Coburn, 5 dy; NH-0002-
387
Robert; m ? & m Margaret
Dinsmore; liv Deering; ch/o
Margaret - James, Adam m
Lydia, Isaac m Hepsibath
Whitten, John, William,
David, Nancy m David
Forsaith; NH-0002-387
MINER,
Rev Alonzo Ames DD; b1814 s/o
Benajah Ames & Amanda Cary;
m1836 Maria S Perley; liv
Lempster & Unity NH, Lowell
MA; NH-0001-16
Solomon; b1786; liv Lyman NH;
ch Annie, Ephraim, Alden M,
John P, William W, 3 others;
NH-0007-514
Thomas; m1765 Eleanor Lamb of
Norwich; liv Norwich CT,

MINER (continued)
Canaan NH; ch Allen b1776;
NH-0007-221
MINOT,
George; b1806 bro/o Hon Josiah;
m --- Clark d/o George
Reynolds of Portsmouth; liv
New London, Bristol, Concord;
NH-0007-69
Josiah; b1819 s/o James & Sally
Wilson; m1843 Abbie P Haines
of Canterbury; liv Bristol,
Concord; NH-0007-69
William; b1814; m Emily Weeks;
liv Bath NH; ch 3 dau, 1 son;
NH-0007-145
MITCHEL,
Daniel; b1848 s/o Abel & Susan
Glover of Bridgewater; m1877
Florence V Nutting d/o John &
Susanna Mitchel; liv Bridge-
water NH; ch Nora Blanche,
Ethel S, Edith Florence; NH-
0007-172
MITCHELL,
Ansel; s/o Isaac & Anable; m
Malinda Flanders of CAN; liv
Campton NH; ch George W m
Annie E Spencer & m Edwina
Caldon, 8 others; NH-0007-207
Rev Daniel; b1697; m Martha
White; liv IRE, Georgetown
ME, Pembroke NH; ch Ruhamah m
Robert Moore, Martha; NH-
0004-584
Dr David; b1782; liv Peter-
borough NH; NH-0002-667
Elijah; s/o Isaac & --- Anable;
m Eliza Webster adopted d/o
Timothy & Susanna; ch Elijah,
Harlan P; NH-0007-629
Francis; m Eliza Kimball d/o
Joseph & Betsy Wilkins & m
Mrs Charlotte Jaqueth; ch/o
Eliza - Charles m Mahala
Coburn, Sarah m Augustus
Wikins & m Francis F Fulton,
James m Almira Twist, Joseph
m Alice Barnes, George,
Albert B; NH-0002-384
Frederick A; s/o Elijah; m
Lucretia M Strong d/o Norman
& Lorena Kitteredge of Port
Hope Ont CAN; liv Campton NH;
ch Frank, Lulu; NH-0007-208
George W; s/o Ansel & Malinda
Flanders of Campton; m Annie
E Spencer & m Edwina Caldon
d/o Benjamin & Martha; liv
Campton Village NH; ch/o ? -
Fred D; NH-0007-207

MITCHELL (continued)

Israel; s/o Ebenezer of ME; m Hepsibah P Blair; liv Campton NH; ch Samuel S m Milla H Homans d/o Gilbert W & Jane C Bryant, Ira C m Mynetta Sweet d/o Sylvester, 5 others; NH-0007-214

John Michael; b1849 s/o John of Derby VT; m1874 Julia C Sonergan; liv Littleton, Concord; ch 1 dau, 1 son; NH-0007-112

Phineas P; m Mary I Swallow d/o Stillman & Nancy Roby Fisk; ch Josephine R m F E Wills, Katie A, Lucy C, Fannie P, Harry S, Howard W, Emily G, Carrie B; NH-0002-217

Stephen; b1780 s/o Benjamin of Peterborough; m Sally Mills d/o Maj Joseph of Deerfield; liv Durham; NH-0003-601

Timothy W; m Mary J Tucker d/o Luther & Mary Dickey of Thornton; ch Luther P, 5 others; NH-0007-208

MONTGOMERY,

John; m Abra Hayes d/o John & Tamsen Wentworth Chesley; liv Strafford NH; ch Jonathan; NH-0003-633

MOODY,

Stephen Esp; liv Gilmanton NH; ch Mary Jane m Dixi Crosby MD & Rebecca Marquand m Judge Nathan Crosby; NH-0001-245

Stephen; b1767; m Frances Coffin; liv W Newbury MA, Lower Gilmanton NH; NH-0004-702

MOONEY,

John; m Susan Chase; liv Loudon & Northfield Centre NH; ch Celestia S m Hon John H Goodale; NH-0004-531

John; liv Gilford & New Durham NH; ch Benjamin, Burnham, Joseph, Stephen, Charles; NH-0004-744

MOORE,

Adams; b1799; m 2 sisters gd/o Moses Little of Newbury MA; liv Bedford & Littleton NH; ch William; NH-0007-478

Andrew G; s/o Stephen & Mary Q Greeley; m Laura A Bachelder d/o Col Zephaniah; ch Charles L m Ida Jameson of Fisherville NH, Herbert G; NH-0004-502

MOORE (continued)

Archelaus; s/o John; ch Abigail, Archelaus Jr m --- Clifford, Lucinda, Abia, Climena, Hannah, Lydia, David, Julia, Jefferson; NH-0004-503

Archelaus Jr; s/o Archelaus; m --- Clifford d/o Joseph of Gilmanton NH; liv Loudon Ridge; ch Daniel L m ? & m Mariane Sleeper of Loudon; NH-0004-503

Coffin; b1739 s/o William & --- Gilman of Stratham; m1760 Comfort Weeks of Greenland; ch Coffin b1768 m Mary Bucknam, 3 sons, 3 dau; NH-0003-241

Coffin; b1768 s/o Coffin & Comfort Weeks; m1789 Mary Bucknam d/o Gen Edward; liv Lancaster NH; ch Edward Bucknam MD b1801 m Elizabeth Lawrence, 7 sons, 3 dau; NH-0003-241

Cyrus; b1823 s/o Nathan & Sally Crosby of Canterbury NH; m1851 Alzina Colburn d/o Ezekial & Jane Bartlet; liv Hebron NH, Groton; ch Albert E b1862, Willie E b1867 dy; NH-0007-388

Maj Daniel; b1777 s/o Robert & Ruhamah Mitchell of Pembroke; m1809 Sally McConnel; liv Pembroke NH; ch McConnel b1809 m1837 Sarah J Sanborn d/o John & Judith Blake of Loudon NH, Samuel E, Sally C, Betsey T; NH-0004-584

Edward Bucknam MD; b1801 s/o Coffin & Mary Bucknam of Lancaster; m1830 Elizabeth Lawrence d/o Hon Samuel of Epping; liv Epping NH, Boston MA; ch Samuel Lawrence MD, 1 son, 1 dau; NH-0003-241

Dr Jacob B; b1772; liv Georgetown ME, Andover NH; ch Henry E, Jacob B; NH-0004-337

Dea James; m Agnes Coolbrath; liv IRE, Concord MA, Pennacook & Suncook NH; ch Robert m Ruhamah Mitchell; NH-0004-584

James G; b1828; m Christiana C Shipman d/o Rev I H of Lisbon; liv Bristol, Franconia, Lisbon NH; NH-0007-459

John; liv Canterbury & Loudon

MOORE (continued)
NH; ch Hannah, Jacob,
Archelaus, Elkins, John,
William, Abia, Betsey, Patty,
Polly, Sally; NH-0004-503
Maj John; d1809; liv Norridge-
wock NH; NH-0002-47
Col Jonathan; ch Jonathan,
William; NH-0003-241
Hon Joseph Clifford; b1845 s/o
Dr D F & Frances S of Loudon
NH; liv Lake Village, Loudon
& Gilford & Manchester NH;
NH-0002-60, NH-0004-783
Leonard; s/o Jesse; m Polly
Huntington of Plainfield VT,
liv Worcester MA, ch
Philander L m Nancy M
Bancroft d/o Pesson & Nancy
Green, 8 others; NH-0007-130
Morrill S; b1798; m Sally
Hancook of Northfield; liv
Canterbury & Northfield NH;
ch Morrill m Lavina A Huse
d/o Daniel M of Compton, 4
others; NH-0004-531
Norman John Macleod MD; liv
Aberdeen SCO, Chelsea MA,
Derry & Nashua NH; NH-0002-
202
Richard R; liv Bow & Monroe NH;
ch Sophronia m --- Paddle-
ford, Nathaniel S, Richard, 3
others; NH-0007-553
Robert; s/o Dea James & Agnes
Coolbrath; m Ruhamah Mitchell
d/o Rev Daniel & Martha
White; liv Pembroke NH; ch
Maj Daniel b1777 m Sally
McConnel, 9 others; NH-0004-
584
Capt Samuel; m twice; liv
Canterbury NH; ch Thomas m
Comfort Perkins, 9 others;
NH-0004-513
Samuel; s/o Thomas & Comfort
Perkins of Loudon NH; m
Charlotte Foster of Canter-
bury; ch Kate m --- Rowe of
Rochester NY; NH-0004-513
Stephen; b1799 s/o Thomas &
Comfort Perkins of Loudon NH;
m Mary Q(L) Greeley d/o
Joseph & Nancy Wells of Gil-
manton NH & m Mrs Mary Bean
Berry d/o Levi Bean of Brent-
wood NH wid/o Alsonson Berry
of Loudon; liv Loudon NH;
ch/o Mary Q(L) - Joseph G
b1827 m Mary A Arlin & m Anne
Nichols, Albert b1831 dy,

MOORE (continued)
Anna Maria b1833 m John O
Hobbs, Andrew G b1836 m Laura
A Ba(t)chelder d/o Zephaniah
& Mary, George L b1838, 1 son
dy, Caroline A b1848 dy, Mary
R b1842; NH-0004-502 & 513
Thomas; s/o Capt Samuel of
Canterbury NH; m1787 Comfort
Perkins; liv Loudon NH; ch
Polly, Samuel m Charlotte
Foster, Joanna, Alexander m
Mary Page of New Hampton,
Samuel (Stephen) m Mary L
Greeley, Sophronia m Jacob A
Potter of Concord, Comfort m
William A W Neal of Concord,
Thomas dy, Myra m Joseph N
Wadleigh of Loudon; NH-0004-
502 & 513
William; s/o Col Jonathan; ch
William m --- Gilman, Coffin,
Harvey, Peter; NH-0003-241
William; s/o William; m ---
Gilman sis/o Col Peter of
Stratham NH; liv Stratham; ch
William, Coffin b1739 m
Comfort Weeks, Peter, Henry,
John; NH-0003-241
William; b1780; m Mary Thomas
of Sanbornton; liv Sanborn-
ton, Dorchester, Wentworth
NH; ch William H b1818, 6
others; NH-0007-640
MOREY,
Benjamin; liv Norton MA, Lyme
NH; ch Gideon b1777 m Ada
Cutting, Lucinda m James
Dayton of Orford; NH-0007-536
Gideon; b1777 s/o Benjamin; m
Ada Cutting; liv Lyme NH; ch
Bethiah, Benjamin, Fanny m
--- Carpenter, 4 others; NH-
0007-536
MORISON,
John; liv Aberdeenshire SCO,
Londonderry IRE, Londonderry
NH; ch Charter James; NH-
0003-564
Lt Samuel; s/o Charter James;
liv Windham; ch Dea Samuel;
NH-0003-564
MORRELL,
Charles; s/o John & Harriet
Brown gs/o John; m Olive C
Dean of Springfield NH; liv
Grafton NH; ch Warren C,
Alfred A, Lucian P, Olive L,
Anna; NH-0007-285
Micajah; s/o Micajah; m Sally
Shaw of Chichester; ch James

MORRELL (continued)
m Lovina Stoning d/o George &
Nancy; NH-0007-558
Theophilus E; s/o Benjamin &
Lovey Drew gs/o Samuel Drew;
m Mary Thorn d/o Nathan &
Elizabeth James; ch Rev
Theophilus E A m Eliza Brown
d/o Jeremiah & Mary Jones;
NH-0007-214
MORRILL,
---; m Annie Lawrence d/o David
& Annie Gordon; ch David
Lawrence, Samuel; NH-0003-243
Aaron; s/o Jacob; ch Elijah
(Abijah), Theodate, Aaron Jr,
Theodate, Susannah, Henry,
Judith, Joannah, Thomas; NH-
0003-203
Amos; b1796 s/o Benjamin &
Sarah Currier of E Kingston;
m Sarah E Nichols d/o Enoch
of Amesbury MA; liv E
Kingston; ch Mary Ann m D E
Eastman of Manchester, George
N, Charles E b1832 m Adeline
S Carter, Sarah E m Andrew
Hoyt of Newton NH, Laura O m
F J Philbrock of E Kingston,
Allan Amos dy; NH-0003-203
Barnard; liv Brentwood & Gil-
ford NH; ch Gen J J; NH-0004-
744
Benjamin; b1707 s/o Elijah
(Abijah) of Salisbury MA; m
Abigail --- b1711; ch Hannah
b1732, Sarah b1738, Benjamin
b1741, John b1743 m Mollie
Rogers, Samuel b1745, Samuel
b1749; NH-0003-203
Benjamin; b1770 s/o John &
Mollie Rogers of E Kingston;
m Sarah Currier of S Hampton;
liv E Kingston; ch Amos b1796
m Sarah E Nichols, Stephen
b1801 m Emily A Barstow,
Benjamin L, George W, Sally m
John Sweatt of Kingston & m
Jeremiah Leavitt of Gilmanton
NH, Betsey m Bernard French,
Emily m John Lovering of
Kensington, Polly dy; NH-
0003-203
Charles E; b1832 s/o Amos &
Sarah E Nichols of E
Kingston; m1857 Adeline S
Carter d/o Ephraim & Susan
Hoyt of Newton NH; liv E
Kingston, Manchester; ch
Allan A b1859, Susie A b1862,
Annie S b1865; NH-0003-203

MORRILL (continued)
David; b1798 s/o Reuben &
Miriam Smith of Canterbury;
m1825 Comfort Merrill d/o
Marsten & m1843 Mrs Sally
Kimball; liv Canterbury NH;
ch/o Comfort - 6 sons, 1 dau;
ch/o Sally - 2 sons; NH-0004-
232
Elijah (Abijah); s/o Aaron; liv
Salisbury MA; ch Ezra, Anne,
Elijah Jr, Mary, Robert,
Benjamin b1707 m Abigail ---;
NH-0003-203
Ezekiel; liv S Hampton, Canter-
bury; ch David, 14 others;
NH-0004-232
Jacob; s/o Abraham; ch Ezekiel,
Hannah, Thomas, Ruth, Jacob
Jr, Aaron, Susannah; NH-0003-
203
Joel Eastman; b1836 s/o Dr
Robert S & Betsey Eastman of
Canterbury; m1863 Caroline
Warren d/o Isaiah & Ann
Walker of Fryeburg; liv
Conway NH; ch Ruth E, Lucia,
Mary, Milton; NH-0006-903
John; m Abigail Knight of
Atkinson; liv Hillsborough,
Deering; ch Joseph m
Catherine Smith, Samuel m
Rachel Sprague, Mary m Joel
Heath, Sarah m William Heath,
Abigail m Elijah Thurson,
Hannah m David Brown, John;
NH-0002-383
John; b1743 s/o Benjamin &
Abigail ---; m1766 Mollie
Rogers; liv E Kingston; ch
Ruth b1768 m --- Bachelor,
Benjamin b1770 m Sarah
Currier, John b1774 m ---
Page, Stephen m --- Martin,
Samuel b1779 m --- Nobles,
Polly b1781 m --- Currier,
Josiah m --- Hutchins; NH-
0003-203
John Barstow; b1828 s/o Stephen
& Emily A Barstow of E
Kingston; m1857 Emeline A
Follett d/o Joseph W & Mary
Bailey of E Kingston; liv E
Kingston; ch Charles B,
George F; NH-0003-203
Jonathan; b1786; liv Brentwood
NH; ch Sarah M b1834; NH-
0003-136
Dr Leonard B; b1865 s/o
Harrison; liv Moultonborough
NH; NH-0006-413

MORRILL (continued)

Reuben; s/o David; m Miriam Smith; liv Canterbury; ch David b1798 m Comfort Morrill & m Mrs Sally Kimball; NH-0004-232

Dr Samuel; bro/o Hon David L; liv Concord, Epsom; NH-0004-97

Samuel; b1803 s/o William & Elizabeth Dudley; m Lydia Sanborn of Brentwood b1802; ch Chester C b1827 m Arvilla O Robinson d/o Jonathan, Caroline F b1831; NH-0003-135

Stephen; b1801 s/o Benjamin & Sarah Currier of E Kingston; m Emily A Barstow d/o Joshua & Hannah Webster of Exeter; liv E Kingston; ch John Barstow b1828 m Emeline A Follett, Hannah L m Henry Willey, Lewis B, Emma S m Moody K Wilson of Pembroke NH; NH-0003-203

William Esq; b1735 m Lydia Trask; ch Abram, William b1768 m Mary Gordon & m Elizabeth Dudley, Nathaniel, Jonathan, Nancy, Sarah, Eleanor, 1 other; NH-0003-135

William; b1768 s/o William Esq & Lydia Trask; m Mary Gordon b1768 & m Elizabeth Dudley b1775; ch/o Mary - Nathaniel b1791 dy, Dolly b1794 m Samuel Dudley, Zebedee b1796 m Lucy Potter, Mary b1798 m Capt John Fifield; ch/o Elizabeth - Sally Dudley b1798 m Henry Marshall, Samuel b1803 m Lydia Sanborn, John Dudley b1805 m Lavinia Robinson & m Ruth Stevens, Anna b1807, William Jr b1810 m Mary Ann Tuck, Washington b1813, Frederick b1815 m Mrs Annie Hungerford; NH-0003-135

William Jr; b1810 s/o William & Elizabeth Dudley; m1838 Mary Ann Tuck; ch Catharine Louise b1839, William Henry b1842; NH-0003-135

MORRIS,

Lewis R; s/o Park & Sophia Morse of W Fairlee VT; m Lucinda B Bliss of Bradford VT; liv Lebanon; NH-0007-95

Royal; liv Orford NH, Schenectady NY; ch George R; NH-0007-566

MORRISON,

Ebenezer; liv Northfield NH; ch Thomas L, Robert G, Amos H, Liva C, Ebenezer; NH-0004-530

Hon George W; b1809 s/o James & Martha Pelton of Fairlee VT; m1838 Maria L Fitch d/o Hon Lyman of Lyme NH; liv Fairlee VT, Manchester NH, Washington DC; NH-0002-13

George; b1821 s/o William; m Susan Ricker of Bath; liv Bath NH; NH-0007-141

Gilman K; m Mary J Ladd of Holderness, liv Bethlehem, Littleton NH; ch 1 son dy, Emma J m Burton Minard; NH-0007-506

James; b1781 s/o Samuel ggs/o Charter Samuel of Londonderry; m1802 Martha Pelton d/o John of Lyme NH; liv Fairlee VT; ch Hon George W b1809 m Maria L Fitch & 1 son & 7 others; NH-0002-13

James MD; b1818; m 2; liv Peterborough NH, San Francisco CA, Quincy MA; NH-0002-668

John C; b1824; m Mary P Edwards of Laconia; liv Bethlehem, Gilmanton, Manchester, St Johnsbury & Vergennes VT, Yonkers NY, Littleton NH; ch 1 dau m Daniel W Ranlet of Bethlehem, J F; NH-0007-505

Joseph; s/o Ebenezer of Sanbornton NH; m Olive Batchelder d/o Abraham & Betsey of Loudon NH; ch Relief R m Thomas J Sanborn, Abram B, Joseph W m Hannah F Giddings; NH-0007-208

Joseph W; s/o Joseph & Olive Batchelder; m Hannah F Giddings d/o William & Sarah; liv Campton NH; ch Emily N m Fisher Ames, Mary J m Dr J M French of Milford MA, Weld, Frank L, Joseph W Jr; NH-0007-209

Leonard Allison; b1843 s/o Jeremiah & Eleanor Reed Kimball of Windham; NH-0003-564

Moses; b1732 s/o John gs/o Samuel; m Rachel Todd; liv Londonderry & Hancock NH; ch Andrew b1770; NH-0002-353

Parker I; m Martha P Marhsall d/o Micajah; liv Fairlee VT,

MORRISON (continued)

Lyme NH; ch Annaline F m Rev J D Graham, Roland M, Edson E; NH-0007-541

Samuel; liv Gilmanton & Bethlehem NH; ch John C, Gillman K, 1 dau m David Oaks, William M, 2 others; NH-0007-166

MORSE,

Alonzo F; b1856 s/o William of Campton; m1882 Mary E Jewell d/o Levi F & Maria Copp of Warren; liv Plymouth NH; ch Lenwood O; NH-0007-598

Alvah L; m Della M Pritchard; ch Myrtie M; NH-0004-504

Arthur T; m Louisa A Hart d/o George & Louisa Bailey; liv Newbury NH; ch George H, Arthur A; NH-0004-216

Caleb; s/o Stephen; liv Haverhill NH; ch Eben F m Laura Ann Whittaker, Caleb; NH-0007-357

Caleb; b1784 s/o Stephen; m1807 Polly Fairbanks b1787; ch Ruth W m Charle Goudy Smith; NH-0007-366

Charles W; b1839 s/o John Webster & Lucy Ann Gove; m1865 P Josephine Merrill of Plymouth; liv Boston; ch Alice J b1860 (1866), Florence b1869; NH-0004-209

Daniel; s/o Rev Timothy & Sally Farmer; m Hannah Gillingham; liv Newbury NH; ch Almira, Huldah, Sarah J, Sprague A; NH-0004-420

Eben F; s/o Caleb of Haverhill NH; m Laura Ann Whittaker d/o Peter; ch Caleb M, Ezra W, 1 dau m T P Blake; NH-0007-357

Edwin T; m Minnie Smith d/o Frank & Harriet B Smith of Lancaster; liv Charlestown MA; ch Frank; NH-0005-394

Gideon; m Hannah Johnson; liv Canaan NH, Haverhill MA; ch Edward, Henry m Eleanor Doton; NH-0007-262

Harris E; s/o Moses Jr & Sally Emery; m1842 Sarah A Eaton; ch Mary A, Sarah A, Harris F, Mary E, Alvah L; NH-0004-504

Harvey C; s/o Joseph & Sarah Sargent; m Helen M Emerson d/o Stephen; ch Sarah L, Frank P, Almira J, Elmer E, Anna G, Page C; NH-0004-420

MORSE (continued)

Henry; s/o Gideon & Hannah Johnson; m Eleanor Doton of Canaan; liv Enfield NH; ch John H, Frank B; NH-0007-262

John C; b1874 s/o Stephen & Sally Kay; m Nancy Wheelock; liv N Haverhill NH; ch Sarah m Amasa P Niles, Louisa K m Moses W Burnham, Mary Ann m W S Cobleigh, Isaac L, Martha L m L T Whitcomb, Alfred, John Nelson b1818 m Kate Southard, Nancy B, Harriet N m Warren J Fisher; NH-0007-357

John Nelson; b1818 s/o John C & Mary Wheelock of N Haverhill NH; m1865 Kate Southard d/o Aaron & Jane Finley; liv N Haverhill NH; ch Katie b1868, John b1872; NH-0007-357

John Webster; b1806 s/o Josiah & Betsey Brown of Henniker NH; m1835 Lucy Ann Gove b1812 d/o Hon Jonathan & Polly Fisher of Acworth NH; liv Weare & Henniker & Bradford NH; ch John G b1836, Charles W b1839 m P Josephine Merrill, Mary E b1843 m1877 Nathaniel F Lund; NH-0004-208 & 209

Joseph; b1795 s/o Rev Timothy & Sally Fisher; m Sarah Sargent d/o William; liv Newbury; ch Joseph Jr m Seba A Thissell, Timothy m Mary Bly & m Hannah Peaslee, Harvey C m Helen M Emerson, Mary J dy, Seth A m Mary A Hoag, Laura L m Ezra Cilley; NH-0004-420

Joseph Jr; s/o Joseph & Sarah Sargent; m Seba A Thissell; ch Sarah C, Mary J; NH-0004-420

Rev Joseph B; b1814 s/o John of Amnesty; m1837 Maria Ripley of Barre VT; liv Hanover NH; NH-0007-333

Josiah; m1773 Lois Webster of Chester NH; ch Josiah m Betsey Brown; NH-0004-209

Josiah; s/o Josiah & Lois Webster; m1798 Betsey Brown d/o Thomas & Persis Gibson; liv Henniker NH; ch John Webster b1806 m Lucy Ann Gove; NH-0004-209

Leonard; m Lydia Walker of Lisbon; liv Windham, Lisbon NH; ch Wilton, Horace, John

MORSE (continued)

dy, John W m Adelia B Dexter, Jane m James Richardson of Littleton, Cordelia m Lowell Moulton of Portland ME, Edina G m Byron A Clark of Easton, Sarah m John H Cameron; NH-0007-445

Moses Sr; b1749; m Abigail Lovejoy b1755 of Andover MA; liv Methuen MA, Loudon NH; ch Abigail, Jonathan, Persis, Moses, Lydia, Moses Jr b1788 m Sally Emery, Deborah, Persis, Levi, Isaac; NH-0004-504

Moses Jr; b1788 s/o Moses Sr & Abigail Lovejoy; m1815 Sally Emery; ch Harris E m Sarah A Eaton, Alvah L, Julianna P; NH-0004-504

Parker; m Love ---; liv Deering; ch Parker, Lovy, Joseph, Josiah, Samuel, Deliverence, Mary, Sarah; NH-0002-385

Seth; s/o Joseph & Sarah Sargent; m Mary A Hoag; ch Sarah O, Marshall W, George M, Laura V, Lilla B, Forestall; NH-0004-420

Stephen; s/o Rev Timothy & Sally Farmer; m Lydia Gillingham; ch David M, Charles M, Sarah E; 3 others; NH-0004-420

Stephen; bro/o Isaac & Jacob of Hebron NH; liv Haverhill NH; ch Marcellus J, 1 dau m A C Foster, 1 dau m George Wells, 1 dau m L C Wells, Melvina m Levi Bisbee; NH-0007-357

Capt Stephen; b1751; m Sarah Bailey of FRA; liv Newburyport MA, Haverhill; ch Moses N; NH-0007-143

Stephen; bro/o Capt Edward; m Sally Kay; liv Bradford MA, Haverhill NH; ch Bryant, John C b1874 m Nancy Wheelock, 10 others; NH-0007-357

Stephen N; m Elizabeth Gordon d/o Moses of Gilmanton & m Mrs Jane L Drew d/o John & Anna Goodwin; ch Lizzie m --- Pulcifer, Amy, William, Henry, Bertha; NH-0007-129.

Timothy; m Sally Farmer; liv Fisherfield NH; ch Susannah B m Moses Morse, Moses m Betsey Cheney, Daniel m Hannah

MORSE (continued)

Gillingham, Joseph b1795 m Sarah Sargent, Timothy m Eliza Adams, Stephen m Lydia Gillingham, Sally dy, Sally m Stephen Emerson; NH-0004-420

Timothy; s/o Joseph & Sarah Sargent; m Mary Bly & m Hannah Peaslee; ch/o Mary - John W, 1 other; ch/o Hannah - Etta; NH-0004-420

MORTON,

Charles F; s/o Leander S & Martha L Hawkes of Conway NH; m Emma O Pratt; ch Martha E; NH-0006-901

Frederick W; b1852 s/o Leander S & Martha L Hawkes of Conway NH; m Fannie M Wiley; ch Annie L, Frederick L, Margaret, Ruth; NH-0006-901

George; liv York ENG, Leyden HOL, Plymouth MA; ch Nathaniel b1613; NH-0006-901

Leander S; b1819 s/o William & Mary Rich of Standish ME; m1844 Martha L Hawkes d/o Benjamin & Lucy Fogg of Buxton ME; liv Conway NH; ch Mary Ellen m Jeremiah Farrington, Frederick W b1852 m Fannie M Wiley, Charles F m Emma O Pratt; NH-0006-901

William H; b1814 s/o William & Sarah Griffith of Portsmouth NH; m1841 Sarah P Merriam of Grafton MA & m1851 Armine Leavitt of York ME & m1867 Mary Shackford of Portsmouth NH; liv Salmon Falls, Somersworth, Blackstone MA; ch/o Sarah - Etta m John Merriam, 2 others; ch/o Armine - Frederick H, William A, Sarah J; NH-0003-678

MOSES,

Eliza L; m Berkley Keysar d/o John & Sarah Clark Wiswall; ch Lula E, Clyde W, Lottie M, Jesse L; NH-0005-695

John F; b1792 s/o Theodore of Exeter; m1815 Mary S Pearson & m Abby C Boyd; liv Exeter; ch/o Mary - 2 sons, 3 dau, 3 others; NH-0003-295

MOSHER,

Ira C; m1878 Mary F Phelps d/o Nathan O & Harriet Lucas of Groton; ch Harvey, Myron H, Gracie M; NH-0007-291

MOULTON,

Dr Albert Alonzo; b1829 s/o Jonathan & Mary Morse of Meredith NH; m1850 Anna Maria Sawyer of Bristol; liv Meredith & Concord & Tilton NH; ch Arthur C; NH-0004-885

Dr Alvah; b1798; m1821 Mary Dalton d/o Mary; liv Parsons-field ME, Ossipee NH; ch 6 son, 6 dau; NH-0006-630

Ausbry C; s/o Lewman G & Mary Marston of Ossipee NH; m Minnie Parsons of Freedom; ch Lisle O; NH-0006-626

Capt Benjamin; b1721; m Sarah --- b1721; liv Hampton Falls; ch Benjamin b1743 m Mary Sanborn & m Elizabeth Rowe, Thomas, Jemima; NH-0003-365

Benjamin; b1743 s/o Capt Benjamin & Sarah; m Mary Sanborn & m Elizabeth Rowe d/o Joseph of Kensington NH; liv Kensington; ch/o Mary - 10; ch/o Elizabeth - Betsey, Capt Benjamin b1795 m Mehitable Brown, Joseph; NH-0003-365

Capt Benjamin; b1795 s/o Benjamin & Elizabeth Rowe of Kensington; m1817 Mehitable Brown b1792 d/o John of Hampton Falls; liv Kensing-ton; ch Elizabeth b1819, Benjamin G b1821, Hannah S b1824; NH-0003-365

Benning; b1761 s/o Gen Jonathan & Abigial Smith; m1782 Sally Lovett(Leavitt); liv Center Harbor NH; ch Nancy m Jonathan Moulton, Jonathan Smith b1785 m Deborah Neal, Thomas L, Benning, John H, Elizabeth m Daniel Hilton; NH-0001-114, NH-0004-825

Edwin Carroll; b1834 s/o Hon John Carroll & Nellie B Senter; m Augusta Ranlet d/o Charles of Laconia; ch Nelly Augusta; NH-0001-117

Gabriel G; b1810; m Sophia Walker of Lyman & m Hannah Hoskins of Lyman; liv Lyman, Littleton NH; ch Moses W, Ansel A, Ellen S m Joel Eastman, Minerva m David Weeks of Concord VT, Louisa W m Augustus Hill of Holden IL; NH-0007-499

Gilman; b1825 s/o Joseph &

MOULTON (continued)

Phoebe Chase; m Abbie T Quimby d/o John S & Nancy & m Lydia A Dearborn d/o Warren & Eliza; liv Sandwich NH; ch/o Lydia - Warren J; NH-0006-675

Jacob; b1688 s/o John & Lydia Taylor; b1714 Sarah Smith; ch Sarah, Lydia, Nathan, Dorothy, Gen Jonathan b1726 m Abigail Smith, John; NH-0004-825

John; bc1599; m Anne ---; liv ENG, Newbury MA, Hampton NH; ch Henry, Mary, Anna, Jane, Bridget, John b1638 m Lydia Taylor, Ruth; NH-0004-825

John; b1638 s/o John & Anne --- ; m Lydia Taylor d/o Anthony; liv Newbury MA; ch Martha, John, Lydia, Daniel, James, Nathan, David, Anna, Lydia, Jacob b1688 m Sarah Smith, Rachel; NH-0004-825

John b1796; m Susan Davis of Newfield; liv Newfield ME; ch Lydia A, Lorenzo D b1827 m Abbie C Merrow, John B, Emily W; NH-0006-620

Hon John Carroll; b1810 s/o Jonathan Smith & Deborah Neal; m1833 Nellie B Senter s/o Samuel M & m1866 Sarah A McDougal; liv Center Harbor, Meredith Bridge & Sandwich & Laconia NH; ch/o Nellie - Edwin Carroll b1834 m Augusta Ranlet, Samuel Moore Senter b1837 m Martha B Thurston, Wiliam Hale b1844 dy, Horatio Francis b1848 m Ella S Melcher 3 ch, Ida Lettice b1850 m Josua B Holden; NH-0001-114, NH-0004-825

Col John Hale; b1795 s/o Benning & Sally Leavitt of Centre Harbor NH gs/o Gen Jonathan; m1832 Susan Sargent d/o Rev Huntington Porter of Rye NH; liv Hampton & Centre Harbor NH; ch Franklin Hale dy, Oliver Porter dy, Susan Huntington m Smith F Emery; NH-0004-727

John S; b1772 s/o John b1731; m Lucy Hubbard; liv Moulton-borough NH; ch John H b1817, 1 dau m George Lee, Hattie; NH-0006-404

Gen Jonathan; b1726 s/o Jacob & Sarah Smith; m Abigail Smith;

MOULTON (continued)
liv Hampton & Moultonborough & Centre Harbor NH; ch Benning b1761 m Sally Lovett; NH-0001-114, NH-0004-825
Jonathan Smith; b1785 s/o Benning & Sally Leavitt; m Deborah Neal; liv Center Harbor NH; ch Hon John Carroll b1810 m Nellie B Senter & m Sarah A McDougall; NH-0001-114, NH-0004-825
Joseph; s/o Robert of Gilford; m Phoebe Chase d/o John Jr; liv Albany, Sandwich; ch Gilman b1825 m Abbie T Quimby & m Lydia A Dearborn, 6 others; NH-0006-675
Lafayette; b1859 s/o Lorenzo D & Abbie C Merrow of Moultonville; m Mattie A Manson; liv Moultonville NH; ch Lorenzo Dow; NH-0006-620
Lewman G; s/o Mark & Sophia Tibbetts; m Mary Marston d/o Jeremiah of W Ossipee; liv Ossipee NH; ch Mary E m Charles Ayers of Wolfeborough, Ausbry C m Minnie Parsons; NH-0006-626
Lorenzo D; b1827 s/o John & Susan Davis; m Abbie C Merrow; liv Moultonville NH; ch Lafayette b1859 m Mattie A Manson; NH-0006-620
Mark; m Sophia Tibbetts; liv Newfield ME, Ossipee NH; ch Lewman G m Mary Marston; NH-0006-626
Noah; liv Lyman & Rye NH; ch William, Noah Jr, Job, Jonathan, Daniel, David, John; NH-0007-513
Oliff Cecil; bc1849 s/o Hon Lewman G; NH-0006-265
Samuel Moore Senter; b1837 s/o Hon John Carroll & Nellie B Senter; m Martha B Thurston d/o Benjamin F; liv Laconia NH; NH-0001-117
Simeon; m Sally Parsons of Parsonsfield ME & m ?; liv Newfield ME; ch/o Sally - Mark, John; ch/o ? - Simeon, Samuel, Lyrena, William m Sally Smith, Charles, Joseph, Francis; NH-0006-626
William; s/o Simeon & ?; m Sally Smith d/o Dea Daniel; liv Ossipee NH; ch Jabez S, Mary C m Dea E W Ambrose,

MOULTON (continued)
Luther, Daniel S, Rhoda M, William H, Alvin A; NH-0006-626
MUCHMORE,
Alonzo D MD; b1840 s/o James & Sarah J Buntin of Orford; m Effie L Cross of Piermont; liv Campton NH; ch James Christie b1871; NH-0007-210
James; s/o James; liv Northfield NH, Orford; ch James; NH-0007-576
James; b1810 s/o James of Northfield NH gs/o James of Isle of Shoals NH; m Sarah J Buntin d/o James; liv Orford; ch Alonzo D MD b1840 m Effie L Cross; NH-0007-210
MUNSEY,
Dr George W; m Hannah Barton of Epsom; liv Centre Harbor & Gilford NH; ch Barton, George W, Benjamin, William, Amos Prescot, David Hall, 1 dau m Rev Josiah Gilman of Lynn MA, 5 dau; NH-0004-745
MURPHY,
Hon Charles M; b1835 s/o John & Mary M Meader of Alton NH; mc1857 Sabrina T Clark d/o Isaac Esq of Barnstead NH & m Mrs Eliza T Hanson wid/o John T of Dover NH; liv Barnstead & Dover NH; NH-0001-67, NH-0003-877
John; m Mary A Meader; liv Alton & Barnstead NH ch Hon Charles M b1835 m Sabrina T Clark & Eliza T Hanson, John E, Frank MD, Albert Warren DDS; NH-0001-67, NH-0003-877
MURRAY,
Charles O; s/o Orlando Dana & Mary J Wetherbee of Nashua; m Lulu Bemis; ch George Bemis, Lilian Cushman; NH-0002-205
David; b1775 s/o Isaac & Elizabeth Durham; m1807 Margaret Forsyth of Chester NH d/o Lt Robert & gd/o Dea Matthew; liv Chester & Nahua NH, Hartland VT, Belfast ME; ch Emeline Johnson b1808 m Dea William Tenney, Laurana Tolford b1810 dy, Marietta b1816 m Charles C Flagg of Mobile AL, Orlando Dana b1818 m Mary J Wetherbee; NH-0002-203
George Washington AM; b1830 s/o John & Mary of Hill; liv E

MURRAY (continued)
Canaan; NH-0007-74
Isaac; m Elizabeth Durham d/o
John gd/o Mary Tolford; liv
SCO, Londonderry NH, Belfast
ME; ch David b1775 m Margaret
Forsyth & m 2 others,
Jonathan b1775, 2 others;
NH-0002-203
Levi Edwin; s/o Orlando Dana &
Mary J Wetherbee of Nashua; m
Jane Russell Hopkins; liv
Springfield MA, Ogdensburg
NY; ch Marie Louise, Charles
Russell, Lizzie Crombie; NH-
0002-205
Orlando Dana; b1818 s/o David &
Margaret Forsyth of Hartland
VT; m1842 Mary J Wetherbee
b1821 d/o Solomon & Sarah;
liv Nashua; ch George Dana,
Sara L m William A Crombie,
Levi Edwin m Jane Russell
Hopkins, Albert C, Clarence
A, Charles O m Lulu Bemis;
NH-0002-203
MUSGROVE,
James; b1796; m1827 Ann Donker
of London ENG; liv ENG,
Boston MA, Bristol NH; ch
Susan, Richard W b1840,
William I, John H, Charles M,
Sarah M C, Abbott C, 4
others; NH-0007-194
MUSSEY,
Reuben D MD LLD; b1780; m Mary
Sewell of Ipswich MA & m
Hitty Osgood of Salem MA; liv
Pelham, Peterborough, Salem
MA; NH-0002-667
MUZZEY,
Craig; m Margaret Anderson d/o
William & Margaret Clark; liv
Weare, Deering; ch Mary Eliza
m Alfred Locke, William m
Mary Griffin, Martha m Horace
Cressey, Sarah, Diamond dy,
Ervin; NH-0002-382

-N-

NASON,
Ephraim; m Sally Wolcott; liv
Eaton NH; ch Newell, Justus,
Alanson, Melvin P, Emily m
Henry Day, Caroline m John W
Perkins, Melvina m Alvin
Snow, Arvilla m Asahel
Barrows, Laura, Maria m
Joseph Valley; NH-0006-791

NEAL,
John; b1777; m Betsey Sawyer of
Lee; liv S Newmarket, London
NH; ch Sarah C b1808 m
Jonathan Burley, 7 others;
NH-0003-403
Moses Leavitt; b1767 s/o John
of Hampton; liv Londonderry,
Rochester, Dover; NH-0003-589
NELSON,
Capt John; m Rachel Franklin
sis/o Jonathan; liv Norton
MA, Lyme NH; ch William C m
Sarah Shapin, George, 5 dau;
NH-0007-535
John; b1778; m Susannah
Brewster d/o Ebenezer of
Hanover & m Lois Everett of
Windsor VT; liv Exeter,
Haverhill; ch/o ? - 11; NH-
0007-82
Levi; m Sarah Evans of Salis-
bury; liv Bridgewater; ch 14;
NH-0007-190
Robert; bro/o William; liv Rye-
gate VT, Lyman & Monroe NH;
ch Hannah m Connor Paddleford
of Monroe, Ruth m --- Paddle-
ford, Nathan, Alice m ---
Clisby, 10 others; NH-0007-
552
William C; s/o Capt John &
Rachel Franklin; m Sarah
Chapin d/o John; liv Lyme NH;
ch John, 6 others; NH-0007-
535
NESMITH,
Arthur; b1721 s/o Dea James &
Elizabeth McKeen; m Margaret
Hopkins; liv IRE & London-
derry NH; ch John, 1 son; NH-
0001-180
Hon George Washington LLD;
b1800 s/o Jonathan & Eleanor
Dickey; m1826 Mary M Brooks
b1799 s/o Samuel & Annie
Bedel of Haverhill gd/o Gen
Timothy Bedel; liv Franklin
NH; ch George Brooks b1831,
Arthur Sidney b1833 m Mary E
Moulder of Washington DC,
Annie b1841; NH-0001-180, NH-
0004-36
Dea James; bc1702 (b1692);
m1714 Elizabeth McKeen d/o
James & Janet Cochran; liv
Antrim IRE, Londonderry NH;
ch Arthur dy, James Jr b1718
m Mary Dinsmore, Arthur b1721
m Margaret Hopkins, Jean
b1723, Mary b1726, John b1728

NESMITH (continued)
m Elizabeth Reed, Elizabeth
b1730, Thomas b1732, Benjamin
b1734; NH-0001-180, NH-0004-
36

James Jr; b1718 s/o Dea James &
Elizabeth McKeen; m Mary
Dinsmore; liv Londonderry NH;
ch James b1744 m Mary
McClure, Dea Jonathan b1759 m
Elenor Dickey & m Mrs Sarah
Wetherbee Hamblin, Robert m
Jane Anderson, Elizabeth m
James Cochran, Mary m James
McClure, Sarah m Daniel
Anderson; NH-0001-180, NH-
0004-36

James III; b1744 s/o James Jr &
Mary Dinsmore; m Mary
McClure; liv Londonderry NH;
ch William M m Harriet
Willis, Robert, Isaac, James,
Martha, Jane W, Margaret; NH-
0001-180

James; b1783 s/o Jonathan &
Elenor Dickey; m1810 Polly
Taylor & m Mrs Susan Clark;
liv Londonderry NH, Solon NY,
Waukon IA; ch Mary b1811 dy,
Mary E b1812 m John Stillman;
Rev John T G b1814 m Harriet
N Taylor, Hannah E b1816 m
John Reed, Abigail S b1818 m
Isaac Barker, Mark W b1820 m
Laura Post, George W b1825 m
Mary C Farrar, Dr Milton W
b1828 m Margaret Donoughue,
Woodbury T b1852; NH-0001-182

John; b1728 s/o Dea James &
Elizabeth McKeen; m Elizabeth
Reed sis/o Gen George of
Londonderry NH; liv London-
derry NH; ch James of Antrim,
John Jr m Susan Hildreth & m
Lydia Sargent; Ebenezer m
Jane Trotter, Thomas, Eliza-
beth m Dea James Pinkerton,
Mary m John Miltimore of
Reading PA, Jane m Hugh
Anderson; NH-0001-180

Jonathan; b1759 s/o James Jr &
Mary Dinsmore of Londonderry
NH; m1781 Elenor Dickey b1761
d/o Adam & Jane Strahan of
Londonderry NH gd/o John &
Margaret Dickey of London-
derry IRE & m Mrs Sarah
Wetherbee Hamblin of Concord
MA; liv Londonderry NH,
Antrim; ch James b1783 m
Polly Taylor & m Mrs Susan

NESMITH (continued)
Clark, Jean/Jane b1787 m John
Dunlap, Thomas b1789 m Martha
Weeks & m Nancy Gregg, Adam
b1792 m Rebecca Dale, Mary D
b1794, Margaret b1796,
Isabell b1798, Hon George
Washington LLD b1800 m Mary M
Brooks; NH-0001-181, NH-0004-
36

Jonathan; b1816 s/o Capt Thomas
D & Martha Weeks; m1841
Marietta F Morrill of
Franklin NH; liv Londonderry
& Hancock NH; ch Jennie
b1842, Thomas S b1848 dy,
Fannie H b1848 m Frank H
Baldwin, Annie M T b1852,
Abbie Isabel b1854 dy, Miles
G b1857, Addie M b1860, John
S b1863; NH-0001-183

Robert W; b1814 s/o Capt Thomas
D & Martha Weeks; m1839 Olive
Dunlap; liv Jefferson TX; ch
Oriette, Sally V m Com
Decatur Morris; NH-0001-183

Thomas; b1732 s/o Dea James &
Elizabeth McKeen; m Annis
Wilson; liv Londonderry NH;
John, Elizabeth, Thomas Jr;
NH-0001-181

Capt Thomas D; b1789 s/o
Jonathan & Elenor Dickey;
m1813 Martha Weeks & m1830
Nancy Gregg; liv Londonderry
NH; ch Robert W b1814 m Olive
Dunlap, Jonathan b1816 m
Marietta F Morrill, Sarah E
b1818 m John W Buttick, Miles
b1821, Harriet F b1823 m
Walker Flanders, Martha J
b1825 m Isaac P Cochran,
Melvin b1830, Hiram G b1833,
Nancy R b1836 m Josiah
Melville; NH-0001-182

William M; s/o James III & Mary
McClure; m Harriet Willis; ch
Hon James W b1820 m Pauline
Goff; NH-0001-180

NEVINS,
William; liv Newton MA, W Dunstable; ch William, Joseph,
Benjamin, John, Phineas; NH-
0002-438

William Jr; b1746 s/o William;
m1768 Rebecca Chamberlain;
liv Hollis; NH-0002-453

NEWELL,
Joseph; b1794; m Lavina Hopkins
d/o Col Samuel of Wilmington
MA; liv Reading MA, Wilton

NEWELL (continued)
NH; ch C H, George A; NH-0002-722
NICHOLS,
Benjamin T; s/o Aaron of Enfield; liv Enfield & Canaan NH; ch Henry A, Helen A, Mandana, Elvin A; NH-0007-263
Frederick Gilman; b1798 s/o Nicholas Jr & Catherine Sanborn; m1823 Sarah Williams d/o N P & Sarah Nichols of Roxbury MA; liv Kingston; ch Sarah W, Stephen Frederic b1829 m Sarah E Chase, Elihu T; NH-0003-387
Jonathan S; b1809; m Myra M Montgomery d/o Gen John & m Elizabeth S Page d/o Samuel; liv Kingston & Haverhill NH; ch/o Myra - George E, Nellie P, 4 others; ch/o Elizabeth - Clara I; NH-0007-366
Nicholas Jr; b1762 s/o Nicholas of Exeter; mc1785 Catherine Sanborn d/o Dea Jonathan & Lydia; liv Kingston; ch True W, Oliver P, Stephen W, Frederick Gilman b1798 m Sarah Williams, Nicholas, Catherine m Nath Brown, Jonathan, 4 others; NH-0003-387
Stephen Frederick; b1829 s/o Frederic Gilman & Sarah William of Kingston; m1861 Sarah E Chase d/o Amos & Hannah P Hook; liv Kingston; ch Perrin W b1865, Clara b1867, Stephen W b1874; NH-0003-387
NICKERSON,
Henry; b1795 s/o Nathaniel; m Nancy Doe b1794 d/o John of Effingham; liv Tamworth NH; ch Hannah m John Shackford & m Jeremiah Marston, Melissa, John H m Clarinda Snell d/o Eleazer of Madison, Alonzo m Melissa Ham d/o James of Albany; NH-0006-765
Nathaniel; liv Cape Cod, Ossipee & Tamworth NH; ch Joshua, Henry b1795 m Nancy Doe, Polly m Stephen Allard, Thankful m Nathaniel Currier; NH-0006-765
NILES,
Benjamin H; b1800 s/o Dea John; m Martha Savage; liv Orford NH, Newbury VT; ch B F, E H,

NICKERSON (continued)
Martha m --- Stone, 1 dau m --- Gardner, 5 others; NH-0007-563
Dea John; liv Portsmouth, Orford NH; ch Capt Nathaniel, Benjamin H b1800 m Martha Savage, 9 others; NH-0007-563
NOIS,
Parker; m Dorcas McCoy & m 2 others; ch Russel T m Mary Currier & m Sarah J Forsaith; NH-0002-382
NORCROSS,
Hon Amasa; b1824 s/o Daniel & Mary Jones; m1852 S Augusta Wallis d/o Benjamin & Rebecca; liv Rindge NH & Fitchburg MA; NH-0001-38
NORRIS,
Benjamin R; b1810; m Pamelia Stark of Hanover; liv Corinth VT, Hanover; ch John A m Phebe Jessaman & m Mrs Hannah Ellenwood, Ira B m Carrie Leavitt, Hattie M m Edward Colburn, Jennie M m L W Aldrich of Westmoreland NH, David P m Emma Wood of Hartland VT, Elvina m Henry H Woodard of Duxbury MA, Abbie m Henry H Bailey of Glover VT; NH-0007-238
Clark C; b1826 s/o March & Polly Sleeman of Corinth VT; liv Colebrook NH; NH-0005-600
James C; b1854 s/o James Shepard & Mary E Palmer; m1876 Minnie Parker Wiggin d/o Augustus & Mary Jane of Concord; ch Mabel Parker b1877, Orra b1878, Ethel b1881, James Shepard b1884; NH-0004-161
James D; b1785 s/o Thomas of Epping NH; m Mary Pike Norris b1785 of Epping; liv Epping; ch Maria H b1809, James Shepard b1812 m Caroline M Hillard & m Mary E Palmer, Mary E b1825; NH-0004-161
James Shepard; b1812 s/o James D & Mary Pike Norris of Epping NH; m1840 Caroline M Hillard d/o Dr Timothy & Sarah of Northwood NH & m1850 Mary E Palmer d/o Wesley & Harriet of Concord; liv Concord & Epping NH; ch/o Caroline - Ellen G b1844 m George W Crockett; ch/o Mary

NORRIS (continued)
- James C b1854 m Minnie Parker Wiggin; NH-0004-161
Rev Josiah; b1779; m Mary Adams of Moultonborough NH; liv Hanover; ch Huldah D m Samuel H Rollins, Josiah, 4 others; NH-0007-190
Samuel; m Sally Fraquier of Nottingham; liv Epping, Salisbury; ch William C m --- Elliott; NH-0007-76
Rev Samuel; b1801; m1823 Elizabeth H Brodhead d/o Rev John; liv Dorchester, S Newmarket NH; ch John Brodhead b1828; NH-0003-539
Thomas; b1743 s/o James gs/o John; liv Epping NH; ch James D b1785 m Mary Pike Norris; NH-0004-161
William C; s/o Samuel & Sally Fraquier; m --- Elliott of Concord; liv Salisbury, Danbury; ch William Taylor b1822; NH-0007-76
NOYES,
Amos; s/o Samuel; liv Landaff NH; ch Michael J; NH-0007-399
Asa; b1804 s/o Sylvanus & Betsey Jewitt; m Lydia Eaton of Landaff; liv Colebrook & Columbia NH; ch 1 dau m Hiram Howe, Eben, Chester, Violetta m Daniel Young, Gilman, Eleazer, Samuel P; NH-0005-617
Bela; b1794 s/o Bela of Norway ME; m Honor Prince of New Gloucester ME; liv Norway ME; ch George W, Capt Warren b1832 m Mary Elizabeth York, Robert P, Aphia E m David Pratt; NH-0005-929
Benjamin; s/o Daniel; liv Landaff; ch Patience, Sabin b1813, 4 others; NH-0007-398
Benjamin; b1797 s/o Samuel; m Olive Tewksbury of Bath; liv Landaff NH; ch Kimball W, Emily m --- Noyes, Ellen, Sarah m --- Durgin, 2 others; NH-0007-399
Benjamin; b1813 s/o David of Landaff; m Mary C Wheeler of Haverhill NH; liv Haverhill NH; ch George H, 5 others; NH-0007-362
Daniel; b1771 s/o James of Kingston; m Nancy Weare d/o Jonathan ofSpringfield NH; ch

NOYES (continued)
Hon John W b1810 m Nancy Aiken & m Clara D McFarland & m Harriet S Bouton, Rev Daniel J DD m Jane M Aiken; NH-0003-158
Rev Daniel J DD; s/o Daniel & Nancy Weare of Springfield; m Jane M Aiken sis/o Nancy; liv Hanover; ch --- m Henry L Smith of NY, --- m Prof Fairbanks, 2 sons; NH-0003-159
Dea Enoch; liv Newbury MA, Hollis; ch Enoch, Elijah; NH-0002-438
Ephraim; m Mary Thurston sis/o Phebe & Moses; liv Webster NH; ch Edna; NH-0004-685
Henry; m1871 Annie L Rogers d/o George W & Sarah Allen of Rumney; liv Rumney NH; ch Allen R b1875; NH-0007-611
James C; b1820 s/o Rufus of Landaff; m Betsey E Coggswell of Landaff & m Maria E Bowles of Lisbon; liv Bath NH; ch/o Betsey - Arabella F m Timothy B Southard of Swiftwater; NH-0007-143
Hon John W; b1810 s/o Daniel & Nancy Weare of Springfield; m1836 Nancy Aiken of Chester & m1842 Clara D McFarland b1822 d/o Rev Dr of Concord NH & m1855 Harriet S Bouton b1832 d/o Rev Dr of Concord NH & gd/o Gov John Bell; liv Chester; ch/o Nancy - Isabella Aiken b1838 m Prof John E Sinclair; ch/o Clara - Elizabeth McFarland b1844 m William S Greenough, Nancy S A b1847, 2 dy; ch/o Harriet - Mary Bell b1858, John Weare b1867 dy; NH-0003-158
Jonathan; liv Plaistow, Landaff NH; ch David W, Moor R b1798, Jacob, 4 others; NH-0007-398
Moor R; b1798 s/o Jonathan; liv Landaff NH; ch Fred P, John B; NH-0007-398
Moses; s/o John of Springfield NH; m Susan C Whitmore d/o Ebenezer & Elizabeth; ch Eben E, Lydia A, Mary J, Charles M, Florilla S, William H m Lucy A Hoyt; NH-0007-120
Rufus; s/o Nathaniel & Mary Harriman; m Hannah Clarke; liv Landaff NH; ch Hon Col Amos C b1818 m Rebecca J

NOYES (continued)
Stewart of Hill Hall PA,
James C, Hannah M, Rufus H,
Charles R, Jane C m W B
Blandin; NH-0007-399
Sabin; b1813 s/o Benjamin of
Landaff; liv Landaff NH; ch
Simon C, 1 dau m --- Kay; NH-
0007-398
Samuel; s/o Samuel; liv Landaff
NH; ch 1 dau m Darius George
of Lisbon, Samuel; NH-0007-
399
Sylvanus; b1769; m Betsey
Jewitt b1770 of Landaff; liv
Maidstone VT, Colebrook &
Plaistow NH; ch John, Mary m
Jeremy George, Michael,
Mehitable m Reuben Ash, Asa
b1804 m Lydia Eaton, Hobart m
Sarah Beecher; NH-0005-617
Capt Warren; b1832 s/o Bela &
Honor Prince of Norway ME;
m1856 Mary Elizabeth York d/o
Joseph & Abigail Cummings of
Norway ME; liv Gorham NE; ch
Abbie F, Fred M, Harry G; NH-
0005-929
William H; s/o Moses & Susan C
Whitmore; m Lucy A Hoyt d/o
Asa & Olive G Hogdon of E
Canaan; liv Alexandria NH; ch
Harry; NH-0007-120
NURSE,
Oliver; b1796; m Polly Fitz-
gerald of Gilmanton; liv
Littleton NH; ch John C,
Albert L, Charles H, Sarah A
m T D Fitzgerald, Samuel P,
William C, Thomas S m Maria C
Streeter of Lisbon, 3 others;
NH-0007-485
NUTE,
Alonzo; b1826 s/o David &
Lovina Cook of Milton; m1850
Mary Pearl b1829 d/o Joseph &
Betsey of Milton; liv
Farmington, Natick MA; ch
Eugene P b1852 m1881 Nellie
Packer of Farmington, Alonzo
I b1853; NH-0003-631
Daniel; liv Jackson NH; ch
Nancy, William (name changed
to Gates), James, John,
Isaac, Daniel; NH-0006-954
David; b1797 s/o Jotham & Sarah
Twombly; m Lovina Cook d/o
Peter of Wakefield NH; liv
Milton; ch Alonzo b1826 m
Mary Pearl, Jeremy O, Leander
M, David H; NH-0003-631

NUTE (continued)
Ezekiel; b1794 s/o Samuel of
Dover; m1815 Dorcas Worster;
liv Milton; ch Cyrus W, Lewis
Worster b1820 m1845 Priscilla
Farrow b1819, Isaac F, Samuel
F; NH-0003-657
James; s/o James of Portsmouth;
m Elizabeth Heard d/o Capt
John & Elizabeth Hull; NH-
0003-772
Jotham; b1760; m1786 Sarah
Twombly of Dover; liv Dover,
Milton; ch John, Jeremy,
Jacob, Sarah m William Allen
of Rochester, David b1797 m
Lovina Cook, Israel, Daniel,
Ivory, Levi, Andrew T,
Sophia; NH-0003-631
NUTTER,
Eliphalet; s/o Maj John of
Barnstead; m1807 Lovey Locke
d/o James; liv Barnstead NH;
ch Eliphalet Simes b1819 m
Sylvania M Blanchard, 1 son;
NH-0004-151
Eliphalet Simes; b1819 s/o
Eliphalet & Lovey Locke of
Barnstead NH; m1845 Sylvania
M Blanchard of Lowell; liv
Barnstead & Concord NH; ch
Ada dy; NH-0004-151
Joshua M; b1818; m Sarah Heath
of Bath; liv Portsmouth,
Boston, Bath NH; ch Joseph M
m Sarah French, William S,
Joshua, Walter, Sarah,
Corinne, Nathan, James H; NH-
0007-143
Matthias; b1740; m Mary Folsom
& m 2 others; liv Newington;
ch/o Mary - Elizabeth,
William White b1808 m Frances
I Dow Brackett, Lovina, Sarah
J, Alfred dy, Alfred, Olive
P; NH-0003-394
William White; b1808 s/o
Matthias of Newington; m1873
Frances I Dow Brackett d/o
Isaac Dow & wid/o Isaac
Brackett; liv Newington; NH-
0003-394

-0-

OAKES,
Henry; m Emily Mann d/o

OAKES (continued)
Solomon; liv Waterford & Fairlee VT; ch Emily Mann m Richard Peabody Kent, & 3 others; NH-0001-22

OBER,
Charles F MD; b1848; m1875 Jennie E Fifield of Milford; liv Nashua, Lowell MA; NH-0002-665

ODELL,
George H; s/o James; m Louisa Barker; ch Mary, George H, James E; NH-0003-550

James; ch James b1785 m Charlotte Hilton, Mary m Zebulon Wiggin, Eliza, George, Charlotte m --- Boyd & m Jonathan Leavitt; NH-0003-550

James; b1785 s/o James; m Charlotte Hilton d/o Daniel; liv Stratham; ch James E b1813 m Sarah E Wiggin, Sarah W m John Smart, William G dy, George H m Louisa Barker; NH-0003-550

James E; b1813 s/o James of Stratham; m1842 Sarah E Wiggin b1823 d/o Daniel & Sarah Clark of Stratham; liv Stratham; ch adopted - Belle; NH-0003-550

Joseph; m Sarah Ingalls d/o Daniel; liv Salem MA, Andover, Conway NH; ch Joseph, Pamela m --- Dresser, Richard, Sarah F m Richard Buswell, Thomas F m Elizabeth Abbott, Daniel J; NH-0006-852

Joseph; s/o Joseph & Sarah Ingalls; ch Richard K, Sarah m Ithamar Seavey, Rhoda m Stephen Shackford, Polly, Nancy, Betsey; NH-0006-852

Richard; liv Centre Conway NH; ch Lary, Fletcher, Arthur, Ruth m Joel Eastman, Almira m Alvah Conant, Hannah m Rev Daniel B Randall; NH-0006-852

Thomas F; s/o Joseph & Sarah Ingalls; m Elizabeth Abbott d/o Jeremiah; liv Conway NH; ch John, Elizabeth m Arnold Floyd, Sarah F m Charles Sparhawk, 7 others; NH-0006-852

ODIORNE,
Hon Jotham; m1720 --- Cutt d/o Robert Kittery; ch --- m Peter Pearse; NH-0003-106

ODLIN,
Elisha; b1640 s/o John of Boston MA; ch Rev John b1681 m --- Woodbridge; NH-0003-288

Elisha; b1709 s/o Rev John & --- Woodbridge of Exeter; m1731 ?; liv Amesbury MA; ch John, Winthrop, William b1738 m Judith Wilson, Anna, Elisha; NH-0003-288

John; liv Boston MA; ch Elisha b1640, John, Peter; NH-0003-288

Rev John; b1681 s/o Elisha; m --- Woodbridge d/o Rev Benjamin & gd/o Rev John of Haverhill MA & wid/o Rev Clarke; liv Exeter; ch John, Elisha b1709, Dudley, Woodbridge; NH-0003-288

William; b1738 s/o Elisha of Amesbury MA; m Judith Wilson; liv Exeter NH; ch William b1767 m Elizabeth Leavitt, 4 dau; NH-0003-288

William; b1767 s/o William & Judith Wilson of Exeter NH; m1791 Elizabeth Leavitt d/o Capt James of Exeter; liv Exeter; ch Woodbridge b1805 m Joanna Odiorne & m Augusta Farley Little; NH-0003-288

Woodbridge; b1805 s/o William & Elizabeth Leavitt; m Joanna Odiorne & m1844 Augusta Farley Little; liv Exeter; ch/o Joanna - Anna O; NH-0003-288

OLCOTT,
Mills; ch Edward R, William; NH-0007-79

ORDWAY,
Abial; b1800 s/o Joses; m Clarissa French; ch Martha S m Joseph C Ordway, Abial C, John F, Mary J; NH-0004-507

Abner; m1656 Sarah Brown d/o Stephen of Newbury MA wid/o Edward Dennis of Boston MA; liv Tower Hill ENG, Watertown MA; NH-0004-507

Daniel; bro/o Joses; m Deborah Lougee of Andover MA & m Ruth Moulton; liv Andover MA, Loudon NH; ch/o Deborah - Daniel b1773, Isaac b1775, Lemuel b1776, Alse b1778, Isaac b1780, Hazen b1783, Polly b1785; ch/o Ruth - Hiram, Chlora, Statira, Eneas, Justus, Jairus, Ruth

ORDWAY (continued)
Ann; NH-0004-507
Hiram; m Sally Blaisdell; ch Myra E m Joseph W Blaisdell; NH-0004-507
James; m1648 Ann Emery; liv Tower Hill ENG, Dover NH; ch Ephraim, James, Edward, Sarah, John, Isaac, Jane, Hannaniah, Annie, Mary; NH-0004-507
Joel S; s/o Lemuel; m M Jane Wiggins; ch Horace F; NH-0004-507
Dr John; m1760 Sarah Robie d/o Samuel; liv Chester; NH-0003-147
John Cassey; s/o Moses gs/o Moses Jr; m Ruth Sanborn; ch Eliza, Augusta A, Benjamin F; NH-0004-507
John F; s/o Abel & Clarissa French; m Georgianna Huckins d/o Samuel of Loudon; ch Della P, Effie L, Lillian M, Cora F; NH-0004-507
Joseph C; m Martha S Ordway d/o Abial & Clarissa French; ch Nellie, Grace, Walter, Henry, Georgianna, Lilla, 1 dy; NH-0004-507
Joses; bro/o Daniel; ch Lucy b1795, Lois b1796, Sophia b1799, Abial b1800 m Clarissa French, John C b1801, Sukey b1803, Harriett b1808; NH-0004-507
Moses; b1721 s/o James gs/o John; m Anna Huntington b1716; liv Amesbury MA; ch Moses Jr m Persis ---; NH-0004-507
Moses Jr; s/o Moses & Anna Huntington; m Persis ---; ch Persis b1776, Moses b1779, Betsey b1781, Amos b1790, Aaron b1792, Hammond b1795; NH-0004-507
Stephen; m Rachel Clifford; ch Mary, Joseph C, Benjamin; NH-0004-507
ORR,
Lt John, bc1758; liv Bedford; NH-0002-48
OSBORNE,
Dr James; b1833 s/o Cyrus & Sally C Thresher of Piermont; m1855 Sally P Stanyan of Wentworth; liv Felchville VT, Sanbornton Bridge NH; ch Flora G b1862; NH-0004-885

OSGOOD,
Ebenezer Esq; liv Raymond & Loudon NH; ch Enoch, James, Polly, Bradley, Ira Esq b1799 m Sally B Parsons, Lamila, Nancy, Ebenezer; NH-0004-502
Ebenezer P; s/o Ira Esq & Sally B Parsons; m Ann Randall of Laconia; ch Charles H; NH-0004-502
Enoch; liv Loudon NH; ch Sally, Molly, Nabby, Deborah, Elanor, Josiah, Dolly, Nancy, Samuel, Clarissa, Betsey; NH-0004-508
Frederic B; b1852 s/o James & Jane Harnden of Fryeburg ME; liv N Conway NH; NH-0006-270
Henry J; b1825 s/o Ira Esq & Sally B Parsons; m Hannah E H Bachelder; ch Mabel, Herbert, Henrietta; NH-0004-502
Ira Esq; b1799 s/o Ebenezer Esq; m Sally B Parsons; liv Raymond & Loudon NH; ch Henry J b1825 m Hannah E H Bachelder, Ebenezer P m Ann Randall, William P m Paulina R Clifford, Charles H m Augusta A Clough of Loudon & m Ann Lamprey of Gilmanton, Annie M, Mary E m Charles C Clough of Canterbury & m Rev A D Smith of Laconia, Martha E m Charles H Bean of Lawrence MA; NH-0004-502
Ira B; s/o Christopher & Annie Abbott; m Alice Prrescott; ch Addison N b1836 m1865 Mary Emma Phelps d/o William A & Julia Upham of Haverhill NH; NH-0004-583
Dr Joseph Otis; b1782 s/o Dr George & Elizabeth Otis of Andover MA; m Elizabeth Boardman; liv Fairhaven & Amesbury & Boston MA, Kensington; ch 2 sons; NH-0003-357
William P; s/o Ira Esq & Sally B Parsons; m Paulina R Clifford; ch Jennie M, George B; NH-0004-502
OTIS,
Joshua; m Mary Hussey of Barrington; ch Nicholas, Elijah, Paul, Micajah m Mary Foss, Joshua, Stephen, Mary, Sarah, Jane, Rebecca; NH-0003-702
Micajah; s/o Joshua & Mary

OTIS (continued)
Hussey; m Mary Foss; liv
Strafford; ch Jon Jacob b1810
m Sally Kimball of Farmington; NH-0003-703

-P-

PADDLEFORD,
Capt Philip; liv Enfield,
Lyman, Monroe NH; ch Seth,
Philip, 4 sons, 2 dau; NH-
0007-553
Philip; s/o Capt Philip; ch 1
dau m Nathan Nelson, Benjamin
F, Curtis, 4 others; NH-0007-
553
PAGE,
Benjamin F MD; b1843; m
Caroline Farr d/o John; liv
Littleton NH, St Johnsbury
VT; ch 1 son, 1 dau; NH-0007-
497
Charles M; s/o John McClary &
Dolly Cram; m Abigail
Blaisdell d/o James; liv Tam-
worth NH; ch Marie m Lowell
Ham, 4 others; NH-0006-770
Daniel; s/o John; m Anna Towle
d/o Samuel of Hampton NH; liv
Kensington NH; ch Daniel m
Sabrina Clement & m Hannah
Wyatt & m Hannah Downing, 7
others; NH-0007-209
Daniel; s/o Daniel & Anna
Towle; m Sabrina Clement of
Center Harbor NH & m Hannah
Wyatt of Campton NH & m
Hannah Downing of Ellsworth;
ch/o ? - Ozias M m Susan
Draper d/o Reuben & Sally
Johnson, 8 others; NH-0007-
209
Capt Daniel D; b1817; m
Charlotte A Boleyn of
Hinsdale NH; liv Benton NH;
ch William B, Harry E,
Harriet E; NH-0007-152
Col David; liv Dunbarton,
Concord; ch Robert b1765,
Edmond b1768, Jeremiah b1770
m Phebe Russell; NH-0006-847
David; b1809 s/o Samuel of
Haverhill MA; m1844 Margaret
Taylor of Derry NH; liv
Groton, Haverhill; ch 2 dy,
Elvira b1847 m Alvin Burleigh
Esq of Plymouth NH, Martha A

PAGE (continued)
m C R Whitney of Keene,
Samuel Taylor m Frances M
Eaton; NH-0007-84 & 87
Capt Enoch; b1772; mc1795 Sarah
Noyes b1774; liv Atkinson &
Sutton NH; ch Susanna b1797 m
Hazen Putney, Enoch b1804;
NH-0004-648
Enoch; b1804 s/o Capt Enoch &
Sarah Noyes; m1846 Hannah C
Colby of Warner NH; liv
Sutton NH; ch Daniel dy,
Josephine b1848 m George
Roby, Eugene b1851 dy, Martha
C b1852 m1882 George H
Littlehale of Sutton s/o
Henry gs/o Isaac, Sarah b1856
dy, Mary b1860 dy; NH-0004-
648
George; s/o David C of Sand-
wich; ch Henry G; NH-0006-730
James; b1834 s/o James of
Benton; m Olive A Hunkings
d/o Jonathan of N Benton; liv
Benton NH; ch 2 sons, 1 dau;
NH-0007-152
Jeremiah; b1770 s/o Col David;
m Phebe Russell; ch Benjamin
R m Achsah Pollard, Harriet m
Isaac Osgood of Conway, Maria
m Nathaniel Potter of
Bridgton ME, Amanda; NH-0006-
847
Rev Jesse; b1805 s/o Col
William; m1837 Ann Poor
Little d/o Ezekiel Esq of
Boston MA; liv N Andover &
Lynn MA, Atkinson; ch Mary
Ann, 3 sons dy; NH-0003-123
John; m Abigail Sanders & m
Abigail Hazeltine of Concord
NH & m Mrs Hannah Green d/o
Samuel Rice of Landaff; liv
Rindge & Haverhill NH; ch/o
Hannah - John b1787 m Hannah
Merrill, William G, Samuel,
Stephen R; NH-0007-350
John; b1787 s/o John & Mrs
Hannah Green; m Hannah
Merrill d/o Maj Nathaniel of
N Haverhill; liv Haverhill
NH; ch Frederick, William,
John Alfred, Henry Harrison
b1816 m1842 Eliza Southard,
Nathaniel Merrill, Stephen
Rice, Sarah Hazen, George
Washington, George Brackett,
Edward Livingston m1855 Laura
M Batchelder of Franklin; NH-
0007-350

PAGE (continued)

John McClary; b1780; m Dolly Cram; liv Deerfield, Tamworth; ch Charles M m Abigail Blaisdell, William P, Clara m Enoch Perkins, 5 others; NH-0006-770

Joseph W; m Dolly Bullock d/o Benjamin & Sybil Drake; liv Grafton NH; ch Sally, Joseph B; NH-0007-278

Samuel; b1772; m Submit Jeffers of Hampstead NH; liv Haverhill MA, Haverhill NH; ch James J b1800, 10 others; NH-0007-152

Samuel Taylor; s/o David & Margaret Taylor; m1872 Frances M Eaton of Manchester; liv Haverhill; ch Gracie M b1874, Donald T b1878; NH-0007-87

Col William; s/o Capt Jesse gs/o Edmund; ch Rev Jesse, Rev William; NH-0003-123

William H; b1824 s/o Samuel of Haverhill; m1854 Mary E Poor d/o Jesse of Orford; liv Piermont; ch 2 sons; NH-0007-350

PALMER,

Fred B; b1827 s/o Asa of Orford; m twice; liv Lyme NH; ch 6; NH-0007-546

Dr Haven; b1843 s/o Lewis & Susan Somers of Jefferson NH; m1875 Lucy G Ellis of Lancaster; liv Plymouth NH; ch Bessie F, Harold H; NH-0007-597

PARKER,

---; liv Lyman NH; ch Solomon, Samuel, Asa, Lemuel, Isaac, Levi, David, Hepsey m William Miner; NH-0007-514

Amos A; s/o Hon Nahum of Fitzwilliam; liv Epping, Newmarket, Kingston, Glastonbury CT; NH-0003-37

Carmi; m Anna Eliza McGaw d/o Isaac; liv Merrimack, Fitchburg MA; ch George L, Harry C, Maurice W; NH-0002-544

Charles Coffin; s/o Edward Lutwyche & Mehetable Kimball; m Sarah J Taylor; liv Derry; ch Frank W, Edward T; NH-0003-181

David Taylor; b1813 s/o Rev Clement & Rachel Taylor of

PARKER (continued)

Bradford VT; m1833 Clara C Chamberlain of Lebanon ME & m1878 Mrs Lucy A Fernald; liv Farmington NH; ch/o Clara - 1 dau dy, 2 sons; NH-0003-636

E George; b1826; m1871 Matilda P Cook of Lyme; liv Rumney NH, Newbury VT, Woodsville; ch 1 son; NH-0007-367

Edward Lutwyche; b1785 s/o Dr Jonathan & gs/o Rev Thomas; m1811 Mehetable Kimball d/o Dea Stephen of Hanover; liv Litchfield & Bradford & Londonderry NH, Topsham ME, Billerica & Salem MA; ch Edward Pinkerton, Charles Coffin m Sarah J Taylor, Caroline P, Harriet dy; NH-0003-180

Edward P; m Margaret Jane McGaw d/o Isaac; liv Derry, Merrimack, Concord MA; ch Caroline Eliza; NH-0002-544

Edward Pinkerton; b1816 s/o Rev Edward L of Londonderry; liv Derry, Merrimac; NH-0003-28

Rev Edward L; s/o Thomas; liv Derry; ch Edward Esq; NH-0002-545

Eleazer B; b1818; m1841 Esther Bowles; liv Lisbon & Franconia NH; ch Phebe A m J A Knapp, Osman, Wilbur F; NH-0007-274

E S; m Phebe Y Keysar d/o John & Sarah Clark Wiswall; ch John R, Otis L; NH-0005-695

Rev Henry E DD; b1821; m1856 Mary Elizabeth Brackett Huntley; liv Keene & Hanover NH; ch Henry Horatio, Alice; NH-0007-336

Henry Rust MD; b1836 s/o John Toppan & Sally L Seavey of Wolfeborough; m1866 Ella M Thompson d/o Moses Esq of Wolfeborough; liv Dover, Wolfeborough; ch Nathalie Sally b1869, Alberta Thompson b1870, Henry Rust b1875; NH-0003-885, NH-0006-363

James; b1806; m Betsey Blakesly of Dalton; liv Lisbon, Littleon NH; ch Lewis H m Eva Aldrich, William F, Hattie m B F Wells, J W, Jane M m Dr Kelsey of Newport VT, Esther A m C M Colburn, Carrie M m G F Abbott, Ellen W m Joseph

PARKER (continued)

Atwood; NH-0007-502

James U; b1797 s/o Dea Matthew & Sally Underwood; m1829 Mary Hawkins of Hanover NH & m1835 Rebecca J Lund d/o Dea Augustus of Merrimack; liv Litchfield, Manchester, Merrimack, New York City; ch/o ? - James U, Charles A; NH-0002-495

John G MD; b1818; liv Peterborough, Dublin, Warner; NH-0002-668

John McGraw; b1822 s/o William & Hannah Adams McGraw of Goffstown NH; m1854 Letita C Stinson b1835 d/o Capt Charles of Dunbarton NH; ch Charles Stinson b1855 m Ella J Hart, Henry Woodman b1859, Frank Adams b1866; NH-0002-326

Hon John McGraw; b1824 s/o William & Hannah Adams; m1854 Letitia C Stinson d/o Capt Charles; liv Goffstown NH; ch Charles Stinson b1855, Henry Woodman b1859, Frank Adams b1866; NH-0001-31

John Toppan; b1804 s/o Henry Rust of Wolfeborough; m Sally L Seavey of Wolfeborough; liv Wolfeborough; ch Henry Rust MD b1836 m Ella M Thompson; NH-0003-885

Hon Levi; b1792 s/o Silas of Richmond NH; m1814 Phebe Ball; liv Lisbon NH; ch Silas, Eleazer B, Levi Pratt, Charles, Chandler B, Phebe Ann m Lindsey Aldrich; NH-0007-447

Matthew; ch James U Esq, Nathan; NH-0002-545

Matthew Stanley; s/o William; m Anna Rust d/o Col Henry of Portsmouth; liv Wolfeborough; ch Henry Rust; NH-0003-885, NH-0006-303

Nathan; b1767; m Mary McQuestin of Litchfield; liv Litchfield, Merrimack; ch William b1797, Frances b1799 m Leonard Walker, Nathan b1801, Matthew b1803 dy, Adeline b1805 m Enoch Merrill, Elkanah Phillip b1807, James b1809, Harriet b1812 m Robert French of Merrimack, Thomas b1815, Marietta b1818 m John

PARKER (continued)

Wheeler; NH-0002-544

Nathaniel; b1760 s/o Judge William Jr of E Kingston; liv Exeter; NH-0003-30

Hon Nathaniel; b1807; m Cynthia L Haines & m Julia B Hoswell; liv Williston VT; NH-0004-621

Prescott; b1821 s/o Prescott gs/o Solomon; m Maria A Fitzpatrick; liv Bath & Benton NH; ch Lebina H, Dora A, Frank B; NH-0007-154

Rev Thomas; b1700 s/o Josiah of Cambridge; liv Dracut MA; ch Thomas, William, John, Matthew, Jonathan, Lydia, Elizabeth, Lucy, Sarah; NH-0002-544

Thomas; s/o Rev Thomas; liv Litchfield; ch Rev Edward L; NH-0002-545

Trueworthy L; b1810; m Dorothea Sawyer of Bethlehem & m Augusta Ramsay of Littleton & m Mrs Mary Turner of Monroe; liv Chichester, Monroe, Littleton NH; ch 14; NH-0007-491

Hon William; b1703 s/o William of ENG; liv Rockingham NH; ch Hon William, John, Samuel; NH-0003-885

William Jr; b1731 s/o Hon William of Portsmouth; liv Exeter; NH-0003-30

William; b1775 s/o John gs/o Thomas ggs/o Josiah; m Hannah Aiken & m Hannah Adams McGraw b1788; liv Goffstown NH; ch/o Hannah Aiken - Rodney, George W, Caroline, Margaret Ann; ch/o Hannah Adams - Hannah A b1819, John McGraw b1822, David Adams, b1824, William H b1831 dy; NH-0002-326

William T; b1822 s/o William & Margaret of Cleethorps ENG; m1846 Abbie N Spaulding d/o Oliver Esq of Merrimack; liv Merrimack; NH-0002-549

PARK,

W R; b1828 s/o William & Lydia of Townsend MA; m Lucy M Ayer d/o Walter H & Nancy; liv Plymouth NH; ch W R Jr b1856 m Elizabeth Dodge d/o Col Joseph A & Sally Tewksbury, Jennie S m Charles R Gilson, Cora L; NH-0007-597

PARKS,
Reuben Sylvester; s/o Sylvester & Laura A Parks of Russell MA; m1870 Ellen Sarah Parsons d/o Hezekiah & Sarah Merrill Bragg of Colebrook NH; liv Washington DC; ch Alice May b1872; NH-0005-633

PARSHLEY,
Sanborn; m Rufina Smith d/o Dea Ebenezer & Mary Smith of Strafford; ch Ethel B, Mary E, Henry G, Ina H, Lula B; NH-0003-716

PARSONS,
Abraham, b1754 s/o Abraham of New Market gs/o Josiah of Cape Breton; m1780 Abigail Burleigh; ch Josiah Esp b1781 m Judith Badger, Sarah, Abraham, James; NH-0002-137

Dea Benjamin; bapt1627 s/o Hugh & Elizabeth Bagshaw Thomkins; m1653 Sarah Vore d/o Richard of Windsor CT; liv ENG, Springfield MA; ch Samuel b1666 m Hannah Hitchock, 4 others; NH-0005-627

Charles; b1811 s/o Hezekiah & Polly (Mary) Bevins; m1860 Augusta Cummings d/o Archelaus & Mary Fletcher; liv Burlington VT, Colebrook NH, Montreal; ch Mary Augusta b1866 m1885 Joseph Smith Pierce, Charles Jr b1871; NH-0005-627

Ebenezer; b1756; m1784 Eunice Potter; ch Ebenezer, Eunice, William, Samuel, Sally, Lucy; NH-0002-137

Edward; b1747 s/o Rev Joseph of Bradford MA; liv Newmarket; NH-0003-37

George; b1815 s/o Hezekiah & Polly (Mary) Bevins; m Clara Lyman Martin; ch Frederick George b1871, Clara Bell dy; NH-0005-627

Capt Hezekiah; b1698 s/o Samuel & Hannah Hitchcock of Enfield CT; m Rebecca Burt & m Anna Evans; liv Enfield CT; ch/o Rebecca - 1 dau; ch/o Anna - Capt Hezekiah b1728 m Sarah Abbee Chapin, 6 others; NH-0005-627

Capt Hezekiah; b1728 s/o Capt Hezekiah & Anna Evans of Enfield CT; m1748 Sarah Abbe Chapin wid/o Nathaniel d/o

PARSONS (continued)
Thomas Abbe; ch Hezekiah b1752 m Margaret Kibbee, Maj Jabez b1754 m Martha Terry; NH-0005-627

Hezekiah; b1752 s/o Capt Hezekiah & Sarah Abbe Chapin; m1775 Margaret Kibbee d/o Isaac & Mary Terry of Enfield CT; liv Enfield CT, Colebrook NH; ch Hezekiah b1776 m Polly (Mary) Bevins, Abdiel b1779, George b1781, Samuel Burt b1783, Jeremiah b1787; NH-0005-627

Hezekiah; b1776 s/o Hezekiah & Margaret Kibbee of Enfield CT; m1802 Polly (Mary) Bevins b1778 d/o Benjamin & Sarah Powers of Middletown CT; ch Margaret b1803 m Jonathan Rolfe, Hezekiah b1805 m Sarah Merrill, William b1807 m Lucy Mooney, Mary b1809, Charles b1811 m Augusta Cummings, Sarah Ann b1813, George b1815 m Clara Lyman Martin, Jane b1817 dy, Samuel b1820; NH-0005-627

Hezekiah; b1805 s/o Hezekiah & Polly (Mary) Bevins; m1832 Sarah Merrill Bragg d/o James Frye & Sallie Chandler; liv Colebrook NH; ch Ellen Sarah b1833 m Reuben Sylvester Parks, Hezekiah Bragg b1835 m1873 Mahala Aldrich d/o George & Sarah Morrison of Colebrook, James Ingalls, 1 dau b1836 dy, 1 dau b1839 dy, 1 dau b1840 dy, 1 dau b1846 dy, Mary Alice b1850; NH-0005-627

Hugh; bapt1563 s/o Thomas & Katherine Hester of Great Milton ENG; m Elizabeth Bagshaw Thomkins; ch Hugh, Dea Benjamin bapt1627 m Sarah Vore, 8 others; NH-0005-627

James Ingalls; b1844 s/o Hezekiah & Sarah M Bragg of Colebrook NH; m1876 Ada A Remick d/o Samuel K & Sophia Cushman of Hardwick VT & m1883 Addie S Marshall d/o John C of Colebrook; liv Colebrook NH, Port Huron MI; ch/o Ada - Cushman Hezekiah b1879; NH-0005-251

John; b1751 s/o William & Hannah Meserve; m1783 Lydie

PARSONS (continued)

Folsom; ch William, Judith, John, Sarah, Hannah, Lydie, Eliza, Joseph Esq b1753 m Ruth Pearson; NH-0002-137

Joseph; d1684; m Mary Bliss; liv ENG, Northampton MA; ch Joseph Jr b1647 m Elizabeth Strong, John, Samuel, Ebenezer, Jonathan, David, Mary, Hannah, Abigail, Hester; NH-0002-137

Joseph Jr; b1647 s/o Joseph & Mary Bliss; m Elizabeth Strong; ch Joseph b1671 m Elizabeth Thompson, John, Ebenezer, Elizabeth, David, Josiah, Daniel, Moses, Abigail, Noah; NH-0002-137

Rev Joseph; b1671 s/o Joseph Jr & Elizabeth Strong; m Elizabeth Thompson; liv Lebanon CT, Salisbury MA; ch Joseph, Samuel, Rev William b1716 m Sarah Burnham, Elizabeth, John dy; NH-0002-137

Joseph Esq; b1753 s/o John & Lydie Folsom; m Ruth Pearson; ch Ruth, Joseph, Sarah, Hannah, Thomas, Mary; NH-0002-137

Josiah Esq; b1781 s/o Abraham & Abigail Burleigh; m Judith Badger d/o Joseph & Sarah Weeks; ch Joseph B, Emily P, Sarah B, Mary E, Lewis N, Dr Joseph, Daniel Jacobs Esq, Sarah Jane Rogers, Hannah Cogswell, William Moody MD b1826 m Marion J Hosley; NH-0002-137

Samuel; b1666 s/o Dea Benjamin & Sarah Vore; m1683 Hannah Hitchcock b1668 d/o John & Hannah Chapin of Springfield; liv Enfield CT; ch Capt Hezekiah b1698 m Rebecca Burt & m Anna Evans, 4 others; NH-0005-627

Thomas; m1555 Katherine Hester; liv Great Milton ENG; ch Hugh bapt1563, 1 son; NH-0005-627

Rev William; b1716 s/o Rev Joseph & Elizabeth Thompson; m Sarah Burnham; liv Gilmanton NH; ch Sarah, William b1745 m Hannah Meserve, Elizabeth, John, Joseph, Ebenezer; NH-0002-137

William; b1745 s/o Rev William & Sarah Burnham; m Hannah

PARSONS (continued)

Meserve; ch William, John b1751 m Lydie Folsom, Joseph, Sarah; NH-0002-137

William; b1807 s/o Hezekiah & Polly (Mary) Bevins; m Lucy Mooney; ch William F b1835, Hiram Charles b1836, Abdiel Charles b1838; NH-0005-627

William MD; b1826 s/o Josiah Esp & Judith Badger; m1882 Marion J Hosley d/o Hon John & Dorothy H Jones of Manchester; liv Gilmanton, Bennington & Antrim & Manchester NH; ch Martha S b1884; NH-0002-136, 137

PARTRIDGE,

Nathaniel; liv Goffstown & Lyman NH; ch Caroline m --- Pike, Ira G, Eliza G m William B Hurd; NH-0007-514

PATCH,

Dea Thomas; m1741 Anna Gilson; liv Groton, W Dunstable; ch Thomas, David; NH-0002-438

PATRICK,

Rev William; b1773 s/o John of Weston MA; m Mary Gerrish d/o Col Joseph of Boscawen & m Mary Mills of Dunbarton; liv Canterbury NH; NH-0004-229

PATRIDGE,

Rev Samuel Hudson; b1827 s/o Lewis & Betsey Fay; m1851 Elvira Fay d/o Joel & Mary Blakesly; liv Sebec & Lebanon & York ME, Hillsborough & Center & Greenfield NH; ch Lizzie M m Warren Lewis, Abbie N, Arlena E; NH-0002-347

PATTEE,

Col Daniel; s/o Capt Asa; liv Canaan NH; ch Barnard m Betsey Howe, Daniel Jr b1799 m Judith Burley; James m Rebecca Currier & m Rosamond Jones, Moses; NH-0007-227

Daniel Jr; b1799 s/o Col Daniel of Canaan; ch Gordon B m Mary Read, 2 sons dy, Louise M m Ithamar P Pillsbury, Eliza D m John Q Perley, James H m Mary E Nye of Monmouth IL, Henry H m Lizzie R Morgan of Canaan & m Anna Willets of Monmouth IL; NH-0007-227

James; s/o Col Daniel of Canaan NH; m Rebecca Currier & m Rosamond Jones; liv Canaan

PATTEE (continued)
NH; ch/o Rebecca - Wyman, James F m Marion F Blake, Ann R m James Currier, Burns W m Tryphena Leeds of Canaan, 1 son; NH-0007-227

Lemuel Noyes; b1804; m1827 Vashti Little d/o Joseph & Margaret of Goffstown; liv Goffstown, Antrim; ch Mary F b1820 m 1849 John B Woodbury of Antrim NH; NH-0002-330

Hon Lewis C; m1858 Rebecca Perley of Enfield; liv Lebanon, ch 6; NH-0007-227

Lewis F; s/o Moses & Jane Gordon of Alexandria; m Mary P Ingles d/o Gilman Jr & Sarah L Roberts; ch Fred L, Charles H, Mary L; NH-0007-117

Moses; s/o William & Judith Worthen of Alexandria; m Jane Gordon of Alexandria; liv Alexandria; ch Jessie, William, Moses, Henry, James, Wilber, Betsey J, Rosa M, Betsey J, Lewis F m Mary P Ingles; NH-0007-117

Wyman; b1826 s/o James gs/o Daniel ggs/o Capt Asa of Canaan; m1857 Mary Jane Burley; liv Canaan & Enfield NH; ch James W, John H; NH-0007-259

PATTEN,
Alonzo; s/o Samuel & Hanna Booes (Bois); m Rhoda Ladd; ch Edwin, Joseph; NH-0002-374

Benjamin A; s/o John & Jane Abbot; m Polly Hastings; ch Emily, Amanda, Jonas, Manson, Seth G; NH-0007-117

Colcord; b1789; ch Hon Wm C, Ichabod B, Claudius B, Ord P, Mehitable C; NH-0003-377

George C; s/o John & Mary Kimball; m Lucy A Roper of Francestown NH; ch William H m Velona E Dodge, Helen L, Susie H m Arthur S Hood of Manchester NH; NH-0002-374

John; s/o Samuel & Hanna Booes (Bois); m Mary Kimball; ch George C m Lucy A Roper, Nancy S m John Currier of Manchester NH; NH-0002-374

Jonathan; s/o Samuel & Priscilla Moore; m Abigail Blood; ch Esther m Hiram Hurd, David m Alice Tubbs,

PATTEN (continued)
Jonathan m Phila Hurd, Mary m Edward Chase, Abigail m David Wilkins, Eliza m Rev Ebenezer Chase; NH-0002-374

Jonathan; s/o Jonathan & Abigail Blood; m Phila Hurd; ch Nyrhe m Joseph Stearns Jr, Phila m David Chase of Henniker NH, Abigail m Benjamin Martin, Edward m Mary Conant, Sarah m Mark Peaslee, John; NH-0002-374

Jonathan; s/o Robert of Londonderry NH; m Margaret Clark d/o Samuel & Margaret Ross; liv Alexandria NH; ch Sophia, Mary Fernald, Samuel S m Etta Bailey; NH-0007-117

Joseph; s/o John; m Sarah Braley of Danbury NH; ch Orlando R, Willie J, Truman T m Etta M Bailey; NH-0007-117

Samuel; m Priscilla More; liv IRE, Marblehead MA; ch Jonathan m Abigal Blood, John, Samuel m Hannah Booes (Bois), Betsy m Aaron Travis, Polly, Jesse m Polly Gove; NH-0002-374

Samuel; s/o Samuel & Priscilla Moore; m Hanna Booes (Bois) of Londonderry; ch John m Mary Kimball, Samuel m Lydia Whitaker, Sophronic m Henry Codman, Hannah, Eliza, Alonzo m Rhoda Ladd, Melissa m Benjamin F Gove; NH-0002-374

Samuel S; s/o Jonathan & Margaret Clark of Alexandria NH; m Etta Bailey d/o William L & Lizzie Bailey; liv Alexandria NH; ch Dora M, Chester S, Lura L, Lena E; NH-0007-117

Truman T; s/o Joseph & Sarah Braley; m Etta M Bailey d/o Isaac H & Maria M Braley; liv Alexandria NH; ch Leroy E; NH-0007-117

William; m1774 Mehitable Colcord d/o Samuel & Mehitable Ladd; ch Aaron b1775, Isaac, Colcord b1789; NH-0003-377

PATTERSON,
Hon George W; b1799 s/o Thomas & Elizabeth Wallace gs/o Peter & Crisel Wilson of Londonderry; m Hannah W Dickey d/o John Esq of

PATTERSON (continued)
Londonderry; liv NY; ch 1 son; NH-0003-582

Joab N; b1835 s/o Joab & Mary Lovering of Contoocook; m1867 Sarah Cilley Bouton d/o Rev Nathaniel DD of Concord; liv Hopkinton, Concord NH; ch 3; NH-0004-409

PAUL,
Amos; b1810 s/o Nathaniel & Mary A Masters of Newmarket NH; m Mary A Randlett d/o Moses of Epping & m Harriet A Randlett d/o Thomas of Newburyport MA; liv S Newmarket; ch/o Mary - Mary H, Amos, Charles R; ch/o Harriet - Isabella, Harriet A; NH-0003-538

Moses; b1797 s/o Edward & Delia of Waterborough ME; m1821 Susan M Hodgdon d/o Shadrock & Elizabeth of Dover; liv Dover; ch Susan E m John A Bickford of Malden MA, Emily J m Russell B Wiggin of Malden MA, Moses A; NH-0003-859

PAYSON,
Hon Moses P; bc1773; mc1798 Hannah Perley; liv Rowley MA, Bath NH; ch Moses P b1806; NH-0007-60

PEABODY,
Amos; m Nancy Messer d/o Stephen; liv Gilead, Randolph, Shelburne NH; ch Aaron, Nancy, Allan, Stephen m Hepzibeth Evans, Enoch m Judith Wheeler; NH-0005-872

Hon Charles Augustus; b1814 s/o Samuel & Abigail Wood; m1846 Julia Caroline Livingston d/o Duane of NYC & m Maria E Hamilton d/o John C gd/o Alexander; liv Sandwich NH, NYC, Beverley MA, Baltimore MD; ch/o Julia - Philip Glendower, 4 others; NH-0001-209, NH-0006-244

Dr Jacob; m Susannah Rogers d/o Rev John of Boxford; liv Topsfield MA, ch Nathaniel b1741; NH-0003-123

James Van Ness; b1841 s/o Noah & Isabella Walker Richards; m1865 Susan Mary Rand; liv Northfield NH; ch Leon b1871; NH-0004-891

John; b1775 s/o Samuel & Eliza-

PEABODY (continued)
beth Wilkins of Andover MA; m Mary Holt; ch John, Samuel, Sargon, Jacob, James, William, Ezekiel, Noah b1810 m Isabella Walker Richards, Joseph; NH-0004-891

Jonathan; m Phebe Kimball of Bethel & m Prudence Patterson; liv Andover & Shelburne; ch/o Phebe - Priscilla m Ben Bean, Phebe, Sally m John Messer, Amos, Oliver m Susy Messer; ch/o Prudence - Mercy m Amos Evans, Philena, Charlotte m Nathan Newell, Asa, Jonathan m Eliza Coffin & m 2 others; NH-0005-875

Jonathan; s/o Jonathan & Prudence Patterson; m Eliza Coffin of Gilead & m 2 others; ch/o Eliza - Warren m Mary Tenny, Augustus m Lydia Tenny, Eliza m Charles Tenny; NH-0005-875

Noah; b1810 s/o John & Mary Holt; m1834 Isabella Walker Richards; liv Sanbornton Bridge & Sutton NH; ch Selwin Bancroft b1839 m Elizabeth S Richards, James Van Ness b1841 m Susan Mary Rand, Georgiana Isabel b1843 m David F Cheney; NH-0004-891

Oliver; s/o Jonathan & Phebe Kimball; m Susy Messer; liv Shelburne NH; ch John, Loammi, Nancy m Noah Gould, Eliza, Betsey, Sally m Peter Runnels, Samuel; NH-0005-875

Oliver; b1753 s/o Oliver of Andover MA; liv Exeter; NH-0003-30

Oliver William Bourne; b1799 s/o Hon Oliver of Exeter; liv Exeter, Boston, Burlington VT; NH-0003-32

Samuel; b1741; m Elizabeth Wilkins of Amherst; liv Andover MA; ch John b1775 m Mary Holt; NH-0004-891

Samuel; s/o Richard of Boxford MA; m Abigail Wood d/o Jonathan of Boxford MA; liv Sandwich, Epsom & Tamworth NH, Andover MA; ch Hon Charles A b1814 m Julia Caroline Livingston & m Maria E Hamilton, Dr William F, George S, Enoch W, 5 others; NH-0001-209

PEABODY (continued)
Selwin Bancroft; b1839 s/o Noah
& Isabella Walker Richards; m
Elizabeth S Richards d/o
Darius M & Elizabeth of New
Bedford MA; liv Tilton NH; ch
Leon Bancroft b1867 dy, 1 dau
b1869, Isabella Weston b1871;
NH-0004-891
Rev Stephen; b1741; liv Andover
MA; m Polly Haseltine of
Bradford MA & m --- Smith
Shaw d/o Rev John Smith of
Weymouth MA & wid/o Rev John
Shaw of Haverhill MA; NH-
0003-123
William H; m Eliza H Woodbury
d/o John & Betsy A Hobbs; ch
Harry O, Frederick H; NH-
0002-648
William H MD; bc1841; liv
Gorham ME, Peterborough NH;
NH-0002-667
PEASE,
Benjamin; b1743; m Anna San-
born; liv Meredith NH; ch
Joseph b1774 m Hannah Folsom;
NH-0004-867
Frank B; s/o Simeon D & Betsey
Batchelder of Meredith; m
Clara Hoyt, liv Meredith NH;
ch Betsey Bertha; NH-0004-867
Joseph; b1774 s/o Benjamin &
Anna Sanborn of Meredith NH;
m1796 Hannah Folsom; liv
Meredith; ch Simeon D b1812 m
Betsey Batchelder, 9 others;
NH-0004-867
Simeon D; b1812 s/o Joseph &
Hannah Folsom of Meredith NH;
m Betsey Batchelder d/o
Nathaniel & Patience Page;liv
Meredith; ch Arzelia Jane m
Edwin Cox, Laura E, Mary R m
Howard Prescott, Hannah A m
Frank Cummings, Frank B m
Clara Hoyt, Simeon Loring m
Ellen Hanson; NH-0004-867
PEASLEE,
Daniel; b1777 s/o Maj Jacob &
Martha Chellis of Kingston;
mc1804 Elizabeth Secomb d/o
Simmons & Mary Tappan; liv
Kingston; ch Sarah T m
Humphrey Nichols of Merrimac
MA, Martha C m Harrison
Pillsbury of Sundown, Simmons
S m Mary Eads of Lowell MA,
Jacob C m Juliette Page of
Danville, Luther Dana b1812 m
Charlotte F Sanborn & m Mary

PEASLEE (continued)
S Clark, John C, Mary S m Dr
N K Kelly of Plaistow, Samuel
S dy, Carrie E; NH-0003-382
Maj Jacob; m Martha Chellis & m
--- Clement; liv Kingston;
ch/o Martha - Daniel b1777 m
Elizabeth Secomb, John m
Hannah Peaslee of Newton,
Moses, Lydia m Samuel
Spofford, Martha m ---
Eastman, Hannah m Jonathan
Bartlett; NH-0003-382
John; s/o Jacob of Ashland; m
Abigail Crawford of Bridge-
water NH; ch Jacob m Ann
Clement; NH-0007-128
Luther Dana; b1812 s/o Daniel &
Elizabeth Secomb of Kingston;
m1846 Charlotte F Sanborn d/o
Jacob & Elizabeth Hoyt of
Kingston & m Mary S Clark d/o
Nath & Betsey Brickett of
Plaistow; liv Kingston; ch/o
Mary - Grace B, Charlotte F,
Carrie Lillie, Mary C; NH-
0003-382
PEASLEY,
Humphrey; m Phebe Dow of Weare;
liv Amesbury MA, Deering NH;
ch Jonathan m Sallie Hook,
Kesiah m Abram Chase, Nancy,
Stephen, Abraham m Eliza
Alcock, Eliza, Humphrey m
Abigail Atwood & m Betsy
Brown, Mary m Dudley Chase,
Phebe m Nathan Bailey; NH-
0002-381
PEAVEY,
John; b1804 s/o Joseph &
Abigail Canney of Tufton-
borough NH; m1825 Hannah
Thing of Ossipee; liv Tufton-
borough NH; ch Emily m George
B Canney, Frank, Charles C,
John L, Lyford, Zebedee,
Lafayette; NH-0006-447
John L; b1835 s/o John & Hannah
Thing of Tuftonborough NH; m
Mary F Wiggin d/o Aaron of
Tuftonborough NH; liv Wolfe-
borough NH; ch Forrest W,
Herman L, Harry B; NH-0006-
391
Joseph; s/o Edward; liv Tufton-
borough NH; ch William,
Edmund, Joseph L, James,
John, Abigail m Trustram
Leighton; NH-0006-440
Maj Peter; liv Wilton & Green-
field NH; ch Peter Jr; NH-

PEAVEY (continued)
0002-344
Dea Peter; b1788 s/o Peter &
Lucy Cummings; m1819 Dorcas
Hold d/o Dea John & m1857
Tamesin Holt; liv Wilton NH;
ch/o Dorcas - Hannah m Nelson
Abbott of Wilton NH, Dorcas A
dy, Lizzie D m Charles Darwin
Fitch, John Peter m Mary J
Patch of Greenfield, Charles;
NH-0002-349
Zebediah; b1795 s/o Capt
Thomas; m1824 Mary B d/o Dea
David Patterson; liv Green-
field NH; NH-0002-344
PEBBLES,
James; d1860; m Martha Haskell;
liv Salem MA, Orford NH; ch
Seth, John m Delia H Weed, 9
others; NH-0007-564
John; s/o James & Martha
Haskell; m Delia H Weed; liv
Orford NH; ch John H,
Lucretia m --- Harris, Delia
m --- Blodgett, Louisa m ---
Porter, William F, Hazen,
George S, Riley, James T; NH-
0007-564
PECK,
John W; s/o Eliel b1768; liv
Lebanon NH; ch Solon A; NH-
0007-419
PEIRCE,
Hon Andrew; b1792 s/o Andrew; m
Betsey Wentworth; liv Dover
NH, Gloucester MA; ch Andrew
b1814 m Rebecca W Dunnaway &
m Mary Frances Gilman, Thomas
Wentworth b1818 m Mary Curtis
& m Catherine Cornelia Cook;
NH-0003-863
Andrew; b1814 s/o Hon Andrew &
Betsey Wentworth of Dover;
m1834 Rebecca W Dunnaway of
Gloucester MA & m1861 Mary
Frances Gilman of Nashua NH;
liv Dover NH, Boston MA, MO,
Clifton Springs NY; NH-0003-
863
Thomas Wentworth; b1818 s/o Hon
Andrew & Betsey Wentworth; m
Mary Curtis of Boston & m
Catherine Cornelia Cook of
Cooperstown NY; liv Topsfield
MA; ch/o Catherine - 1 son, 1
dau; NH-0003-868
PENDEXTER,
Hon John; b1752; m Martha
Jackson b1753; liv Ports-
mouth, Lower Bartlett; ch

PENDEXTER (continued)
Alice b1776 m Col Jonathan
Meserve, Nancy b1778 dy,
Sally b1780 m Benjamin
Pitman, Susanna b1782 m
Stephen Rogers, John b1784 m
Susan Eastman, Joseph b1786 m
Lydia Dinsmore, Betsey b1789
m Daniel Meserve, George
b1790 dy, Martha b1792 m
William Stilphen, Samuel
b1794 m Lydia T Meserve; NH-
0006-934
John; b1784 s/o Hon John &
Martha Jackson; m1806 Susan
Eastman b1786; ch George
b1808 m1839 Ursula Cushman of
New Gloucester ME, Alice M
b1812 m1834 Rev Henry Butler
of Cornish ME, Hannah Eastman
b1814 m Rev Thomas Hillman,
Susan b1816 m Dr J S Farnum,
Amelia Ann L b1819 m1844
Hasket D Eastman, Daniel E
b1822 m Harriet Cushman,
Benjamin b1824 m Esther P
Dinsmore, Lydia P b1827 m1848
Samuel Shackford; NH-0006-934
Joseph; b1786 s/o Hon John &
Martha Jackson; m Lydia Dins-
more; ch Solomon Dinsmore
b1813 m1838 Mary D Meserve,
Eliza D b1817 m1850 Cyrus A
Tasker, Martha J b1819, Nancy
m1837 George P Stilphen, John
b1822 m1840 Melinda Chase of
Fryeburg ME, Mary D (Polly) m
Hazen Pitman, Abigail m James
C Willey, H Augustus b1834;
NH-0006-934
Samuel; b1794 s/o Hon John &
Martha Jackson; m Lydia T
Meserve b1800 d/o Silas; liv
Bartlett NH; ch Silas m b1819
m1850 Lydia D Hale, Betsey M
b1822, Charles Carroll b1828
m1866 Caroline P Gale d/o Rev
Jonathan & Caroline Persis
Staples of Guildhall VT; NH-
0006-937
PENNIMAN,
Caleb D; b1804 s/o Nathan &
Bridget Blodget gs/o James
Blodget; m1829 Clarissa
Chesley d/o Thomas & Eliza-
beth Brewster of Rumney; liv
Plymouth NH; ch Adna L,
Charles D, Caroline m William
Harriman, James A, Justus B,
Clara C, Nathan; NH-0007-589

PENNOCK,
Human; b1791; m Mary Barnes of Haverhill; liv Strafford VT, Lisbon NH; ch Elbridge, Francis, Harley C, Mary m Charles W Bedell; NH-0007-453

Jefferson; b1808 s/o Human; m Ann Clark of Bath & m Jane Crouch of Dalton; liv Monroe, Haverhill NH; ch 1 dau m Edwin C Rowe, Jonathan C, Capt William, Ira W; NH-0007-359

PEPPARD,
J W; b1827; m1854 Mary G Merrill & m Nancy H Hutchins d/o David & Lucy; liv Londonderry Nova Scotia, Rumney NH; ch/o Mary - John E, William; NH-0007-620

PEPPERELL,
William; b1647; mc1680 --- Bray d/o John; liv Cornwall ENG, Shoals, Kittery; ch Sir William; NH-0003-79

Sir William; s/o William; m1722 --- Hirst of Boston; liv Kittery; NH-0003-79

PERKINS,
Lt ---; liv Waterville ME; ch John; Joseph; Stephen m Lydia Smith; NH-0003-292

Abraham; bro/o Isaac & John; m Mary Wise d/o Humphrey; liv Ipswich MA, Hampton NH; NH-0006-779

Dr Asa; b1793 s/o William of Dover; liv Rochester & Dover NH; NH-0003-847

Benjamin; b1680 s/o Caleb; ch Jonathan b1723 m Miriam True; NH-0006-779

Benjamin Rollins; b1807 s/o Stephen & Lydia Smith; m1831 Mary Jane Dolloff of Exeter & m Elmira J Kimball of Haverhill MA; liv Exeter, Rockingham, Dover; ch/o Mary - Lydia F, Benjamin J m Sarah Giles, William H, Jacob S, Irene E; NH-0003-293

David K; b1797 s/o John & --- Keniston of New Durham; m Margaret Runnels d/o Margaret Randall gd/o Elder Benjamin Randall; liv Middleton, Whitefield, Manchester; ch Nathaniel, Samuel R, Mary Ann m James Eastman, Manasseh H, Hon Nathan Randall b1828 m Elizabeth C Hicks, William

PERKINS (continued)
Dana, Joan m Moses Drew, David, 1 dy; NH-0005-421

Edwin R; b1833 s/o True & Mary A Chapman; m1858 Harriet Pelton d/o Asahel of La Grange NY; liv Tamworth NH, Cleveland OH; ch Mary Witt b1866, Harriet Pelton b1868, True b1873, Edwin Ruthven b1879; NH-0006-780

Isaac; bro/o Abraham & John; m Susannah Wise d/o Humphrey; liv Ipswich MA, Hampton NH; ch Caleb b1648, 11 others; NH-0006-779

Isaac; m Olive Leonard; liv Middleboro MA, Lyme NH; ch 4 dau, 5 sons; NH-0007-531

Israel; s/o Fredon & Lydia Cressey; m Emma B Ford d/o George N & Amanda M Davis of Danbury NH; liv Grafton NH; ch Annie S, Paul G H; NH-0007-287

James; bro/o Daniel; m Lucy Wilder d/o Maj Jonas; liv Lancaster NH; NH-0005-362

Capt John; m Hannah Hall d/o Ralph; liv Jackson NH; ch Col Joseph, 7 others; NH-0006-953

John; m --- Keniston; liv New Durham; ch David K b1797 m Margaret Runnels; NH-0005-421

Jonathan; b1723 s/o Benjamin; m1752 Miriam True; ch True b1753 m Sally Hunt; NH-0006-779

Jonathan Chesley; m1787 Hannah Dennett of Portsmouth NH; liv Wells ME, Loudon NH; ch Mary m David Morrill Carpenter; NH-0001-44

Col Joseph; s/o Capt John of Jackson NH; ch James M, Clinton; NH-0006-953

Joseph M; b1815 s/o Enos M b1784 & Judith Colby; m Maria P Jewett; liv Chelsea VT, Lebanon NH; ch George C, Helen M; NH-0007-421

Matthew; b1788; m Jane Little; liv Sanbornton NH; NH-0004-702

Hon Nathan Randall; b1828 s/o David K & Margaret Runnels; m1854 Elizabeth C Hicks; liv Lancaster & Jefferson NH; ch Manasseh b1855; NH-0005-421

Paul; s/o Timothy & Sarah of Center Harbor NH; m Frances O

PERKINS (continued)
Baker d/o James & Jane Smith; liv Ashland NH; ch Ella F; NH-0007-126

Solomon J; b1804 s/o Stephen & Lydia Smith; m1831 Armine Goodwin d/o Moses & Sally Lord of S Berwick ME; liv Exeter, Dover, Pittsfield NH; ch Rev George G, Solomon S, Moses A, Augusta m H E Parsons, Albert M, Robert Hamilton, Jennie S; NH-0003-292

Stephen; m Philomela ---; liv Wells, Eaton NH; ch Lucinda m John Gray, Harriet m Charles T Hatch, John W; NH-0006-791

Stephen; b1789; liv Wells ME, Eaton NH; ch John W b1813; NH-0006-793

Stephen; s/o Lt ---; m Lydia Smith; liv Exeter; ch John, Stephen, Solomon J b1804 m Armine Goodwin, Benjamin Rollins b1807 m Mary Jane Dolloff & m Elmira J Kimball; Joseph W; Sarah A m John F Merrill; Adeline A m George Merrill; NH-0003-292

Timothy; m Mary Gentleman; liv Jackson NH; ch Lemuel, John Y; NH-0006-953

True; b1753 s/o Jonathan & Miriam True; m Sally Hunt; liv Gilford, Tamworth; ch Nathaniel, Enoch, True b1806 m Mary A Chapman, Daniel; NH-0006-779

True; b1806 s/o True & Sally Hunt; m1831 Mary A Chapman b1810 d/o Andrew McC of Parsonsfield ME; liv Tamworth NH; ch Edwin R b1833 m Harriet Pelton, Mary A, Winslow T, George W, Andrew C; NH-0006-779

PERLEY,
Ira; b1799; m1840 Mary L Nelson of Haverhill; liv Boxford MA, Hanover, Concord; NH-0004-14

J Samuel; b1818 s/o Jacob b1775; m1850 Harriet E Fellows; liv Hanover NH; ch 1 dau; NH-0007-322

PERRYMAN,
Nicholas; b1692; mc1717 Joanna Dudley d/o Stephen; liv Devonshire ENG, Exeter; ch Joanna m Noah Emery Esq; NH-0003-29

PETERS,
John; s/o William gs/o William; liv Boston, Hebron CT; ch Margaret m John Mann; NH-0006-722

PETTENGILL,
Benjamin AM; b1789; m Betsey Pettengill d/o Lt Benjamin; liv Salisbury NH; ch Hon John W b1835 m Margaret W Dennitt & m Emma M Tilton & m Mary Dennitt; NH-0004-620

Hon James O; b1810; m Emaline Woodbury & m Mrs Harriet B Howard; liv Rochester NH; NH-0004-620

Hon Moses; b1802; m Lucy Pettengill d/o Amos & m Mrs Hannah W Bent Tyner; liv Rochester & Brockport NY, Peoria IL; NH-0004-620

Thomas Hale Esq; bc1780 s/o Benjamin & Polly of Salisbury; m Aphia Morse; liv Canaan, Salisbury; NH-0004-620, NH-0007-72

PEVERLY,
Thomas Jr; m Almira Everett d/o Hon Richard C; liv Northumberland; ch Richard Everett, Helen m Antipas Marshall; NH-0005-210

PHELPS,
Ephriam; liv Hebron CT, Orford NH; ch Elihu, 9 others; NH-0007-564

Henry; m Hannah Nevins d1806 & m Hannah Blodgett; liv Hollis, Groton; ch/o Nevins - Nathan b1788 m1810 Rebecca Otis; ch/o Blodgett - 2 sons, 5 dau; NH-0007-291

Nathan O; b1814 s/o Nathan & Rebecca Otis; m1841 Harriet Lucas; liv Groton NH; ch Charles O, Ruth Ann b1850, Mary F m Ira C Mosher; NH-0007-291

Samuel; b1742; m1764 Lydia Morey; liv Orford, Hebron CT; ch Samuel b1776 m Patience Cook & m Fanny Stevens & m Anna Bartholomew, 12 others; NH-0007-547

Samuel; b1776 s/o Samuel & Lydia Morey; m Patience Cook & m Fanny Stevens & m Anna Bartholomew; ch/o ? - Abner, Anna m Oliver Mitchell of Orford, Timothy B b1801 m Lydia B Rood & m Harriet N

PHELPS (continued)
Dickey; NH-0007-547
Timothy B; b1801 s/o Samuel;
m1849 Lydia B Rood of Lyme &
m Harriet N Dickey of Windham
NH; liv Lowell MA, Lyme NH;
ch/o ? - Nellie H; NH-0007-
547
PHILBRICK,
Daniel; m Ruth Morrill; liv
Hampton & Epsom NH; ch Daniel
m Polly Locke, 11 others; NH-
0004-475
Daniel; s/o Daniel & Ruth
Morrill; m Polly Locke; liv
Epsom NH; ch Abigail dy, Ruth
m --- Mason & m --- Merrill,
Mary, Asenath, Abigail m E B
Sargent, Betsy m Stephen F
Ring, David Morrill b1823,
Peggy Almira m George Buffum;
NH-0004-475
David; m Jennie Masten & m
Hannah Graves; liv Old
Campton NH; ch/o ? - David m
Eliza Dockham & m Abigail
Roberts, 6 others; NH-0007-
213
David Morrill; b1823 s/o Daniel
& Polly Locke of Epsom; m1850
Sarah A Stearns d/o John &
Margaret Wallace of Deerfield
NH; liv Epsom NH; 1 dy, Clara
I m Frank Buffum of Berwick
ME, Daniel, David F dy, Mary
A m George Giles of Pitts-
field NH, John S, Susan M,
George H, Augustus T; NH-
0004-475
Hon Emmons B; b1833 s/o Josiah
Webster & Sarah A Brown;
m1859 Vianna M Dalton of N
Hampton & m1875 Mary C Seavey
of Rye; liv Rye; ch/o Vianna
- 2 sons; ch/o Mary - 1 son,
1 dau; NH-0003-468
Harrison; b1822 s/o David of
Ware NH; m Sylvia A Brown & m
Ann C Dow d/o Elijah & Eunice
Robbins; liv Plymouth NH;
ch/o Sylvia - Adin; ch/o Ann
- Hattie m George S Pierce of
CA, Sylvia C m Albert C
Whittemore of Concord, Willis
F, Belle A; NH-0007-593
Jedediah; b1700 s/o Thomas Jr &
Mehitable Ayers; m1721 Mary
Taylor; liv Kingston; ch
Jeremiah b1722 m Mary
Stevens, Samuel b1739 m1767
Sarah Sanborn; NH-0003-375

PHILBRICK (continued)
Josiah; m Sarah Quimby d/o
Elisha & Hannah Badger; ch
Almon Q, Luella B b1824 m
John Elkins, Almira, Madison;
NH-0003-164
Josiah Webster; s/o Ephraim &
Sally Webster; m Sarah A
Brown; liv Rye; ch Emmons B
b1833 m Vianna M Dalton & m
Mary C Seavey, Horace F, Ella
F; NH-0003-468
Stephen G; b1771 s/o Jonathan;
m Ruth Rowe of Kensington;
liv Tamworth, Brentwood; NH-
0006-771
Sylvester; s/o David & ?; m
Sarah Wallace d/o Edward &
Betsey Pease; ch Nellie E,
Alice M, Byron J, Lizzie G;
NH-0007-213
Thomas Jr; b1659; m1681
Mehitable Ayres; liv Hampton,
Kingston; ch Jedediah b1700 m
Mary Taylor; NH-0003-375
PHILLIPS,
Alvah A; b1803 s/o John & Annie
Cummings; m Ruth A Sleeper
d/o Peter & Sally Atwood; ch
John F m Sarah A Pattee & m
Sarah A Ferrin; NH-0007-122
Jeremiah; b1813; m Lois Fisher
of Dalton; liv Bethlehem; ch
Warren, Clement J m Etta M
Benn of Lisbon, Lucy Ann m
Charles Cole, Lemuel; NH-
0007-497
Jesse; liv Bethlehem NH; ch
Reuben, Jeremiah, Moses, 6
others; NH-0007-165
John; m1783 Annie Cummings of
Plymouth NH; ch Alvah A b1803
m Ruth A Sleeper, 5 sons, 6
dau; NH-0007-122
John F; s/o Alvah A & Ruth A
Sleeper; m Sarah A Pattee d/o
William S & Betsey McMurphy &
m Sarah A Ferrin d/o Jonathan
& Mary V Hall of Plymouth NH;
liv Alexandria NH; ch Ella R,
Henry C, Willie A, Levi H,
Lou B; NH-0007-122
Moses; s/o Jesse; liv Bethlehem
NH; ch Amanda m --- Taylor,
Martha m --- Jesseman, Frank
B, Dennis, Willie B; NH-0007-
165
PHIPPS,
James M; b1816 s/o Elisha &
Dorcas Harriman of Chatham;
m1839 Lydia G Wheeler d/o

PHIPPS (continued)
  Amos of Milan; liv Milan NH;
  ch James S, 6 others; NH-
  0005-851
  Peter A G W; b1824 s/o Elijah &
  Dorcas of Chatham NH; m1845
  Abby W Kingsbury d/o Rev
  Leonard of Milan; liv Milan
  NH; ch 2 son, 3 dau; NH-0005-
  852
PICKERING,
  Daniel; b1795 s/o William &
  Abigail Fabyan, bro/o John;
  m1822 Sarah C Farrar d/o
  Joseph Esq of Wolfeborough;
  liv Wolfeborough NH; ch
  Joseph W dy, Eliza M dy,
  Caroline D m Charles Rollins
  Esq; NH-0006-309 & 380
  Frank T; s/o Thomas & Martha P
  Brackett of Newington; m
  Sophia DeWitt; ch Thomas,
  James B, Mary S, Adelia; NH-
  0003-311
  James A; s/o Thomas & Martha P
  Brackett of Newington; m
  Susan Mathes; ch Frederick,
  Alice B, Sarah; NH-0003-311
  John; liv ENG, MA, Portsmouth
  NH; ch John, Thomas; NH-0006-
  380
  John B; b1821 s/o Thomas &
  Martha P Brackett of Newing-
  ton; m1868 Sarah J Hodgdon;
  ch Edwin C, John B; NH-0003-
  311
  Joshua B; s/o Thomas & Martha P
  Brackett of Newington; m Jane
  Pickering; ch Deborah B,
  Joshua B Jr; NH-0003-311
  Nicholas; s/o Thomas of Newing-
  ton NH; m ? & m --- Langdon
  of Portsmouth; ch/o Langdon -
  Thomas m Martha P Brackett, 3
  others; NH-0003-311
  Thomas; liv Newington; ch
  James, Joshua, Thomas b1703 m
  Mary Downing & m Mary
  Janvrin, 9 dau; NH-0006-380
  Thomas; b1703 s/o Thomas of
  Newington; m Mary Downing &
  m1743 Mary Janvrin d/o Jean
  of Portsmouth; ch/o Mary J -
  William b1745 m Abigail
  Fabyan; NH-0006-380
  Thomas; s/o Nicholas & ---
  Langdon; m Martha P Brackett
  d/o Joshua of Greenland; liv
  Newington; ch Edwin A b1808,
  James A m Susan Mathes,
  Joshua B m Jane Pickering,

PICKERING (continued)
  Frank T m Sophia DeWitt,
  Martha P, John B b1821 m
  Sarah J Hodgdon; NH-0003-311
  William; s/o William of Green-
  land; liv Greenland; NH-0003-
  36
  William; b1745 s/o Thomas &
  Mary Janvrin; m Abigail
  Fabyan of Newington; liv
  Newington, Greenland; ch
  John, Stephen, Daniel b1795 m
  Sarah C Farrar, 7 others; NH-
  0006-380
PIERCE,
  Charles Warren; b1837 s/o
  Jerediah & Deborah Heath of
  Fairlee VT; m1866 Sarah C
  Dimick & m1876 Martha Abbie
  Howard; liv Concord; NH-0007-
  112.7
  Cummings; b1803 s/o Nathan &
  Phebe Cummings; m1833
  Caroline Dowlin of Bradford;
  liv Bradford NH; ch Lucetta
  b1838 m John Herbert Ewins of
  Warner, Anna b1849 m Freeman
  H Gillingham of Bradford; NH-
  0004-207
  Daniel; liv Watertown, Newbury
  MA; ch Daniel, Joshua m
  Dorothy Pike; NH-0003-105
  Daniel; b1709 s/o Joshua &
  Elizabeth Hall of Portsmouth
  NH; m1743 Anna Rindge d/o
  John of Portsmouth; liv
  Portsmouth; ch John m Mary
  Pearse, 1 son, 2 others; NH-
  0003-105
  David; s/o William & Dorothy
  Barnard; m Mary A Fuller d/o
  John & Eliza Rogers of
  Bridgewater; liv Ashland NH;
  ch Clara E; NH-0007-129
  Pres Franklin; b1804 s/o Gen
  Benjamin; m Mary A Appleton;
  liv Hillsborough, Concord,
  Washington DC; ch Frank dy,
  Benjamin; NH-0002-10
  Joel; m Hannah F Rowe; liv
  Petersham MA, Campton NH; ch
  Nathan m Caroline M Foss d/o
  Greenlief & Rebecca Mitchell
  of Campton; NH-0007-210
  John; s/o Daniel & Anna Rindge
  of Portsmouth; m Mary Pearse
  d/o Peter; liv Portsmouth; ch
  Col Joshua Winslow b1791 m
  Emily Sheafe, 3 sons, 2 dau;
  NH-0003-105
  John; b1799; m Sarah Oakes of

PIERCE (continued)
Bethlehem & m Rebecca Cush-
man; liv Gardner MA,
Bethlehem, Littleton NH; ch/o
Sarah - John Jr, Edward; ch/o
Rebecca - Sarah m E D Sawyer,
Eliza m Horace Woodard of
Cold Water MI, Mary m John G
Sinclair, Franklin, 1 other;
NH-0007-502

Joseph Rindge; s/o Col Joshua
Winslow & Emily Sheafe; m1859
Marcia Robinson; ch Mark
Wentworth, Emily Milnor, Anne
Burroughs, Joseph Parish,
Elizabeth Wentworth; NH-0003-
107

Joshua; s/o Daniel; m Dorothy
Pike d/o Maj Robert of Salisbury MA; liv Woodbridge NJ;
ch Sarah, Joshua b1670 m
Elizabeth Hall; NH-0003-105

Joshua; b1670 s/o Joshua &
Dorothy Pike of Woodbridge
NJ; m Elizabeth Hall d/o
Joseph of Greenland NH; liv
Portsmouth NH; ch Daniel
b1709 m Anna Rindge, 3 sons,
5 dau; NH-0003-105

Col Joshua Winslow; b1791 s/o
John & Mary Pearse of Ports-
mouth; m1823 Emily Sheafe d/o
William Esq & Anna Wentworth
of Portsmouth; liv Ports-
mouth, Greenland, Salmon
Falls; ch Sarah Coffin m1877
William M Kennard, Ann Went-
worth, Joseph Wentworth m1879
Annie L Sise, Joseph Rindge m
Marcia Robinson, William
Augustus m Mrs Susan M Smith,
Robert Cutts m1877 Marianna
Hackett, John, Peter, Emily
Sheafe, May Pease, James
Sheafe, Mark Wentworth,
Daniel Rindge; NH-0003-105

Martin; m Frances Martin; liv
Grafton NH; ch Ellen L,
Mattie V; NH-0007-279

Nathan; b1765; m Phebe Cummings
b1768; liv Hillsborough,
Antrim, Bradford; ch Nathan
b1787 m Abigail Graves, Susan
b1792 dy, Mary b1794,
Cummings b1796 dy, Susan
b1799 m Enos Collins of
Warner, Daniel b1801,
Cummings b1803 m Caroline
Dowlin, Stephen Chapin b1807
m Martha Collins; NH-0004-206

Nathan; b1787 s/o Nathan &

PIERCE (continued)
Phebe Cummings; m Abigail
Graves of Washington; ch
Benjamin Franklin, Cynthia m
Leonard Jameson; NH-0004-207

Stephen Chapin; b1807 s/o
Nathan & Phebe Cummings; m
Martha Collins d/o Enos of
Warner; ch Daniel; NH-0004-
207

Col Thomas P; b1820; m1842
Asenath R McPherson of Bed-
ford NH; liv Chelsea MA,
Manchester & Nashua NH; ch
Julia M m William N Johnson,
Frank; NH-0001-127

William; s/o Nathan & Jane
Steele of Francestown NH; m
Dorothy Barnard d/o Currier &
Samson of Plymouth; ch David
m Mary A Fuller; NH-0007-129

William Augustus; s/o Col
Joshua Wentworth & Emily
Sheafe; m1878 Mrs Susan M
Smith; ch Joshua Winslow; NH-
0003-107

PIKE,
Charles J; s/o Drewry & Louise
Burbank; m Ellen S Talbert;
ch Frederick b1869, Harry H
b1870, Bertha M b1876; NH-
0007-370

Chester; b1829 s/o Eben & ---
Bryant; m1862 Amanda M Fay
d/o Hon Levi Chamberlain; liv
Cornish NH; ch Chester Fay, 3
others; NH-0001-123

Elder Daniel Prescott; b1815
s/o Sewell & Mary Prescott of
Hampton Falls; liv Kensington; NH-0003-356

Drewry; b1811 s/o Moses & Mary
Ball; m Louise Burbank; ch 1
dau m John Goodwin of Man-
chester, 1 dau m Robert
Arnold, 1 dau m E R Morrill,
Burns H, Charles J m Ellen S
Talbert, Oscar B; NH-0007-370

Eben; s/o Ebenezer & Mary
Marcy; m1827 --- Bryant d/o
Capt Sylvanus & Sarah Chase
of Cornish NH; liv Cornish
NH; ch Chester b1829, John B;
NH-0001-123

Edward A; b1853 s/o Austin F &
Caroline White of Franklin;
m1879 Ida T Smith d/o
Jeremiah & Ellen of Fran-
conia; liv Hebron NH; NH-
0007-391

Edwin B; b1845 s/o Isaac &

PIKE (continued)
Sally Morse Noyes of Haverhill; m Addie A Miner of Salem MA; ch E Bertram b1866, Winifred A b1869, Archie F b1873; NH-0007-370

Eli; bro/o Newhall & Asher; m Mary A Sennott of Saco ME; liv Haverhill NH; ch Amos M, 2 sons, 4 dau; NH-0007-376

Harwood; b1808 s/o Robert & Deborah Smith of Stark NH; m --- Cole; liv Stark NH; ch Joseph A, William T; NH-0005-579

Isaac; b1799 s/o Moses & Mary Ball; m Irena Dole & m Sally Morse Noyes; liv Haverhill NH; ch/o Sally - Isaac b1829, Alonzo Franklin b1835 m Ellen M Hutchins, Edwin B b1845 m Addie A Miner, 3 sons, 2 dau; ch/o Irena - John D b1822; NH-0007-370

Isaac; b1829 s/o Isaac & Sally Morse Noyes of Haverhill; ch John D Hilliker, 1 dau m George Wilson of Bradford, Bion W dy, 1 dau; NH-0007-370

John D; b1822 s/o Isaac & Irena Dole of Haverhill; ch 1 dau m George Hatch, Samuel P, 1 dau m George Perkins, 1 dau m A A Knapp, Emma, Ephriam; NH-0007-370

John Gilman MD; b1817 s/o Nathaniel G gs/o John ggs/o Rev James of Somersworth NH; liv Durham & Salmon Falls & Dover NH, Boston MA; NH-0003-850

John Henry; b1829 s/o William & Elizabeth Folsom Hilton of New Market NH; m1850 Eliza J Thompson d/o William & Deborah Davis of Middleton NH; liv Epping; ch William H, John Q, Charles Edward, Albert Hilton; NH-0003-238

Moses; m Mary Ball; ch Isaac b1799 m Irena Dole & m Sally Morse Noyes, Drewry b1811 m Louise Burbank, Samuel b1814, 10 others; NH-0007-370

Robert; b1766 s/o Nathaniel & Betsey Bush of Portsmouth; m Deborah Smith; liv Stark NH; ch Harwood b1808 m --- Cole; NH-0005-579

Samuel; b1814 s/o Moses & Mary Ball; ch Charles W, Andrew J,

PIKE (continued)
William E; NH-0007-370

PILLSBURY,
Caleb; liv Loudon NH; ch Nathan, Ruth, Sarah, Judith, Elizabeth, Mary, Caleb, Benjamin, Martha; NH-0004-508

Caleb; b1681 s/o Moses & Mrs Susanna Whipple of Newbury; m1703 Sarah Morss; liv Newbury; ch Caleb b1717 m Sarah Kimball; NH-0004-147

Caleb; b1717 s/o Joshua of Newburyport MA; liv Amesbury MA; ch Micajah b1763 m Sarah Sargent; NH-0001-39

Caleb; b1717 s/o Caleb & Sarah Morss of Newbury MA; m1742 Sarah Kimball of Amesbury MA; liv Amesbury; ch Micajah b1761 m Sarah Sargent, 3 sons, 3 others; NH-0004-147

Caleb; b1786 s/o Capt Caleb; m1808 Nancy Nelson; liv Bridgewater NH; ch Randall J b1830 m Emeline L Fletcher, 5 sons, 6 dau; NH-0007-172

Hon George Alfred; b1816 s/o John & Susan Wadleigh of Sutton NH; m1841 Margaret S Carleton; liv Sutton & Warner & Concord NH, Minneapolis MN; ch Charles A b1842, Mary Ada b1848 dy, Frederick C b1852; NH-0001-39, NH-0004-147

John; b1789 s/o Micajah & Sarah Sargent; m1811 Susan Wadleigh d/o Benjamin of Sutton NH; liv Sutton NH; liv Sutton NH; ch Simon Wadleigh b1812, Hon George Alfred b1816 m Margaret S Carlton, Dolly W b1818 m Enoch P Cummings, John Sargent b1827, Benjamin Franklin b1831; NH-0001-39, NH-0004-147

Micajah; b1763 s/o Caleb; m Sarah Sargent; liv Amesbury MA, Sutton NH; ch Stephen, Joseph, John b1784 m Susan Wadleigh, Moses, 1 dau m Nathan Andrews; NH-0001-39

Moses; s/o William & Dorothy Crosby; m1668 Mrs Susanna Whipple of Newbury; liv Newbury; ch Caleb b1681 m Sarah Morss, 1 son, 4 others; NH-0004-147

Hon Oliver; b1817 s/o Dea Oliver & Anna Smith of Henniker NH; m Matilda Nevius

PILLSBURY (continued)
d1847 & m1850 Sarah Wilkins
of Henniker NH; liv Henniker
& Concord NH, Bound Brook
NJ; ch/o Matilda - 1 dau m
J S Eveleth of Beverly MA;
NH-0001-191, NH-0004-45
Randall J; b1830 s/o Caleb &
Nancy Nelson of Bridgewater;
m1856 Emeline L Fletcher d/o
S G & Dorothy S Prescott; liv
Manchester, CA; ch Geo I,
Henry F, Ida G, S G, Fred R;
NH-0007-172
Rev Stephen; b1781 s/o Micajah
of Amesbury MA; m Lavinia
Hobart b1795 d/o Dea Josiah
of Plymouth NH; ch Mary
Bartlett m --- Weston,
Lavinia Hobart m Samuel
Andrews of Bradford NH, Hon
Josiah Hobart m Elnora
Pevear, Stephen Jr m Sarah A
Bailey, Edwin m Mary Ann
Reid, Ann Judson m Andrew B
Marshall of Weare NH, A
Judson, Col William Staughton
b1833 m Sarah A Crowell & m
Martha Silver Crowell; NH-
0003-181
William; b1615; m Dorothy
Crosby; liv ENG, Dorchester &
Newbury MA; ch Moses m Mrs
Susanna Whipple, 6 sons, 3
dau; NH-0004-147
Col William Staughton; b1833
s/o Rev Stephen & Lavinia
Hobart; m1854 Sarah A Crowell
of Londonderry & m Martha
Silver Crowell; liv London-
derry; ch/o Martha -
Rosecrans Williams b1863,
Charles Hobart b1866, Hattie
Lavinia b1870, Ulysses Grant
b1876; NH-0003-181
PINGREY,
Col Stephen; b1835 bro/o Col
Samuel E AM b1832; m Mary
Foster of Bethel VT, liv
Hartford; NH-0004-620
Hon William M AM; b1806; m Lucy
G Brown & m Mrs Lucy C
Richardson; liv Weathers-
field, Springfield, Perkins-
ville; NH-0004-620
PINKHAM,
Rev George H; s/o Rufus & Mary
Trickey; ch Grace, Fred,
Carrie; NH-0006-950
Capt Joseph; liv Madbury,
Jackson; ch Joseph D m Mary

PINKHAM (continued)
Tuttle, George m Mary Gray,
Daniel m Esther Chesley,
Rufus m Mary Trickey, Betsey
m Isaac Meserve; NH-0006-950
Richard; ch Richard m Elizabeth
Layton d/o Thomas, John m
Rose Otis d/o Richard,
Thomas; NH-0003-772
Rufus; s/o Capt Joseph; m Mary
Trickey; ch Cyrus F, Rev
George H, Rufus U; NH-0006-
950
PIPER,
Benjamin; m1817 Sarah Currier
d/o Amos & Mary Sargent of
Hopkinton NH; ch Mary m Wyer
Gove; NH-0004-414e
John; liv Wolfeborough &
Tuftonborough NH; ch 1 dau m
Joseph Ayer of Barnstead, 1
dau m Abel Haley, 1 dau m
Nathaniel Mason, 1 dau m Levi
Hersey of Wolfeborough, 1 dau
m Lyman Allen of Nottingham,
Benjamin Y, 8 dau, 7 son; NH-
0006-440
John H; b1815 s/o John Jr; liv
Tuftonborough NH; NH-0006-443
Nathan; m Hannah Smith of Brad-
ford; liv Hopkinton & Bridge-
water & Bradford NH; ch True-
worthy b1805, Sally b1809,
Keziah bc1812 dy, Henry
b1816; NH-0004-207
Samuel; liv Loudon NH; ch
Jonathan, Benjamin, Sally,
Jane, Betsey, Samuel, David,
Elisha, Enoch; NH-0004-508
Thomas; liv Suncook, Wolfe-
borough; ch Thomas, David,
John; NH-0006-304
PITMAN,
Benjamin; m Sally Pendexter;
liv Jackson, Bartlett; ch
John P; NH-0006-916
Hon George W M; b1819 s/o
Joseph & Joanna Meserve of
Barlett; m1840 Emeline
Chubbuck d/o Levi & Ann M
Davis; liv Bartlett; ch Joan
M m Lyman Charles, Mary A,
Angevine, Winthrop M,
Lycurgus, William, Adnah m
Charles E Wingate, Levi C,
Joseph H, Emma m George A
Carson, Andrew J; NH-0006-270
John; s/o Joseph; m Abby
Carlton d/o Woodman; ch Hazen
b1806 m Mary Pendexter d/o
Joseph & m Eliza H Tasker d/o

PITMAN (continued)
Ebenezer & Polly Huson; NH-0006-915
John; s/o John & Susan Keniston; m Shuah Lougee of Gilmanton NH; ch John m Fannie B Miles, 5 sons; NH-0007-119
John; s/o John & Shuah Lougee; m Fannie B Miles d/o William & Hannah Batchelder of Alton; liv Alexandria NH; ch Warren L m Julia E Tappin; NH-0007-119
Jonathan M; b1814 s/o Hon Joseph & Joanna Meserve of Bartlett; m Mary Hodge; ch Georiana m Charles Chandler, Mary A m S D Meserve, Lucretia m W Chandler, William H; NH-0006-939
Joseph bc1759; m Alice Pendexter sis/o John; liv London ENG, Bartlett NH; ch William, Samuel, John, Hon Joseph b1788 m Joanna Meserve, Walter A, Sally m Joseph Philbrick, Rebecca m A D Gardner, Alice m Woodman Carlton, Dorcas A dy, Susan m J T Wentworth, Polly dy; NH-0006-939
Hon Joseph; b1788 s/o Joseph & Alice Pendexter; m Joanna Meserve b1786; liv Bartlett NH; ch Ezra M b1812, Jonathan M b1814 m Mary Hodge, Dorcas A b1816 m Joseph K Garland, George W M b1819, Joseph b1823, Frances E b1826 m Edward C Sinclair; NH-0006-939
Joseph P; b1809 s/o Ebenezer Jr of Meredith NH; m1841 Charlotte Abby Parker d/o Charles & Abigail; liv Laconia NH; ch Elizabeth W m Charles U Bell of Lawrence MA, Helen M m --- Bell, Charles F, Joseph W, Walter H; NH-0004-831
Hon Lycurgus; b1848 s/o Hon G W M & Emeline Chubbuck of Bartlett; m1870 Lizzie I Merrill d/o Caleb & Emeline B Kenney of Conway; liv Conway NH; ch Minnie E, Lena E, Millie I; NH-0006-903
PLAISTED,
Benjamin Hunking; b1808; m Rebecca ---; liv Jefferson

PLAISTED (continued)
NH; ch Charles, Philip C; NH-0005-420
Benning E; s/o Benning M & Phebe Eaton of New Hampton; m Nancy B Merrill d/o Moses & Sarah Chandler of Ashland; ch Oscar A m Ellie J Clough, Pamelia m --- Hogdon, Georgeanna m --- Stephens; NH-0007-128
Benning M; s/o William; m Phebe Eaton of Candia; liv New Hampton NH; ch Benning E m Nancy B Merrill, 2 others; NH-0007-128
Cyrus C; s/o Stephen; m Eliza Rowe; liv Ashland NH; ch Samuel, Clark, Ai; NH-0007-129
Oscar A; s/o Benning E & Nancy B Merrill; m Ellie J Clough; liv Ashland NH; ch Blanche M; NH-0007-128
PLATTS,
George; m Mary F Manter d/o Francis & Harriet Crowningshield of Londonderry & m Elizabeth A Smith; ch/o Mary - Ida, George, Frederick, Nathaniel, Floyd; NH-0003-586
James; m Harriet Manter d/o Francis & Harriet Crowningshield of Londonderry; liv Londonderry; ch Clarence b1856, Harriet b 1858, Mary b1867, Florence b1870; NH-0003-585
PLUMER,
Bard B; s/o Enoch W & Orinda Ayers; m Eliza D Wentworth; ch Lutia C, Fanny W, Bard B; NH-0003-657
Hon Bard; b1754 s/o John of Rochester; m --- Ham & m --- Page of Dunbarton; liv Milton; ch/o Ham - Jonathan, Enoch, Joseph b1786 m Sally Brown, Betsey m Joshua G Hall of Wakefield, Susan m Adam Brown of Wolfborough; NH-0003-657
Enoch W; b1815 s/o Joseph & Sally Brown of Milton; m1840 Orinda Ayers b1817 of Wakefield NH; liv Milton; ch John T, Joseph E, Mary B m Samuel W Wallingford, Bard B m Eliza Wentworth, Sarah m Rev Frank Haley, Fanny W m Dr J H Twombly, Susan m John

PLUMER (continued)
Roberts; NH-0003-657
George Washington; b1796 s/o
Gov William & Sally Fowler of
Epping NH; m1824 Betsey
Plumer d/o Samuel & Betsey
Cilley; liv Epping; ch George
W, Sarah E m F V Noyes of
Billerica MA, Catherine J m
James B Pierson of Epping;
NH-0003-230
John; liv Rochester; ch Joseph;
Hon Bard b1754 m --- Ham; NH-
0003-657
Joseph; b1786 s/o Hon Bard &
--- Ham; m Sally Brown b1785
d/o Nathan of Hampton Falls;
liv Milton; ch Jonathan dy,
Caroline m David P Wentworth
of Ossipee, Enoch W b1815 m
Orinda Ayers, Bard, Joseph
b1820 m Adaline F Baker & m
Hannah D Clark, Sarah m
George A Neal of Wakefield;
NH-0003-657
Joseph; b1820 s/o Joseph &
Sally Brown of Milton; m1844
Adaline F Baker b1820 d/o Hon
Moses of Somersworth NH &
m1863 Hannah D Clark b1830
d/o John N; liv Milton; ch/o
Adaline - Moses B, Joseph Jr
m Carrie Fall; NH-0003-657
Gov William; m Sally Fowler;
liv Epping NH; ch George
Washington b1796, Samuel; NH-
0003-230
William; b1759 s/o Samuel of
Newbury MA; liv Epping NH; ch
William Jr b1789; NH-0003-28
William Jr; b1789 s/o William
of Epping NH; liv Portsmouth,
Epping; NH-0003-29
PLUMMER,
Bitfield; m1769 Priscilla
Richardson of Chester NH; liv
ENG, Boscawen NH; ch Ephraim
b1771 m Rachel Choate
Cogswell; NH-0004-184
Ephraim; b1771 s/o Bitfield &
Priscilla Richardson; m1792
Rachel Choate Cogswell of
Essex MA; liv Boscawen NH; ch
Ephraim b1793 m Lucy Gerrish
of Boscawen; NH-0004-184
John H; s/o Richard J & Nancy
Swayne of Campton Village; m
Nellie Russell d/o Pelatiah &
Mary A Woodman of Plymouth
NH; liv Campton Village NH;
ch Carrie E; NH-0007-212

PLUMER (continued)
Dr Nathan; b1787 s/o Nathan &
Mary Palmer; m Sarah Colby
d/o Rev Zaccheus & m
Mehitabel Dinsmore d/o
Robert; ch Dr Albert MD; NH-
0003-147
Richard J; s/o Richard & Mary
Boynton; m Nancy Swayne d/o
Samuel & Abigail Hunter; liv
Campton Village NH; ch Sarah
A, John H m Nellie Russell;
NH-0007-212
POLLARD,
Jonathan Webster; b1808; m
Sarah H Marston d/o Dea John
of Tamworth & m --- Fellows
d/o Capt John of Sandwich & m
Mary R Brown of Moulton-
borough; liv Gilford, Tam-
worth; ch/o Sarah - Albert;
ch/o Mary - Albert S, Edward
S m --- Remich d/o Joseph S &
Julia A of Tamworth; NH-0006-
770
Milo C; b1842; m Climena
Blakeslee of Littleton, liv
Ryegate VT, Bath, Littleton
NH; ch 2 dau; NH-0007-505
Thomas; m Sarah ---; liv
Billerica; ch John b1727,
Ebenezer b1728, Thomas b1732,
Dorcas b1735 dy, Amos b1737,
Rachel b1739, Mary b1741 dy,
Samuel b1743, Timothy b1745;
NH-0002-460
POMFRETT,
William; liv Dover; ch Eliza-
beth m Thomas Whitehouse,
Martha m William Dam; NH-
0003-772
POOL,
Dr Jonathan; b1758 s/o Eleazer
of Woburn; m1780 Elizabeth
Hale d/o Col John; liv
Hollis; NH-0002-453
William; m1751 Hannah Nichols;
liv Reading MA, Hollis NH; ch
William W, James, Hon
Benjamin b1771, 11 dau; NH-
0002-438
POOR,
Benjamin; b1795 s/o Ebenezer &
Sarah Brown; m1816 Alice
Moore d/o Lt William of
Chester; liv Raymond; ch
Sarah J m Stephen Moar,
Rufus, Melinda K, George S;
NH-0003-454
Ebenezer; b1752 s/o Samuel; m
Sarah Brown d/o Capt Nathan

POOR (continued)
of Poplin; liv Newbury MA,
Raymond; ch Mary m John
Prescott, Nathan, Sally m E
Thatcher, Ebenezer, Rebecca m
Moses Stuart, Ruth m Reuben
Whittier, Benjamin b1795,
Dennis; NH-0003-454
Eri; b1800 s/o Samuel & Anna
Bridges; m1825 Susan Salt-
marsh of Goffstown; ch
Samuel, Eri; NH-0004-378
Jonathan; liv Atkinson &
Landaff NH; ch Betsey m ---
Simonds, John b1801; NH-0007-
401
Samuel; s/o Samuel; m Rachel
Bailey; liv Newbury MA; ch
Rebecca, Samuel, Judith,
Sarah, Eleanor, Rebecca; NH-
0003-454
Samuel; b1758; m1784 Anna
Bridges b1762 of Rowley MA;
liv Rowley MA, Goffstown NH;
ch Eri b1800 m Susan Salt-
marsh; NH-0004-377
PORTER,
John; s/o Asa & Mehitabel
Crocker of Haverhill; m ---
Webster of Chester liv
Chester, Newbury VT, CAN; NH-
0003-148, NH-0007-82
John Jr; s/o John Esq of
Londonderry; liv Bedford,
Manchester, Derry; NH-0003-28
Joseph Thyng; b1815 s/o Dudley
& Lydia Swasey Thyng of
Exeter NH; m1843 Abby P Fogg
d/o Josiah of Exeter & m1861
Anna M Wiggin d/o James J &
Nancy P; liv Georgetown KY,
Exeter NH; ch/o Abby - Ella m
Hazen Churchill; NH-0003-294
POTTER,
Col Chandler Eastman; b1807 s/o
Joseph & Anna Drake; m1832
Clara A Underwood d/o John of
Portsmouth & m1856 Frances
Maria McNeil d/o Gen John of
Hillsborough; liv E Concord &
Manchester NH, Hillsborough;
ch/o Clara - 4; NH-0001-302,
NH-0002-136
POWERS,
Clark W; b1824; m Clarissa E
Allen of Burke VT; liv
Newfane VT, Littleton NH; ch
Scott W, Allen, Clark W Jr,
Survillan, William A, Abel R,
Henry, Flora m John Thompson,
Rosette, 4 dy; NH-0007-505

POWERS (continued)
Ezekiel; b1745 s/o Lemuel &
Thankful Leland; m1767 Hannah
Hall d/o Lt Edward & Lydia
Brown; liv Croydon NH; ch
Ezekiel b1771 m Susannah
Rice; NH-0001-51
Ezekiel; b1771 s/o Ezekiel &
Hannah Hall; m1790 Susannah
Rice; liv Croydon NH; ch
Hannah b1795 m Bezaleel
Barton; NH-0001-51
Lemuel; b1714 s/o William &
Lydia Perham; m Thankful
Leland d/o Capt James of
Grafton MA; liv Northbridge &
Grafton MA; ch Ezekiel b1745
m Hannah Hall; NH-0001-51
Martin C; b1806 s/o Walter of
Bath gs/o Aaron; m1826 Mary
Weeks d/o David & Matilda
Child; ch Charles, Ellen M m
H B Denning, Laura W m Reuben
Dow, John M m Fanny Mande-
ville, Walter m Ellen
Cheever, H H m Lucie Weeks, 1
other; NH-0007-140
Capt Peter; m1728 Anna Keyes of
Chelmsford; liv Littleton MA,
Hollis, W Dunstable; ch
Stephen, Whitcomb, Levi,
Francis, Nahum, Samson; NH-
0002-439
Walter; b1639; m1660 Trial
Shepherd d/o Dea Ralph; liv
Salem & Littleton MA; ch
William b1661 m Mary Banks;
NH-0001-50
William; b1661 s/o Walter &
Trial Shepherd; m Mary Banks;
liv Littleton MA; ch William
b1691 m Lydia Perham; NH-
0001-51
William; b1691 s/o William &
Mary Banks; m1713 Lydia
Perham; NH-0001-51
William; m Mary Thompson; liv
Groton NH; ch Hon Joseph
b1802 m1825 Betsey Blood; NH-
0007-363
PRATT,
John; b1806 s/o Joseph & Lydia
Mann; m Sabra Tory & m Mrs
Myra B Bufton of Topsham; liv
Post Mills VT, Vershire,
Orford NH; ch/o Sabra - Alma,
1 other; NH-0007-566
Joseph; m Lydia Mann d/o John;
liv Salem, Orford NH; ch
Joseph, John b1806 m Sabra
Tory & m Mrs Myra B Bufton;

PRATT (continued)
NH-0007-566
PRAY,
T J W AM MD; s/o Maj Moses &
Lydia Worcester of Lebanon
ME; m1851 Sarah E Wheeler d/o
John H Esq & m1870 Martha A
Matthews d/o Rev S S; liv
Dover; ch/o Sarah - John
Wheeler, Thomas M; ch/o
Martha - Mary E; NH-0003-879
PRESCOTT,
Asa, b1787 s/o Nathan & Anna
Wells; m Polly Clark of
Greenland; liv Deerfield,
Epsom; ch Nathan Gove b1807 m
Betsey Hills Richards, 5
sons, 3 dau; NH-0001-281
Gov Benjamin Franklin; b1833
s/o Nathan Gove & Betsey Hill
Richards; m1869 Mary Little
Noyes d/o Jefferson & Nancy
Peart of Concord; liv Concord
NH; ch Benjamin Franklin
b1879; NH-0001-282, NH-0003-
227
Chase; s/o Enoch; m Nancy
Blackman d/o Adam & Betsey
Thurston of Gilmanton NH; ch
James S m Sarah Dean; NH-
0007-282
Daniel R; m Julia A Claflin d/o
Preston Williams of Lyme NH;
liv Manchester; ch George W;
NH-0007-542
David S MD; b1823; m Olive J
Ladd Knowles d/o Jonathan &
Betsey Lawrence Ladd; liv
Franklin & Temple & Laconia
NH; NH-0004-829
Fred S; m Ellen (Lill) Gilman
d/o James & Susan Mead of
Meredith NH; ch Leo F, Harry
S, Frank G; NH-0004-868
James; m Mary Boulter d/o
Nathaniel & Grace; liv Dryby
ENG, Hampton Falls & Kingston
NH; ch Jonathan b1675, 4
sons, 4 dau; NH-0001-281
James Sr; m1668 Mary Boulter of
Exeter; liv Lincolnshire ENG,
Kingston NH; ch James b1761 m
Maria Marston, Joshua b1769,
Jonathan, Mary b1677 m Jabez
Coleman, John b1681 m1701 Abi
Marston, Nathaniel m Ann
Marston, 2 others; NH-0003-
375
James; s/o Elisha gs/o James
ggs/o James; m Sarah Lane; ch
Simon, James b1779 m Margaret

PRESCOTT (continued)
Baab, 7 dau; NH-0003-351
James; b1761 s/o James Sr &
Mary Boulter; m Maria
Marston; liv Hampton Falls;
ch Samuel; NH-0003-375
James; b1779 s/o James & Sarah
Lane; m Margaret Babb d/o
James of Epsom & m Sarah
Sanborn; ch/o Margaret - True
M b1804 m Sarah M Pike, Lucy
M m Aaron Prescott, Eliza m
Emory Stevens of Eppingham;
NH-0003-351
James B; b1838 s/o Samuel &
Mary E Robinson; m1860 Hannah
D Clifford; ch George B
b1862; NH-0003-136
James S; s/o Chase & Nancy
Blackman; m Sarah Dean; ch
Clara E, Harry L; NH-0007-282
Jeremiah; m --- & m Elizabeth
Chase; ch/o --- 7; ch/o
Elizabeth - Samuel b1809 m
Mary E Robinson, 1 other; NH-
0003-136
Jonathan; b1675 s/o James &
Mary Boulter; liv Hampton; ch
Jonathan m Judith Gove, 3
sons, 2 dau; NH-0001-281
Jonathan; s/o Jonathan; m1721
Judith Gove d/o Ebenezer &
Judith Sanborn; ch Nathan
Gove b1735 m Patience Brown,
Micah, 2 sons, 7 dau; NH-
0001-281
Joshua; b1740 s/o Joshua of
Chester; m1762 Ruth Carr d/o
Bradbury & Anna; liv Sandwich
NH; ch Bradbury b1765, Ruth
b1767 m Samuel Burleigh,
Dolly b1773 m John Atwood,
Anna b1775 m Rev David Bean,
Joshia; NH-0006-673
Judson V B; s/o Charles; m
Lizzie J Webster d/o Iddo &
Sally Buswell of Wilmot; ch
Fred W, Laura A, Myra E,
Bertha J, Blanche E; NH-0007-
282
Nathan Gove; b1735 s/o Jonathan
& Judith Gove; m1757 Patience
Brown of Kensington; liv
Epping; ch Nathan b1759 m
Anna Wells, 2 sons, 2 dau;
NH-0001-281
Nathan Gove; b1807 s/o Asa &
Polly Clark; m1832 Betsey
Hill Richards b1811 d/o Capt
Benjamin & Mehitable Hills of
Nottingham; ch Gov Benajmin

PRESCOTT (continued)
Franklin b1833 m Mary Little Noyes; NH-0001-282
Nathan; b1759 s/o Nathan Gove & Patience Brown of Epping; m Anna Wells; liv Monmouth ME; ch Asa b1787 m Polly Clark, 3 sons, 5 dau; NH-0001-281
Samuel; s/o James & Maria Marston; liv Hampton Falls; ch John, Joseph, William; NH-0003-375
Samuel; b1809 s/o Jeremiah & Elizabeth Chase; m1838 Mary E Robinson b1818 d/o Eliphalet of Brentwood; liv Newport ME, Brentwood NH; ch James B b1838 m Hannah D Clifford, Samuel C b1843 dy, Mary E b1849 m Charles Snyder, --- b1859 dy, Howard L b1864; NH-0003-136
True M; b1804 s/o James & Margaret Babb; m Sarah M Pike b1808 d/o Joshua of Hampton Falls; ch Harriet A M, Warren J b1842 m Lavina F Hoyt; NH-0003-351
Warren J; b1842 s/o True M & Sarah M Pike; m1864 Lavina F Hoyt; ch Edwin J b1865, Nellie L b1868; NH-0003-351
PRESSEY,
Carlos G; m Mary N Putney d/o Hazen & Susan Page; ch George H; NH-0004-646
PRESTON,
Clinton F; b1826 s/o Joseph & Betsey Burnham; m1867 Rachel Abbott d/o Hazen; liv Rumney NH; NH-0007-613
Henry C; s/o William & Eliza Bradford of Cabot VT gs/o John; m Selina Houston d/o Henry C & Eliza Packard of Thornton; liv Campton NH; ch 1 dau m Bugbee of Hartford VT, Charles M, Fred H, Herbert R; NH-0007-216
James M; m1866 Louisa C Grant Demeritt s/o Charles & Salome V Center Grant & wid/o John Y Dermitt; ch Mabel S b1867, Emma F b1868, Marion P b1874, 2 dy; NH-0003-128
John; s/o Capt Samuel of Littleton MA, m1764 Rebecca Farrar sis/o Rev Stephen; ch John b1770 m Elizabeth Champney, 10 others; NH-0002-628

PRESTON (continued)
John; b1770 s/o John & Rebecca Farrar; m1798 Elizabeth Champney d/o Judge Ebenezer; ch John b1802 m Elizabeth French Smith, 9 others; NH-0002-628
John; b1802 s/o John & Elizabeth Champney; m1828 Elizabeth French Smith b1808 d/o Abram & Elizabeth Kidder of Boston; ch 2 sons, 1 dau, 4 others; NH-0002-628
PRICE,
Rev Ebenezer; b1771; m1799 Lucy Farrar of Hanover NH; liv Newburyport MA, Webster NH, Belfast ME; NH-0004-692
PRIEST,
Dr Jabez B; m1820 Fanny Moore; liv Pelham; ch 2; NH-0002-664
PROCTOR,
Thomas; liv Loudon NH; ch Lydia, Fanny, Sally, Thomas, Rebecca, Peter, Joseph, William, James, Benjamin, Priscilla; NH-0004-508
William W MD; b1807; m Mary Hale; liv Hill, Pittsfield; NH-0004-621
PULSIFER,
Charles W; s/o Maj John & ?; m Melvina Cook d/o Thomas & Martha Bartlett; liv Campton NH; ch Willard C, Lizzie G; NH-0007-206
David B; s/o Moses & Mary Bartlett; m Isabella W Draper d/o Reuben & Sally Johnson; liv Campton NH; ch Flora L, Joseph W, George E; NH-0007-206
Maj John; b1781 s/o Joseph & Mary Brown; m1806 Mary Palmer d/o Joseph & Martha Taylor & m Martha L Foss d/o Stephen & Keziah Stearns; ch/o ? - Thomas S m Hannah P Cook, Charles W m Melvina Cook, Phebe m Benjamin F Stickney; NH-0007-206
Joseph; b1745 s/o Joseph b1705 & Sarah Lovell; m1769 Mary Brown; liv Ipswich MA, Campton NH; ch Maj John b1781 m Mary Palmer & m Martha L Foss, Moses m Mary Bartlett; NH-0007-206
Moses; s/o Joseph & Mary Brown; m Mary Bartlett d/o Dea David & Joanna Hazeltine; ch David

PULSIFER (continued)
B m Isabella W Draper, 8
others; NH-0007-206
Thomas S; s/o Maj John & ?; m
Hannah P Cook d/o Col Moody &
Lucy Eaton; liv Campton NH;
ch John M; NH-0007-206
PURINGTON,
John; m Phoebe Beede; ch
Patience m Gen Montgomery;
NH-0006-676
PURMONT,
Charles W; m Susan E Gage d/o
Converse & Cerlania Carroll;
liv Enfield NH; ch Frank M,
Herbert C, George C, Mabel M;
NH-0004-650
Hiram; s/o Nathaniel; liv
Enfield NH; ch Nathaniel,
Minor T m Hannah C Day d/o
David; NH-0007-259
PUSHEE,
David P; s/o David; m Amy
Carpenter; liv Lyme NH; ch
Sylvester, Lucy, David C,
Miriam, Jesse C, Sidney A,
Mary, David P Jr, Alfred W m
Edna Steele d/o David, Albert
J; NH-0007-530
PUTNAM,
Alonzo W; b1828 s/o David of
Hanover; m1850 Hannah Cole of
Lebanon; liv Haverhill NH; ch
Parker A, John, Hiram M,
Walter E, Susie H m William H
Prescott, Carrie m Thomas
Morris, Mary, Nellie M m F P
Winn; NH-0007-373
PUTNEY,
Hazen; s/o Joseph of Hopkinton;
m Susan Page; ch Mary N m
Carlos G Pressey, Lydia E m
Walter W Stone, Almira M m
Jacob S Harvey, Truman b1828
m Lydia A Woodward & m
Frances E Gile & m Mrs Lydia
M Nelson; NH-0004-646
Truman; b1828 s/o Hazen & Susan
Page; m Lydia A Woodward d/o
Jonathan of Sutton & m
Frances E Gile d/o P S H &
m1880 Mrs Lydia M Nelson d/o
Emery Bailey; liv Sutton NH;
ch Cora Belle dy, Fred b1855;
NH-0004-646

-Q-

QUARLES,
Joseph V; s/o Hon Samuel &
Lydia Very; liv Ossipee NH,
WI; ch Joseph V, Charles; NH-
0006-637
Hon Samuel; b1764; m1795 Lydia
Very b1774 of Danvers MA &
m1810 Abigail Knight; liv
Wenham MA, Ossipee NH; ch/o
Lydia - Fanny m Benjamin
Sceggell, Joseph V, Lydia V m
Moses P Brown, Jerusha m
Charles Brooks, Capt Samuel
Jefferson b1807 m Sarah S
Dalton; ch/o Abigail -
Belinda K m Josiah Dearborn
of Effingham, Francis, Mary
Francis m Ebenezer French
Esq, Abigail Ann Caroline m
Asa Beacham; NH-0006-637
Capt Samuel Jefferson; b1807
s/o Hon Samuel & Lydia Very;
m Sarah S Dalton d/o Samuel
of Parsonsfield ME; liv
Ossipee NH; ch Maria, Lydia,
Samuel Dalton b1833 m1866 S
Augusta Brown d/o Moses P,
Sarah M m Aldo M Rumery,
William C; NH-0006-637
QUIMBY,
Aaron; s/o Jeremiah; m --- & m
Mary Towle; ch/o Mary -
Ziporah, Rebecca, Elisha m
Hannah Badger, Joanna, Lucy,
Mary, Aaron; NH-0003-164
Prof Elihu T; b1826; m Nancy A
Cutler of Hartford VT; liv
Danville NH; NH-0007-327
Elisha; s/o Aaron & Mary Towle;
m Hannah Badger; ch Nicholas,
Col Aaron b1799 m Mary A
Blake, Stephen, Sarah m
Josiah Philbrick; NH-0003-164
Enoch; liv Sandwich NH; ch
Nathaniel bc1801, John S; NH-
0006-247
Enoch; b1769 s/o Aaron b1733;
liv Weare & Sandwich NH; ch
John Smith b1793; NH-0006-674
Col Henry B; m Octavia M Cole
d/o Hon Benjamin James &
Mehitable A Batchelder; ch
Harry Cole, Candace E; NH-
0004-775
Jeremiah; ch Jacob, Moses,
Aaron m --- & m Mary Towle,
Jeremiah; NH-0003-164
John C; b1818; m Jane Rowell of
Bath; liv Lisbon, Littleton
NH; ch Ella m William B
Bowman, Sarah m Scott W

QUIMBY (continued)
Powers, Henry m Nellie Fisher, 1 other; NH-0007-495
William; d1804; m Martha Jesseman; liv Whitfield, Franconia; ch Mary Ann, James, Phebe; NH-0007-270

QUINCY,
Hon Josiah; b1793 s/o Samuel of Lenox MA; m1819 Mary Grace Weld d/o Jabez H of Plymouth & m1845 Harriet Tufts of Rumney & m1868 Mrs Mary H Dix of Boston & Woburn MA; liv Rumney; ch/o Weld - Martha Grace m --- Sleeper, Samuel Hatch, Elizabeth Frances m --- Dix, Josiah; ch/o Harriet - Mary Ann m --- Kinsman; NH-0007-112.18

QUINN,
Patrick; b1815 s/o Patrick & Catharine Clarke of Ballygar IRE; m1841 Mary Roach b1823 d/o William & Joanna Cumberford of Newfoundland; liv IRE, Providence RI, Boston, S Newmarket NH; ch William J, Sarah E m Matthew Carney, Laura A, Martha E, Charles E; NH-0003-539

QUINT,
Alonzo H; b1828 s/o George & Sally W Hall; b1854 Rebecca P Putnam d/o Allen & Eliza Page of Salem MA; liv New Bedford MA, Dover NH; ch George Putnam dy, Clara Gadsden, Wilder Dwight, Katherine Mordantt, John Hastings; NH-0003-881

-R-

RAND,
Charles White; b1819 s/o Hamlmn of Bath; m1847 Jane M Batchelder d/o Otis; liv Littleton; NH-0007-105
Edward Dean; b1821 s/o Hamlin of Bath; m Jennie Stevens d/o Truman of Littleton; liv Littleton, Lisbon; NH-0007-97
Hamlin; liv Bath; ch Charles White b1819 m Jane M Batchelder, Edward Dean b1821 m Jennie Stevens; NH-0007-97 & 105

RAND (continued)
Joseph J; b1844; m1874 Helen A Fife d/o Capt William & Mary D Gault of Pembroke; liv Rye NH; ch Mary A b1875; NH-0004-584

RANDALL,
James Emery Esq; m Arabella Chandler d/o Capt Isaac & Elizabeth Downing Furber; liv Great Falls; ch Mary C, Lizzie A; NH-0003-700
Moses; liv Sanbornton, Conway; ch William, John, Hannah, Polly, Nathaniel; NH-0006-850
Nathaniel; s/o Moses; liv Conway NH; ch George K, Agnes m Samuel Forrest, Susan m Charles S Whitaker, Hannah m Abiel C Lovejoy, Betsey m Luther Whitaker; NH-0006-850
William; m Betsey Lovejoy d/o Dea Abiel & Anna Stickney; ch Mary, Eliza m Samuel W Thompson; NH-0006-849

RAMSAY,
Ira Allen; b1827 s/o Robert of Wheelock VT; m Sarah L Merrill d/o Sherburn Rowell & Sarah B Merrill; liv Guildhall VT, Colebrook NH, St Paul MN; ch Sherburn R M, Ira A, Louis; NH-0005-249 & 643

RAMSEY,
David; s/o James Jr & Mary Nesmith of Greenfield; m Hannah Marshall; ch John M b1809, David b1811, 7 others; NH-0002-343
James Jr; m Mary Nesmith; liv Greenfield; ch David m Hannah Marshall, John m Margaret Steele of Antrim, James m Nancy Tenney, Elizabeth B m Thomas Holmes, Margaret, Mary Nesmith m Ebenezer Hopkins of Francestown; NH-0002-343
Capt John; liv Greenfield; ch William, Lt John, Samuel, Ebenezer, Mary m --- Boyd of Francestown, Margaret m David Parker of Antrim, Anne m John McKeen of Deering, Jane; NH-0002-343
Dr John; b1784 s/o William & Jemima Smith gs/o John; m1818 Ophelia Davis of Westford MA & m1829 Janet Steele d/o Thomas & Ann Moore of Peterborough NH; liv Greenfield & Mont Vernon NH; ch John

RAMSEY (continued)
Milton, Mary Davis m Dr
Leonard French of Manchester,
William Henry; NH-0002-347
William; s/o Capt John; ch John
MD; NH-0002-343
RAWLINS,
James; m Hannah ---; liv Dover;
ch Ichabod, Thomas m Rachel
Cox, Samuel, James, Benjamin,
Joseph, Deborah; NH-0003-551
& 674
Joseph; s/o Thomas; liv
Stratham; ch Mary, Joseph,
Hannah, Elizabeth, Charity,
Mercy, Rachel, Mary, Joshua m
Mary Clark; NH-0003-551
Joshua; s/o Joseph of Stratham;
m1735 Mary Clark of Stratham;
liv Stratham; ch Hannah,
Jonathan, David, Elisha,
Nicholas (Rollins) m Abigail
Tilton, Sarah, Anna; NH-0003-
551
Thomas; s/o James & Hannah;
mc1670 Rachel Cox; liv Dover,
Exeter; ch Thomas, Moses,
Joseph, Mary, Benjamin,
Aaron, Samuel, John, Alice,
Rachel; NH-0003-551
RAWSON,
Jonathan; b1759 s/o Rev
Grindall of Yarmouth MA; liv
Dover; NH-0003-588
RAY,
George; s/o William & Abigail
Wyman; m1834 Hannah Greene
d/o Capt James & Mercy
Nelson; liv Hinesburg &
Waterbury VT; ch Ossian b1835
m Alice A Fling & m Mrs
Sallie Emery Small Burnside,
Orman P, Elizabeth m ---
Bridges, Amelia m ---
Corrigan of Ogden UT, Hannah
m --- Baker of Waterbury VT;
NH-0005-222
Ossian; b1835 s/o George &
Hannah Greene; m1856 Alice A
Fling d/o Henry & m1872 Mrs
Sallie Emery Small Burnside;
liv Hinesburg VT, Lancaster
NH; ch/o Alice - Edward
b1858, Alice b1866; ch/o
Sallie - Helen b1873, Ossian
Jr b1878; NH-0005-222
William; m ? & m Abigail Wyman;
liv Hartford NY, Hinesburg
VT; ch/o Abigail - George m
Hannah Greene; NH-0005-222

REDING,
John R; b1805; m Rebecca R Hill
sis/o Hon Isaac of Concord &
m1846 Jane Martin of St
Johnsbury VT; liv Portsmouth
& Haverhill NH, Boston; NH-
0007-359
REED,
David S; m Huldah Moulton of
Lyman; liv Barnet VT, Bath
NH; ch Horace E m Emma Lang,
Elmer E, Albert M, Abiel S,
Henry S L, James B; NH-0007-
142
Joseph; m Martha Fletcher; liv
Westford MA, Plymouth NH; ch
Martha, Mary, Joseph b1792 m
Susan Cummings, 6 dau; NH-
0007-584
Joseph; b1792 s/o Joseph &
Martha Fletcher; m Susan
Cummings d/o Jonathan; liv
Plymouth NH; ch George C
b1814 m1844 Phebe C Currier
d/o Aaron & Anna Hoag,
William b1822 m Mary E Moses,
2 sons, 2 dau; NH-0007-584
William H; b1822 s/o Joseph &
Susan Cummings; m1861 Mary E
Moses of Campton; ch Charles
W b1863 m1885 Mary E Currier
d/o Edward & Mary Smith,
Henry W b1865, George C b1867
dy, Jennie May b1869, Joseph
M b1872; NH-0007-584
REID,
George; b1774 s/o Col George of
Londonderry; liv Londonderry,
MA; NH-0003-37
REMICH,
Daniel Clark; b1852 s/o Samuel
K Remick of Hardwick VT;
m1879 Belle Loverin d/o
Alfred of Colebrook & m1886
Mrs Lizzie M Jackson d/o
Benjamin W of Littleton; liv
Hardwick VT, Littleton &
Colebrook NH; NH-0005-256,
NH-0007-112.3
REMICK,
Capt Enoch; s/o John & ---
Evans of Tamworth NH; liv
Tamworth NH; ch Levi,
Charles, Edwin, Sarah m
Nathaniel Hubbard; NH-0006-
773
James; s/o John & --- Evans of
Tamworth NH; liv Tamworth NH;
ch Samuel Evans, Mary, John,
Joseph, 1 son; NH-0006-773
James Waldron; b1860 s/o Samuel

REMICK (continued)
K of Hardwick VT; liv Colebrook & Littleton NH; NH-0005-256

John; s/o Capt James & Sarah Edgell gs/o Capt Samuel Edgell; m Mary Jane Pease d/o John of Meredith; ch Harriet m Uriah Copp Esq of Lodi IL, Francis P; NH-0006-771

John; m --- Evans; liv Tamworth NH; ch Francis, True, James, Capt Enoch, Sarah; NH-0006-773

Levi E; b1823; m Harriet Beede of Tamworth; ch Charles Hayward, Edwin, Alice B; NH-0006-773

Samuel E; m Hannah Hatch d/o Gamaliel; ch Frank; NH-0006-775

Samuel Kelly; b1815; m1838 Sophia Cushman; liv Danville & Hardwick VT; ch Daniel Clark Remich b1852, James Waldron b1860, Kate O m Edwin Small; NH-0005-256 & 648

Simeon; m Hannah Bowman d/o Walter; ch James W m Ellen Goss of Waterford VT; NH-0007-485

REYNOLDS,
Dr Joseph; b1800 s/o Rev F of Wilmington MA; liv Chester, Gloucester, Concord MA; NH-0003-148

Thomas Osgood MD; b1842 s/o Rev Thomas F & Mary Currier of Chester NH; m1870 M Fanny Smith d/o William & Mary A Holman of Raymond NH; liv Kingston; ch Mabel; NH-0003-383

RICE,
Edward C; m Ianthe Blanchard d/o Daniel; liv Northfield NH; ch Laura, Fannie m --- Purdy, Inez m Artemus Tirrell Burleigh; NH-0004-532

Rev George M; m1855 Persis Fayette Weeks d/o James Brackett & Elizabeth Stanley; liv Dublin NH; ch Laura W m H H Piper, George B, Mary Nye, William; NH-0005-385

RICHARDS,
Dexter, b1818 s/o Capt Seth & Fanny of Newport NH; m1847 Louisa Frances Hatch d/o Dr Mason of Newport; liv Newport; ch Seth Mason b1850,

RICHARDS (continued)
Josephine Ellen b1855, William Francis b1867, Elizabeth d1868, 2 others; NH-0001-271

Edward; m1638 Susan Hunting; liv Cambridge MA; ch John; NH-0001-271

Capt Seth; b1792 s/o Sylvanus & Lucy of Newport; m1817 Fanny of Dedham MA; liv Newport NH; ch Dexter b1818, 1 son, 6 dau; NH-0001-271

Sylvanus; s/o Abiathar; m Lucy; liv Newport & Newport Village NH; ch Capt Seth b1792 m Fanny of Dedham MA, 3 sons; NH-0001-271

RICHARDSON,
Charles; b1809 s/o Jacob Esq & Sarah Lewis; liv Greenfield; ch Edward A b1843; NH-0002-346

E Coolidge MD; b1821; liv Peterborough NH, Ware MA; NH-0002-668

David; s/o Ebenezer; m Sally Walker; liv Lisbon NH, Littleton; ch Horace m Sarah Elliott & m Marinda H Dutton, 3 others; NH-0007-446

Edward; m --- Ellis of Sutton MA; liv Bethel ME, Milan NH; ch 3 son, 4 dau; NH-0005-833

Henry; b1821; m Mary J Clark d/o James; liv Lisbon, Bethlehem, Littleton NH; ch Israel C m Nellie E Williams of Lyndon VT, Leroy D H, Albert J; NH-0007-501

Horace; s/o David & Sally Walker; m Sarah Elliott & m Marinda H Dutton; liv Lisbon NH; ch/o Marinda - 2 dau, David F, Isaac; NH-0007-446

Jacob Esq; b1769; m1793 Sarah Lewis d/o Benjamin; liv Billerica MA, Milford & Greenfield NH; ch Jacob Jr b1794, Col Lewis b1801, Albert Louis b1803, Charles b1809, Col Cyrus b1812; NH-0002-345

James; b1814; m Jane Morse of Lisbon; liv Lisbon; ch 5; NH-0007-506

Jeremiah D; b1809 s/o Thomas & Nancy Odiorne; m Martha Place d/o John & m1849 Mary C Hopkinson b1822 d/o Moses & Elizabeth of Bruxton ME; liv

RICHARDSON (continued)
Rochester; ch/o Martha - Caroline m Edward C Hurd of Rochester, George A dy; ch/o Mary - N Bradbury b1851, Charles T b1853, Louis M b1860, J Sherman b1865; NH-0003-757
John Adams; b1797 s/o Joseph of Durham; liv Durham; NH-0003-601
Lucian; b1813 s/o Eliphalet b1785 of Moultonborough gs/o Col Bradbury of Bradford; liv Moultonborough; ch Orlando b1843; NH-0006-441
Thomas; s/o John gs/o William; m Nancy Odiorne, liv Rochester; ch Jeremiah D b1809 m Martha Place & m Mary C Hopkinson, Caroline, Mary Ann; NH-0003-757
William Merchant; b1774 s/o Capt Daniel of Pelham; liv Groton MA, Portsmouth NH, Chester; NH-0003-38
RIDDLE,
John; s/o James & Sally Ford; m Polly Robinson of Springfield NH; ch James, Ira, Andrew J, Neriah m Charlotte S Davis d/o Timothy & Hannah of Springfield NH; NH-0007-282
William P; b1789 s/o Isaac gs/o Gaen of Bedford NH; m1824 Sarah Ferguson d/o Capt John of Dunbarton; liv Piscataquog, Bedford & Manchester NH; ch 7; NH-0001-307
RITTERBUSH,
---; m Sophia Carlton d/o Timothy; liv Merrimack; ch Eliza, Sophia m --- Dodge, Mary Ann m Jerry Kittredge, Henry; NH-0002-543
Zebulon; m Sarah Wilkins d/o Andrew; liv Merrimack; ch Stephen W, Lucy Jane m John Collins of Nashua, William, Nelson; NH-0002-546
ROBBINS,
George A; m Mary C Goodale d/o Thomas Newton & Caroline G Calkins; ch Thomas G b1874; NH-0002-429
ROBERTS,
---; m Susanna Burnham; ch Timothy b1759 m Betty Hayes, John b1761, Joseph b1762 m --- Dam of Rochester, Susanna b1764 dy, Child b1765 dy,

ROBERTS (continued)
Relief b1767 m Daniel Horne; NH-0003-634
Amasa; b1814 s/o Ephraim of Farmington; liv Dover; NH-0003-598
Amos Main; s/o Timothy & Betty Hayes of Milton; ch Charles Wentworth; NH-0003-634
Andrew K; b1853 s/o William N; liv Tuftonborough NH; NH-0006-444
George T; s/o John; liv Kennebunk & Deering ME, Milan NH; ch Benjamin T, John, Burleigh, Marcia A, Lizzie W; NH-0005-832
Hiram R; b1806; m1831 Ruth Ham d/o John of Dover; liv Somersworth; ch John Ham, Stephen, Elizabeth, Edward H, Walter S Hall, Frank W, Susan J m Samuel H Rollins, Joseph Doe; NH-0003-674
Thomas; m Rebecca ---; ch John b1629 m Abigail Nutter d/o Elder Hatevil, Thomas b1636 m Mary Layton d/o Thomas, Hester m1673 John Martyn, Anna m James Philbrick of Hampton, Elizabeth m Benjamin Heard of Cochecho, Sarah m Richaird Rich; NH-0003-772
Timothy; b1759 s/o --- & Susanna Burnham; m Betty Hayes d/o Wentworth & Mary Main of Rochester; liv Milton; ch Amos Main, 7 others; NH-0003-634
ROBERTSON,
Robert; b1812 s/o William & Lydia Allard; m Lydia Nickerson d/o Joshua; liv Eaton NH; ch Charles, Orra m John Snow, Mark, Henry H; NH-0006-790
William; b1759 s/o Robert of SCO; m Elizabeth Conway & m Lydia Allard d/o David; liv Eaton NH; ch/o Elizabeth - Richard, William dy, Enoch m Hepzibah Bryant; ch/o Lydia - George, James, Samuel, Robert b1812 m Lydia Nickerson; NH-0006-790
ROBIE,
Henry; liv ENG, Dorchester MA, Hampton; ch John; NH-0003-352
Henry; b1714 s/o Ichabod; ch Nathan; NH-0003-352
Henry; b1797 s/o Nathan; ch

ROBIE (continued)
Nathan b1835; NH-0003-352
Ichabod; s/o John; liv Dover & Hampton Falls NH, ch Henry b1714; NH-0003-352
John; s/o Henry; liv Haverhill MA, ch Ichabod; NH-0003-352
John; s/o Lowell & Margaret Keniston; m Almira Dolloff d/o Abraham & Rachel Locke; liv Alexandria, Bristol; ch Gustavus, Sarah m A J Ferrin, Kathleen m George H Robinson; NH-0007-187
Lowell R; b1825 s/o Lowell & Margaret Kenniston; m Nancy S Flanders; liv Hebron NH; ch Fidelia J m John W Sanborn, Margaret A, Lurette K, Oscar S, Sadie E, George D; NH-0007-389
Nathan; s/o Henry; ch Henry b1797; NH-0003-352
Reuben; b1833 s/o Richard of Corinth; m1854 Eveline B Church of VT; liv Rumney NH; ch George W, Reuben W; NH-0007-613
Thomas; m Jennie McDermitt; liv Thornton; ch Archie m1853 Sally S Plummer d/o Mark & Nancy Clark of Sanbornton NH, 6 others; NH-0007-214
ROBINSON,
Addison R; s/o John G & Lucinda A Roberts; m Nellie M Swazey of Tamworth; liv Tamworth NH; ch Henry B; NH-0006-776
Don A MD; b1836 s/o Dr Elijah of W Charleston VT; liv Milan NH; NH-0005-846
Ezekiel; s/o George of SCO; m Hannah Hutchins of Killingly CT; ch Preserved m Betsey Gillis & m Mahaley Kimball, 5 others; NH-0007-211
John F; s/o Noah of Brookfield NH; liv Brookfield NH; ch Walter; NH-0006-457
John G; m Lucinda A Roberts of Meredith; liv Meredith, Tamworth; ch Addison R m Nellie M Swazey, Angeline m John D Hidden; NH-0006-776
Josiah; liv Epping, Brookfield; ch Josiah, Walter b1761, 1 son, 3 others; NH-0006-457
Noah; s/o Walter of Brookfield; liv Brookfield NH; ch George, John F, Albert O; NH-0006-457
Preserved; s/o Ezekiel & Hannah

ROBINSON (continued)
Hutchins; m Betsey Gillis of Bedford NH & m Mahaley Kimball of Concord NH; ch/o - ? William P m Julia W Foss, 3 others; NH-0007-211
Walter; b1761 s/o Josiah; liv Brookfield NH; ch Richard, Henry, Ebenezer C, Noah, 4 others; NH-0006-457
William P; s/o Preserved & ?; m Julia W Foss d/o Carter & Mahaley of Thornton; ch George, Charles, Julia, Jennie, Frank; NH-0007-211
ROBY,
George; b1834 s/o Samuel gs/o Ichabod ggs/o Samuel; m1868 Josephine Page d/o Enoch & Hannah C Colby of Sutton; liv Sutton NH; ch Eva B b1870; NH-0004-649
John; m Mary Garland; liv N Hampton; ch Thomas b1783 m Betsey Elkins, Bashaba, Betsey, Mary, Simon; NH-0003-423
Thomas; b1783 s/o John & Mary Garland of N Hampton; m1826 Betsey Elkins d/o Jeremiah of Hamilton; liv N Hampton; ch John H dy, Jeremiah H b1828 m1852 Hannah P Seavey b1831 d/o Ephraim & Betsey, Mary E A b1830 Washington Parker; NH-0003-423
ROGERS,
Benjamin; b1780 s/o Dea Samuel; m Lucy Hoegg of Bow; liv Northfield NH; ch Fannie m Simeon Kimball of Sanbornton Bridge, Betsy R m John T Gilman of Columbia, Lucy H m Gilbert L Frizzell, Rebecca L m Thomas J Emerton, Sally K m Ebenezer Thurston, Abigail dy, Samuel B m Susan K Forrest, Benjamin A b1823; NH-0004-525
Benjamin A; m Viola E Rundlett & m Adeliza S Rundlett sis/o Viola; liv Northfield & Sanbornton Bridge NH, TX; NH-0004-702
Charles; s/o Enoch & Lydia Moors; m Mary L Gordon of Pittsfield NH & m Tryphena French; liv Ashland NH; ch Gardner F m Myra A Brown d/o John S & Mara Robinson of Groton NH; NH-0007-127

ROGERS (continued)
  Charles C Esq; b1834; m1860
  Sophia T Curry; liv Bloom-
  field VT, Tilton NH; ch John
  W b1861, Carrol B b1863 dy,
  Arthur b1870 dy, George Bell
  b1874, Herbert S b1877; NH-
  0004-702 & 885
  Daniels Allen; b1828 s/o Rev
  Daniel & Phoebe Tibbetts of
  Columbia; m1855 Sarah A
  Cooper d/o Samuel B & Amanda
  Bicknel of Beloit WI; liv St
  Johnsbury VT, Wells River;
  NH-0004-248
  George W; b1796 s/o Dr John of
  Plymouth; m1833 Sarah Allen
  d/o John of Salem NH; liv
  Rumney NH; ch George S b1835,
  Hamilton K b1837 m Addie E
  Fales, Annie L b1844 m Henry
  Noyes; NH-0007-611
  Hamilton K; b1837 s/o George W
  & Sarah Allen of Rumney;
  m1876 Addie E Fales; liv
  Rumney NH; ch Willie H b1877,
  Walter M b1879; NH-0007-611
  Herbert E; m Lillian Sanborn
  d/o Hon John W & Almira J
  Chapman of Wakefield; ch
  Herbert Sanborn; NH-0006-524
  James; liv Barlett NH; ch
  Daniel, Joshua, Jonathan; NH-
  0006-916
  John; s/o Dea Samuel; m Sally
  Cofran; liv Northfield NH; ch
  Joanna m Walter Bailey,
  Jeremiah, 2 others; NH-0004-
  525
  Nathaniel P; b1794 s/o Dr John
  & Betsey Mulliken; m1832 Mary
  Porter Farrand of Burlington
  VT; liv Plymouth & Concord
  NH; NH-0007-112.9
  Dea Samuel; bc1745; liv Bow &
  Northfield NH; ch Enoch,
  Samuel, John m Sally Cofran,
  Benjamin b1780 m Lucy Hoegg,
  Jesse, Rebecca, Mehitable;
  NH-0004-525
  Thadeus; liv Lemington VT,
  Piermont NH; ch Elisha b1807;
  NH-0007-575
ROLFE,
  Benjamin; m Sarah Walker d/o
  Rev Timothy; liv Concord; ch
  Paul; NH-0004-411
  Benjamin; s/o Benjamin & Lydia
  Pearsons of Newbury MA; m
  Margaret Searle d/o Rev
  Jonathan of Salisbury; liv

ROLFE (continued)
  Boscawen NH; ch Henry
  Pearsons b1821 m Mary Rebecca
  Sherburn; NH-0004-624
  Henry Pearsons; b1821 s/o
  Benjamin & Margaret Searle of
  Boscawen NH; m1853 Mary
  Rebecca Sherburn d/o Robert H
  of Concord; liv Concord NH;
  ch Marshall Potter b1854 dy,
  Margarett Florence b1858 dy,
  Henrietta Maria b1861 dy,
  Robert Henry b1863, George
  Hamilton b1866; NH-0004-624
  Jonas; b1793; m1819 Martha P
  Sloan; liv Lyme, Colebrook
  NH; ch Mariel W b1822,
  William Smith b1824 m Lois
  Hobart, Mary E m George S
  Leavitt, Morton B b1832, Fitz
  C b1834, Frank M; NH-0005-623
  Jonathan; m1824 Margaret
  Parsons d/o Hezekiah & Polly
  (Mary) Bevins; ch Susan Jane
  b1831 m Allen Hatch Forbes,
  Almera B b1828 m George
  Brower, Charles E b1826 m
  Ellen Faulkner, Harriet A
  b1833 m Daniel Munroe Smith
  of Brunswick VT, 2 others;
  NH-0005-631
ROLLINS,
  Amos L; b1826 s/o Ichabod Jr of
  Alton gs/o Ichabod of Newing-
  ton NH; m1851 Sarah E Kimball
  & m1872 Permelia A Pendergast
  of Barnstead NH; liv Alton
  NH; ch/o Sarah - 3 sons, 2
  dau; NH-0004-709
  Augustus; b1797 s/o Capt Hiram
  & Joanna Wentworth of Somers-
  worth; m1824 Abiah Winkley of
  Barrington NH; liv Rollins-
  ford; ch Samuel Winkley,
  Oliver E, Augustus W m Mary A
  Livy d/o Dr D T of Wolf-
  borough NH, Mary, Ellen,
  Lydia Hale; NH-0003-678
  Charles Esq; m Caroline D
  Pickering d/o Daniel & Sarah
  C Farrar of Wolfeborough; liv
  Boston, Rollinsford; ch Helen
  M, Sarah P m Harry Ashmead
  Lewis, Charles H; NH-0006-383
  Hon Daniel G; b1796 s/o John &
  Betsey Shapleigh gs/o John
  ggs/o Hon Ichabod gggs/o
  Jeremiah; m1825 Susan Binney
  Jackson of Watertown MA; liv
  Portsmouth & Great Falls NH;
  ch Franklin J, Hon Edward

ROLLINS (continued)

Ashton, Daniel G, George F, --- m Thomas C Parks of Newton MA, --- m Oliver W Shaw of Austin MN, --- m John P Pope, Carrie E, Mary P, 2 dy; NH-0003-394 & 674 & 693

Daniel; b1797 s/o James of Rollinsford NH; m Mary Plumer d/o Ebenezer of Rollinsford; liv Rollinsford, ME; ch Hon Edward Henry b1824 m Ellen E West, 3 sons, 2 dau; NH-0001-215, NH-0003-674

Hon Edward Atherton; b1828 s/o Hon Daniel G; liv Wakefield & Somersworth NH; NH-0001-143

Hon Edward Henry; b1824 s/o Daniel & Mary Plumer; m1849 Ellen E West d/o John & --- Montgomery of Concord NH; liv Rollinsford & Concord NH, Boston MA; ch Edward W b1850, Mary Helen b1853 m Henry Robinson, Charles Montgomery b1856 dy, Frank West b1860, Montgomery b1867; NH-0001-217, NH-0003-674

Elijah; m Mary Prescott of kensington & m Mary Chase of Deerfield; liv Deerfield NH; ch/o ? - Ebenezer m Betsey Rollins of Deerfield, 10 others; NH-0007-281

Ephraim F; s/o Paul & Deborah Pickering; m Abigail Frink; ch Margaret m --- Prescott of Boston, William; NH-0003-394

George A; s/o Joseph & Harriet K Simons; m Edna J Scribner d/o Lowell & Charlotte Bean of Franklin; ch Harry D (adopted); NH-0007-122

Gilbert W; s/o Ebenezer & Betsey Rollins; m Savalla Barney d/o John; liv Grafton NH; ch Helen A, Albion W; NH-0007-281

Henry O; s/o Horace R & Hannah M Wadleigh of Grafton; m Arrolin Clifford d/o Samuel & Sally Sanborn of Enfield; liv Grafton NH; ch Arthur H, Weston C, Bessie A, Willis H, Belle M; NH-0007-281

Capt Hiram; s/o John gs/o Ichabod ggs/o Jeremiah; m1790 Joanna Wentworth d/o Paul gd/o Col John & m1804 Mary H Simes of Portsmouth; liv Somersworth; ch/o Joanna -

ROLLINS (continued)

Augustus b1797 m Abiah Winkley; NH-0003-678

Horace R; s/o Aaron; m Hannah M Wadleigh; liv Grafton NH; ch Henry O m Arrolin Clifford; NH-0007-281

Ichabod; s/o James; ch Jeremiah; NH-0003-394

Ichabod; s/o Jeremiah of Dover & Somersworth NH; liv Rollinsford NH; d1800; ch John, Daniel G, James; NH-0001-218, NH-0003-674

James; liv ENG, Ipswich MA, Newington NH; ch Ichabod, Thomas; NH-0001-217

James; bc1605; liv ENG, Ipswich MA, Dover; ch Ichabod; NH-0003-394

James; s/o Ichabod of Rollinsford; liv Rollinsford; ch Daniel b1797 m Mary Plumer, 6 sons, 6 dau; NH-0003-674

James; s/o Nicholas & Ann Fifield of Stratham; m1823 Sophia Moore of Stratham; liv Stratham; ch Benjamin F, James W b1825 m Abby A Smith, Sophia A, Augusta H, Albert N; NH-0003-551

James W; b1825 s/o James & Sophia Moore of Stratham; m1874 Abby A Smith d/o L B & Betsey Dole of Newmarket NH; liv Stratham; ch Florence F, James W Jr; NH-0003-551

Jeremiah; s/o Ichabod; liv Dover & Somersworth NH; ch Ichabod, several others; NH-0001-217

Jeremiah; s/o Ichabod gs/o James Rawlins; liv Somersworth; ch Ichabod, several dau; NH-0003-674

John A; b1791; m1823 Mary Randlett & m Mary Copp of Tuftonborough & m Elizabeth Lee; liv Andover, Moultonborough; NH-0006-414

Col Jonathan; liv Loudon NH; ch Joanna, Huldah, Sophronia, Judith, John, Sally, Jeremiah, Ai, Judith, Trueworth; NH-0004-508

Joseph; s/o David & Judith Leach; m Harriet K Simons d/o Caleb & Lois Phelps of Hebron; ch George A m Edna J Scribner, 9 others; NH-0007-122

ROLLINS (continued)
Joseph; b1789; m1812 Mary Huckins; liv Sanbornton & Bristol NH; Bridgewater; ch Eliza m Putnam Spaulding, Samuel H m Irena Whipple & m1876 Mrs Huldah B Walker, Sarah Jane m John F Tilton, Mary S m Samuel Fellows, Richard B m Martha Gray, Joseph m Amanda Ingalls, Lyman m Augusta Flanders of Concord; NH-0007-186
Moses; liv Loudon NH; ch Samuel, Anna, Thomas, Moses, William, Eliza, Sarah, Abigail, Jonathan, John, Dorothy; NH-0004-508
Nicholas; s/o Joshua (Rawlins) & Mary Clark of Stratham; m1761 Abigail Tilton d/o Abraham of Stratham; liv Stratham; ch Hannah, Elisha, Nicholas m Ann Fifield, Daniel, Mary, Levi, Mark, Asa, Ann, Elisha, Abigail; NH-0003-551
Nicholas; s/o Nicholas & Abigail Tilton of Stratham; m1795 Ann Fifield of Stratham; liv Stratham; ch Clarissa, James m Sophia Moore, Hannah, Levi, Mary, Ann, Martha, Abigail, Nicholas F, Louisa; NH-0003-551
Paul; m Deborah Pickering d/o Ephraim & Martha Coleman; ch Martha C, Ephraim F m Abigail Frink, Lydia, Daniel; NH-0003-394
Reuben B; m Mary Smith; ch John m Mrs Wiggins & m Ruth B Sargent d/o John & Nancy of Holderness, 12 others; NH-0007-129
William; s/o Ephraim F & Abigail Frink; ch Alice A; NH-0003-394
ROOD,
Rev Herman DD; b1795 s/o Thomas D & Sarah Bradley of Jericho VT; m1827 Frances Susan Moody d/o Stephen Esq of Gilmanton; liv Gilmanton & Haverhill NH; New Milford CT, Quebec & Hartland VT; NH-0004-796
ROSEBROOK,
Capt Eleazer; b1747; m Hannah Haines of Brimfield; liv Grafton MA, Lancaster NH,

ROSEBROOK (continued)
Guildhall VT; ch Phineas bc1778 m Hannah Stillings; NH-0005-443
Phineas; bc1778 s/o Capt Eleazer & Hannah Haines; m Hannah Stillings b1780 of Bartlett; liv Carroll NH; ch Franklin, Leander, Phineas b1807 m Sophronia Tuttle, Mitchell dy, Mitchell, Louisa m Robert Tuttle, Mary, Laura, Lee, Eleazer, James F D; NH-0005-443
Phineas; b1807 s/o Phineas & Hannah Stillings of Carroll NH; m1827 Sophronia Tuttle d/o Benjamin & Jane Folsom; liv Carroll NH; ch Lee, Jennie m Augustus Hodgkins, Amasa, Mark P, Frank B, Eliza J m Nelson A Glines, Laura A m Frank Hobbs, John W; NH-0005-443
ROSS,
Harvey P; s/o Samuel & Fanny Smith; m Eliza Balch of Bath & m Lucia W Eastman of Littleton; ch/o Eliza - Elwood J, Samuel m Mary Chamberlin d/o Phineas, Mary m F H Rollins of Plymouth; NH-0007-144
Samuel; m Fanny Smith d/o Jonathan & m --- Smith wid/o Oliver of Lebanon; liv Gilmanton, Bath NH; ch/o Fanny - Julia m Cyrus Eastman of Littleton, Seraphina m D K Jackman, Harvey P m Eliza Balch & m Lucia W Eastman, 3 sons; NH-0007-144
Thomas; liv Billerica MA, Hanover NH; ch Nathan, Benjamin, Hon Isaac, David, 2 sons, 3 dau; NH-0007-320
William C; b1834 s/o Elam of Groton; m1860 Mary A Nutting d/o Arthur & Mary Ann Noyes; liv Hebron NH; NH-0007-389
ROWE,
Benjamin; liv Brentwood & Gilford NH; ch Hon John M, Benjamin F; NH-0004-746
Dr Benjamin; b1719 s/o Robert; liv Kensington; ch Dr Benjamin b1750; NH-0003-357
Benjamin MD; b1750 s/o Hon Benjamin & Susanna Figg of Kensington; m Joanna Tilton b1751; liv E Kingston; NH-

ROWE (continued)
0003-189
George R; b1849 s/o Robert &
Sally T Sinclair; m1870 Betsy
J Gordon d/o Lewis B; ch
George Russell; Robert G; NH-
0003-135
James H; b1844 s/o Robert &
Sally T Sinclair; m1868 Emma
P Little d/o David; ch Annie,
John M; NH-0003-135
Jonathan; b1777 s/o Simon &
Mary Morrison; m1805 Anna
Robinson d/o Joseph of Brent-
wood; liv Brentwood; ch Simon
b1806, Robert b1810 m Sally T
Sinclair, Joseph b1813; NH-
0003-134
Joseph F; s/o Dr Benjamin MD of
E Kingston; m Mary Thayer
b1782 d/o Rev Elihu DD of
Kingston; ch Martha T m
George Webster, Rev Elihu
Thayer b1813, 2 others; NH-
0003-190 & 189
Joseph R; b1846 s/o Robert &
Sally T Sinclair; m1871 Abby
Robinson d/o John R; ch
Lillian; NH-0003-135
Robert; liv Kensington NH; ch
Robert b1726 m Abigail
Tilton, 9 sons, 2 dau; NH-
0003-134
Robert; b1726 s/o Robert of
Kensington NH; m1749 Abigail
Tilton; liv Brentwood; ch
Robert, Simon b1751 m Mary
Morrison, Lovey, Aphia; NH-
0003-134
Robert; b1810 s/o Jonathan &
Anna Robinson; m1834 Sally T
Sinclair b1813 d/o Henry of
Brentwood; liv Lynn MA,
Brentwood; ch Harriet E m
Aaron Brown, Jonathan S,
James H b1844 m Emma P
Little, Joseph R b1846 m Abby
Robinson, George R b1849 m
Betsy J Gordon; NH-0003-134
Simon; b1751 s/o Robert of
Brentwood; m1776 Mary
Morrison of Haverhill MA; ch
Jonathan b1777 m Anna
Robinson, Simon, David,
Benjamin, Anna, Miriam; NH-
0003-134
Smith; b1814; m1835 Elvira
Wheet of Canaan & m1838
Caroline A Sanborn of
Andover; liv Landover & Ply-
mouth NH; ch/o Elvira - Eliza

ROWE (continued)
m Stephen B Kendrick; ch/o
Caroline - Joseph B, Caroline
E m John Bullard, George D,
Abbie E m W L Horner of
Thornton, Frank L, Asa M,
Fred S, Ralph B; NH-0007-596
ROWELL,
---; m Abigail Prescott d/o
Jeremiah; liv E Kingston; ch
Philip; NH-0003-190
Daniel; liv Stark NH; ch Piercy
b1790, Lydia b1792; NH-0005-
570
Irving G; m Mary E Fulton d/o
Joseph W & Lucy A Sargent;
liv Weare NH; ch Alice M,
Charles W; NH-0002-390
Jonathan; liv Stark NH; ch
Jonathan b1800; NH-0005-570
Moses; liv Gilford NH; ch
Jacob, Philip; NH-0004-746
Moses Sr; b1764 s/o Christopher
of Amesbury MA; m Alice
Currier of Amesbury & m Nancy
Leavitt of Chichester NH; liv
Loudon NH; ch/o ? - Capt
John, Moses Jr b1793 m Sophia
French, Nancy, Micajah, Ruth,
Asa T, Harris, Cyrus, Rufus,
Sally L; NH-0004-505
Moses Jr; b1793 s/o Moses Sr &
?; m Sophia French d/o John
Leavitt of Loudon; ch Perley
W b1823 m Caroline Clark,
John F b1826, Sarah Ann; NH-
0004-505
Perley W; b1823 s/o Moses Jr &
Sophia French; m1869 Caroline
Clark of Pittsfield NH; ch
Sarah W, George W; NH-0004-
505
RUGGLES,
Edward R; b1837; m Charlotte
Blaisdell d/o Hon Daniel; liv
Norwich VT; NH-0007-327
RUMERY,
Aldo M; b1842 s/o John M &
Sarah of Effingham; m1870
Sarah M Quarles Wiggin wid/o
Thomas B of Ossipee; liv
Ossipee NH; ch Howard C
b1873, Laura M b1874; NH-
0006-632
RUNDLET,
Abraham; b1769 s/o James &
Sarah Rowell of Epping NH;
m1793 Hannah Lawrence b1770
d/o Edward; liv Epping; ch
John b1795, James L b1805 m
Elsie Plumer & m Olive B

RUNDLET (continued)
Rundlet & m Mrs Harriet Sanborn Winslow; NH-0003-242
James; b1735; m Sarah Rowell b1742; liv Epping; ch James, John, Mercy, Sarah, Abraham b1769 m Hannah Lawrence, Anna, Molly, Rhoda, Dorothy, Jemima, Honor; NH-0003-242
James L; b1805 s/o Abraham & Hannah Lawrence of Epping; m Elsie Plumer b1804 d/o Samuel & m1840 Olive B Rundlet d/o John S & m1861 Mrs Harriet Sanborn Winslow wid/o George Winslow d/o Zebulon Sanborn; liv Epping; ch/o Elsie - Elizabeth P m Rufus Sanborn; ch/o Olive - Albert S dy, Clara H m Alvin R Thompson of Epping; NH-0003-242

RUNNELLS,
John Sumner; b1846 s/o Rev John & Huldah Staples of Effingham NH; liv IA; NH-0006-262

RUSSELL,
Dr Ai S; b1857 s/o Stephen & Eunice C Hanson of Lincoln; m1884 Clestia A Elliott wid/o Joseph Pease; liv Rumney NH; NH-0007-619
Frank W; b1847 s/o William W; b1873 Louisa Hall d/o Philander & Louisa Augusta Webster; liv Plymouth NH; ch William Wallace b1876, George Moor b1878, Susan Carleton b1879, Walter Hall b1882, Louise Webster b1885, 1 dau dy; NH-0007-586
Moor; b1757; m1790 Betsey Webster; liv Derryfield & Plymouth NH; ch Nancy b1793, David M b1795, Catherine M b1797, Eliza b1799 m Benjamin G Edwards of Brooklyn NY, William W b1801, Mary b1804, Walter W b1806, Jane A b1808 m Milo P Jewett of Milwaukee WI, Julian b1810, Charles J b1813, Julia A b1815, Alfred; NH-0007-586
Nathaniel; b1811; liv Pelham & Orford NH; ch 1 dau m --- Trussell, 1 dau m Franklin Eaton, George N; NH-0007-568
William W; b1801 s/o Moor & Betsey Webster; liv Plymouth NH; ch William W Jr m Clara J Smith d/o Stephen & m Martha C Ward d/o Arthur & Hannah

RUSSELL (continued)
Dudley, Frank W b1847 m Louisa Hall; NH-0007-586

RUST,
Capt Henry; liv Wolfeborough NH; ch Henry, Richard, Anna m Matthew S Parker, 1 dau m Isaiah Horne, 1 son, 2 dau; NH-0006-302

-S-

SANBORN,
Arthur V; s/o James MD & Harriet L Chase; m1879; liv Rochester; ch James F; b1880; NH-0003-748
Benjamin; liv Gilford NH; ch Benjamin Jr Esq, Abial; NH-0004-746
Caleb T; b1797 s/o Hilliard & Sarah Tilton; m1824 Polly M Melcher b1798 d/o Joseph & Mary Rowell of Hampton Falls; ch George W b1825, Eliza S b1827, Mary H b1830 m David C Hawes, Hiram E b1834, Martha J b1840; NH-0003-352
Calvin; m Amy W Hodsdon d/o Ebenezer & Sally Wentworth of Ossipee NH; liv Wakefield; ch Henry S, Asa F; NH-0006-625
Charles; s/o Simeon & Lucy Palmer; m Elizabeth Cram & m Ann Rowe; ch/o ? - Carroll G m Hattie G Moulton d/o Gideon & Esther W Perkins; NH-0007-213
Charles W; b1849 s/o Hon John W of Wakefield; m1872 Addie E Smith; NH-0006-260
Daniel; ch Josiah Sullivan, Braley, James, Daniel, Samuel C, John; NH-0004-531
Daniel Hall; b1796 s/o John & Hannah Hall of Wakefield; m1821 Lydia Dorr b1796 d/o Joseph of Acton ME; liv Wakefield NH; ch Hon John W b1822 m Almira J Chapman, Joshua H, Enoch E, Daniel H, Lydia S m F N Dixon; NH-0006-521
Daniel L; s/o Edmund & Ruth Griffin; m Ada Moore; ch Jacob O, Ruth J, Joseph T m Fanny Peverly of Canterbury NH, Charles E, Mary E; NH-0004-503

SANBORN (continued)

David E; m Hannah Cook d/o Capt Dyer of Chichester; liv Gilmanton NH; ch Dyer H, Edwin David LLD b1808 m Mary Ann Webster & m Mrs Sarah F Clark, 7 others; NH-0007-328

Dyer H; b1799 s/o David E & Hannah Hook of Gilmanton; m Harriet W Tucker of Deerfield & m Mrs Abigail Glidden of Sanbornton Bridge; liv Hopkinton; ch/o Harriet - 1 son; NH-0004-409

Edmund; b1788 s/o Capt John & Ruth Rand; m Ruth Griffin; ch William, Sally, Daniel L m Ada Moore, Clarissa, James S m Mary E Yeaw, Jeremiah C m Betsy French, Eliza J, John m --- Thorndike of Pittsfield NH, True H m Adaline Green; NH-0004-503

Edwin David LLD; b1808 s/o David E & Hannah Cook of Gilmanton; m1837 Mary Ann Webster d/o Euhoit & m1868 Mrs Sarah F Clark of Detroit; liv Hanover NH; ch/o Mary - Kate, Mary Webster m Paul Babcock Esq of NY, Edward W; NH-0007-328

Frederick G; b1836 s/o Eliphalet Glidden & Abigail of Sanborton Bridge; (adopted by Abigail's second husband Dyer H Sanborn); m1880 Sophia W Rogers of Hopkinton; liv Hopkinton NH; Chicago IL, Sherbrook CT, Portland ME; NH-0004-410

Hilliard; s/o Richard & Eliza Hilliard; m Sarah Tilton d/o Caleb; liv Kensington; ch Caleb T b1797 m Polly M Melcher, 4 others; NH-0003-352

Israel; liv Gilford NH; ch Dea Levi, Mary; NH-0004-746

James Fletcher; b1853 s/o James Monroe & Elizabeth H Fletcher of E Kingston; m1874 Mary J d/o Elbridge & Mary Judkins of Kensington; ch Winifred J, Henry C; NH-0003-200

James Monroe; b1819 s/o John & Abigail of E Kingston; m1842 Julia A Currier d/o Reuben W & Lois Stevens & m1850 Elizabeth H Fletcher d/o Jonathan & Lydia Hammond; liv E

SANBORN (continued)

Kingston; ch/o Julia - Areanna Evelyn b1845 m Edward A Holmes, James M dy; ch/o Elizabeth - James Fletcher b1853 m Mary J, Julia Augusta b1855 m Rev John Wentworth Sanborn, Sherman Hammond b1857 m Clara T Stevens d/o Atherton H & Emily E Bradley of E Cambridge MA, Mary Abbie dy, John Munroe b1863 m Clara N Chase of Kingston, Moses Manson b1865; NH-0003-199

James S; s/o Edmund & Ruth Griffin; m Mary E Yeaw of RI; ch John B, Hattie B, Byron; NH-0004-503

Jeremiah C; s/o Edmund & Ruth Griffin; m Betsy French of Gilmanton; ch Ida B m James S Tilton; NH-0004-503

Jesse A; b1820 s/o Dr John & Susan Hubbard of Meredith; m1842 Sarah Sanborn d/o Dr Nathan of Henniker NH; liv Gardner MA, Wolfsboro, Campton, Plymouth NH; ch Sarah E, John A, Fred M; NH-0007-597

John; m --- Bachilor d/o Rev Stephen; liv ENG; ch John; NH-0004-775

Lt John; bro/o Stephen & William; liv ENG, Hampton; ch Richard, Josiah, John, Joseph; NH-0006-521

John; m Hannah Hall d/o Daniel & Patience Taylor; ch Daniel Hall; NH-0006-475

John Sr; bc1600; liv ENG; ch John b1620 m Mary Tuck & m Mrs Margaret Moulton, William m Mary Moulton, Stephen; NH-0003-345

John; b1620 s/o John Sr of ENG; m Mary Tuck d/o Robert & m Mrs Margaret Moulton d/o Robert Page; liv ENG; NH-0003-345

John; mc1706 Mehitable Fifield; ch Tristram b1710, Abigail, Paul bc1714; NH-0003-376

Capt John; b1747; m1774 Ruth Rand b1751; ch Elisha b1775 m --- Ladd, Lydia b1777, Betty b1779, Thomas b1781, Sarah b1783, John Jr b1785 m Judith Blake, Edmund b1788 m Ruth Griffin, William b1791 m Susan Haines; NH-0004-503

SANBORN (continued)
John; b1767 s/o Joseph & Sarah Lane of Brentwood; m1792 Hannah Hall b1772 d/o Daniel & Patience; liv Wakefield NH; ch Daniel Hall b1796 m Lydia Dorr, Joseph W, Sarah L, Susan, Ann, John G; NH-0006-521

John Jr; b1785 s/o Capt John & Ruth Rand; m Judith Blake; ch Stephen, Jane, Judith, Edmund, Almira, Joseph B m Sarah Ann Sanborn; NH-0004-503

John; b1800 s/o John & Abigail Rowell of E Kingston; m1842 Mercy E Morrill d/o Ebenezer & Eunice Merrill of Salisbury MA; liv the South, Amesbury MA; NH-0003-198

Hon John W; b1822 s/o Daniel Hall & Lydia Dorr of Wakefield; m1849 Almira J Chapman d/o Thomas & Almira Robinson of Wakefield; liv Wakefield NH; ch Charles W b1849, Lillian m Herbert E Rogers; NH-0006-521

Hon John W; b1845 s/o John of Hebron; m1870 Delia J Rolins of Hebron; liv Hebron NH; ch Ada Grace, Norman W, Katie; NH-0007-389

Rev John Wentworth; m1873 Julia Augusta Sanborn d/o James Monroe & Elizabeth H Fletcher of E Kingston; ch Elizabeth ME, John W Jr? NH-0003-200

Dea Jonathan; liv Gilford NH; ch Jonathan, Jacob, Joseph; NH-0004-746

Joseph; s/o Shubael of Canterbury NH; m Cyrene Cofran of Northfield NH; liv Holderness; ch Benjamin m Nettie D Cone d/o Edmond & Sally Bartlett, Shubael m Lizzie Russell of Thornton; NH-0007-213

Joseph B; s/o John Jr; m Sarah Ann Sanborn d/o Jonathan gd/o Jesse; liv Loudon; ch Joseph E m Lizzie Adams of Pittsfield NH, Jennie M; NH-0004-503

Joseph T; s/o Thayer S & Deborah Ward of Hampton Falls; m1876 Eliza B Janvrin b1843 d/o Jefferson & Mary Wadleigh of Seabrook; liv

SANBORN (continued)
Hampton Falls; ch Fannie Ward b1877; NH-0003-345 & 347

Lowell; liv Gilford NH; ch Lowell, Richard, Elisha; NH-0004-746

Mesheck; liv Brentwood & Gilford NH; ch 1 dau m Gen J J Morrill, 1 dau m Dr A G Weeks, 3 dau; NH-0004-747

Samuel Gilman; b1787; m Sally Mason d/o Capt Lemuel B & Molly Chamberlain of Durham NH; liv Gilford NH; ch Winborn Adams b1810 m Lavinia Peaslee Hoyt, 3 sons; NH-0004-775

Sewell S; m Elizabeth Batchelder; liv Hampton Falls; ch Thayer S m Deborah Ward; NH-0003-345

Simeon; b1793 s/o Ebenezer; m Lucy Palmer; ch Charles m Elizabeth Cram & m Ann Rowe; NH-0007-213

Thayer S; s/o Sewell S & Elizabeth Batchelder of Hampton Falls; m Deborah Ward of Hampton; liv Hampton Falls; ch Harriet W m Dr Edward Grosvenor of Newburyport, Thomas L, Joseph T, Marcia W, Helen E dy, Joseph H; NH-0003-345

Thomas Jefferson; b1812 s/o Charles T & Martha P Haines; m1841 Relief Rogers Morrison d/o Joseph & Olive Batchelder of Plymouth; liv W Campton & Sanbornton NH; ch Edward H m Julia E Robinson d/o William & Julia Foss; NH-0007-209 & 216

William; b1791 s/o Capt John & Ruth Rand; m Susan Haines; ch Richard P, William H; NH-0004-503

Winborn Adams; b1810 s/o Samuel Gilman & Sally Mason of Gilford; m1835 Lavinia Peaslee Hoyt d/o James Jr & Ruth Ayer Gordon of Gilford; liv Gilford NH; ch 1 son dy, Ellen E m Capt John S Wadleigh; NH-0004-775

SANDBURN,
Benjamin; s/o John; m Mary Tuck d/o John; liv Lynn, Hampton; ch Benjamin b1668 m Sarah --- & m Wid Margaret Moulton d/o Robert Page, 9 others; NH-

SANDBURN (continued)
0003-375
SANDERS,
George; m --- Martin d/o Richard'; liv Gilford NH; ch George W; NH-0004-747
George Sr; s/o John; m Polly Twombly of Barrington; liv Epsom NH; ch George Jr b1832 m Nancy A White, Mary b1832 m Nathaniel Twombly of Barrington, John; NH-0004-473
George Jr; b1832 s/o George & Polly Twombly of Epsom NH; m1875 Nancy A White d/o David & Mary Ann Carr of Antrim NH; liv Epsom; NH-0004-473
John; s/o George of Rye NH; m Anna ---; liv Epsom & Concord NH; ch George Sr m Polly Twombly; NH-0004-473
Orrin Strong MD; b1820 s/o Col Job & Polly of Epsom NH; m1843 Drusilla Morse d/o Silas M Esq & Huldah Morse of Effingham NH; liv Effingham, Chichester, Epsom NH, Boston MA; NH-0004-248 & 471, NH-0006-554
SANDERSON,
Morrison; m Hannah d/o Samuel; liv Merrimack; ch Nancy J, Lorenzo, Ellen, Dana, Orrin; NH-0002-542
SANGER,
Thaddeus Ezra MD; b1832 s/o Ezra & Sarah M Brown of Troy VT; m1856 Ianthe C Kneeland of Victory VT; liv Toledo OH, Hardwick VT, Littleton NH; ch Ellen I, Lillian E, Katie F; NH-0007-479
SARGEANT,
Cyrus; b1824 s/o Rufus of Candia gs/o Moses ggs/o Capt John; m1856 Sarah J Emerson & m1873 Mary E McQuesten d/o James; liv Boston, Plymouth NH; ch/o Sarah - Caroline m1883 Dr Robert Burns of Plymouth; ch/o Mary - 4; NH-0007-594
SARGENT,
Amos; s/o Thomas Jr; m --- Beck; ch Elbridge G, David S, Albert B, Mary A; NH-0004-505
Andrew B; b1797; m1819 Betsey Alexander d/o Enoch & Merriam Colby; ch Merriam E b1822 m1843 Daniel Messer, Samuel A b1826 m1863 Adaline B Holt of

SARGENT (continued)
Wilton, Simeon b1828 m1858 Mary E Thorndike, Enoch A b1831, Lucy Jane b1833 m1852 John Morgan, Philip J b1839 m1870 Sarah E Messer; NH-0004-286
Rev Christopher; s/o Thomas II, bro/o Christopher; liv Methuen MA; ch Nathaniel Peaslee; NH-0001-93, NH-0004-18
Ebenezer; b1768 s/o Peter & Ruth Nichols; m1792 Prudence Chase d/o John & Ruth Hills of Sunapee NH; liv Hopkinton & New London NH; ch Anna, Rebekah, Ruth, Seth Freeman, Aaron Lealand, Sylvanus Thayer, Lois, Laura, Jonathan Kittredge dy, Hon Jonathan Everett LLD b1816 m Maria C Jones & m Louisa Jennings (Jennie) Paige (Page); NH-0001-93, NH-0004-18, NH-0007-112.21
Harmon L; b1833 s/o Sylvanus & Emeline Crockett of New London CT; m1866 Almira Randall d/o Samuel & Nancy Carter of Canterbury NH; liv ·Plymouth NH; ch Herbert, Fannie E, Mary T, Ellie M, Grace O, Alice P; NH-0007-596
Jonathan Everett LLD; b1816 s/o Ebenezer & Prudence Chase; m1843 Maria C Jones d/o John Esq of Enfield NH & m1853 Louisa Jennings (Jennie) Paige (Page) d/o Dea James K of Wentworth NH; liv Concord, New London, Canaan & Wentworth NH, Washington DC; ch/o Maria - John Jones, Everett Foster dy; ch/o Louisa - Maria (Marie) Louise, Annie Lawrie dy, George Lincoln; NH-0001-93, NH-0004-18, NH-0007-112.21
Moses; b1803 s/o Moses & Nancy Morrill of Amesbury MA; m1824 Judith Hoyt d/o Stephen & Esther Reynolds & m1850 Mrs Mary Seavey Huntington & m Sarah Thyng d/o Gilman & Sally; liv Amesbury, Lake Village & Upper Gilmanton NH; ch/o Judith - Mary m H O Heywood, Stephen H, Moses, John, David, Frank S; NH-0004-782

SARGENT (continued)
Peter; b1740 (b1736) s/o Dea
Stephen & Judith Ordway of
Amesbury MA; m Ruth Nichols
of Amesbury or Newbury MA;
liv Hopkinton & New London
NH, Amesbury MA; ch Anthony,
Abigail, Ruth, Judith, Peter,
Ebenezer b1768 m Prudence
Chase, Amasa, John, Molly,
Ezekiel, Stephen, William,
Lois; NH-0001-93, NH-0004-18,
NH-0007-112.21
Dea Stephen; b1710 s/o Thomas
II, bro/o Christopher; m1730
Judith Ordway of W Newbury
MA; liv Amesbury MA; ch
Amasa, Ezekiel, Thomas,
Moses, James, Peter b1740 m
Ruth Nichols, Nathan,
Stephen, Abner, Ebenezer, 4
daus; NH-0001-93, NH-0004-18
Maj Sterling; b1794 s/o Philip
& Sally Peirce; m1815 Sally
Gault of Hooksett; liv
Allenstown NH; ch Philip,
Warren, Sallie S m George
Hirsch & m Rev H H Hartwell,
Elsie K m Henry W Forbush Esq
of Philadelphia, Mary H m W F
Head Esq of Hookset, Abbie H
m Natt B Emery of Suncook, 3
sons dy, 2 sons; NH-0004-166
Thomas; b1643 s/o Wiliam &
Elizabeth; mc1667 Rachel
Barnes; liv Amesbury; ch
Thomas II b1676 m Mary
Stevens, Rev Christopher; NH-
0001-93, NH-0004-18
Thomas II; b1676 s/o Thomas &
Rachel Barnes of Amesbury;
m1702 Mary Stevens; liv Ames-
bury MA; ch Dea Stephen b1710
m Judith Ordway, Christopher;
NH-0001-93, NH-0004-18, NH-
0007-112.21
Thomas Sr; m1772 Abigail
Blaisdel; liv Loudon NH; ch
Dolly b1772, Charles b1774,
Thomas Jr b1778, Josiah
b1780, Sarah b1782, Susannah
b1785, Timothy b1786, David
b1789, John b1791; NH-0004-
505 & 508
Thomas Jr; b1778 s/o Thomas Sr
& Abigail Blaisdell; ch
Hannah, Amus m --- Beck,
Maria, Susan, John; NH-0004-
505
Walter H; b1825 s/o Isaac &
Rebecca of Boscawen; m1852 S

SARGENT (continued)
L Farrington; liv Plymouth
NH; ch Ellen, Arthur W, Anna
J, Flora, Mary, Walter H; NH-
0007-596
William; bc1602 s/o Richard of
ENG; m Judith Perkins & m
Elizabeth ---; liv ENG,
Ipswich, Newbury, Salisbury &
Amesbury MA, Hampton NH; ch/o
Judith - several daus, ch/o
Elizabeth - Thomas b1643 m
Rachel Barnes, William; NH-
0001-93, NH-0004-18, NH-0007-
112.21
SAUNDERS,
Horace; s/o Joel & Phebe Scott;
m Hannah Challis d/o Thomas &
Betsey of Parsonfield; liv
Alexandria NH; ch Imogene,
Inez F; NH-0007-120
James W; s/o Joel & Phebe
Scott; m Mary J Ackerman d/o
John & Abigail Gray; liv
Alexandria NH; ch Alice,
Horace, Ida; NH-0007-120
Joel; s/o Rev William & Comfort
Drew; m Phebe Scott d/o
James; ch Horace m Hannah
Challis, James W m Mary J
Ackerman, 1 other; NH-0007-
120
SAVAGE,
Capt Benjamin; liv New Durham
NH; ch Maj George D b1818,
Henry; NH-0004-708
Maj George D; b1818 s/o Capt
Benjamin of New Durham NH;
liv Alton NH; ch 1 dau m John
W Currier, 1 dau m George F
Jones, 1 dau m Charles H
Downing, George Frank,
Jessie; NH-0004-708
George; d1876; liv Deerfield
MA, Orford NH; ch Charles T,
John A, George F, Thomas W;
NH-0007-564
Seth; b1807; m Martha
Spaulding; liv Lancaster NH;
ch Edward, Hubbard, Sarah m
Alden Lewis, Lucy m James
Bain, Henry, John, Charlotte,
Mattie, Cyrus; NH-0005-363
SAVORY,
Col Jonathan; b1812 s/o Thomas
& gs/o Jonathan; m1836
Abigail Scribner Coffin
b1814; liv Londonderry; NH-
0003-584
SAWYER,
Hon Aaron Flint; b1780; m1811

SAWYER (continued)
Hanna Locke gd/o Rev Samuel
DD; liv Westminster MA, Mont
Vernon & Nashua NH; ch Samuel
L, Aaron Worcester b1818, 1
other; NH-0002-36

Hon Aaron Worcester; b1818 s/o
Hon Aaron Flint & Hannah
Locke of Mont Vernon NH; m
Mary Frances Ingalls of New
York City & m1855 Fanny Winch
d/o Francis & Almira Stetson
of Nashua; liv Nashua; ch/o
Fanny Fanny Ingalls dy, Fanny
Locke, Aaron Frank, William
Merriam; NH-0002-36

Alonzo Havington; b1827 s/o Hon
Daniel & Tamson Walker of
Alton; m1850 Martha J Shap-
leigh d/o Samuel & Eunice of
Lebanon; liv Alton & Great
Falls NH; ch Fred Shapleigh
b1853 dy; NH-0004-709

Capt Bela; s/o Jared ggs/o
Thomas; m Deborah P Josselyn;
liv Lyme NH; ch Arthur H; NH-
0007-546

Caleb; b1659 s/o Thomas & Mary
Prescott of Lancaster; m
Sarah Houghton (Houston); liv
Lancaster; ch Seth b1705 m
Hepsabeth Whitney, 1 son, 2
dau; NH-0001-240, NH-0003-860

Caleb; b1737 s/o Seth &
Hepsabeth Whitney; m1766
Sarah Patch; liv Harvard MA;
ch Phineas b1768 m Hannah
Whitney, Jonathan; NH-0001-
240, NH-0003-860

Col Charles Henry; b1840 s/o
Jonathan & Martha Perkins;
m1865 Susan Ellen Cowan d/o
Dr James W & Elizabeth; liv
Watertown NY, Dover NH; NH-
0001-250, NH-0003-862

Hon Daniel; d1869 s/o Enoch; m
Tamson Walker; liv Alton NH;
ch Alonzo Havington b1827 m
Martha J Shapleigh, Ellen m
Jeremiah Jones of Alton,
Frank P m Jennie Farnham; NH-
0004-709

Enoch; liv Alton NH; ch Hon
Daniel m Tamson Walker, Seth,
1 dau m Judge Ira Mooney of
Belmont, 1 dau m --- Cate of
Alton; NH-0004-709

Ezra A J; b1828 s/o John &
Clarissa Chesley gs/o David
ggs/o Josiah; m1853 Sarah
Collins Bean b1830 d/o Joseph

SAWYER (continued)
& Lydia H Collins; liv Deer-
field NH; ch Fred B b1854,
John F b1856, Mabel J b1861;
NH-0003-168

John; liv Lincolnshire ENG; ch
William, Edward, Thomas m
Mary Prescott; NH-0001-240,
NH-0003-860

John; b1815; m1842 Louisa
Johnson; liv Dorchester,
Rumney, Bath NH; ch John M,
George H, Charles N, Joshua
W, Amanda L m Ezra A Rodimon,
3 others;NH-0007-145

Jonathan; b1817 s/o Phineas &
Hannah Whitney of Marlborough
MA; m1839 Martha Perkins of
Barnard VT; liv Marlborough &
Lowell MA, Dover NH, Water-
town NY; ch Charles Henry
b1840 m Susan Ellen Cowan,
Mary Elizabeth, Francis
Asbury, Roswell Douglas,
Martha Frances, Alice May,
Frederic Jonathan; NH-0001-
240, NH-0003-860

Josiah; m --- Eastman sis/o
Jeremiah; liv Nottingham; ch
Josiah, 2 others; NH-0003-168

Josiah; liv Gilford NH; ch
Israel, Dr Josiah, John,
Joseph; NH-0004-747

Luther Dearborn; b1803 s/o
Timothy of Wakefield; liv
Ossipee, Wakefield, Dover;
NH-0003-598, NH-0006-258

Rev Moses AM; b1776 bro/o
Nathaniel AM; m Fanny Kimball
d/o Capt Peter of Boscawen;
liv Henniker, Saugus &
Ipswich MA; NH-0004-621

Moses; b1803; m Rebecca B
Morrill of Seabrook NH & m
Hanah Bassett Jones of
Gilmanton; liv Henniker & N
Weare NH; ch/o ? - Henry
Abbott, Ellen Rebecca m J
Fred Smith of Fishkill NY,
Mary Elizabeth; NH-0002-694

Nathaniel AM; b1784 bro/o Rev
Moses AM; m Palemia Bacon;
liv Newburyport & Boston MA,
Cincinnati OH; NH-0004-621

Phineas; b1768 s/o Caleb &
Sarah Patchof Harvard MA; m
Hannah Whitney of Harvard MA;
liv Marlborough & Lowell MA;
ch Jonathan b1817 m Martha
Perkins, Alfred Ira, Zenas;
NH-0001-240, NH-0003-860

SAWYER (continued)
Reuben; b1798 s/o Rev Isaac; m1819 Laura Wyman; liv Monkton & W Haven & Chester VT; New London NH; Leyden NY; ch Rev A W DD; NH-0004-440
Seth; b1705 s/o Caleb & Sarah Houghton (Houston); m Hepsabeth Whitney; liv Harvard MA, Lancaster; ch Caleb b1737 m Sarah Patch, 1 son; NH-0001-240, NH-0003-860
Symmes; liv Newburyport MA, Woodstock NH; ch Sylvestrus, Symmes, Mary, Eliza, Barnard, Lois, Walter H, Moses, John; NH-0007-643
Thomas; s/o John of Lincolnshire ENG; m1647 Mary Prescott d/o John of Lancaster MA; liv Rowley & Lancaster MA; ch Ephraim, Thomas, Caleb b1659 m Sarah Houghton (Houston), Elias, 7 others; NH-0001-240, NH-0003-860, NH-0004-709
Thomas Ellwood; b1798 s/o Stephen of Dover; liv Dover; NH-0003-592
SCALES,
James; m Susanna ---; liv Boxford MA, Rumford, Canterbury, Hopkinton; ch John b1737 dy, Joseph b1740 dy, Stephen b1741, Susanna b1744; NH-0004-406
SCOFIELD,
John; m Sarah ---; liv CT, Canaan NH; ch Eleazer, John Jr, Miriam m Maj Samuel Jones; NH-0007-220
SCOTT,
Jonathan; m --- Bowles d/o Rev Nathaniel; liv Richmond, Dalton NH; ch Nathaniel m Margaret Harriman; NH-0005-526
Dr N Harvey; b1851 s/o Nathaniel & Margaret Harriman of Dalton; m Lizzie Moulton d/o Daniel of Sandwich; liv Sandwich, Wolfeborough, Maynard MA; ch Margaret E, Ruth B; NH-0006-363
SCRIBNER,
Benjamin; m Huldah Tappan d/o Christopher; liv Brentwood & Sandwich NH; ch Peggy b1772 m Paul Bunker, Hannah b1776 m Joshua Hoag, Abigail b1778 m Timothy Varney, Samuel b1780,

SCRIBNER (continued)
Sarah b1784, Huldah b1786 m Elisha Hanson, Stephen b1794, Ruth b1795, Benjamin b1799; NH-0006-673
Eugene William; b1852 s/o William P & Catherine Burbank of Gilead; m1871 Sara E Wheeler d/o Dexter & Elizabeth F Hodgdon; liv Berlin NH; ch Claude Dexter, Leona, Isola Genieve; NH-0005-827
Franklin; s/o John & Abigail Emery; m Marcia E Hackett d/o Chase T & Susan of New Hampton; ch Ida m --- Fellows, Carrie A, George E; NH-0007-130
John; s/o Capt Josiah & Phebe Cross; m Abigail Emery d/o Josiah of Loudon NH; liv Andover, Ashland; ch Franklin m Marcia E Hackett, John C, Asentha, Ambrose b1817, 2 others; NH-0007-130
Capt Josiah; s/o Samuel & Hannah Webster; m Phebe Cross; ch John m Abigail Emery, 12 others; NH-0007-130
Leander D; b1804; liv Essex VT, Bartlett, Ossipee NH; ch William C; NH-0006-631
SCRUTON,
David; s/o Jonathan & Sarah Otis; m Lydia C Reed; liv Holderness NH; ch Lydia N m True Garland, Edward S m Emma E Tate; NH-0007-396
Edward S; s/o David & Lydia C Reed of Holderness; m Emma E Tate d/o Josiah C & Arnor Hill of Tuftonboro NH; liv Holderness NH; ch Lydia A, Joseph O; NH-0007-396
Jonathan; s/o Thomas & Molly Hutchins; m Sarah Otis; ch David m Lydia C Reed, 3 sons; NH-0007-396
Michael; b1774 s/o Thomas gs/o William; liv Strafford; ch Thomas b1804; NH-0003-703
Thomas; b1804 s/o Michael of Strafford; liv Strafford; ch Dea Charles; NH-0003-703
William; liv IRE, Barnstead; ch 1 dau m --- Drew, Thomas; NH-0003-703
SEAMANS,
Job; b1748 s/o Dea Charles of Rehoboth MA; m Sarah Esterbrooks d/o Valentine Esq of

SEAMANS (continued)
Sackville Nova Scotia & m1819 Mrs Mary Everett wid/o Jonathan; liv N Attleborough MA, New London NH; NH-0004-438

SEARLE,
Rev Jonathan; b1746; m Mrs Margaret Sanborn Tappan; liv Rowley MA, Salisbury NH; NH-0004-606

SEAVEY,
Elijah; liv Bartlett NH; ch Lavina m Walker George, Eliza m John Wentworth, Lucy m John George; NH-0006-916

SELDEN,
Samuel; m1811 Louisa Parkhurst of Royalton VT & m --- Parkhurst sis/o Louisa; liv Royalton VT, Liberty MI; NH-0007-93

SHACKFORD,
Charles B; b1840 s/o Samuel B of Conway; m1869 Caroline Cartland d/o Moses A of Lee; liv Barrington, Dover; NH-0006-269
Maj Samuel B; m --- Hale & m Lydia Poindexter; liv Canaan, Conway; ch/o Hale - Onslow, Charles B, Martha S m Richard Thom; ch/o Lydia - Lucy m F W Davis; NH-0006-854

SHANNON,
Dr Thomas; b1783 s/o Nathaniel of Moultonborough; m1808 Margaret Vaughn Moses; liv Pittsfield, Moultonborough; ch Nathaniel, 7 others; NH-0006-411

SHAW,
Hon Albert M; b1819 s/o Francis & Olive Garland; m1848 Caroline Dearborn Emery of Andover NH; liv Poland ME, Lebanon NH; ch Mary Estelle, William F, Albert O; NH-0001-268, NH-0007-425
Asa; s/o Moses of Holderness; m Diodama York; ch William H m Charlotte E Marden d/o Timothy & Esther Cox, 8 others; NH-0007-215
Asa; d1861 s/o Dan & Joanna Perkins; m Elizabeth T Slade of Hanover; liv Lyme NH; ch Thomas Asa, Eliza T; NH-0007-533
Benjamin; b1766; m Abigail Paige b1773 & m Ruth Sher-

SHAW (continued)
burne; liv Hampton & Chichester NH; ch/o Abigail - John, David P b1797 m Clarissa Carpenter; NH-0004-254
Charles C; b1830 s/o David P & Clarissa Carpenter; m1861 Sophia F Whittemore d/o Hon Aaron & Arieannah S Barstow of Pembroke NH; liv Chichester; ch John Langdon (adopted); NH-0004-254
Dan; b1758; m1780 Joanna Perkins d/o Dea Isaac of Middleboro MA; liv Bridgewater MA, Lyme NH, Bradford VT; ch Asa m Elizabeth T Slade, 2 dau; NH-0007-533
David P; b1797 s/o Benjamin & Abigail Paige; m1823 Clarissa Carpenter d/o Rev Josiah & Hannah Morrill of Chichester; ch John, Josiah C, David C, Charles C b1830 m Sophia F Whittemore, Benjamin; NH-0004-254
Elder Elijah; b1793 s/o Elijah & Deborah Nudd; liv Kensington; NH-0003-356
Rev John; m --- Smith d/o Rev John of Weymouth MA; liv Haverhill MA; ch William, Abigail Adams m Rev Joseph B Felt; NH-0003-123
Rev Naphtali; b1764; m --- Craft; liv Kensington, Bridgewater MA, Bradford VT; NH-0003-354

SHEAFE,
John Lane; b1791 s/o Jacob of Portsmouth; liv Lancaster & Colebrook NH, New Orleans; NH-0004-246

SHED,
Eliza A; b1857 ch/o John & Mary E Tuttle; m Ruthven Childs of Hillsborough NH; ch Carrie May b1879; NH-0002-262
John S; m Mary E Tuttle d/o Hon Jacob & Betsey Cummings; ch Mary J b1854 dy, Eliza A b1857 m Ruthven Childs; NH-0002-262

SHELTON,
R H; m Anna T Barker d/o Josiah H & Adeline Godfrey; liv Boston & Worcester MA; ch Emma D, Richard B; NH-0003-330

SHEPARD,
George L; s/o William B & Lucy
Beck of Holderness; m Nancy
Shepard d/o John M & Lydia;
liv Holderness NH; ch
Hastings M, Emeline O, Edna;
NH-0007-394
Henry H; s/o George W & Sarah
Fowle; m Mary Calley d/o
Jeremiah M & Mary; liv Ash-
land NH; ch Martha M; NH-
0007-128
Jacob; s/o John of Canterbury
MA; m Jane Blair of London-
derry NH; liv Holderness NH;
ch William B m Lucy Beck, 9
others; NH-0007-394
John; m Eleanor Shepard d/o
Richard; liv Holderness; ch
George W m Sarah Fowle, 10
others; NH-0007-128
John; m Susanna Smith of
Nottingham NH; ch John b1767;
NH-0007-394
William B; s/o Jacob & Jane
Blair of Holderness; m Lucy
Beck d/o John & Abigail
Slade; liv Holderness NH; ch
George L m Nancy Shepard, 8
others; NH-0007-394
SHERBURNE,
Henry C; b1830 s/o Reuben B &
Sally Rackleyft Staples; liv
Charlestown & Boston MA,
Concord NH; ch Henry A
bc1871; NH-0001-699
John Samuel; b1757 s/o John &
Elizabeth Moffat of
Portsmouth; m1791 Submit Boyd
d/o Hon George; liv
Portsmouth; NH-0003-19
Reuben B; m Sally Rackleyft
Staples of Newmarket NH; liv
Charlestown MA, Pelham NH;
ch Henry C b1830; NH-0001-69
SHERMAN,
Langdon; b1806 s/o William of
Waitsfield VT; m Pamelia P
Smith; ch Lucy J, Celia, Emma
m Wilton M Lindsey of Warren
PA; NH-0007-333
Peter; s/o Jotham of Lisbon;
liv Lisbon; ch 1 dau m ---
Noyes, John B, Moses; NH-
0007-402
Smith; b1805; s/o Benjamin; m 3
times; liv Lyman NH, Lisbon;
ch J R, 15 others; NH-0007-
515
SHIPMAN,
Rev Isaiah; b1810; m1835

SHIPMAN (continued)
Charlotte R Cook of N Spring-
field VT; liv Westminster & N
Springfield VT, Lisbon NH; ch
Christina m James G Moore,
Emily R m Arthur C Wells,
Sylvia A m Moses N Howland,
James F m Julia Sargent,
Charles H m Ellen F Keith,
Mary Ellen m William P
Dillingham; NH-0007-456
SHIRLEY,
Daniel M; b1791 s/o James &
Abigail McCutchins; m Jane
Moore d/o Robert of Bristol;
ch Robert M b1819 m Margaret
Dodge of Goffstown, Nancy
b1823 m Gilman Shirley, Mary
b1826 m Ephraim Heald, Joseph
b1831 m Nellie Niles, Harriet
b1835 m Sylvanus D Johnson,
Daniel b1838 m De Ette
Sackett, Horace b1841; NH-
0002-328
Daniel; b1838 s/o Daniel M &
Jane Moore; m De Ette Sackett
of Potsdam NY; ch James
b1876, Emma De Ette b1879;
NH-0002-328
Edward Carlton; b1834 s/o
Robert & Sophia McCutchins;
m1862 Amanda Malvina Baldwin
d/o Dea Nahum of Manchester;
ch Mary Vicksburg b1863,
Robert Lawrence b1868,
Florence Sophia b1871; NH-
0002-329
Gilman; m Nancy Shirley d/o
Daniel M & Jane Moore; ch
Alma b1849, Frank b1854,
Clinton b1857; NH-0002-328
James; b1759 s/o Thomas of IRE,
m Mary Moore d/o Col Daniel &
m Mrs Abigail McCutchins; liv
Chester; ch/o Abigail - Nancy
b1784 m Joshua Vose, Jane
b1785 m William McKinney,
Thomas b1789, Daniel M b1791
m Jane Moore, James b1794 m
Harriet Walsworth & m Adeline
Quincy, John b1797 m Margaret
Houston, Gilman b1799,
William b1802, Robert M b1808
m Sophia McCutchins & m
Lucretia Houston; NH-0002-328
James; b1794 s/o James &
Abigail McCutchins; m1820
Harriet Walsworth d/o James
of Norwich CT & m1835 Adeline
Quincy d/o Abraham of Boston
MA; liv Florence, Huntsville

SHIRLEY (continued)
AL, Vicksburg; ch/o Harriet - James Jay b1825 m Harriet ---; ch/o Adeline - Frederick b1836, Quincy b1848 m Margaret Parks, Alice b1844 m Gen John Eaton; NH-0002-328

James Jay; b1825 s/o James & Harriet Walsworth; m Harriet ---; ch Emma m Andrew Criddle; NH-0002-329

John; b1797 s/o James & Abigail McCutchins; m Margaret Houston; liv Suspension Bridge NY; ch Alfred b1819 m Jane Woodbury, Maria b1827 m Andrew Kimball, Gilman b1823 m Nancy Shirley, John d1885 m Susan Parker, Mary Jane b1823 m Griggs Holbrook & m Joseph Stevens & m Andrew Kimball, Sarah b1836 m Matthew Dolphin, Margaret b1840 m James Cooper; NH-0002-329

John; d1885 s/o John & Margaret Houston; m Susan Parker of Hooksett; ch Josephine b1849, Charles b1850, Quincy b1858, Susey b1862; NH-0002-329

Joseph; b1831 s/o Daniel M & Jane Moore; m Nellie Niles of Bombay NY; ch Ardello b1859 dy, Delbert b1861, Jennie b1869, Delmay b1871, Hattie b1875; NH-0002-328

Robert; b1808 s/o James & Abigail McCutchins; m Sophia McCutchins b1805 & m Lucretia Houston m1820; liv Manchester NH; ch/o Sophia - James Quincy b1829 m Elmira McPherson of Bedford, Mary Helen b1839 m Frederick Eaton, Abigail Frances b1844 m Col James David, Edward Carlton b1834 m Amanda Malvina Baldwin; NH-0002-329

SHURTLEFF,
William Henry; b1840 s/o Otis & Eliza of Compton PQ; m Mary J Merrill d/o Sherburn Rowell & Sarah B Merrill; liv Lancaster & Colebrook NH; ch Merrill, Harry; NH-0005-250 & 643

SHUTE,
Nathaniel; b1801; m Maria Smith of Sanbornton; liv Sanbornton, Littleton NH; ch Gilman D m Lucy Whiting of Lyman, 2 dy; NH-0007-491

SIMES,
George; s/o John; m Nancy Hardy; liv Portsmouth; ch William b1806 m Olourn Laighton, 7 others; NH-0003-104

John; liv ENG, Portsmouth NH; ch Joseph, 5 dau; NH-0003-104

Joseph; s/o John; ch John, Thomas, Mark, William, George m Nancy Hardy, Joseph, 4 dau; NH-0003-104

William; b1806 s/o George & Nancy Hardy of Portsmouth; m1831 Olive Bourn Laighton d/o Capt James of Portsmouth; liv Portsmouth; ch James T, Joseph S, William, 3 dau; NH-0003-104

SIMMONS,
Bartlett; s/o John & Lydia Bartlett; m Almira Stuart of Henniker; ch Garvin, Ellen m Samuel Sprague, Lydia m Bartlett S Brown; NH-0002-379

Daniel; s/o John & Lydia Bartlett; ch Daniel, Lovilla m --- Davis, Nancy Jane m Matthew Forsaith; NH-0002-379

John; m Lydia Bartlett d/o John & Hepzibath Stevens; ch Daniel m Huldah Loveren, Hannah m Stephen Brown, Bartlett m Almira Stuart, Garvin, Eliza m Eaton Sleeper of Francestown; NH-0002-379

SIMONDS,
Darius W; b1809; m1834 Betsey Poor of Landaff; liv Landaff, Bath NH; ch Lizzie d1881, William m Sarah Snow; NH-0007-143

John; s/o James & Lydia Morrison Simons; liv Franklin; ch Hon John Wesley; NH-0004-524

Robert; s/o William; m Phebe Hastings of Bristol; liv Alexandria NH; ch Robert Jr m Margaret Simons, 7 others; NH-0007-118

Robert Jr; s/o Robert & Phebe Hastings of Alexandria NH; m Margaret Simons d/o Caleb & Lois Phelps; ch Scott H, Emma M, Preston F, Walter F m Tirza Ladd & m Sarah A Sanburn; NH-0007-118

Stephen P; m Susan Stokes of Ossippee; liv Landaff, Lisbon NH; ch 4 sons, 1 dau m ---

SIMONDS (continued)
Prescott, 1 dau m --- Howland; NH-0007-444

Walter F; s/o Robert Jr & Margaret Simons; m Tirza Ladd & m Sarah A Sanburn d/o Jacob & Emily Terrill; liv Alexandria NH; ch/o ? - Perley H, Flossie E; NH-0007-118

SIMONS,
Abram; b1774 s/o John & Dorothy Bachelder of Northfield; m Nancy Forrest & m Mrs Lucy Rundlett; ch Joseph; NH-0004-524

Hiram; b1805 s/o Christopher & Nancy Locke of Weare NH; m1842 M Almeda Chase d/o John & Lydia of Weare; liv Weare NH; ch Hiram Augustus b1843, George Frank b1847; NH-0002-691

James; b1763 s/o John & Dorothy Bachelder of Northfield; m1782 Lydia Morrison of Northfield; liv Andover; ch John Simonds, 7 others; NH-0004-524

John; b1739 s/o Joseph & --- Knox; m Dorothy Bachelder of Canterbury; liv Northfield; ch James b1763 m Lydia Morrison, Nathaniel, John, Sarah b1770 m John Forrest of Northfield, Dorothy m --- Foss, Abram b1774 m Nancy Forrest & m Mrs Lucy Rundlett, Thomas b1783 m --- Hancock of Northfield & m ?, Comfort b1786 m Eben Abbott; NH-0004-523

Joseph; s/o Abram; liv Northfield NH; ch Joseph m Simonds; NH-0004-524

Joseph; b1688; m1735 --- Knox; liv ENG, CT, Canterbury NH; ch William, John b1739 m Dorothy Bachelder; NH-0004-523

Langdon; b1841 s/o Lewis & Hannah Gove; ch Minot; NH-0002-692

Lewis; b1815 s/o Christopher of S Weare; m1840 Hannah W Gove d/o Charles of Weare NH & m Mary J Gilmore; liv Weare, Manchester; ch/o Hannah - Langdon b1841, Almeda b1842 m Darwin A Simons, Minot b1849, 3 sons dy; NH-0002-691

SIMPSON,
Clinton B; b1840 s/o Hugh B & Sarah A Edmonds of Rumney; m1862 Elvira Smith d/o Timothy P & m1882 Augusta L Valentine; liv Rumney NH; ch/o Elvira - Edward H, Charles A, Carrie M, Arthur E; ch/o Augusta - Edith Mabel; NH-0007-608

Daniel L; b1807 s/o George; m1829 Angeline L Kneeland d/o Edward & Charity B; liv Rumney NH; ch Henry C, Edward A, Minerva J m J M Douglass, Helen M m A G Hobbs, Charles D, Mary S m J R Fessenden of MA, Evelyn L m Henry Clark, Oliver E, Hattie F m D C Smalley, Susan C, Alice O m A M Hamblet, Lizzie m W F Flynn, Frank E; NH-0007-608

Hugh B; s/o Samuel & Sarah; m1836 Sarah A Edmonds; liv Rumney NH; ch Clinton B b1840 m Elvira Smith & m Augusta L Valentine, Charles E b1845, Mary C b1849; NH-0007-608

Samuel; m Sarah ---; liv Greenland, Rumney NH; ch Hugh B m Sarah A Edmonds, Benjamin, Samuel, David, James M, Albert; NH-0007-608

William F; b1848 s/o Capt Edward & Harriet M Johnson of Middle Haddam CT; m1880 Abbie J Sheldon d/o Capt J H & Clarissa A Russell; liv Groton NH; ch William Edward b1881; NH-0007-294

SINCLAIR,
Charles G; s/o Richard Jr & Betsey Hodgdon of Barnstead NH; m Martha G Norris; liv Barnstead; ch Hon John G b1826 m Tamar M Clark & m Mary E Blandin; NH-0004-714

Prof John E; m1864 Isabella Aiken Noyes d/o Hon John W & Nancy Aiken; ch Annie N, Isabella A; NH-0003-159

Hon John G; b1826 s/o Charles G & Martha G Norris of Barnstead NH; m1847 Tamar M Clark d/o Col Daniel of Landaff & m1872 Mary E Blandin d/o John Pierce Esq of Littleton NH; liv Landaff & Manchester & Bethlehem NH, Lawrence MA, Orlando FL; ch/o Tamar - Charles A, Emma S, Martha A;

SINCLAIR (continued)
NH-0004-714
John T; s/o Zebulon & Mary
Seavey; m Mary Hilliard d/o
Christopher & Martha E; liv
Holderness NH; ch Jennie M;
NH-0007-395
Richard; m Polly Cilley sis/o
Col Joseph; liv Gilmanton NH;
ch Richard Jr m Betsey
Hodgdon; NH-0004-714
Richard Jr; s/o Richard & Polly
Cilley of Gilmanton NH; m
Betsey Hodgdon; liv Barnstead
NH; ch Charles G m Martha G
Norris; NH-0004-714
SKINNER,
Capt Cyrus; s/o Dea Joseph; m 3
times; ch Heman, Thirza, Mary
E m Royal Storrs, Joshua G,
Cyrus B; NH-0007-528
Daniel Moulton; b1825 s/o
Elijah & Abigail Moulton;
m1845 Sarah P Stratton d/o
Samuel & Lois gd/o Cornelius
Dinsmoor; liv Manchester; ch
Clara M m David Hammond,
Flora S m Charles A Hammond,
Cyrus E, Daniel W, Walter L,
Lucien C, Olive L; NH-0006-
727
Elijah; b1786 s/o Jedediah;
m1807 Lydia Page & m1810
Abigail Moulton b1782 d/o
Daniel; liv Lyme CT, Sandwich
Centre NH; ch/o Lydia - Eliza
m George W Mann; ch/o Abigail
- Polly m Hosea Pettingill,
Lydia m James M Smith, Cyrus,
Daniel Moulton b1825 m Sarah
P Stratton; NH-0006-727
Jedediah; liv CT, N Sandwich
NH; ch Elijah b1786 m Lydia
Page & m Abigail Moulton,
Clark; NH-0006-727
SLACK,
John Hancock AM; b1789 s/o John
& Betsey Ide of New London;
m1825 Lydia Hastings d/o Levi
of Wilton; liv Canaan NH,
Fairfax VA; NH-0007-73
SLEEPER,
Aaron; b1661 s/o Thomas &
Johannah S; m1682 Elis Shaw &
m Sarah ---; ch/o Elis - 17;
ch/o Sarah - Daniel b1715,
Edward b1719 m Anne Clough;
NH-0003-377
Edward; b1719 s/o Aaron; m1746
Anna Clough b1722; liv
Kingston; ch John bc1746,

SLEEPER (continued)
Sarah b1750, Jonathan b1754 m
Mary Clark, Ann b1762, Aaron,
Abigail Hannah b1767; NH-
0003-377 & 385
John M; s/o Peter & Wealthy
Corless; m Clara S Merrill of
Appleton WI; ch Jessie M,
Clarence M, Myrtle, Archie L;
NH-0007-121
Jonas; m --- Bean d/o Farmer of
Gilmanton; liv Gilford NH; ch
Dr Francis, Jonas, Sarah m
--- Smith; NH-0004-747
Jonathan; b1754 s/o Edward &
Anna Clough; m Mary Clark; ch
Anna b1798 m Joseph Wadleigh;
NH-0003-385
Justin M; s/o Samuel T W &
Bethana Seavey; m Louisa
Berry of Moultonborough NH;
ch Eva L m Joseph H Legallee;
NH-0007-180
Peter; s/o Gideon; m Sally Wood
of Alexandria; liv Grafton;
ch Peter m Wealthy Corless, 7
others; NH-0007-121
Peter; s/o Peter & Sally Wood;
m Wealthy Corless d/o John &
Abigail Bowen; ch James, John
M m Clara S Merrill, Marcus O
m Minnie E Vose; NH-0007-121
Dea Samuel; liv Loudon NH; ch
Hannah, Susannah, Elizabeth,
Molly, Molly, Anna, Stephen,
Samuel, Chase, Gilman, Sarah,
Sarah, Mahala, Abigail; NH-
0004-508
Samuel; m Elizabeth Sanborn of
Chester; liv Sandown &
Bristol NH; ch Samuel T W
b1796 m Bethana Seavey,
Aaron; NH-0007-180
Thomas; bc1607; m Johannah S;
liv ENG, Hampton; ch Aaron
b1661 m Elis Shaw & m Sarah
---; NH-0003-377
Rev Walter; b1790; m1814 Nancy
Plaisted; liv Bristol, New
Chester; ch Hon Solomon S
b1815, Horace L; NH-0007-191
& 193
SLOAN,
William Spencer; b1770; m
Martha Palmer of Orford & m
Lydia Felshaw Post wid/o
Aaron; liv Lyme NH; ch/o
Martha - William S, Hiram B,
Naomi W, Martha P m Jonas
Rolfe, Asenath B, Mary W,
Esther S; ch/o Lydia - Henry

SLOAN (continued)
C, Harriet G m John Clark, John L; NH-0007-524
SLOANE,
Daniel; b1780; m --- Johnson d/o Capt Thomas of Newbury VT; liv Pehlam MA, Haverhill NH; NH-0007-82
SMALLEY,
Dr Adoniram; b1803; m Rosamond Wood of Lebanon; liv Randolph & Brookfield VT, Corinth, Lebanon, Lyme NH; NH-0007-522
SMART,
Charles C; b1834 s/o Richard & Asenath Clark of Rumney; m1860 Jennie M Merrill d/o Jeremiah & Mary Ann George; ch Achsah b1861 m Ira M Abbott, Mary A, Hattie B b1865; NH-0007-607
Daniel; bro/o Moses; liv Canterbury, Rumney NH; ch Richard b1795 m Asenath Clark, 1 son, 3 dau; NH-0007-607
Lewis B; s/o Caleb & Hannah Libby gs/o Elijah of Coryden NH; m Amanda J Dearborn d/o Jonathan & Amanda F of Thornton; liv Campton Village NH; ch Willis E, Amy A, Bertha M; NH-0007-208
Richard; b1795 s/o Daniel; m1818 Asenath Clark; liv Rumney NH; ch Harriet N b1819 m Francis Cushman, Daniel R b1821, Mary E b1826 m Jeremiah Chapman, Caroline A b1828 m Jonathan Greenough of Canterbury NH, Sarah dy, Lydia M b1832 dy, Charles C b1834 m Jennie M Merrill, Mark C b1836, William H b1840; NH-0007-607
SMILEY,
David; s/o William; m Mary Harkness d/o Elizabeth Putnam; liv Plymouth, Grafton, Bristol NH; ch Mary Harkness b1806 m1834 Dea David Fosdick, James Robinson MD b1808, 3 dy; NH-0004-650
Dr David; b1760; m Rachael Johnson of Peterborough; liv Haverhill MA, Peterborough NH; NH-0002-664
James Robinson MD; b1808 s/o David & Mary Harkness; m1837 Elizabeth Lane; liv Bristol & Grafton NH; ch Adelaide Lane,

SMILEY (continued)
Mary Elizabeth, Frances Farley, Susan Ela, Pamelia Tarbell, Robert Lane; NH-0004-650
William; b1728; liv IRE, Jaffrey NH; ch David m Mary Harkness, Robinson, 8 others; NH-0004-650
SMITH,
Aaron Jackson; b1810; m Lucinda Cole & m Louisa Cole; liv Stark NH; NH-0005-580
Albert MD LLD; b1801; m1828 Fidelia Stearns of Jaffrey; liv Peterborough; NH-0002-664
Dr Alpheus; m Mehitable Foster of Saulsbury NH; liv RI, Lebanon NH; ch Foster, Solomon K, Josephine dy, Rev Alpheus D b1813 m Emily B True; NH-0004-231
Rev Alpheus D; b1813 s/o Dr Alpheus & Mehitable Foster; m Emily B True of Corinth & m1874 Mrs Mary E Clough of Canterbury; liv Corinth & W Fairlee VT, Dover & Concord & Laconia NH; ch/o Emily - Josephine E m S W Sanders of Laconia NH, Alpheus D; NH-0004-231
Ami; b1800 s/o David & Eleanor Giddings; m Lydia F Butler d/o Dr Elijah of Weare; liv Acworth, Saxton's River VT, Hillsborough Bridge; ch John Butler b1838 m Jennie M Knowles & m Emma E Lavender; NH-0002-430
Arthur Noel MD; b1851 s/o Samuel M MD of Baring ME; liv Silver City ID, Dover NH; NH-0003-850
Asa Dodge AM DD LLD; b1804 s/o Dr Rogers & Sally Dodge of Amherst NH; m Sarah Ann Adams d/o Capt John of N Andover MA; liv New York City NY, Hanover NH; ch William Thayer AM MD; NH-0007-326
Asahel; s/o Edward & Hannah Chandler of Hanover NH; m Anna Owen; liv Hanover NH; ch Cyrus Pitt m Abbie Wilson of Fitzwilliam, Adaline E m Franklin W Smith, Laura P m Horace P Brown, Asahel A m Mary Benning & m Mary Stanton, Edward W, Noah W; NH-0007-316

SMITH (continued)
Asahel A; s/o Asahel & Annie Owen of Hanover; m Mary Benning & m Mary Stanton; liv Boston; ch/o Benning - Frank H; NH-0007-316
Ashbel; s/o Edward & Hannah Chandler of Hanover; m Esther Camp & m Lucinda Tenney; liv Hanover NH; ch/o ? - Roswell T, Esther R m --- Parsons, Ann W, Hannah E, Adaline L, Newton J, Noah Payson, Charles E, Chandler P, Mary F, William H; NH-0007-316
Benjamin; liv Stark NH; ch Sally b1787, Nancy b1789, Benjamin b1792, Nathan b1794, Hannah b1798; NH-0005-570
Benjamin F; s/o Benjamin H; m Sarah A Wheat d/o Joshua R & Huldah Kidder; liv Plymouth NH; ch Jennie A, Joshua W, Frankie H, Iza J; NH-0007-594
Charles B; b1814; liv Belgrade ME, Union Village VT; ch George F, Henry M; NH-0007-367
Charles Goudy; b1822 s/o Eleazer & Anne Peters; m1847 Ruth W Morse d/o Caleb; liv Haverhill NH; ch William Peters, Anna M; NH-0007-365
Dr Cheney; m Eunice Baker d/o Capt Thomas of Dover; liv Dover; ch Cheney, 5 dau; NH-0003-773
Daniel; m Mary Mudgett; liv Gilmanton NH; ch Johm M m Fanny Edgely & m Sarah Watson, 1 dau m James Mudgett of New Hampton, 6 others; NH-0007-215
Dr Daniel; liv Waterborough ME; ch Dryden MD b1822, Jefferson MD; NH-0003-848
David; s/o Ean John & ?; m Eleanor Giddings; ch Ami b1800 m Lydia F Butler, 12 others; NH-0002-430
Judge Ebenezer; liv Meredith NH; ch Ebenezer Esq, John Esq, Daniel, Washington; NH-0004-747
Ebenezer Esq; s/o Judge Ebenezer; ch John, Isaac, Daniel, Joseph P, Ebenezer Jr; NH-0004-748
Ebenezer; b1774 s/o Garland & Mary Brown; m1796 Patience Brown d/o Nicholas; liv

SMITH (continued)
Barrington & Strafford NH; ch Elizabeth, Daniel, Mary, Lydia, Sarah A, Hannah, Patience, Dea Ebenezer b1810 m Mary Smith, William P; NH-0003-715
Dea Ebenezer; b1810 s/o Ebenezer & Patience Brown; m Mary Smith b1813 d/o John & Sarah Clark gd/o Remembrance Clark of Madbury NH; liv Strafford; ch Sarah C m Daniel Otis, Olive A m Garland Brown, Rufina m Sanborn Parshley, Anna P m Paul P Brown, May Ella m Frederick I Foss, Ebenezer Romanzo, Athelinda L; NH-0003-715
Edward; s/o Timothy & Esther Webster; liv Hanover NH; ch John, Edward m Hannah Chandler; NH-0007-316
Edward; s/o Edward of Hanover NH; m Hannah Chandler; liv Hanover NH; ch Asahel m Anna Owen, Noah, Ashbel m Esther Camp & m Lucinda Tenney, Cyrus Porter, Chandler P, Irene m John Wright, Russell m Mary Richardson, Hannah m Jerome Canfield, 3 dy; NH-0007-316
Eleazer; b1797 s/o Shubael of Washington VT; m Anne Peters d/o Andrew B of Bradford VT; liv Haverhill, Wentworth; ch Charles Goudey b1822, William Peters; NH-0007-365
Elias; b1796; m Matilda Stiles of Hillsboro; liv Beverly MA, Hanover NH; ch James Madison, Stephen D, Alonzo A, 3 sons, 6 dau; NH-0007-332
Elijah L; b1828 s/o Josiah & Hannah Morse of Brookfield VT; m Martha J R Glover d/o Benjamin & Polly Smith & m Cynthia D Glover sis/o Martha J R; liv Haverhill & Plymouth NH; ch/o Martha - Emogene, Benjamin F, Lydia L, Leonard H; NH-0007-593
Elisha; m Nancy Meader of Nantucket; liv Barnstable, Nantucket MA, Littleton NH; ch Mary m Isaac R Wilson of Trenton NJ; NH-0007-499
Elmer G; s/o John R & Mary E Wadleigh of Grafton NH; m

SMITH (continued)
Viola A Spaulding; ch Burnice E, Henry J; NH-0007-285
Ethan; b1784; liv Lyman, Monroe; ch Stebbins, Horace, Frances m --- Emery; NH-0007-552
Francis Peter; b1795 s/o Rev Isaac; liv Boston, Kingston, Ossipee; NH-0003-36
Frank; b1833 s/o Chester & Betsey Hutchins of Lunenburg VT; m1855 Harriet B Smith d/o Fielding & Mary Bingham & m1877 Esther J Rhodes d/o Benjamin & Eunice Bennett of Cairo NY; liv Lancaster NH; ch/o Harriet - Minnie; ch/o Esther - Florence J, Frank C; NH-0005-392
Frank R; s/o Israel & Mary Reed gs/o Eleazer; m Sarah E Kilton d/o Lovel & Sally Currier of Enfield; liv Grafton NH; ch Lillian A, Carrie L; NH-0007-281
Frederick A MD; b1830; m1856 Frances Gregg of Bellville NJ; liv Peterborough NH, Leominster MA; NH-0002-668
Freeman C; s/o Stephen & Hannah Foss; m Marinda C Jewell d/o Daniel & Mercy Priest; liv Campton Village NH; ch Lucius D, Wilfred; NH-0007-212
Garland; b1744; m1767 Mary Brown d/o John & --- Nevins; liv Somersworth & Barrington NH; ch Patience, James, John, Ebenezer b1774 m Patience Brown, Lydia, Joseph, Garland, David, Mary, Hannah; NH-0003-715
George S; m Emma McClure d/o George W & Mary Ann Merrill; ch Roy M; NH-0007-390
Hazen D; b1828 s/o John & Sarah Gilson of Sanbornton NH; m1859 Lydia B Walker of Campton; liv Campton, Plymouth NH; ch Charles C dy, Helen m J C Storey; NH-0007-594
Isaac; s/o Ichabod; m Nancy Codman; ch Isaac m Amelia Stevens, Catherine m Joseph Morril, Rene m --- Jones, Agnes m William Campbell, Henry m Mary Tuton, Turner, Loraine m Samuel Gibson, Jail Smith dy, Princess m ---

SMITH (continued)
Fletcher, Achasa m --- Spaulding, Larnard; NH-0002-383
Isaac; s/o Isaac & Nancy Codman; m Amelia Stevens; ch Matilda m Alvah Loveren, Nancy S m Robert Tuton, William T m Mary Ann Morgan, Calvin S m Maria, Isaac m Josephine Whittle, Ester m Adam Dickey, Francis G m Mary A Peaslee, Theresa m William Dickey & m Dea Christie of New Boston & m John McCollom of Mont Vernon, Ellen M dy, George D m Margaret ---; NH-0002-383
Isaac; b1793 s/o Joseph & Mary Sawyer of Plaistow NH; m1822 Mary Clarke d/o Nathaniel & Abigail Woodman & m1834 Sarah Clement b1795 d/o Moses & Mary & m1867 Abigail Clarke b1795 sis/o Mary & wid/o David Clarke of Sandown NH; liv Hampstead NH; ch/o Mary - Isaac William m Amanda W Brown, 2 others; ch/o Sarah - 2; NH-0002-27
Isaac William; b1825 s/o Isaac & Mary Clarke of Hampstead NH; m1854 Amanda W Brown d/o Hon Hiram of Manchester NH; liv Manchester NH, Lowell MA; ch Mary Amanda b1855, William Isaac b1857, Arthur Whitney b1860, Julia Brown b1862, Edward Clark b1864, Daniel Clark b1866, Jennie Patterson b1868, Grace Lee b1870; NH-0002-28
Jefferson MD; b1808 s/o Dr Daniel of Berwick ME; liv Springvale ME, Dover NH; NH-0003-847
Jeremiah; b1759 s/o William of Peterborough; liv Peterborough, Exeter; NH-0003-31
Jeremiah; b1770 s/o William & Dilly Clough of Old Hampton NH; m Betsy Glidden b1778 d/o Squire Charles Sr of Northfield NH; liv Northfield; ch Alice G b1804 m Charles Mills Glidden, Nancy C b1806 m William Gilman, Joseph M G b1807, Warren H Esq b1817 m Elizabeth Glines, Mary Elizabeth b1822 m Ephraim S Wadleigh; NH-0004-532 & 543

SMITH (continued)

Jesse MD; m Eliza Bailey of Charlestown; liv Peterborough, Cincinnati OH; NH-0002-667

John Esq; s/o Judge Ebenezer; liv Meredith NH; ch John P; NH-0004-748

Rev John; liv Weymouth MA; ch 1 dau m Rev John Shaw & m Rev Stephen Peabody, 1 dau m Pres John Adams; NH-0003-123

Dea John; s/o Lt Thomas; m --- McNeil d/o William & m Ann Brown of Francestown; liv New Boston; ch/o McNeil - 5, ch/o Ann - 14; ch/o ? - David m Eleanor Giddings; NH-0002-430

John; s/o Dea Christopher & Mary Page of N Hampton NH gs/o Benjamin; m Martha Drake d/o Abram & Martha; liv New Hampton NH; ch Hannah P m William E Merrill s/o David & Sarah Lee; NH-0007-396

John Jr; b1771 s/o John of Ipswich MA; m Betsey Burnham; liv Enfield NH; ch Betsey Ann b1799 m Nehemiah Dustin, Lucy dy, Daniel L, Ziba H, John B, George W, Lucy W, Joslina P; NH-0007-262

John Butler; b1838 s/o Ami & Lydia F Butler; m Jennie M Knowles of Manchester & m1883 Emma E Lavender d/o Stephen of Boston; liv Hillsborough, Saxton's River, Boston, Weare; NH-0002-430

John M; s/o Daniel & Mary Mudgett; m Fanny Edgely & m Sarah Watson of Guilford NH; liv Laconia, Campton; ch/o ? - J Frank m Fannie C Smith, 3 others; NH-0007-215

John P; s/o John Esq of Meredith NH; ch Daniel K, John P Jr, 1 dau m Richard Gove of Laconia; NH-0004-748

John R; s/o Joseph & Polly Russell; m Mary E Wadleigh d/o Samuel & Harriet Lane; liv Grafton NH; ch Elmer G m Viola A Spaulding, Alvin L, Mary m --- Tinkham, Hattie m --- Walker, Sam J, J Warren, Grace O; NH-0007-285

Jonathan; b1798 s/o Jonathan of Peterborough NH; m --- Payson d/o Hon M P; liv Lisbon NH, Bath; ch 1 dau, 3 sons; NH-

SMITH (continued)
0007-62

Jonathan M; s/o Jonathan of New Hampton gs/o Jonathan; m Elizabeth A Mason d/o Caleb & Sarah Godfrey; liv Ashland NH; ch Jonathan E; NH-0007-128

Joseph; s/o Peter & Molly Taylor; m Polly Russell d/o John & Achsah; ch John R m Mary E Wadleigh, 4 others; NH-0007-285

Joseph; b1740 s/o Samuel & Sarah of Haverhill MA; m1762 Hannah Harriman b1744, m1784 Mary Sawyer b1758 d/o Jonathan of Atkinson NH & m1803 Mrs Phebe Runnels; liv Plaistow & Hampstead NH; ch/o Hannah - 11; ch/o Mary - Isaac b1793 m Mary Clarke, Sarah Clement, Abigail Clarke, 4 others; NH-0002-27

Joseph Haven MD; b1805 s/o John of Rochester NH; liv Dover NH; Lowell MA; NH-0003-847

Joseph M G; b1807 s/o Jeremiah & Betsy Glidden of Northfield; ch Joseph W, Jacob H, Mary E, Josephine m Orin Murfin; NH-0004-543

L B; m Betsey Dole & m Mary Folsom of Laconia; liv Andover MA, Newmarket NH; ch/o Betsey - Abby A, 3 others; ch/o Mary - 3; NH-0003-552

Luke; b1804 s/o David & Ellen Giddings of Acworth NH; m1831 Wealthy Eyres d/o Dea James & Susan Senter & m1860 Mrs Sarah G Sargent d/o Issachar & Mindwell Sillsby Mayo of Lempster; liv Boston MA, Hillsborough, New Boston, Milford; ch Wealthy dy, George Luke b1837, Mark J, Charles H V; NH-0002-608

Moses; b1799; m Mehitable Ward of Hanover; liv Canaan & Lyme NH; ch Baxter P, H Ellen m ? & m C B Dow of Hanover, Otis F m Sarah D Waite, Sarah H m Charles Townsend, Abigail J C m L Richardson, Elizabeth, Rosella A, Mehitable W, 1 other; NH-0007-544

Noah; s/o Edward & Hannah Chandler of Hanover; ch Edward P; NH-0007-316

SMITH (continued)
Perley; liv Chesterfield & Lyman NH; ch Amos, Julius; NH-0007-516

Lt Robert; m1768 Sarah Eaton; liv Salisbury NH; NH-0004-621

Robert MD; gs/o Lt Robert & Sarah Eaton; m Susan Fifield d/o Joshua & m Hannah Marston & m Abigail Pettengill; liv Amesbury MA, Hampton NH; NH-0004-621

Samuel; m Julia A E Chamberlin; liv Bath NH; ch Elizabeth, 2 sons, 3 dau; NH-0007-142

Samuel; b1800; m Phoebe Noyes; liv Sandwich, Lisbon NH; ch David m Durilla Priest & m Katie Knight, 1 dau m George Brummer, 7 sons, 2 dau; NH-0007-452

Rev Samuel H; b1811; m1832 Hannah P Field of Rutland VT & m1854 Ellen M Copps & m1860 Hannah Kendall of Chester VT; liv Conway MA, Hanover NH, Lyme; ch/o Hannah P - Bertha A, Charles E dy, 1 dy, Delia H m F F Flint of Lyme; ch/o Ellen - 1 dy; ch/o Hannah - Edmund J dy, Edmund H dy; NH-0007-337

Simeon S; b1799; m Rhoda Jesseman; liv Gilmanton, Lisbon NH; ch Ezra G, Lizzie m Charles Watson of Franconia, 1 other; NH-0007-454

Solomon; s/o Solomon; m Esther Porter; liv Lyme NH; ch Lyman, Porter, Joseph, Esther m Thomas Hall, Ebeta m George Franklin; NH-0007-530

Stephen; s/o Stephen; m Hannah Foss d/o John & Mehetable Worthing; ch Freeman C m Marinda C Jewell, 5 others; NH-0007-212

Lt Thomas; liv IRE, Chester, New Boston; ch Dea John m --- McNeil & m Ann Brown; NH-0002-430

Hon Thomas J; b1830; m1854 Sarah S Kelley of Wentworth; liv Dorchester & Wentworth & Dover NH; ch 2 dau, 1 son; NH-0007-112.24

Timothy; b1702; mc1724 Esther Webster of Glastonbury CT; liv Hadley MA, Hanover NH; ch Edward, Rebecca m Gideon Smith, Timothy, Mary, Esther,

SMITH (continued)
Abijah, Jemima, Hannah m Isaac Walbridge, John; NH-0007-316

Rev Uriah; liv Woodstock, Barnard, Enfield; ch Catharine m --- Cox of Barnard VT, Elias, Melinda, Amanda m --- Snow of Mound City MN, Susan A m J W Johnson; NH-0007-261

Warren H Esq; b1817 s/o Jeremiah & Betsy Glidden of Northfield; m Elizabeth Glines of Northfield; liv Northfield; ch Charles Glidden, Jeremiah Eastman; NH-0004-543

William; b1737 s/o William & Betty Cilley of E Kingston; liv Kensington & Gilmanton NH; NH-0003-189

William; bc1800 s/o Jeremiah of Exeter; liv Exeter; NH-0003-32

SMYTH,
Alexander G; b1817 s/o Joshua of Holderness; m1847 Caroline Flanders of Plymouth; liv Plymouth NH, Holderness; ch Rodney E, Cora H; NH-0007-595

Gov Frederick; b1819; m1844 Emily Land b1822 d/o John & Nabby Emmerson gd/o Col Nathaniel; liv Candia & Manchester NH; NH-0001-106, NH-0002-67

SMYTHE,
Horatio N; s/o Joshua; m Eliza Smythe d/o Caleb & Abiah Colburn; liv Ashland NH; ch Charles W m Margaret Harris d/o Dr Charles & Mary of NC, 5 others; NH-0007-128

SNOW,
Alvan, b1820 s/o Joseph & Sally Atkinson; ch Frank, Will; NH-0006-799

Edwin; b1836 s/o Joseph & Sally Atkinson; m1857 Maria H Perkins d/o John W & Caroline Nason gd/o Stephen Esq; liv Eaton, ch Nellie H m A J White, Isabel S m Dr L W Atkinson of Cherry Valley MA, Leslie P b1862 m Susie Elsie Currier, Bertha; NH-0006-799

John; b1831 s/o Joseph & Sally Atkinson; liv Eaton NH; ch Mark; NH-0006-799

Joseph; b1791 gs/o Thomas; m

SNOW (continued)

Sally Atkinson d/o John; liv Gorham ME, Eaton NH; ch Silas b1816, Hannah m Noah Thompson & m Jonathan Nickerson, Alvan b1820, Apphia m Henry Mason, Joseph Jr, Susan m Mayhew Patch & m Red Edmund Dudley, Sally dy, John b1831, Mary A m William F Brooks, Edwin b1836 m Maria H Perkins, Jane m Charles Robertson; NH-0006-799

Joseph; b1798; m Hannah Noyes of Landaff; liv Landaff, Bath Upper Village; ch 10; NH-0007-142

Leslie P; b1862 s/o Edwin & Maria H Perkins of Eaton; m Susie Elsie Currier of Haverhill; liv Haverhill; ch Conrad Edwin b1889; NH-0006-779

SNYDER,

Charles; b1837; m1870 Mary E Prescott d/o Samuel & Mary E Robinson; liv New York City; ch Charles B b1872, Byron P b1874; NH-0003-136

SOULE,

David F; s/o Samuel; m Elizabeth McMurchie Dole wid/o Cyrus d/o Archibald & Elizabeth Holbrook McMurchie; liv Woolwich ME; ch Capt Gilbert b1820 m Eliza A Mills, Hannah, Sarah m James Bailey, Lewis, Augusta m Alden P Goudy, Lemuel; NH-0005-559

Ezekiel; b1711 s/o Joshua & Joanna Studley; m Hannah Delano; liv Woolwich ME; ch John b1735; NH-0005-559

George; m Mary Becket; liv ENG, Plymouth, Disbury, Bridgewater, ch John; NH-0005-559

Capt Gilbert; b1820 s/o David F & Elizabeth McMurchie Dole of Woolwich ME; m1853 Eliza A Mills b1829 d/o John & Mercy Adams of Detroit ME; liv Bath & Brewer ME, St Anthony MN, Groveton; ch Gilbert Mills, Annie Laurie m Augustus Thayer MD of Portland, Edward Beecher, James Bailey; NH-0005-559

Joshua; s/o John; m Joanna Studley; ch Ezekiel b1711 m Hannah Delano; NH-0005-559

Samuel; b1769 s/o John; ch

SOULE (continued)

David F m Elizabeth McMurchie Dole; NH-0005-559

SOUTHARD,

Aaron; b1784 s/o Thomas & Rachel; m Jane Taylor Finley d/o Dea Samuel of Acworth; liv Walpole & Haverhill NH; ch Samuel Finley b1813, Eliza m Henry H Page s/o Gov John, Ann Jane m Nathaniel M Page s/o Gov John, Joseph dy, Kate m John N Morse; NH-0007-374

Marshall; s/o Nathaniel Southworth; m Sarah Abbott d/o David of Newbury; liv MA, Newbury; ch Lydia m J M Woodward, Elizabeth S, Emily, Mary E m Preston Claflin, Nathaniel, Abbie C; NH-0007-542

Moses; b1784 s/o Thomas & Rachel; m Nancy King of Acworth; liv Walpole & Haverhill NH; ch Solon S, Lyman M m Jane Bachop & m Hetty Kimball d/o Dudley of Newbury V.T, 3 dy; NH-0007-374

Thomas; b1750; m Rachel ---; liv Plainfield CT, Acworth NH, Hanover, Charlestown; ch James, Moses b1784 m Nancy King, Aaron b1784 m Jane Taylor Finley, Eliza, Lucinda; NH-0007-374

William; b1805; m Annie Brown of Bath; liv Fairlee VT, Bath NH; ch Lemuel J, Timothy B, 4 dau, 2 sons; NH-0007-140

SOUTHWORTH,

Nathaniel; m Patience Shaw sis/o Col Dan & m Abigail Robbins & m Elizabeth Hobart; liv MA, Lyme NH; ch/o ? - Marshall Southard m Sarah Abbott, Martha m Micajah Marshall, Anson m Phebe Steele, Harriet m David Steele, Nathaniel, Chestina, Zibeon, David, Benjamin; NH-0007-542

SPALDING,

Asa; s/o Samuel; liv Merrimack; ch Asa, Ephraim dy, Samuel Woods dy, Joanna dy, Sophia m Timothy Fry of Lowell MA, Cynthia m Gilbert Colburn of Pelham, Albert Jefferson, Lucy Davis m Jacob Carlton of Lowell MA, John Langdon dy, Sarah m Jacob Carlton of

SPALDING (continued)
Lowell MA, Dorcas m Andrew J
Nute of Lowell MA; NH-0002-
545
Asa; s/o Asa; liv Merrimack; ch
Samuel Woods, Joanna m
William Lyon of Pelham, Asa
Langdon, Albert Jefferson;
NH-0002-545
Charles; b1827 s/o Daniel;
m1862 Eliza S Hall wid/o W J
Greenough; liv TX, CA, Rumney
NH; ch Charles P b1863,
Edward P b1864 dy, Mary S
b1868, George P b1870 dy,
James C b1872, Warren A b1873
dy, Sarah E b1880; NH-0007-
611
Ebenezer; b1783?(1683?) s/o
Edward of Chelmsford; m Anna
---; liv Chelmsford; ch
Edward b1708, Bridger b1709,
Experience b1711, Reuben
b1715 dy, Stephen b1717,
Sarah b1719, Esther b1722,
Mary b1724, Reuben b1728,
Anna b1731; NH-0002-462
George Burley DD; b1835 s/o Dr
James & Eliza Reed of Mont-
pelier VT; m Sarah Livingston
Olmstead d/o Rev Dr John W &
Mary Livingston gd/o Richard
Montgomery Livingston of
Saratoga NY; liv Dover; ch
Mary Livingston, Martha Reed,
Catherine Olmstead dy,
Gertrude Parker, George
Brown; NH-0003-883
George D; b1858 s/o Benjamin D;
m1880 Sarah M Pillsbury &
m1882 Florence E Field d/o
Lawrence & Imogene; liv
Rumney NH; ch/o Sarah -
Lilian S; NH-0007-612
George Franklin; s/o Ira; liv
Merrimack; ch Caribella
Frances, Frank Clarence; NH-
0002-545
Ira; s/o Samuel; liv Merrimack;
ch Ira dy, William Moore,
Ephraim Heald, Nancy Isabella
m William Kimball of Temple,
Eliza Jane dy, George
Washington dy, George
Franklin, Betsy Chandler m
John G Kimball of Nashua,
Catherine Mears m Chancy C
Kuler, Ellen Maria m Albert
Gay of Boston MA, Henry
Harrison dy; NH-0002-545
Hon Isaac; b1796 s/o Capt Isaac

SPALDING (continued)
of New Ipswich NH; m1828 Lucy
Kendall b1796 d/o Nathan of
Amherst; liv Wilton, Amherst,
Nashua; ch Edward Francis
b1831 dy, Isaac Henry b1840
dy; NH-0002-199
Dr James; s/o Reuben & Jerusha
Carpenter; m Eliza Reed; liv
Montpelier VT; ch George
Burley DD b1835 m Sarah
Livingston Olmstead, 9
others; NH-0003-883
John Lund; s/o Oliver; liv
Merrimack; ch Sarah Frances,
John Oliver; NH-0002-545
Oliver; s/o Samuel; liv Merri-
mack; ch Abigail dy, Oliver,
1 other; NH-0002-545
Oliver; s/o Oliver; liv Merri-
mack; ch Abigail Nourse m
William T Parker, John Lund,
Hosea Ballou, Oliver Perry
dy; NH-0002-545
Reuben; s/o Reuben of CT gs/o
Ephraim of CT ggs/o Edward
of Canterbury CT; m Jerusha
Carpenter; liv Sharon VT; ch
Dr James m Eliza Reed, 11
others; NH-0003-883
Samuel; liv Chelmsford MA,
Merrimack NH; ch Samuel,
Abijah, Sarah, Henry, Oliver,
Isaac, Silas, Asa; NH-0002-
545
Samuel; s/o Samuel; liv Merri-
mack; ch Ephraim dy, Sarah m
Luther Abbott of Andover VT,
Abijah, Betsey m Isaac Blood
of Hollis, Luther, Meriel m
John Thomas of Goffstown,
Ira, Josiah, Eleanor; NH-
0002-545
William W; m Lizzie Etta Leach
d/o Walter S & Lizzie S
Durrell; liv Lawrence MA; ch
Helen D, John W; NH-0004-217
SPARHAWK,
George; liv Conway NH; ch
George, Andrew, David,
Charles; NH-0006-854
SPAULDING,
Daniel; b1737 s/o Phineas of
Chelmsford MA; m Phebe
Dustin; liv Hudson, London-
derry & Northumberland NH; ch
Edward m Martha Weeks,
William Dustin; NH-0005-387 &
544
Edward; s/o Daniel & Phebe
Dustin; m Martha Weeks; liv

SPAULDING (continued)
Northumberland & Lancaster NH; ch John Wilson m Electa Stebbens; NH-0005-387

Edward; b1635 s/o Edward; liv Chelmsford MA; ch Edward b1674; NH-0004-387

Edward; b1674 s/o Edward of Chelmsford; ch Phineas b1706; NH-0005-387

Hon Edward MD; b1813 s/o Dr Matthias; m1842 Dora Everett Barrett d/o Joseph & Mary Appleton; liv Amherst & Nashua NH; ch Edward Atherton, 2 daus; NH-0001-81

George Burley DD; s/o Dr James; m Sarah Livingston Olmstead d/o Rev Dr John W & Mary Montgomery d/o Richard of Saratoga NY; liv Montpelier VT, Vergennes VT, Hartford CT, Dover NH; ch Mary Livingston, Martha Reed, Catherine Olmstead dy, Gertrude Parker, George Brown; NH-0001-291

John Hubbard; b1821 s/o John Wilson & Electa Stebbens of Lancaster; m1848 Emeline Corser of Guildhall VT; liv Lancaster NH; ch John H Jr, Debby Ann; NH-0005-387

John Wilson; s/o Edward & Martha Weeks; m Electa Stebbens; ch John Hubbard b1821 m Emeline Corser; NH-0005-387

Dr Matthias; b1767 s/o Col Simeon & Abigail (Johnson) Wilson; m Rebecca Wentworth Atherton d/o Hon Joshua; liv Amherst NH; ch Hon Edward MD b1813 m Dora Everett Barrett, 7 others; NH-0001-81

Oliver; b1816 s/o Oliver & Sarah Greenough gs/o Lt Joseph; m1840 Sarah Ann Hawkins d/o Amasa & Sarah Merrill; liv Rumney NH; ch Edgar O, Phebe A, Charles A; NH-0007-606

Phineas; b1706 s/o Edward; liv Chelmsford; ch Daniel b1737 m Phebe Dustin; NH-0005-387

Phineas AM MD; b1799 s/o Reuben & Jerhusha Carpenter of Sharon VT; m1826 Caroline B Lathrop & m1843 Charlotte Merrill of Haverhill; liv Lyndon VT, Haverhill NH; ch/o

SPAULDING (continued)
Caroline - Caroline A, Mary G m James H Tolle; ch/o Charlotte - Ada L m Henry D James, Frank M; NH-0007-360

Reuben; s/o Ephraim gs/o Edward ggs/o Benjamin gggs/o Edward; ch Reuben m Jerhusha Carpenter; NH-0007-360

Samuel; b1763; liv New Marlboro, Stockbridge CT, St Johnsbury & Charleston VT; ch Susannah m --- Harvey, Carlton b1805; NH-0007-517

Col Simeon; m2nd Mrs Abigail (Johnson) Wilson; liv Chelmsford MA; ch Dr Matthais b1769 m Rebecca Wentworth Atherton, others; NH-0001-81

SPENCER,
Uel; b1839 s/o James b1784; m Ruth Emerson d/o M C of Hanover; ch 4; NH-0007-324

SPOKESFIELD,
John; m Abigail Furnald & m Betsey Crosby of Alexandria NH; liv Thornton, ME; ch Jonathan C m Keziah Foss of Thornton & m Jane Chase d/o William & Susan of Deerfield NH; NH-0007-208

SPRAGUE,
Alden; m ? & m Eunice Stoddard; liv Rochester MA, Haverhill NH; ch/o ? - 1 dau m James I Swan; ch/o Eunice - 5; NH-0007-81

SPRING,
John Langdon; b1830 s/o John Clark of Newport NH; m1856 Ellen Melvina Fountain; liv Wilton, Milford, Lebanon; ch Arthur Langdon, Clarence Walker, Carrie Melvina, John Roland; NH-0007-96

STACKPOLE,
Joshua; m1740 Lucy Baker & m Abigail Hobbs; liv Somersworth; ch/o ? - 12; ch/o Abigail - Tobias b1766 m Eunice Roberts; NH-0003-680

Lorenzo; b1824 s/o Moses & Nancy Leighton of Somersworth; m1849 Elvira C Wentworth of Rollinsford; liv S Berwick ME, Rollinsford; ch Annie Wentworth b1850 m1869 Joshua H Lane of NJ & m Bernhard Baer, Edgar C b1852 dy; NH-0003-680

Moses; s/o Tobias & Eunice

STACKPOLE (continued)
Roberts of Somersworth; m Nancy Leighton of Somersworth; liv Somersworth; ch Lorenzo b1824 m Elvira C Wentworth, 2 others; NH-0003-680

Paul A AM MD; b1817 s/o Samuel & Rosanna of Rochester; m1845 Elizabeth G Hills d/o Charles P of Haverhill MA; liv Dover; ch Charlotte E, Charles H, Harry H; NH-0003-878

Tobias; b1766 s/o Joshua & Abigail Hobbs of Somersworth; m Eunice Roberts; liv Somersworth; ch Moses m Nancy Leighton, 11 others; NH-0003-680

STANLEY,
Clinton Warrington; b1830 s/o Horace C & Mary Ann Kimball of Hopkinton; m1857 Lydia A Woodbury d/o William Esq of Weare NH; liv Hopkinton & Manchester; NH-0002-22

Lt Dennis; m Sarah Bishop of Boscawen NH; liv Kittery ME, Lancaster NH; NH-0005-360

Horace C; m Mary Ann Kimball; liv Hopkinton; ch Clinton Warrington b1830 m Lydia A Woodbury, Helen Isabel Scribner, Edward W, Benton M; NH-0002-22

STANTON,
Benjamin; b1700; m --- Ricker, liv ENG; ch William m --- Brock, 4 others; NH-0003-703

Ezra; s/o William Jr & --- Holmes; m --- Otis; liv Barrington; ch Joshua O MD, William P m --- Brock, 5 others; NH-0003-703

William; s/o Benjamin & --- Ricker; m1761 --- Brock; liv Barrington; ch William Jr m --- Holmes; NH-0003-703

William Jr; s/o William & --- Brock; m --- Holmes; liv Barrington; ch Ezra m --- Otis, 7 others; NH-0003-703

William P; s/o Ezra & --- Otis; m --- Brock; liv Strafford Corner; ch Fred T; NH-0003-703

STARBUCK,
Edward; b1604; m Katherine ---; liv Nantucket; ch Nathaniel b1636 m Mary Coffin d/o Tristram, Dorcas m William

STARBUCK (continued)
Gayer, Sarah m William Storey of Dover & m Joseph Austin & m Humphrey Varney, Abigail m Judge Peter Coffin, Jethro; NH-0003-773

STARK,
Capt Albert; b1811 s/o Zephaniah & Susanna Porter of Hanover; m Alice Dodge; ch Reuben P, Dolly R m J R Hewes of Lyme, Alice D m William West of Boston, Mary E m Thomas H Bruce; NH-0007-325

Archibald; b1693; m Eleanor Nichols; liv Londonderry IRE, Glasgow SCO, Londonderry, Harrytown MA; ch William, John, Archibald, Samuel, 3 dau; NH-0002-40b

Maj Caleb; b1759 s/o Capt John & Elizabeth Page; m1787 Sarah McKinstry d/o William of Taunton MA; liv Boston MA, Pembroke NH, OH; ch Caleb Jr b1804, 4 sons, 6 dau; NH-0004-302

Frederick G; s/o John 3rd; liv Manchester NH; ch George b1823 m Elizabeth A Parker & m Mary G Bowers; ch/o ? - Juliet d1840 m Henry C Gillis, Emma d1859 m J G Cilley, William d1873; NH-0001-9

Gen George; b1823 s/o Frederick G; m1845 Elizabeth A Parker d/o Daniel & m1848 Mary G Bowers d/o Col Joseph; liv Manchester NH; ch John F, Emma G; NH-0001-9

Isaac D; b1805 gs/o Nathan; m Rhoda Fitts of Hanover; liv Lyme NH; ch Alonzo, Irenus, Isaac G, Alfred D m1853 Diadema Quint of Lyme; NH-0007-531

Capt John; m1758 Elizabeth Page d/o Caleb Esq; liv Derryfield NH; ch Maj Caleb b1759 m Sarah McKinstry; NH-0004-302

Maj-Gen John; s/o Archibald Esq of Derryfield d1822; NH-0002-46

STEARNS,
Isaac; liv ENG, Watertown; ch John m Sarah Mixer, 2 others; NH-0003-228

Hon Isaac; liv Billerica MA; ch John, William; NH-0004-138

John; s/o John & Ruth; m

**STEARNS** (continued)

Margaret Wallace; liv Deerfield NH; ch Sara A m David Morrill Philbrick; NH-0004-475

John; s/o Isaac; m Sarah Mixer d/o Isaac & Sarah of Watertown; ch Lt John m Elizabeth Bigelow; NH-0003-228

John; s/o Isaac; liv Billerica MA; ch Franklin, Hon Onslow, John O; NH-0004-138

Lt John; s/o John & Sarah Mixer; m Elizabeth Bigelow d/o John & Mary Warren of Watertown; ch John m Esther Johnson; NH-0003-228

John; s/o Lt John & Elizabeth Bigelow; m Esther Johnson; liv Billerica; ch Hon Isaac, Rev Josiah b1732 m Sarah Abbott & m Sarah Ruggles; NH-0003-228

Rev Josiah; b1732 s/o John & Esther Johnson; m Sarah Abbott & m Sarah Ruggles; liv Epping; ch/o Sarah A - 6; ch/o Sarah R - Rev Samuel, William b1773 m --- & m Abigail Richards Howe, 4 others; NH-0003-228

Rev Josiah Howe; b1812 s/o William & Abigail Richards Howe; m Eliza Kilby d/o John Esq of Dennysville ME; liv Dennysville ME, Epping NH; ch Abby Thayer m Frank W Spaulding MD, William Charnock dy; NH-0003-228

Nathan B; s/o Oliver & Lois Lathrop; liv Lebanon NH; ch Frederick O, Arlington C, Sophia F m Dr Carl Allen, Hattie A m Dr Henry Powers of Hopkinton NH; NH-0007-422

Hon Onslow; s/o John of Billerica MA; m1845 Mary A Holbrook d/o Hon Adin of Lowell MA; liv Concord NH; ch Charles O, Mary m John R Brooke, Margaret m --- Ingalls of N Adams MA, Sarah, Grace; NH-0004-138

Oliver; b1776; m1798 Lois Lathrop; liv Mansfield CT, Lebanon NH; ch 3 dy, Oliver L m Betsey Wood of Lebanon, Nathan B, 7 others; NH-0007-422

William; b1773 s/o Rev Josiah & Sarah Ruggles of Epping; m

**STEARNS** (continued)

--- & m Abigail Richards Howe d/o Lemuel of Templeton MA; liv Exeter & Epping NH; ch/o Abigail - William Ruggles, Rev Josiah Howe b1812 m Eliza Kilby, Mary Elizabeth, Samuel Richards dy; NH-0003-228

**STEELE,**

David; b1767; m1793 Phebe Edgerton; liv Tolland CT, Lyme NH; ch David, Daniel, Phebe m Col Anson Southard, Ruth, Azel, 7 others; NH-0007-542

David; b1793 s/o Thomas of Peterborough; liv New Durham, Dover; NH-0003-602

Eleazer; b1784; m1826 Eunice Hodgdon; liv Tolland CT, Bath ME, Bradford NH; ch Julia Minerva b1827 dy, Eliza S b1828 dy, Julia M b1830, Emily M b1831, George b1833 dy, George b1835 dy, Ellen Ophelia b1837 dy, George Harvey b1839 m1876 Mary Augusta Jones d/o Timothy Peaslee of Bradford, Eliza Ann b1841 dy, Caroline Kimball b1844, Harriet Clara b1847; NH-0004-209

Jonathan; m Elizabeth Harvey; liv Peterborough; ch Michael McClary; NH-0004-467

Jonathan; b1760 s/o David of Peterbrough; m Lydia Sullivan; liv Durham; NH-0003-600

Richard MD; b1797 s/o Judge Jonathan of Durham NH; liv Portsmouth & Dover NH; NH-0003-848

Thomas; liv Peterborough; ch David b1793, Hon Jonathan; NH-0003-602

**STEESE,**

Edward; m Ellen B Sturtevant d/o John D & Adeline Bradley; liv Boston; ch Edwin S, Gertrude; NH-0003-749

**STEPHENS,**

Andrew; s/o Moses Sr; m Lucinda Sargent; ch Moses E m Nettie P Bachelder, John, Hannah; NH-0004-507

Moses Sr; ch Joseph, Jonathan C, Elizabeth, Hannah, Eliza, Andrew m Lucinda Sargent; NH-0004-507

Moses E; s/o Andrew & Lucinda

NEW HAMPSHIRE GENEALOGICAL DIGEST

STEPHENS (continued)
Sargent; m Nettie P Bachelder
d/o William; ch Winnie M,
William G; NH-0004-507
STEPHENSON,
Turner; m Eluthera Porter of
Charlestown & m Phebe Oakes;
liv Lyme & Lancaster NH; NH-
0005-212
STEVENS,
Gen Aaron Fletcher; b1819 s/o
Capt John F & Martha; m1861
Adelaide M Johnson of Lynn
MA; liv Londonderry,
Manchester, Peterborough,
Nashua; NH-0002-37
Alonzo W; s/o Jotham & Ruth
Cross; m Rhoda Hoyt d/o Asa &
Lucy Whittier; liv Grafton &
Orange NH, E Canaan; ch
Alfred A, George O; NH-0007-
556
Alvah; s/o Josiah & Rachel
Homan of Grafton; m Harriet E
Hutchinson d/o David & Polly
Curtis; liv Grafton NH; ch
Fred A, Albert B, 2 others;
NH-0007-282
Asa; b1787; s/o Calvin & Esther
Wilkins; m1811 Mary Ann
Appleton d/o Rev Joseph of
Brookfield MA & sis/o Hon
William of Boston; ch William
b1816 m Louisa W Dye & m Mrs
Helen L Ober Whipple, 2 sons,
4 others; NH-0002-744
Caleb; b1782; m Sally Dewey
b1793 of Piermont; liv
Hampstead & Piermont NH; ch
Lyman Dewey b1821 m Achsah
Pollard French & m Frances
Child Brownell; NH-0004-40
Calvin; b1753 s/o Isaac &
Abigail Parling; m1773 Esther
Wilkins; liv Carlisle,
Hillsborough & Mont Vernon
NH; ch Asa b1787 m Mary Ann
Appleton, 4 sons, 8 others;
NH-0002-743
Cyprian; s/o Col Thomas of ENG;
m1672 Mary Willard d/o Maj
Simeon of Lancaster MA; liv
Lancaster MA; ch Joseph
bc1682 m Prudence Rice, 4
others; NH-0002-743
Maj Ebenezer; m1710 Elisabeth
Colcord; liv Kingston; ch
Benjamin bc1712, Col Ebenezer
b1715 m Mary Colcord & m
Doley Stevens, 1 other; NH-
0003-376, NH-0004-863

STEVENS (continued)
Col Ebenezer; b1715 s/o Maj
Ebenezer & Elisabeth Colcord
of Kingston NH; m1736 Mary
Colcord & m1768 Doley Stevens
of Newburyport; liv Kingston;
ch/o Mary - Capt Ebenezer
b1739 m Sarah Emerson & m
Sarah Stevens; ch/o Doley -
John b1770, Moses b1771,
Peter Colcord b1773, Paul
b1775 m Sally Howe; NH-0003-
376, NH-0004-863
Capt Ebenezer; b1739 s/o Col
Ebenezer & Mary Colcord;
m1760 Sarah Emerson & m Sarah
Stevens; ch/o ? - Samuel
b1761, 1 dau b1805, 10
others; NH-0003-376
Col Ebenezer; b1810 s/o Paul &
Sally Howe; m1831 Therina
Osgood d/o John S & Leah
Prescott gd/o Col Prescott of
Gilmanton & m1846 Cassandra
d/o John B & Alice Ladd of
Meredith; liv Gilford &
Meredith NH; ch/o Therina -
Cyrus A, Celestine A m Edward
Stowell, Ebenezer dy; ch/o
Cassandra - Alice S m Henry W
Lincon of Norton MA; NH-0004-
863
Elbert Carroll; b1847 s/o Grove
S & Lydia Wilson of Piermont
NH; m1875 J Augusta Stevens
of Littleton; liv Littleton;
NH-0007-112.1
Sgt Ephraim; bc 1762; liv
Derryfield; NH-0002-48
Col George AM; b1814; m Sarah A
Davenport; liv Lebanon; NH-
0004-621
George W; b1804; liv Piermont
NH; ch George H, Octavia A,
Charles E, Velina J, Leverett
E; NH-0007-574
Isaac; b1719 s/o Joseph &
Prudence Rice; m1743 Mercy
Hubbard of Rutland MA & m1748
Abigail Parling; liv Rutland
& Carlisle MA; ch/o Mercy - 1
son, 1 dau; ch/o Abigail -
Calvin b1753 m Esther
Wilkins, 2 sons, 1 dau; NH-
0002-743
John; liv Loudon NH; ch
Harriet, Polly, William,
John, Jonas, Parmelia,
Betsey, Ruth, Jemima; NH-
0004-508
John; liv Loudon NH; ch Edna,

239

STEVENS (continued)
Abel, Elizabeth, Martha, Dolly, John, Charity, Richard, Jesse, David; NH-0004-508

John; liv Gilford NH; ch Sherburn, Hubbard, Sickum; NH-0004-748

Joseph; bc1682 s/o Cypria & Mary Willard; m Prudence Rice d/o John of Sudley MA; liv Sudbury, Framingham, Lancaster, Rutland MA; ch Phineas b1707, Isaac b1719 m Mercy Hubbard & m Abigail Parling, Samuel dy, Joseph dy, 1 son, 5 dau; NH-0002-743

Joseph H; m Mary Jane Shirley d/o John & Margaret Houston; ch Margaret Abbie b1866, Alice Maria b1868, John Hadley b1870, Fred Hodgman b1873; NH-0002-329

Joshua; m Hannah Harriman & m Sarah Marshall of Hamstead & m Sarah French; liv Hamstead, Enfield; ch/o Hannah - Ruth, Jeremiah, Hannan, Mehetable, Susannah, Jotham, Samuel, Sarah, Mary, Judah, Joshua, 1 other; NH-0007-252

Josiah; s/o Josiah; m Rachel Homan; liv Grafton NH; ch Alvah m Harriet E Hutchinson, Wyman; NH-0007-282

Jotham; m Ruth Cross of Ellsworth; liv Grafton, Enfield; ch Alonzo W m Rhoda Hoyt, Samuel H; NH-0007-556

Lyman Dewey; b1821 s/o Caleb & Sally Dewey; m1850 Achsah Pollard French d/o Capt Theodore of Concord & m1875 Frances Child Brownell of New Bedford MA; liv Piermont & Concord NH; ch/o Achsah - Margaret French, Henry Webster; ch/o Frances - Fanny Brownell b1876, William Lyman b1880; NH-0004-40

Paul; liv Gilford NH; ch Col Ebenezer, William, 1 dau m Benjamin Wadleigh Esq, Paul Jr, Smith, John, Moses; NH-0004-748

Paul; b1775 s/o Col Ebenezer & Dolly Stevens of Kingston; m Sally Howe; liv New Chester & New Hampton & Gilford NH; ch Dolly, William, Mark, Sarah, Fanny, Nancy, Fifield, Peter

STEVENS (continued)
F, Col Ebenezer b1810 m Therina Osgood & m Cassandra Swasey, Moses, John, Paul, James S, 2 dy; NH-0004-863

Samuel G; b1797 s/o David; m Betsey Davis; liv Goffstown, Nashua, Weare, Derry; ch Eliza m Charles Lund; NH-0002-216

Samuel H; b1802 s/o John & Ruhamah Fifield of E Kingston gs/o Col Ebenezer ggs/o Maj Ebenezer; m1840 Serephina (Sophronia) Sanborn d/o Moses of Kingston; liv Bristol & Exeter NH, Lawrence MA, ME; ch 1 dau; NH-0003-190, NH-0007-69

Sherburn; s/o John; liv Gilford NH; ch Frank, John; NH-0004-748

Col Thomas; liv Devonshire & London ENG; ch Mary, Cypria m Mary Willard, 2 sons; NH-0002-743

Truman; b1803; m Malvina A Carlton of St Johnsbury VT; liv Barnet & St Johnsbury VT, Littleton NH; ch Joan H m E D Rand of Lisbon; NH-0007-490

William; b1816 s/o Asa & Mary Ann Appleton; m Louisa W Dye of Newark NJ & m1876 Mrs Helen L Ober Whipple wid/o John of New Boston NH; liv Mont Vernon, Boston; ch/o Louise - Mary Ann m Charles F Wilkins of Omaha NE, Ella L, Catherine m C Henry Hobbie of Omaha, Frances E; ch/o Helen - Helen Willette Stevens b1880; NH-0002-744

Zelotes; m Susan M Morse d/o Silas; lif Orford, PA, Rutland VT, Littleton NH; NH-0007-505

STEVENSON,
James; s/o Thomas; m Polly Remick d/o William; ch David, Lucinda m Dr James Norris of Sandwich, John Milton b1801 m Martha Boyden, Dolly m J B Smith; NH-0006-777

John Milton; b1801 s/o James & Polly Remick; m1824 Martha Boyden d/o Dr Joseph; liv Tamworth NH; ch Elizabeth W m David F Miller of Manchester, Julia M H m Benjamin F Colby, Augusta A; NH-0006-777

STEVENSON (continued)
Thomas; liv Durham, Tamworth; ch John m Abigail Remick, James m Polly Remick; NH-0006-777

STICKNEY,
Benjamin F; m Phebe Pulsifer d/o Maj John & ?; liv Newbury MA, Campton NH; ch William H m Sarah O Hogdon d/o Joseph & Almira, Benjamin F m Laura A Eaton, 7 others; NH-0007-206 & 210

Benjamin F; s/o Benjamin F & Phebe Pulsifer; m Laura A Eaton d/o Alvina & Roxanna Chamberlain; liv Campton NH; ch Annie E, Henry E; NH-0007-207

Charles; s/o Benjamin & Annie Poor of Newbury MA; m Abigail Noyes d/o Samuel & Abigail Burbank; ch Samuel N m Sarah A Smith d/o Samuel P & Sally Judkin, 4 others; NH-0007-210

Dr Jacob E; m Martha Goss d/o Nathaniel & Mary Nye; liv ME, Lancaster NH; NH-0005-349

Hon William Weir; b1801 s/o Daniel & Sarah Morse of Enfield NH; m1850 Frances A Hough d/o Clark of Lebanon NH; liv Concord & New Market & Exeter NH; ch 2 dau, 1 other; NH-0003-34

STILLINGS,
Isaac G; b1799 s/o Rock; m Mary G Colby d/o Ichabod; liv Ossipee NH; ch Rev Alonzo m Mary J Hyde d/o William & Joanna Mason; NH-0006-629

Capt Nicholas Tuttle; b1818 s/o Samuel & Martha Tuttle of Bartlett; m1839 Patience Stanton b1817 d/o William & Patience Jenkins of New Durham; liv Bartlett, Jackson; ch Sophronia m Silas M Thompson, Alonzo, Emeline m James Nute of Bartlett; NH-0006-972

Rock; liv Sanford ME, Ossipee NH; ch Richard, Isaac G b1799 m Mary G Colby, 3 others; NH-0006-628

Samuel; b1790 s/o Samuel; m Martha Tuttle d/o Benjamin & Jane Folsom; liv Bartlett; ch Capt Nicholas Tuttle b1818 m Patience Stanton, Alfred, Benjamin F, Clarinda J m

STILLINGS (continued)
Elias M Hall of Bartlett; NH-0006-972

STILPHEN,
William; m Martha Pendexter d/o Hon John & Martha Jackson; ch George P m1837 Nancy Pendexter, Charles, Cornelius, Betsey A m Charles Morse, Martha P, Mary m John B Foote, Lavinia S; NH-0006-937

STINSON,
Capt Charles; b1800 s/o William Jr & Jane Cochran of Dunbarton NH; m1831 Susan Cochran b1803 d/o Robert & Prudence of Sharon VT & m1839 Mary Ann Poore b1811 d/o Moses & Sally of Goffstown NH; liv Dunbarton NH; ch/o Susan - Jane b1833 m1858 Wallace Caldwell of Byfield MA, Letitia C b1835 m1854 John M Parker of Goffstown, Susan C b1837 m1860 George Bryan Moore & m1877 Judge Edwin S Jones of Minneapolis MN; ch/o Mary - Mary A b1841 m1866 Charles A Pillsbury of Minneapolis MN; NH-0002-327, NH-0004-307

Col John; b1789 s/o James & Janette Allison of Dunbarton NH; m1819 Betsey Stinson; liv Dunbarton; ch Mary Jane m David Story, Nancy Chase m David Story, John Chase m1867 Alice B Cogill of Gloucester City; NH-0004-306

William; b1725; m1754 Agnes Caldwell b1734; liv IRE, Londonderry NH, Starkstown; ch William Jr b1762 m Jane Cochran, 11 others; NH-0002-327, NH-0004-307

William Jr; b1762 s/o William & Agnes Caldwell; m Jane Cochran b1776 of New Boston NH; liv Dunbarton NH; ch Capt Charles b1800 m Susan Cochran & m Mary Ann Poore, 4 others; NH-0002-327, NH-0004-307

STONE,
George Washington; s/o Maj Uriah & Hepzibah Hadley; ch Malvina m Rev William Arthur DD; NH-0007-576

STONY,
Capt Alexander; liv Salem MA, Orford NH; ch Sally m George Riley; NH-0007-565

STORER,
William; m Sarah Starbuck; ch
Samuel b1640 dy, Sarah b1642
dy, Hancock b1644, Sarah
b1645, Joseph b1648, Benjamin
b1648, Samuel bc1653; NH-
0003-773
STORRS,
Abel; s/o Constant of Lebanon
NH gs/o Nathaniel; m1839
Sarah A Storrs & m Eliza C
Hoyt of Craftsbury CT; liv
Lebanon NH; ch Nellie E
b1853, Alice C b1855, Jennie
L b1865; NH-0007-418
Augustus; b1762; liv Mansfield
CT, Hanover NH; ch Dan m Mary
Hurlbutt & m Marcia Haskell &
m Caroline H Haskell sis/o
Marcia, Royal m Mary E
Skinner; NH-0007-528
STORY,
Abraham B; b1777 s/o David of
Dunbarton; liv Northwood,
Washington; NH-0003-38
STRAW,
Ezekiel Albert; b1819 s/o James
B & Mehitable Fisk; m1842
Charlotte Smith Webster; liv
Manchester NH, Salisbury; ch
Albert dy, Charlotte Webster
m William H Howard, Herman
Foster, Ellen m Henry M
Thompson; NH-0002-80
James B; m Mehitable Fisk; liv
Lowell & Salisbury MA; ch
Ezekial Albert b1819 m
Charlotte Smith Webster,
Miranda m Benjamin F Manning,
Abigail, James B Esp, 3
sons; NH-0002-80
STREETER,
Frank S; m1877 Lillian
Carpenter d/o Hon A P; liv E
Charleston VT, Concord; ch 1
son, 1 dau; NH-0007-112.8
John; b1787; m Lucy Beemis of
Brattleboro VT; liv Landaff,
Lisbon; ch Stephen B m Sally
Howe, Julia b1820, 4 others;
NH-0007-495
Stephen B; s/o John & Lucy
Beemis; m1840 Sally Howe of
Benton; liv Littleton NH; ch
Mary mGeorge Colby of Warner,
Lucy A; NH-0007-495
STUART,
Charles J; b1788; m Eliza
Austin; liv Peterborough,
Sanbornton Square; NH-0004-
702

STURTEVANT,
John D; b1816 s/p Perez &
Dorothy Kimball; m1841
Adeline Bradley b1819 d/o
Joshua & Dorcas Jones; liv
Bath NH, Lowell MA; ch Edwin
A, Frances A m Amasa Clarke
of Boston, Ellen B m Edward
Steese; NH-0003-748
Perez; bc1765-7 bro/o Hosea,
John, Benjamin, Joseph; m
Dorothy Kimbal bc1785 d/o Rev
Josiah of Sandwich NH; liv
Centre Harbor NH, Danville
VT, Sterling IL; ch Starrett,
Josiah, Hezekiah Field,
Isaac, John D b1816 m Adeline
Bradley, Albert P, Rosette m
C A Giles, Mary m Moody
Clarke; NH-0003-748
SULLINGHAM,
Henry; m Amy ---; liv Stewarts-
town NH; ch Katharine b1803,
Jacob b1804, Elizabeth b1806,
Susanna b1808, Polly b1810;
NH-0005-664
SULLIVAN,
Eugene; m Ann Sullivan of
Lowell; liv IRE, Plymouth NH;
ch William dy, Nellie F, John
C, Joseph A D; NH-0007-593
George; b1771 s/o Gen John of
Durham; liv Exeter; NH-0003-
30
John; s/o Hon George of Exeter;
liv Exeter; NH-0003-32
M B MD; b1856 s/o Jeremiah &
Rebecca of Winthrop ME, liv
Lewiston ME, Dover NH; NH-
0003-850
SULLOWAY,
Hon Alvah Woodbury; b1838 s/o
Isreal W & Adeline Richard-
son; m1866 Susan K Daniell
d/o J F; liv Framingham MA,
Enfield & Franklin NH; ch
Alice b1871, Richard Woodbury
b1876, Frank Jones b1883; NH-
0001-119, NH-0004-322
Cyrus A; b1839 s/o Greeley &
Betsey L of Grafton NH; m1864
Helen M Fifield d/o Jonathan
W & Theodora L Dickinson of
Franklin; liv Plymouth, Man-
chester NH; ch Belle H b1868;
NH-0002-32
Isreal W; b1812 gs/o Capt
Isreal Woodbury; m Adeline
Richardson; liv Boston &
Waltham MA, Enfield NH; ch
Hon Alvah Woodbury b1838 m

SULLOWAY (continued)
Susan K Daniell, 1 dau m Herbert Bailey Esq of Claremont, 2 dau; NH-0001-119, NH-0004-322

SUMNER,
George; liv Deering; ch George, Charles, William, Eben, Thomas, Lucy, Sybil, Mary, John, Eben m Martha Merrill; NH-0002-387

SUTHERLAND,
Rev David; b1777; m1803 Anna Waters b1774 of SCO; liv Edinburgh SCO, Barnet VT, Bath NH; ch 7; NH-0007-147

SWAIN,
James R; b1826 s/o William; m1851 Ruth W Morse d/o Joshua & Ruth White; liv Rumney NH; ch Hattie N m Eugene G Dole, Ellen M, Charles H dy; NH-0007-611
Nathan; liv Gilford NH; ch Moses, Silvester; NH-0004-748

SWALLOW,
Archelaus; s/o Peter & Sibbil of Dunstable MA; m Susanna Kendall; liv Dunstable MA; ch Stillman b1816 m Nancy Roby Fisk, 5 others; NH-0002-217
Clarence H; s/o Stillman & Nancy Roby Fisk; m Mary H Barr; ch James C, Geo W, Willie C; NH-0002-217
Louis M; s/o Stillman & Nancy Roby Fisk; m Amanda A Smith; ch Lucy E, Frank H, Fred W; NH-0002-217
Peter; m Sibbil ---; liv Dunstable MA; ch Nahum, Larnard, James, Moody, Abijah, Archelaus, Prudence, Lucy; NH-0002-217
Stillman; b1816 s/o Archelaus & Susanna Kendall of Dunstable; m1837 Nancy Roby Fisk d/o James & Lucy Cutter Roby of Amherst wid/o Ralph Fisk of Boston; liv Nashua NH; ch Mary F m Phineas P Mitchell, Clarence H m Mary H Barr, James R, Anna A, Louis M m Amanda A Smith; NH-0002-217

SWAN,
Hon James I; b1780; m Elizabeth Sprague d/o Alden Esq of Haverhill; liv Haverhill NH; NH-0007-61

SWASEY,
Benjamin; b1752 s/o Ebenezer of

SWASEY (continued)
Exeter; m1777 Jane Bond; liv Meredith NH; ch John B b1782 m Alice Ladd; NH-0004-865
Henry; liv Gilford NH; ch Henry; NH-0004-748
John B; b1782 s/o Benjamin & Jane Bond of Meredith NH; m Alice Ladd d/o Eliphalet & Mary Park; liv Meredith; ch Cassandra m Col Ebenezer Stevens; NH-0004-865
Nathaniel Merrill; s/o Obadiah & Nancy Merrill; m Mary M Angiers; liv Haverhill NH; ch Mary m --- Brooks; NH-0007-352
Obadiah; b1775 bro/o Moses; mc1798 Nancy Merrill of Haverhill; liv Haverhill MA, Newbury VT, Haverhill NH; ch Samuel, John H, Nathaniel Merrill m Mary M Angiers, 10 others; NH-0007-352

SWEAT,
Nathan C; m1863 Lora T Kingsbury of Hanover NH; liv Canaan & Lebanon NH, Washington DC, Toledo IA; NH-0007-95

SWETT,
Isaac; b1784; m1817 Nancy Brown b1791 d/o Stephen T & Anna; liv Thornton, Bristol; ch Benjamin m Sarah Todd, Roswell D, Mary, Sylvester m Emma Jaquette & m Marcia A Smith, Marinda L m Thomas H Wicom; NH-0007-185
Noah; d1869; m Sarah ---; liv Gilmanton & Bethlehem NH; ch Elisha, 7 others; NH-0007-166
Hon Peter; b1801; m Frances Trumbull; liv Brockport NY, Peoria IL; NH-0004-621
Stephen R; b1820; m Sarah Cheney of Sutton & m Sarah Clough of Canaan; liv Salisbury, Andover, Wilmot, Canaan; NH-0007-230

SYMONDS,
Joseph; b1746; m Mittie Cummings of Hollis; liv Shirley MA, Hancock; ch Capt Joseph m Hannah Dodge, Mellia m Capt Jacob Ames, Charles m Sallie Dennis; NH-0002-354
Capt Joseph; s/o Joseph & Mittie Cummings; m Hannah Dodge d/o Lt Joseph of Hancock; ch Nancy m James Bowers, Hannah m Rev Syl-

SYMONDS (continued)
vester Cochrane, Amelia m
Capt Gardner Nay, Joseph dy,
Joseph m Annais Cavender,
Rebecca m James Davis, Lewis
m Persis Robinson; NH-0002-
355
Lewis; s/o Capt Joseph & Hannah
Dodge; m Persis Robinson of
Hancock; liv Hancock; ch
William F m Abbie M Washburn;
NH-0002-355
William F; s/o Lewis & Persis
Robinson of Hancock; m Abbie
M Washburn d/o Elijah & Mary
Hills; liv Hancock; ch Henry
A, Annie L, Herbert W; NH-
0002-355

-T-

TAFT,
Richard; b1812; m1839 Lucinda
Knight of Hancock NH; liv
Barre VT, Franconia NH; ch 1
dau m Charles F Eastman; NH-
0007-270.1
TALPEY,
Charles W; b1835 s/o Jonathan &
Elizabeth Carlisle of York;
m1863 Mary Abbie Berry d/o
Elder Nathan & Mary of New
Durham NH; liv Dover,
Farmington NH; NH-0003-632
Henry; s/o Richard; liv York
ME; ch Jonathan b1793 m
Elizabeth Carlisle; NH-0003-
632
Jonathan; b1793 s/o Henry;
m1817 Elizabeth Carlisle
b1796 d/o Daniel of York ME;
liv York; ch Charles W b1835
m Mary Abbie Berry; NH-0003-
632
TALLMAN,
Thomas; liv New Bedford MA,
Vershire VT, Lyme NH; ch
Hannah b1798, William m Phila
Culver; NH-0007-540.
TAPPAN,
John; m Abigail Weare; ch
Jonathan MD b1772, Weare
b1790 m Lucinda Atkins; NH-
0003-189
Mason Weare; b1817 s/o Weare of
Newport; m Emeline M Worth of
Sutton & m Mary E Jenkins of
Boston & m Imogene B Atwood

TAPPAN (continued)
of Lisbon; liv Bradford; ch/o
Emeline - Frank M Esq; ch/o
Imogene - Helen L; NH-0004-
22, NH-0004-192
Weare; b1790 s/o John & Abigail
Weare; m1816 Lucinda Atkins
of Claremont; liv Bradford;
ch Hon Mason W; NH-0003-189
TARBELL,
Joel; b1793 s/o Thomas & Sarah
Barrett; m Betsey Shattuck
d/o Jonathan of Pepperell MA
& m1831 Mary Mansfield of
Temple; liv Mason; ch/o
Betsey - Joel Harrison b1816
m Esther Putnam, Mary Eliza-
beth b1820, William b1824;
ch/o Mary - Charles, Solon,
Hiram, Alonzo, Joseph; NH-
0002-511
Joel Harrison; b1816 s/o Joel &
Betsey Shattuck; m1839 Esther
Putnam d/o Ephraim; liv
Lyndeborough; ch Sanford P
b1839, Charles F b1843, Sarah
Adeline b1850 m Byron Stacy;
NH-0002-512
Thomas; b1751 s/o Capt Thomas
Jr; m1778 Sarah Barrett; ch
Sally b1778, Esther b1780,
Thomas b1782 dy, Reuben
b1784, Lemuel b1786, Thomas
b1788, Eunice b1791, Joel
b1793 m Betsey Shattuck,
Lydia b1797; NH-0002-511
TARLETON,
Col Amos; s/o Col William &
Mary Melville of Piermont; m
Theodora Ladd d/o James; liv
Piermont; ch Henry, Horace,
Arthur, Mary J m Thomas A
Barstow; NH-0007-379
Elias; liv Rye; ch Stillman,
William, Joseph; NH-0003-541
Samuel; b1769 s/o Stillman gs/o
Elias; m Jerusha Hopkins
b1774; ch Stillman b1794 m
Martha Warner, Martha M b1796
m Samuel Paul, Mercy H b1799
m H J Jenness, Sarah b1802 m
David Manson, Samuel Hopkins
b1806 m Mary J Pickering,
Mary A b1808 m Dana Bullard,
John W dy; NH-0003-541
Samuel Hopkins; b1806 s/o
Samuel & Jerusha Hopkins;
m1838 Mary J Pickering d/o
Gee of Newington; liv S New-
market NH, Newington; ch
George m Mary Webb, Sarah;

TARLETON (continued)
NH-0003-541
Col William; m Mary Melville &
m ?; liv Piermont; ch/o Mary
- William, Col Amos m
Theodora Ladd, Betsey, Mary;
NH-0007-379
TASKER,
Ebenezer; s/o John; ch
Ebenezer, Jonathan; NH-0006-
914
Gilbert; b1805; m Eliza Durgin
d/o Jonathan & Susan Bick-
ford; liv Barrington, Barn-
stead; ch Elvira m Nehemiah
Caverly Twombly; NH-0003-715
John; liv ENG, Madbury; ch
Ebenezer, Samuel, John,
William; NH-0006-914
Jonathan; s/o Ebenezer; liv
Bartlett NH; ch Jonathan,
Ebenezer, Polly m Elder
Hasletine, Lucretia m Daniel
Rogers, Lurana m Joshua
Rogers, Comfort m Benjamin F
George; NH-0006-914
TAYLOR,
Chester; m Hannah Sherman; liv
CT, Lisbon NH; ch Chester m
Clementine Stebbins, 7 sons,
4 dau; NH-0007-454
Hon Cyrus; b1818 s/o Nicholas M
& Sally Eastman of New
Hampton; m Martha Minot d/o
James; liv Bristol NH; ch
Henry A b1848 m Helen A White
of Bristol, Abbie M b1851
m1882 Ira A Chase; NH-0007-
189
John; s/o Thaddeus gs/o Dea
Samuel ggs/o Abraham gggs/o
William; m Sally Jones; liv
Lempster; ch Matilda R m
Horace Childs; NH-0004-360
Joseph; m A M Ketchum of Pier-
mont; liv Springfield &
Hanover NH; ch 1 dau m C B
Walker; NH-0007-319
Oliver; s/o Gilman R; m Polly
Baker; ch George C m Amanda P
Huckins d/o John B & Dorcas H
Smith of Holderness, 3
others; NH-0007-202
William MD; b1761 bro/o Dr
Benjamin; m Mehitable Low of
Stratham; liv N Hampton,
Effingham, Parsonsfield ME;
NH-0006-553
TEBBETS,
Noah; b1802 s/o James of
Rochester; liv Parsonfield

TEBBETS (continued)
ME, Rochester; NH-0003-603
Samuel; b1780 s/o Maj Ebenezer
of Rochester; liv Dover; NH-
0003-589
TENNEY,
David; liv Hanover NH; ch
David, John, Andrew; NH-0007-
313
David; s/o John & Olive Arm-
strong; m Anna Jacobs; ch
Elisha, Shelden, Seth, David,
Elijah, Joseph m Ann H Davis,
Eunice m Elijah Miller Esq,
Susan m Orange Woodward, Lucy
m Harby Morey, Vina m Alba
Hall, Anna m Benjamin Ross,
Olive m Isaac Ross, Percy m
Benjamin Smith; NH-0007-313
Elisha; b1785 s/o David Jr;
m1814 Phebe Freeman & m1829
Sarah Freeman of Lebanon; liv
Hanover NH; ch/o Sarah -
Reuben A b1841 m1866 Jennie
Wardrobe of Campton CAN, 5
others; NH-0007-313
George; b1821 s/o Benjamin &
Betsey Taylor of Groton NH;
m1852 Eluthera Malvina
Bissell d/o Isaac of Hanover;
liv Bristol, Concord; NH-
0007-70
John; m Sophia ---; liv Dalton
& Alstead NH; ch Lucy Ann m
John Blakesle, Hon Asa W; NH-
0005-525
John; b1729 s/o Joseph & Anna
of Woodbury CT; m1755 Olive
Armstrong; liv Norwich CT,
Hanover NH; ch Silas, Reuben,
Andrew, Truman, David b1759 m
Anna Jacobs; NH-0007-313
Capt John; b1767 s/o John &
Anna Armstrong; m Lucinda
Eaton; ch Capt John m
Tryphena Dow, Lucinda m
Achbel Smith, Adna; NH-0007-
313
Capt John; s/o Capt John &
Lucinda Eaton; m Tryphena
Dow; liv Randolph VT, Hanover
NH; ch Ulysses Dow, John
Francis, Lemuel D, Roswell A;
NH-0007-313
Hon Ralph E; b1790 s/o Capt
William & Phebe Jewett of
Hollis; m1812 Olive Brown of
Hollis & m1818 Phebe C Smith
of Dracut MA b1790; liv
Hollis; ch/o Olive - 1 dau;
ch/o Phebe - 9; NH-0002-453

TENNEY (continued)
Dr Richard Perley Jewett; b1810 s/o Dr William of Rowley MA; m1834 Hannah A Sanborn of Gilmanton NH sis/o Prof E D; liv Loudon & Pittsfield NH; ch Abby; NH-0004-505 & 598
Dr William; m Abigail Rollins & m Peggy Flanders; liv Loudon; ch/o ? - Abigail, Richard P J m Hannah A Sanborn, William D B, Joseph J M; NH-0004-505
Capt William; b1755 s/o William & Anna; m1776 Phebe Jewett; liv Hollis; ch Caleb Jewett, William, Hon Ralph E b1790 m Olive Brown & m Phebe C Smith, 2 sons, 5 dau; NH-0002-453
William; b1785 s/o Capt William of Hollis; liv Pepperell MA, Salem & Newmarket NH; NH-0003-37
TEWKSBURY,
Isaac; b1795; liv W Newbury & Lawrence MA, Hampstead NH; NH-0003-317
THAYER,
Ephraim; b1806; m Ezuba Quimby of Franconia; liv Lisbon, Bath NH; ch Willis, Lydia m Levi Bisbee, Henry, Hibbard, Levi G; NH-0007-142
Henry L; b1817; m Mary Ann Cox of Holderness; liv Keene, Littleton NH; ch Henry, Frank; NH-0007-496
William F; b1846 s/o Calvin & Sarah Wheeler Fiske gs/o Rev Elihu Thayer DD of Kingston; m1874 Sarah Clarke Wentworth d/o Col Joseph; liv Concord; ch Margaret, William Wentworth; NH-0004-92
THING,
Jeremiah; liv Gilford & Brentwood NH; ch Jeremiah Jr, Morrill; NH-0004-748
THISELL,
Samuel; m Polly Wyatt; liv Beverly MA; ch Samuel, Eben, Andrew, Mary, William m Sarah A Davis & m Sarah T True; NH-0007-121
William; s/o Samuel & Polly Wyatt; m Sarah A Davis of Orford & m Sarah T True of Wentworth; ch/o ? - Charles C, Martha; NH-0007-121
THOM,
John W; s/o James of Conway;

THOM (continued)
liv Conway NH; ch Frank, Frederick; NH-0006-853
Samuel; s/o William; m Ann Buswell d/o Richard & Anne; liv Conway Corner NH; ch Richard, Alpha, George, Winfield; NH-0006-853
William; liv Derry, Conway; ch James, Samuel m Ann Buswell; NH-0006-853
THOMPSON,
Alexander; b1819 s/o Daniel & Persis Ladd of Corinth VT; m ? & m Ellen Armington & m1866 Alice Twitchell d/o Hiram & Alice Child of Randolph VT; liv Boston, St Johnsbury & Paddocksville VT, Lancaster NH; ch/o Ellen - 1 dau; ch/o Alice - Mary, Mabel C, Alice T, Grace, Sarah Agnes, Persis A; NH-0005-396
Allen; b1814; m Lucinda Barrett of Bethlehem & m Harriet Chase Phillips; liv Woodstock VT, Bethlehem NH; ch/o Lucinda - Mary P, Luella A, Ellen E, Frances, 4 others; NH-0007-167
Charles; b1776; m Sally Holton b1777 d/o Timothy; liv E Windsor CT, Colebrook NH; ch Mary H b1803 m Grant Fuller of Stratford, Harriet b1805 m1826 William Loomis, Charles H b1807, Elizabeth M; NH-0005-619
Charles E; b1807 s/o Hon Thomas W; m Mary Olcott d/o Hon Miles; liv Haverhill MA, Creskill NY; NH-0004-621
David; liv Gilford NH; ch Jonathan Jr, Levi B; NH-0004-749
Henry M; m Ellen Straw d/o Ezekial Albert & Charlotte Smith; liv Manchester; ch Albert W, Herman Ellis; NH-0002-80
John; liv Newfield ME, Eaton NH; ch James, Samuel dy, Noah, John, Isaac, David, Eli; NH-0006-793
Jonathan; s/o Joseph & Sally Chesley; m Polly Willey d/o Samuel; ch James W, Samuel W m Eliza Randall, Zebulon M P, Elizabeth G m Jonathan Dow; NH-0006-851
Joseph; m --- Randall & m Sally

THOMPSON (continued)
Chesley; liv Lee, Conway; ch/o Randall - Joseph, Miles, 1 dau m Solomon Dinsmore; ch/o Chesley - John, Jonathan m Polly Willey, Jeremiah, Ebenezer, Hannah m Theophilus Hall, Sally m Daniel Cheney; NH-0006-851

Rev Leander; m1839 Anne Eliza Avery d/o Samuel & Mary Moody Clark of Wolfeborough; liv Woburn & S Hadley & W Amesbury MA; ch Everett Augustine b1847, Samuel Avery b1850 m Harriet Ella Carter; NH-0006-379

Moses; liv Deerfield, Wolfeborough; ch Benjamin F, William, Moses; NH-0006-309

Samuel; s/o Theodore of Ossipee; m --- Canney; ch Samuel J; NH-0006-626

Samuel Avery; b1850 s/o Rev Leander & Anne Eliza Avery; m1879 Harriet Ella Carter d/o Dexter Esq of Woburn; liv Woburn MA; ch Amy Carter b1881, Everett Leander b1884; NH-0006-380

Samuel W; s/o Jonathan & Polly Willey; m1830 Eliza Randall; ch William F, Samuel D, James W, Frederick, Anna m L J Ricker, Carrie C m Frank Grover; NH-0006-851

Silas M; m Sophronia Stillings d/o Capt Nicholas Tuttle & Patience Stanton; ch Harry Alonzo b1884; NH-0006-973

Thomas W; b1766 s/o Dea Thomas of Boston; liv Salisbury, Concord; NH-0004-5

William Coombs; b1802 s/o Hon Thomas W; m Martha H Leavett & m Susan B Nelson; liv Concord, Plymouth, Worcester MA; NH-0004-621

THORNTON,
Achia; s/o Joshua; m Betsey Moulton d/o Jonathan of Lyman; liv Plymouth & Lyman NH; ch Hannah m --- Stevens, Sidney, 2 sons, 2 dau; NH-0007-515

James; s/o Matthew & Hannah Jackson; m Mary Parker; liv Merrimack; ch Matthew, James Bonaparte, Thomas, Hannah, Mary; NH-0002-546

James Bonaparte; s/o James &

THORNTON (continued)
Mary Parker; liv Merrimack; ch James Shepard m --- Wood d/o Rev Henry, Mary Parker m Dr Charles A Davis & m Judge W S Gardner of MA; NH-0002-546

Matthew; s/o James & Mary Parker; ch Margaret Ann; NH-0002-546

Matthew; b1714 s/o James & Elizabeth Jenkins of ENG; m Hannah Jackson; liv Londonderry; ch James m Mary Parker, Andrew, Mary m Hon Silas Britton of Salem NH, Hannah m John McGaw of Newburyport MA, Matthew; NH-0002-545

Matthew; s/o Matthew & Hannah Jackson; liv Merrimack; ch 1 dy, Abby m Capt David MacGregor of Derry; NH-0002-546

William; m1859 Emma Elizabeth Keniston d/o George Washington & Deborah Davis; ch William Elmer b1863 dy, George Keniston b1865; NH-0007-206

THURSTON,
Asa; liv Lyme NH; ch Charles, Nellie m L D Warren; NH-0007-546

Horace L; s/o Josiah & Martha M Marsh; m Stella L Baker d/o William & Asenath Scales; liv Campton Village NH; ch Lillie M; NH-0007-213

Josiah; b1814 s/o Oliver & Anstress Cross; m1840 Mary Ann Thurston d/o William & Mary Robinson of Eaton & m1877 Julia Anna Roberts b1843 d/o Daniel & Abigail Pierce of Hiram ME; liv Freedom NH; ch/o Julia - Hattie P; ch/adopted - Nathaniel H m Georgia A Sias, Sarah A m Edwin Towle; NH-0006-576

Nathaniel H; adopted s/o Josiah of Freedom; m Georgia A Sias of Ossipee; ch Mary Bell, Addie, Winfield O; NH-0006-576

Oliver; b1773; m1792 Anstress Cross b1775 of Exeter; liv Brentwood & Freedom NH; ch Mary, Oliver, William, William, Sally, Martha m Hale

THURSTON (continued)
Watson, Nathaniel, Josiah, Sally, Josiah b1814 m Mary Ann Thurston & m Julia Anna Roberts, Eunice, Isaac; NH-0006-576

TIBBETTS,
Frank E; b1857 s/o Daniel; m1880 Lizzie Whitehouse; ch Sara E b1880; NH-0003-643

Israel; s/o Daniel gs/o Jeremiah; ch Daniel b1809; Joannah Chesley, Lydia S m Paul Snell; NH-0003-643

TICKNOR,
Col Elisha; liv Scituate MA, Lebanon CT, Lebanon NH; ch Dea Elisha; NH-0007-418

George; b1822 s/o Benjamin & Hannah Gardner; m Lucy A Stone; liv Lebanon, Marlow, Claremont, Keene; ch Clara, Anna; NH-0007-94

TILDEN,
Joseph; liv CT, Lebanon; ch Joseph, Stephen, Elisha, Joel; NH-0007-337

TILTON,
Alexander Hamilton; b1804 s/o Jeremiah & Mehitable Hayes of Sanbornton NH; m1837 Abigail B Baker d/o Mark & Abigail; liv Meredith & Sanbornton Bridge NH; ch Albert Baker b1845 m1866 Abbie Gardner Day of Boxford MA, Alfred Edwin b1846 dy, A Evelyn b1854; NH-0004-890

Charles Elliott; b1827 s/o Hon Samuel; m1882 ---; liv Sanbornton NH, South America, San Francisco CA, Portland OR; NH-0001-110

Maj Daniel; ch Sally, Nathan, Harriett, Newell, Joseph, Mary A, John S R, Samuel; NH-0004-505

Dea Daniel; ch Nathan F b1797, Shuah b1779?, Abigail b1801, Betsey b1804, Daniel Jr b1805 m Olive Sargent; NH-0004-505

Daniel Jr; b1805 s/o Dea Daniel; m Olive Sargent; ch Charles S, Daniel, John, James S m Ida B Sanborn d/o Jeremiah C of Loudon, Olive E; NH-0004-505

Elbridge; b1822 s/o Silas B & Abigail of Andover NH; m1847 Alice Cummings d/o Daniel & Lois Kidder of Groton; liv

TILTON (continued)
Groton, Canaan, Gilford, Laconia, Bristol; ch Zerah, Della; NH-0007-187 & 189

George T; s/o Joseph & Mary Rowe; m Mary H Glidden d/o Jasper E & Eliza F Rowe; liv Alexandria NH; ch Willie G; NH-0007-117

Henry L; b1828 s/o Joseph & Sally B of N Danville VT; liv Littleton NH, CA; NH-0007-494

Horace F; s/o Timothy & Mary McMurphy; m Jennie E Lewis of Malden MA & m Flora Noys d/o Moses & Susan of Springfield NH; ch/o ? - Bertha M, Edith M; NH-0007-117

Col Philip; m Molly Batchelder; ch Rev Nathan b1772, Joseph b1774; NH-0003-189

Dr James A; b1815; m Sarah T Stanyan d/o Abram; liv Chichester & Pembroke NH; Amesbury MA, Newburyport; NH-0004-247

James S; m Ida B Sanborn d/o Jeremiah C & Betsy French; ch Maud; NH-0004-504

Jeremiah; b1762 s/o Nathaniel & Abigail Gilman of Sanbornton; m1786 Mehitable Hayes; liv Sanbornton NH; ch John b1787 m Eunice Jacques, Samuel b1789 m1815 Myra Ames & m1858 Mrs Elizabeth Haven, Sally b1791, Jeremiah Jr b1793 m1816 Nancy Carter, James P b1796 m1820 Mary G Cross, Abigail b1798, Mahala b1800 m1818 Hon D C Atkinson, Mary P b1802 m1832 Parson Whidden, Alexander Hamilton b1804 m Abigail B Baker, Mehitable b1807 m1828 Hon D C Atkinson, Sophronia b1810; NH-0004-890

Jonathan; s/o Sherburn & Huldah; m Sarah Clifford; liv Bridgewater, Alexandria; ch Timothy m Mary McMurphy, 8 others; NH-0007-117

Joseph; s/o Samuel of Andover NH; m Mary Rowe d/o Jessie & Mary of Campton NH; ch George T m Mary H Glidden, 11 others; NH-0007-117

Joseph Sr; m ? & m 1783 Coziah Bagley; ch/o ? - Joseph b1781, Martha b1783; ch/o Coziah - Anna b1784, Dolly b1787, Timothy b1791; NH-

TLTON (continued)
0004-504
Nathan; b1755; m Susannah Gail b1761; ch Betty b1781, Timothy b1783, Susannah b1785, Daniel b1787, Nathan b1791, Stephen b1793, Newell b1795, David b1798, Joseph b1801; NH-0004-504
Nathaniel; d1818; m Abigail Gilman; liv Sanbornton NH; ch Jeremiah b1762 m Mehitable Hayes, 6 others; NH-0004-890
Samuel; b1789 s/o Jeremiah b1762 gs/o Nathaniel; m1815 Myra Ames d/o Samuel of Canterbury; liv Tilton NH; ch Hon Charles Elliott b1827, 4 others; NH-0004-877 & 887
Timothy; s/o Jonathan & Sarah Clifford; m Mary McMurphy of Alexandria; ch Jeriah, Sarah E, Horace F m Jennie E Lewis & m Flora Noys; NH-0007-117
William; ch Eliza b1788, William J b1790, Timothy b1792, Hannah b1794, Patty b1796, Amos; NH-0004-505
William Jr; m Abigail Brown; ch Louisa A m Jeremiah Blake Esq, Charles S; NH-0004-505
TINKHAM,
Ebenezer; b1755; liv Lyme NH; ch Ruel, Cyrus m Betsey Kemp; NH-0007-539
Fayette; s/o Cyrus & Betsey Kemp gs/o Ebenezer; m Clarissa S Williams d/o Rufus & Lettice Smith; ch Charles C, Edwin L, John W m Mary J Smith, Susan K, Lettie J; NH-0007-287
John W; s/o Fayette & Clarissa S Williams; m Mary J Smith d/o John R & Mary E Wadley; liv Grafton NH; ch Anna J, Frank A, Ada B, Lena E, Florence A; NH-0007-287
TITUS,
Calvin; b1777 s/o Samuel; liv Lyman NH; ch Lucy m --- Moulton, Calvin, Betsey m --- Young, Moses, Calvin J b1802; NH-0007-515
David; bro/o Eleazer; liv Colebrook NH; ch Moses, 1 dau m Gilman Corser, 1 dau m David Young, 1 dau m David Hodge; NH-0005-617
Eleazer; bro/o David; liv Colebrook NH; ch Samuel; NH-0005-

TITUS (continued)
617
TOPPAN,
Edmund; b1777 s/o Hon Christopher of Hampton; liv Deerfield; NH-0003-36
TORR,
John F; b1829 s/o Simon & Betsey Davis; m1868 Mary C Downs b1840 of Farmington; ch Charles C, Simon A, George A; NH-0003-756
Simon; s/o Vincent; m Sarah Ham; liv Rochester; ch Betsey, Polly, Abigail, Sarah, John Greenfield (name changed) m Phebe ---, Simon b1789 m 'Betsey Davis, Jonathan H; NH-0003-756
Simon; b1789 s/o Simon & Sarah Ham of Rochester; m Betsey Davis d/o Thomas; ch Charles dy, Simon A dy, John F b1829 m Mary C Downs, Sarah E m Lewis E Hanson; NH-0003-756
TOWLE,
Amos; m Susan Moulton; liv Freedom NH, Hollis & Limington ME; ch Amos, William, Roley, Lovell, Lucinda, Almira, Elias b1807 m Lois Swett, Uriah, Jonah; NH-0006-574
Edwin; m Sarah A Thurston adopted d/o Josiah of Freedom NH; liv Freedom NH; ch Amos C, Josiah Thurston; NH-0006-577
Elias; b1807 s/o Amos & Susan Moulton; m1831 Lois Swett b1811 d/o Stephen & Lois; liv Freedom NH; ch Orin b1833 dy, Stephen S b1836, Elias Irving b1845 m Vesta M Merrill; NH-0006-574
Elias Irving; b1845 s/o Elias & Lois Swett of Freedom NH; m1871 Vesta M Merrill d/o Henry & Diantha Parks of Cornish ME; liv Freedom NH; ch Harold Irving b1887, 1 other; NH-0006-574
TRACY,
Oren; b1798 s/o Cyrus & Hannah Lillie of Tunbridge VT; m Marcia Billings of Royalton VT; liv E Stoughton & Townsend & Greenfield MA, New London & Newport & Concord NH; ch 1 dau m --- Elliott of Boston; NH-0004-439

TRAVIS,
Aaron; m Betsy Patten d/o
Samuel & Priscilla More; ch
Priscilla m Daniel Hook,
Jesse m Sarah Lucy, Samuel m
Hannah Lacy, Mary m Caleb
Philbrook, Gilman m Lucretia
Brown, Reuben m Eunice
Stearns; NH-0002-374
Luther; m Nancy Shearer; ch
John, James, Levi m Amra
Hall, William m Eliza Heath;
NH-0002-385
William; s/o Luther & Nancy
Shearer; ch Lucinda m Albert
Heath, Dexter, Giles; NH-
0002-385
TRICKEY,
Ephraim; liv Durham, Jackson;
ch Joseph, Ephraim; NH-0006-
951
James; b1770; m1791 Mary
(Polly) Burnham b1771 d/o
Pike G; liv Durham & Jackson
NH; ch Sally m Nathaniel
Meserve, James C b1794, Capt
Joshua b1802 m Martha P
Meserve, Ann N b1805 m Daniel
Bean, Samuel b1811 m Sarah A
Johnson d/o George; NH-0006-
951 & 967
James C; b1794 s/o James &
Polly Burnham; ch Joseph B,
Martha D, Emily S m George
Pinkham; NH-0006-951
Joseph; m Joanna Chesley d/o
Nathaniel; ch Nathaniel C, W
H H; NH-0006-952
Joseph B; b1820; m Alice P
Meserve d/o Gen George P; liv
Barltett, Jackson; ch James
C, George P, Nelson I, C
Lilian, S Alice, Josie G; NH-
0006-952
Capt Joshua; b1802 s/o James &
Mary Burnham of Jackson;
m1826 Martha P Meserve d/o
Col Jonathan & Alice Pen-
dexter; liv Jackson NH; ch
Alice, Mary, Martha A,
Georgia A m Gen Marshall
Wentworth; NH-0006-967
Nathaniel C; s/o Joseph of
Jackson; m Elizabeth Johnson;
liv Jackson NH; ch Ransom D,
Cheston; NH-0006-951
TRUE,
Ezekiel; s/o Dea John & Martha
Morrell; m Mary Morrell; liv
Salisbury Plain MA; ch Sarah,
Jacob b1748 m Lydia Dow,

TRUE (continued)
Lydia, Martha, Ezekiel, Mary,
Jabez, Dr John, William,
Paul; NH-0003-753
Henry; m Israel Pike d/o Capt
Robert of Salem MA; liv ENG,
Salem MA; ch Capt Henry
bc1644 m Jane Bradbury,
Joseph; NH-0003-753
Capt Henry; bc1644 s/o Henry &
Israel Pike; mc1667 Jane
Bradbury; liv Salem MA; ch
William, Ens Henry, Dea John
b1678 m Martha Morrell, Dea
Jabez; NH-0003-753
Jacob; b1748 s/o Ezekiel & Mary
Morrell of Salisbury Plain
MA; m1773 Lydia Dow; liv
Salisbury MA; ch Daniel,
Polly, Jacob, Ezekiel b1780 m
Nancy Nutting, Lydia, Dr
John; NH-0003-753
Dea John; b1678 s/o Capt Henry
& Jane Bradbury; m1702 Martha
Morrell; ch Jacob, Ezekiel m
Mary Morrell, Daniel, Moses,
Thomas; NH-0003-753
Dr John AB; b1789 s/o Dea
Jacob; liv Haverhill MA, TN;
NH-0004-621
Samuel M; m --- Bachelder d/o
Dea Harmon E & Clarisa San-
born of Loudon; ch Nellie,
Blanche, Mary; NH-0004-501
TRUELL,
Hiram; s/o David & Abigail
Phillips; m Nancy Russell of
Rindge; liv Grafton NH; ch
Sumner R m Susan Hutchinson &
m Mrs Florina W Felch, 6
others; NH-0007-284
Sumner R; s/o Hiram & Nancy
Russell of Grafton; m Susan
Hutchinson of Bristol & m Mrs
Florina W Felch; liv Grafton
NH; ch/o Susan - Charles P,
Alfred H; NH-0007-284
TRUESDELL,
Edmund Erskine; b1845 s/o
Thomas & Mary Boydon of
Jewett City CT ggs/o Darius;
m1872 Mary Wilkins Austin d/o
David; liv Suncook NH; ch 1
son; NH-0004-579
Ichabod; liv SCO, S Woodstock
CT; ch Asa, Darius, Thomas,
John; NH-0004-579
TRUSSELL,
Benjamin; mc1820 Sophia Derby &
m Aseneth French; liv
Boscawen & Orford NH; ch/o ?

TRUSSELL (continued)
- Benjamin F, 6 others; NH-0007-568
TUBBS,
Dr Mical; bro/o Russell; m Esther ---; liv Deering; ch Hiram, Alice m David Patten, Mical m --- Stewart, Eben L, Russell m Mary Gordon, Desire m Richard Cilley; NH-0002-387
Russell; bro/o Dr Mical; m Desire Healy of Washington; liv Alstead, Deering; NH-0002-387
Russell; s/o Dr Mical & Esther ---; m Mary Gordon; ch Alvin m Lucy J Hadlock; NH-0002-387
TUCK,
Charles E; b1835 s/o Jonathan & Sally Philbrick; m Sarah J Eaton of S Hampton; liv Kensington; ch Charles F, Lizzie E, Frank L, Anna; NH-0003-363
Edward; s/o Robert & Joanna; mc1648 Mary Philbrick d/o Thomas Sr; ch Edward, John b1652 m Bertha Hobbs; NH-0003-363
Dr Henry; b1808 s/o Jonathan & Dorothy Webster; liv Barnstable MA; NH-0003-358
John; b1652 s/o Edward & Mary Philbrick; m1678 Bertha Hobbs b1659 d/o Morris & Sarah Eastow of Hampton; ch Dea Jonathan b1697 m Tabitha Towle, 8 others; NH-0003-363
Jonathan; b1697 s/o John & Bertha Hobbs; m1721 Tabitha Towle b1697 d/o Benjamin & Sarah Borden of Hampton; ch Samuel b1731 m Martha Blake, 9 others; NH-0003-363
Jonathan; m Dorothy Webster; liv Kensington; ch Dr Henry b1808, Rev Jeremy Webster b1811; NH-0003-358
Jonathan b1771 s/o Samuel & Martha Blake; m1792 Dorothy Webster b1769 d/o Jonathan Ladd of E Kingston NH; liv Kingston; ch Jonathan b1799 m Sally Philbrick, 7 others; NH-0003-363
Jonathan; b1799 s/o Jonathan & Dorothy Webster; m1829 Sally Philbrick b1799 d/o Stephen G of Kensington & Tamworth NH; ch Henry C b1833, Charles E b1835 m Sarah J Eaton; NH-

TUCK (continued)
0003-363
Robert; m Joanna ---; liv Gorlston ENG, Watertown, Salem; ch Edward m Mary Philbrick, 3 others; NH-0003-363
Samuel; b1731 s/o Jonathan & Tabitha Towle; m1754 Martha Blake b1733 d/o Philemon & Lydia Boulter of Kensington; ch Jonathan b1771 m Dorothy Webster, 10 others; NH-0003-363
Samuel; m Martha Fogg; liv Kensington; ch Ebenezer Franklin b1822, Edward Prentice b1825; NH-0003-358
TUCKER,
William; s/o William of Rye NH; m Sarah Nutlir of Rochester NH; ch Charles W m Alice Gilchrist of Methuen MA, 6 others; NH-0007-121
TUFTS,
Charles Augustus; b1821 s/o Asa Alford of Dover; liv Dover; NH-0003-849
TURNER,
David; bro/o Jacob; m1781 Rhoda Porter; liv Lyme NH; ch Col Philip, 5 sons, 3 dau; NH-0007-533
Jacob; b1749 bro/o David; m1779 Rachel Cushing; liv Scituate MA, Lyme NH; ch Jacob; NH-0007-533
James; s/o Samuel; m Mrs Parker; liv Bernardston MA, Bethlehem NH; ch Timothy P b1795, 2 others; NH-0007-165
TUTTLE,
Benjamin; b1764; m Jane Folsom; liv Lee, Eaton; ch Sophronia b1807 m Phineas Rosebrook, 9 others; NH-0005-445
Elijah Jr; b1774 s/o Elijah of Barrington; m1798 Sally Tasker; liv Strafford; ch Samuel, William, Mary, Jehoah, Sarah, Asa, Ester; NH-0003-704
George; s/o Col John; m Judith Mason Davis; liv Barnstead NH; ch Hiram A b1837 m Mary C French; NH-0001-14
Hon Hiram A; b1837 s/o George & Judith Mason Davis gs/o Col John ggs/o John of Barnstead; m1859 Mary C French d/o John L Esq; liv Barnstead & Pitts-

TUTTLE (continued)
field NH; ch Hattie French
b1861; NH-0001-14, NH-0004-
597
Hon Jacob; b1767 s/o Sampson &
Submit Warren of Littleton
MA; m1795 Betsey Cummings d/o
Isaac & Elizabeth Trowbridge
of Westford MA; liv Antrim,
Branch Village; ch Betsey
b1796 dy, Jacob b1798 dy,
Nancy b1800 dy, Betsey b1801
dy, Nancy b1803 dy, Submit R
b1805 m James Steel, Lucetta
b1807 m John Sargent, Louisa
b1809 m Andrew C Cochran,
Lydia S b1811 m Hiram
Griffin, James M b1813 m
Hannah Shedd, Susan b1815 m
Henry Pierce, Harriet b1817 m
David W Grimes, Isaac C b1820
m Louisa J Love, Mary E b1823
m John S Shed; NH-0002-261
Col John; s/o John of Dover &
Barnstead NH; liv Barnstead;
ch George m Judith Mason
Davis; NH-0001-14
Sampson; b1738 s/o Samuel &
Martha Shattuck; m Submit
Warren b1742; liv Littleton
MA; ch Hon Jacob b1767 m
Betsey Cummings, 13 others;
NH-0002-261
Samuel; b1709; m1729 Martha
Shattuck b1712 d/o Rev
Benjamin of Littleton MA; ch
Sampson b1738 m Submit
Warren, 8 others; NH-0002-
261
TWITCHELL,
Abel; b1751; m Sarah Adams; liv
Sherborn, Dublin NH; ch Cyrus
b1788 m Eunice Belknap; NH-
0005-848
Adams; b1812 s/o Cyrus & Eunice
Belknap; m1843 Lusylvia Bart-
lett d/o Ebenezer & Lois
Powers of Bethel ME; liv
Milan NH, Bethel ME; ch
Claudius A, Virtue F, Lois A,
Helen Mar m P G Evans,
Cassius M C; NH-0005-848
Gen Albert S; b1840 s/o Joseph
A & Orinda L of Bethel ME;
m1862 Emma A Howland d/o
Parker; liv Gorham NH; ch
Harold P dy; NH-0004-229
Cyrus; b1788 s/o Abel & Sarah
Adams; m Eunice Belknap b1788
d/o Nathaniel of Dublin NH;
liv Dublin & Milan NH, Bethel

TWITCHELL (continued)
ME; ch Ransom, Gilman,
Sullivan, Cyrus, Hannah B m
Nathan Bickford, Adams b1812
m Lusylvia Bartlett, Clayton,
Harvey; NH-0005-848
Virgil V; b1842 s/o Joseph A &
Orinda L Mason of Bethel ME;
m1866 Georgie E Cary d/o
Benjamin W of Portland ME;
liv Portland ME, Gorham NH;
ch Helen May, Ora Lee, Willie
C; NH-0005-933
TWOMBLY,
Daniel; b1811 s/o Samuel &
Olive Huntress of Strafford;
m Julia Reed of New Bedford
MA; ch Maria, W; NH-0003-715
Harrison; b1826 s/o Silas &
Sally Caverly; m1855 Harriet
A Caverly; ch Charles H; NH-
0003-715
Moses; s/o William; m Elizabeth
Holmes sis/o Ephraim; ch
Samuel b1766 m Olive Hunt-
ress, Anthony, William,
James, Hannah, Deborah,
Phebe; NH-0003-715
Nehemiah Caverly; b1835 s/o
Silas & Sally Caverly; m1878
Elvira Tasker d/o Gilbert &
Eliza Durgin of Barnstead NH;
liv Strafford; NH-0003-715
Ralph; m Elizabeth ---; liv
Cocheco (Dover) NH; ch John,
Ralph, Joseph, Mary, Eliza-
beth, Hope, Sarah, Esther,
William; NH-0003-715
Samuel; b1766 s/o Moses &
Elizabeth Holmes; m Olive
Huntress & m ?; liv Straf-
ford; ch/o Olive - Hannah m
James Roe, Silas b1798 m
Sally Caverly, William m
Betsey Rollins, Deborah m
Nicholas Evans of Holderness,
Samuel m Susan Durgin, Enoch
m Lucretia Daniels, Moses m
--- Parker of Holderness,
Daniel b1811 m Julia Reed,
John m Sarah Berry, Smith,
Mesheck; ch/o ? - Andrew J;
NH-0003-715
Silas; b1798 s/o Samuel & Olive
Huntress of Strafford; m1822
Sally Caverly; liv MA, Straf-
ford; ch John W b1822, Hazen,
Harrison b1826 m Harriet A
Caverly, Silas H b1829 m Ann
H Twombly, Sally A, Nehemiah
Caverly b1835 m Elvira

TWOMBLY (continued)
Tasker, Viany S; NH-0003-715
Silas H; b1829 s/o Silas &
Sally Caverly; m Ann H
Twombly; ch Roxana m William
Shepard; NH-0003-715
William; s/o Ralph; liv
Madbury; ch Moses m Elizabeth
Holmes, Nathaniel, Joshua,
John; NH-0003-715

-U-

UNDERHILL,
Stephen; b1806 s/o Nathaniel; m
Sarah A Stevens; liv Piermont
NH; ch 4; NH-0007-575
UNDERWOOD,
Thomas; m Mehitabel Gage; liv
Merrimack; ch Thomas, John,
Peter, Sally, William,
Charles; NH-0002-543
UPHAM,
Nathaniel Gookin; b1801 s/o
Hon Nathaniel & Judith
Cogswell of Rochester; m
Betsy W Lord of Kennebunkport
ME & m Eliza W Burnham of
Pembroke; liv Deerfield NH,
Bristol, Concord; ch/o Betsy
- Rev Nathaniel L, 1 dau m
Joseph B Walker of Concord;
ch/o Eliza - 1 dau dy,
Francis A; NH-0004-5, NH-
0007-68
UPTON,
Daniel; m ? & m1822 Asenath
Teel of Goffstown NH; liv
Wilmot NH; ch/o Asenath - Hon
Samuel b1824 m Jennie L
Merriman; NH-0002-34
Hon Peter; m Sarah Miller
Duncan d/o Hiram; ch Hiram
Duncan; NH-0002-354
Hon Samuel; b1824 s/o Daniel &
Asenath Teel of Wilmot NH; m
Jennie L Merriman of Man-
chester; liv Meriden, Cornish
Flatt, Ashland & Ashby MA,
Manchester, Deering & Goffs-
town NH, Corinth VT, Western
IA; ch 1 dy; NH-0002-34

-V-

VAN DYKE,
George; m1836 Abigail Hatch
Dixon d/o Capt Joseph gd/o
Capt Thomas of S Hero VT; liv
Highgate VT, Stanbridge PQ;
ch George b1846, Eva; NH-
0005-390
VARNEY,
Benjamin; s/o Peter; m Mary
Hussey; ch Moses bc1724 m
Esther Chick; NH-0003-598
Caleb; s/o Ebenezer of
Rochester; m Huldan Hussey of
Rochester; liv Rochester,
Farmington; ch William m Anna
Varney, Job, John, Mary m
Moses Hanson of Rochester,
Elizabeth m James Austin of
Dover Neck; NH-0003-638
Humphrey; s/o William (Varnie)
of Ipswich MA; m Sarah Star-
buck d/o Elder Edward &
Catharine; liv Dover; ch
Peter bc1666; NH-0003-598
James Bowdoin; b1784 s/o Moses
& Mercy Cloutman; m1812 Sarah
Byles Riley d/o John & Mary
of Dover; liv Dover; ch John
Riley b1819; NH-0003-589
Moses; bc1724 s/o Benjamin &
Mary Hussey; m1750 Esther
Chick; ch Moses b1762 m Mercy
Cloutman; NH-0003-598
Moses; b1762 s/o Moses & Esther
Chick; m1782 Mercy Cloutman;
ch James Bowdoin b1784 m
Sarah Byles, 9 others; NH-
0003-598
William; s/o Caleb & Huldah
Hussey; m Anna Varney d/o
Enoch & Abigail of Milton;
liv Farmington; ch Job b1826,
Mary m William P Tuttle of
Dover, Hannah E m Alfred F
Ware of Salem MA, 1 dy; NH-
0003-638
VOSE,
Joshua; m Nancy Shirley d/o
James & Abigail McCutchins;
liv Bedford; ch Joshua,
Daniel, James, Nancy; NH-
0002-328

-W-

WADDELL,
William; b1806; m1840 Emaline
Bass of Lyman; liv Barnet VT,

WADDELL (continued)
Bath NH; ch Emma m Lemuel Southard of Bath, Emily m Payson Newcomb of Orford, Harry m Katie Moore of Haverhill, 4 others; NH-0007-143

WADLEIGH,
Benjamin; d1817 s/o Thomas; m Hannah Kezar d/o Ebenezer; liv Sutton NH; ch Benjamin Jr b1783 m Polly Marston; NH-0004-643 & 644

Benjamin Jr; b1783 s/o Benjamin & Hannah Kezar of Sutton NH; m Polly Marston d/o Jacob of Sutton; liv Sutton NH; ch Eliphalet b1804, Luther b1806, Erastus Esq b1808 m Almira Challis & m Mary W Flanders & m Olive Holmes, Milton, Hannah b1814 m Nathaniel A Davis, Lydia F, Benjamin d1868, Gilbert, 2 dy; NH-0004-644

Charles F; m1877 Annie S Lane d/o Levi E & Cynthia S Lane; ch Mabel F, Fannie M; NH-0003-348

Daniel; b1758; m1788 Dolly Bartlett b1751; liv Kingston; ch John b1789, Joseph b1790, Daniel b1793 m Sally Davis, Hannah b1797 dy; NH-0003-385

Daniel; b1793 s/o Daniel & Dolly (Polly) Bartlett; m1839 Sally Davis d/o John & Betsey Kimball; ch Elizabeth C m William Davis of Hampstead, Joseph B; NH-0003-386

Dearborn; s/o John & Mollie; m Polly Hayes of Sanbornton; liv Meredith NH; ch Gen John b1806 m Mary Ann Wentworth; NH-0004-857

Ephraim S; m Mary Elizabeth Smith d/o Jeremiah & Betsy Glidden of Northfield; ch Addie P, Annie E, Charlotte B, Olive A m Peter Gile of Franklin Falls, Smith G; NH-0004-546

Erastus Esq; b1808 s/o Benjamin Jr & Polly Marston of Sutton; m1839 Almira Challis b1815 d/o Timothy & m Mary W Flanders & m Olive Holmes wid/o Dr Dimond Davis; liv Sutton NH; ch/o Almira - Milton B; NH-0004-644

Henry; liv Gilford NH; ch William, Benjamin; NH-0004-

WADLEIGH (continued)
749
John d1842; m Mollie ---; liv Epping & Meredith NH; ch Dearborn m Polly Hayes; NH-0004-857

Gen John; b1806 s/o Dearborn & Polly Hayes of Meredith NH; m1831 Mary Ann Wentworth; liv Meredith; ch Le Roy B, Abbie m Dr G F Brickett, John Dearborn m Annie Leffingwell wid/o Frank P of Chicago IL, 1 other; NH-0004-857

John D; s/o Moses; liv Bradford; ch Hon Bainbridge; NH-0004-643

Joseph; m Anna Sleeper d/o Jonathan & Mary Clark; ch Jonathan S b1817, Daniel dy, Hannah b1820, Nancy b1822, Daniel b1824 m1854 Maria E Hoyt; NH-0003-385

Moses; s/o Thomas; ch Thomas J, John D; NH-0004-643

Thomas; liv Hampstead; ch Benjamin m Hannah Kezar, Thomas, Moses, John, 5 sons, 3 dau; NH-0004-643

WAITE,
Nathaniel; liv Lyme NH; ch Nathaniel, John, Reuben, Solomon; NH-0007-540

WALDRON,
Aaron; b1749; m Hannah Boodey b1758 d/o Azariah gd/o Zechariah; ch Azariah, Aaron, Isaac, John, Abram, Robert, Abram, William, Hannah, Richard, Lovey, Zachariah, Sarah b1802 m James B Foss; NH-0003-704 & 714

Jesse; s/o John & Sarah Collins; m Mary Ann Martin d/o James & Jeanette of Grafton; liv Grafton NH; ch Gilbert, Charles E, Jane m --- Masten, Lennie; NH-0007-285

WALKER,
Alden; m Susan Grimes d/o John & Elizabeth Wilson; ch John Grimes; NH-0002-423

Franklin; s/o Simeon & Clarissa; m Caroline Colton of Cabot VT & m Martha Gile of Littleton; liv Littleton NH; ch/o Caroline - 3; ch/o Martha - George E; NH-0007-501

Joseph B; b1822 s/o Capt Joseph

WALKER (continued)
& ggs/o Rev Timothy of Concord; liv Concord; NH-0004-33
Simeon; m Clarissa --- b1787 of Middletown CT; liv Cabot VT, Littleton NH; ch Franklin m Caroline Colton & m Martha Gile, 4 others; NH-0007-501
Rev Timothy; b1705 s/o Dea Samuel of Woburn MA; liv Concord; ch Judge Timothy, 1 dau m Benjamin Rolfe Esq; NH-0004-58
Hon Timothy; b1737 s/o Rev Timothy of Rumford; m Susannah Burbeen d/o Rev Joseph of Woburn MA; liv Concord; ch 14; NH-0004-2
William B; m Eliza Chase d/o Edward & Mary Patten; ch Eliza; NH-0002-381
WALLACE,
Alonzo Stewart MD; b1847 s/o David & Margarett; m Mary F Maynard d/o Charles & Harriett of Lowell MA; liv Boston, Brookline; ch Arthur Lowell, 2 others; NH-0002-394
Amos; b1797; m Polly Hildreth & m Clarinda Atherton; liv Franconia, Littleton NH; ch/o Polly - Abigail m Erastus D Emerson of Thetford VT, Mary A m Solomon Ladd, Elmira m Ephraim Rowe of Newbury VT, Amos P m Betsey A Durham of Concord VT, Cordelia m Isaac B Hoyt of Bethlehem, Bernice H m Ira Goodall of Littleton, John A, Andrew M, 1 other; NH-0007-488
David; b1797 s/o David (Wallis) & Susannah Conn; m1821 Roxanna Gowen of New Ipswich; liv Rindge NH, Fitchburg MA; ch Rodney b1823 m Sophia Ingalls & m Sophia Bailey; NH-0001-56
Ebenezer G; b1823 s/o Linzey & Abigail Gowell; m1853 Sarah E Greenfield of Rochester; liv Berwick ME, Rochester NH; ch Albert, Sumner, Carrie Helen, Annie, Emma Josie, Henry Ernest dy; NH-0003-750
Edwin; b1823 s/o Linzey & Abigail Gowell; m Susan R Whitehouse d/o William of Rochester & m --- Lander d/o Seneca of Woodstock ME; liv

WALLACE (continued)
Rochester; ch/o Susan - 1 dau m H D Jacobs of Brooklyn NY; ch/o Lander - 1 son, 2 dau; NH-0003-751
Gideon A; m Eliza V Knowles d/o John & Olive A Chadwick; liv Campton Village NH; NH-0007-216
Dr John; m Eliza Burns; liv Milford NH; ch John J; NH-0002-365
Linzey; m Abigail Gowell; liv Berwick ME, Littleton NH; ch Linsy, Ebenezer G b1823 m Sarah E Greenfield, Edwin b1823; NH-0003-750 & 751
Hon Rodney; b1823 s/o David & Roxanna; m1853 Sophia Ingalls d/o Thomas Esq of Rindge NH, m1876 Sophia F Bailey of Woodstock VT; liv New Ipswich NH, Fitchburg MA; ch Herbert I b1856, George R; NH-0001-56
William; liv Dalton NH; ch Ira m Keziah Southwick of MA, Asahel; NH-0005-526
William; s/o William; m Julia M Starks d/o Elisha of Hanover; liv Portsmouth NH; ch William m Hannah B Burbeck d/o James & Ruth Pulsifer, 9 others; NH-0007-215
WALLINGFORD,
David; s/o Peter of Rochester NH; liv Milton NH; ch Samuel m Sallie Wooster; NH-0001-70
John; b1659 s/o Nicholas (Wallington) & Sarah Travis; m Mary Tuttle d/o Judge John & Mary of Dover NH; liv Rowley MA; ch John b1688, Hon Thomas; NH-0001-70, NH-0003-869
John; b1688 s/o John & Mary Tuttle; liv Rochester NH; ch Peter; NH-0001-70
Nicholas; m1654 Sarah Travis b1636 d/o Henry & Bridget; liv London ENG, Newbury MA; ch John b1659 m Mary Tuttle, 7 others; NH-0003-869
Peter; s/o John of Rochester NH; liv Rochester & Milton NH; ch David; NH-0001-70, NH-0003-869
Samuel; s/o David of Milton NH; m Sallie Wooster; liv Milton NH; ch Zimri Scates b1816 m Alta L G Hilliard; NH-0001-70, NH-0003-869

WALLINGFORD (continued)
Zimri Scates; b1816 s/o Samuel & Sallie Wooster of Milton; m1840 Alta L G Hilliard d/o Rev Joseph of Berwick ME; liv Milton & Dover NH; ch John O, Mary C m Sidney A Phillips Esq of Framingham MA, Julia; NH-0001-70, NH-0003-869
WALLINGTON,
Nicholas; m1654 Sarah Travis d/o Henry & Bridget; liv ENG, Newbury MA; ch John (Wallingford) b1659 m Mary Tuttle; NH-0001-70
WALLIS,
Benoni; m1755 Rebecca Brown of Lynn MA; liv Ipswich & Lunenburg MA; ch David b1760 m Susannah Conn; NH-0001-56
David; b1760 s/o Benoni & Rebecca Brown; m Susannah Conn; liv Ashburnham MA; ch David (Wallace) b1797 m Roxanna Gowen; NH-0001-56
WARD,
Enoch; b1786 s/o Enoch & Mary Carter gs/o Rev Nathan; m1815 Lydia Church d/o Jabez & Dorothy Bartlett of Thornton; liv Plymouth NH; ch Artemas, Thomas C, Judith C m David Connell, Esther C m James Harrison, Catharine W m Charles Morrill, Philema C, Mary Ann, Enoch; NH-0007-590
Simon Jr; m Eliza Hoyt d/o Horace F & Caroline E Hardy; liv Hanover; ch Cora, Florence, Josephine; NH-0007-325
WARDEN,
David; liv Ryegate VT, Bath; ch Alexander, 8 others; NH-0007-554
WARE,
Ebenezer; m Esther Hunting; liv Needham MA; ch Ebenezer m Alice Eaton; NH-0002-356
Ebenezer; s/o Ebenezer & Esther Hunting of Needham MA; m Alice Eaton; ch Ebenezer m Martha E Lakin; NH-0002-356
Ebenezer; s/o Ebenezer & Alice Eaton; m Martha E Lakin; liv Hancock NH; ch 10; NH-0002-356
WARREN,
Asa, gs/o Ezra; m Mary A Derby; ch Martha A m H H Holt, Leander D, Lewis W, Arad J, 1

WARREN (continued)
dau m George Melvin, 1 dau m Charles Stetson; NH-0007-535
Benjamin F; b1829 s/o Benjamin L of Weathersfield VT; m1851 Mary L Stearns of Haverhill; liv Haverhill & Warren NH; ch Sarah E b1858 dy; NH-0007-635
Benjamin L; m Lucy Barton; liv Wethersfield VT, Haverhill NH; ch Asahel L m Lucia Heath, Benjamin F; NH-0007-360
Daniel; b1768; m Sally --- b1767; liv Rochester; ch Joseph, Rev James b1802 m Lydia Perkins, Mary, Hannah, Emily; NH-0003-758
Rev James; b1802 s/o Daniel & Sally; m Lydia Perkins b1812 of Sanford ME; liv Lebanon ME, Rochester NH; ch Horatio H b1837, Arethusa K, Melvin M dy, Sarah F dy, Osman B b1845 m Luella J Brown, Wilbur F b1848; NH-0003-758
Osman B; b1845 s/o Rev James & Lydia Perkins; m1870 Luella J Brown d/o Ephraim H & Jane of Norway ME; ch Frank S, Fannie C, Alice dy; NH-0003-758
WASHBURN,
Alden; b1758; m1782 Sally Allen; liv Bridgewater MA, Moultonborough; ch Abigail b1783, Oliver m Nancy Stevenson d/o Dea John, Eliezer, Sally b1796 m Nicholas Ham, Alden, John, Ephraim, Jane; NH-0006-766
John; s/o Libeus & Mary Sloan; m Sarah Tucker; liv Lyme NH, VA; ch John, Benjamin T m K Josephine Oakley, Mary E m L H Richards; NH-0007-532
Libeus; m Mary Sloan d/o Capt John; liv Bridgewater MA, Lyme NH; ch Salmon, Libeus m Anna Culver, John m Sarah Tucker, William, 3 dau, 6 sons; NH-0007-532
WASON,
Elbridge; s/o Robert & Nancy Bachelder; m Mary Stickney d/o Samuel of Lyndeborough NH & m Mary Isabella Chase d/o Hon Leonard of Milford NH; ch/o Mary I - Mary Isabell, Leonard Chase; NH-0002-605
Dr Franklin L; b1834; m1852 Amanda C Colby d/o Ebenezer &

WASON (continued)
m1872 Mrs Carrie Philbrick W
Meeks; liv Freedom, Tilton &
Meredith NH; NH-0004-885
James; b1711 bro/o Thomas;
m1736 Hannah Caldwell of
Portsmouth NH; liv Ballymanus
IRE, Portsmouth NH; NH-0002-
605
Robert; b1781 gs/o James; m1808
Nancy Bachelder of Mont
Bernon; liv Nottingham West,
New Boston; ch Elbridge, 8
others; NH-0002-605
WATERMAN,
Silas; s/o Thomas gs/o Silas;
liv Lebanon NH; ch Thomas P;
NH-0007-420
WATSON,
David; liv Meredith & Gilford
NH; ch Jonathan, Job; NH-
0004-749
Henry P MD; b1845 s/o Dr Henry
L of Guildhall VT; m1867
Evelyn Marshall of North-
umberland NH; liv Groveton &
Haverhill NH; ch 3; NH-0007-
379
Irving A MD; b1849; m Lena A
Farr of Littleton; liv
Northumberland, Concord; NH-
0004-622
WAUGH,
William; m Sunnah Walker; liv
Londonderry, Deering; ch
Nancy m Benjamin Masterman,
Rebecca m Joseph Stevens,
Susannah, Joseph m Sally
Kendall & m Fanny Down, Achsa
m Charles Butrick, Robert;
NH-0002-386
WEARE,
John; b1696 s/o Nathaniel &
Hulda Hussey; m1720 Deborah
Taylor; ch Joseph, Taylor,
Susannah, Jonathan b1724 m
Sarah Lane & m Mary French,
Huldah, Jemima, Deborah; NH-
0003-513
John; b1775 s/o Jonathan &
Sarah Lane of Seabrook; m1780
Thankful Hubbard; ch Joseph
Hubbard b1781 m Betsy
Mitchell, Sarah Lane, John;
NH-0003-513
John Mitchell; b1819 s/o Joseph
Hubbard & Betsy Mitchell of
Seabrook NH; m1836 Mary
Morrill Gove d/o David of
Seabrook gd/o Winthrop; liv
Chichester & Concord & Sea-

WEARE (continued)
brook NH; NH-0003-513
Jonathan; b1724 s/o John &
Deborah Taylor; m1747 Sarah
Lane & m Mary French; liv
Seabrook; ch/o Sarah -
Hannah, Abigail, Peter,
Jonathan, John b1775 m
Thankful Hubbard; NH-0003-513
Jonathan; liv Andover NH; ch
Nancy b1785 m Daniel Noyes &
m Nathan Stickney Esq; NH-
0003-158
Joseph Hubbard; b1781 s/o John
& Thankful Hubbard; m1804
Betsy Mitchell b1784 d/o Bela
gd/o William Swett; liv Sea-
brook NH; ch Joseph Hubbard,
Mary Ann, Elizabeth Brown,
Sarah Lane, John Mitchell
b1819 m Mary Morrill Gove,
Benjamin Swett; NH-0003-513
Nathaniel; m Sarah ---; liv
ENG, Newbury MA, Nantucket;
ch Nathaniel bc 1631 m Eliza-
beth Swayne, Hester, Robert,
Daniel, Peter; NH-0003-513
Nathaniel; bc1631 s/o Nathaniel
& Sarah; m1656 Elizabeth
Swayne of Hampton; liv
Newbury, Hampton; ch Eliza-
beth, Peter, Mary, Sarah,
Nathaniel b1669 m Hulda
Hussey & m Mary Wait, Hannah,
Abigail; NH-0003-513
Nathaniel; b1669 s/o Nathaniel
& Elizabeth Swayne; m1692
Hulda Hussey & m1703 Mary
Wait; ch/o Hulda - Daniel,
Peter, John b1696 m Deborah
Taylor, Hannah, Huldah; ch/o
Mary - Nathan, Mary, Marcy,
Sarah, Elizabeth, Mesheck,
Abigail, Mehitable; NH-0003-
513
WEATHERBEE,
Smith; b1803; m Sally Jesseman;
liv Manson MA, Lisbon NH; ch
Warre, Horace O, David, 1 dau
m Horace Aldrich, 1 dau m
Francis Locke; NH-0007-453
WEBER,
Luther; s/o Edward; m Pauline A
Small; liv Holderness NH; ch
2; NH-0007-395
WEBSTER,
Col David; s/o Col John of
Conway NH; ch David, James,
Samuel; NH-0006-853
David; m Olive A Smith & m
Phebe F Clark; liv Holder-

WEBSTER (continued)

ness, Campton; ch/o ? - Alfred m Susan E Kendall d/o Jesse & Louisa Fellows & m Lydia M Wallace d/o George W & Julia M Durgan of Thornton NH; NH-0007-209

Sergt Ebenezer; b1667; m1709 Hannah Judgkins; liv Kingston; ch Ebenezer b1714 m Susan Batchelder; NH-0003-375

Ebenezer; b1714 s/o Sergt Ebenezer & Hannah Judgkins; m Susannah Batchelder d/o Benjamin & Susannah Page of Hampton Falls NH; ch Col Ebenezer; NH-0003-345 & 375

Col Ebenezer; s/o Ebenezer & Susannah Batchelder of E Kingston; m1761 Mehitable Smith & m Abigail Eastman of Salisbury MA; liv Salisbury NH; ch/o ? - Hon Ezekiel b1780 m Alice Bridge & m Achsah Pollard, Hon Daniel b1781 m1808 Grace Fletcher & m1832 Caroline Bayard Le Roy; NH-0003-345, NH-0004-622

Ebenezer; b1711 s/o Stephen & Mary Cook; m Mehitable Kimball of Bradford MA; ch Lydia, Isaac, Mary, Ebenezer b1744 m Elizabeth Bradford & m 2 others; Jonathan, Stephen, Moses, John; NH-0002-482

Ebenezer; b1744 s/o Ebenezer & Mehitable Kimball; m Elizabeth Bradford of Beverly MA & m 2 others; liv Pelham; ch/o Elizabeth - Rebecca, Nancy, Moses, Simon, Isaac, Asa, John b1791 m Hannah Cummings, Benjamin, Betsy; NH-0002-482

Capt Ebenezer; liv Salisbury; ch Hon Ezekiel b1780, Daniel b1782; NH-0004-7

Humphrey; b1821; m Eliza Hamilton Emery d/o Lucius A; liv Springfield & Worcester MA, NC; NH-0004-623

James; s/o Col David; ch William E; NH-0006-853

James P; s/o Moses; m1838 Rebekah M English; liv Landaff, Haverhill NH; ch Eliza m --- Kellam; NH-0007-363

John; liv Ipswich ENG, Ipswich MA; ch John, Mary, Hannah, Elizabeth, Abigail, Stephen m Hannah Ayer & m Judith Brown,

WEBSTER (continued)

Israel, Nathan; NH-0002-482

John; b1710; m Susannah Snow; liv Salisbury NH; NH-0004-623

John; gs/o Jeremy; m1803 Judith Brown b1775 d/o Elijah & Susanna of S Hampton; ch George B, 3 sons; NH-0003-190

John; b1791 s/o Ebenezer & Elizabeth Bradford of Pelham; m1815 Hannah Cummings d/o Eleazer & Sarah Hale of Nottingham West & ggd/o Dea Henry & Mary Hale; liv Pelham, Amherst, Hudson; ch Elizabeth B m Warren Blodgett, Sally Hale m Simeon C Titcomb, Eleazer C, Louisa U m John H Baker, Lucy Ann m Daniel B Cluff, Kimball b1828 m Abiah Cutter, Hannah J, John C, Nathan P, Willard H, Milton E, Orrin P; NH-0002-482

Kimball; b1828 s/o John & Hannah Cummings of Pelham; m1857 Abiah Cutter d/o Seth & Deborah Gage of Pelham; liv Hudson NH, West; ch Lizzie Jane m Horace A Martin, Ella Frances m Frank A Walch, Eliza Ball m Charles C Leslie, Latina Ray, Julia Anna, Mary Newton; NH-0002-483

Moses; liv Landaff; ch James P m Rebekah M English, Moses K; NH-0007-363

Col Moses; b1780; m Sarah Kimball; liv Haverhill MA, Landaff NH; ch 10; NH-0007-401

Samuel C; m1816 Catherine Russell; liv Plymouth NH; NH-0007-112.9

Stephen; s/o John; m1663 Hannah Ayer d/o John of Salisbury & m Judith Brown; liv Ipswich MA, Haverhill; ch/o Hannah - Hannah, John, Mary, Stephen b1762 m Mary Cook, Nathan, Abigail; NH-0002-482

Stephen; b1762 s/o Stephen & Hannah Ayer of Haverhill; m Mary Cook; ch Samuel, John, Stephen, William, Ebenezer b1711 m Mehitable Kimball, Mary; NH-0002-482

WEED,

Henry; liv Sandwich NH; ch Henry b1751 m --- Eastman,

WEED (continued)
Elisha, Susanna, Phebe,
Jacob; NH-0006-246
Henry; b1751 s/o Henry of
Sandwich; m --- Eastman; ch
Hannah, Sally m Roby French,
Phebe m --- Drake, William
b1774 m Rebecca Foss, Henry;
NH-0006-246
William; b1774 s/o Henry & ---
Eastman; m1801 Rebecca Foss
b1775 d/o Jacob & Margaret
McClary; ch Hannah, Melinda,
Jacob, Harvey M, William
McGaffey b1814 m Eliza N
Hanson, Grace E; NH-0006-246
William McGaffey; b1814 s/o
William & Rebecca Foss of N
Sandwich; m1850 Eliza N
Hanson d/o Elisha of
Sandwich; liv Sandwich Lower
Corner; ch Herbert F, Clara
Belle dy; NH-0006-246
WEEKS,
Alonzo; b1819; m Caroline A
Harris of Danville VT; liv
Danville VT, Littleton NH; ch
John A, Mabel I; NH-0007-497
Benjamin Esq; bro/o John & Dea
Noah; liv Gilford & Burton
NH; ch Daniel, Matthias,
Elisha, William, Benjamin,
Levi R, Sally m Henry Wad-
leigh; NH-0004-749
David; s/o David b1745 & Ruth
Page; m Matilda Childs; liv
Bath; ch 1 dau m --- Powers,
1 dau m William Minot, 1 dau
m George Chamberlain, Moses M
m Sally Minot, 7 others; NH-
0007-369
Enoch R; liv Piermont, Warren
NH; ch Ira M b1817; NH-0007-
634
George; s/o John & Mary Coffin
of Greenland; m1856 Caroline
Avery d/o Maj John of Green-
land; liv Greenland NH; NH-
0003-309
George William; b1841 s/o
William & Louisa Porter of
Greenland NH; m1878 Sarah L
Robinson of Exeter; ch
William b1880; NH-0003-310
Dr Ichabod; b1738; m Sarah C
Cotton d/o Rev Ward of
Hampton & m Comfort Johnson
of Greenland & m Abigail
March d/o Col Clement of
Greenland; liv Greenland &
Hampton NH; ch/o Abigail -

WEEKS (continued)
Stephen March m Mary
Shackford Gookin, 2 dau; NH-
0003-312
James Brackett; b1784 s/o Capt
John & Deborah Brackett;
m1810 Elizabeth Stanley d/o
Lt Dennis; liv Greenland &
Lancaster NH; ch James
Wingate b1811 m Martha W
Hemmenway & m Mary E Burns,
Mary Nye b1813 m Richard H
Eastman, Sarah Stanley b1815
m Edmund C Wilder of Cole-
brook NH, William Dennis
b1818 m Mary Helen Fowler,
John, Martha Eliza b1824,
Persis Fayette b1831 m Rev
George M Rice; NH-0005-378
James Wingate; b1811 s/o James
Brackett & Elizabeth Stanley;
m1842 Martha W Hemenway d/o
Solomon & Clarissa & m1859
Mary E Burns d/o Dr Robert of
Plymouth sis/o Hon William;
liv St Johnsbury VT, Lan-
caster NH; ch/o Martha -
Sarah m --- Oxnard, George,
James W Jr, Clara H; NH-0005-
378
Dr John; b1716 s/o Capt Joshua
& Comfort Hubbard of Green-
land; m Martha Wingate sis/o
Hon Paine; ch Joshua Wingate
b1738 m Sarah Treadwell,
Sarah (Sally) m Rev Jacob
Bailey, Capt John b1749 m
Deborah Brackett, 3 others;
NH-0004-378
Capt John; b1749 s/o Dr John &
Martha Wingate; m1770 Deborah
Brackett d/o James & Martha
Wingate; liv Hampton & Lan-
caster NH; ch Martha b1771 m
Edward Spaulding, Deborah
b1776 m William Ayers & m
Jacob Emerson, Elizabeth
b1778 m Azariah Webb of
Lunenburg VT, John Wingate
b1781 m Martha Brackett & m
Persis F Everett, James
Brackett b1784 m Elizabeth
Stanley, Mary Polly Wiggin
b1787 m Adino N Brackett,
Sally Brackett b1789 m
Edwards Bucknam; NH-0005-378
John P; b1844 s/o William &
Louisa Porter of Greenland;
m1870 Ellen R Hatch & m1876
Laura A Foss; ch/o Laura -
Mabel Porter b1878, Carrie F

WEEKS (continued)
b1881; NH-0003-310
John Wingate; b1781 s/o Capt
John & Deborah Brackett;
m1805 Martha Brackett; m1824
Persis F Everett d/o Hon
Richard C; liv Greenland &
Lancaster NH; NH-0005-378
Capt Joshua; b1674 s/o Leonard
& Mary Haines; m1690 (1699)
Comfort Hubbard sis/o Thomas
of Boston; liv Greenland NH;
ch Martha m Capt Benjamin
Randall, Comfort m Dr Coffin
Moore, Mary, Ichabod, Dr John
b1716 m Martha Wingate,
Thankful, Maj William m
Eleanor March, Richard,
Margaret; NH-0003-309, NH-
0005-378
Joshua; s/o Leonard of Green-
land NH; ch William b1723 m
Eleanor Marsh; NH-0003-310
Leonard; liv Greenland NH; ch
John, Samuel, Jonathan,
Joshua, Mary, Margaret,
Sarah; NH-0003-310
Leonard; b1635; m1667 Mary
Haines d/o Dea Samuel of
Portsmouth; liv Wells ENG,
Greenland & Portsmouth NH; ch
John, Samuel, Joseph, Capt
Joshua b1674 m Comfort
Hubbard, Mary, Jonathan,
Margaret, Sarah; NH-0003-309,
NH-0005-378
Moses M; s/o David & Matilda
Childs of Bath; m Sally
Minot; liv Bath, Haverhill
NH; ch Hattie P m J L Bell,
Elbridge; NH-0007-369
Nathan H; b1825 s/o Benjamin &
Betsey Hoit of Guilford NH;
m1845 Harriet A Hacket &
m1860 Martha G Philbrick; liv
Thornton, Woodstock, Plymouth
NH; ch/o Harriet - Emerette L
m Thomas J Gilman, Edwin S,
Clara J m Frank P Field; ch/o
Martha - Anna M, Fred P,
Lelia G, Scott N, Martha F;
NH-0007-595
Dea Noah; bro/o John & Benjamin
Esq; ch Noah, Ira, Mathias;
NH-0004-750
Rufus W; s/o Stephen March &
Mary Shackford Gookin; m1861
E Jenette Belknap d/o William
of Lisban NH; ch Belknap,
Goldwin Ichabod, Arthur Hale,
Rufus W Jr; NH-0003-312

WEEKS (continued)
Dea Stephen; s/o Stephen &
Betsey Weed of Gilmanton NH;
m Mary A Stevens & m Eliza-
beth W Haines of Canterbury;
liv Loudon NH; ch/o Elizabeth
- Adaline, William H, Martha,
Abby, Mary J, Dora V; NH-
0004-509
Stephen March; s/o Dr Ichabod
of Abigail March; m Mary
Shackford Gookin d/o
Nathaniel & Mary Shackford of
Portsmouth NH; ch Charles M,
Stephen M, Caroline,
Nathaniel Gookin, Ichabod,
Rufus W m E Jenette Belknap;
NH-0003-312
William; b1723 s/o Joshua &
Comfort Hubbard of Greenland;
m1748 Eleanor Marsh (March)
d/o Dr Clement Sr of Green-
land; liv Greenland NH; ch
William b1755 m Nabby Rogers
& m Sarah Cotton Weeks, John
m Mary Coffin, J Clement; 6
sons, 7 dau; NH-0003-310 &
309
William; b1755 s/o William &
Eleanor Marsh of Greenland;
m1780 Nabby (Abigail) Rogers
& m Sarah (Sally Cotta)
Cotton Weeks d/o Dr Ichabod
of Greenland; liv Hopkinton
NH; ch/o Nabby - William
b1781 m Louisa Porter,
George; ch/o ? - Charles,
Abigail Rogers, Mary, Jacob,
Washington, Thomas Jefferson,
Sarah Ann, Susan, Hannah,
Emily, John; NH-0003-310, NH-
0004-407
William; b1781 s/o William &
Nabby Rogers; m1835 Louisa
Porter d/o Rev Huntington of
Rye NH; liv Greenland; ch Ann
Louisa b1836, Ellen Maria
b1838, Sarah Porter b1839,
George William b1841 m Sarah
L Robinson, John P b1844 m
Ellen R Hatch & m Laura A
Foss; NH-0003-310
William Dennis; b1818 s/o James
Brackett & Elizabeth Stanley;
m1848 Mary Helen Fowler; liv
Lancaster NH, St Johnsbury
VT; ch Emma F m Burleigh
Roberts, John W, William C;
NH-0005-378
William Pickering; b1803 s/o
Brackett & Sarah Pickering of

NEW HAMPSHIRE GENEALOGICAL DIGEST

WEEKS (continued)
Greenland; m1833 Mary Elizabeth Doe of Derry; liv Canaan NH; ch 1 son, 2 dau, Joseph Doe b1837, William Brackett b1839 m1866 Henrietta Bridgeman of Hanover; NH-0007-74 & 75

WELCH,
Jonathan; d1880; m Ruth Merrill; ch Silas M m Nancy Albert, Ezra B; NH-0007-151
Silas M; s/o Jonathan & Ruth Merrill; m Nancy Albert; ch George H, Edgar S, Ella m Charles Cutting of Piermont; NH-0007-151
William H; b1852 s/o William of CAN; m1875 Marietta Fogg d/o David H & Emeline L; ch Henry W, Harry W; NH-0007-598

WELLES,
Henry; b1804 s/o Winthrop & Polly Marsh of Plymouth NH; m1826 Elizabeth Edson & m1852 Lovina Gordon; ch/o Lovina - Henry N, Fred A, Frank E, Flora J m George Richardson, 1 son; NH-0007-584
Winthrop; s/o Winthrop & Dorothy Ely; m Polly Marsh d/o Samuel; liv Plymouth NH; ch Henry b1804 m Elizabeth Edson & m Lovina Gordon, 4 sons, 6 dau; NH-0007-584

WELLS,
Artemas; b1808; m Abigail Bowles of Lisbon; liv Lisbon NH; ch Climena dy, Phebe m George S Pike of Franklin, Franklin m Harriet Parker of Littleton, Arthur C m Emma R Shipman, Curtis A m Emma P Wellman, Alma m Henry Eastman of Concord, George W m Maria Bowles, Flora m Phineas S Gordon; NH-0007-453
Dr Charles; b1817 s/o Horace & Betsy Heath; m1847 Mary M Smith; liv Chili NY, Manchester NH, Westminster VT; NH-0002-127
Capt Enos; s/o Ephraim; m Lois Hibbard & m1824 Sally Clark of Landaff; liv Canaan, Haverhill NH; ch/o Sally - Caleb m Martha H Gordon of Landaff & m Lucy Gordon sis/o Martha, George, Enos C, 1 son; NH-0007-377
Capt Hezekiah; b1736; m Sarah

WELLS (continued)
Trumbull; liv Windsor CT; ch Horace b1776 m Betsy Heath; NH-0002-127
Horace; b1776 s/o Capt Hezekiah & Sarah Trumbull of Windsor CT; m Betsy Heath of Warehouse Point CT; liv Westminster & Bellows Falls VT, Windsor CT; ch Dr Charles b1817 m Mary M Smith, Dr Horace, Mary E W m Capt John Cole; NH-0002-127

WENTWORTH,
Bartholomew; b1788 s/o Bartholomew & Ruth Hall; m1811 Nancy Hall d/o Capt William & Sarah Roberts; liv Rollinsford; ch Arioch, Catherine m Charles Ela of Dover, Ruth m John B Griffiths of Durham, William Hall, Selucus, Sally, Rebecca Ann; NH-0003-673
George Thomas; b1814 s/o Isaac of Dover; liv Dover; NH-0003-598
James F; s/o James M & Elizabeth P Humphrey of Grafton NH; m Mary A Champion d/o Levi & Nancy B Doe of Jamaica Plain; ch Levi F, Anna M; NH-0007-285
James M; s/o James & Lydia Perse; m Elizabeth P Humphrey of Dorchester MA; liv Grafton NH; ch James F m Mary A Champion, 9 others; NH-0007-285
Gov John AM LLD; s/o Mark Hunking gs/o Lt Gov John; m Frances Atkinson wid/o Theodore Jr; liv Wolfeborough NH; NH-0006-293
John Jr; b1745 s/o Hon John; m1771 Margaret Frost of New Castle; liv Dover; ch Paul b1782 m Lydia Cogswell; NH-0003-587, NH-0006-713
Col Joseph; m Sarah J ---; liv Sandwich NH; ch Paul m Ellen F Dunckle, Moses J; NH-0006-253
Col Joseph; b1818 s/o Paul & Lydia Cogswell; m1845 Sarah Payson (Jones?) d/o Moses & Sarah C Jones of Brookline MA; liv Sandwich & Concord NH; ch Paul, Moses, Sarah C, Lydia C, Susan J, Dolly F; NH-0004-157, NH-0006-713

WENTWORTH (continued)
Paul; b1782 s/o John Jr of
Dover gs/o Judge John; m1814
Lydia Cogswell d/o Col Amos;
liv Dover & Sandwich NH; ch
Hon John LLD b1815, Lydia C,
Col Joseph b1818 m Sarah
Payson Jones, George, William
B, Mary F, Margaret J, Samuel
H; NH-0004-157, NH-0006-713
Paul; s/o Col Joseph & Sarah J
of Sandwich NH; ch Louisa C,
Joseph, John Paul; NH-0006-
253
Samuel H; b1805 s/o Spencer; m
Hannah Gray; ch Lowell M, Ira
H E; NH-0006-954
Sewell F; s/o William H H &
Mary Clark; liv Parker
DAKOTA; ch Paul; NH-0006-954
Spencer; s/o Ephraim gs/o
Ephraim ggs/o Ephraim gggs/o
Elder William; m Eunice
Smith; liv Wentworth,
Jackson; ch Charles B; NH-
0006-969
Spencer; liv Meredith, Jackson;
ch Charles B b1801, Samuel H
b1805 m Hannah Gray, Lydia H
b1809 m Daniel Smith, Warren
C b1833; NH-0006-954
Tappan; b1802 s/o Isaac of
Dover; liv Somersworth,
Lowell MA; NH-0003-603
Thomas; bro/o Isaiah F, Richard
O, Ephraim F; m Melissa
Sessions; liv Dummer NH; NH-
0005-858
William H H; b1818 s/o Charles
B of Jackson; m Mary Clark of
ME; liv Jackson NH; ch Gen
Marshall Clark b1844 m1869
Georgia A Trickey d/o Capt
Joshua & Martha P Meserve,
Frances E m Robert Fowle,
Sewell F, Luceba W m J Colman
Trickey; NH-0006-954 & 969
WESLEY,
John; d1869; liv Kent ENG,
Bethlehem NH; ch 1 dau m ---
Shattuck, John L, 1 dau m ---
Merrell, 1 dau m Frank Blake;
NH-0007-166
WEST,
Elijah; liv Henniker & Bradford
NH; ch Betsy m Joseph
Shattuck, Polly m James Pres-
bury, Timothy Kendall b1800,
John b1802 dy, Sally b1804
dy, Emily b1806 m Joshua
Wright of Warner, Leonard

WEST (continued)
b1808 m Mary Ayers, Elijah
b1810 m Jane Albe of VT; NH-
0004-207
Timothy Kendall; b1800 s/o
Elijah; ch Daniel F b1824 dy,
Abigail Eaton b1825, Rufus
Fuller b1828, Timothy Kendall
Jr b1830 m Polly Wright, Mary
Elizabeth b1832 m Addison
Cressy, Daniel Fuller b1834,
John b1836; NH-0004-207
WESTCOTT,
Stephen; m1855 Abbie A Fuller
d/o John Gibson & Ann Jones
of Hillsborough; liv Boston
MA; ch Everett Fuller b1858,
Edith b1870; NH-0002-426
WESTGATE,
Hon Nathaniel Waite; b1801 s/o
Earl & Elizabeth Waite of
Plainfield NH; m Lydia J
Prentiss of Springfield &
m1842 Louise Tyler d/o Austin
of Claremont; liv Enfield
Center; ch/o Louise - Tyler
b1843 m Lucretia M Sawyer,
Nathaniel W Jr b1846, William
Francis, Jennie L, George H,
1 other; NH-0007-85
WESTON,
Amos; liv Reading & Derryfield
NH; ch Amos Jr b1791 m Betsy
Wilson; NH-0002-121
Amos Jr; b1791 s/o Amos of Man-
chester NH; m1814 Betsy
Wilson d/o Col Robert of
Londonderry NH & gd/o James;
liv Manchester NH, Derry-
field; ch James Adams b1827 m
Anna S Gilmore, 4 others;
NH-0001-85, NH-0002-121
Hon James Adams, b1827 s/o Amos
Jr & Betsy Wilson, m1854 Anna
S Gilmore d/o Mitchel S Esq
of Concord NH, liv Manchester
& Concord NH; ch Herman dy,
Grace Helen b1866, James
Henry b1868, Edwin Bell
b1871, Annie Mabel b1876,
Charles Albert b1878; NH-
0001-85, NH-0002-121
WETHERBEE,
Charles; bc1790-94; m Nancy
Ralph & m Nancy Hale & m
Abigail Woodward d/o Jacob
gd/o Judge James; liv
Weathersfield MA, Haverhill
NH; ch/o Abigail - Dr Myron
S, 5 others; NH-0007-353

WEYMOUTH,
Dr Henry A; m Louisa Young; liv Andover NH; ch George W m Minnie T Morgan d/o Jerry & Mary J Strong, 2 others; NH-0007-284

WHEELER,
Abel; liv Haverhill & Newport NH; ch 1 dau m Benjamin Noyes, 1 dau m J G Marcy; NH-0007-362

Alonzo F; b1835 s/o William O & Betsey Fletcher of Plymouth; m1857 Lucia N Worthen d/o Samuel; liv N Groton, Bridge-water NH; ch Nellie F b1859, Roscoe b1865, George H b1873; NH-0007-175

Daniel C; b1815 s/o William N & Hannah Odell of Plymouth; m Malinda French & m Harriet Randall; liv Plymouth NH; ch/o Malinda - Mary, Lenora A; ch/o Harriet - Daniel B m Anna Howe, William O m Rosa B Avery; NH-0007-590

Daniel P; b1810; m Mary Ann Wheeler; liv Fairlee VT, Orford NH; ch Daniel b1836, Charles b1839; NH-0007-569

Dexter; b1816 s/o Thomas & Sally Blodgett of Gilead ME; m1847 Elizabeth F Hodgdon d/o Moses of Milan; liv Berlin NH; ch Sara m E W Sribner; NH-0005-822

Gilman; b1822; m Eliza E Brooks of Dalton; liv Littleton NH; ch Edward O, Charles D, Galen H, Albert P; NH-0007-488

Ira; b1826 s/o William & Annie Davis; m1852 Harriet E Holt & m1878 Lizzie E Hazelton d/o Rufus & Martha; liv Sutton & Groton NH; ch/o Harriet - Alfretta m E K Follansbee, Susan J m Charles Thisell, Martin; ch/o Lizzie - Anna May b1883; NH-0007-294

John A; s/o Richard; m1822 May Stevens d/o Rev William of MA; ch Abraham M, J W b1826 m Phoebe Dow; NH-0003-482

J W; b1826 s/o John A & May Stevens; m1849 Phoebe Dow d/o Richard of Windham NH; ch Minnie A b1852 dy, William R b1854, Ethel May b1871; NH-0003-482

James Henry; b1831 s/o John H of Dover; liv Dover; NH-0003-

WHEELER (continued)
849
Peter; liv Salem MA?, Monson (Hollis) NH; ch Ebenezer, Lebbeus; NH-0002-439

Reuben Hobart; b1819 s/o Thomas & Sally Blodgett of Gilead ME; m1844 Daphne Chandler d/o Hazen & Betsey Lary; liv Berlin NH; ch Viola m John W Greenlaw, Hazen C b1847, Ozman T b1851; NH-0005-824

Samuel; liv Shelburne NH; ch Samuel m Lydia Austin & m Hannah Austin, Lucy, Amos; NH-0005-874

Samuel; s/o Samuel of Shelburne NH; m Lydia Austin & m Hannah Austin sis/o Lydia; ch Austin, Joseph, Samuel m Eliza Burbank, Hannah m Reuben Hobart, Margaret, Judith m Enoch Peabody; NH-0005-874

Thomas; s/o Samuel; liv Gilead ME, Temple & Berlin NH; ch Thomas, Amos, Cyrus, Polly m Daniel Green, Sarah m Benjamin Thompson, Dexter, Hiram, Reuben H, Daniel, Jonathan; NH-0005-790

WHEET,
Alonzo W; b1849 s/o Capt Joseph & Lucette Kidder of Groton; m1881 Georgiana Kelly wid/o Joseph Adams d/o Rev Paul Chase; liv Groton NH; ch Willie F; NH-0007-291

Capt Joseph; b1813 s/o Josiah & Hannah Reed; m1834 Lucette Kidder d/o John & Lois Buel; liv Groton NH; ch Charles F b1835 m Annie A Bacon wid/o Charles P Fish, Elizabeth m Charles Johnson of Campton NH; Emily A dy, Lafayette b1844 m Emma F Colburn, Alonzo W b1849 m Georgiana Kelly, Ella J b1851 m Luther Bradley, Lura L m Elias Bailey; NH-0007-291

Josiah; b1761; m Sarah Hayes & m Hannah Reed; liv Hollis, Groton; ch/o Sarah - 2 sons, 6 dau; ch/o Hannah - Col Joseph, Betsey m John Bartlett of MO, Lucy m Reuben H Colburn, Capt Joseph b1813 m Lucette Kidder; NH-0007-291

Josiah; s/o Joshua R & Huldah Kidder of Groton; m1863

WHEET (continued)
Hannah W Southwick & m1880
Abbie A McClure d/o A J; liv
Groton NH; ch/o Hannah - Fred
E, Harvey A, 3 sons; ch/o
Abbie - Ava; NH-0007-291
Joshua R; b1807 s/o Josiah;
m1830 Huldah Kidder d/o John
& Lois Buel; liv Groton NH;
ch Caroline B b1832 m J
Cummings Hall, Sarah A b1834
m Frank Smith, Sylvester
b1836 m Cynthia J Whitcher &
m Mary L Merrill, Josiah m
Hannah W Southwick & m Abbie
A McClure, Dr John C b1840,
Alonzo J dy, Huldah A b1843 m
A J McClure, Mary Ann b1850
dy; NH-0007-291
Lafayette; b1844 s/o Capt
Joseph & Lucette Kidder of
Groton; m1871 Emma F Colburn;
liv Groton NH; ch Marion J,
Lucy J, Sadie L, Carl R; NH-
0007-291
Sylvester; b1836 s/o Joshua R &
Huldah Kidder of Groton;
m1858 Cynthia J Whitcher &
m1880 Mary L Merrill d/o
Arthur L & Mary E; liv Groton
NH; ch/o Cynthia - Hattie A,
Mary J, Edith F, Hattie C;
ch/o Mary L - Carrol S, Ethel
M; NH-0007-291
WHIDDEN,
Benjamin Franklin; m1851 Eliza
Turner Spaulding of Lancaster
& m1874 Kate J Brooks of
Cincinnati OH; liv Greenland
& Lancaster NH; ch/o Eliza -
John W; NH-0005-220
WHIPPLE,
David C; m Clemantine Chandler
d/o Henry H of Hanover; ch
Henry C, Margaret P m A R
Brewer of NY; NH-0007-261
Edwards; m Milly ---; liv
Dalton NH; ch Abigail b1802,
Matthew W b1803, Benjamin
b1804, Louisa b1806, Mary
b1808; NH-0005-520
Gilman C; b1837 s/o Moses &
Heiress Cooper of Corydon NH;
m1864 Clara P Wood d/o
Samuel; liv Lebanon NH; NH-
0007-430
Rufus; b1748; m Mary Comstock
b1750; liv Richmond; ch 1 dau
m Silas Parker, David, Sally
m Elkanah Hildreth, Lewis;
NH-0007-447

WHIPPLE (continued)
Stephen; m Hannah Kingsbury d/o
Joseph & Silence Richards of
Francestown; liv New Boston;
ch Joseph K; NH-0002-301
Col Thomas J; b1816 s/o Dr
Thomas of Wentworth; m1842
Belinda Hadley of Rumney; liv
Laconia; NH-0007-112.21
WHITAKER,
Caleb; s/o William of Weare; m
Mrs Nancy Mathis White; liv
Deering; ch Hannah m James
Gregg, Lydia m Samuel Patten,
Roxiana m George Smart,
Daniel m Hannah Blodgett,
Joseph Wheeler dy, Charlotte;
NH-0002-383
James; m Susannah Simons of
Haverhill MA; liv Deering; ch
Isaac, Sarah, James m Mary
Chase, Susannah m Jesse
Whitaker of Weare, Joseph,
Peter m Sarah Alcock, John m
Lydia Chase & m Anah Bickford
& m Ruth Killom, Bette,
Nehemiah m Phebe Bryant,
Jonathan; NH-0002-378
James; s/o James & Susannah
Simons of Deering; m Mary
Chase; ch William C m Sarah J
Collins, James S m Abigail
Collins, Charles, Lydia dy,
Gilman m Lydia Neal; NH-0002-
378
James S; s/o James & Mary
Chase; m Abigail Collins; ch
Mary E; NH-0002-378
Nehemiah; s/o James & Susannah
Simons of Deering; m Phebe
Bryant; ch Hiram m Ellen
Monroe & m Harriet Tuttle,
David, Susannah m Samuel
Osborne of Weare NH, Abbie m
Daniel Buxton of Henniker NH,
Aurelia, Ophelia m Monroe
Blood; NH-0002-378
William C; s/o James & Mary
Chase; m Sarah J Collins; ch
Francis, John J dy; NH-0002-
378
WHITCHER,
David; b1827; m Nancy R Knight
of Landaff; liv Benton,
Landaff, Bath NH; ch 9; NH-
0007-146
David; b1828 s/o William of
Coventry; m1853 Sally A Noyes
of Landaff; ch Hattie
Blanche; NH-0007-366
Ira; b1815 s/o William of

WHITCHER (continued)
Benton NH; m1843 Lucy Royce;
liv Benton NH, Woodsville; ch
William, Mary m Chester
Abbott; NH-0007-366

WHITCOMB,
Clark; m1844 Harriet Maria
Melvin d/o Richard & Betsy
Straw; liv Hillsborough; ch
Frank Lawton b1851 m Ida
Jennett of Rockport MA, 2
dau; NH-0004-206
Lindsey; liv Easton, Bethlehem
NH; ch C L, H E; NH-0007-166

WHITE,
A J; m Nellie H Snow d/o Edwin
& Maria H Perkins of Eaton;
liv Grand Rapids MI; ch
Walter J, Wallace, Leonard;
NH-0006-800
Dr Charles; b1795 s/o Samuel &
Mary Williams; m1820 Sarah
French b1795 Ezekiel; liv
Sandwich NH; ch Eliza F b1820
m1840 Rev L P Frost, Laura C
b1822 m1840 Timothy Varney,
Sarah F b1824 m1843 Dr David
Huckins, Mary Jane b1826,
Emily M b1828 m1851 John F
Coffin, Henrietta b1830 m1857
Frank Davis & m1866 Levi
Guptil, Susan Frances b1832
m1855 Luther Mooney & m1870
Norman G French, Dr Charles
Henry b1838 m1875 Mary K
Connor; NH-0006-706
David; s/o Patrick gs/o John of
IRE; m Sarah Dutton of Peter-
borough; NH-0004-473
James; s/o John & Susannah
Eaton; m Susannah Flint; liv
Framingham MA, Deering NH; ch
Sophona, Rhoda m Moses Roach,
James m Abigail Coburn,
Artemas m Sarah Case & m
Charlotte Burley, Susan m
Joel Bixby, Cyntha m Hiram
Smith, Eliza A m William
Brown, Jason m Mary Case; NH-
0002-384
Jeremiah; b1775 s/o Josiah of
Pittsfield NH; liv Pittsfield
NH; ch Jeremiah Wilson b1821
m Caroline G Merrill & Anna M
Prichard; NH-0001-140, NH-
0002-205
Jeremiah Wilson Esq; b1821 s/o
Jeremiah of Pittsfield NH;
m1846 Caroline G Merrill d/o
Caleb Esq of Pittsfield NH &
m1881 Mrs Anna M Pritchard of

WHITE (continued)
Bradford VT sis/o Caroline G
Merrill; liv Pittsfield &
Nashua NH, Boston MA; cn
Caroline Wilson dy, James
Wilson b1849; NH-0001-140,
NH-0002-205
John; m Susannah Eaton; ch
James m Susannah Flint,
Nathan m Dorcas Wilson & m
Hannah Ordway; NH-0002-385
John Hubbard; b1802 s/o Amos &
Sarah of Dover; liv Dover;
NH-0003-592
Maj Moses; liv Rutland MA,
Lancaster NH; ch John H; NH-
0005-362
Nathan; s/o John & Susannah
Eaton; m Dorcas Wilson & m
Hannah Ordway; liv Deering
NH; ch/o Dorcas - Ann m John
Sterrett, Dorcas m Samuel
Kimball, Nathan m Jane Smith,
Mary m William Matten; ch/o
Hannah - Harrison m Esther
Burley & m Amelia Morrison,
Nancy dy, Harriet m David Mc-
Alister, Lovine dy, Nancy dy;
NH-0002-385
Nathaniel; b1811 s/o Samuel &
Sarah Freeman of Lancaster
NH; m1836 Armenia S White
b1817 d/o John; liv Concord
NH; ch John A, Armenia E m
Horatio Hobbs, Lizzie H,
Nathaniel Jr, Benjamin C,
Annie Frances dy, Seldon F
dy, Hattie S (adopted) m Dr D
P Dearborn of Brattleborough
VT; NH-0001-172, NH-0004-136
P; m Hannah Libbey d/o James;
ch George G; NH-0003-424
Samuel; bc1750; m1773 Mary
Williams of Mansfield; liv
Mansfield MA, Nelson NH; ch
Dr Charles b1795 m Sarah
French, 7 others; NH-0006-706
Timothy; liv Ossipee NH; ch
Josiah G, Lucinda m ---
Tibbetts; NH-0006-628
William; m Nancy Mathis; ch
Nancy m Levi Brown, Aaron m
Louisa Cram, William m Mary
Wilson, James m Lovinia
Clough, Judith m Enos Bailey,
Mahala m Luke Otis; NH-0002-
383
William; m Susanna ---; liv
ENG, MA; ch Peregrine; NH-
0006-706

WHITEHOUSE,
Charles C; s/o George L; ch Charles Walter; NH-0003-628

George L; b1797 s/o Nathaniel & Anna Leighton; m1822 Liberty N Dame d/o Paul of Rochester; liv Dover, Farmington, Middleton; ch George W, Charles C, Laura Ann m James E Fernald Esq, Walter Scott dy; NH-0003-628

Nathaniel; b1767 s/o Turner & --- Hanson; mc1795 Anna Leighton b1775 d/o Samuel of Farmington; liv Farmington & Middleton NH; ch George L b1797 m Liberty N Dame; NH-0003-628

Thomas; m Elizabeth Pomfrett d/o William; ch Pomfret; NH-0003-772

Turner; m --- Hanson; liv Dover & Rochester NH; ch Nathaniel b1767, 9 sons, 1 dau; NH-0003-628

WHITFORD,
Elliot; b1809 s/o William & Lucy Dale; m1840 Elizabeth Bowman d/o Abel & Hannah F Hunniwell; liv Nashua; ch Alfred J, Josephine E, Frederick E, Maria K m James H Hall; NH-0002-215

William; b1773; m1798 Lucy Dale b1778 of Beverly MA; liv Salem MA, Hillsborough NH; ch Elliot b1809 m Elizabeth Bowman; NH-0002-215

WHITING,
David; b1810 s/o Oliver & Fany Stiles; m1830 Emma Spalding d/o Isaac of Wilton; liv Wilton NH, Fitchburg MA; ch Harvey A, George O, Frances m --- Spencer of Lexington MA, Maria m --- Van Alstine of Louisville KY, Lizzie m --- Bradley of Chicago IL; NH-0002-723

George W; s/o Stephen H; m Mindwell P Kendall of Landaff; liv Lisbon NH; ch Horace A m Emily J Gray of Jackson, George W, Julia H m David S Richardson of Lisbon, Angeline E m Albert Gray of Lowell MA, Martha A m Orrin C Gordon of Royalstown MA; NH-0007-446

Oliver; m Fany Stiles; liv Temple & Wilton NH; ch David

WHITING (continued)
b1810 Emma Spalding, 3 dau; NH-0002-723

Solomon; b1791; m Maria Charlton of Littleton; liv Manchester, Littleton NH; ch Robert; NH-0007-486

WHITMAN,
David; liv Bridgewater MA, Lyme; ch Rhoda m --- Morey, David, 6 others; NH-0007-570

WHITNEY,
Joshua; m Esther ---; liv Dalton NH; ch Abigail b1788, John b1792; NH-0005-519

Joshua; m Electa ---; liv Dalton NH; ch Joshua Jr b1795, Obadiah b1799, George b1800, Sally b1803; NH-0005-519

Kimball; b1810 s/o Otis & Sarah Taylor of Campton; m Eliza Elliott; liv Plymouth NH; ch Anna P m1859 Hon Manson S Brown b1834 of Bridgewater, Sarah T, Emma J; NH-0007-596

Manning; m1818 Dolly Brooks; liv Stowe MA, Franconia NH; ch Emeline, Daniel, Henry B, Lydia, Jane, Sally H; NH-0007-270

Nathan; b1828 s/o Smyrna & Ruth Whitney of Westminster MA; m1850 Mary S Tolman & m1864 Charlotte M Belcher; liv Bennington; ch/o Mary - Frank E b1853, Caroline L b1856 m Dr Hadley of Block Isl; ch/o Charlotte - William B b1866, Samuel E b1867; NH-0002-288

Orlando; m Mary S Couch d/o Enoch & Jane O Stickney; ch Herbert C; NH-0004-694

Smyrna; m Ruth Whitney; liv Westminster MA; ch Samuel b1821, Nathan b1828 m Mary S Toleman & m Charlotte M Belcher; NH-0002-288

WHITTEMORE,
Rev Aaron; b1711 s/o Benjamin & Esther Brooks of Concord MA; m1743 Abigail Coffin b1718 of Newbury MA; liv Groton MA, Suncook NH; ch John b1744 dy, Aaron b1746 m Sarah Gilman, Judith b1748 dy, Benjamin b1750 m Abigail Abbott, Esther b1752 m Jeremiah Hall & m Rev Joseph Woodman, Sarah b1754 dy, Ruth b1756 m Dea David Kimball, Peter b1758

WHITTEMORE (continued)
m1783 Elizabeth Baker; NH-0004-585
Aaron; b1746 s/o Rev Aaron & Abigail Coffin; m1770 Sarah Gilman b1745 d/o Peter of Exeter; liv Suncook NH; ch 1 b1770 dy, Judith b1771 m1793 James Baker of Bow, John b1772 dy, 1 b1773 dy, Hon Aaron b1774 m Lydia Fisk, Richard b1776 m Nancy Brickett, Sarah b1777 m1796 Jesse Baker, Abigail b1781, Peter b1783, Polly b1785 dy; NH-0004-585
Hon Aaron; b1774 s/o Aaron & Sarah Gilman of Suncook NH; m1800 Lydia Fisk b1776 of Derry; liv Pembroke NH; ch Benjamin b1801, Louisa b1802 m1847 Charles P Hayward, Mary F b1804 m1820 Daniel Parker, Adaline b1806 dy, Hon Aaron b1808 m Ariannah S Barstow, Hiram b1811 m1823 Elizabeth J Hoit of Exeter & m1856 Alma M Pugalls, Lydia b1813, Sarah b1815 m Jacob Sawyer, Dolly D b1819 m David H Burnham; NH-0004-585
Hon Aaron; b1808 s/o Hon Aaron & Lydia Fisk of Pembroke; m1840 Ariannah S Barstow b1821 of Exeter; liv Pembroke NH; ch Sophia F b1842 m1861 Charles C Shaw, Ariannah B b1844 m1870 John H Sullivan, Aaron b1846, Adaline G b1850 m1870 John G Tallant, John Cambridge b1852, Charles Barstow b1854, Arthur Gilman b1856, Frederick B b1857, Annie Brewster b1859, Elizabeth M b1861; NH-0004-585
Aaron Jr; b1849 s/o Hon Aaron of Pembroke; liv Pittsfield; NH-0004-39
Maj Amos; b1746; liv Greenfield; ch William Esq b1781; NH-0002-342
Hon Amos; b1802; m1825 Ruth Bullard; liv Bennington; NH-0002-287
Benjamin; b1669 s/o John & Mary Upham; m1692 Esther Brooks; liv Concord & Cambridge MA; ch Mary b1694, Benjamin b1696, Nathaniel b1698, Grace b1700, Esther b1707, Rev Aaron b1711 m Abigail Coffin;

WHITTEMORE (continued)
NH-0004-585
Benjamin; b1799; m Almira Chandler d/o Joseph; liv Rumford ME, Colebrook NH; ch Harvey, Sidney B m Emeline Corbett; NH-0005-622
Rev David R; b1819; m Eliza I Gilbert; liv N Providence RI; NH-0004-623
George R; m1870 Helen D Grimes d/o Francis & Mary Chase; liv Antrim NH; ch Francis Grimes b1872 dy, Henry Ernest b1872; NH-0002-423
Dr Jacob P; b1810 s/o Jacob & Rebecca Bradford of Antrim; liv Hartford VT, Gilmanton, Chester, Haverhill MA; NH-0003-148
John; b1638 s/o Thomas of Kitchen Parish Hartfordshire ENG; m Mary Upham of Weymouth & m1677 Mary Miller; ch/o Upham - Thomas b1664, Joseph b1666, Benjamin b1669 m Esther Brooks, Nathaniel b1673; ch/o ? - Joel b1677; ch/o Miller - Mary b1678 dy, Pelatiah b1680, Amos b1681, Mary b1683, Daniel b1685, Rebecca b1687, Hannah b1689; NH-0004-585
John; liv Rumford ME, Dixville NH; ch John b1805; NH-0005-594
John J; b1810; m1834 Sarah Bullard b1809; ch John, 1 son, 1 dau; NH-0002-287
WHITTIER,
Elijah; s/o Elijah; m Nancy Kineston of Canaan & m Lucretia Aldrich; ch/o ? - Nathaniel m Sophia Hastings; NH-0007-557
John; b1818 s/o Aaron & Lydia Worthen of Raymond NH; m1849 Mary A Lovering b1825 d/o Daniel & Ruth Atwood; liv Fremont; ch Hattie A; NH-0003-298
Nathaniel; s/o Elijah; m Sophia Hastings d/o Jonas of Bristol; liv Orange NH; ch Julia m --- Hoyt; NH-0007-557
WHITTLE,
Thomas; m Mary Folsom d/o Joshua & Mary Brackenbury of Deering; liv Weare & Deering NH; ch William m Eliza P Gove, Thomas Parker m Mrs

WHITTLE (continued)
Almira Lock, Joshua F m
Amanada Roby & m Mrs Sarah C
Wallace, David F m Charlotte
Nichols, Hannah m Charles
Farnsworth, Martha A m Reuben
Loveren, Mary E m Joseph
Loveren, Emma J m Lewis
Goodall; NH-0002-381

WHITTON,
Charles A; s/o Hon Thomas
Lupton & Sally Morse of
Wolfeborough NH; m Annie E
Prescott; ch Annietta Lilian,
Abbie Anna, Ellie B; NH-0006-
389

David E; s/o Hon Thomas Lupton
& Sally Morse of Wolfeborough
NH; m Anetta A Tibbetts; ch
Thomas Edwin; NH-0006-389

George; bro/o Margaret m Daniel
Raynard Esq; m Esther Copp
d/o Capt David of Wakefield;
liv Wakefield & Wolfeborough
NH; ch George Washington, Hon
Thomas Lupton b1811 m Sally
Morse, David Copp; NH-0006-
389

Oscar F; s/o Hon Thomas Lupton
& Sally Morse of Wolfeborough
NH; m Clarissa Blake; ch
Sarah M, Esther C, Clara L;
NH-0006-389

Hon Thomas Lupton; b1811 s/o
George & Esther Copp; m Sally
Morse b1812 d/o Ebenezer &
Elizabeth Page of Kingston;
liv Wolfeborough NH; ch
Charles A m Annie E Prescott,
Oscar F m Clarissa Blake,
David E m Annetta A Tibbetts,
William M m Susan Haines; NH-
0006-389

WIGGIN,
Arthur Elliott; b1842 s/o Jacob
C & Mary S Cogswell; m1863
Mary F Drown of Newington;
liv Tamworth NH, Lawrence MA;
ch Mary L b1871; NH-0006-768

Benjamin; m Elizabeth Clement &
m Mrs Sarah Holt; liv
Stratham, Hopkinton NH; ch
Timothy, Benjamin, Mary,
Ellen m Baruch Chase, Joseph,
Elizabeth; NH-0004-407

Jacob C; b1803 s/o Henry &
Elizabeth Clark of Wakefield;
m Mary S Cogswell d/o Dr
Joseph; liv Tamworth NH; ch
Joseph C b1826, Colby S,
Emily C m Alvin W Stevens,

WIGGIN (continued)
Almira J, Mary J, Cordelia A,
Mayhew C b1839, Arthur
Elliott b1842 m Mary F Drown,
Hannah S, Amanda F; NH-0006-
768

Joseph; m Ancie Bachelder; ch
Nattie, Gertrude; NH-0004-501

Joseph A; b1833 s/o Henry; m
Frances Hutchins of ME; liv
Wakefield & Tamworth NH; ch
James H b1865, Arthur E
b1875; NH-0006-775

Josiah Bartlett; b1811 s/o Capt
Andrew & Dolly Wiggin gs/o
Andrew ggs/o Bradstreet;
m1842 Eleanor Hilton Smith of
Epping; liv Stratham & Dover
& S Newmarket NH; ch Andrew
C, Clara E m Ephraim Gordon
of Brentwood, Linnie B dy, 1
dy; NH-0003-552

Col Mark; b1746; m Betsey
Brackett b1748; liv Stratham,
Wolfeborough; NH-0006-309

Richard; s/o Andrew & Judith
Varney; m1829 Mehitable Beede
b1800 d/o Jonathan & Anna
Winslow; ch Jonathan B,
Andrew B, Anna H, Samuel B,
Elizabeth, George W, Richard
H, Eliphaz O; NH-0006-717

WIGGLESWORTH,
Dr Samuel; b1734 s/o Rev Samuel
of Ipswich MA, m1779 Mary
Waldron d/o George of Dover;
liv Dover; NH-0003-846

WIGHT,
Aaron; b1795 s/o Daniel of
Needham MA; m1827 Rebecca
Carlton d/o Isaac & Sarah
Messer; liv Milan & Dummer
NH; ch Isaac Carlton b1830 m
Philantha L Howard, Sarah, 5
others; NH-0005-863

Isaac Carlton; b1830 s/o Aaron
& Rebecca Carlton; m1865
Philantha L Howard d/o Joseph
of Hanover ME; liv Dummer NH;
ch Joseph Howard, Aaron
Carlton, Rebecca Carlton,
Adam Willis, Isaac Henry,
Daniel Roberts, Mary
Philantha, Alice Iantha; NH-
0005-863

Nahum MD; b1807; m1833 Mary Ann
Straw d/o Lt Gideon of Newfield ME; liv Gilead ME,
Gilmanton NH; ch 8; NH-0004-
797

WILCOMB,
Daniel; b1783; m1812 Betsey Page & m1816 Hannah Eaton; liv Atkinson MA, Bethlehem NH; ch/o ? - Daniel P, Moses K, 4 others; NH-0007-167

WILCOX,
Leonard; b1799 s/o Hon Jeduthan b1769; liv Hanover & Orford NH; ch Samuel M b1829; NH-0007-112.6

WILDER,
Marshall Pinckney PhD; b1798 s/o Samuel Locke & Anna Sherwin; m1820 Tryphosa Jewett d/o Dr Stephen & m1833 Abigail Baker d/o Capt David & m1855 Julia Baker sis/o Abigail; liv Rindge NH, Boston MA; NH-0001-25

Samuel Locke; m1797 Anna Sherwin d/o Jonathan & Mary Crombie; liv Rindge NH; ch Marshall Pinckney b1798 m Tryphosa Jewett & m Abigail Baker & m Julia Baker; NH-0001-25

WILKINS,
Alexander; m Lydia Gage d/o Phineas; liv Merrimack; ch Olive, Fanny m Levi Fisher; NH-0002-543

Alexander McCalley (McCauley); b1806 s/o Levi & Ann McCauley; m1834 Caroline Richmond Stearns d/o James of Amherst; liv Merrimack; ch Lucy Ann, Franklin A, James M, Gustine, Mary C; NH-0002-547 & 550

Amos; s/o Andrew; liv Merrimack, VT; ch Joanna A, Sally N, Amos A; NH-0002-546

Andrew; s/o Capt Stephen Jr; liv Merrimack; ch Amos, Mehitable m Samuel McClure, Andrew, Sarah m Zebulon Ritterbush, Samuel, Asa, John; NH-0002-546

Bray; m Mrs Lucy Blanchard; liv Deering; ch Lucy, Sally m Robert Fulton, Anna m Nathaniel Merrill & m Stephen Carr, Betty m Joseph Kimball, Rebecca m Alexander Gregg, David m Abigail Patten, Isaac m Nancy Chase, James m Abigail Chase & m ?, John m Lucinda Forsaith; NH-0002-381

Hezekiah; m Margaret Armor; liv Deering; ch Gawn, Polly m

WILKINS (continued)
Benjamin Huntington, Sally m Robert McFerson, Isaac m Roxanna Eaton, Rodney m Harriet Ellingwood, Andrew; NH-0002-386

Isaac; m Rosanna Eaton d/o James & --- McClure; ch Gawn dy, Lucinda m Sewell Packhard, Malvina m William Forsaith, Elzira m Mathew Forsaith, Andrew A m Calista Goodhue, Augustus m Sarah Mitchell, Frances m Charles J Taft; NH-0002-386

James; s/o Capt Stephen Jr; liv Merrimack, NY; ch Eliza, Charles A, Mary A, Jane McC; NH-0002-547

John; s/o Andrew; liv Merrimack; ch Martha H m Amos A Wilkins, Charlotte m Edward Colburn, Augusta, Adeline, Frances, Alma P, 1 son dy; NH-0002-547

Levi; s/o Capt Stephen Jr; liv Merrimack; ch Ann dy, Alexander McCalley b1806 m Caroline Richmond Stearns, Roxana, Levi F dy, Lucy A m Thomas H Hall, Hannah m Ira Roby, Levi W, 1 son dy; NH-0002-547

Phineas; m Abigail Ellingwood; liv Deering; ch Louisa m Benjamin Roberts, Nathan; NH-0002-386

Samuel; s/o Andrew; liv Merrimack, Amherst; ch Samuel; NH-0002-546

Capt Stephen Jr; s/o Stephen of Salem; liv Merrimack; ch Andrew, Stephen dy, Hannah m Elijah Chubbuck, Lucy, Stephen, Levi, James; NH-0002-546

WILLARD,
Steadman; m1828 Mary Wilder Harwood d/o Joseph & Pattee Gilbert; ch Alma Harwood b1828 m1864 George Kendall, Mary Almeda b1831, Steadman Alfred b1834 m1865 Annette Putnam, Lydia S b1837 m1862 William G Barrows; NH-0002-434

Stedman; b1798; m Meriel Wheeler d/o John Brooks; liv Saxton's River VT, Orford NH; ch David E b1829, Isaac b1832, Hannah m John W

WILLARD (continued)
Sanborn, John, William A, Meriel m T D Rowell, Sarah S m Rev T F W Clary; NH-0007-567

WILLEY,
Diodate; s/o Abel; m1778 Lydia Church; liv Campton NH; ch Diodate m Mary Butler; NH-0007-202

Isaac; s/o Darius & Mary Willey; m Susan Ryan of Plymouth; liv Campton NH; ch Allen m Mehitable W Foss d/o William of Thornton; NH-0007-207

James; s/o Capt Samuel & Betsey Glazier; ch James C; NH-0006-850

Capt Samuel; m Betsey Glazier; liv Lee, Bartlett, N Conway; ch Polly m Jonathan Thompson, James, Samuel b1788 m Polly Lovejoy, Hannah m John M Barnes, Betsey m Jacob Bray, Rev Benjamin G, Stephen, Sally; NH-0006-850

Samuel; b1788 s/o Capt Samuel & Betsey Glazier; m1812 Polly Lovejoy; liv Bartlett; ch Eliza Ann b1813, Jeremiah b1815, Martha G b1817, Elbridge G b1819, Sally b1822; NH-0006-850

Selden C; s/o Diodate & Mary Butler; m Elizabeth Denison of Gloucester MA & m Melvina Harvey d/o Daniel & Fanny Ferry of Colebrook NH; ch/o Elizabeth - Elizabeth; ch/o Melvina - Milton H, Esther E; NH-0007-202

WILLIAMS,
Alexander; s/o Samuel; m Candace Martin; liv Taunton MA, Grafton NH; ch Martin m Angeline Caswell, 9 others; NH-0007-279

Benjamin; s/o Samuel & Jean Bullock; m Serepta Barney & m Deborah J Storey; ch/o Serepta - Horace B, Ellen H; ch/o Deborah - Benjamin, Josephine m --- Whitford; NH-0007-279

Hon Charles; b1816 s/o Lt Seth & Sarah Mitchael; m1846 Eliza A Weston d/o Sutheric of Antrim NH; liv Easton & Chelmsford MA, Springfield IL, Manchester & Nashua NH;

WILLIAMS (continued)
ch Seth Weston b1849; Charles Alden b1851 m Kate N Piper, Marian b1854 m Herbert Allen Viets; NH-0001-47

Edward; s/o Seth & Susannah Forbes; m 1772 Sarah Lothrop of Bridgewater MA; liv Bridgewater MA; ch Lt Seth b1776 m Sarah Mitchael; NH-0001-47

George Canning; b1827 s/o Hon Jared W of Lancaster; liv Lancaster NH; NH-0005-221

George L; m Emma F Marshall d/o Anderson J & Frances Perkins; liv Concord; ch Jessie, Ethelyn; NH-0005-395

James; m Candace Billings of Waterford VT; liv N Littleton NH; ch Franklin B m Ellen Artler of Liverpool ENG; NH-0007-506

Jared Irving; b1832 s/o Hon Jared W of Lancaster NH; m1857 Mary Hamilton Morse; liv Lancaster NH; NH-0005-220

Hon Jared Warner; b1796; m1824 Sarah Hawes Bacon of Woodstock CT; liv W Woodstock CT, Lancaster NH; ch George Canning b1827, Jared Irving b1832 m Mary Hamilton Morse; NH-0005-212 & 221

Leroy D; s/o Martin & Angeline Caswell; m Ellen Philbrick d/o Jeremiah & Jane Sanborn of Springfield NH; liv Grafton NH; NH-0007-279

Peleg; m Sarah Wheeler of Charlestown NH; liv RI, Littleton NH; ch 1 dau; NH-0007-485

Rufus; s/o Samuel & Jean Bullock; m Lettice Smith d/o Eleazer; ch Alfred S m Sarah Ann Sanburn, 5 others; NH-0007-279

Samuel; m Ursula Day of Enfield; liv Canaan NH; ch Jennie m Rev Francis Parker, Lewis M, Miriam Elizabeth, Susan Augusta, Frank B; NH-0007-264

Samuel; s/o Samuel & Mercy Case; m Jean Bullock of Grafton; ch Annie m --- Walker, Benjamin m Serepta Barney & m Deborah J Storey, Rufus m Lettice Smith, 6 others; NH-0007-279

WILLIAMS (continued)
  Seth; b1722 s/o Josiah of
  Bridgewater MA; m Susannah
  Forbes of Bridgewater; liv
  Bridgewater & Easton MA; ch
  Edward m Sarah Lothrop; NH-
  0001-47
  Lt Seth; b1776 s/o Edward &
  Sarah Lothrop; m1800 Sarah
  Mitchael d/o Col Mitchael of
  Bridgewater MA; liv Easton
  MA; ch Seth, Charles b1816 m
  Eliza A Weston; NH-0001-47
  Stephen; m Elizabeth Longfellow
  of Byfield MA; liv Enfield,
  Canaan; ch Samuel, Stephen,
  Lorenzo D, William, Susan m
  James Eastman, Mary m Leonard
  Hadley, Abraham L m Chastina
  Burnham of Hanover; NH-0007-
  230
WILLOUGHBY,
  John; liv Billerica, W Dun-
  stable; ch John W Jr; NH-
  0002-439
WILMOT,
  Haron; s/o Timothy; m Lydia
  Martin of Bradford VT; liv
  Haverhill NH; ch Frank L,
  Nellie B, George E; NH-0007-
  359
  Timothy; liv Norwich VT, Haver-
  hill NH; ch Haron m Lydia
  Martin, Harvey B, Mary m
  Daniel Sargent, Betsey m
  Henry Tower, Harriet m
  Charles Snow; NH-0007-359
WILSON,
  Adams Brock; b1842; m1866 Lou M
  Little d/o William of Little-
  ton; liv Newbury VT, Little-
  ton NH; NH-0007-480
  David; liv Deering NH; ch James
  m Mary McNeil, Betsy m John
  Grimes, Jenny m Josiah Morse,
  Nancy m Hugh Bell, Hannah m
  Robert Gibson & m James
  Cochran, Sally m --- Hill & m
  --- Dustin, Susan m Nathan
  Murdough, David Jr m Jenny
  Dickey & m Margaret Dinsmore;
  NH-0002-375
  David Jr; s/o David; m Jenny
  Dickey & m Margaret Dinsmore;
  ch/o Jenny - Eliza dy, Sally
  dy, Hannah m James Forsaith,
  Sarah M m Luther Aiken, David
  F m Electa Aiken, Susan m
  George Smart, Mary dy, James,
  William D m Sarah F Chase;
  ch/o Margaret - Eliza D m

WILSON (continued)
  George A Ramsdell of Nashua
  NH; NH-0002-375
  Ephraim F MD; b1817; m Rhoda
  Barnard; liv Sanbornton, E
  Concord, Rockville CT; NH-
  0004-623
  Rev Geo P; m Emily Fisk d/o
  Ralph & Nancy Roby; liv
  Lawrence MA; ch Geo H,
  Francis A, Anna F; NH-0002-
  217
  George L; s/o Isaac P & Rhoda
  Brainard; m1857 Marion M
  Morrison; liv Haverhill NH;
  ch Carrie S, Lillie M; NH-
  0007-356
  Humphrey; s/o Jeremiah Esq of
  SCO; ch Thomas b1677 m Mary
  Light; NH-0004-792
  Humphrey; b1699 s/o Thomas &
  Mary Light of Gilmanton; m
  Mary Leavitt; ch Capt
  Nathaniel b1739 m Elizabeth
  Barber; NH-0004-792
  Isaac P; b1805 s/o Nathaniel &
  Sarah Pearson of Haverhill
  NH; m1826 Rhoda Brainard; ch
  George L m Marion M Morrison,
  Edward B; NH-0007-356
  James Ladd; b1834 s/o William &
  Sally Morse of Morgan VT;
  m1859 Lydia B Long of Andover
  NH; liv Holderness; NH-0007-
  91
  Joseph; m Eliza Carlton d/o
  Timothy & Rebecca Fields; ch
  Eliza Ann, Henry; NH-0002-543
  Capt Nathaniel; b1739 s/o
  Humphrey & Mary Leavitt; liv
  Epping & Gilmanton NH; m1762
  Elizabeth Barber; ch Jeremiah
  b1781 m1803 Abigail Prescott
  Sanborn d/o Dea Abraham, 8
  sons; NH-0004-792
  Nathaniel; b1777 s/o Jesse of
  Pelham; m Sarah Pearson d/o
  Capt Joseph of Haverhill; liv
  Haverhill NH; ch Isaac P
  b1805 m Rhoda Brainard,
  Nathaniel Jr b1808 m1834
  Adeline Boardman & m Abbie A
  Colburn, 1 other; NH-0007-356
  Hon Nathaniel; b1808; liv
  Haverhill & Lancaster NH;
  Orono ME; NH-0004-341
  Thomas; b1677 s/o Humphrey;
  m1698 Mary Light; liv Gilman-
  ton; ch Humphrey b1699 m Mary
  Leavitt; NH-0004-792
  Thomas W MD; b1806; m Amanda M

WILSON (continued)
Sawyer; liv Salisbury NH; ch
Moses S MD m Mary S Harvey;
NH-0004-623
Wesley; b1810; m1834 Rachel
Caldwell; liv Bennington; ch
Orville b1838, Orline A
b1840; NH-0002-287

WINKLEY,
Daniel; s/o John & Mary Swain
of Strafford; m1816 Sarah
Otis d/o Hon Job; liv Oxford
& Strafford NH, Malden MA; ch
Otis P, John A, Daniel S; NH-
0003-707
Francis; b1689 s/o Samuel; m
Mary Emerson d/o Rev John of
Portsmouth; liv Kittery ME;
ch John b1726, Elizabeth
b1728, Samuel b1731 m Mary
Brewster, Francis b1733, Mary
b1736, Emerson b1738, Sarah
b1740; NH-0003-707
John; b1766 s/o Samuel & Mary
Brewster of Barrington; m1791
Mary Swain d/o Richard of
Barrington; liv Strafford; ch
Daniel m Sarah Otis, Mary A m
D K Montgomery of Portsmouth,
7 others; NH-0003-707
Samuel; m1684 Sarah Trickey d/o
Francis; liv Lancashire ENG,
Kittery ME, Portsmouth; ch
Samuel, Francis b1689 m Mary
Emerson, Nicholas, William,
Sarah m Tobias Langdon,
Elizabeth m Samuel Weeks of
Boston; NH-0003-707
Samuel; b1731 s/o Francis &
Mary Emerson of Kittery ME; m
Mary Brewster b1734 d/o
Samuel & Margaret Waterhouse
of Portsmouth; liv Barring-
ton; ch Samuel, Francis,
Mehetable, William, John
b1766 m Mary Swain, Eliza-
beth, Benjamin, David, Mary;
NH-0003-707

WINSLOW,
Zebulon; liv Loudon NH; ch
Moses, George, David,
Sleeper, Elizabeth, Lucy,
Mary, Zebulon, Clarissa,
Almira, Ann; NH-0004-508

WISWALL,
Benjamin Clark; b1808 s/o
Joseph & Sally Clark gs/o
Capt Norman Clark; m1830
Susan Sawyer b1808 of Foxboro
MA; liv Newton MA, Clarks-
ville NH; ch Mary m Moody B

WISWALL (continued)
Haines, Albert C b1835,
Joseph N b1837, William H,
Charles W b1846, George O
b1853; NH-0005-692

WOOD,
Eliphalet; bro/o Enoch; m1788
Elizabeth Tilton; liv Concord
NH; ch Eliphalet, Betsey,
William, Sophia, Harry, Mary,
Jonathan, Julia; NH-0004-502
Joseph; b1725; m Anna Palmer
b1728; liv Mansfield CT,
Lebanon NH; ch Rev Samuel
b1753, Mariam b1755, Joseph
b1759 m Sarah Gerrish,
Ephraim b1761, Anna; NH-0007-
425
Joseph; b1759 s/o Joseph & Anna
Palmer; m1782 Sarah Gerrish
of Boscawen; liv Lebanon NH;
ch Mary b1789 m1806 Samuel B
Gerrish, 10 others; NH-0007-
425
Roger; m Achsah Tilden; ch
Achsah m Russell Risley,
Samuel, Luther, Rosamond m Dr
A Smalley, Hannah, Roger m
Emily Willard; NH-0007-425

WOODBURY,
Isaiah; s/o John of Salem; m
Lois Woodbury d/o Capt Israel
of Salem; liv Cornish NH; ch
John b1819 m Betsy A Hobbs;
NH-0002-648
John; liv Salem; ch Isaiah m
Lois Woodbury; NH-0002-648
John; b1819 s/o Isaiah & Lois
Woodbury; m1843 Betsy A Hobbs
d/o Capt Samuel of Pelham;
liv Haverhill & Methuen MA,
Pelham; ch John Otis, Alice A
m Ezekiel C Gage, Frank M,
Eliza H m William H Peabody;
NH-0002-648
Dr Jonathan; b1791 s/o Dr
Robert of Barrington NH; liv
Dover NH, Union NY; NH-0003-
847
Josiah A; m Polly Knowles d/o
Joseph & Sarah Locke; liv
Northfield; ch Mary, Cyrene,
William; NH-0004-546a
Levi; b1789 s/o Hon Peter of
Francistown; m1819 Elizabeth
W Clapp of Portland ME; liv
Litchfield CT, Boston,
Exeter, Francistown,
Portsmouth; ch Charles Levi,
--- m Hon Montgomery Blair,
--- m Capt Gustavus V Fox;

WOODBURY (continued)
NH-0003-22
Peter; liv Francestown NH; ch James Trask, Hon Levi; NH-0007-63

WOODMAN,
Charles; b1792 s/o Rev Joseph; liv Dover; NH-0003-589
Charles; b1822 s/o Isaac & Mary E Locke of Woodstock; m1848 Jemima Avery d/o Jacob & Jemima Cook; liv Bridgewater NH; ch Jacob A, Lyman B, Charles S, Addie C, Corydon E, Cora M dy, Austin W; NH-0007-175
Charles William; b1809 s/o Jeremiah H Esq of Rochester; liv Dover; NH-0003-597
Hon Edgar H; b1847 s/o John Kimball & Mary Jane Drew of Gilmanton NH; m1878 Georgiana Hodges of Boston MA; liv Concord, Boston; ch George Edgar dy; NH-0004-40
Jeremiah Hall; b1775 s/o Rev Joseph of Sanbornton; liv Warner, Meredith, Rochester; NH-0003-602
John Smith; b1819 s/o Nathan of Durham; liv Charleston SC, Dover, Rollinsford, Durham; NH-0003-603

WOODS,
Andrew Salter; b1803 s/o Andrew of Bath; m Eliza Hutchins d/o James; liv Bath; ch Eliza Isabella b1830 m Hon George A Bingham, Rebecca Newell b1833 m T J M Smith of Boston MA, Edward b1835 m Mary Carlton d/o John, Katherine Jane b1837, Harriet Jameson b1840, Helen Adelaide b1842 dy, Andrew Salter Jr b1845 dy; NH-0007-63 & 136
Edward; b1835 s/o Hon Andrew S of Bath; m1863 Mary Carlton d/o John L; liv Littleton, Bath; ch Edward, Katherine E, Thomas Smith, Andrew Salter; NH-0007-67
William A; m Martha Minot d/o Samuel of Bath; ch Arthur m Adaline B Weeks d/o Dudley, Andrew J, Luella W m Charles W Leighton, 2 dy, Emily; NH-0007-139

WOODWARD,
Daniel S; s/o Jesse gs/o Stephen; m Dorcas Adams d/o

WOODWARD (continued)
Enoch; liv Salisbury & Fisherville & Franklin NH; ch Frank R b1845; NH-0004-558
Frank R; b1845 s/o Daniel S & Dorcas Adams; liv Manchester Hill NH; ch Edwin Chase b1867 dy, May F b1871 dy, Flora A b1874, Lillia Gordon b1875 dy, Eugene S b1878 dy; NH-0004-558
George; m --- Leverett of Windsor VT & m --- Webster of Plymouth; liv Hanover, Haverhill; NH-0007-82
George; m Mary A Lake; liv Springfield VT, Haverhill NH; ch Mary J, Henry L, George J; NH-0007-369
Myron S; b1803 gs/o Hon James of Haverhill; m1829 Caroline Hutchins of Bath Upper Village; liv Swiftwater; ch Ira E, Mary J m James Williams, Horace J, Laura E m O J Gifford of Haverhill, 1 son; NH-0007-148
Nathaniel; m twice; liv CT, Hanover NH; ch Polly m George Perkins, Nathaniel Jr m Joann Perkins, Marhsall; NH-0007-318
Nathaniel Jr; s/o Nathaniel; m Joann Perkins; liv Hanover NH; ch John Marshall, 1 dau m Asa Camp, 1 dau m Cyrus Camp, 1 dau m Lysander T Woodward of Hanover, 2 dau; NH-0007-318

WOOLSON,
Amos; s/o Elijah gs/o Asa b1727 ggs/o Joseph b1699 gggs/o Joseph b1677; m Hannah D Temple; liv Lisbon NH; ch 1 son b1831 dy, John b1832, Hon Augustus A b1835, Charles E b1836, Mary R b1838, Jennie L b1841; NH-0007-449
Thomas; bc1626; liv Cambridge MA, Watertown; ch Joseph b1677; NH-0007-449

WOOSTER,
Hazen F; b1846; m Chestina H Hutchinson d/o Hoah B; liv Maidstone VT, E Canaan NH; ch David H, 2 sons; NH-0007-231

WORCESTER,
Joseph E LLD; b1784 s/o Jesse & Sarah Parker of Bradford NH; m1841 Amy Elizabeth McKean d/o Joseph DD; liv Hollis NH,

WORCESTER (continued)
Salem & Andover & Cambridge MA; NH-0002-455
Samuel T; b1804 s/o Jesse & Sarah Parker; m1835 Mary F C Wales d/o Samuel Esp of Stoughton MA; liv Norwalk OH, Weymouth MA, Nashua NH; NH-0002-39
Rev Thomas; b1768 s/o Noah & Lydia Taylor of Hollis; m1792 Deborah Lee; liv Salisbury NH; NH-0004-606
WORTHEN,
Daniel; m Harriet Shepard d/o Jacob; liv Amesbury MA, Holderness NH; ch Daniel C, 2 others; NH-0007-396
George W; b1822; m Eveline Dustin of Claremont NH; liv Enfield, Lebanon NH; ch 4 sons, 2 dau; NH-0007-423
WORTHLEY,
Alonzo H; b1839 s/o Moses & Cynthia Marshall; m1865 Ruth Perkins d/o D B; liv Hebron NH; ch Alonzo H b1867; NH-0007-389
Hiram M; b1848 s/o Moses & Cynthia Marshall; m Sarah G Leavitt d/o Gillman; liv Hebron NH; ch Lena Blanche b1879; NH-0007-389
Moses; b1807; m Cynthia Marshall; liv VT, Hebron NH; ch Alonzo H b1839 m Ruth Perkins, Hiram M b1848 m Sarah G Leavitt, Mary Ella m James Gill Patrick of Bristol; NH-0007-389
WRIGHT,
Col Carroll D; b1840 s/o Rev Nathan R; liv Dunbarton NH, Reading MA; NH-0004-301
David; s/o John; m Lydia Tenney; liv Hanover NH; ch David Jr m Irena Ladd of Haverhill; NH-0007-319
Capt Joshua; liv Woburn MA, Hollis, W Dunstable; ch Lemuel, Uriah; NH-0002-439
WYMAN,
Daniel; s/o Timothy & Elizabeth Shattuck; m Louisa Moore; ch Squiers Clement, Louisa Maria, Ann Sophia, Laura Fidelia, Andrew Jackson, Martin Van Buren, Loella Matilda; NH-0002-386
Ebenezer; s/o Timothy & Elizabeth Shattuck; m Mehitable

WYMAN (continued)
Clement & m Betsy Stanly; ch/o Betsy - Elizabeth, Mehitable, John S, Charles, Daniel dy, Abigail Dow, Daniel, Almira, Almena, Moses; NH-0002-386
Timothy; m Elizabeth Shattuck; liv Deering, Hollis; ch Timothy m Abigail Dow, Nathan m --- Stuart & m ? & m Patty Howard, Elizabeth m Jesse Emery, Ebenezer m Mehitable Clement & m Betsy Stanly, Sybil m Jonathan Sargent, Reuben m Rhoda Hartwell, Abel dy, Sally m Josiah Killom, Polly m Isaac Merrill, Hannah m John Smith, Daniel m Louisa Moore; NH-0002-385
Timothy; s/o Timothy & Elizabeth Shattuck; m Abigail Dow; ch Lot dy, Stephen Dow m Ursula Forsaith; NH-0002-386


-X-


-Y-


YEATON,
James; m Annie R Crockett d/o --- & S Rebecca Randall; ch John C, Helen E P, George H; NH-0004-471
YORK,
Daniel G; b1818 s/o Solomon & Patience Giles; m1842 Betsey P Nudd b1819 of Kensington; liv Brentwood & Deerfield & Kensington NH; ch Oren S dy, Mary A b1848 m Arthur W Gooch, John W b1850 m Marcia E Godfrey; NH-0003-364
Jasper Hazen MD; b1816 s/o John of Lee NH; liv S Boston MA, Dover NH; NH-0003-850
John W; b1850 s/o Daniel G & Betsey P Nudd; m1871 Marcia E Godfrey b1854 d/o Jonathan & Theodatie of Hampton; liv Kensington; ch Grace G, Frank N, Katie E dy, Arthur S, Mary F; NH-0003-364
Manson R; b1832 s/o Stephen of Holderness; m1861 Catherine Fadden d/o James & Emily

YORK (continued)
Rowles of Franconia NH; liv Plymouth NH; ch Orissa A, Effie E; NH-0007-593
Solomon; m Patience Giles; liv Allenstown NH, ME; ch Daniel G b1818 m Betsey P Nudd, 7 others; NH-0003-364
YOUNG,
Aaron; s/o William & Charity Howe; m Lydia Daniels d/o Clement & Esther Danielson; liv Barrington NH; ch Col Andrew b1827 m Susan Elizabeth Miles, Esther m John E Buzzell of Durham NH, Sophia A m George S Hanson of Ashland MA, Hon Jacob D, Aaron, George W; NH-0003-872
Col Andrew H; b1827 s/o Aaron & Lydia Daniels of Barrington NH; m1853 Susan Elizabeth Miles d/o Col Tichenor Miles of Madbury NH; liv Dover; ch Andrew Hamilton b1856 dy, Mary Hale b1861, Haldimand Putnam b1863, Richard Batchelder b1869; NH-0003-872
Benjamin; liv Dover, Strafford; ch Elder Winthrop b1753, 6 others; NH-0003-703
Charles Edward; b1821 s/o Israel & Esther Stevens; m1848 Sarah D Gilcrest b1816 d/o David & Sarah Davis of Londonderry; liv Londonderry; NH-0003-586
Gen Ira; b1794 (b1797) s/o Col Samuel of Lisbon NH; mc1836 Mrs Sarah D F Smith wid/o John A of Cuba d/o Mills Deforest of Lemington VT; liv Bath, Colebrook & Lancaster NH; ch Mary, Capt Harry D F, Richard O; NH-0004-245, NH-0007-61
Israel; s/o James of Manchester; m1819 Esther Stevens; liv Manchester, Londonderry; ch Charles Edward b1821 m Sarah D Gilcreast; NH-0003-586
James; m Margaret Sloan; liv SCO, Philadelphia; ch William m Charity Howe; NH-0003-872
Dr John; b1739; m twice; liv Peterborough NH, Worcester MA; ch 10; NH-0002-663
Jonathan; ch Stephen, John F, 6 others; NH-0003-703
Parley; s/o Peleg & Ruth Albee;

YOUNG (continued)
m Susan B Lawton of Fall River MA; liv Grafton NH; ch Albert L, Charles, Harriet, Ella, 7 others; NH-0007-286
Peleg; s/o Othaniel & Esther Phillips; m Ruth Albee of Mendon MA; ch Parley m Susan B Lawton, 6 others; NH-0007-286
Priest; b1797; m1818 Mary Oakes; liv Lisbon, Franconia; ch Eliza, Adaline, George, Harriet, Charles B, Herbert, Adelaide, 5 others; NH-0007-270
YOUNGMAN,
David MD; b1817; liv Peterborough NH, Winchester & Boston MA; NH-0002-668

--Z--

INDEX

All surnames mentioned within the text of another surname are indexed here. For example, references to the Abbott surname on page 1 of the text are not indexed, but all references to Abbott not found under that heading are indexed. Women are indexed under maiden as well as married names whenever known. References without given names are listed with ---, and some are listed under titles (such as Dr, Prof, Hon, Elder, etc.) without the ---.

AMES, Alice 83 Clara 45 David
144 Emily N 174 Fisher 174
Martha Jane 45 Mary 148 Mellia
243 Myra 248 249 Persis 23
Phebe 144 Ruth 144 145 Samuel
249 Capt Thomas R 23
AMROSE, --- 122
AMSDEN, G P 69 Lucinda D 69 Mary
55 Dr W W 55
ANABLE, --- 170
ANDERSON, Alexander 110 159
Daniel 180 Frances M 110
Francis M 110 Hugh 180 Jane 180
Margaret 179 Martha 159 Sarah
180 William 179
ANDREWS, Alice 132 Almira R 118
Elizabeth 58 133 140 George H
159 Hattie 37 Isaac Esq 160
Israel 132 J N 159 Janet Cole
79 Julia C 139 Lavinia Hobart
201 Lucy 160 Mary 34 Mary E 50
159 Nathan 200 Samuel 201 Susie
A 159
ANGIERS, Mary M 243
ANIN, Ruth 5 Sally 5
ANNIS, J B 31 Maria 31
APPLEBEE, Rev Warren 9
APPLETON, Harriet 4 Rev Joseph
239 Josette Alcock 4 Mary 236
Mary A 198 Mary Ann 239 240 Hon
William 239
ARBUCKLE, --- 160
ARLIN, Mary A 172
ARLING, Abigail M 157 Augustus A
157
ARMINGTON, Ellen 246
ARMOR, Margaret 269
ARMSTRONG, Minerva 75 Olive 245
ARNOLD, Abigail 72 Hon Jonathan
72 Robert 199
ARTHUR, Rev William DD 241
ARTLER, Ellen 270
ARWIN, Elizabeth 50
ASH, Betsey 137 David 137
Mehitable 183 Reuben 183
ASHMEAD, Sarah P 213
ATHERTON, Catherine 165 166
Clarinda 255 Hon Joshua 165 236
Lydia 119 Rebecca Wentworth 236
ATKINS, Lucinda 244
ATKINSON, Hon D C 248 Frances
261 Isabel S 233 John 234
Josephine B 105 106 Dr L W 233
Mahala 248 Mehitable 248 Sally
233 234 Theodore Jr 261
ATTWILL, Mrs Ann 96 Mrs Ann
Burrows 94 102
ATWELL, Bridget 129
ATWOOD, Abigail 193 Dolly 205
Ellen W 187 Hannah 53 Imogene B
244 Jacob 114 John 205 Joseph

187 Lizzie M 25 Mahala 50 Moses
91 Nancy 120 Rebecca H 18 Ruth
267 Sally 197 Sarah 114 128
AUGUSTA, Harriet 5
AUSTIN, A E 105 Mrs Amelia Allen
88 Ann 32 Anna 31 David 249
Eliza 242 Elizabeth 253 Hannah
263 James 253 Joseph 237
Lucretia 82 Lydia 263 Mary
Wilkins 249 Mercy H 105
AVERILL, Alma 138 Anna 138
Bernard 152 Betsy 131 Ebenezer
138 Elijah 29 Harriet 152 Lois
F 77 Relief 29 Sophia 152
AVERY, --- 131 Anne Eliza 247
Caroline 259 Caroline S 1
Daniel 59 Elizabeth 131 Hannah
69 Huldah 68 167 Ira 1 Jacob
273 Jemima 273 Maj John 259
Louisa 22 Mary 32 46 Mary Moody
247 Olive Light 59 Rosa B 263
Rosilla 23 Ruth 30 Ruth B 29
Samuel 46 247
AYER, Hannah 26 258 John 258
Joseph 201 Lucy M 188 Mary
Greene 99 Nancy 188 Hon Richard
H 99 Roena F 79 Walter H 188
AYERS, Augustine R 145 Charles
178 Clara Maria 145 Deborah 259
Mary 262 Mary E 178 Mehitable
197 Orinda 202 203 William 259
AYRES, Jonathan 6 Mehitable 197
Myra 5 6

BAAB, Margaret 205
BABB, Alice 92 93 James 205
Jemima 93 Margaret 205 206
William 93
BABCOCK, Mary Webster 218 Paul
Esq 218
BABSON, Adelia 148 Isaac 129
Mehitable 129
BACHELDER, --- 249 Ancie 268
Betsy 8 9 Clarisa 249 Clarissa
9 Cyrus T 9 Dorothy 227
Elizabeth 30 72 Hannah E H 185
Dea Harmon E 249 Henry F 151
Josiah 147 Laura 172 Laura A
171 Lorenzo 78 Lydia S 151
Marion 151 Mary 172 Mary E 9
Nancy 256 257 Nettie P 238 239
Sally 147 Susan 78 Col
Zephaniah 171 Zephaniah 172
BACHELDOR, Amos 30 Harriet S 27
30
BACHELOR, --- 173 Ruth 173
BACHILOR, --- 218 Rev Stephen 9
218
BACHOP, Jane 234
BACON, Annie A 263 Henry E 101
Jane Appleton 101 Louisa 54

Martha M 38 Palemia 222 Sarah
Hawes 270
BADGER, --- 133 Hannah 93 1 97
207 Hannah Pearson 52 Jennie 8
Gen Joseph 52 93 Hon Joseph Sr
52 Joseph 1 90 Judith 10 47 51
52 189 1 90 Ruth 51 Sarah 106
107 1 90 Sophronia 84 Stephen C
84 Susan 133 156 Gov William 52
William 107
BAER, Bernhard 236
BAGLEY, Coziah 248 David 166
Harriet 166 Nancy 72 Rhoda 38
Susan 28 29 30
BAILEY, --- 161 Abbie 181 Abel
61 Addie T 35 Alfreda 61 Betsey
52 Cyrus 119 Daniel 2 7 David
43 Edwin 121 Edwin M 162 Elias
263 Eliza 232 Elizabeth 2 Elsie
163 164 Elvira 161 Emeline 121
Emery 119 Emery 207 Emma R 99
Enos 265 Etta 1 91 Etta M 1 91 G
H 35 Georgia 121 Hannah 1 52 61
Henry H 181 Herbert Esq 243 Maj
Isaac 99 Isaac H 1 91 Rev Jacob
259 James 234 Joanna 213 Josiah
34 Judith 265 Lizzie 1 91 Louisa
119 175 Luella 162 Lura L 263
Lydia M 207 Maria 43 Maria A 34
Maria M 1 91 Martha 80 119 Mary
43 161 173 Mary Anna 99 Moses
66 Nancy 161 Nathan 1 93 Orlando
121 Osman 80 Pamelia 119 Phebe
1 93 Polly C 140 Rachel 204
Rebecca 1 44 77 78 Richard 52
Sally 259 Sarah 176 234 259
Sarah A 201 Solomon 161 Sophia
255 Sophia F 255 Susan 2 7 66
Walter 213 William L 1 91
BAILY, Clarissa M 134
BAIN, James 221 Lucy 221
BAKER, --- 209 Abigail 248 26 9
Abigail B 248 Adaline F 203
Adis 134 Angeline 57 Asenath
247 Maj Benjamin 142 Chastina L
123 Col Moses 55 Capt David 26 9
Col Davis 142 Deborah Davis 142
Dorcas 72 82 Elizabeth 267
Esther J 134 Eunice 230 F W 126
Frances O 195 Hannah 142 20 9
Hepsibeth 17 James 1 96 267
James A 152 Jane 1 96 Jesse 267
John H 258 Judith 267 Julia 26 9
Lois 23 Louisa U 258 Lucy 1 46
236 Mark 248 Mary 75 142 Molly
55 Hon Moses 203 Polly 245
Rebecca 55 Ruth 82 S H 123
Samuel S 134 Sarah 267 Sarah F
126 Stella L 247 Capt Thomas
230 William 247
BALCH, --- 89 Abigail 16 Eliza

215 Julia 146 Mary 89 Nancy 7 4
Samuel 16
BALDWIN, Alger 155 Amanda
Malvina 225 226 Betsey 21
Charles 139 Edward F 125 Eliza
155 Eunice 124 125 Fannie H 180
Frank H 180 Hannah 3 Dea Nahum
225 Samuel 21 Sarah 125 Sarah A
125 Sarah P 139
BALES, Charles 37 Mary Ann 37
BALL, Bettie 6 Laura A 107 Mary
1 99 200 Phebe 188 S F 107
BALLARD, Mary 110 Penelope 1
BALLOU, Achsah 66
BANCROFT, Emily 18 Fanny 167 168
J S 18 Nancy 172 Nancy M 172
Pesson 172
BANFIELD, Joanna 41
BANKS, Ann 18 57 Fanny 18 Joseph
18 Mary 204
BARBER, Catharine 89 90
Elizabeth 271 Capt John 79 Mary
93 Miriam 79 Sarah W 2
BARKER, --- 35 53 Abigail S 180
Alma 7 Anna 169 Benjamin 7
Eliza 55 Elizabeth 149
Elizabeth L 21 Emeline 161 Dea
Ephraim 26 Gilman 161 Isaac 180
Jane 55 Jared 24 Josiah H 104
Judith 57 58 Levi 149 Louisa
184 Lucy 24 Martha 35 Mary 149
Mary Manning 26 Sarah 161
BARLETT, Anne S 16 Hannah 65
Henry C 39 Joseph A 48 Lavinia
K 65 Levi 65 Mabel M 39 Mary S
R 48
BARNARD, Almira 108 Anna 43
Arvilla 89 Charles 89 Currier
1 99 Dorothy 1 98 1 99 Elizabeth
17 George 108 John 43 Maria H
14 Maria H 140 Mary 141 Mary J
168 Morrill 168 Nancy 168 Rhoda
271 Samson 1 99
BARNES, Alice 170 Amos 78 Ann 25
155 Anna 37 Betsey 37 Buel 37
Electa 4 Elizabeth 37 Dr Enoch
B 8 Hannah 166 270 Joanna 96
John M 270 Mary 1 95 Polly 78
Rachel 221 Lt Reuben 96 Reuben
155 166 Sally 159 160 Susan R 8
William L 37
BARNET, Mary 141
BARNETT, Nehemiah 126 Sally 126
BARNEY, --- 15 Alanson W 1 46
Aramintha 164 Ellen F 132 John
214 Savalla 214 Serepta 270
BARNHAM, Susanna 130
BARNUM, Rev S W 153 Rev Samuel H
153 Susan Paulina 153
BARR, Mary H 243
BARRELL, Abby 26 Charles C 26

BARRETT, Dora Everett 236 Isabel
38 Joseph 236 Julia 151 Lucinda
246 Luther 38 Lydia 160 Mary
236 Sarah 244
BARRON, Abigail 85 Dolly 15
Martha V 69 Solomon 15
BARROWS, --- 127 Arvilla 179
Asahel 179 E P 127 Lydia S 269
Rachel 82 William G 269
BARSTOW, Ariannah S 267
Arieannah S 224 Betsey 161
Emily A 173 174 Ezekiel 54
Hannah 174 Joshua 174 Mary 54
Mary J 244 Thomas A 244
BARTHOLOMEW, Anna 196
BARTLET, Abiah 52 Jane 171
Johanna 52 Joseph 52
BARTLETT, --- 147 Abigail 36 156
Anna 154 156 B F 36 Betsey 34
135 136 263 Betsy 154 Caroline
147 Charlotte 99 Daniel 69
Daniel Jr 156 Dea David 206
Dolly 254 Dorothy 256 Ebenezer
252 Eleanor 17 Elinor 16
Elizabeth 59 135 Erastus H 43
Esther 156 Evan 59 Dr Ezra 21
George E 107 Greely 109 Hannah
109 193 Hannah Thomas 61 Hattie
I 36 Huldah 69 Isaac 135 Joanna
206 Johanna 138 Col John 154
John 263 Jonathan 193 Joseph 39
Gov Josiah 21 36 111 Hon Josiah
36 Laura 21 Lois 252 Lucy 154
Lusylvia 84 252 Lydia 226 Maria
P 82 Martha 206 Martha A 107
Mary 17 111 206 Miriam 36 78
Parker 16 Dr Peter 99 Polly 254
Rhoda 39 Ruth 69 Sally 25 219
Sarah 43 109 154 Solomon 109
154 Sukey 78 Susan 107
BARTON, Bezaleel 204 Hannah 178
204 Lucy 256
BASS, David 79 Polly 79
BASSET, Daniel 109 Huldah 109
BASSETT, Huldah 109
BATCHELDER, --- 95 96 Abigail 74
Abraham 174 Almira 49 Ann 57
Ann A 117 Anna 150 Benjamin 258
Betsey 57 61 174 193 Charlotte
45 Dea David 150 David S 117
Dolly 68 Dr 51 Ebenezer 49 Dea
Elisha 95 Eliza A 100 Elizabeth
18 219 Ella E 105 Emery 68
Fanny C 57 Hannah 202 Increase
100 Jane M 208 John 18 Jonathan
157 Dea Joseph 130 Laura 172
Laura M 186 Lydia 46 68 Martha
B 51 Mary 68 81 172 Mary M 5
Mehitable A 53 207 Molly 248
Moses 74 Nathan 53 Nathaniel
193 Olive 174 219 Otis 208

Patience 193 Peace 53 Phebe 130
Polly 76 S 36 Sally 18 157
Samuel 73 Sandborn 68 Sarah 73
157 Simeon 57 Susan 100 258
Theodate 95 Zephaniah 172
BATCHELDOR, Anna 149
BATCHELLOR, --- 27 Stillman 27
BATEY, Fanny 57
BATTELLE, Lucy 146
BAXTER, Abigail 2
BAYLEY, Rev Abner 141 Elizabeth
168 Judith 84 Lavinia 141
BEACH, Anna 155 Heman 155 Rispah
5
BEACHAM, Abigail Ann Caroline
207 Asa 207 Eunice 28 George A
37 Mary Frances 37
BEAMAN, --- 152 Abigail 152 Lucy
73
BEAN, --- 228 Ann N 250 Anna 94
205 Ben 192 Rev Beniah 13
Benjamin 23 83 Charles H 185
Charles W 84 Charlotte 214
Daniel 249 Rev David 205
Deborah C 23 Dorothy 113 Ella S
146 Emma 106 107 Farmer 228
George 59 Hannah 50 Dr J Walter
146 James 23 Joseph 53 222 Levi
172 Lizzie 169 Louisa 145 Lydia
H 222 Margaret 9 Martha E 185
Mary 23 59 172 Mrs 1 Priscilla
192 Sally 146 Sarah 83 Sarah
Collins 222
BEASOM, --- 89 Persis 89
BECK, --- 220 221 Abigail 225
John 225 Lucy 225
BECKET, Mary 234
BEDEE, Daniel S 81 Irene 85
Laura E 81 Mary 85 Taylor 85
BEDEL, Ann Smith 155 Annie 179
Hazen 155
BEDELL, Charles W 195 Helen 152
Mary 195 Rosanna H 82 William
152
BEECHER, Elizabeth 97 Esther 168
Frances 97 Laban 97 Sarah 183
BEEDE, Aaron 133 Anna 104 132
133 268 Elijah 104 Harriet 39
210 Horatio 96 Jane R 104
Jonathan 268 Mary 39 Mary Ann
91 Mehitable 268 Moses 91
Phoebe 207 Thomas 39
BEEMIS, Lucy 242
BELCHER, Charlotte M 266 Martha
H 78
BELDEN, Emily A 42 Haynes W Esq
42 Lizzie J 44 S W 44
BELKNAP, Burke 121 E Jenette 260
Eunice 252 Helen 121 Nathaniel
252 William 260
BELL, --- 202 Betsey G 13 Carrie

E 59 Charles U 202 Elizabeth W
202 Hattie P 260 Helen M 202
Hugh 13 271 J L 260 Gov John
182 Letitia 75 Mary 45 Nancy 13
271
BELLOWS, Catharine 21 Eliza 3
Elizabeth 17 Hon Henry A 3 Mrs
Sarah 126 William J 3
BEMIS, Amarintha 7 Lulu 178 179
BENEDICT, Ephraim 57
BENJAMIN, E M Esq 121 Jessie B
121
BENN, Etta M 197
BENNETT, Betsy 50 Emily 152
Eunice 231 Jane 65 Mary 159 Mrs
Ruth 105 106 Stephen W 152
BENNING, Mary 229 230
BENSON, Rev Almon 146 Julitta
146
BENT, Hannah W 196 Martha 166
BERRY, --- 92 Abigail 28 29 74
Alsonson 172 Charles F 65
Elizabeth 74 Elizabeth D 65
Emma J 1 Josephine 38 Judith 92
Louisa 228 Mary 244 Mrs Mary
172 Mary Abbie 244 Mary J 132
Elder Nathan 244 Nathan 42
Rachel 92 S P 132 Sally J 42
Sarah 252 Sarah J 42 Tamson 22
Dea Thomas 22 Thomas 149
Woodbury 38
BEVERLEY, Julia Etta 102
BEVERLY, Julia Etta 102
BEVINS, Mary 189 190 213 Polly
189 190 213
BIATHROW, Frank 135
BICKFORD, Alfred Porter 108 Dr
Alphonzo 28 Anah 264 Bridgett
98 Fannie 28 Hannah 69 Hannah B
252 John 69 98 John A 192 Mary
91 Nathan 252 Rebeckah 156
Susan 245 Susan E 192 Thomas 98
BICKNEL, Amanda 213
BIGELOW, Elizabeth 238 John 238
Mary 238 Mrs H A 161
BILLINGS, Candace 270 Marcia 249
BINGHAM, Eliza Isabella 273
Elsea 97 Hon George A 273
Jeremiah 103 Lemuel 97 Lydia
103 Mary 231 Orinda 97
BIRDIN, Nancy 112
BISBEE, Drusilla M 46 Levi 176
246 Lydia 246 Melvina 176 Sarah
T 161
BISHOP, Sarah 237
BISSELL, Anna 155 Aurelia 26 75
Eluthera Malvina 245 Isaac 245
BIXBY, --- 87 Betsey 55 Dorothy
160 Elizabeth W 136 Joel 265
Maria 35 Mary 64 Samuel 136
Susan 265

BLACK, Frank 169 Martha 37 Sarah
130
BLACKMAN, Adam 205 Betsey 205
Eunice 15 Nancy 205
BLACKMER, Ellen E 73 Orlando C
73
BLAINER, --- 4
BLAIR, Eliza 72 Hepsibah P 171
Jane 225 John L 7 Lois 12
Louisa C 2 Mary 159 Hon
Montgomery 272 Sarah E 7 Sarah
E 72 Walter 2 Judge Walter 72
William H 12
BLAISDEL, Abigail 221 Mary 142 W
D 142
BLAISDELL, --- 53 Abigail 53 186
187 Abra 64 Adeline F 64
Charlotte 216 Hon Daniel 216
James 186 Joseph W 185 Martha
133 Mary E 185 Moses 64 Sally
185 Zenas 133
BLAKE, --- 137 Abigail 89 90 164
Abigail D 25 Albert Jr 164
Bathsheba 24 Betsy 35 Clarissa
268 David 169 Deborah 81 Dolly
14 Elvira 142 Emeline 135 Frank
262 George B 142 Gideon 135
Hannah 151 169 Hannah E 140 141
Jasper 81 Jeremiah Esq 249
Jethro 14 Johanna 135 Judith
171 218 219 Louisa A 249 Louisa
H 87 Lucy 83 Lydia 251 Marion F
191 Martha 251 Mary A 207 Moses
24 Philemon 251 Polly 82
Roswell 69 Sally 24 Sarah E 69
T P 175
BLAKESLE, John 245 Lucy Ann 245
BLAKESLEE, Bathsheba 24 Caroline
146 Climena 203 H F 146 John 24
Sally 24
BLAKESLY, Betsey 187 Mary 190
BLAKSLEE, --- 143 Josephine W
143
BLANCHARD, --- 44 131 Abigail
131 Augustus 132 Betsey 43
Catharine H 132 133 Clarissa A
142 Daniel 210 Capt Ebenezer
142 Ianthe 210 Lucy 43 Mrs Lucy
269 Orissa 82 Pamelia A 69 70 S
Stillman 58 Susan E 58 Sylvania
M 183
BLANDIN, Jane C 183 John Pierce
Esq 227 Mary E 227 W B 183
BLISS, --- 126 Dolly P 106
George W 106 John W 106 Louise
154 Lucinda B 174 Mary 190
Nancy B 106 Sarah 1
BLODGET, Bridget 194 James 194
BLODGETT, --- 194 A Maria 127
Abigail C 127 Atassa 103 Delia
194 Eben 166 Rev Ebenezer 103

Eliza 135 Elizabeth B 258
Hannah 1 96 Hannah 26 4 Rev
Julius C 127 Marcena 135 Roancy
F 112 Rose 167 Sally 111 Sally
263 Warren 258
BLOOD, --- 63 Abigail 1 91 Abigal
1 91 Betsey 204 235 Catherine
129 Henry T I 155 Isaac 235
Julia A 35 Martha 43 Mary 58
Monroe 26 4 Ophelia 26 4 Rebecca
63 Sarah 155 Sarah Ann 5
BLY, John 103 Mary 175 176
Rebecca 103
BOARDMAN, Adeline 271 Elizabeth
185 John 162 Laura A 162 Mary
162 Mary Webster 110 Col
William 110
BODGE, James 92 Mollie 92
BOIS, Hannah 1 91
BOLEYN, Charlotte A 186
BOND, Clara L 47 Elvina 169 Jane
243
BONNEY, Dr C F 44 Emily 144
Hattie O 44
BONZIE, Mary 48
BOODEY, --- 40 Azariah 254
Hannah 254 Zechariah 254
BOOES, Hannah 1 91
BORDEN, Sarah 251
BORNTON, Mary 4 5
BOSWELL, James 161 Lucy F 161
Mary 161 Moses P 161
BOSWORTH, Abigail 81 Alice 135
136
BOULD, Polly 81
BOULTER, Grace 205 Lydia 251
Mary 53 205 Nathaniel 205
BOURNS, Hon Jesse 20 Mary
Augusta 20
BOUTON, Harriet S 182 Rev
Nathaniel DD 1 92 Rev Dr 182
Sarah Cilley 1 92
BOUTWELL, Mary A 116 Maj
Nehemiah 116 Reuben 103
BOWEN, Abigail 228 Fanny 164
Peggy 60 Sarah 125
BOWERS, Chloe 130 Clara 159 Capt
Francis 130 James 243 Col
Joseph 237 Mary 161 Mary A 110
Mary G 237 Nancy 243
BOWLES, --- 15 56 223 Abigail 56
261 Mrs Almina 126 Esther 187
Leonard 109 Levina 126 Maria
261 Maria E 182 Miles 58 Rev
Nathaniel 223 Sally 15 Vienna
109
BOWMAN, Abel 266 Mrs E M 85
Elizabeth 115 266 Ella 207
George 77 Hannah 210 Hannah F
266 Lydia 134 Maria 77 Walter
210 William B 207

BOYCE, Nettie E 80
BOYD, --- 151 168 184 208 Abby C
176 Charlotte 184 Hon George
225 Harriet 153 Mary 208 Submit
225
BOYDEN, Dr Joseph 240 Martha 240
BOYDON, Mary 249
BOYLSTON, Susanna 2
BOYNTON, Alfred L 114 Almira 57
Eliza C 85 Ella L 57 James W 57
Louisa 57 Mary 203 Sarah J 114
BRACE, Judith 12
BRACKENBURY, Mary 91 267
BRACKETT, Adino N 259 Ambrose S
29 Betsey 268 Carrie A 167
Deborah 259 260 Elizabeth 78
Frances I 183 Isaac 183 James
78 259 Joshua 1 98 Mrs Julia
Ross 77 Martha 259 260 Martha P
1 98 Mary Polly Wiggin 259 Nancy
29
BRADBURY, Dolly 106 E W 106 Jane
249 Mary 165
BRADFORD, Aurelia 75 Dr Austin
75 Eliza 206 Elizabeth 258 Lucy
3 4 Lucy A 75 Rebecca 267
BRADLEY, --- 266 Adeline 238
Adeline 242 Ann Matilda 3
Apphia 85 Betsey 115 116
Clarisa 8 9 Dorcas 242 Ebenezer
116 Ella J 263 Emily E 218
Isaac 3 Jane 167 Joshua 242
Lizzie 266 Luther 263 Ruth 101
Sara 116 Sarah 19 215
BRADSTREET, --- 73 Louisa
Catharine 73 Rebecca 82
BRAGG, James Frye 189 Sallie 189
Sarah M 189 Sarah Merrill 189
BRAIDON, Mary Ann 136 Robert 136
BRAINARD, Affie 1 Daniel 1 Rhoda
271
BRALEY, Emma L 125 Harriet M 102
Helen L 102 John W 102 Maria M
1 91 Sarah 1 91
BRAND, Ella F 82
BRAY, --- 1 95 Betsey 270 Ida 70
Jacob 270 John 1 95 Samuel L 70
BRECK, Emily 116 117
BREED, Amos 109 Annie 109 Lydia
A 96 William J 96
BREWER, A R 26 4 Margaret P 26 4
Mary 150 Thomas 150
BREWSTER, Betsey 121 Ebenezer
179 Elizabeth 1 94 George 122
Margaret 40 272 Mary 272 Peggy
122 Samuel 272 Susannah 17 9
BRIARD, Maria 37
BRICKETT, Abbie 254 Adelia W 118
Betsey 1 93 Dr G F 254 Jonathan
118 Lydia 118 Nancy 267
BRIDGE, Alice 258 Eunice 73

BRIDGEMAN, Henrietta 261
BRIDGES, --- 209 Anna 204
Elizabeth 209
BRIDGMAN, Charles 64 Elder Isaac
36 Julia 64 Theoda 36 37 138
BRIGGS, Mrs Dora J 84 Elizabeth
125 Lovina 93 Nathaniel 5
BRIGHAM, Capt Levi 101 Susan Ann
101 Wealthy C 117
BRINLEY, Deborah 89
BRITTON, --- 150 Mary 247 Hon
Silas 247
BROAT, Eliza 30
BROCK, --- 139 237 George W 92
Martha C 139 Sarah A 92
BROCKWAY, Erastus F 29 Hannah 29
John 80 Mary 80 Phebe 79
BRODHEAD, Elizabeth H 182 Rev
John 182
BROOKE, John R 238 Mary 238
BROOKS, --- 63 243 Addie 87
Annie 179 Charles 207 Dolly 266
Eliza A 63 Eliza E 263 Ella
Cora 147 Emeline R 12 Esther
266 267 Gardne 108 Hannah 152
Jemima 108 Jerusha 207 John 75
Hon John W 147 Kate J 264 Lucy
154 Mary 243 Mary A 234 Mary M
179 180 Rev Nahum 12 Samuel 179
Susan 75 William F 234
BROUGHTON, --- 167 Harriet 167
Mark 167
BROWER, Almera B 213 George 213
BROWN --- 4 29 66 231 Aaron 216
Abbie E 10 Abby C 18 Abigail 24
91 94 249 Adam 2 202 Albert 22
Amanda W 231 Ann 29 232 233 Ann
E 164 Anna 10 60 97 124 243
Anna M 159 Anna P 230 266 Anna
S 163 Anne E 164 Annie 234
Asenath 97 Bartlett S 226
Benjamin 73 160 Betsey 175
Betsy 193 Catherine 181
Catherine Babson 51 Clarissa 53
121 Cyrus L 18 Daniel 3 61
David 173 David A 6 Dora A 167
Drucilla 71 Dudley 121 Edmun 88
Electa 141 Elijah 258 Eliza 173
Eliza A 265 Eliza J 88
Elizabeth 28 29 74 Elizabeth W
151 Ephraim H 256 Eunice 7
Ezekiel 34 Fanny 67 68 143
Frank S 159 Garland 230 George
62 Hannah 84 173 226 Hannah
Sargent 84 Harriet 95 127 172
Harriet E 216 Helen A 6 Henry
133 Hon Hiram 231 Horace P 229
Ida 22 Irena 95 Isabella 160 Dr
J G 62 James 151 Jane 256 Janet
160 Jeremiah 173 Jesse 17
Joanna 164 John 26 95 177 231

John G 164 165 John S 10 212
Jonas 110 Dea Jonathan 49
Josiah 130 Judith 133 258 Julia
126 Langdon 163 Laura P 229
Levi 96 265 Louisa C Barrett 11
Louisa Frances 16 17 Lucretia
249 Lucretia B 111 Lucy 3 95
Lucy G 201 Luella J 256 Lydia
96 97 115 130 141 204 226 Lydia
V 207 Hon Manson S 266 Mara 212
Maria 83 Martha 41 106 Martha A
6 Mary 17 65 66 67 115 173 206
230 231 Mary Ann 49 Mary
Lawrence 34 Mary R 203
Mehitable 177 Moses 71 91 Moses
P 207 Myra A 212 Nancy 3 26 61
116 243 265 Nath 181 Nathan 203
Capt Nathan 203 Nellie M 8 9
Nicholas 230 Olive 245 246
Olive A 230 P M 135 Patience
205 206 230 231 Paul P 230
Persis 175 Persis H 98 Mrs
Phebe A 15 Polly 95 100 Rebecca
256 Rosetta C 62 S Augusta 207
Sabrina 156 Sally 39 202 203
Sarah 26 62 63 73 88 89 97 98
184 203 Sarah A 197 Sarah F 106
107 Sarah J 165 Sarah M 220
Silence 125 Stephen 184 226
Stephen T 97 243 Susan 2 202
Susan A 13 Susan M 31 Susan P 2
Susanna 73 130 258 Sybil 124
Sylvia A 197 Taft 29 Thomas 74
175 Thomas M 106 Vernelia S 110
William 111 124 265
BROWNE, Rev Arthur 154 Jane 154
Rebecca 10 Sarah A 138 Rev W W
138
BROWNELL, Frances Child 239
Frances Child 240 Phebe 102
BRUCE, Mary E 237 Thomas H 237
BRUMMER, George 233
BRUNSON, Azubah 140 Susanna 163
BRYANT, --- 199 Enoch 211
Hepzibah 211 Col J S 33 Jane C
171 Lenora J 35 Louise H 33
Phebe 264 Sarah 199 Susan 167
Capt Sylvanus 199
BUCK, Clarissa 35 N Della 37
Sally 65
BUCKINGHAM, Anna 60 John 60
BUCKLIN, Mrs Calista 31
BUCKMAN, Caroline 12 John 12 Gen
Edward 171 Edwards 259 Mary 171
Sally 259
BUEL, Asahel 59 Capt Benjamin
140 Emeline E 59 Lois 59 263
264 Minerva 140 Violetta 140
BUFFUM, Clara I 197 Frank 197
George 197 Peggy Almira 197
BUFTON, Mrs Myra B 204 Myra B

204
BUGBY, Amos 32
BULLARD, Caroline 21 Caroline E
216 Clarissa 3 Dana 244 Joel 3
John 216 Mary A 244 Ruth 267
Samson 21 Sarah 267
BULLOCK, Benjamin 74 187 Dolly
187 Jean 270 Mary 108 Philip
108 Sybil 74 187
BUMFORD, Abigail 74 156 Martha
35
BUNCHER, James 2 Mary Jane 2
BUNDY, Rebecca 161 Susan 12
BUNKER, Mary A 82 Paul 223 Peggy
223 Rebecca J 104
BUNTIN, James 178 Sarah 48 Sarah
J 178
BUNTON, Elizabeth 100 101
BURBANK, Abigail 241 Catherine
223 Eliza 263 Hattie 82 John 82
Judith 40 Lizzie Wheeler 45
Louise 199 200 Hon Robert I 45
Ruth A 82
BURBECK, Hannah B 255 James 255
Ruth 255
BURBEEN, Rev Joseph 255 Susannah
255
BURGESS, Dr 51 Mary C 51
BURLEIGH, Abigail 189 190 Alvin
Esq 186 Artemus Tirrell 210
Belinda 129 Christine S 23
Daniel R 23 Ellen M 42 43
Elvira 186 Eunice K 23 Harry W
33 Hollis 129 Isabella 3 Nannie
33 Ruhamah 155 Ruth 205 Samuel
205 Sarah 5 6 William 5
BURLEY, Capt Benjamin 45
Charlotte 265 Elizabeth Ann 45
Esther 265 Fannie E 53 54
Harrison G 54 John 129 Jonathan
179 Judith 190 Mary Jane 191
Nathaniel Jr 95 Phoebe 95 Sally
129 Sarah 115 Sarah C 179
Thomas 115
BURNAP, Orril 106
BURNHAM, Betsey 76 206 232
Chastina 271 David H 267 Dolly
D 267 Eliza W 253 Hannah 51 117
Hortense 34 Irene 89 90 Jacob
89 Jane 86 Louisa K 175 Mary
249 Moses W 175 Phebe 14 91
Pike G 249 Polly 249 Sarah 87
190 Solomon 44 Susanna 211
BURNS, Caroline 220 Charles 135
Eliza 255 Elizabeth 135 Mrs
Francis A 76 Maj John 145 Maria
L 160 Mary E 259 Dr Robert 220
259 Sarah 145 Thomas Esq 160
Hon William 259
BURNSIDE, Mrs 57 Mrs Sallie
Emery 209

BURPEE, Cora 38 Dolly 66 Dudley
38 Ellen F 85 Heman 66 Judith
53 Perley 53
BURRALL, John 133 Lydia 133
BURROWS, Ann 96 George 16 Lydia
16 Rebecca S 16
BURT, Rebecca 189 Rebecca 190
BURTON, Louisa Partridge 60 Col
Oliver 60
BUSH, Betsey 200 Hepsebeth 63
Lovina 117
BUSWELL, Abigail 156 157 Ann 246
Ann Elizabeth 116 Anne 246 Dr
Caleb 116 Eliza 116 Richard 184
246 Sally 205 Sarah F 184
BUTLER, Alice M 194 Dr Elijah
229 Elizabeth 61 Enoch 117 Rev
Henry 194 James 114 Jane 114
John 72 162 Lydia 162 Lydia F
229 230 232 Mary 162 Mary 270
Mary A 147 148 Rebecca 117
Sarah 71 72 Sarah N 168 Susan
117
BUTMAN, D H 35 Mary 35
BUTRICK, Achsa 257 Charles 257
BUTTERFIELD, Caroline 108 Desire
115 Desire 116 Emma E 146
George P 146 Hannah 159 Thomas
108
BUTTICK, Sarah E 180
BUTTRICK, Sally 81
BUXTON, Abbie 264 Daniel 264
BUZZEL, Mehitable 133
BUZZELL, Esther 274 Henry 69
John E 275 Sarah 82
BYER, John 10 Ladena 10
BYLES, Sarah 253

CALDON, Benjamin 170 Edwina 170
Martha 170
CALDWELL, Agnes 241 Elizabeth 92
Hannah 257 Jane 241 Mary 127
Rachel 272 Wallace 241
CALEF, Joseph 78 Mary 42 Miriam
77 78 79 William 42
CALKINS, Caroline G 41 104 105
211 Mehitabel 141 Mehitable 141
CALL, --- 43 Ann 109
CALLEY, David 107 Dorcas D 107
Jeremiah M 225 Louisa 57 Mary
225 Mary M 107 N S 57
CAMERON, Alice 83 John H 176
Sarah 176
CAMP, Asa 273 Cyrus 273 David
138 Esther 138 230 Sally 37
Theoda 138
CAMPBELL, --- 87 Agnes 231 Jane
4 Lewis A 135 Viola 135 William
231 Judge William 135 Wilson 4
CANFIELD, Hannah 230 Henry 119
Jerome 230

CANNEY, --- 247 Abigail 193
Aphia 19 Betsey 19 Emily 193
George C 193 James 19 Mary
Abbott 19 Mary Frances 19 Moses
B 19
CAPEN, Nancy 135
CARBARY, Catherine E 112
CARBEE, Sarah 152
CARGIL, Janet 45
CARHEN, Ann Elizabeth 150
CARLETON, C M 10 Dr Charles 39
Hannah 50 Kate Elizabeth 39
Margaret S 200 Mehitable 144
CARLISLE, Daniel 244 Elizabeth
244
CARLTON, Abby 201 Alice 202
David 45 Eliza 271 Elizabeth 63
Isaac 170 268 Jacob 234 James
63 Jane 45 John 45 273 John L
273 Lucy 234 Lucy Ann 69 Lydia
1 Malvina A 240 Margaret S 200
Maria 48 Mary 273 Peter 87
Phebe 17 Ralph 50 Rebecca 87
268 271 Sally 87 Sarah 170 234
268 Sophia 211 Timothy 87 211
271 Woodman 201 202
CARMON, Phebe 161 W F 161
CARNEY, Matthew 208 Sarah E 208
CAROLTON, Sally 45
CARPENTER, --- 172 Hon A P 242
Amy 207 Charles H 108 Clarissa
224 Daniel W 106 David Morrill
195 Electa Ann 108 Fanny 172
Frank P 25 Hannah 224 Jerusha
235 236 Josiah 74 Rev Josiah
224 Lillian 242 Mary 195 Miriam
55 Nora 25 Persis 106
CARR, Anna 205 269 Bradbury 205
Caroline L 37 Clara 105 106
Daniel 37 David S 114 Elizabeth
139 Elizabeth H 105 Ellen 137
Ellen M 143 Emma M 88 Frank 53
H F 137 Helen Frances 53 J K
143 Kate Elizabeth 37 Maria L
114 Mary 114 Mary Ann 220 Mary
Turner 139 Nathan 139 Robert
105 106 Robert D 105 Ruth 205
Stephen 269
CARROLL, Cerlania 98 99 207 John
P 98 Rachel 98
CARSON, Emma 201 George A 201
CART, Naomi 1
CARTER, Adeline S 173 Angeline
93 Betsey 113 Dexter Esq 247
Ephraim 173 Hannah D 139
Harriet Ella 247 John Jr 139
Margaret 139 Mary 256 Nancy 220
248 Susan 173
CARTLAND, Caroline 224 Moses A
224
CARY, Amanda 170 Benjamin W 252

George 39 Georgie E 252 Mary 39
CASE, Anna L 106 Ellen M 11 Mary
265 Mercy 270 Sarah 265
CASS, Augusta C 108 Betsey 87
Elva 71
CASWELL, A D 91 Abbie 91 Abraham
100 Angeline 270 Mrs Anna S 164
Charlotte 100 Polly 100 Ruth 69
CATE, --- 222 Eliza 94 95
Margaret 121 122 Sophia 122
Susanna 108 Polly 130
CATON, Mrs Sarah 166 167 168
CAVENDER, Annais 244
CAVERLY, Elizabeth 67 Elizabeth
O 92 Harriet A 252 John 25 Rev
John 92 Nancy 92 Mrs Nancy L
Smith 67 Rebecca Marquand 60
Sally 252 253 Dea Samuel 67 Z B
60
CAVERNO, Horace F 65 Rebecca B
65
CAWELL, Lucretia R 132
CENTER, Frederick L 160 Jennie F
160 Lucy 110 Salome V 110 206
Thomas 110
CHADBOURNE, Betsy 106 107 Dr 160
Martha 77 78 160 Dr William 77
CHADWICK, Betsy 4 Ida 28 L M 28
Olive A 255
CHALLIS, Almira 254 Betsey 221
Hannah 221 Thomas 221 Timothy
254
CHAMBERLAIN, Abigail 35 112
Clara C 187 Edmund 52 169
Ephraim 164 George 259 Mary 52
164 Molly 219 Rebecca 180
Roxanna 241 Susan 169 Sybil 107
CHAMBERLIN, John 77 Julia A E
233 Mary 215 Phineas 215
Rebecca 40 Tamson A 152
CHAMPION Levi 261 Mary A 261
Nancy B 261
CHAMPNEY, Judge Ebenezer 206
Elizabeth 206
CHANDLER, Almira 267 Amos 151
Arabella 208 Betsey 263 Charles
202 Christabel 101 Clementine
264 Daphne 263 Elizabeth
Downing 208 Ellen 76 Emily 128
Fanny R 163 Hon George B 163
Georgiana 202 Hannah 1 229 230
232 Hazen 263 Henry 66 71 Henry
H 264 Capt Isaac 208 J H 128
John 76 Joseph 267 Laura A 101
Laura A 105 Levee 127 151 Lois
144 Lucretia 202 Lucy 168 Molly
77 Nathan 14 Nathaniel L 101
104 Oliver 162 Phebe M 66 Ruth
151 Sallie 189 Sally 14 155 156
Samantha S 144 Sarah 120 121
202 Timothy 144 W 202 William

156
CHAPIN, Hannah 1 90 John 17 9
Nathaniel 189 Sarah 179 Sarah
Abbee 189
CHAPMAN, Almira 219 Almira J 213
217 219 Andrew McC 1 96 Huldah
131 Jeremiah 229 Joseph 131
Lucinda 138 Mary 137 138 Mary A
195 1 96 Mary E 229 Nathaniel 22
Rebecca 65 Sallie J 22 Sarah M
162 Thomas 219
CHAPPOTIN, Leon 53
CHARLES, --- 169 Joan M 201
Lyman 201 Sarah 169
CHARLTON, Maria 266
CHASE, --- 33 Abbie M 245
Abigail 26 9 Abram 84 1 93
Adaline 11 Amos 181 Baruch 26 8
Belinda 117 Betsey S 118
Charles 62 Charles K 159
Charlotte 117 Clara N 218 David
1 91 Dorothy 113 160 Dudley 1 93
Rev Ebenezer 1 91 Edward 72 1 91
255 Eliza 72 160 1 91 255
Elizabeth 38 39 92 205 206
Ellen 26 8 Maj Francis 160 H S
29 Hannah 10 9 117 Hannah P 181
Hannibal 137 Harriet L 85 217
Judge Henry B 113 Herod 10 9 Ira
A 245 Irena 78 Jane 236 John
10 9 220 227 John Esq 220 John
Jr 178 Jonathan E 78 Judge
Jonathan T 1 Kexiah 1 93 Laura A
1 Hon Leonard 256 Lucy 129
Lydia 227 264 Lydia A 43 M
Almeda 227 Margaret A 160
Marinda 137 Martha 11 Martha E
154 Mary 11 72 113 114 134 138
1 91 1 93 214 255 264 267 Mary A
2 9 Mary Abbie 159 Mary Isabella
256 Mehitable 105 Mehitable
Ambrose 49 Melinda 1 94 Moody
154 Moses 92 1'29 Nancy 75 88
26 9 Nathaniel 108 Oliver 117
Parker 75 Patience 73 Patty 16
Rev Paul 263 Phila 1 91 Phoebe
177 178 Polly 75 Priscilla 166
168 Prudence 220 221 Roanna 72
Ruth 78 7 9 220 Sally 73 84
Sarah 16 62 108 1 99 Sarah E 1 81
Sarah F 271 Simon 118 Stephen
12 49 105 Susan 154 236 Thomas
Sr 24 Dea William 72 William
236
CHATMAN, Oliver 15
CHEANY, --- 133 Cordelia 133
CHEDEL, Laura A 6 9
CHEENEY, Abiah 52 George C 104
CHEEVER, Ellen 82 204 Ezekiel 82
Orissa 82
CHELEY, Susan 7

CHELLIS, Judith 36 Martha 16 77
1 93
CHENEY, Alonzo 5 Anna B 5
Antoinette 58 Betsey 176
Charlotte 3 Daniel 247 David F
1 92 Frederick 94 Georgiana
Isabel 1 92 Luther 82 Mary E 1 43
Polly 145 Ruth S 82 Sabrina A
94 Sarah 243 Savory 58 Stephen
94 Theodate 5 Thomas P 143
CHESLEY, Abigail 16 9 Adeline 16 9
Andrew 16 9 Charlotte 120
Clarissa 1 94 222 Comfort 121
122 123 Elizabeth 1 94 Esther
201 James 122 Joanna 249
Joannah 248 John 16 9 Nancy 123
Nathaniel 249 Sally 2 46 Samuel
123 Susan 2 Tamsen 122 Tamsen
Wentworth 122 123 171 Thomas
1 94
CHICK, Esther 253
CHILD, Alice 2 46 Hannah 44
Lorietta C 136 Lucinda 45 Mary
45 Matilda 204 Nancy 44 William
45
CHILDS, Horace 245 Kate M 114
Matilda 259 260 Matilda R 245
Richard L 114 Ruthven 224
CHOATE, Abby Parker 51 Hon
George F 51 Mary Jane 132
Ruhamah 67 Ruhamah 68 Susie V 28
CHRISTIE, Dea 231 Emma Josephine
128 Jane 75 9 7 Jane W 116 Mary
112 113 159 167 Theresa 231
Rebecca C 70 71
CHRUCH, Lydia 270
CHUBBUCK, Elijah 26 9 Emeline 202
Hannah 26 9
CHURCH, Dorothy 256 Eveline B
212 Hannah 11 12 142 Jabez 256
Lydia 256 Mary 12 Mary L 73
Miranda C 153 Rev Selden 12
CHURCHILL, Ella 204 Hazen 204
CILLEY, Abby Hawks 73 Ann
Elizabeth 34 Bartlett G 6
Betsey 1 48 203 Betty 233 Desire
251 Elizabeth Ann 33 Emma 237
Ezra Dow 73 Greenleaf 33 J G
237 Jane 33 Gen Joseph 93 148
Laura L 175 Martha Jane 6 Polly
93 228 Richard 251 Robert 93
CILLY, Ezra 175
CLADON, Edwina 170
CLAFLIN, Celinda 83 Isabel 155
Julia A 205 Lydia B 83 Mary E
234 Preston 83 155 234 Preston
Williams 205
CLAPP, Alice J 1 43 E G 143
Elizabeth W 272 Judith 139
CLARISSA, French 185
CLARK, --- 103 170 Angie L 88

Ann 160 195 Asenath 229
Benjamin 60 Betsey 2 193 Byron
A 176 Calvin D 71 Caroline 216
Comfort 8 Col Daniel 227 Edina
G 176 Elida 163 Elizabeth 160
268 Evelyn 227 Ezekiel 166
George A 118 George Reynolds
170 Hannah 8 60 Hannah D 203
Harriet G 118 229 Harry S 68
Isaac Esq 178 J A 132 James 210
Jane 59 Joanna W 1 2 John 117
229 John N 203 Jonathan 60
Joseph 8 Josephine L 43 Judy 5
Lewis N 112 Lucinda 134 Lucy
109 Lydia 59 117 132 Margaret 6
86 179 191 Maria Pierce 109
Martha 73 Martha L 134 Martha S
41 Mary 95 153 209 215 228 254
262 Mary Anna 68 Mary J 210
Mary Moody 7 8 247 Mary S 193
Mehitable 14 Morris 109 Moses
103 Nancy 155 156 212 Nath 193
Nathan 103 Nathaniel 95 Ninian
Esq 59 Capt Norman 272 Persis
Georgianna 112 Phebe 7 Phebe F
257 Polly 205 206 Priscilla 166
Remembrance 230 Robert 59 160
Sabrina T 178 Sally 85 103 261
272 Samuel 2 191 Sarah 50 118
126 184 230 Sarah A 71 Mrs
Sarah F 218 Sarah Hidden 44 Mrs
Susan 180 Tamar M 227 Wilber 50
CLARKE, Abigail 231 Amasa 242
Anna Maria 111 Catharine 208
David 231 Frances A 242
Greenleaf 52 Hannah 182 Julia
52 Mary 231 232 242 Moody 242
Nathaniel 231 Rev 184 Mrs
Ruhama 43 Sarah 42 62 79 80 Hon
William C 111
CLARY, Sarah S 270 Rev T F W 270
CLAY, Caroline C 78 Ithiel E 78
CLEMENS, Phila 84
CLEMENT, Abigail 100 Ann 193
Belinda 52 Betsey 47 Mrs
Carleton 48 Charlotte Lucretia
168 Dolly 100 101 Elizabeth 268
Jonathan 168 Joshua 100 Mary
231 Mehitable 110 274 Moses 231
Rachel P 101 Sabrina 29 186
Sarah 231
CLEMENTS, Jacob 78 Mary 37
Phoebe 48 78 Phoebe W 77 78
CLIFFORD, --- 171 Arrolin 214
Mrs Charlotte 130 Hannah D 205
206 Joseph 171 Lucinda 126 Mary
36 Paulina R 185 Pauline R 185
Peace 53 Rachel 185 Sally 214
Samuel 214 Sarah 248 249 Susan
84
CLISBY, --- 179 Alice 179

CLOUGH, --- 92 151 160 Amos 87
Anna 228 Anne 228 Augusta A 185
B W 116 Betsy 49 Calista 150
Caroline M 116 Charles C 185
Clara 49 Dilly 231 Dorothy 104
Ellie J 202 Elsie 87 Emma 7
Ephraim 7 Ezekiel 19 Gillman
154 Jeremiah 49 Joseph 151
Leavitt 49 Lovinia 265 Lucinda
7 Mary 65 67 Mary A 19 Mary E
70 185 Mrs Mary E 229 Nancy E
154 Nathan C 70 Orissa 77 Rose
160 Ruth 151 Sabrina 49 Sally
19 25 49 Sarah 151 243 Sarah M
87 Susan 49 Susan J 132
Susannah 81 82 William 150
CLOUTMAN, Almira 70 Joseph A 70
Mercy 253
CLUFF, Daniel B 258 Lucy Ann 258
COATES, Minnie R 132
COBLEIGH, Hannah 71 Lydia 85 M D
85 Mary Ann 175 W S 175
COBURN, Abigail 265 Catharine
107 Elizabeth 87 Fanny 170
Harriet 55 James 107 John H 87
Mahala 170 Paulina A 22 22
Sybil 107
COCHRAN, Andrew C 252 Elizabeth
180 Hannah 271 Isaac P 180
James 180 271 Jane 241 Janet
179 Letitia 47 Louisa 252
Martha J 180 Mary Abbie 37
Nancy 47 Prudence 241 Robert
241 Sarah 113 Susan 241 Susan G
10 11
COCHRANE, Alice 41 Charlotte M
41 Hannah 164 243 Harriet 50
Leila C 50 Levi 41 Sally 163
164 Rev Sylvester 243 William C
50
CODMAN, --- 4 Baxter 166 Ephraim
109 Esther Maria 166 Hannah 50
109 Henry 191 Nancy 231 Peter 4
109 Polly 109 Rhene 156
Sophronia 191
COE, D W 149
COFFIN, Abigail 237 266 267
Betsey 110 Deborah 53 Demaris
101 Eliza 192 Emily M 265
Eunice K 23 Frances 171 Hattie
S 110 John F 265 Mary 67 74 237
259 260 Mary Kilburn 67
Nathaniel 101 Judge Peter 237
Phoebe 78 Rose 7 Stephen 74
Thomas 110 Tristram 53 237
COFRAN, Cyrene 219 Sally 213
COGGSWELL, Betsey E 182 Mary 102
COGILL, Alice B 241
COGSWELL, Abiah 57 Col Amos 262
Hannah 169 Hannah Pearson 10 Dr
Joseph 268 Judith 10 47 253

Julia 47 48 Lydia 261 262 Mary
137 Mary S 268 Rachel Choate
203 Dr William 10 47 Rev
William DD 137
COLBATH, Hannah 152 John K 152
COLBURN, Abbie A 271 Abiah 233
Alzina 171 C M 187 Charlotte
26 9 Cynthia 23 4 Edward 181 26 9
Emma F 263 264 Esther A 187
Ezekial 171 Frances E 47
Gilbert 234 Hattie M 181 Jane
171 Josiah 47 Lucy 263 Mary 117
Reuben H 263 Sarah 121
COLBY, --- 159 A P 56 Abigail 7 9
Amanda C 256 Augusta 79 80
Belinda 48 Benjamin 79 129
Benjamin F 240 Clara I 103
Ebenezer 256 Elizabeth 56 Ella
Frances 73 Ethean 40 Fidelia
106 George 242 George W 106
Hannah 30 Hannah A 3 Hannah C
186 Hannah D 166 Harriet 160
Helen Marie 121 Ichabod 241
Jacob 30 Jane 159 Jesse P 103
Jonathan 5 Col Joseph 1 46
Judith 4 51 1 95 Julia M H 240
Levi O 76 Lucinda 84 Mrs Lydia
A 144 Martha 5 Mary 36 76 82
242 Mary G 241 Merriam 4 5 104
120 220 Miriam 4 5 Moody 42
Nancy 42 Nathan 82 Nathan S 84
Polly P 58 76 Prescott 103 121
Priscilla 129 Sally 76 1 46
Samuel 76 Sarah 4 30 142 162
203 Susan 3 William 30
COLBY Willoughby 4 Rev Zaccheus
35 203
COLCORD, Edward 68 Elisabeth 23 9
Hannah 16 17 68 Mary 1 47 23 9
Mary O 38 Mehitable 1 91 Olivia
38 Samuel 147 1 91 William 38
COLE, --- 200 Almira 108 Ann M
132 Hon Benjamin James 207
Charity 71 Charles 1 97 Choice
31 Emerson 112 Hannah 207
Harriet 55 Helen Elizabeth 112
Janet 79 Jesse 115 John 55 Capt
John 261 Louisa 22 9 Lucinda 22 9
Lucy Ann 1 97 Mary E W 261 Mary
J 55 Mehitable A 207 Octavia M
207 Richard 15 Sally 115 Sarah
A 115 Sylvia 15 Victoria 15
COLEMAN, Alice 41 Jabez 205
Martha 215 Mary 205
COLGATE, James 52 Mary 52
COLLEY, Nancy 138 Richard 138
Sarah 138
COLLINS, Abigail 26 4 Benjamin 99
Eliza 99 108 109 Elizabeth 73
Enos 132 199 Ester Pierce 3 9
Esther Pierce 162 Eunice 132

Eva M 85 Freeman 85 Helen
Frances 39 Jesse 17 John 211
John H 39 John Harriman 162
Lucy A 120 Lucy Jane 211 Lydia
H 222 Martha 199 Nelly A 15
Rebecca 17 Sarah 254 Sarah J
26 4 Susan 199
COLTON, Caroline 254 255 Lovina
P 71
COMSTOCK, Mary 264 Mary G 48
CONANT, --- 98 127 Almira 184
Alvah 184 Catherine 108 Emily A
40 Ezra 103 Hannah 127 Mary 1 91
Rachel 34 Rhoda 55 Sally 98 127
CONE, Edmond 21 9 Jonathan 142
Nettie D 21 9 Sally 21 9 Sarah
142
CONER, William 54
CONN, Sally 97 Sarah 97 Susannah
255 256 William 97
CONNARY, Betsy 15 John 15
CONNELL, David 256 Judith C 256
CONNER, Jeremiah 128 Joseph 118
Lucinda 128 Sarah 118
CONNOR, Fannie E 33 Jewett 33
Lydia 33 Mary K 26 5
CONOVER, Harriet 33 Sarah P 33
William 33
CONVERSE, Elvira 1 43 Jane 97
Josiah 97 Lyman 142 Polly 1 42
Sally 97
CONWAY, Elizabeth 211
COOK, --- 24 Abigail 68
Catherine Cornelia 1 94
Charlotte R 225 Clarissa 12 102
Coffin 12 Capt Dyer 218 Edward
76 Emma 162 Eunice 16 Fidelia
76 George M 82 Hannah 218
Hannah P 206 207 Maj James 6
102 Jemima 273 Julia 24 Lois 23
Dr Lot 95 Lovina 183 Lucy 71 72
207 Martha 206 Mary 6 12 167
258 Matilda P 187 Melvina 206
Moody 12 71 72 Col Moody 207
Patience 105 106 1 96 Peter 183
Rebecca 12 Samantha 71 72 Sarah
Frances 82 Sarah P 55 56
Susanna 95 Thomas 206 Zebedee
12
COOLBRATH, Agnes 171 172
COOLEDGE, Anna 139 1 40 Nathaniel
13 9 Sarah 13 9
COOLEY, Dorothy 128 138 Zediah 4
COOPER, Amanda 213 Gilman 1 4
Heiress 26 4 James 226 Julia A
137 Margaret 226 Samuel B 213
Sarah A 213 Sarah D 1 4
COPELAND, Harriet A 1 9
COPP, Capt David 268 Esther 268
Harriet 210 Maria 175 Mary 214
Uriah Esq 210

COPPS, Ellen M 233
CORA, Lomira 42
CORBETT, Emeline 267 Hannah 57
COREY, Eliza 56 George 170
  Hattie E 104 Sarah J 56
CORLES, --- 106 Mehitable 106
CORLESS, Wealthy 228
CORLIS, --- 105 John 105
  Mehitable 105 Nancy 105
CORLISS, Abigail 144 Alma 168
  Gen Cyrus 168 Elizabeth 7 Emily
  167 Mary 32
CORNING, Mary Jane 162
CORRIGAN, --- 209 Amelia 209
CORSER, Emeline 236 Gilman 249
CORSON, Luella 106 William 106
CORY, Relief 17 Willard 17
COSSITT, Judge Ambrose 109
COTTON, Alvin S 133 Ann 133
  Betsy 136 Dorothy 107 Rev John
  107 Margaret 40 Molly 18 Sarah
  C 259 Rev Ward 259
COUCH, Eliza 49 Enoch 266 Jane O
  266 Mary S 266
COUGH, Dorothy 103
COULT, Abigail 55
COUSINS, Huldah 132
COVIL, Isaac 57
COWAN, Elizabeth 222 Dr James W
  222 Susan Ellen 222
COWELL, Maria H 106
COWEN, Lucy 52
COWLES, Mary 116
COX, --- 126 233 Adaline 5
  Arzelia Jane 192 Betsey 126
  Catharine 233 Catherine S 157
  Edwin 193 Esther 224 Louisa A
  119 Mary Ann 246 Rachel 209
CRAFT, --- 224 Charles 15 Hannah
  15
CRAFTS, Anette 145 Pliny E 145
CRAGIN, Augustus 57
CRAGON, Francis 57
CRAIG, Edna 17 Fanny 17 Hugh 17
  Parker 17 Rosilla A 17
CRAM, Annah E 18 Aurilla 109
  Celenda 156 Daniel 62 David 10
  Dolly 186 187 Elizabeth 217 219
  Hannah 74 Homer B 18 Humphrey
  78 Jonathan 74 Levi 147 Loiel
  74 Louisa 265 Lydia 74 Marinda
  132 Mary 10 Mary F 147 Nathan
  74 Phebe 78 Sarah 62 74
CRANE, Daniel 148
CRAWFORD, Abigail 193 George 104
  Mary Y 104 Susan 141 Susanna
  119
CREES, Hannah 50
CRESSEY, Daniel 79 Horace 179
  Lydia 195 Martha 179 Mehitable
  79

CRESSY, Abigail 94 95 96 Addison
  262 Edward 140 Eliza 140 John
  94 Mary Elizabeth 262 Phebe 132
CRIBBS, --- 50 Abby 50
CRIDDLE, Andrew 226 Emma 226
CRIPPEN, Helen F G 76 J J 76
CROCKER, Mehetable 168 Mehitabel
  204 Roland 168
CROCKETT, --- 274 Annie R 274
  Elizabeth 134 Ellen G 181
  Emeline 220 George W 181 Mrs S
  Rebecca 108 S Rebecca 274
CROMBIE, Harriet 50 Mary 269
  Nannie Moor 115 Ninia Clark 115
  Rebecca 115 Sara L 179 William
  A 179
CROMWELL, Elizabeth 151 Capt
  Philip 151
CROOKER, Stephen 98
CROOKS, Hester 25
CROSBY, --- 21 Abigail 127
  Betsey 64 236 Dixi MD 171
  Dorothy 200 201 Esther 24 Grace
  Beede 95 96 Jacob 127 John 95
  Judge Nathan 171 Phoebe 95
  Sally 171 Sarah D 124 William
  124
CROSS, Abigail C 84 Amanda 87
  Anstress 247 Effie L 178
  Ephraim 84 Judith 56 Margaret
  75 Mary G 248 Phebe 223 Ruth
  239 240 Sarah 114 Sarah J 178
CROUCH, Jane 195
CROWE, Susan 156
CROWELL, Celestia E 62 Elizabeth
  166 167 Martha Silver 201 R T
  62 Sarah A 201
CROWNINGSHIELD, Harriet 161
  Harriet 202
CUBBUCK, Ann M 201 Emeline 201
  Levi 201
CULVER, Anna 256 James 46 Maria
  H 46 Phila 244
CUMBERFORD, Joanna 208
CUMINGS, Hannah Farwell 138 Ens
  Jerahmael 138
CUMMINGS, Abigail 183 Adaline C
  134 Alice 248 Alvah 114
  Angeline 57 Annie 197 Archelaus
  189 Augusta 189 Betsey 224 252
  Daniel 134 140 248 Dolly W 200
  Edward N 168 Effie 10 Eleazer
  258 Eliza 2 Elizabeth 252
  Elmira 101 Elvira 61 Enoch P
  200 Frank 193 George F 57
  George J 118 Hannah 258 Hannah
  A 192 Helen M 155 Henry 25 Ida
  F 57 Ira 10 Isaac 252 Jane 25
  Jonathan 209 Joseph 26 Hon
  Joseph 2 Lois 134 140 248 Lois
  A 140 Louisa 57 Lucretia F 168

Lucy 194 Lucy E 118 Mary 26 189
Mary E 31 Mary H 26 Mittie 243
Noah 101 Phebe 198 199 Polly
114 Sally 25 Sarah 57 102 258
Sumner 155 Susan 209
CUMMINS, Lucinda 117
CURRIER, --- 62 65 109 173 Aaron
209 Alice 216 Amos 140 201 Ann
R 191 Anna 209 Belle 53 David
70 Deborah 33 Edward 209
Elizabeth 3 Helen C 166 167 J
53 James 191 Jane H 88 John 28
42 191 John W 221 Julia A 130
218 Lois 218 Lydia L 138
Margaret 47 Marinda 142 Mary 3
28 70 113 140 181 201 209 210
Mary A 27 29 Mary E 209 Nancy S
191 Nathaniel 181 Persis H 65
Phebe C 209 Polly 173 Rebecca
190 Rebecca F 24 Reuben W 218
Rhoda 70 Rosetta C 28 Sally 62
231 Samuel 88 Sarah 14 42 94
140 173 174 201 Sophia 27 Susie
Elsie 233 234 Thankful 181
William 27 William 142
CURRY, Sophia T 213
CURTIS, Chauncey 35 Mrs Cora M
143 Ed 36 Jennie 36 Lucy 76
Mary 194 Polly 239
CUSHING, Daniel 122 Jael 152 153
Maria B 104 Mary 104 Nancy 122
Rachel 251 Tamsen 122 William
104 122
CUSHMAN, Francis 229 Harriet 194
Harriet N 229 Rebecca 199
Sophia 4 189 210 Ursula 194
CUTLER, Abigail Grant Jones 59
Elizabeth 127 Rev Lyman 127
Mary E 15 Nancy A 207 Samuel 15
CUTT, --- 184 Robert Kittery 184
CUTTER, Abiah 258 Deborah 258
Elizabeth 142 Emma 72 Harriet
42 Leonard F 72 Lucy 88 243
Lucy S 11 Seth 258
CUTTING, --- 48 Ada 172 Bernice
48 Charles 261 Ella 261 Lucy 23
Col Zebedee 23
CUTTS, Nancy 143 Maj William 143

DADMAN Sarah 135
DAGGETT, Elizabeth 28 29 Martha
A 6
DALE, Lucy 266 Maria 21 22
Rebecca 180
DALOFF, Hannah 5 6
DALTON, Dorothy 68 Louisa 67
Mary 177 Philemon 68 Samuel 207
Sarah S 207 Vianna M 197
DALY, Nancy 58 Polly 58
DAM, --- 211 Elizabeth 98 John
98 Leah 122 123 Martha 123 203

William 123 203
DAME, Charity 118 159 Katharine
165 Liberty N 86 266 Mehitable
81 Paul 266
DAMON, Carrie B 116 Galen 55
Jane 55 Jane B 55 Otis S 116
DANA, --- 21 Hon Samuel 21
DANFORTH, Betsy 4 Elizabeth 88
Jonathan 4 Orpah 157 Timothy 88
William 157
DANIELL, J F 242 Susan K 242 243
DANIELS, Abigail 92 Albert H 40
Charity M 63 Charles T 119
Clement 92 275 Hon Darwin J 41
Elizabeth T 40 Esther 275 Flora
A 41 Isaac 92 Joseph 5 Lucretia
252 Lydia 92 275 Rebecca B 40
Susanna 5
DANIELSON, Esther 275
DARLING, Benjamin 125 Betsey 166
167 Maria L 125 Mary J 54
DARWIN, Lizzie D 194
DASCOMB, Caroline 34 Caroline M
34 George 34 Mary 34
DAVENPORT, Sarah A 239
DAVID, Abigail Frances 226 Col
James 226
DAVIS, --- 65 81 226 Abbie J 113
Abby 70 71 Abigail 65 Abigail
94 Abram 62 Amanda 50 Amanda M
50 144 195 Amos 71 Andrew 153
Ann 45 Ann H 245 Ann M 201 Anna
29 30 97 151 Annie 263 Asa 81
Benjamin 50 66 144 Benjamin A
104 Betsey 69 122 157 240 249
254 Betsy 66 Mrs Betsey Jones !
Dr Charles A 247 Charlotte S
211 D K 132 Dr Dana D 17
Dearborn 69 Deborah 11 12 142
200 247 Delia 40 Dr Dimond 254
Eleazer 14 50 Elizabeth 92
Elizabeth A 71 Elizabeth C 254
Emily 118 Emma 18 Ephraim 12
Eva M 51 F W 224 Frank 265
George E 123 Hannah 211 254
Helen A 64 Henrietta 265 Horace
Miles 18 Huldah L 69 Ida 50 J A
64 Jacob 151 James 50 244
Jemima 50 John 254 Joshua 66
Judith Mason 251 252 Laura P
151 Lavinia K 17 Lawrence A 80
Mrs Lizzie B 86 Lovilla 226
Lucinda B 144 Lucy 66 224 Lucy
L 153 Margaret 25 Martha 50
Martha J 80 Mary 89 169 Mary A
104 Mary Parker 247 Mehitable P
71 Moses 70 Nancy 15 71
Nathaniel A 254 O B 118 Olive
68 Ophelia 208 Priscilla 62
Rebecca 81 244 Sally 13 14 26
254 Samuel 94 122 Sarah 69 157

275 Sarah A 144 246 Sarah W 104
Seviah 18 Dr Silas W 142
Sophronia 66 Susan 177 178
Susanne 132 Thomas 249 Timothy
211 W P 50
DAVISON, Emily 93 F W 93 H C 137
Lydia H 69 70 Mary 137
DAWES, Sarah 57 58
DAY, Abbie Gardner 248 Betsey
162 Carlos P 71 David 207
Eliphalet 162 Emily 179 Emma 94
George 43 Hannah C 207 Henry
179 Joseph 15 Moses 106 Nancy
15 Phebe A 57 Samuel E 57 Sarah
43 Tirzah 162 Ursula 270 Ward
94
DAYTON, James 172 Lucinda 172
DE FOREST, Mills 275 Sarah 275
DE, MARY Abigail 64
DE, ROCHEMONT Annie M L S 22
DE, WITT Sophia 198
DEAN, Charles F 167 Elizabeth S
136 Grace 67 Isabella 167 Lucy
H 36 Martha 31 Olive C 172
Sally 97 Sarah 124 205
DEANE, Grace 67
DEARBORN Abigail 57 Abigail N
167 Amanda F 229 Amanda J 229
Asa 143 Asaph 88 Belinda K 207
Benjamin 74 Betsey 157 Dr D P
265 Dorothy A 18 19 Eliza 177
Elizabeth 17 Ellen S 23 Esther
74 Fanny 128 H Jennie 55 Hannah
53 Harriet 55 Hattie 24 Hattie
S 265 Huldah 167 J L 167 Jacob
28 John 46 128 143 John S 23
Jonathan 229 Joseph 55 Joseph
Freese 163 Josiah 207 Lucretia
J 131 Lucy A 143 Lydia 46 Lydia
A 177 178 Mary 28 47 Mary Ann
163 Mary Anna 46 Miriam 57
Nancy 167 Oliver 131 Polly 12 R
R 143 Ruhamah 143 Sally 155 157
Samuel 17 57 Sarah 18 19 29 88
104 119 162 163 Simon N 18 163
Thomas 53 Warren 177
DEDMAN, Hannah 135
DEFRIES, Henry 145 Isabella 145
DELANO, Augusta B 120 Clarence E
121 Hannah 234
DELAPLAINE, Eugenia C 119
DEMARY, Rebecca 115
DEMERITT, Abigail 152 Emma B 129
John Y 110 206 Louisa C 110 206
Mark 129 152 Susan 129
DENISON, Elizabeth 270
DENNETT, --- 1 110 111 Hannah 38
1 95 Harriet 43
DENNING, Ellen M 204 H B 204
DENNIS, Edward 184 Sallie 243
DENNITT, Margaret W 196 Mary 196

DENNY, George 58
DERBY, J H 107 Mary A 256 Ruhama
E 107 Sophia 249
DEWAR, Henry 145 Mary 145
DEWEY, Sally 239 240 Sarah J 93
DEXTER, Adelia B 176
DICKEY, A W 160 Adam 48 180 231
Angeline 159 Clara 170 Eleanor
179 Elenor 180 Eliza W 22 Ester
231 Hannah 22 Hannah W 191
Harriet N 196 Jane 180 Jenny
271 John Esq 191 Kesiah D 48
Margaret 180 Mary 157 Mary 171
Naomi 157 Mrs Relief 109 Robert
22 Sarah 70 160 Theresa 231
Vienna 48 William 231
DICKINSON, Jonathan 36 Louisa 94
Lucy H 36 Mary A 36 Theodora L
242
DIKICK, Abigail 102
DILLINGHAM, Mary Ellen 225
William P 225
DIMICK, --- 64 Dea Adolphus 103
Betsey 103 John 102 Mary F 162
Rachel 64 S C 162 Sally 103
Sarah C 198 Shubael 70
Sophronia 64
DIMOND, Mary 144
DINSMOOR, Cornelius 228
DINSMORE, Dr 120 Esther P 194
Hannah 120 Joseph 119 Lydia 119
194 Mrs Lucinda E 13 Margaret
170 271 Mary 179 180 Mehitabel
203 Rhoda 45 Robert 203 Sarah
70 Solomon 247 Tobias 45 Wilbur
F 13
DIVOL, Roxana 52
DIX, --- 208 Elizabeth Frances
208 Mrs Mary H 208
DIXON, Abigail Hatch 253 F N 217
James P 155 Capt Joseph 253
Lydia S 217 Mary A 155 Capt
Thomas 253
DOANE, Hon Elisha 51 Elizabeth
51 52 Susan 51 52
DOCKHAM, Eliza 197
DODGE, --- 1 131 211 Abigail 27
Alice 237 Anna L 88 Betsey 70
Betsy 113 Caroline 127 128
Elizabeth 188 Flora A 7 Hannah
25 50 243 244 Hazen G 88 John
70 128 Jonathan 115 Lt Joseph
243 Col Joseph A 88 Rev Joshua
133 Lydia 7 97 113 Margaret 113
225 Martha 102 133 Mary 3 79 80
Mrs Nancy 156 Ninian C 27 Polly
71 130 131 Rachel 131 Sally 188
229 Sarah 1 115 Sarah L 17
Sarah P 148 Dea Solomon 7
Sophia 115 211 Triphena 72 73
DOE, Betsey 115 116 Horace B 33

Jefferson 115 John 181 Joseph
128 Lavina 128 Lavina J 33 Mary
Elizabeth 261 Nancy 181
DOEG, Augustus 132 Huldah 132
Sarah A 132 133
DOLBY, Albert T 1 Frances V 83
Mrs Vasta Morrison 1
DOLE, Betsey 214 Cyrus 234
Elizabeth 234 Eugene G 243
Hattie N 243 Irena 200 Mary 93
Polly 93
DOLLIVER, Jane L 57 John 57
Lucette 57
DOLLOFF, Abraham 30 212 Almira
212 Levi 154 Mary Jane 195 196
Rachel 30 212 Roxy 154 Sally
154 Susan 30 Susanna 30
DOLPHIN, Matthew 226 Sarah 226
DONKER, Ann 179
DONOGHUE, Margaret 180
DONOVAN, Mary J 24
DORR, Joseph 217 Lydia 217 219
DORTHEY, --- 142 Hannah 142
DOTON, Eleanor 175
DOTY, Cynthia 143
DOUGLASS, Margaret 78 Minerva J
227
DOW, Abigail 274 Abram 42 Ann C
197 Anna 141 C B 232 Christy 75
Daniel G 42 Ebenezer 165 Elijah
197 Eliza 42 48 Elizabeth A 129
Elizabeth G 246 Eunice 197
Freeman 3 H Ellen 232 Hannah 39
43 109 Hannah M 95 Isaac 183 J
B 157 John Esq 141 Jonathan 30
246 Julia 44 Kesiah 48 Laura W
204 Lois 75 Lorenzo 95 Louisa
157 Louisa Dwight 21 Lydia 249
Margaret 95 139 Margaret 162
Martha E 137 Mary 3 Gen Neal 21
Ora 48 Phebe 193 Phoebe 263
Polly 108 Reuben 204 Richard
263 Rosa J 8 Sarah 68 Sophia R
62 Susan 76 Tryphena 245
DOWE, Eliza 36 Ellen E 23 Esther
23 Ulysses 23
DOWLIN, Caroline 103 198 199
Catharine 121 Timothy L 121
DOWN, Fanny 257
DOWNER, Hannah 124 John 124
DOWNING, Adaline 52 Charles H
221 Hannah 186 John 43 Joshua
156 Lydia 86 Mary 198 Sally 43
Sarah 156 Stephen 109
DOWNS, Areline B 112 Gershom 112
Mary C 249 Sally P 112
DRAKE, --- 152 259 Abigail 18
Abram 232 Anna 204 Clara B 95
Capt Daniel 32 Dorothy 4
Elizabeth 67 90 Elizabeth J 128
Dea Francis 128 Georgianna

Butters 38 Harriet 154 Col
James 38 Martha 232 Mary E 90
125 126 Mehitable 90 Olive A
128 Phebe 259 Phillip S 154
Rhoda 120 Samuel 18 90 Samuel J
128 Susan 152 Sybil 32 187
DRAPER, Hattie E 42 Isabella W
206 207 Rev L 42 Prudence 19
Reuben 186 206 Sally 186 206
Susan 186
DRESSER, --- 184 Jane 32 Pamela
184 Samuel 79 Sarah 79
DREW, --- 12 29 152 223 Adis 134
Hon Amos W 156 Avis 12 Caroline
H 168 Comfort 221 Edwin W 156
Elizabeth 90 Hannah 163 Harriet
55 I W 168 J G 132 Mrs Jane L
176 Jesse 111 Joan 195 Julia A
132 Julia Esther 156 Levi 12
Lovey 173 Lucy 156 Mary Jane
273 Mehitable 152 Moses 195
Samuel 173 Sarah 111 Sophronia
11 William 90
DROWN, Mary F 268
DUDLEY, A T 133 Dolly 174
Elizabeth 174 Hannah 217 Jason
Henry 26 Joanna 196 Lucy A 26
Minnie 154 Polly 133 Red Edmund
234 Samuel 174 Sarah 87 Stephen
196
DUNAVAN, Electa 40
DUNCAN, Christie 74 Hannah 161
Hiram 253 James 97 Jane 97
Letitia 97 Mehitable 157 Sarah
Miller 253
DUNCKLE Ellen F 261
DUNHAM, --- 43 Louisa 43
DUNLAP, Hon Archibald 90 John
180 Lucy Jane 90 Mary 32 73
Mary A 125 Olive 180 Samuel 73
DUNNAWAY, Rebecca W 194
DUNNING, Lydia 86 Sally 26
DUNSACK, Sarah 109
DURGAN, Julia M 258
DURGIN, --- 56 182 Betsey 22
Eliza 245 252 Harriet 56
Jonathan 245 Lydia 40 Sarah 182
Susan 77 245 252
DURHAM, Betsey A 255 Elizabeth
178 179 John 179
DURRELL, Benjamin 83 David 58
Helen F G 58 Judith 83 Lizzie S
235 Lydia 82 83 Polly P 58
DUSHONG, Sally 38
DUSTIN, --- 271 Betsey Ann 232
Eben R 51 Emily A 51 Eveline
274 Lucy Ann 148 Nancy 11 12
Nehemiah 232 Phebe 235 236 Ruth
89 90 Sally 271
DUSTON, Abiah 76 Susan 101
DUTTON, Marinda H 210 Mary 117

Sarah 265
DWIGHT, Josiah E 127
DWINELLS, Sylvia 53
DWINER, Sylvia 15
DYE, Louisa W 239 240
DYER, Sarah 94 Thankful 139

EADS, Mary 193
EASTBROOK, --- 115 Mary O 115
EASTERBROOKS, Sarah 223
 Valentine Esq 223
EASTMAN, --- 46 193 222 258 259
 Abiathar 168 Abigail 258 Addie
 D 66 Alma 261 Amelia Ann L 194
 Anna 154 Anna Quackenbush 60
 Annette 64 Azubah 31 140 Betsey
 173 Caroline C 48 Charles F 244
 Cyrus 215 D E 173 Capt Ebenezer
 39 Elizabeth 127 Elizabeth R
 112 Ellen S 177 Elsie 156
 Esther 77 Eunice 127 George F
 31 Hannah 157 Hannah M 16
 Harriot 169 Hasket D 194 Henry
 261 Hon Ira Allen 60 James 195
 271 Jane B 117 Jeremiah 222
 Joel 177 184 Dea Jonathan 155
 Jonathan K 48 Dr Joseph 36
 Julia 215 Laura L 157 Lucia 1
 Lucia W 215 Martha 193 Mary 8 9
 42 43 46 Mary Ann 173 195 Mary
 Nye 259 Mehitable 61 Miriam 36
 Mollie 154 Moses 1 Nancy 57 155
 Nancy L 169 Nellie F 69 Dr O D
 66 O E 69 Phebe 14 168 Phoebe
 48 155 Polly 14 Rebecca 140
 Rebecca W 31 Richard 14 169
 Richard H 259 Ruth 10 11 14 39
 184 Sally 1 74 245 Rev Stephen
 157 Susan 194 271 Thomas 127 W
 P 117 William 140 155 169
EASTON, Mary 163 William 163
EASTOW, Sarah 251
EATON, --- 165 269 Abiel C 133
 Alfred 48 Alice 226 256 Alvina
 241 Alzada 132 Alzina 132
 Amanda 140 Ann 133 Augusta 159
 Charlotte M 79 80 Clara 135
 David 56 Dr 84 Elizabeth 106
 Frances M 186 187 Franklin 217
 Frederick 226 George 32 Hannah
 96 269 Horace 167 Huldah 14
 James 269 Jane 95 96 109 John
 144 Gen John 226 Joshua 132
 Laura A 241 Louie Frances 67 68
 Louisa S 67 Lucy 55 56 71 72
 207 Lydia 182 183 Martha 32 Mrs
 Mary 134 Mary 144 Mary Helen
 226 Mehitable 48 Moses 67 Phebe
 96 98 202 Rosanna 269 Roxanna
 241 269 Sarah 88 233 Sarah A
 175 176 Sarah J 251 Stephen 159

Susan 84 Susannah 265 Dr Thomas
 67
ECELESTON, Lucy A 61
EDGELL, Capt Samuel 210 Sarah
 210
EDGELY, Fanny 230 232
EDGERLEY, Susan 33
EDGERLY, --- 43 Andrew 50 Mary K
 152 Nancy 43 Patience T 50
EDGERTON, Phebe 238 Philda 121
EDMANDS, Ormacinda 135
EDMONDS, Sally 20 Sarah A 227
EDMUNDS, Betsey 45 Edward 108
 Hannah Y 108 Jefferson 108
 Nancy L 108 Nathaniel 108 Sally
 108
EDSON, Elizabeth 261
EDWARDS, Benjamin G 217 Eliza
 217 Mary P 174
EGERTON, Lucy 41
EGERY, Abigail 31 Daniel 31
EGLESTON, Lucinda 114 Mrs
 Lucinda 113
ELA, Catherine 261 Charles 261
 George W Esq 150 Joseph 20
 Laura E 20 Sally 20
ELEA, Maria 59
ELIOTT, Lucy 58 Susan 58 Thomas
 58
ELKINS, Anna 89 Betsey 212
 Henrietta A 12 Jeremiah 212
 Johanna 95 John 197 Luella B
 197 Mary 68 Sarah 111
ELLENWOOD, Mrs Hannah 181 Nancy
 71
ELLINGWOOD, Abigail 269 Harriet
 269 John 4 Ora 4
ELLIOT, Caroline 148 Clarinda 72
 Daniel 72 Dorcas 72 Frank H 72
 Josephine 115 117 Mary 57
 Mehitable 167 Roxana 137
 Susanna 91
ELLIOTT, --- 182 249 Caroline
 149 Charlotte 29 30 Clestia A
 217 Eliza 30 266 Ephraim 30 Ira
 E 69 John F 125 Kate V 125 Mary
 69 Sally 146 Sarah 210
ELLIS, --- 210 Hannah M 94 96
 Louisa 94 Lucy G 187 Mary 56
 Stephen 56 Susan F 56 William B
 94
ELLSWORTH, Jonathan 3 Lucy 3
 Mary 119
ELWELL, Benjamin 48 Ithiel 48
 Olive 48
ELWYN, Thomas Esq 150
ELY, Dorothy 261
EMERSON, --- 131 Abigail 81 255
 Annie 168 Catharine 54 Deborah
 259 Elizabeth 92 Ellen 142
 Erastus D 255 Etta F 166 Frank

166 Helen M 175 Jacob 259 Rev
John 272 Joseph 120 Julia A 83
M C 236 Marcus M 142 Mary 28
272 Mary Ann 161 Mary E 20 N W
168 O T Esq 83 Phebe 72 Polly
45 Rachel 131 Ruth 236 Sally
176 Samuel 92 Samuel Esq 68
Sarah 81 239 Sarah G 82 Sarah J
220 Stephen 175 176 Susan 120
Susannah 68 William P 161
EMERTON, Rebecca L 212 Thomas J
212
EMERY, --- 52 127 231 Abbie H
221 Abigail 223 Ann 185
Caroline Dearborn 224 Eliza
Hamilton 258 Eliza Pendexter
169 Elizabeth 274 Eunice 83
Florinda 169 Frances 231 George
F 98 James 41 Jesse 274 Joseph
O 169 Josiah 223 Lucius A 258
Martha 49 Mary 18 19 Moses 83
Natt B 221 Noah Esq 196 Sally
175 176 Sarah A 175 Smith F 177
Susan A 98 Susan Huntington 177
William 169
EMMERSON, Nabby 233
EMMONS, Benjamin Jr 120 Dorothy
120 Electa T 119 Harriet 67
Mary 27 30 Sally 78 Sarah 141
ENGLISH, Andrew 46 Celinda 46
Lois 115 Rebekah M 258
ERWIN, Mary E 128
ESDEN, James 89 Julia M 89
ESTES, Huldah B 109 James B 109
ESTEY, D 35 Lydia H 35
ETHRIDGE, Dorothy 20 Capt
Nathaniel 20
EVANS, --- 100 209 Dr A S 127
Amos 192 Anna 189 190 Mrs Clara
N 132 Deborah 252 Emma 165
Eunice 112 Hazen 100 Helen Mar
252 Hepzibeth 192 Isaac P 32
Jonathan 100 Lydia Fairbanks
111 Mehitable 170 Mercy 192
Nicholas 252 P G 252 Sarah 100
179 Simeon 112 Simon 170
Sophronia 10 Susan 58 Susan A
127 Tirzah 13
EVELETH, J S 201
EVENS, Edwin B 62 Jessie M 62
EVERETT, Almira 196 Betsey 146
Drusilla 134 Eleazer 19 146
George 111 Jonathan 224 Lois
179 Lucy 146 Mary 52 53 Mrs
Mary 224 Persis F 259 260 Hon
Richard C 134 196 260 Sally 24
138 146 Sarah 111
EWEN, Ruth 24 William 24 William
Jr 24
EWINS, John Herbert 198 Lucetta
198

EYRES, Dea James 232 Susan 232
Wealthy 232

FABYAN, Abigail 198
FADDEN, --- 56 Catherine 274
Emily 274 James 274
FAIRBANKS, Polly 175 Prof 182
FAIRFIELD, --- 156 Almos 113
Lydia Ann 113 Phoebe 156
FALES, Addie E 213 Ella J 7
Laura J 8 Mary A 7 William W Sr
7 8
FALL, Carrie 203 Clara Bell 169
Judith 5
FARLEY, Louisa 165
FARMER, Col Isaac W 118 Jane G
153 Jessie B 118 Prof M G 51
153 Sallie R 51 Sally 175 176
FARNHAM, Jennie 222 Laurilla H
12 Lucy H 12 Lydia S 120 Mary
88 Mary J 101 Moses 88 Peter F
12
FARNSWORTH, Charles 268 Hannah
268
FARNUM, --- 167 Eliza 72 Dr J S
194 Ruby 7 Susan 194
FARR, Caroline 186 Corydon 155
Isabel A 155 John 186 Lena A
257
FARRAND, Mary Porter 213
FARRAR, Joseph Esq 198 Mary C
180 Rebecca 95 206 Dea Samuel
96 Rev Stephen 206 Sarah C 198
213
FARRINGTON, --- 162 Betsey 146
Hiram 119 Dr James 118 157 159
Jeremiah 176 Mary 62 Mary D 118
Mary Ellen 176 Nellie 157 159 S
L 221
FARROW, Priscilla 183
FARWELL, Caroline 48 Hannah 60
FAULKNER, Ellen 213 Hannah 97 98
Mary 155
FAVOR, Hannah 154
FAY, Amanda M 199 Betsey 190
Elizabeth 119 Elvira 190 Joel
190 Hon Levi Chamberlain 199
Mary 190
FEARING, Dr J W 59 Matilda 59
FELCH, --- 16 Anna 104 Mrs
Florina W 249 John 16 Mary 11
Susan 71
FELLOWS, --- 203 223 Anna 128
Asa W 37 Belle F 139 Benjamin F
128 Betsey 31 145 Betsey J 115
F W 115 Hannah 78 Harriet E 196
Ida 223 Capt John 203 Jonathan
78 Lorana 22 Louisa 258 Lydia
22 31 Mary 57 Mary S 215 Milo
154 Otis 139 Peter 22 Prescott
31 Ruth 144 Sally 154 Samuel

215 Winthrop R 154
FELSHAW, Lydia 228
FELT, Abigail Adams 224 David
145 Rev Joseph B 224 Ruth Burge
145 Susan 145
FERGUSON, Capt John 211 Patty
170 Sarah 211
FERNALD, James E Esq 266 Laura
Ann 266 Mrs Lucy A 187
FERRIN, A J 212 Abigail 164
Elisha B 38 Elizabeth 65 66
Jonathan 66 197 Marietta 66
Mary V 197 Orpha 164 Sarah 66
212 Sarah A 197 Zebulon 164
FERRIS, Aseneth D 131
FERRY, Fanny 270
FERSON, Horace 50 Lucy 50 Nancy
160
FESSENDEN, Huldah Perley 42 Mary
S 227
FIELD, Clara J 260 Elizabeth 140
Florence E 235 Frank P 260
Hannah P 233 Imogene 235
Lawrence 235 Phebe 93 94
FIELDS, Benjamin 53 Elizabeth 50
Henry 38 John 50 Mary 53
Rebecca 38 271
FIFE, Helen A 208 Mary D 208
Capt William 208
FIFIELD, --- 136 Ann 214 215
Betsey 19 David 87 Eliza E 87
Elizabeth 11 Helen M 242 Jennie
E 184 Capt John 174 Jonathan W
242 Col Joseph 11 Joshua 233
Lucy A 104 136 Mary 174 Mary J
114 Mehitable 218 Rebecca 8 9
Ruhamah 240 Sarah 87 Shuah 20
Susan 233 Theodora L 242
FIGG, Susanna 215
FILMAN, Betsey 62
FINLEY, Jane 175 Jane Taylor 234
Dea Samuel 234
FISH, Ann J 7 Charles P 263
Clarissa A 35 Rev J L A 7 S 35
FISHER, Aaron J Anna L 71
Annette 7 Fanny 71 Fanny 269
Harriet N 175 Jane W 116 Levi
71 269 Lois 197 Lucy 109 Mary J
116 Matthew A 116 Nellie 208
Polly 24 175 Sally 175 Col
Samuel C 45 Sarah Jane 45
Warren J 175
FISK, Alonzo 88 Emily 271 Lucy
Cutter 243 Lucy W 88 Lydia 267
Mehitable 242 Nancy 243 271
Nancy Roby 171 Ralph 243 271
William 132
FISKE, Harriet 57 Sarah 124 125
Sarah Wheeler 246
FITCH, Ann 107 Charles Darwin
194 Hon Lyman 174 Maria L 174

Sara 59
FITE, Elizabeth 132
FITTS, Rhoda 237
FITZGERALD, --- 86 Councilor 86
Polly 183 Sarah A 183 T D 183
FITZPATRICK, Maria A 188
FLAGG, Amy 163 Charles C 178
Hannah 163 Joseph 163 Marietta
178 Ruth 77 Sarah 84
FLANDERS, --- 4 73 123 152 Alice
I 5 Anna 62 Ardell I 36 Augusta
215 Caroline 233 Clarissa 4
Elsie 87 George L 5 Hannah C 54
Harriet F 180 L C 36 Malinda
170 Maria J 32 Maria J 95 Mary
Ann 73 Mary Eliza 152 Mary W
254 Moses 62 Nancy S 211 212 P
M 54 Peggy 246 Polly 123
Susannah 99 Walker 180
FLETCHER, --- 120 231 Almira B
149 Anna 83 Betsey 263 Carrie
103 Dorothy S 201 Elizabeth H
218 219 Ellen W 95 Emeline L
201 George W 95 Grace 258
Hannah 49 Hiram A 60 Hiram A
149 Jesse 30 Jonathan 218
Jotham H 134 Lucinda 134 Lucy
84 Lydia 218 Martha 209 Mary 60
189 Mary A 30 Patience 30
Persis 149 Princess 231 Rebecca
141 Ruth 115 116 S G 201 Susan
156 Susan E 134
FLING, Alice A 209 Henry 209
Sarah E 21
FLINT, Benjamin 132 Betsey 55 56
Clarissa 106 Denia H 233
Elizabeth 136 Fanny 106 Hannah
36 John W 106 Mary 80 0 S 106
Persis 106 Sally 132 Samuel 106
Susannah 265
FLOOD, Mary H 5 Mary H 6
FLOYD, Affa E 27 Affa E 30
Arnold 184 Betsey A 30 Daniel
32 Elizabeth 184 Joseph S 30
Lizzie 32
FLYNN, Lizzie 227
FOGG, --- 109 Abby P 204 Ann F
39 David 90 David H 261 Eleanor
146 Elizabeth 74 Emeline L 261
John 74 Maj Josiah 75 Josiah
204 Josiah Raymond 75 Lucy 176
Lucy Jane 75 Marietta 261
Martha 251 Mary 23 Mehitable 89
Ruth 89 90 Col Seth 146
Sherburne 89
FOLLANSBEE, Alfretta 263 Anna
129 E K 263 Eliza 116 Minnie
111
FOLLETT, Emeline A 173 Emeline A
174 Joseph W 173 Mary 173
FOLLINSBEE, Hannah J 91

FOLSOM, --- 107 Abigail 103
Abigail Peasley 118 Agnes 57
Andrew 129 Ann Elizabeth 20
Benjamin 57 Betsey 26 Elis 53
Elizabeth 57 Ellen 155 George
76 Hannah 1 93 James 128 Jane
215 241 251 Joanna W 164 165
John 20 Joshua 267 Col Levi 164
Lydie 189 1 90 Mary 125 183 232
267 Mary E 127 Mary Gordon 148
Miriam 19 Nancy 156 Lt Peter 53
Sally 129 Samuel 156 Sarah A 76
Sophia 127 Thomas 127
FOOT, Elizabeth 10
FOOTE, John B 241 Mary 241
FORBES, --- 30 Allen Hatch 213
Elizabeth 145 George W 145
Susan 30 Susan Jane 213
Susannah 270 271
FORBUSH, Elsie K 221 Henry W Esq
221
FORD, George N 1 95 Harriet 108
Janet 163 164 Lamar 144 Lydia
78 79 Mary 101 Sally 144 211
William C 78
FOREST, Deborah 1 42 Isaiah 1 42
Miranda S 142
FORIST, Elizabeth L 41 Merrill C
41
FORNUM, Ruby 6
FORREST, Agnes 208 Isaiah 123
John 227 Nancy 227 Samuel 208
Sarah 123 227 Susan K 212
FORSAITH, Amanda 1 19 Clarissa
113 114 David 170 Elzira 26 9
Hannah 271 James 113 271 Jane
159 226 Lucinda 26 9 Lydia 73
Malvina 26 9 Mathew 26 9 Matthew
226 Nancy 113 170 Sarah 109
Sarah J 181 Ursula 27 4 William
73 26 9
FORSYTH, Margaret 178 179 Dea
Matthew 178 Lt Robert 178
FOSDICK, Dea David 229 Mary
Harkness 22 9
FOSS, --- 227 Abiah W 92 Abigail
165 Alvira 54 Caroline M 1 98
Carter 212 Cotton H 93 Deborah
55 Dora B 55 56 Dorothy 227
Eliza 93 Elizabeth 18 19
Frederick I 230 George 55
Greenlief 1 98 Hannah 231 233
Harriet 93 J G M 54 Jacob 259
James B 254 John 233 Joshua 93
Julia 21 9 Julia W 212 Keziah
206 236 Laura A 259 260 Mahaley
212 Margaret 259 Martha L 206
Mary 92 185 1 86 May Ella 230
Mehetable 233 Mehitable W 270
Rebecca 1 98 259 Sally 93 Sarah
254 Stephen 206 William 92 93

270
FOSTER, --- 113 A C 176 Abigail
135 Alfreda 10 Alfreda 61
Betsey 2 Charlotte 172 E B 72
Isaac 130 Rev Jacob 113 John A
157 Laura 157 Mary 97 130 167
201 Mary E 167 Mehitable 229
Samuel 167 Stearns 97
FOUNTAIN, Ellen Melvina 236
FOWLE, Frances E 262 Robert 262
Sarah 225
FOWLER, Anna 106 Clarissa 130
Elizabeth 125 Ellen Lizette 102
Enoch 106 Esther 108 Mary 105
106 Mary Helen 259 260 Moses
Field 102 Philip 125 Sally 203
FOX, David P 118 Capt Gustavus V
272 Sally 118 Samuel 75 Sarah
75 118
FOYE, Mary E 137 Nathaniel G 137
FRANCIS, --- 140 Charles 60
Fanny 1 40 164 James 60 Joseph G
164 Louisa B 164 Susan Coffin
60
FRANK, Abigail 215
FRANKLIN, Ebeta 233 George 233
Jonathan 179 Nancy 27 Patty 45
Rachel 179
FRAQUIER, Sally 182
FRARY, Lucy 163
FRECH, Aseneth 249
FREEMAN, Asa 1 42 Elizabeth P 1 42
James O Esq 95 Phebe 245 Sally
127 Sarah 125 126 245 26 5
Susanna 95
FREESE, Sarah 68
FRENCH, --- 19 97 Abi 82 Abigail
101 Achsah Pollard 23 9 240
Adaline 4 Almira 124 Alonzo 124
Amos 13 9 Annette C 131 Annie D
128 Asenath 83 Augusta 95 Aura
3 Bernard 173 Betsey 173 Betsey
B 86 Betsy 218 248 C A 131
Charles H 131 Clarissa 184 185
Daniel 83 Deborah 122 123
Ebenezer Esq 207 Elsie 19
Hannah 44 79 95 Harriet 188
Harriet N 111 Henry K 111 Dr J
M 174 Jane 109 138 John 32 John
F 128 John L Esq 251 John
Leavitt 216 Rev Jonathan 85
Joseph 97 Josiah 118 Josie 97
Lemira 128 Dr Leonard 20 9
Malinda 263 Maria J 32 Mary 137
1 41 257 Mary C 251 Mary Davis
20 9 Mary Francis 207 Mary H 131
Mary J 174 Mary Jane 162 Mercy
163 164 Nancy 92 Norman G 265
Pamelia 118 Phineas 109 Polly
77 Rebecca 85 Robert 188 Roby
259 Sally 259 Sarah 112 183 240

265 Sarah M 32 Sophia 216 Susan
E 108 109 Susan Frances 265
Susan Matilda 139 Capt Theodore
240 Tirzah 162 Tryphena 212
William 3 Capt William 44
FRETTS, Henry 14 Joanna 14
FRINK, Abigail 214
FRIZZELL, --- 140 Gilbert L 212
Lucy H 212 Nancy 140
FROST, --- 107 Dorcas S 117
Ebenezer 124 Eliza F 265
Elizabeth Burrows 102 Henry 102
Jane N 84 Judith 84 Laura E 153
Lucy 117 Lydia 29 Margaret 261
Mary A C 17 Mary Susan 124
Newell 84 Pepperell 29 Reuben
117 Rev L P 265
FRY, --- 91 Mary 91 Mehitable 70
Sophia 234 Timothy 234
FRYE, Elisha 42 Fanny 105 Lizzie
42 Peter Y 105
FULLER, --- 35 Abbie A 262 Ann
262 Asenath 30 Calvin 30 Eliza
198 Grant 246 Isabelle 57 John
198 John Gibson 262 Letitia 75
Martin 75 Mary A 198 199 Mary H
246 Rebecca 75 Susan 98 Susan
99 Hon T P 75
FULLERTON, Betsey 48 William 48
FULLSIFER, Mary 56
FULTON, Betsy 11 Eunice 113
Francis F 170 James 113 Jane 11
Joseph W 216 Lucy A 216 Mary 11
Mary E 216 Robert 11 269 Sally
269 Sarah 170
FURBER, Alice C 41 Elizabeth 64
Elizabeth Downing 41 208 Sarah
56 Sarah A 13 William 41 64
FURBUR, Elizabeth 125 William
125
FURBUSH, Catharine 22 Daniel 22
Nancy 22
FURGURSON, Betsy 69
FURNALD, Abigail 236 John 162
Sarah Knowlton 162

GACHON, Leontine Augustine 157
GAFNEY, Charles B Esq 110 Mary
Ellen 110
GAGE, Dea Aaron 53 59 Alice A
272 Cerlania 207 Converse 207
Deborah 258 Eva M 144 Ezekiel C
272 Hannah 48 Lydia 88 269
Mehitabel 253 Phineas 269
Roswell 144 Sally 53 59 127
Sarah 144 Susan E 207 Susannah
249
GALE, --- 39 Abigail 78 Dr Amos
G 8 Bartholomew 138 Caroline P
194 Caroline Persis 194 Clara A
32 Col 78 Mrs Edna Little 81

Rev Jonathan 194 Louisa A 32
Lovina 32 Luke 32 Mary 138 Mary
G 8 Sarah Folsom 138
GANNET, Charlotte 60 Susan 104
William 60
GANNETT, Consider 131 Keziah 131
Miranda 111 Philena 123 Sophia
123 Susan 123
GARDNER, --- 69 70 181 A D 202
Hannah 248 Mary Parker 247
Rebecca 202 Shubael Dimick 70
Judge W S 247 William 69
GARFIELD, Saloma 100 Sarah 155
GARLAND, Abigail 149 Anna D 26
Betsey 126 D Jennie 22 David 71
Dorcas A 202 Eliza 126 Hannah
163 Rev J W 26 John 71 126
Joseph K 202 Louisa 22 Lydia N
223 Mary 212 Mary J 71
Mehetable 126 Nancy 71 Olive
224 Sally 92 Samuel P 163
Sophia 87 True 223 William P 22
GARLIN, Mary 124
GARMAN, Deborah 55 James 55
Sarah J 55 Olive 76
GARRISON, Josephine Emma 55
GATES, William 183
GATHERCOLE, John 144 Maria C 144
GAULT, Andrew 87 Dolly 48 Jesse
48 Mary D 87 208 Sally 221
Sarah 87 Sarah S 47 William 47
GAY, Albert 235 Ardenia 157
Ellen Maria 235 George E 157
Nancy 15
GAYER, Dorcas 237 William 237
GAYLORD, Caroline 134
GENISON, Rebecca 144
GENTLEMAN, Mary 196
GEORGE, --- 113 Benjamin F 245
Charles 65 Charles S 41
Christabel 41 Clara 5 6 45
Comfort 245 Darius 183 David
Esq 113 Elizabeth 161 Ella 65
67 Rev Enos 83 Fanny 16
Gilliman 16 Jane 65 Jeannette
McKeith Wilson 65 Jeremy 183
John 224 Julia A 83 Lizzie H
154 Lucy 224 Mary 183 Mary Ann
229 Medora 121 Sarah H 143
Walker 224
GEORGG, Medora 121 Willman 121
GEROULD, Cynthia S 25 Rev Moses
25 Sarah A 25
GERRISH, --- 49 Almira C 100
Enoch 151 Eunice M 126 Harlan P
100 Col Joseph 190 Joseph W 126
Lucy 153 Martha 153 Mary 190
272 Nancy Thompson 106 Ruth 151
Sally 85 Samuel B 272 Sarah 272
GERRY, Jemima 109 Joseph 109
Ruth 4

GIBSON, --- 92 Hannah 271
Loraine 231 Nancy M 125 Persis
175 Robert 271 Samuel 231
GIDDINGS, --- 54 Anne 54 Eleanor
229 230 232 Ellen 232 Hannah F
174 Sarah 174 William 174
GIFFIN, Jane 113
GIFFORD, Anable 82 Elmira 15
Ezra T 15 Laura E 273 O J 273
GILBERT, Abigail 69 70 Alvira
149 Mrs Ann 96 Mrs Ann Burrows
94 Betsey 70 Betsy 69 Clarissa
56 Clarrissa 55 Eliza I 267
Elizabeth Burrows 96 Ellen
Lizette 93 94 John 94 96 Joseph
120 149 Lydia 23 Pattee 120 269
Sarah 120 Susan Page 149 Col
Thomas 23 55
GILCHRIST, Alice 251 Sarah D 275
GILCREST, David 275 Sarah 275
Sarah D 275
GILE, Elizabeth 85 Frances E 207
Martha 254 255 Mary A 140 Noah
85 Olive A 254 P S H 207 Peter
254
GILES, C A 242 George 197 Mary A
197 Patience 274 275 Rosette
242 Sarah 129 195
GILLINGHAM, Alzina 132 Alzina E
80 Anna 198 Benjamin 16 Clara
53 Elizabeth 80 Freeman H 198
Hannah 175 176 James 80 Lydia
176 Moody 53 Sarah 16
GILLIS, Betsey 212 Henry C 237
John 97
GILLMAN, Betsey 89
GILMAN, --- 70 155 171 172
Abigail 54 71 248 249 Benjamin
19 Benjamin 56 Betsy R 212
Bridget 117 Caroline 118
Deborah 13 14 Ednah 81 Emerette
L 260 George E 81 Hannah 19 26
Henry H 45 James 96 James M 111
Jane W 147 Jeremiah 117 Col
Jeremiah 165 John T 71 212
Jonathan C 126 Rev Josiah 178
Laura 111 Lavinia F 56 Livona
117 Mary 26 Mary C 119 Mary
Frances 194 Mary O 155 Nancy C
231 Nathaniel 155 Col Peter 172
Peter 267 Sarah 70 164 165 266
267 Sceera 96 Sophia 126 Susan
154 Thomas J 260 Virgil C 103
Ward 26 William 231
GILMORE, --- 42 Anna S 262 Gov
Joseph A 42 Martha 75 76 Mary J
227 Mitchel S Esq 262
GILSON, Anna 190 Charles R 188
Jennie S 188 Sarah 231 Sarah W
104 Solomon 117 Tamar 117
GLAZIER, Betsey 270

GLEASON, Elsea 97
GLIDDEN, Mrs Abigail 218 Alice G
58 231 Betsy 104 231 232 233
254 Squire Charles Sr 231
Charles Mills 58 231 Eliza F
248 Jasper E 248 Mary H 248
Mary Y 58
GLINES, Eliza J 215 Elizabeth
231 233 Isaac 99 Nelson A 215
Phebe 99
GLOVER, Benjamin 230 Cynthia D
230 Diana 40 Elizabeth 97 Lucy
Ann 96 Martha J R 230 Polly 230
Seth 96 Susan 170
GLYNN, Martha J 142 Thomas F 142
GODFREY, Adeline 14 224 Capt
James 14 Jonathan 274 Marcia E
274 Sarah 232 Theodate 14
Theodatie 274
GODRON, Sarah 115
GOEWEY, Hester 94 95
GOFF, Pauline 180
GOOCH, Arthur W 274 Mary A 274
GOODALE, Caroline G 41 211
Celestia S 171 Elbert 105 Eliza
Ann 109 Elizabeth 156 Hannah
156 Hon John H 171 Jonathan 109
154 Laura A 41 101 Lucy 154
Mary 139 Mary C 211 Mehitable
43 Polly 108 109 Robert 156
Sarah 109 Thomas Newton 41 211
GOODALL, Bernice H 255 Emma J
268 Ira 255 Ira Esq 38 Julia R
38 Lewis 268 Lucretia 38
GOODELL, Anna 139 Asa 139
Clarissa 89 Dolly P 24 Emeline
L 134 Fanny 89 John 24 John 89
Dea Jonathan 83 Lucy S 54
Luther 89 Mary 83 Nancy B 24
Persis 89
GOODHUE, Alvin 35 Andrew A 269
Calista 269 Deborah 103 Eva E
35 Hannah 51 52 Martha A 117
GOODRICH, Lucy 24
GOODWIN, --- 4 15 Anna 176
Armine 196 Betsy 15 Eben 5
Elizabeth 148 Elizabeth J 153
John 199 Judith S 70 Lydia 137
Moses 196 Persis 5 Sally 4 155
196 Sally S 28 29 Sarah T 43
COOKIN Mary 260 Mary Shackford
259 260 Nathaniel 260
GOOKINS, Anne 68
GOOLD, Alice 85 Marcus L 85
GORDON, --- 48 Annie 151 173
Betsy J 216 Charlotte 48 Clara
E 268 Cyrus 13 Deborah 133
Edwin 107 Elizabeth 176 Ephraim
268 Eunice 156 Flora 261
Frances 107 108 Francis A 159
Ida May 69 Jacob 156 Jane 191

John B 69 Laura A 13 Lewis B
216 Lovina 261 Lucy 261 Martha
A 266 Martha Dickinson 159
Martha H 261 Mary 174 251 Mary
D 107 Mary L 212 Moses 176
Nathaniel 107 Orrin C 266
Phineas S 261 Ruhama E 69 Ruth
Ayer 219 Sarah 34 Thomas 107
GOSS, Abbie M 31 Ashley 35
Calista 31 Elizabeth (Lizzie) J
22 Ellen 210 Irena 32 Laura A
35 Lizzie J 23 Martha 241 Mary
98 99 241 Maryett 22 Nathaniel
241 Reuben 31 Susan 31 William
22
GOTT, Mary 144 Mary 145
GOUDY, Alden P 234 Augusta 234
GOUGH, Anna G 87
GOULD, Alice M 165 Augustine 118
Benjamin 116 Mrs Caroline 43
Charlotte 48 Dea Daniel 2 Col
Daniel C 2 David 81 Elizabeth 2
79 148 Elizabeth Collins 73
Ephraim 169 Eunice 118 Hannah
116 Horace 48 John 75 Leonora
160 Lydia 75 133 Moses E 73
Nancy 192 Nathaniel 79 Noah 192
Roxana 146 Sarah A 25
GOVE, Almira 161 Ann 54 Benjamin
F 191 Charles 227 Daniel 156
David 257 Ebenezer 205 Edmund
54 Eliza P 267 Ella 53 Enoch 42
Hannah 43 227 Hannah J 97
Hannah Philbrick 159 Hannah W
227 Henry 97 Hon Jonathan 24
175 Jonathan 16 105 Judith 205
Lucy Ann 175 Marcia E 25 Martha
16 Mary 16 201 Mary Morrill 257
Melissa 191 Moses B 96 Polly 24
105 161 175 191 Polly E 24
Rachel 42 Richard 232 Sally 156
Sarah Ann 17 Susan E 96
Winthrop 257 Wyer 201
GOWELL, Abigail 255
GOWEN, Roxanna 255 256
GRACE, Lucy 156 157
GRAHAM, Ann Annaline F 175
Esther 92 Francis 113 114
Francis Jr 113 114 Rev J D 175
Col James D 101 Robert 92
Salvadora Meade 101
GRANDIN, Grace H 58 J L 58
GRANT, --- 4 84 Caroline Carter
97 Charles 206 Charlotte M 129
Charlotte S 129 Deliverance 40
Louisa C 206 Dr Nathaniel 129
Salome V 206
GRANVILLE, Joseph F 120 Susie C
120
GRAPES, Nancy 98
GRAVES, Abigail 199 Abigail M 36

Abram 1 Hannah 197 James 103
Phebe J 1 Phineas 103
GRAY, --- 81 99 Abigail 1 2 221
Albert 266 Angeline E 266
Daniel 81 Emily J 266 Hannah
262 Capt James 30 John 196
Lucinda 196 Lucretia B 30
Martha 215 Mary 201 Miranda 99
Olive 44 Sally 168 169
GREELEY, Abigail 156 Almeda 57
Anna Maria 48 Clarissa 91
Daniel Esq 149 Eliza Gibbs 149
Jonathan Esq 88 Joseph 172
Martha 54 Mary L 128 172 Mary Q
171 172 Nancy 172 Stephen Esq
48 Susan E 88 Wilder 91
GREELY, Elizabeth 166 Merrill
166
GREEN, --- 8 40 133 Adaline 218
Daniel 47 53 128 263 Dr Ezra
123 George 133 Mrs Hannah 186
Helen Elizabeth 53 Jemima 79 80
Lucinda Angelina 128 Mary 81
Nancy 172 Persis Georgianna 47
Peter Esq 8 Dt Peter 40 Polly
47 53 128 263 Susanna 5 123
GREENE, Alpha 157 Hannah 209
Capt James 209 Mary L 62 Mercy
209 Thomas 157 William E 62
GREENEY, Elizabeth 75
GREENFIELD, Ebenezer G 255 John
249 Sarah E 255
GREENLAW, John W 263 Viola 263
GREENLEAF, Elizabeth 10 Mary 105
106 Nathaniel 48 Sarah 48
GREENOUGH, Caroline A 229
Elizabeth McFarland 182
Jonathan 229 Louisa R 81 Lucy A
129 130 Mehitable 129 Sarah 236
W J 235 William 129 William S
182
GREENSLADE, Joanna 8
GREENWOOD, Bellona 67 Gilman 67
Lucy 67 Martha 52
GREGG, Abial 73 Alexander 167
269 Anna 167 168 Asanath 156
Bessie 35 Betsey 24 Catherine
113 Cristy 168 David 73
Elizabeth 77 Eunice 97 Frances
231 Hannah 264 James 109 264
Capt James 45 Janet 45 John 24
Judith 109 Lydia 24 97 Mary 45
167 Mary 168 Mr 35 Nancy 180
Rebecca 269 Sally 159 Samuel 45
Capt Samuel 97 Sarah 26 29
GRIFFIN, Augusta 76 Hiram 252
James 146 Jerusha 146 Lydia S
252 Mary 179 Mary Jane 146
Nancy E 31 Ruth 217 218 Sarah
131
GRIFFITH, Sarah 176

GRIFFITHS, John B 261 Ruth 261
GRIMES, Ann 159 160 Betsy 271
David 139 David W 252 Elizabeth
254 Francis 138 160 267 Harriet
252 Col James F 139 Jane 134
John 254 271 Mary 138 267 Mary
E 139 Nathan 132 Sarah A 139
Sarah F 138 Susan 254
GRISWOLD, --- 157
GROSVENOR, Dr Edward 219 Harriet
W 219 Mary 41
GROUARD, Hannah L 29 John P 29
GROUT, Col Ebenezer 60 Polly 60
61
GROVER, --- 39 A J 130 Anna A
130 Carrie C 247 Clarissa 15
Ephraim 138 Frank 247 Mary A
138
GUILD, Mary A 7
GUPTIL, Henrietta 265 Levi 265
Mary 100
GUPTILL, Frank 129 Rebecca 56
GURDY, Nancy 86 154
GUTTERSON, John 45 Kate M 44
Mary A 73 S Frances 45

HACKET, Harriet A 260 Jude 106
Mary 106
HACKETT, Chase T 223 Marcia E
223 Marianna 199 Mary 39 Sally
3 Susan 223
HADDOCK, --- 144 Henry 120
HADLEY, Abigail Elizabeth 135
Arabella 62 Belinda 264
Caroline 62 Dr 266 Enoch 108
Esther 74 Helen M 52 Hepzibah
241 Leonard 271 Lois P 4 Mary
271 Mary Ann 108
HADLOCK, Albert 105 Eliza Ann
105 Elizabeth 62 Eunice 156
Hannah 17 Hezekiah 154 Judith
113 Lucy 154 Lucy J 251 Lydia
159 160 Sarah 105 106 Susan 119
HAGAR, Susan 157
HAGGET, Abigail 87 Benjamin 87
John 87 Thursay 87
HAGUE, Sarah W 58 William W 58
HAINES, --- 62 147 Abbie P 170
Cynthia L 188 Elizabeth W 260
Hannah 49 116 147 215 Capt John
118 Josiah 49 Martha P 219 Mary
57 260 272 Mary Bean 118 Moody
B 272 Dea Samuel 260 Sarah 166
167 Susan 218 219 268
HALE, --- 42 124 224 Clara E 47
Eliza J 159 Elizabeth 203
Elvira 15 Maj Ezra 142 Hannah M
91 Henry 258 Jacob 92 James 159
Jane 15 Col John 203 Hon John P
42 Capt Josiah 47 Livonia 142
Lydia D 194 Mary 206 258 Mary S

156 Mindwell 161 Nancy 262
Royal 91 Hon Salma 126 Dr
Samuel 161 Sarah 126 258 Simeon
15 Susanna 91
HALEY, Abel 201 Rev Frank 202
Samuel 33 Sarah 34 202 Sarah E
33 Thomas 34
HALL, --- 64 74 123 128 Alba 245
Alpheus 23 Amra 249 Annette 59
Betsey 110 202 Caroline B 264
Catherine 16 Mrs Charlotte 117
Clarinda J 241 Daniel 128 218
219 David 34 Dorcas 2 Ebenezer
70 Ebenezer L D 1 Lt Edward 204
Elias M 241 Eliza S 235 Hannah
204 217 218 219 247 Henry 59
Isaac W 83 J Cummings 264 James
H 266 Jeremiah 266 Capt John
137 Sergt John 64 Jonathan 1 34
Joseph 199 Joshua G 202 Julia
23 Julia T 88 Kinsley 150 Lois
83 Louisa 217 Louisa Augusta
217 Lucy A 269 Luther F 75
Lydia 1 70 204 Margaret T 1
Maria G 96 97 Maria K 266
Marietta 74 75 Martha 155 Mary
31 72 75 90 137 150 151 152
Mary Christiner 120 Mary E 110
Mary V 1 97 Nancy 76 261 Nannie
Moor 59 Patience 123 218 219
Philander 217 Ralph 1 95 Rev
Ralph 120 Rosilla 23 Ruth 27
261 Sally W 208 Salome 34 Sarah
261 Susan 34 Theophilus 247
Thomas 233 Thomas H 269 Vina
245 William 88 Capt William 261
HALLOWELL, Hannah 76 John 76
HAM, --- 202 203 Ann Sophia 123
Israel P 39 James 181 John 125
211 John S F 123 Lowell 186
Marie 186 Martha J 39 Mary 26
122 123 125 Melissa 181
Nicholas 256 Ruth 211 Sally 256
Sarah 112 157 249
HAMBLET, Abigail 157 Alice O 227
Osni P 157
HAMBLETT, David 3 Emma 3
HAMBLIN, Mrs Sarah 180
HAMILTON, Alexander 192 Betsey
139 Emily M 60 Jennie 157 John
C 192 Maria E 192 Ziba 139
HAMM, Mary 122
HAMMOND, Charles A 228 Clara M
228 David 228 E B 2 Elizabeth
124 Esther D 117 Flora S 228
Lydia 218 Mary L 117 Mary N 138
Nathan 117 Rodney 138 Sarah Ann
2 Sarah N 117
HAMMONDS, Lucinda 127
HANCOCK, --- 227 Sally 172
HANDLEY, Rebecca 55

HANKS, --- 114 Helen M 103 Sarah 114
HANNAFORD, Jabez R 117 Lettice T 61 Lucy M 117 Ruth 117
HANSOM, Abigail 122 Ichabod 122
HANSON, --- 266 Abigail M 91 Charity 159 Cynthia J 48 Elisha 223 259 Eliza 37 Eliza N 259 Eliza T 178 Ellen 193 Eunice C 217 George S 275 Huldah 223 Joanna 157 159 John T 178 Joseph 159 Lewis E 249 Lizzie 157 159 Mary 43 253 Moses 253 Otis 114 Sarah 42 43 115 Sarah E 249 Sophia A 274 Timothy 91
HARBOUR, Mary E 161
HARDEY, Annette M 115 David 115 Sarah 115
HARDIN, Hitty 99 Jacob 99
HARDING, Louise 65
HARDY, Annette M 116 Betsey 96 Caroline E 22 132 133 256 Daniel 96 132 Dorcas 169 Elbridge 143 Emeline F 144 Georgia C 143 Israel 96 Johnson 139 Laura J C 147 Lois 59 Lovinia 94 139 Marcus A 147 Mary 48 139 Nancy 226 Oliver 139 Pamelia 96 Sally 139
HARKNESS, Elizabeth 229 Mary 229
HARLOW, Joseph 97 Sarah Jane 97
HARNDEN, Jane 185 Laura A 98
HARNDON, Laura A 97
HARPER, Mary 89
HARRAN, Judith B 29
HARRIMAN, Caroline 194 Dorcas 197 Elizabeth 107 108 Elvira 61 Hannah 232 240 Hubbard 169 James D 63 John 74 Margaret 223 Mary 169 182 Mary M 63 Mehitable 93 Milton 61 Nancy 38 Sally 74 75 Sophia 5 William 194
HARRINGTON, Judith 43 Moses 43
HARRIS, --- 194 Caroline A 259 Dr Chalres 233 Daniel 25 Electa J 25 Hannah H 131 Jason Esq 113 Dr Jerome 77 Joshua Esq 131 Lucretia 194 Lydia 124 M W 124 Margaret 233 Mary 28 29 77 233 Mary Helen 77 Mary Helen 78 Ursula J 113
HARRISON, Esther C 256 James 256
HART, Betsey 26 Ella J 188 Ellen A 54 Emma W 54 George 175 Hannah 99 Louisa 175 Louisa A 175 Lydia 70 Marcy 155 Orin F 54 Susan 100
HARTNESS, Elizabeth 35
HARTSHORN, Abbey 64
HARTSHORNE, Mary L 39

HARTWELL, Rev H H 221 Rhoda 274 Sallie S 221
HARVEY, --- 236 Almira M 207 Daniel 270 Elizabeth 157 238 Eva 56 Fanny 270 Jacob S 207 John L 155 Maria E 155 Mary S 272 Melvina 270 Susannah 236
HARWOOD, Joseph 102 Joseph 269 Mary Wilder 269 Pattee 269 Sarah 61 William 61
HASELTINE, Margaret 158 Polly 193 245 Rev 157
HASELTON, Mary H 85 Capt Samuel 85 Sarah 49
HASKELL, Caroline H 242 Hannah 51 Marcia 242 Martha 194
HASLETINE, Elder 245
HASSELTON, Nancy J 131
HASTINGS, John 126 Jonas 267 Kezia 24 Levi 228 Lydia 228 Mary C 126 Phebe 226 Philinda 35 Polly 191 Sophia 267
HATCH, Alfred 44 Benjamin 64 Charles 196 Charlotte 44 Ellen R 259 260 Gamaliel 210 George 200 Hannah 131 210 Harriet 196 Jerusha 64 Louisa Frances 210 Lydia 85 Martin 85 Mary 101 Dr Mason 210 Newlon S 131 Rowena 6 Samuel 101
HATHORN, Lydia 4
HAUFT, Kitty 5
HAVEN, Mrs Elizabeth 248 John 68 Martha 68 Rev Dr Samuel 68
HAWES, David C 217 Mary H 217
HAWKES, Benjamin 176 Clarissa 53 Colburn 53 David Knowlton 21 Helen 21 Helen Maria 53 Lucy 176 Martha L 85 176 Susan 21
HAWKINS Amasa 236 Carrie B 153 Lewis A 153 Mary 188 Sarah 236 Sarah Ann 236
HAWKS, Abigail 10 53 146 162 Catharine 73 Farrington 73
HAYDEN, Eunice 112
HAYES, Betsey 67 Betty 211 Clementine E 35 Elihu 67 Elisabeth 122 Elizabeth 122 Ichabod 122 John 122 157 John H 62 Jonathan 63 Joseph 69 83 Kate W 62 Lois 69 Lydia 100 Marcia 83 Maria 13 Mary 63 211 Mary Fannie 157 159 Mehitable 248 249 Patience 13 Polly 254 Reuben 13 112 Sarah 263 Dea Solomon 122 Susanna 112 Tamsen 63 Tamsen Wentworth Chesley 122 Wentworth 211
HAYFORD, David 6 Elizabeth 6 Joanna 5 6 Nathaniel 99 Philena 99 Priscilla 99 Seth 99 Susan

99
HAYNES, Adaline B 4 Charlotte 57
David 44 Lusena 10 Olive 22 23
Rebecca 44 Reuben 129 Roxanna
129 Sarah 129 T C 10
HAYWARD, Charles P 267 Charlotte
146 Louisa 267
HAYWOOD, --- 46 Caroline E 10 E
10 Ellen 46 Emily 72 Parthena
66 Rebecca 160
HAZELTINE, Abigail 186 Joanna
206
HAZELTON, Betsey 136 Eliza A 136
Ellen D 25 F R 148 Hannah 101
James 136 Johanna 16 Lizzie E
263 Martha 25 263 Rufus 263
Rufus B 25 Ruth 103 Sylvia W
148
HAZEN, Harriet A 134 J V 134
HEAD, Abbie 48 Abigail 100 Anna
31 Col John 31 Lydia J 62
Margaret 101 Mary H 221 Gen
Nathaniel 48 Ruth 151 W F Esq
221
HEALD, Ephraim 225 Mary 152 225
Sadie 146 Sibyl 152 153 Capt
Thomas 152
HEALEY, Nellie L 95 Newell W 95
HEALY, Catharine 11 Desire 251
HEARD, Anne Elizabeth 163
Benjamin 211 Elizabeth 98 183
211 Emily Maria 163 Capt John
98 183 Susan 161 Tristram 121
William 161 Hon William A 163
HEATH, Albert 249 Anne 52 53
Betsy 261 Deborah 198 Dorothy
56 Eben 62 Eliza 249 Elizabeth
158 Judith 124 Leuella 62 Liva
54 Lovina 30 Lucia 256 Lucinda
250 Mary 173 Mrs Mary A 162
Mary Ann 111 Priscilla 91
Relief 66 67 Sally 74 77 Sarah
13 106 107 173 183 Capt Simon
157 Solomon 54 Susan 136
William 173
HEATON, Mary 45
HEITH, Philena 135
HEMENWAY, Clarissa 259 Solomon
259
HEMMENWAY, Martha W 259
HENDERSON, Charles 108 Lois S 69
Olive A 108 William 69
HENRY, Catherine M 65
HERBERT, Ellen 105 George C 109
Henry W 65 Lucy T 109 Susan 65
HERRICK, Editha 94 Elizabeth 94
Henry 94 Jonathan 53 Sara 53
HERSEY, Edward 128 Elizabeth 128
Levi 201
HESTER, Katherine 189 190
HEWES, Dolly R 237 J R 237 Sarah

F 11 Sylvanus 11
HEYWOOD, H O 220 Mary 220
HIBBARD, Charles F 144 Hon David
126 Hannah E 44 John 150 Lois
261 Martha Jane 150 Mary C 120
Susan 126 Susan M 144 Timothy
120
HIBBERT, Dorcas 1
HICKEY, Elizabeth 15
HICKINS, Almira 48 Ellen M 48
Joseph 48
HICKOK, --- 24 Mary 24
HICKS, Elizabeth C 195 Rebecca
57
HIDDEN, Angeline 212 John D 212
HIGGINS, Caroline 134
HIGHT, Betsey 126
HILDRETH, --- 18 Abigail 82
David B 18 Elkanah 264 Polly
255 Rhoda 135 Sally 264 Susan
180
HILL, --- 271 Abigail 117
Adeline W 92 Ann C 72 Anna
Blaisdell 79 80 Arnor 223
Augustus 177 Benjamin 117
Betsey 78 117 Charles A 92 Ella
H 139 Esther 121 Eunice 77
Freeman 53 George A 18 George W
45 Gilbert P 72 Hannah 53
Hannah H 9 Hiram 150 Hon Isaac
209 Isabella 81 Johanna 7 John
78 Mrs Lavosier 77 Louisa W 177
Lucina P 101 Lydia 90 Maria 18
Martha 140 Martha E 95 Mary
Eliza 145 Mary Elizabeth 150
Patty 41 Rebecca R 209 Rhoda
150 151 Sabrina 45 Sally 48 154
271 Samuel 145 Susan 84 Susan A
157 Susan S 45 William 95
William W 139
HILLARD, Caroline M 181 Sarah
181 Dr Timothy 181
HILLIARD, Alma P 137 Alta L G
255 256 Christopher 228 Eliza
218 Capt H S 137 Rev Joseph 256
Joseph C 29 Martha E 228 Mary
228 Sarah 29 156
HILLMAN, Hannah Eastman 194 Rev
Thomas 194
HILLS, Charles P 237 Elizabeth G
237 Mary 244 Mehitable 129 205
Rowena 136 Ruth 220
HILTON, Charlotte 184 Daniel 177
184 Dorothy 148 Elizabeth 177
Elizabeth Folsom 200 Polly 86
Winthrop 148
HINCKLEY, Caroline 151 Col
Oramel 151
HINES, Barzilla 20 Patience 20
HINKLEY, James F 154 Lucina 154
HINMAN, Blanche 72

HIRSCH, George 221 Sallie S 221
Mrs Sally 119
HIRST, --- 195
HISCOCK, Clara M 27 Ora S 27
HITCHCOCK, --- 151 Hannah 190
John 190
HITCHOCK, Hannah 189
HOAG, Mary A 175 176 Mary E 91
Stephen 20 Susannah 20 21
HOBARD, Lucy 35
HOBART, Albert 35 Elizabeth 234
Emily 55 Hannah 263 Ida A 35
Dea Josiah 201 Lavinia 201 Lois
213 Reuben 263 Sally 138
HOBBIE, C Henry 240 Catherine
240
HOBBS, Abigail 236 237 Anna
Maria 172 Annie D 95 Armenia E
265 Bertha 251 Betsy A 98 193
272 Catherine 110 Charlotte S
110 129 Dorothy 138 Dorothy C
128 Emma Josephine 45 Esther 73
74 Frank 215 Frank Esq 45 Helen
M 227 Henry 37 Horatio 265
James 74 John 53 128 John F 95
John O 172 Joseph 138 Laura A
215 Mary M 51 Morris 251 Nancy
143 Nathaniel 143 Olive A 128
Phebe 72 Capt Samuel 272 Sarah
53 74 100 251 Sarah Frances 169
Thomas 128 William 110 William
Esq 51
HOBERT, Patience 30
HOBNAN, Mellie 71
HOBSON, Lucy 3 4
HODGDON, Betsey 227 228
Deliverance 49 Elizabeth 192
Elizabeth F 223 263 Eunice 238
Hanson 127 Lucinda Angeline 112
Mary 127 Moses 263 Moses Jr 112
Mrs Rebeckah 156 Russel 156
Sarah J 198 Shadrock 192 Susan
M 192
HODGE, --- 67 David 249 Maria 67
Mary 202
HODGES, Georgiana 273
HODGKINS, Augustus 215 Jennie
215
HODGSKIN, Eunice 126
HODSDON, Amy 129 Amy W 217
Arthur L 110 Charlotte M 110 Dr
Daniel 143 E P 69 Ebenezer 217
Emma B 69 Nancy 143 Sally 217
HOEGG, Lucy 212 Lucy 213
HOFFMAN, Catherine 91
HOGDON, --- 202 Almira 241
Joseph 241 Olive G 183 Pamelia
202 Sarah O 241
HOGG, Rebecca 129
HOGSDON, Sarah 88
HOIT, --- 147 Capt Benjamin 34

Betsey 59 60 260 Clarissa 30
Gen Daniel 19 Eliza 19
Elizabeth J 267 Nancy 33 34
Judge Nathan 59 Thomas 30
HOITT, Charles W 104 Elizabeth
123 Hariet Louise 104
HOLBROOK, Hon Adin 238 Elizabeth
234 Griggs 226 Lydia 43 Mary A
238 Mary Jane 226
HOLD, Dorcas 194 Dea John 194
HOLDEN, Joanna 27 Josua B 177
HOLLISTER, Dr H H 44 Myra 44
HOLMAN, Mary A 210 Nelly 89
William A 89
HOLMES, --- 166 237 Abra 64 B B
37 Edward A 218 Elizabeth 252
253 Elizabeth B 208 Ephraim 252
Esther T 37 John 13 John L 24
Lydia 78 Margaret F 166 Maria
Jane 12 13 Mary 28 Mary E 24
Rev Obadiah 28 Olive 254 Sarah
13 Susan 39 Thomas 208
HOLT, Abiah 78 Abigail 87 Dorcas
88 Capt Ephraim 130 Frye 77 H H
256 Hannah 12 77 78 130 Harriet
E 263 Joshua 12 Lydia 77 Maria
A 168 Martha A 256 Mary 192
Mary R 24 Mrs Sarah 268 Tamesin
194
HOLTON, Sally 246 Timothy 246
HOMAN, Rachel 239 240
HOMANS, Gilbert W 171 Hannah 66
Jane C 171 Milla H 171
HOOD, Susie H 191
HOOK, Daniel 249 Hannah 218
Hannah P 42 181 Jacob 7 Josiah
42 Mary 7 Polly 49 Priscilla
250 Sallie 193 Sarah 42
HOPE, Mary Harriet 26
HOPKINS, Ebenezer 208 Jane
Russell 179 Jerusha 244 Lavina
180 Margaret 179 Mary Nesmith
208 Sally 154 Col Samuel 180
HOPKINSON, Elizabeth 210 Mary C
210 211 Moses 210
HORN, James W 20 Nellie 20
HORNE, --- 122 123 Daniel 211
Isaiah 217 Mary 121 122 123
Mary B 155 Nathaniel 122 Relief
211 Sarah 122
HORNER, Abbie E 216 W L 216
HORTON, L H 69
HOSFORD, J T 143 Julia L 143
HOSKINS, Hannah 177 Phila 93
HOSLEY, Hon John 190 Marion J
190
HOSWELL, Julia B 188
HOUGH, Clark 241 Frances A 241
HOUGHTON, Elizabeth T 72 Ellen
46 Lucy L 144 Sarah 222 223
HOUSTON, --- 113 Eliza 206 Henry

C 206 John 121 Laura 93
Lucretia 225 226 Margaret 56 72
121 144 225 226 240 Mary 21
Sarah 222 223 Selina 206
HOVEY, Beulah 131 Minnie 80
Myron 80
HOWARD, Ann J 41 Charlotte
Webster 242 Ezra P 94 Hannah
120 Hannah M 120 Mrs Harriet B
1 96 Joseph 268 Maria 9 Martha
Abbie 198 Mary 94 Mary H 94
Patty 5 6 274 Philantha L 268
Wealthy 151 William H 242
HOWE, Abigail Richards 238 Ada
Elizabeth 142 Anna 263 Betsey
1 90 Charity 275 Ebenezer 78
Elizabeth 142 Frances 6 Hannah
6 Hiram 182 Isaac 6 Kate 3
Lemuel 238 Lucius M 142 Lucy 58
Mary 161 Phebe 163 Sally 23 9
240 242 Sarah 78 Susanna E 66
Tabitha 39 40 Theresa 4
HOWLAND, --- 126 227 Emma A 252
Moses N 225 Parker 252 Phebe
126 Rhoda 6 Sylvia A 225
HOWLET, Mary A 62 Sarah 61
HOWLETT, Mary 105 106 Thomas 105
HOYET, John 109 Sarah 109
HOYT, --- 92 267 Alzada 80
Andrew 173 Apphia K 118 Asa 183
239 Dea Benjamin 157 Benjamin F
80 Betsey 59 Caroline E 22 256
Clara 193 Cordelia 255 Dolman C
80 Eliza 256 Eliza C 242 Eliza
J 23 Elizabeth 193 Elizabeth A
71 Ella M 30 Enos 141 Esther
220 Flora E 71 72 Francelia 141
Hannah 157 Hannah B 47 Horace F
22 256 Isaac B 255 James Jr 219
John P 30 Joseph 35 75 Judith
86 220 Julia 267 Lavina 156 157
Lavina F 206 Lavinia Peaslee
219 Louisa L 80 Lucy 239 Lucy A
182 183 Lydia 35 Maria E 254
Mary 35 75 Mary J 22 Miriam C
86 Olive G 183 Dr Peter L 71
Phebe 5 6 144 Polly 75 Rhoda 32
239 240 Rhoda H 32 Ruth Ayer
219 Samuel 86 Sarah 79 80 Sarah
E 173 Stephen 220 Capt Stephen
118 Susan 173 Thomas 5 Thomas C
32 William G 47
HUBBARD, Allen T 5 Betsey 170
Catherine R 126 Comfort 259 260
Eliza Jane 5 Dr George H 140
Laura 156 Leah 61 Lucy 177 Mary
150 Melissa 83 Mercy 239 240
Nathaniel 209 Sally Martin 140
Sarah 117 209 Susan 218
Thankful 257 Thomas 170 260
HUCKINS, Amanda P 245 Caroline

118 Dr David 265 Dorcas H 245
Georgianna 185 Hannah 104 Jane
H 39 John B 245 Mary 215 Nancy
1 Samuel 185 Sarah F 265
HUGHES, Eleanor 86 Elenor 86
Michael 86
HULL, Elizabeth 125 183 Rev
Joseph 125
HULTH, Virginia 43
HUMPHREY, Elizabeth P 261 Lydia
134
HUNGERFORD, Mrs Annie 174
HUNKING, Dr Benjamin 89 Persis
89 149 Persis E 89
HUNKINGS, Jonathan 186 Olive A
186
HUNKINS Adaline C 60 Dr Benjamin
84 Drusilla S 84 Romanzo J 60
HUNNIWELL, Hannah F 266
HUNT, --- 24 Deborah 24 Eliza
Ann 157 Hannah 107 Harriet 76
John N 76 Joshua W 157 Mary 20
Sally 195 196
HUNTER, Abigail 203
HUNTING, Esther 256 Susan 210
HUNTINGTON, Anna 185 Benjamin
269 Betsey 160 Elizabeth 20
Esther 11 Fanny 11 12 Hezekiah
11 Mrs Mart 220 Miriam 20 Polly
172 269 Sarah 109
HUNTLEY, Mary Elizabeth Brackett
187
HUNTON, Flora E 39
HUNTOON, Anna 104 Celia 86
Charles 4 Persis 4 Stephen 119
HUNTRESS, Olive 252
HURD, Caroline 211 Edward C 211
Eliza G 190 Esther 191 Hiram
191 Phila 191 William B 190
HURLBURT, --- 76 Angie 156 Anna
76 David 106 Elihu 106 Emeline
L 106 Mary 106 Willard 156
HURLBUTT, Betsey 36 Bettie 36
David J 37 Delia M 37 Edna 37
Mary 242 Rebecca 86
HUSE, Abigail 62 Daniel M 172
Hattie N 29 John 78 Lavina A
172 Mary 26 61 78
HUSON, Polly 202
HUSSEY, Christopher 10 Hulda 257
Huldan 253 Mary 185 186 253
Theodate 10
HUSTON, Mary 89
HUTCHIN, Nancy 48
HUTCHINS, --- 5 173 Betsey 49
231 Caroline 273 David 195 Rev
Elias 5 Eliza 273 Ellen M 200
Frances 268 Hannah 212 James
273 Laura 104 Lucy 195 Mary 32
Molly 223 Nancy H 195 Nancy J
32 Nathaniel 160 Ruth 164 165

Sally 160 Stephen 32
HUTCHINSON, --- 131 Abel 34
Betsey 34 Catherine Frances 7
Chestina H 273 David 239
Elizabeth 34 35 105 Ella 36
Esther 76 Frank 36 Harriet E
239 240 Hoah B 273 Jerry 76 Dr
Jonas 7 Levi 76 Martha 131
Pamelia 142 Polly 76 239 Sarah
76 Susan 249
HYDE, Abigail 146 Betsey A 146
Joanna 241 Mary J 241 William
241
HYLANDS, Jane 37

IDE, Betsey 228
ILLSLEY, Louisa H 84
INGALLS, --- 238 Amanda 215
Betsey 133 Daniel 184 Fletcher
33 H L 59 Margaret 238 Mary
Frances 222 Mary P 59 Mehitabel
93 Polly 33 Sarah 30 184 Sophia
255 Thomas Esq 255
INGALS, Harriet E 64 Josiah 64
Lucy 64
INGLES, Gilman Jr 191 Mary P 191
Sarah L 191
INGRAHAM, Sarah Jane 73
INNIS, Asa F 27 Elizabeth C 27
28 Sally 27
IRISH, Nancy A 13 Hon Stephen 13
IRVING, Ellen P 18
IRWIN, --- 55 Nancy 55
ISHAM, Orinda 97 Samuel Jr 97

JACKMAN, D K 215 Judith 162
Polly 66 Samuel 66 Seraphina
215
JACKSON, --- 39 Betsey 122
Charles R 104 Cora 39 Hannah
247 Joseph 106 Mrs Lizzie M 209
Lucy D 24 Lydia B 104 Martha
169 194 241 Mary 41 141 Nancy
106 Phillip 141 Polly 141 142
Samuel 122 Sarah 122 Stephen
122 Susan Binney 213
JACLARD, --- 152
JACOB, Joseph 94 Susanna 94
JACOBS, Anna 245 H D 255
JACQUES, Eunice 248
JAMES, Ada L 236 Elizabeth 173
Fanny 18 Henry D 236
JAMESON, --- 21 Cynthia Rev E O
52 199 Ida 171 Leonard 199 Mary
Joanna 52 Nancy 21
JANVRIN, Eliza B 219 Jean 198
Jefferson 157 219 Mary 157 198
219 Miranda 157
JAQUETH, Mrs Charlotte 170
JAQUETTE, Emma 243
JARED, Mary 161

JARVIS, Abigail Adkins 154
JEFFERS, Alvah 116 James 123
Lucretia 123 Mary 116 Roxana 82
Silvester 82 Submit 187
JENKINS, Elizabeth 54 Elizabeth
247 Mary E 244 Patience 241
JENNESS, Abby O 18 19 Abigail 74
Almira 18 Deborah 128 H J 244
John 74 Joseph 74 Judith 127
128 Mary 19 74 Mercy H 244
Samuel 127 Sarah 18 Sheridan 18
Theodate 74 Thomas 18
JENNETT, Ida 265
JENNEY, Jane 146 Stillman 146
JERVETT, Ennie 130
JESSAMAN, Phebe 181
JESSEMAN, --- 197 Martha 197 208
Olive 107 Rhoda 233 Sally 257
JEWELL, --- 157 Anna M 35 Annie
158 Benjamin 35 Daniel 231
Dorothy 128 Elizabeth 163 Fanny
O 35 Hannah 163 Rev Jacob 96
Levi 163 Levi F 175 Maria 175
Marinda C 231 233 Mark F 128
Martha 96 Mary E 175 Mary L 35
Mercy 231 Noah L 35
JEWETT, Abigail 74 Eunice 83
Harriette N 146 J S 85 Jane A
217 Lizzie F 17 Lois 36 Maria P
195 Mary 54 Milo P 217 Pegga 53
Phebe 245 246 Rebecca 77 78 79
140 Ruth 26 Dr Stephen 269
Sylvanus 146 Tryphosa 269
JEWITT, Betsey 182 183
JILLSON, Martha 132
JOHNSON, --- 99 151 229 Abel D
36 Abigail 12 236 Adelaide M
239 Alfred 113 Alma 7 Anna 7
138 Anna S 91 Annie 151 Betsey
116 Catharine C 99 Charles 263
Clara E 82 Comfort 259 D S 117
Daniel 7 David 97 Eleanor 124
Eliza 25 Elizabeth 249 263
Ellen Frances 124 Emma F 30
Esther 36 238 Frank 124 George
249 Hannah 118 175 Harriet 225
Harriet M 227 J W 233 Jane 99
John 91 Joseph 30 Julia M 199
Louisa 222 Lovinia 94 Lucy F
116 Lydia 154 Mary Ann 11 Mary
N 117 Moses 94 Myron E 82
Perley M 11 Phebe 132 Rachael
229 Sally 96 97 186 206 Samuel
25 116 Sarah A 249 Sarah F 113
Sarah G 25 Sophronia Clement
147 Susan 144 Susan A 233 Susan
Matilda 94 Sylvanus D 225 Capt
Thomas 229 William 116 William
N 199
JONES, --- 32 91 95 108 231
Abigail 34 35 125 Abigail M 91

Alice 44 Allie 17 Ann 97 262
Ann B 42 Benjamin H 91 Betsey
35 Betsy 97 Daniel Sr 67 Dollie
67 Dorcas 242 Dorotha H 131 190
Eben 114 Judge Edwin S 241
Eliza 58 Elizabeth 25 58 133
Ellen 222 Emily E 93 George 105
George F 221 H H 44 Hannah
Bassett 222 Hiram 139 Jacob 66
Jenkin 125 Jeremiah 222
Jonathan 62 Lucy T 91 Maria C
220 Mary 67 114 173 181 Mary
Augusta 238 Mary Jane 66 Mina O
111 Miriam 109 223 Nancy 108
Nanna 108 Nathaniel 97 Nicholas
118 Rene 231 Rosamond 190 Sally
45 245 Sally Martin 133 Samuel
58 133 Maj Samuel 223 Samuel H
42 Sarah 62 71 261 262 Sarah
Ann 113 114 Sarah C 261 Sophia
32 Susan C 241 Timothy Peaslee
238
JORDAN, Johnson 31 Minerva 31
JOSLIN, Lucretia 39 40 Ruth 32
JOSSELYN, Deborah P 222
JOURDAINE, Susanna 166 168
JOY, Charles 82 Mary Ann 82
JUDD, Azubah 31 79 Nathan 31 79
JUDCKINS, Hannah 258
JUDKIN, Sally 241
JUDKINS, Alden 60 Anna 8 9 Eliza
H 132 Lois 62 Lois A 60

KASSON, Lucia W 31
KAY, --- 182 Sally 175 176
KEAY, Abby Jane 102 Lizzie Lake
102
KEELY, Rev George 71 Mary 70
KEILEY, Harriet 72 Lawrence 72
KEITH, Ellen F 225 Mrs Sarah
White 44
KEIZER, Tuba 24
KELLAM, --- 258 Eliza 258
KELLEY, Rev G W 162 Jonathan 129
Mary 129 162 Nancy 43 Sarah S
233
KELLY, Eliza 30 Eliza C 30
Georgiana 263 Hannah 17 65
Harriet S 101 Judge Israel 89
James H 101 Joseph 263 Mary S
193 Dr N K 193 Rebecca 89 Ruth
A 167 William 167 Rev William
17
KELSEY, Dr 187 Jane M 187 Jennie
E 108 Mary 149
KELSO, Sarah 140
KEMP, Abigail 27 Betsey 249
Martha 65 66
KENDALL, Alma Harwood 269
Aurilla E 35 George 269 Hannah
233 Harriet C 154 Jesse 258

Jesse F 86 Joshua 133 Lemuel 35
Louisa 86 258 Lucy 235 M L K 25
Maria 133 Mindwell P 266 Nathan
235 Philinda 35 Rensellaer 35
Sally 257 Sarah 35 Susan E 258
Susanna 243
KENDRICK, Abigail 27 Alden 93
Benjamin Esq 27 Celina 93 Eliza
216 Elizabeth 81 Mary 151
Nathaniel 106 Patty 106 Stephen
B 216 Thomas 151
KENERSON, Arvilla R 92 John 92
KENISTON, --- 195 Deborah 247
Deborah Davis 11 Eliza 11 Emma
Elizabeth 247 George W 11
George Washington 247 John 11
Margaret 212 Mary 11 Samuel 11
Susan 202
KENNARD, Sally 100 Sarah Coffin
199 William M 199
KENNEDY, Mary 108 Ziba Gray 108
KENNEY, Emeline B 202 Lorenzo C
77 Martha A 77 Mary 15 William
15
KENNISON, Jonathan 64 Lorinda 64
KENNISTON, Margaret 212
KENRICK, --- 24 Alexandria 55
Eliza 55 Eliza A 55 56 John 162
KENT, Abigail 166 Emily Mann 184
John 67 128 166 Lydia 118 Mary
114 Nancy 128 Polly 55 Richard
Peabody 184 Ruhamah 67
Temperance 128
KENYON, Martha J 109
KERN, Julia 31
KETCHUM, A M 245 Martha 23
KETTERAGE, Abigail 21
KEYES, Anna 204 Emma 151 Lewis
36 Luther H 151 Mary E 36
KEYSAR, Berkley 176 John 100 126
176 Maria C 100 Sarah 100 126
Sarah Clark 176 Susan M 126
KEZAR, Ebenezer 254 Hannah 254
KIBBEE, Gaius 85 Isaac 189
Margaret 85 189 Mary 189
KIDDER, Almira J 61 Elizabeth
206 Emeline 157 Hannah 139
Huldah 115 230 263 264 John 263
264 Jonathan 157 Julia A 57
Lois 60 61 134 140 248 263 264
Lucette 263 264 Mrs Maria 24
Mary 24 Mary J 116 Dr Samuel
24 Susan 157 Uriah H 116
KIDNEY, Frances E 105
KILBURN, Hannah 51 Phebe 153
KILBY, Eliza 238 John Esq 238
KILHAM, Daniel 102 Elizabeth 102
KILLHAM, --- 152 Nancy 152
KILLOM, Josiah 274 Ruth 264
Sally 274
KILLROY, Hannah 152 John 152

KILTON, Annie 164 Lovel 231 Mrs
Mary A 145 Polly 15 Sally 231
Sarah E 231
KIMBAL, Dorothy 242 Rev Josiah
242
KIMBALL, --- 91 157 Abel 96
Abiah 96 Abigail 96 Almira 102
Andrew 226 Apha 165 Benjamin 5
96 97 Bethia 130 Betsey 254
Betsy 170 Betsey Chandler 235
Betsy Jane 43 Betty 269 Caleb
79 104 157 Caroline 114
Charlotte P 162 Clara Maria 8
Clarissa 43 Dea Daniel 130
David 266 Dorcas 265 Dorothy
242 Drucilla 71 Dudley 234
Eleanor Reed 174 Eliza 170
Elizabeth 42 43 96 Elizabeth T
161 Ellen E 50 Elmira 15 Elmira
J 195 196 Eunice 135 Fannie 212
Fanny 222 George 161 Hannah 97
144 Hannah R 144 Hetty 234
Jacob 112 Jane 165 Jane H 150
John 102 Hon John 8 John G 235
Joseph 170 269 Kesiah 102
Keziah 97 L 71 Lydia 27 29
Mahaley 212 Maria 226 Maria H 8
Martha 94 Mary 79 80 116 191
Mary Ann 237 Mary Jane 226
Mehetable 187 Mehitable 104 258
Molly 77 78 Nancy 4 Nancy
Isabella 235 Olive 60 Capt
Peter 222 Phebe 192 Richard 94
Ruth 5 266 Ruth H 93 Sally 186
Mrs Sally 173 174 Samuel 4 265
Samuel A 50 Samuel O 104 Sarah
15 79 96 157 200 258 Sarah A
144 Sarah E 213 Sarah F 104
Sarah P 112 Simeon 212 Stephen
144 Dea Stephen 187 Susanna 54
Theophilus 43 Thomas 60 Ursula
94 William 235
KINESTON, Hannah 135 Nancy 267
KING, Charles 107 Clarissa 111
George 15 Hannah 150 Martha A
71 Mary 63 Nancy 234 Olive 107
Sarah 15 Thomas 63
KINGMAN, Col John W 45 Joseph
Esq 59 Martha 59 Mary Spalding
45 Molly 131
KINGSBURY Abby W 198 Caroline H
24 George 24 138 Hannah 264
Harriette N 138 Joseph 264 Rev
Leonard 198 Lora T 243 Mrs Mary
23 Sally 24 138 Silence 264
KINSMAN, --- 208 Mary Ann 208
KITTEREDGE, Lorena 170
KITTREDGE, Bertha 140 Eleanor 90
Dr George 90 Jerry 211 Mary 162
Mary Ann 211 Sumner 162
KNAPP, A A 200 J A 187 Nancy 36

Phebe A 187
KNEELAND, Ianthe C 220
KNIGHT, Abigail 173 207 Allen
137 Artemas 35 Betsy 132 Caleb
119 Elizabeth 137 141 Katie 233
Louisa K 137 Lucinda 244
Melrose V 52 Nancy R 264
Nehemiah 132 Sarah 52 Susannah
35
KNOW, --- 27 70 Marianda B 79
KNOWLES, Betsey Lawrence 205
David 163 Eliza V 255 Hannah
138 162 163 Jennie M 229 232
John 255 Jonathan 205 Rev
Jonathan A 23 Joseph 9 272 Mary
149 Olive A 255 Olive J Ladd
205 Polly 272 Sally 9 Sarah 9
272 Susan G 23
KNOWLTON, Anna 11 12 David 121
Helen M 47 Hosea C Esq 74
Sallie S 74 Sarah 121 Capt
William 47
KNOX, --- 167 227 Anna 124 137
Daniel M 153 Elizabeth A 153
Emma J G 42 Mary Dole Cilley 93
Miranda B 80 Nehemiah 42
Timothy 124
KULER, Catherine Mears 235
Chancy C 235
KYSER, Emma J 163 164 Hiram 163
Patience 163

LACY, Hannah 249
LAD, Mehitable 53
LADD, --- 218 Abigail 60 Alice
239 243 Almira 89 Augusta 71
Betsey Lawrence 205 Eliphalet
243 Hannah 79 Irena 274 James
244 Jerusha 93 John 93 Dea John
79 Mrs Judith 91 Lois Folsom
119 Lucy 64 Lydia 22 Mary 1 243
Mary A 255 Mary J 174 Mehitable
93 94 191 Persis 246 Rhoda 191
Solomon 255 Theodora 244 245
Tirza 226 227 Capt Trueworth 93
W S 89
LAIGHTON, Capt James 226
Marianna 70 71 Olive Bourn 226
Olourn 226 Dr Wm 70
LAKE, Mary A 273
LAKIN, Betty 108 Martha E 256
Moody 108 Rodney S 102 Susan
Page 102
LAMB, Eleanor 170
LAMBERT, Angie F 132 George W
132
LAMPER, Mary 151
LAMPREY, Ann 185 Hannah 28 149
Irving H 18 Morris 28 Reuben 28
Ruth 28 30
LAMSON, Margaret R 113 Susan C

153
LAND, Emily 233 John 233 Nabby
233 Col Nathaniel 233
LANDER, --- 255 Seneca 255
LANE, Abigail 68 Adna 68 Annie S
254 Annie Wentworth 236 Betsey
103 Cornelia T 123 Cynthia S
150 254 Dearborn 150 Edmond J
14 Elizabeth 14 229 Ellen T 84
Elvira B 163 Capt George 14
Hannah 94 146 150 Harriet 232
Harriet N 79 Huldah 74 Joshua H
10 236 Joshua J 167 Levi E 254
Louis Clement 167 Mary 2 14 81
118 Mary Adelaide 81 Mary J 146
Meribah A 30 Rev Dr 81 Richard
146 Samuel G 163 Sarah 205 219
257 Scott W 146 Susan 167
LANG, Almira 100 David 160
Deborah 163 Edward 163 Elmira
100 Emma 209 Henry H 150 Jane
41 Lydia 100 Martha 150 Mary B
160 Samuel 100
LANGDON, --- 198 Eliza 82 Sarah
272 Tobias 272
LANGFORD, Ann 28 Dea Anthony 28
Elizabeth W 28 Nancy 28
LANGLEY, Patience 71
LAPHAM, Betsey 127
LAPISH, Capt Robert 143
Temperance 128 143
LARCOM, Emily 7
LARY, Andrew G 127 Anna 88
Betsey 263 Dawn 127 Eliza 64
Emeline 136 Joseph Jr 7 Capt
Joseph 136 Lettie A 120 Levee
127 Mary 84 Mercy 112 136
Richard 88 Sally 7 Susannah 112
W H 120 William 64
LASKIN, Editha 94 Editha 125
LASSEY, Sarah 129
LATHAM, --- 99
LATHROP, Caroline B 236 Lois 238
Lydia 102 Susan 31
LATHROPE, Emily M 135
LATTIMER, Betsey 120
LAURENCE, Samantha 96
LAVENDER, Emma E 229 232 Stephen
LAVOSIER, Mrs 77
LAW, Elizabeth 57 Elizabeth 58
LAWRENCE, --- 49 119 Annie 173
Caroline 101 102 David 173
Edward 216 Elizabeth 171 Fred 9
Gordon 34 Hannah 63 216 217
Harriet N 101 Joseph S 101
Marion 9 Mary 34 Mary J 80
Miranda O 101 102 Nicholas 119
Phoebe 93 Prudence 60 Hon
Samuel 171 Tamar 117 Col
William 93
LAWTON, Susan B 275

LAYTON, Elizabeth 201 Mary 211
Thomas 201 211
LE CONSTEUR, Elizabeth 137
LE ROY, Caroline Bayard 258
LEACH, B C 132 E P 54 Eunice C
54 Josephine 150 Judith 214
Lizzie Etta 235 Lizzie S 76 235
Orlando 150 Sarah B 132 Walter
S 76 235
LEAR, Mrs Martha Gregg 13
LEARNED, Susan 58
LEAVETT, Martha H 247
LEAVIT, Abihail 128
LEAVITT, --- 128 Andrew 135
Armine 176 Belle 110 Betsey 69
Carrie 181 Chase 142 Dolly 95 E
E 151 Elizabeth 65 110 184 Ella
S 112 Frances 168 George S 213
Gillman 274 Harriet A 28 30
Helen 41 Henrietta 11 Capt
James 184 Jeremiah 11 110 173
John 7 Jonathan 184 Joseph 68
Justin M 112 Lavinia 68 Lemira
95 128 Mahala 41 Martha Sophia
139 Mary 111 135 163 271 Mary E
213 Moses 30 Nancy 7 Nancy 216
Sally 177 178 Sarah 30 69 142
Sarah G 274 Sarah M 29 30 Sarah
W 166 167 Simon 95 Thomas 29
Ware 41 William 168
LEE, Deborah 274 Elizabeth 214
George 177 Harriette S 136
Maria E 59 Nathan M 136 Sarah
77 232
LEECH, Elijah 15 Jane 15
LEEDS, Maria 32 Tryphena 191
LEEMAN, Elizabeth 52 Samuel 52
LEESON, Georgia 118 Joseph R 118
LEFFINGWELL, Annie 254 Frank P
254
LEGALLEE, Eva L 228 Joseph H 228
LEIGHTON, Abigail 193 Abigail E
69 Anna 266 Betsey 98 Charles W
273 Frances 82 83 Joseph 69
Luella W 273 Mary 39 98 Nancy
236 237 Samuel 266 Gen Samuel
82 Trustram 193 William 98
2LELAND, Capt James 204 Josephine 32
43 Thankful 204
LEMIST, Annie E 149 John 149
LEONARD, Olive 195
LESLIE, Charles C 258 Eliza
Ball 258
LEVERETT, --- 273 Lucretia 24
Hon William 24
LEWIS, --- 67 Alden 221 Benjamin
210 Frances 97 Harry Ashmead
213 Irene 67 Jennie E 248 249
Lizzie M 190 Mary 16 Sarah 210
221 Warren 190 William M 16
LIBBEY, Benjamin 69 Dorcas 17

Hannah 96 265 James 17 96 265
Mary 149 150 Susan 69
LIBBY, Dudley Leavitt 7 8 Elijah
229 Hannah 229 Helen Maria 8
Nancy 71 Sarah Ann 7 8 Sarah
Elizabeth 7 8
LIDDELL, Mary 93
LIGHT, Mary 271
LILAND, Thankful 204
LILLIE, Hannah 249
LILLIS, Lorette 23
LINCOLN, Sarah 134
LINCON, Alice S 239 Henry W 239
LINDSEY, Emily 5 Emma 225
William 5 Wilton M 225
LINFIELD, Mary 165
LINSCOTT, Elizabeth 110
LINZEE, Hannah R 6
LITE, Josiah 143
LITTLE, Abraham 20 Ann Poor 186
Augusta Farley 184 Catharine
118 Christine P 94 David 216
Elbridge G 99 114 Elizabeth 119
Emma P 216 Ezekiel Esq 186 Mrs
Harriet B 120 Jane 195 John 143
Joseph 191 Lou M 271 Margaret
191 Martha 20 Moses 171 Nancy
99 114 Polly 103 Relief 124
Roene 114 Sarah 144 Sarah F 99
143 Selina 13 Silas 120 Thomas
94 Timothy Wiggin 119 Vashti
191 William 271
LITTLEFIELD, Phebe 72
LITTLEHALE, George H 186 Henry
186 Isaac 186 Martha C 185
LIVERMORE, Hon Samuel 29
LIVINGSTON, Caroline 101 Duane
192 Jane 45 Julia Caroline 192
Mary 235 Richard Montgomery 235
William 101
LIVY, Dr D T 213 Mary A 213
LOCK, Mrs Almira 268 Anna 16
Benjamin 86 Ebenezer 17 Lucy 17
109 Nancy 86 Rachel 1 Sarah 17
Susan D 86
LOCKE, --- 123 Alfred 179 Ann L
94 Capt Arthur 22 Capt Arthur C
23 Belle 162 Benjamin 72
Ephraim 92 94 Francis 257
George S 162 Hanna 222 James
183 Lovey 183 Lucy 105 Lydia 93
Lydia M 109 110 Mary E 273 Mary
Eliza 179 Nancy 227 Polly 197
Rachel 72 212 Roxia 72 Roxy 72
Salina O 23 Sallie 92 Samuel
123 Rev Samuel DD 222 Sarah 9
94 147 272 Sarah J 11 12 Simon
93 Susan 43 Tamsen 123
LOMBARD, Ann S 20 Betsey 155 168
Ellen L 168 Emma 168 J E 168 Dr
Lyman 20 155 168

LONG, --- 82 Lydia B 271 Mary 45
Nancy 82
LONGA, Ann 15 25 Charles 16
Nelson 15 25 Sarah 16 25
LONGFELLOW, Elizabeth 271
LOOMER, Ethalinda 153
LOOMIS, Anna 155 Betsey 154 155
168 Harriet 246 Hattie I 46
Horace 35 Joseph 155 Julia 35
Gen Lewis 5 Marian Wallace 5
Rispah 5 William 246
LORD, Betsy W 253 Joseph W 44
Nancy Dearborn 158 Ruth E 44
Sally 196 Samuel 157
LOTHROP, Huldah 5 Huldan 12
Sarah 270 271
LOUGEE, Annetta 152 Deborah 184
Hayes Esq 152 Nancy 147 148
Shuah 202
LOVE, Louisa J 252
LOVEJOY, --- 30 Abiel 78 Dea
Abiel 208Abiel C 208 Abigail
175 176 Anna 208 Clara 50
Hannah 208 Jerusha 93 Molly 77
78 Nancy 78 Olive 60 Phebe 78
Polly 270 Sabatha 50 Sabrina 30
Sally 78 Sarah 206
LOVEREN, Abigail 16 Abigail 156
Alvah 231 Anna 16 Asenith 113
Benjamin 17 Ebenezer 109
Elizabeth 105 Esther 17 Eunice
109 Hannah 105 Hilliard 105
Huldah 226 Joseph 268 Josiah
113 Martha A 268 Mary E 268
Matilda 231 Nancy 91 Reuben 6
16 268 Sarah 73
LOVERIN, Abbie 139 Alfred 139
209 Belle 209
LOVERING, Abigail 9 74 Anna 127
Daniel 267 Dolly 137 Emily 173
Hubbard 74 John 173 Julia
Esther 74 Lydia 28 29 96 Mary
192 Mary A 267 Polly 4 Ruth 267
Thomas 29
LOVETT Mary T 71 Sally 177 178
LOVJOY, Lydia 91 William 91
LOW, Grace 31 Martha 13
Mehitable 245
LOWD, Elmira 157
LOWE, Clovis 112 George Ann 108
George Anne 107 John Jr 108
LOWELL, Molly 120
LUCAS, Edmund D 167 Elizabeth
167 Harriet 176 196 Nancy A 162
LUCY, Joanna 81 John T 81 Sarah
249
LUFLIN, Edward 14 91 Jane 91
Phebe 14 91 Sarah 14 Susan 146
LUND, Dea Augustus 188 Charles
134 240 Eliza 134 240 Eliza Ann
134 Jennie L 85 Joseph S 1

Nathaniel F 175 Olive 166 168
Phebe E 1 Rebecca J 188 Sally
15
LUNT, Jane 73
LUSCOMB, Aaron N 110 Margaret
110
LUTHER, Charlotte 57 Ruth 102
LYFORD, --- 54 Abigail 144 145
Ann 53 88 Hannah 117 J 88
Judith 147 148
LYMAN, Justus 4 Lois P 4
LYON, Maj Alexander McD 59
Joanna 235 Maria Stocker 59
William 235
LYSSON, Mary 107 Mary 108
Nicholas 107

MAC GREGOR, Abby 247 Capt David
247
MACK, Jeremiah 108 Nancy L 108
MADISON, Flora 13
MAGOON, Fanny 110 Henry C 110
Mehitable 110 Sophia Ann 73
MAIN, Rev Amos 123 Mary 122 123
211
MALDER, --- 108 Luella 108
MALEHAM, Charlotte J 100 Nancy
100 William A 100
MALLARD, Ephraim 14 Mercy 14
MALOON, Mehitable 89 90
MANAHAN, Almira 109 Esther 42 43
Mary 11 Nancy 11 Polly 109
Richard 109 Stephen 11 Thompson
109
MANDEVILLE, Fanny 204
MANN, Eliza 228 Emily 143 183
George W 228 John 196 Lydia 204
Margaret 196 Solomon 184 Susan
124 125
MANNING, Benjamin F 242 C A MD
77 Martha J 77 Miranda 242
MANSFIELD, Mary 244
MANSON, David 244 Mattie A 178
Sarah 244
MANTER, Francis 202 Harriet 202
Isabella 83 Mary Ann 83 Mary F
202 Rebecca 58 Samuel 83
MARBLE, Sarah 13 William C 13
MARCH, --- 7 Abigail 259 260 Col
Clement 259 Dr Clement Sr 260
Eleanor 260 Hannah 109 121 John
7 Sarah 125
MARCY, J G 263 Mary 199
MARDEN, --- 110 Charlotte E 224
Dolly 70 110 Dorothy 106 107
Esther 224 Hannah 107 Harriet 1
Jonathan 108 Capt Joseph 163
Mary A 163 Mehitable 151 Nancy
L 108 Thomas 107 Timothy 224
MARDON, --- 28
MARLAND, Abraham 51 Mary S 51 52

MARONG, Elizabeth 3
MARRIAN, Elizabeth 68
MARRION, Carrie E 139 Dr Otis
139
MARSDEN, Patience 22
MARSH, Adaline W 103 Dr Clement
Sr 260 Edmond 16 Eleanor 260
Eunice 16 Fitch P 103 Hannah 12
Joshua 166 Martha 166 Martha M
247 Polly 261 Samuel 12 261
Sarah Abby 4 Susan 117
MARSHALL, Abigail 10 53 121 146
Addie S 189 Anderson J 154 270
Andrew B 201 Ann Judson 201
Antipas 196 Belle 154 Caroline
149 Cynthia 274 Emma F 270
Esther 166 Esther Pierce 53
Eunice P 114 Evelyn 257 Frances
154 270 Hannah 149 208 Helen
196 Henry 149 174 John C 189
Joshua P 94 Luella 10 Martha
234 Martha P 174 Mary 146 Mary
Jane 94 Micajah 174 234 Nathan
R 121 Nathan Richardson 10 53
146 Richard 166 Sally Dudley
174 Sarah 240
MARSTON, --- 5 Abi 205 Abihail
128 Ann 205 Ann M 120 Anne
Elizabeth 125 Annie A 155
Augusta M 29 Caleb 5 Charles E
155 David 29 68 Elisha 73 Emily
Maria 125 Fannie 127 128 Hannah
90 138 181 233 Jacob 254
Jeremiah 178 Jeremiah 181 Dea
John 203 Judith 94 96 Lucretia
M 13 Maria 205 206 Mary 73 127
177 178 Dr Moses 127 Hon
Moulton H 125 Polly 254 Robert
90 Sarah 29 Sarah H 203 Simeon
128 Susan 130 Thomas 138
William 90
MARTIN, --- 41 173 220 Abigail
191 Col B F 41 Benjamin 191
Betsey 87 Candace 270 Caroline
Salome 66 Charles 15 Clara
Lyman 189 Daniel 87 Eliza 118
Elmira 87 Frances 199 Frances
Coffin 59 Frederick 66 Harriet
15 39 Harriet Maria 39 Dr Henry
A 59 Horace A 258 James 254
James H 133 Jane 209 Jeanette
254 Lizzie Jane 258 Lois 79
Lydia 271 Mary 18 32 92 93 164
Mary Ann 254 Mary N 161 Mary R
133 Nancy 15 Richard 220 Sally
65 66 Sarah 15
MARTYN, Hester 211 John 211
MASON, --- 155 197 Almira 17 157
Ann J 41 Apphia 234 Caleb 232
Daniel 13 Deborah 142 Elijah 17
Elizabeth A 232 Emma F 84

310

Fannie E C 112 Dr George L 84
Harriet 154 Henry 234 Ira 41
Joanna 241 Josie M 46 Kinsley
157 Laurinda 13 Capt Lemuel B
219 Maria H 41 Molly 219
Nathaniel 201 Orinda L 252
Peggy 49 Ruth 1 97 Sally 99 219
Sarah 232
MASSEY, Carrie 160
MASTEN, --- 254 Comfort 5 Jane
254 Jennie 1 97 Martha 36
MASTERMAN, Benjamin 257 Nancy
257
MASTERS, Mary A 1 92
MATHER, Addie L 105
MATHES, Ruth 151 Susan 1 98
MATHIS, Nancy 26 4 265
MATTEN, Mary 265 William 265
MATTHEWS, Martha A 205 Rev S S
205
MAUD, Elinda 103 John 103
Marriott 103 Mary 103
MAXFIELD, Anna 109 Joanna 38
MAYNARD, Charles 255 Elmira 166
Harriett 255 Mary F 255
MAYO, Issachar 232 Mindwell 232
Sarah G 232
MC ALISTER, David 265 Harriet 265
MC ALLISTER, James 2 Sally 41
Sara 2 Sarah 2
MC AUSTIN, James 157 Sarah B 157
MC CARTER, Robert 16 9 Sophia 16 9
MC CAULEY, Ann 26 9
MC CLARY, Margaret 259 Gen
Michael 155 Nancy Dearborn 155
Sally 155 Sara 2
MC CLAVE, Harriet N 106 John 106
MC CLINTOCK, Alexander 13 9 Anna
13 9
MC CLURE, --- 7 9 26 9 A J 26 4
Abbie A 264 Emma 231 George W
231 Huldah A 26 4 Mary 1 80 Mary
Ann 231 Mehitable 26 9 Samuel
26 9
MC COLLOM, John 231 Theresa 231
MC CONNEL, Sally 171 172
MC COY, Caroline 3 Dorcas 181
Elizabeth 4 Milton 4 Susan 129
MC CRILLIS, --- 144 Elizabeth
157
MC CUTCHINS, Abigail 13 9 160 225
226 253 Mrs Abigail 225 Sophia
65 7 9 225 226
MC DERMID, Abigail 101 M Ellen
101 William 101
MC DERMITT, Jennie 212
MC DEVITT, Henry 137 Miranda 137
MC DOLE, Mrs Sarah N 168
MC DONOUGH, Delia 152 153
MC DOUGAL, Sarah A 177
MC DOUGALL, Sarah A 178

MC DUFFEE, George 85 Joanna 118
John 118 Nellie F 85
MC FARLAND, Clara D 112 Clara D
182 Elizabeth 36 Mary 10 Rev Dr
182
MC FERSON, Robert 26 9 Sally 26 9
MC GAFFEY, Mary 20
MC GAFFY, Jane 158 157
MC GAW, Anna Eliza 187 Hannah
247 Isaac 107 187 John 247
Margaret Jane 187 Martha
Dickinson 107
MC GOON, Rebecca 133
MC GRAW, Hannah Adams 188
MC GREGGOR, Joseph 64 Laura 64
MC GREGOR, --- 165 Rev Alexander
87 Rev David 165 Rev James 35
Susan 35 Susanna 18
MC GREGORY, Emma J 87 Hannah P
109 Joel 109
MC KEAN, Amy Elizabeth 273 Anne
110 Joseph DD 273 Dea William
110
MC KEEN, Angeline 6 9 Anne 208
David 159 Elbridge 53 Elizabeth
179 180 James 17 9 Janet 17 9
Jennie 50 John 208 Leonard 6 9
Lydia 109 Mary 53 Nancy 53 159
Robert 15 Sally 15 Sarah 6 9
William 109
MC KINLEY, Martha 106
MC KINNEY, Jane 225 Nancy 99 114
William 225
MC KINSTRY, Sarah 237 Dr William
237
MC MAHON, Louise T 37 Lydia 4
Samuel 4
MC MILLAN, --- 70 Almira 70 Rev
James 70
MC MURCHIE, Archibald 234
Elizabeth 234
MC MURPHY, Betsey 1 97 Mary 248
249 Mary Ann 88 Nancy 87
MC NEIL, --- 232 233 Betsy 160
Frances Maria 204 Gen John 20 4
Mary 271 William 160 232
MC PHERSON, Asenath R 1 99 Elmira
226
MC QUESTEN, Almira 56 Caroline L
71 Charles 56 Edward 160
Harriet 160 James 220 Marcia V
160 Mary E 220 Mary 188
MEAD, Abigail 91 Abigail V 148
149 Adelaide 111 Eunice 103
Fannie P 64 Joseph 111 Loanna
Sherburne 16 9 Rhoda 88 Mrs
Sally T 92 Samuel 88 Susan 103
104 205 William 103
MEADER, Almira 39 Mary A 178
Mary M 178 Moses 10 Nancy 230
MEARS, David B 65 Hannah 14 Ira

14 Lydia 65
MEDBURY, Fannie G 134 George 134
MEEKS, Mrs Carrie Philbrick 257
MELCHER, Ella S 177 Esther 76
Joseph 217 Mary 217 Polly M 121
217 218
MELLEN, Christine Van Ness 65
James Jr 65
MELLIGAN, Carrie 142
MELOON, Sally 47
MELVILLE, Josiah 180 Mary 244
245 Nancy R 180
MELVIN, Betsy 265 Dorothy 25
Esther 162 George 256 Harriet
Maria 265 Josiah 162 Lovina 25
Lydia 24 Mary 162 Richard 265
Walter 25
MERRELL, --- 262
MERRIAM, Etta 176 Fletcher 56
Harriet 56 John 176 Sarah P 176
MERRIL, Emma J 17
MERRILL, --- 153 197 Abigail 38
127 Abigail N 68 Adeline 188
Adeline A 196 Albert 62 170
Alvin I 126 146 Ambrose 127
Anna 113 269 Anna M 265 Annie
150 151 Arthur L 264 Augusta 29
126 Betsey E 78 Caleb 202 Caleb
Esq 265 Caroline (Carrie) H 75
Caroline G 265 Charlotte 236
Charlotte L 48 Christie 113
Clara A 38 Clara S 228 Clarissa
78 Comfort 173 David 77 80 168
232 Delia A 170 Dexter 142
Diantha 249 Dorcas 78 Eben 91
Eliza A 168 Ellen L 154 Emeline
96 Emeline B 202 Emily 55 56
Emma E 155 Enoch 188 Enos 113
Esther 146 Eunice 219 George 96
196 George W 29 Hannah 78 150
186 Hannah P 232 Harriet 27
Henry 249 Isaac 78 274 J B Esq
129 Jane 25 Jennie M 229
Jeremiah 229 John F 196 Judith
55 79 80 153 Julia A 77 Lizzie
I 202 Lucretia 60 Lucretia F 61
Lydia 168 Lyman 68 Maria 91
Mark 27 Marsten 173 Martha 243
Martha G 133 Martin 56 Mary 58
113 142 157 Mary A 58 Mary Ann
117 157 229 231 Mary E 264 Mary
G 195 Mary J 226 Mary L 62 Mary
L 264 Moody 55 Moses 202 Nancy
243 Nancy B 202 Nathaniel 269
Maj Nathaniel 186 P Josephine
175 Phebe 77 78 168 Polly 274
Priscilla 66 Reuben 58 Ruth 79
80 197 261 S S 155 Sally 27
Samuel 78 Samuel C 38 Sarah 77
189 202 232 236 Sarah A 196
Sarah B 61 75 155 168 208 226

Sarah L 208 Sherburn Rowell 61
75 155 208 226 Rev Stephen 78
Stillman 117 Thomas 77 Uriah
157 Vesta M 249 William E 232
MERRIMAN, Jennie L 253
MERROW, Dr A D 155 Abbie C 177
178 Edith 155
MESERVE, Abigail 44 Alice 194
249 Alice P 249 Betsey 169 194
201 Daniel 194 George 111 Gen
George P 78 169 249 Hannah 189
190 Harriot 78 Isaac 201 Joanna
169 201 202 Col Jonathan 194
249 Lorinda 111 Lydia T 194
Martha 42 169 Martha P 249 262
Mary A 202 Mary D 194 Nathaniel
249 S D 202 Sally 250 Silas 194
MESSER, Betsey 133 Daniel 220
Frederick A 80 Frederick G 40
Hannah M 80 John 192 Merriam E
220 Nancy 192 Sally 192 Sarah
268 Sarah E 220 Stephen 133 192
Susan 40 Susy 192
METCALF, Calvin 105 Hannah 132
Mary 105
MILES, Fannie B 202 Hannah 202
Susan Elizabeth 275 Col
Tichenor 275 William 202
MILLEN, Dorcas 50
MILLER, Benjamin 166 Delia 166
168 Elijah Esq 245 Elizabeth W
240 Eunice 245 Mary 60 267
Miriam S Pushee 69 Prosper 69
Sally 20 Sarah 75
MILLET, Martha 119
MILLINGTON, Annie 72 73
MILLS, Achsa A 29 30 Amos H 140
Anna 159 Betsey 116 Clara W 69
Clarissa 57 David 116 Eliza A
234 Ella Z 140 Gawn W 69 James
11 Jane 11 57 John 234 Maj
Joseph 171 Mary 113 115 116 190
Mercy 234 Robert 159 Sally 171
Sarah N 34 35
MILTIMORE, John 180 Mary 180
MINARD, Burton 174 Emma J 174
MINER, Addie A 200 Caroline T 65
Elisha 65 Hepsey 187 Thomas 65
William 187
MINOT, Sally 259 260 Samuel 273
William 259
MITCHAEL, Col 271 Sarah 270
Sarah 271
MITCHEL, Susanna 170
MITCHELL, --- 61 Anna 196 Bela
257 Betsey 29 257 Rev Daniel 172
David 61 Eliza 145 Francis 145
Lettice 46 Margaret 164 Martha
172 Mary F 243 Oliver 196
Phineas P 243 Pork 119 Rebecca
198 Ruhamah 171 172 Sarah 269

MIXER, Isaac 238 Sarah 237 238
MOAR, Sarah J 203 Stephen 203
MODICA, Georgie A 3
MOFFAT, Elizabeth 225
MONROE, Ellen 264
MONTGOMERY, --- 214 Anna 109 D K
272 Gen 207 Gen John 181 John
122 Mary 236 Mary A 272 Myra M
181 Patience 207
MOODY, Frances Susan 215 Rev
Howard 50 Mary Jane 59 Rebecca
Marquand 59 Stephen 59 Stephen
Esq 59 215
MOOERS, Florence 52 R D 52
MOONEY, Betty 122 Celesta S 106
Celestia S 105 Daniel M 118 E P
152 Hester Ann 118 Judge Ira
222 Maj Joseph 122 Lucy 189 190
Luther 265 Susan Frances 265
Tamson A 152
MOOR, John 37 Mary 45 Matilda 37
Sabrina 37 Rev Solomon 37
MOORE, --- 144 Ada 217 218 Alice
203 Alivra 102 102 149 Alzina
52 Amanda A 164 Ann 208 Anna
Maria 128 Christina 225 Coffin
31 Dr Coffin 260 Comfort 260
Cyrus 52 Col Daniel 225 Dr
Ebenezer 126 Dr Edward B 151
Eliza Ann 47 Elizabeth 126
Fanny 206 Frances 86 George
Bryan 241 James G 225 Jane 124
225 226 John B 70 Katie 254
Louisa 274 Lucy M 70 Robert 170
225 Ruhamah 170 S Anna 44
Sophia 214 215 Stephen 128
Susan C 241 Thankful 88 Lt
William 203
MOORS, H C W 153 Hannah M 153
Lydia 212
MORDOUGH, Anna 133
MORE, Priscilla 191 249
MOREY, --- 266 Annie 116 Harby
245 Lucy 245 Lydia 196 Rhoda
266 William P 116
MORGAN, James 1 Jerry 263 John
220 Lizzie R 190 Lucy Jane 220
Mary 28 62 Mary Ann 231 Mary J
263 Minnie T 263 Sarah 1
MORRELL, Elizabeth 109 110
Harriet 125 Jabez 106 Jennie
125 Lydia 106 Martha 249 Mary
249 Samuel 125
MORRIL, Catherine 231 Joseph 231
MORRILL, --- 151 Abigail 49 50
Annie 151 Benjamin 94 Betsey 94
Catharine W 256 Charles 256
Comfort 174 Dea David 49 E R
199 Ebenezer 219 Elmira 78 Emma
T 49 Ephraim 91 Hannah 27 30 38
120 224 Gen J J 219 Jabez 105

Judith 163 Louisa 78 Lydia 105
Marietta F 180 Mary 91
Mehitable 91 Mercy E 219 Nancy
220 Rebecca B 222 Ruth 197
Samuel 120 Sarah 94 Sophia 91
127
MORRIS, Almira 121 Carrie 207
Com Decatur 180 Harriet 33
Sally V 180 Thomas 207
MORRISON, --- 148 Abigail 44
Amelia 265 Anna P 2 Clara A 56
Davenport 89 Elvira S 4 Isabel
115 116 J H 56 John C 4 Joseph
219 Lucy Maria 89 Lydia 227
Marion M 271 Martha P 162 Mary
216 Mary J 119 Olive 219 Parker
I 162 Relief Rogers 219 Sally
142 Sarah 4 101 142 189
MORSE, --- 147 Almira 141 142
Amelia 14 Aphia 196 Arthur T
119 Betsey A 241 Caleb 133 230
Charles 241 Christiana Colcord
147 Daniel 168 Drusilla 220
Ebenezer 268 Elizabeth 268
Fanny 147 George 108 Hannah 80
116 230 Huldah 220 Jane 210
Jenny 271 John H 98 John N 234
Joseph 45 Joshua 243 Josiah 271
Kate 234 Laura L 45 Loisa 17
Louisa A 119 Lucinda 74 Lucy 98
Lydia 126 Mary 177 Mary C 108
Mary Hamilton 270 Mehitable 133
Moses 142 176 Rachel 166 168
Rhoda 70 Ruth 243 Ruth W 230
243 Sally 268 271 Samuel W 147
Sarah 45 88 241 Silas 240 Silas
M Esq 220 Sophia 174 Sophronia
14 Susan M 240 Susannah B 176
Tryphena 85 Rev William 14
William C 116
MORSS, Sarah 200
MORTON, Hon Hamilton E 93
Harriet 93 Leander S 85 Martha
L 85 Mary Ellen 85
MOSES, Eliza L 144 Hannah 18 Dea
John F 167 Margaret Vaughn 224
Mary E 166 167 209 Theodore 167
MOSHER, Ira C 196 Mary F 196
MOSHIER, Asceneth 154
MOTT, Lizzie C 155
MOULDER, Mary E 179
MOULTON, --- 133 249 Abigail 228
Benjamin 145 Betsey 247
Cordelia 176 Daniel 223 228
Edward 126 Ellen 78 Esther W
217 Eveline A 95 Gideon 217
Hattie G 217 Huldah 209 Col
John 83 Jonathan 81 177 247 Gen
Jonathan 163 Julia 49 106 107
120 Lizzie 223 Lowell 176 Lucy
133 249 Mrs Margaret 218 219

Mary 83 127 218 Mehitable S 165
Nancy 163 177 Nathan 120 Reuben
49 Ruth 184 Sally 77 78 Sally
Miller 81 Sarah 126 144 145
Simon 95 165 Susan 249 Susan
Greeley 47 Susan Huntington 83
William E 127
MUCHMORE, Mary 13
MUDDGETT, Abigail 133
MUDGETT, --- 70 Clara A 157
Elisha 70 Herman W 157 James
230 Mary 230 232 Sarah 11 12
MULLIKEN, Betsey 213
MUNSON, Catharine L 72
MURDOUGH, Katherine 159 Nathan
271 Susan 271 Thomas 159
MURFEY, Mrs Oliver 97
MURFIN, Josephine 232 Orin 232
MURRAY, Emeline 149 Mary J 59
Orlando Dana 59 Sarah L 59
MUZZEY, Cora A 144 Craig 6
Margaret 6 Mary 6 Mary E 154 0
J 144 Patty 53
MUZZY, Daniel 98 John D 105
Jonathan 96 Louisa 105 Phebe 96
Ruana 96
MYRECK, Abbie L 105

NASON, Caroline 233 Gee 72 Phebe
72
NAY, Amelia 244 Capt Gardner 244
NEAL, Annis J 157 Betsey 33
Comfort 172 Deborah 177 178
George A 203 George W 157 John
33 Joseph 75 Lydia 264 Martha
75 Sarah 203 Sarah C 33 34
William A W 172
NEALLY, Elizabeth 114
NEALY, Jane 33 Jane 45
NELSON, --- 43 Abigail 68 Eliza
23 Elizabeth 86 Louisa 43
Lovinia 43 Mrs Lydia M 207 Mary
L 196 Mercy 112 209 Moses 112
Nancy 200 201 Nathan 186 Sarah
23 Susan B 247
NESMITH, Jennie 75 76 Jonathan
113 Dea Jonathan 76 Mary 208
Nancy 113
NEVINS, --- 29 231 Hannah 196
Susannah 101
NEVIUS, Matilda 200
NEWCOMB, A W 40 Benjamin 46
Emily 254 Gideon Esq 104 Hannah
46 Harriet Sprague 61 John 46
Maria T 61 O P 61 Payson 254
Sarah Louisa 104 Sarah Louise
103
NEWELL, Charlotte 192 Dr H C 124
Eunice 71 Hannah M 124 Martha
135 Nathan 192
NEWHALL, Ellen Pitkin 89 Rev

Matthew 89
NEWMAN, Abigail 108 109 Harriet
109 Martha L 105 Mary 105
NICHOLS, --- 4 Alice 125 Anne
172 Charlotte 268 Eleanor 237
Enoch 173 Hannah 156 203
Humphrey 193 Humphry 156 John
20 Mary L 54 Mary Tevey 4 Mary
W 31 Polly 146 Ruth 20 220 221
Ruth P 20 Sarah 20 181 Sarah E
42 173 Sarah S 72 Sarah T 193
Stephen F 42
NICKERSON, Benjamin 82 Eliza 82
Hannah 234 Jonathan 234 Joseph
82 Joshua 211 Lydia 211 Mary
Jane 82
NIGHTINGALE, James 128 Mary
Folsom 128
NILES, Amasa P 175 Nellie 225
226 Polly 130 Sarah 175
NOBLES, --- 173
NORCROSS, Ellen Grant 60 N G Esq
59
NORRIS, Betsey 54 Daniel L 30
Israel 91 Dr James 240 Josiah R
54 Lucinda 240 Lydia 33 54
Martha G 227 228 Mary Pike 181
182 Sarah 73 91 Sarah G 29 30
Sophia 30
NORTHEY, Martha 80
NORTON, Dr Bishop 111 George 94
Mary 94 Nancy 111
NOYES, --- 27 182 225 Abigail
241 Amanda 101 Annie L 213
Benjamin 263 Carrie 75 Clara D
112 Daniel 257 David 132 Dolly
P 23 Elijah 138 Eliza J 132
Elizabeth 25 Elizabeth L 11
Elizabeth McFarland 112 Emily
182 Dea Enoch 25 F H 75 F V 203
Hannah 234 Henry 213 Huldah 27
Isabella Aiken 227 Jefferson
205 Johanna 138 Johanna B 138
Hon John W 112 227 Kimball W 25
Martha 167 Mary 51 Mary 163
Mary Ann 215 Mary L 117 Mary
Little 205 206 Mary Lizzie 65
Mehitable 18 Nancy 205 227
Phoebe 233 Polly 52 Ruth 117
Sally 59 60 99 Sally A 264
Sally Morse 200 Samuel 101 241
Samuel Jr 65 Sarah 186 Sarah E
203 Sarah L 11 Sophia 62
Susanna 80 Timothy 18
NOYS, Flora 248 249 Moses 248
Susan 248
NUDD, Betsey P 104 274 275
Deborah 224 Mary 19 108 109
Ruth P 133 Simon 19
NURS, Martha 107
NURSE, Mary 135

NUTE, Andrew J 235 Aurilla 70
Dorcas 235 Eliza 111 Elizabeth
125 Elizabeth M 155 Emeline 241
James 98 125 241 Col John 111
Joseph 70 Jotham 123 L S 155
NUTLIR, Sarah 251
NUTT, Mary 5
NUTTER, Abigail 211 Elizabeth
151 Elder Hatevil 151 211 Ida R
140 Martha 165 Oliver 140
Roxannah C 140 Sarah 164 Sarah
D 162 163
NUTTING, Arthur 215 Eunice 83
Florence V 170 John 170 Mary A
215 Mary Ann 215 Nancy 249
Susanna 170 Thomas 83
NYE, Mary 241 Mary E 190
NYLAND, Mary 5

OAKES, Abigail 63 Eliza 132
Emily 143 161 Emily Mann 143
Henry 143 161 Mary 275 Phebe
239 Sarah 198
OAKLEY, K Josephine 256
OAKS, David 175
OBER, Helen L 239 240
ODELL, Charlotte 25 Charlotte
151 Hannah 263 James 25 151
Ruth G 77 Ruth Gerrish 77
ODIORNE, Joanna 184 Nancy 210
211
OLCOTT, Catharine 21 Mary 246
Hon Miles 246 Mills 21
OLMSTEAD, Mary 235 236
OLMSTEAD, Rev Dr John W 235 236
Sarah Livingston 235 236
ORDWAY, --- 29 89 Abial 185
Annie 89 Clarissa 185 Esther
170 Hannah 265 Harriet A 98
Joseph 170 Joseph C 184 Judith
221 Martha S 184 185 Polly 120
Relief 27 29 30 Reuben 98
Stephen 29
ORNE, Jennie 17
ORSBORN, Mehitable 157
OSBORN, Chloe 5 Jemima 39
OSBORNE, Mrs Mary A 111 Samuel
264 Susannah 264
OSGOOD, Aaron 24 Christopher 94
Clara A 72 Eliza 72 George W
130 Hannah 22 Harriet 186 Hitty
179 Ira Esq 49 Isaac 186 John S
239 Leah 239 Luther 72 Margaret
94 Mary 62 63 Mary E 49 Mary S
130 Polly 148 Polly 149 Relief
24 Sophia 30 Susan 130 Therina
239 240 William 63
OTIS, --- 237 Abigail 93
Charlotte 39 Daniel 230
Elizabeth 185 Experience 125
Ezra 237 Hon Job 272 Joshua 39

Luke 265 Mahala 265 Micajah 39
93 Rebecca 196 Richard 125 201
Rose 201 Sarah 223 272 Sarah C
230
OTTERSON, Isaac C 101 Margaret
101 Martha A 100 101
OWEN, Anna 229 230 Annie 230
Esther 23 72 73
OXNARD, --- 259 Sarah 259

PACKARD, Eliza 206 Elizabeth 5
Esther 25
PACKER, Nellie 183
PACKHARD, Lucinda 269 Sewell 269
PADDLEFORD, --- 172 179 Connor
179 Hannah 179 Ruth 179
Sophronia 172
PAGE, --- 4 108 113 173 202
Abigail 99 141 Amanda F 51 Ann
Jane 234 Dr B F 85Dea Benjamin
99 Betsey 269 Caleb Esq 237
Caroline 85 Cora T 141 Daniel
29 141 157 David 31 Dolly 32
Dorothy 154 Eleanor 154 Eliza
208 234 Eliza Ann 28 29
Elizabeth 73 163 237 268
Elizabeth S 181 Elvira 33 Enoch
212 Evatine 82 Hon Ezekiel
Morrill 6 George W 166 Gideon 4
Hannah 99 150 Hannah C 212
Harriet 4 Henrietta 166 Henry H
234 Dea James K 220 Jeremiah 73
John 63 Gov John 234 Jonathan
154 Joseph W 32 Josephine 212
Juliette 193 Louisa Jennie 220
Lydia 6 228 Lydia B 145 M H 154
Margaret 218 219 Maria 108
Marietta C 162 Mary 90 91 104
113 172 232 Mary C 82 Mollie
158 Nathaniel M 234 Patience 18
19 193 Phebe 63 Rachel 81
Rebecca 63 Robat (Robert) 90
Robert 218 219 Ruth 259 Sabrina
29 Samuel 74 181 Sarah 18 19 22
29 32 Sarah E 131 Susan 119 206
207 Susanna 18 Susannah 31 258
PAIGE, Abigail 224 Dea James K
220 Louisa Jennings 220
PAINE, Eliza Brigham 149 Maj Gen
Holbert E 149 Vienna 159 160
PALMER, Anna 272 Aurelia 148 149
Charles E 80 Ellen M 80 Harriet
181 Jerusha 146 Joseph 206 Lucy
217 219 Martha 206 228 Mary 160
203 206 Mary E 181 Mary Eliza
66 Rhoda 43 Samuel 43 Vianna
162 163 Wesley 181
PARINGTON, Dr Josiah R 106
Persis 106
PARK, Lizzie 71 Mary 148 243
William R Jr 71

PARKER, --- 93 127 252 Abiah 131
Abigail 23 41 44 51 52 202
Abigail Nourse 235 Adeline A 11
Anna 217 Anna Eliza 159 Annis C
C 50 Benjamin F 127 Carmi 159
Charles 202 Charles H 127
Charlotte Abby 202 Clarie F 159
Clementine 64 Cynthia 32 Daniel
237 267 David 208 E G 56 E P
157 E S 144 Edward P 159
Elizabeth 83 Elizabeth A 237
Everett E 159 Rev Francis 270
Frank I 140 Hannah 97 117
Harriet 261 Helen M 150 Hollis
M 27 Jennie 270 Jerusha 25 John
32 130 John M 241 John O 50
Leora A 11 Letitia C 241
Margaret 208 Margaret Jane 159
Martha 130 Mary 111 158 247
Mary F 267 Matilda P 56 Matthew
S 217 Mrs 251 Nancy 93 Nancy J
3 Peter Esq 51 Phebe Y 144
Rebecca 84 Robert 157 Sabra 157
Samuel 84 Sarah 139 273 274
Sarah J 79 80 Sarah M 41 Silas
264 Susan 226 William T 235
Zachariah 83
PARKHURST, --- 224 Louisa 224
PARKS, Diantha 249 Ellen Sarah
189 Laura A 189 Margaret 226
Reuben Sylvester 189 Thomas C
214
PARLING, Abigail 239 240
PARMENTER, Elsie B 76
PARSHLEY, Rufina 230 Sanborn 230
PARSLEY, John 112 Mary F 112
PARSONS, --- 10 230 Augusta 196
Augusta P 60 Charles 60 Daniel
J 112 Elizabeth 90 Ella G 112
Ellen Sarah 189 Esther R 230 H
E 196 Hezekiah 189 213 Hezekiah
B 4 Louisa 134 Mahala 4
Margaret 213 Marion J 131 Mary
213 Minnie 177 178 Rev Moses
111 Polly 213 Sally 178 Sally B
185 Sarah 13 Sarah Merrill 189
Susannah 111 William MD 131 Rev
William 10
PATCH, Fannie B 135 Mary J 194
Mayhew 234 Sally 76 Sarah 222
223 Susan 234
PATRICK, James Gill 274 Mary
Ella 274
PATRIDGE, Harry M 167
PATTEE, Betsey 197 Hannah E 107
Jane 107 Judith 107 Sarah A 197
William 107 William S 197
PATTEN, Aaron 42 Abby 135
Abigail 269 Alice 251 Betsy 249
Clarissa 156 David 251 Hiram G
156 Jesse 108 Jonathan 86

Ludlow 135 Lydia 264 Margaret
86 Mary 42 72 255 Mary E 86
Mehitable 53 Melissa 108 Nancy
62 Phila 42 Polly 108 Priscilla
249 Rebecca 59 115 Samuel 249
Samuel 264 Capt Samuel 59 Sarah
42 Sophronia 50 Wm 53
PATTERSON, Dea David 194 Hannah
161 Jane Duncan 161 Joab 156
John D Esq 34 Lizzie H 34 Mary
35 75 132 133 156 Mary B 194
PATTIE, Susan 90 91
PAUL, Martha M 244 Samuel 244
PAYSON, --- 232 Mrs Ann 134 Hon
M P 232 Sarah 261
PEABODY, --- 133 Amos 133 170
Eliza H 272 Enoch 263 Dea
George W 116 James 101 James H
47 Judith 263 Lizzie R 66 Mary
F 116 Nancy 156 170 Oliver 169
Rebecca 135 136 Lt Richard 143
Roxanna 47 Sophronia Phelps 153
Rev Stephen 232 Susannah 169
Tabitha 143 William 136 William
H 272
PEARL, Betsey 183 Eliza 122 123
Joseph 123 183 Mary 183
PEARSE, Mary 198 Peter 184 198
PEARSON, Abigail 157 Anna 102
Dorcas 87 George 145 Hannah 10
James 102 Jane 145 Capt Joseph
271 Mary S 176 Ruth 190 Sarah
149 271
PEARSONS, Lydia 213
PEART, Nancy 205
PEASE, Arzelia Jane 57 Betsey 19
57 61 197 Hannah A 61 John 210
Joseph 217 Mary Jane 210 Simeon
D 19 57 61
PEASLEE, Abigail 91 Francis G
231 Hannah 10 16 175 193 Maj
Jacob 16 18 77 John 91 Jonathan
96 109 Judith 51 52 Keziah D
154 Mrs Margaret Temple 13
Maria 70 Marion 103 Mark 191
Martha 16 77 Mary A 231 Mary S
141 Phebe 109 Ruth 20 21 Sarah
154 191 Susan 96
PEASLEY, --- 113 Abigail 79 80
Betsy 16 Manly 16 Phebe 11
PEAVEY, Abigail 37 Alvin 81
Dorcas 88 Jeremiah 88 Joseph 37
Lizzie D 88 Louisa 88 Dea Peter
88
PEBBLES, Nellie 25
PECK, Angeline M 26
PEEBLES, --- 25
PEIRCE, Annie 103 Caroline 103
Cumming 103 Sally 221
PELTON, Asahel 195 Harriet 195
196 John 174 Margaret 125 126

Martha 174
PENDERGAST, Parmelia A 213
PENDEXTER, Alice 169 202 249
  Betsey 169 C C 99 Caroline P 99
  Hon John 169 241 John 202
  Joseph 201 Martha 169 241 Mary
  169 201 Nancy 241 Sally 201
  Solomon D 169
PENNIMAN, Adeline 143 Bethuel
  143 Caleb D 118 Caroline S 118
  Clarissa 118 Mary 5 Sophia 143
PENNOCK, Mary 20
PERASON, Hannah 52
PERHAM, Lydia 204 Mary 115 116
PERKINS, --- 27 47 48 92 111
  Abbie 111 Abigail 35 92 Ann 37
  Anna 5 Caroline 179 233
  Catharine 152 Clara 187
  Clarissa Bartlett 101 Comfort
  172 Cyrus F 111 D B 274
  Drucilla 27 Elias 99 Elizabeth
  126 Enoch 187 Estha 102 Esther
  W 217 Fanny 62 Frances 154 162
  270 Frances O 12 George 162 200
  273 Hannah 38 116 152 Hannah P
  25 Hannah P McCoy 2 Hon
  Hamilton E 101 Dea Isaac 224
  Dea James 47 Joann 273 Joanna
  224 John 116 John W 179 233
  Jonathan Chesley 38 Judith 73
  221 Laura 48 Louisa A 32 99
  Lydia 112 256 Mabel 118 Maria H
  233 234 265 Martha 222 Mary 38
  111 162 N R 126 Paul 12 112
  Peter 5 Polly 273 Rebecca 99
  Ruth 274 Sally 70 111 Stephen
  Esq 233 Susan 34 111 Thomas 2
  Timothy 152
PERLEY, Benjamin 99 Eliza 99
  Eliza D 190 Hannah 192 John Q
  190 Louise S 2 Maria S 170
  Rebecca 191
PERRIMAN, Frances 6
PERRY, Rev Baxter 45 Eunice 88
  Lydia A 45 Mary Ann 20 Mary C
  93 Roxana M 10
PERRYMAN, Joanna 83 Nicholas 83
PERSE, Lydia 261
PERVERT, Mary 167
PETERS, Andrew B 230 Anne 230
  Charlotte E 66 Henry M 66 John
  161 Margaret 161
PETTENGILL, Abigail 233 Amos 196
  Lt Benjamin 196 Betsey 77 196
  Charlotte E 99 Eleanor 16 Lucy
  196 Phebe 131 Susannah 134
  William 131
PETTINGILL, --- 129 Ann 16
  Eleanor 17 Hosea 228 Polly 228
PEVEAR, Elnora 201
PEVERLY, Almira J 84 Fanny 217

Thomas Esq 84
PHELPS, Drusilla 117 Harriet 176
  Henry 25 59 Joseph 117 Lois 214
  226 Louis 13 Mahala 25 Mary
  Emma 185 Mary F 176 Mason 85
  Mercy D 120 Mira J 85 Nathan O
  176 Pauline 59 60 136 Sarah 25
  59 William A 185
PHILBRICK, --- 89 90 Andrew 20
  Anna 211 Annie M 95 David
  Morrill 238 Ellen 270 Hannah
  109 James 211 James M 42 Jane
  270 Jeremiah 270 Joseph 202
  Josiah 82 207 L B Esq 95 Luella
  B 81 82 Martha G 260 Mary 251
  Mary S 42 Sally 82 202 251 Sara
  A 238 Sarah 82 207 Stephen G
  251 Susan L 20 Thomas Sr 251
PHILBROCK, F J 173 Laura O 173
PHILBROOK, Caleb 249 Eliphalet
  100 Mary 14 Mary 250 Nancy 100
  Sarah 74
PHILIPS, Maria H 8
PHILLIPS, --- 34 Abigail 249
  Caroline M 1 Dorothy 25 Esther
  275 Harriet Chase 246 Jane 135
  136 Joanna 34 Lillie 135
  Margaret 135 Maria H 144 145
  Mary C 256 Sidney A Esq 256
  Walter 135
PHIPPS, --- 122
PICKENS, James 59
PICKERING, Abigail 137 Caroline
  D 213 Charlotte 132 133 Daniel
  213 Deborah 214 215 Ephraim 215
  Eunice T 157 Gee 244 James 132
  Jane 198 Joseph W 114 Maria G
  57 Martha 215 Mary J 244
  Mehitable 90 Molly 137 Olive
  114 Polly 27 Richard 27 Sarah
  260 Sarah A 27 29 Sarah C 213
  Sophia L 127 Thomas 137
  Winthrop 133
PIERCE, --- 131 160 Abigail 247
  Betsey 131 Caroline 73 141
  Carrie D 40 Cummings 73 Esther
  162 Frances H 164 George S 197
  Gov 160 Hannah 109 Hannah E 109
  Hattie 197 Henry 252 Hiram 109
  Joseph Smith 189 Lucy 89 90
  Luella S 141 Maria D 107 Martha
  131 Martin 164 Nancy W 92
  Oliver 92 Rexford 40 Sarah A
  146 Sophia 92 Susan 252
PIERCOE, Mary Augusta 189
PIERSON, Abbey 64 Catherine J
  203 George 83 James B 203 Mary
  83 Nancy 64 Samuel 64
PIKE, --- 190 Caroline 190
  Charles P 105 Dorothy 198 199
  George S 261 Israel 249 Joshua

206 Mary A 17 Nancy 100
Nicholas 122 Phebe 261 Capt
Robert 249 Maj Robert 199 Sarah
121 Sarah M 205 206
PILLSBURY, Charles A 241 Dolly W
61 Emeline L 89 Harrison 193
Ithamar P 190 John 61 Mrs
Louisa F 36 Louise M 190 Martha
C 193 Mary A 241 Nancy 89
Randall J 89 Sally 65 Sarah C
65 Sarah M 235 Susan 61
Tristram 65
PINGHRAM, Amanda 15 Moses 15
PINGRY, Polly 134
PINKERTON, --- 144 Elizabeth 180
Dea James 180
PINKHAM, Abigail 123 Mrs
Catharine C 99 Daniel 44 84
Emily S 250 Esther 44 George
249 Martha 84 Tristram 123
PINNER, Nancy 128
PIPER, Arvilla 168 Benjamin 62
140 Esther 168 H H 210 Hannah
11 12 John 125 Kate N 270 Laura
W 210 Mary 13 14 75 Nancy S 136
Polly 55 R Bruce 136 Reuben 78
Sally 78 Sarah 62 Sarah A O 87
Thomas 168
PITCHER, Andrew 32 Experience 32
PITKIN, R A 103 Samuel P 168
PITMAN, --- 19 Angevine 118
Benjamin 194 Emeline 45 Hon G W
M 45 Hazen 194 Joanna 169
Jonathan 129 Joseph 169 Mary D
194 Polly 194 Sally 194
PLACE, James A 55 John 210
Martha 210 211 Mary 141 Mary
Jane 55
PLAISTED, Louisa 133 Margaret S
27 28 Nancy 28 228 William 28
PLATTS, George 161 Harriet 161
James 161 Mary F 161
PLIMPTON, Flora 44 S W 44
PLUMER, Betsey 148 203 Ebenezer
214 Elsie 216 217 George 46
Hannah Jane 105 106 Jesse T 105
Mrs Louisa A 80 Mrs Louisa A
Niel 80 Mary 214 Priscilla 153
Rebecca 148 Samuel 148 203 217
Sarah 122 Sarah F 46
PLUMMER, --- 133 Henry 162 Mark
212 Mary 133 Nancy 212 Richard
122 Sally S 212 Sarah 122 166
167 168 Susan 2 27 29
POINDEXTER, Lydia 224
POLAND, Chastina 146 D A 146
Rachel 71
POLK, Lydia 70
POLLARD, Achsah 186 258 Benjamin
102 Margaret 88 Sally 67 Susan
102 145

POMEROY, Mary F 43
POMFRET, Martha 64 123 William
64
POMFRETT, Elizabeth 266 William
266
POOL, Mary 141
POOLE, Bethia 13
POOR, Alfred 62 Annie 241 Betsey
226 Eliphalet 119 Eliza A 144
Elizabeth 119 Jesse 187 Mary
119 162 Mary E 187 Mary L 62
POORE, Anna 71 Mary Ann 241
Moses 241 Sally 241
POPE, --- 4 Edwin Esq 62 John P
214 Nellie B 62
PORTER, --- 194 Abigail 84
Bathsheba 100 Clarrissa 55
Elizabeth 102 Elizabeth J 108
Eluthera 239 Emerson 82 Esther
233 Rev Huntington 260 Isaac
142 Joseph 103 Louisa 194 259
260 Lydia 161 Maria 100 Mary 54
55 Mary E 154 Mrs Rebecca 82
Reuben 84 Rhoda 251 Sally 103
142 Susanna 237
POST, Aaron 228 Dinah 60 Laura
180 Lydia 228 Mary 151 Peter
151
POTTER, Hon Charles E 160 Eliza
A 90 91 Eunice 189 Frances 160
George 90 Honora 70 Jacob A 172
Lemuel 70 Lucy 174 Maria 186
Nancy A 90 Nathaniel 186
Sophronia 172
POTTS, John L 25 Nellie E 25
POWELL, Betsey 139 140
POWERS, --- 259 Ezekiel 115
Hannah 17 115 Hattie A 238 Dr
Henry 238 Leonia 131 Lois 252
Rachel 98 Sally 118 Sarah 189
207 Scott W 207
PRADDEX, E Minnie 166 H A 166
PRATT, Aphia E 182 C Waterman 5
David 182 Emma O 176 F W Esq
159 Louisa A 159 Mary A 5
PRAY, Capt Samuel 14 Sophronia
14
PRENTISS, Lydia J 262
PRESBURY, James 262 Phebe 133
Polly 80 262 Dea William 133
PRESCOTT, --- 214 226 Aaron 205
Abigail 99 216 Alice 185 Almira
48 Annie E 268 Betsey 1 Col 239
Daniel R 46 Dorothy S 88 89 201
Edna 67 Ellen 103 Fred S 103
Hannah 39 Hannah B 38 Howard
193 J D 86 James 25 James Sr 53
Jedediah 116 Jeremiah 216 John
204 223 John H 67 Jonathan 49
Julia A 46 Leah 239 Lill 103
Lucy M 205 Lydia 88 89 Mary 25

34 53 67 199 204 214 222 223
Mary A 40 Mary E 234 Mary F 86
Mary R 193 Merinda 49 Patience
20 Ruth 115 116 Samuel 234
Susie H 207 William H 207
PRESSEY, Carlos G 207 Mary N 207
PRESTON, Ann Eliza 167 Anna 48
Fannie M 167 George P 167 James
M 110 Louisa C 110 Mary J 138
Mrs Sarah A 2 Wingate T 138
PRICE, Betsey 126 Mary 55 56
PRICHARD, Anna M 265
PRIEST, Durilla 233 Irena 154
James 154 Mercy 231 Sally 97
Sarah 54
PRIME, Noble 89 Sally 88 89
PRINCE, Hannah 119 Honor 182 183
PRITCHARD, Della M 175
PROCTOR, Addie G 3 Clara 40 Emma
Thorndike 51 Hannah 88 Dr John
111 Katharine L 111 Mary E 39
Rachel 61 Roxellana 25
PROUTY, Esther 21
PUGALLS, Alma M 267
PULCIFER, --- 176 Lizzie 176
PULSIFER, Maj John 241 Phebe 57
241 Ruth 255
PURDY, --- 210 Fannie 210
PURINGTON, Mrs Betsey Ambrose 24
Eunice 126 Hannah 126 James 126
John 20 Phebe 20
PURMORT, Charles W 98 Susan E 98
PUSHEE, Albert J 137 Mary 143
Sarah F 137
PUTNAM, Allen 208 Annette 269
David 30 Eliza 208 Ella H 111
Ephraim 244 Esther 244 Gen
Israel 63 Rebecca P 208 William
H 111
PUTNEY, --- 17 Abigail 17 Almira
M 119 Eliza 3 Hazen 119 186 206
Louise 98 Mary N 206 Nancy 17
Nellie H 62 Nellie M 31 Polly 5
Susan 119 206 Susanna 186

QIGGIN, Zebulon 184
QUACKENBUSH, Jane 77 John N Esq
77
QUARLES, Abigail Ann Caroline 19
Sarah M 216
QUIGG, --- 74 Abel 74 Abbie T
177 178 Celia 126 Elisha 197
Ellen L 51 Enoch 86 Ezuba 246
George 160 Hannah 197 Col Henry
B 53 Jemima 86 John S 177 Col
Joseph L 86 Lydia 160 Mary 4
Mary E 86 Mary J 86 Miriam 77
Nancy 177 Octavia M 53 Dr S J
51 Sarah 82 197
QUINCY, Abraham 225 Adeline 80
225

QUINT, Hannah 27 Lydia 29

RALPH, Nancy 262
RAMSAY, Augusta 188 Ira A 168
Sarah L 168
RAMSDELL, Eliza D 271 George A
271
RAMSEY, Ann 160 Henrietta 143
Mary 16 17
RAND, E D 240 Elizabeth 137
Hamlin 61 Harriet 61 Harriet
Sprague 61 Helen A 87 Joan H
240 John 111 Joseph J 87 Judith
Parsons 111 Ruth 147 218 219
Sarah B 52 Susan Mary 192
William 137
RANDALL, --- 108 246 Agnes 92
Almira 220 Ann 185 Arabella 41
Capt Benjamin 260 Elder
Benjamin 195 Betsey 155 Daniel
B 184 Eliza 246 247 Hannah 184
Harriet 263 Margaret 195 Martha
260 Nancy 220 Polly 164 165 S
Rebecca 58 274 Samuel 220
William 155
RANDLETT, Hannah 115 116 Harriet
A 192 Mary 214 Mary A 192 Moses
192 Thomas 192
RANKIN, Joan 59
RANLET, Augusta 177 Charles 177
Daniel W 174
RAWLINS, --- 54 Elizabeth 147
Hannah 53
RAWSON, Nizaulla 136
RAY, Alice S 27 Ann L 77
Benjamin F 77 Edward 27 Emma P
77
RAYMOND, Jennie 72 Mary 105 106
REA, Calvin 92 Clara C 92
READ, Mary 190
REDDINGTON, Henry 48 Stella L 48
REDLOW, George 16 Mary F 16
REED, Alma 56 168 Alsea 88 Anna
56 Bellona 67 Eliza 235
Elizabeth 180 Elsie 4 Eunice
164 Gen George 180 Hannah 97
263 Hannah E 180 J T 35 John 97
180 Julia 252 Lucy 35 Lydia C
100 223 Mary 231 Persis 130
Samuel 56 Sarah 64 65 73 139
Sybil 131 Capt Wm 131
REID, David 161 Isabella 83 161
Mary Ann 201
REMICH, --- 203 Joseph S 203
Julia A 203
REMICK, Abigail 241 Ada A 189
Charles 133 Elizabeth Gardner
133 Ella 88 Capt Enoch 133
Henry 131 Louise M 4 Polly 131
240 241 Samuel 4 Samuel K 189
209 Sarah 133 Sophia 4 189

William 240
REVALL, Harriet 161
REYNOLDS, Esther 220
RHODES, Benjamin 231 Capt Elisha
  H 28 Esther J 231 Eunice 231
  Mary Eliza 28 29
RICE, Hon Alexander H 163 Rev
  Daniel 75 Edwin 17 Elijah 45
  Rev George M 259 Hannah 6 186
  John 240 Louisa 77 78 Martha 45
  Mary Ann 163 Persis Fayette 259
  Prudence 239 240 Samuel 186
  Sarah 17 75 Sarah Parker 107
  Susannah 204 Willard 163
  William 107 Zilpha 63
RICH, Mary 176 Richaird 211
  Sarah 211
RICHARDS, Abigail 95 96 Benjamin
  95 Capt Benjamin 205 Betsey
  Hill 205 Betsey Hills 205
  Darius M 193 David 163
  Elizabeth 193 Elizabeth S 192
  193 Hannah 163 Isabella Walker
  192 193 L H 256 Martha 163 Mary
  E 256 Mary Ella 128 Mehitable
  205 Nancy M Silence 146 264 W
  Eugene 128
RICHARDSON, --- 34 48 156
  Abigail J C 232 Adeline 242
  Charlotte 45 Clarissa 156
  Daniel 134 David 127 David S
  266 Edward 58 Eliza J 76 Eliza
  Messenge 52 Elizabeth 34 58
  Flora J 261 George 261 Harriet
  152 Henry 45 Hiram 76 James 176
  Jane 176 Julia H 266 L 232 Mrs
  Lucy C 201 Maria 22 Mary 97 134
  230 Mary Currier 22 Mary F 127
  Miriam 2 Nancy 156 Patience 91
  Phebe 61 Priscilla 203 Sarah 14
  Sarah B 45 Mrs Tryphena T 64
  Hon William M 14 Wm Gray 22
RICHFORD, Nancy 82
RICHMOND, Sarah R P 29
RICKER, --- 237 Anna 247 Harriet
  134 L J 247 Mehitable 150 Susan
  174
RIDDLE, Ann Lincoln 44
RIDEOUT, Mary 138
RILEY, George 241 John 253 Mary
  253 Sally 241 Sarah Byles 253
RINDGE, Anna 198 John 198
RING, Betsey 27 30 Betsy 30 197
  Page Esq 27 Stephen F 197
RIPLEY, Maria 175
RISLEY, --- 84 Achsah 272
  Russell 272
RITTERBUSH, --- 38 146 Mary Ann
  146 Sarah 269 Sophia 38 146
  Zebulon 269
RIX, Lucretia 77

ROACH, Joanna 208 Mary 208 Moses
  265 Rhoda 265 William 208
ROADES, Rebecca 160 Sarah E 160
  Silas 160
ROBBINS, Abigail 99 234 Betsy 97
  139 Emily R 111 Eunice 197
  Francis 99 Capt George A 105
  Hannah W 46 Harriet Elizabeth
  55 Jane 6 Mary C 105 Philemon
  Wadsworth 55 Sarah 102 120
ROBERTS, --- 123 130 Abigail 197
  247 Alice J 28 29 Ann E 27 30
  Benjamin 269 Betty 123 Burleigh
  260 Daniel 247 David 120
  Elizabeth 125 Emma F 260 Eunice
  103 165 236 237 John 202 Rev
  Joshua 152 Julia Anna 247 248
  Louisa 269 Lucinda A 212 Mary
  122 151 Relief 130 Sarah 261
  Sarah L 191 Sarah M 120 Susan
  100 152 202 Susan Burnham 122
  123 Susanna 130 Tamson 140
  Thomas 125 151 Timothy 123
  Watkins 30 Zerviah 131
ROBERTSON, Charles 51 234
  Elizabeth 103 Emma J 51 H D 84
  Jane 234 Robert 103 Sarah 84
ROBIE, Annie H 135 Batsheba 149
  Caleb T 135 Hannah 135 Samuel
  185 Sarah 86 185
ROBINSON, Abby 216 Almira 219
  Angelina P 126 Anna 10 216
  Arvilla O 174 Belinda 86
  Eliphalet 206 Emma 9 Frank E 9
  Franklin 86 George H 212 Henry
  214 John R 216 Jonathan 174
  Joseph 216 Julia 219 Julia A 65
  66 Julia E 219 Kathleen 212
  Lavinia 174 Mahaley 64 Mara 212
  Marcia 199 Mary 89 90 247 Mary
  E 205 206 234 Persis 244 Polly
  211 Profinda 148 Mrs Sarah 154
  Sarah L 259 260 Sarah Pratt 147
  Theodora 67 William 219
ROBY, Amanda 268 George 186
  Hannah 269 Ira 269 James 88 243
  Josephine 186 Lucy 88 243 Nancy
  88 243 271 Theodate 73 74
ROCKWELL, --- 87 Abbie 167 Laura
  J 87 R E 167
RODIMON, Amanda L 222 Ezra A 222
ROE, Hannah 252 James 252
ROGERS, --- 68 Abigail 260 Annie
  L 182 Daniel 245 Eliza 198
  George W 182 Hannah 93 Herbert
  E 219 Rev John 192 Joshua 245
  Lillian 219 Lucretia 245 Lurana
  245 Lydia 116 Lydia S 9 151
  Mary S 156 157 Mollie 173 Nabby
  260 Sarah 182 Sophia W 218
  Stephen 194 Susanna 194

Susannah 192 Thomas 116
ROLF, Catherine 139
ROLFE, Benjamin Esq 255 Jonas
  228 Jonathan 189 Margaret 189
  Martha P 228
ROLINS, Delia J 219
ROLLINGS, Nancy 90 Ruth Jane 89
  90 Sherburne 90
ROLLINS, Abigail 147 246 Amy L
  134 Betsey 214 252 Caroline D
  198 Charles Esq 198 F H 215
  Huldah D 182 John A 134
  Jonathan 70 Joseph 86 Joshua 48
  Lydia 48 Martha 31 Mary 48 215
  Mary S 86 Polly 31 Ruama 56
  Sally 50 70 Samuel H 182 211
  Sewell 31 Susan J 211
ROOD, Lydia B 196 197
ROPER, Lucy A 191
ROSEBROOK, --- 58 Eleazer 58
  Phineas 251 Sophronia 251
ROSS, Anna 245 Annette A 120 121
  Benjamin 245 Elam 60 Elizabeth
  60 H P 77 Isaac 72 245 James 74
  Jane 50 Julia A 155 Lucia W 77
  Lucy G 108 Margaret 191 Olive
  245 Sarah 74 Thomas 155 Vina H
  72 73
ROUSE, Fannie H 38
ROWAN, Phebe 168
ROWE, --- 172 Alexander 146 Ann
  217 219 Belinda 146 Edwin C 195
  Eliza 202 Eliza F 248 Elizabeth
  177 Elmira 255 Ephraim 255
  Hannah F 198 Harriet E 27
  Jessie 248 Joseph 177 Kate 172
  Keziah 4 Lucy 95 Margaret 120
  Mary 248 Oren 87 Robert 27 Ruth
  197 Sally 146 Sally T 27
ROWELL, Aaron 170 Abigail 219
  Annie 156 Belinda 109 Berenice
  A 143 David 190 156 David O 137
  Dolly 156 Esther 170 Irena 17
  Irving G 98 Jane 207 Judith 105
  Kerenhappuch 16 Lucia J 169
  Mary 166 217 Mary E 98 Meriel
  270 Nancy 108 Sally L 164
  Samuel 143 Sarah 216 217 Sarah
  C 137 Stephen 16 17 T D 270
  Thomas 153 Urvin G 98
ROWLES, Emily 274
ROYCE, Lucy 265 Merab 132 Samuel
  132
RUGGLES, Sarah 238
RUMERY, Aldo M 207 Sarah M 207
RUMRILL, Mary 15 Peter 15
RUNDLET, John S 217 Olive B 216
  217
RUNDLETT, Adeliza S 212
  Elizabeth D 64 65 Mrs Lucy 227
  Viola 212 Viola E 212

RUNNELLS, Myra 126
RUNNELS, Margaret 195 Peter 192
  Mrs Phebe 232 Sally 192
RUSS, Eliza 162
RUSSEL, Rebecca G 58
RUSSELL, Achsah 232 Acy 249
  Addie A 97 Armena 82 Armena H
  82 Caroline Carter 97 Catherine
  258 Clarissa A 227 Elizabeth 53
  Frank 53 George E 97 John 232
  Lizzie 219 Lucy Ann 13 14 Mary
  67 Mary A 203 Mary Frances 33
  Nancy 249 Nellie 203 Pelatiah
  203 Phebe 186 Polly 232 Sarah
  127 Selestie 82 Thomas K 13
RUST, Anna 188 Col Henry 188
RUTTER, Jane 6
RYAN, Hannah 63 Martha Louise 63
  Samuel 63 Susan 270
RYDER, --- 126 Betsey 11 Ezekiel
  11 Mary D 11

SABIN, Huldah 130
SABINS, Huldah 31
SACKETT, De Ette 225
SAFFORD, Caroline H 151 Noah B
  Esq 151
SALTER, Anne W 46 John 63 Maria
  J 63
SALTMARSH, Susan 204
SAMPSON, Mary 111 Mary A 111
  Priscilla 120 William 111
SANBORN, --- 152 Abbie 167 Dea
  Abraham 271 Alcina Eveline 107
  108 Almira J 213 Amy W 129 Anna
  193 Areanna Evelyn 130 Aroline
  E 17 Arthur V 85 Betsy 248
  Caleb T 121 166 Calvin 129
  Caroline 135 Caroline A 216
  Catherine 133 181 Charles 133
  Charles P Esq 21 Charlotte F
  193 Clara N 42 Clarisa 9 249
  Comfort 150 Cynthia P 13 Capt
  Daniel L 35 Dr 90 133 Dyer H
  218 E A 27 Prof E D 246 Edmund
  9 Elisha 147 148 Eliza 98 137
  Eliza J 9 Elizabeth 11 193 228
  Elizabeth H 219 Elizabeth P 217
  Elizabeth Prescott 271 Etta C
  27 Fanny 21 Fidelia 212 Flora M
  135 Freeman 54 Georgianna 90
  Gould 50 Hannah 99 122 123 269
  Hannah A 246 Harriet 217 Herman
  19 Ida B 248 J N 42 J Warren 89
  Jacob 193 James Monroe 130 219
  Jane 270 Jeremiah C 248 Jesse
  219 Johanna 135 John 115 171
  Capt John 147 John Peverly 145
  John W 212 269 Hon John W 213
  Rev John Wentworth 218 Jonathan
  219 Dea Jonathan 181 Joseph 13

Lt Joseph 149 Joseph O 135
Joseph T 137 Josephine C 85
Josiah 73 Judith 171 205 Julia
A 130 Julia Augusta 218 219
Lillian 213 Louisa 8 Lydia 174
181 Margaret 224 Mary 73 148
149 150 177 Mary A 19 Mary Ann
19 Mary E 35 50 54 Mary H 121
Mehitable 23 152 Moses 17 108
240 Nancy 90 Dr Nathan 218
Polly M 121 166 Rebecca F 89
Relief R 174 Rufus 217 Ruth 147
185 Sally 50 145 214 Samuel 135
Sarah 13 17 133 197 205 218
Sarah Ann 219 Sarah J 16 171
Serephina 240 Sophronia 240
Stella 21 Susan 86 Theodate 73
Thomas J 174 Violet S 119
Zebulon 217
SANBURN, Abigail 91 Eliza 72
Emily 227 Jacob 227 Margaret 99
Sarah A 226 227 Sarah Ann 270
SANDERS, Abigail 186 Elizabeth
152 I L 152 Israel L 152
Josephine E 229 S W 229
SANDERSON, Hannah 15 Mrs Lizzie
Carleton 59 Morrison 15
SANFORD, Abbie M 124
SANGER, Abbie A 64 65
SANGLETERY, Eunice 79 80
SARGENT, --- 16 17 Abigail 127
197 Asa 162 B F 69 Catharine L
93 Daniel 271 Dorothy A 82 E B
197 Ella 69 Hannah 49 120 123
Mrs Hannah Hubbard 90 Harriet
Newell 66 Rev Huntington Porter
177 Ira 66 Joanna 115 116 John
215 252 Jonathan 274 Joshua 127
Julia 225 Lucetta 252 Lucinda
238 Lucy A 97 98 216 Lydia 180
Margaret 1 Mary 9 62 140 201
271 Mary H 124 Nancy 215 Dea
Nathan 62 Olive 248 Polly 136
Ruth B 215 Sarah 45 162 175 176
200 Mrs Sarah G 232 Maj
Sterling 119 Susan 83 177 Susan
E 132 Sybil 274 William 175
SARJEANT, Elizabeth 166 168
SARTWELL, Anna E 159 Joel M 159
SAUNDERS, Annie 6 George 164
Richard Lang 114 Sarah B 19
Susan 114 Tabitha 146 147
SAVAGE, Hannah 107 Martha 181
SAWYER, Abigail 5 Alzina M 114
Amanda M 271 Anna Maria 177
Arianna 144 Betsey 33 179
Cynthia 151 David 91 Dorothea
188 E D 199 Frances 65 Hannah
38 58 Hannah F 91 Jacob 267
Jeannette McKeith Wilson 65
Jonathan 232 Capt Josiah 5

Lucretia M 262 Lucy 110 Mary
167 231 232 Mary C Cox 26
Rachel 114 Richard 144 Ruth 60
Sarah 69 79 144 157 199 267
Susan 272 Susanna 5 William 65
SAYLES, Anna 56
SCALES, Asenath 247
SCAMON, John 14 Mary G 14
SCARRIOTT, Elder 95 Phoebe 95
SCATES, Oliver 152 Sally 152
SCEGGELL, Benjamin 207 Fanny 207
SCHENCK, Delia P 44 Martin L 44
SCHOFF, Kate 12
SCIRBNER, Catherine 33
SCOTNEY, Elizabeth 15 Francis 15
Jane 15
SCOTT, Eliza 150 Rev G R W 72
James 221 Mary 72 Phebe 221
Ursula 94
SCRIBNER, Abbie 28 Ann 28
Charlotte 214 Daniel 28 Edna J
214 Franklin Esq 86 Helen M 3
Ida G 86 Lowell 214 William P
33
SCRUTEN, Betsey 1 Betsey 2
SCRUTON, David 100 Lydia C 100
Lydia N 100
SCULLY, Irene 73 Patrick 73
SEAMAN, Marianna 47 Prof W H 47
SEARLE, Rev Jonathan 213
Margaret 213
SEARLES, Elizabeth 78 79 Mary 77
78 79
SEARS, Anna P G 6 David 6 Electa
B 41
SEAVEY, Bethana 228 Betsey 147
212 Daniel 74 Elijah 169
Ephraim 212 Hannah P 212
Ithamar 184 Jonathan 14 Mary
169 220 228 Mary C 197
Mehitable 74 Moses Esq 147
Polly 14 Sally L 187 188 Thomas
Lewis 129
SECOMB, Elizabeth 193 Mary 193
Simmons 193
SEDY, Rebecca 100
SEDY, Mary A 200
SENNOTT, Mary A 200
SENTER, Frances H 139 140
Georgiana V 139 140 Lavinia T
50 Mary 161 Nellie B 177 178
Samuel 161 Samuel M 51 Samuel M
177 Susan 232
SESSIONS, Melissa 262 Violetta
31 140
SEVERANCE, John 96 105 Sarah A
105
SEWELL, Mary 179
SEYMOUR, Edward D 50 Ellen F 50
SHACKFORD, --- 97 Abigail 123
Hannah 181 John 181 Lydia P 194
Mary 72 107 176 260 Nancy

Walker 137 Nathaniel C 72 Rhoda
184 Samuel 194 Samuel Esq 137
Stephen 184
SHANNON, Lucy E 58 S A 58
SHAPIN, Sarah 179
SHAPLEIGH, Betsey 213 Eunice 222
Hannah T 85 Martha J 222 Samuel
222
SHATTUCK, --- 262 Rev Benjamin
252 Betsey 244 Betsy 262
Elizabeth 274 Francis 152
Harriet N 106 Jonathan 244
Joseph 262 Martha 252 Mary 152
Mary Heald 153 Sarah 80 Simeon
80 Vashti P 157 Hon Zebadiah
157
SHAW, --- 12 95 Abigail 95
Abigail C 25 Amiah 82 Anne 90
Bethsheba 22 Charles C 267
Clarissa 38 Col Dan 142 234
David P 38 Rev Elijah 25 Elis
228 Emma A 26 Gilbert 92 Joanna
142 John 12 Rev John 193 232
Mary A 92 Mrs 193 Oliver W 214
Patience 234 Roger 90 Sally 70
172 Sarah 90 Sophia F 267
William 127
SHEAFE, Anna 199 Emily 198 Jacob
64 James Esq 121 Louisa 121
Mary Hurke 64 William Esq 199
SHEARER, Mattie 4 Nancy 249
SHED, John S 252 Mary E 252
SHEDD, Adaline F 36 Hannah 63
252 Malvina 139
SHELDON, Abbie J 227 Clarissa A
227 Capt J H 227
SHELDRON, Elizabeth W 54 Hon
Parker 54
SHELTON, Anna T 14 R H 14
SHEPARD, Anna 96 Eleanor 225
Elizabeth 27 28 Elizabeth A 134
Elmira 134 Frances M 68 Harriet
274 Jacob 17 274 Jane G 151
John C 134 John M 225 Lydia 225
Mary 36 Mercy 17 Nancy 225
Richard 225 Roxana 253 Sarah 17
18 Thomas 17 William 253
William H 151
SHEPHERD, Dea Ralph 204 Trial
204
SHEPHERDSON, Adella 161 E E 161
SHERBORN, Sarah 68
SHERBURN, Mary Rebecca 213
Robert 79 Robert H 213 Ruth 79
SHERBURNE, --- 25 128 Adaline B
147 Anna N 84 Elizabeth 150
Hattie 25 Henry 150 Joseph 84
Mary 90 Ruth 224 Sarah 68 90
SHERMAN, --- 134 Elizabeth T 40
65 Hannah 245 John 65 Lucy R
134 Sibyl 124 125

SHERWIN, Anna 269 Elizabeth 63
Jonathan 269 Mary 269
SHIPMAN, Christiana C 171 Emma R
261 Rev I H 171
SHIRLEY, Abigail 139 160 253
Abigail Frances 65 Adeline 80
Alice 79 Daniel M 124 139 225
Gilman 225 Harriet 139 James 80
160 253 Jane 124 160 225 John
56 72 144 240 Margaret 56 72
144 240 Maria 144 Mary 124 Mary
H 79 Mary Helen 79 Mary Jane
240 Nancy 225 226 253 Robert 65
Robert M 79 Sarah 72 Sophia 65
79
SHOALS, Horatio 4 Merriam A 4
SHORES, Mary 157
SHURBORNE, Jane 73 John 73
SHURTLEFF, Anna P 83 Mary J 168
W H 168
SHUTE, Augusta S 28 Mary 28 159
Nathaniel 14 Susannah G 14
Thomas 28
SIAS, Georgia A 247 Joseph 151
Lydia 151 Ruth 151
SILLSBY, Mindwell 232
SILVER, Mehitable 62
SIMES, Mary H 214
SIMMONS, Abigail M 157 George
157
SIMONDS, --- 204 Arabel A 11
Arad 11 Betsey 204 Cordelia 43
Cordelia P 43 Daniel 30 Martha
J 30 Orpha 32 Polly 40 Rebecca
99 Sophronia 11 Vilona L 162
SIMONS, Almeda 227 Caleb 13 214
226 Christopher 154 Daniel 156
Darwin A 227 Harriet K 214
Huldah 156 John 16 Lois 214 226
Louis 13 Lydia 16 Lydia
Morrison 226 Margaret 226 227
Mary 13 16 79 80 Nancy 154
Orpha 32 Polly 16 17 Susannah
264
SIMPSON, --- 24 Elizabeth P 2
Francis T 29 Maj John 2 Livonia
29 Martha 24 Dea Samuel 2
SINCLAIR, Charles A 139 Edward C
202 Emma I 139 Frances E 202
Henry 216 Isabella Aiken 182
Prof John E 182 John G 199 Mary
199 Sally T 27 216 Sarah 55
SISE, Annie L 199
SKELTON, Deborah 57 58 Elizabeth
64 Rev John 64
SKINNER, Dorcas S 117 Joseph 117
Mary E 242 Melissa 46
SLADE, Abigail 225 Elizabeth T
224 Esther 12
SLAPP, Maj John 11 Mehitable 131
Nancy 11 Simon 11

SLEEMAN, Polly 181
SLEEPER, --- 71 163 208 Ann 16
Anna 20 21 254 Cyrus 89 Eaton
226 Eliza 226 Hezekiah H 71
Huldah 16 Jonathan 254 Levi H
168 Lydia 168 Mariane 171
Martha Grace 208 Mary 81 254
Mary C 88 Mary L 88 89
Mehitable 20 21 Moses W 89
Peter 197 Polly 36 Ruth A 197
Sally 163 197 Thomas 81
SLOAN, Capt John 110 256
Margaret 275 Martha P 213 Mary
256 Sarah 110
SMALL, Edwin 210 Elvira L 27 30
Gilbert 154 Kate O 210 Leila J
70 Pauline A 257 Sabra 154
Sallie Emery 209
SMALLEY, Dr A 272 Hattie F 227
Rosamond 272
SMART, George 264 271 John 184
Mrs Mary A 129 Mary G 68
Roxiana 264 Sarah W 184 Susan
271
SMILEY, Almira A 4
SMITH, --- 16 43 60 193 215 224
228 A Augusta 33 Rev A D 185
Abby A 48 214 Abigail 177 Abram
206 Achbel 245 Adaline 159
Adaline E 229 Addie E 217 Mrs
Addie L Mather 105 Alfred
Colburn 73 Alice G 58 104 Alma
66 Amanda A 243 Andalucia P 15
Ann Jennette 128 Anna 15 200
Col Ashbel 37 Benjamin 245
Benjamin B 152 Benjamin H 110
Betsey 76 129 133 214 Betsey
Ann 76 Betsy 104 254 Catherine
173 Celestia T 105 Chandler P
36 Charle Goudy 175 Charles E
33 Charlotte 57 132 246 Clara J
58 92 217 Crosley 62 Cynthia
265 Daniel 262 Dea Daniel 13
178 Daniel B 105 Daniel Munroe
213 David 57 Deborah 10 18 19
200 Dolly 240 Dorcas H 245
Dorothy 148 Dea Ebenezer 28 189
Edna 12 Eleanor Hilton 268
Eleazer 270 Elias 52 Eliphalet
95 Elivra 152 Eliza 2 27
Elizabeth 52 139 164 206
Elizabeth A 202 Elizabeth
French 206 Ellen 72 73 199
Ellen A 26 Ellen Rebecca 222
Elvira 37 227 Elvira E 36
Emeline 13 14 161 Emma 158
Esther 37 69 Esther A 132
Eunice 262 Fannie C 232 Fanny
215 Fielding 231 Francis 48
Frank 2 175 264 Frank J 55
Franklin W 229 Frederick P 61

Galusha 159 Garland 29 George
77 George S 157 Gideon 233
Hannah 201 274 Harriet 36
Harriet A 213 Harriet B 175 231
Harriet C 132 Helen M 165 Rev
Henry 129 Henry L 182 Hiram 265
Huldah 68 Ida T 199 Irene 85
Isaac 15 48 Rev Isaac 10 Isabel
117 Israel O 132 J B 240 Col J
C 92 J Fred 222 J P F 44 James
M 152 228 Jane 11 12 196 265
Mrs Jane 47 Jemima 208 Jeremiah
12 104 199 254 John 68 128 230
274 Rev John 193 224 John A 275
John Jr 76 John R 249 Jonathan
177 215 Dr Joseph H 118
Josephine R 150 Joshua 133
Josiah 95 Julia A E 41 Kate G
148 L B 214 Laura 60 Leona 50
Lettice 249 270 Louisa B 62
Lucinda 245 Lydia 15 115 132
195 196 228 Lydia H 262 M Fanny
210 Mahala 12 Marcia A 44 243
Maria 226 Marian 110 Martha 10
28 Mary 1 28 29 48 189 209 215
230 231 Mrs Mary 139 Mary A 62
210 Mary E 185 249 Mary
Elizabeth 254 Mary F 77 Mary H
105 Mary J 249 Mary Jane 19 Mrs
Mary Jane 47 Mary Lizzie 60 61
Mary M 107 261 Mary S 133
Matilda 156 Mattie 103 104
Mehitable 258 Meribah 118
Minnie 175 Minnie D 108 Miriam
173 174 Miriam E 55 Mrs 90 146
Nancy 109 Mrs Nancy 20 Nancy S
142 Obadiah 27 Olive A 28 A 257
Oliver 164 215 Pamelia P 225
Peddy 89 Peggy 12 Percy 245
Phebe C 245 246 Polly 29 230
Rebecca 95 136 233 Rebecca
Newell 273 Reuben 115 Robert MD
153 Roxana 27 Rufina 189 Ruth
165 Ruth W 175 S P 26 Sally 1
77 78 178 241 Sally M 110
Samuel 12 41 Samuel P 241 Sarah
139 145 177 228 230 Mrs Sarah
275 Sarah A 241 264 Sarah F 36
Sarah Jane 73 Sophronia 20
Stephen 217 Susan 139 165 Susan
E 153 Mrs Susan M 199 Susan
Morton 153 Susanna 225 T J M
273 Theresa 69 Thomas P 16
Timothy P 227 Rev Uriah 139
William 29 210 William Barry
148 William R 132
SMYTHE, Harriet C 1
SNELL, Clarinda 181 Eleazer 181
Jane 121 Lydia S 248 Paul 248
SNOW, --- 233 Alvin 179 Amanda
233 Azubah 79 Charles 271 Dora

Richardson 22 Edwin 265 Hannah 32 Harriet 271 Jacob 99 Joseph 7 Lydia 131 Maria H 265 Mary 46 Nellie H 265 Orra 211 Sally 7 Sarah 226 Susan 99 Susannah 258
SNYDER, Charles 206 Mary E 206
SOMERLY, Elizabeth 47 Henry 47 Judith 47
SOMERS, Susan 187
SONERGAN, Julia C 171
SOUTHARD, Aaron 175 Col Anson 238 Arabella F 182 Eliza 186 Emma 254 Jane 175 Kate 175 Lemuel 254 Rev Marshall 46 Mary E 46 Melissa 78 Phebe 238 Solon S 78 Timothy B 182
SOUTHMAYD, Benjamin 166 Hannah 166
SOUTHWICK, Hannah W 264 Keziah 255
SOUTHWORTH, Cynthia 65 Eliza 162 Martha P 162 Nathaniel 162
SPALDING, Emma 266 Eunice 7 Isaac 266 Rev Levi 45 Mary Christie 45 Oliver 7
SPARHAWK, Charles 184 Sarah F 184
SPAULDING, --- 74 231 Abbie N 188 Abby Thayer 238 Annette 130 Catharine R 152 Edward 259 Eliza 215 Elizabeth 89 Florence E 87 Frank W 238 George C 130 George D 87 Hannah 74 Dea Isaac 124 Jackson 37 Joshua 165 Kate 111 Lydia 124 Martha 221 259 Mary A 165 Mary Anne 133 Mary T 37 Dr Matthew 7 Oliver Esq 188 Putnam 215 Rebecca 7 Sarah A 20 Viola A 231 232
SPEAR, --- 43 Alphonzo A 129 Robert 116 Sarah 116 Sarah E 129 W T 43
SPEARS, Mary 2
SPENCER, --- 266 Annie E 170 Carrie 15 Frances 266 Gardner 11 Hannah 11 Marinda 134 Statira 11
SPILLER, Catharine 56 Deborah H 56 John 56 Judith 56 Mary 56 William W 56
SPINGER, Sally 23
SPLAIN, Elizabeth 67
SPOFFARD, Alden E 82 Lucy 95 Mary Ellen 82 Osmond 95
SPOFFORD, Harret 54 Lydia 193 Miranda 18 Samuel 18 Samuel 193
SPOKESFIELD, Betsey 117
SPOONER, Betsey 58 Hannah 32 James 32 Mary 32
SPRAGUE, Alden Esq 243 Elizabeth 243 Ellen 226 Harriet 61 Helen

M 54 Rachel 173 Samuel 226
SPRINGER, Elmira 57 Mack 57
SPURLIN, Elcy 87 John 87
SRIBNER, E W 263 Sara 263
STACKPOLE, Annie Wentworth 10 Rev E S 23 Elvira C 10 Lizzie 23 Lorenzo 10
STACY, Adeline 244 Byron 244 Rebecca 26 33 34 Susannah 33 Thomas 33
STALBIRD, --- 146
STANLEY, Betsy 274 Cynthia 112 Lt Dennis 259 Elizabeth 78 210 259 260
STANTON, Hannah 57 Isaac W 57 Mary 229 230 Patience 241 247 William 241
STANYAN, Abram 248 Sally P 185 Sarah T 248
STAPLES, Caroline Persis 99 194 Catharine 164 165 Clarissa 165 Elva N 155 Huldah 217 Rev L T 155 Nicholas W 164 Sally Rackleyft 225 Susan B 55 56
STARBIRD, Abbie 169 George 169
STARBUCK, Abigail 51 Catharine 253 Dorcas 101 Edward 51 101 Elder Edward 253 Katherine 51 101 Sarah 242 253
STARK, -- 125 Albert 125 Alonzo 156 Mary 142 Nancy 156 Pamelia 181 Phineas 142
STARKS, Elisha 255 Julia M 255
STARRETE, Henrietta M 68
STARRETT, Betsy 106 Henry G 107 Mark 106 Rhoda C 107
STEARNS, Caroline Richmond 269 Eunice 249 Eunice P 114 Fidelia 229 Dr Isaac 114 James 269 John 197 Joseph Jr 191 Keziah 206 Lucius 135 Lydia 70 Margaret 197 Mary L 256 Nyrhe 191 Rachel 135 136 S Frances 45 114 Sarah A 197
STEBBENS, Electa 236
STEBBINS, Clementine 245
STEEL, James 252 Submit R 252
STEELE, Ann 208 David 207 234 Edna 207 Elder Eleazer 140 Elizabeth Harvey 158 George Harvey 140 Harriet 234 Jane 199 Janet 208 Jonathan 157 Margaret 208 Mary 34 Mary Augusta 140 Olivia 38 Phebe 234 Thomas 208
STEESE, Edward 242 Ellen B 242
STEPHENS, --- 202 Georgeanna 202 Sally 27
STERRETT, Ann 265 Betsy 105 John 265 Mark 105
STETSON, --- 82 Almira 222 Charles 256 Florence 22

STEVEN, Eliza 170 J 170
STEVENS, --- 247 Abigail 16 65
66 67 166 168 Alvin W 268
Amelia 231 Anna 16 17 Atherton
H 218 Augustia L 93 Benjamin 62
Betsey 157 Cassandra 243 Clara
T 218 David 136 Doley 239 Dolly
240 Dorcas 132 Col Eben 53 Col
Ebenezer 243 Ebenezer C 78
Eleanor 124 Elinor 16 Eliza 125
134 157 205 Emily C 268 Emily E
218 Emory 205 Esther 275 Fanny
1 96 Grove S 93 Hannah 124 247
Hannah A 124 Hannah P 96 Helen
M 71 Hepzibath 16 17 226 J
Augusta 239 James 11 Jennie 208
John 157 168 Jonathan Ackerman
124 Joseph 226 257 Col Josiah
Jr 124 Lois 62 218 Lois Sanborn
62 Louisa 168 Mary 53 96 1 97
221 Mary A 260 Mary Jane 226
Mary W G 155 May 263 Mehitable
53 Nancy 158 Nathaniel 53
Phineas 3 Priscilla M 78
Rebecca 257 Roxa 11 Ruth 66 174
Sally 3 136 Samuel G 157 Sarah
239 Sarah A 253 Solomon 16
Theodore 65 Truman 208 Dr
Whiting 155 Rev William 263
William L 96
STEVENSON, Dea John 256 Nancy
256 Nellie H 146
STEWART, --- 251 Rebecca J 182
STICKNEY, Alexander H 31 Anna
155 208 Anne 25 Benjamin F 206
C Thomas 1 Charlotte E 31 32
Elizabeth 1 137 Jane O 57 266
Jonathan 78 Mary 256 Capt Moses
137 Nathan Esq 257 Patty 78
Phebe 206 Samuel 256
STILES, Fany 266 Hannah W 92
Joseph 92 Matilda 230 Olive 111
STILLINGS, Hannah 215 Isaac 53
Mary 53 Capt Nicholas Tuttle
247 Patience 247 Sophronia 247
STILLMAN, John 180 Mary E 180
STILPHEN, Charles 169 George P
1 94 Martha 1 94 Nancy 1 94
William 194
STINSON, Betsey 241 Capt Charles
188 Letita C 188 Letitia C 188
Mary S 119
STOCKWELL, Hannah F 56 Sylvester
56
STODDARD, Rev David 124 Mary G 6
Mary Graves 5 Sophia 124
STOKER, Sally 18
STOKES, Irena 95 Moses 95 Susan
226
STONE, --- 113 181 Addie 37
Calvin 124 Dorcas 63 Eliza P 2

Elvira 124 Hannah 27 Ira 2
Jedediah 27 Rev L H 97 Lucy A
248 Lydia 113 Lydia A 75 Lydia
E 207 Martha 181 Mary E 124
Pierce 139 Rev 75 Samuel 63
Sarah 63 Walter W 207
STONECLIFFE, Anable 82 David 82
Mary B 82
STONING, George 173 Lovina 173
Nancy 173
STOREY, Deborah J 270 Helen 231
J C 231 Sarah 237 William 237
STORRS, Augustus 106 Laura 93
Lucy 106 Mary E 228 Mehitable
115 Royal 228 Sarah A 242
STORY, David 241 Elizabeth D 50
Hannah 163 Rev Isaac 82 Lucy 62
Mary Jane 241 Susan 37 W W 50
STOWELL, Celestine A 239 Clara
105 Edward 239 P F 105
STRAHAN, Jane 180
STRATTON, Aaron 102 Abigail 131
Elizabeth 102 George W 148 Lois
228 Lucy 148 Samuel 228 Sarah P
228
STRAW, Betsy 166 265 Charlotte
132 246 Charlotte Webster 132
Daniel 114 Ellen 246 Ezekial
Albert 246 Ezekiel Albert 132
Lt Gideon 268 Hepzibath 17
Jonathan 17 Mary Ann 268 Mary E
114 Rhoda 42 Samuel 42 Susan 21
121
STREETER, Betsey 58 Frank S 38
Joel 69 Lillian 38 Maria C 183
Mercy 69 Phebe 104
STRONG, Amanda 69 Asa 4
Elizabeth 23 190 Joanna 52 Rev
Jonathan 52 Lorena 170 Lucretia
M 170 Mary J 263 Norman 170
Phebe 64 Rosantha A 4
STUAIART, Almira 226
STUART, --- 274 Almira 226
Elijah 27 Mary 27 Moses 204
Polly 3 4 Rebecca 204
STUDLEY, Joanna 234
STUMP, Augusta 106 John 106
STURDEVANT, Charlotte 149 John
149 Mary 148 149
STURTEVANT, --- 19 57 Adeline
238 Ellen B 238 John D 238
Josiah C 19 Sylvia 61 Sylvia 62
SULLAWAY, Joseph 126 Lucinda 126
Salome C 126
SULLIVAN, Ann 242 Ariannah B 267
John H 267 Lydia 238
SULLOWAY, Alvah Woodbury 64
Susan K 64
SUMNER, Eben 168 Hattie M 71
Lewis 138 Louise 138 Martha 168
SWAIN, Annie Martha 89 90 Hattie

M 71 Jonathan 119 Mary 119 272
Richard 90 272 Sarah 90 119
SWALLOW, Mary I 171 Nancy Roby
171 Stillman 171
SWAN, James I 236 Molly 85
SWARTZ, Lydia 165
SWASEY, Alice 148 Ambrose 163
Cassandra 240 John B 148
SWAYNE, Abigail 203 Elizabeth
257 Nancy 203 Samuel 203
SWAZEY, Nellie M 212
SWEAT, Esther 141
SWEATLAND, Hannah T 98 99
SWEATT, Flora Ann 119 John 173
Mary 81 Sally 173 Sarah 18
SWEET, Mynetta 171 Nancy 83
Sylvester 171
SWEETSER, --- 35 Eliza 78 Loisa
35
SWETLAND, Hannah 98
SWETT, Caroline R 145 Hattie F
58 Lois 249 R R 58 Stephen 249
William 257
SYLVESTER, Lucy 126
SYMONDS, Hannah 25 50 Capt
Joseph 25 50 Nancy 25 Gov
Samuel 94 Susanna 94

TABER, Lydia 91
TAFT, Charles J 269 Frances 269
TAINTOR, Asa 55 Betsey 54
TALBERT, Ellen S 199
TALBOT, Betsey 70 Mary H 29
TALLANT, Adaline G 267 John G
267 John L 19 Sarah Jane 19
TALLENT, Mrs Caroline Gibson 49
TALMER, Lucinda 87
TANDY, Clara 3 John 3
TAPPAN, Caroline L 37 39
Christopher 223 Huldah 223 Mrs
Margaret 224 Mary 193 Weare 39
TAPPIN, Julia E 202
TARBELL, John 135 Mary 135 Sarah
135
TARLETON, --- 65
TARLETON, Col Ames 65 Mary 4
TASKER, Cyrus A 194 Ebenezer 202
Eliza 252 Eliza D 194 Eliza H
201 Elvira 252 Gilbert 252
Lillie E 92 Mary 162 163 Polly
202 Sally 251
TATE, Alice J 126 Arnor 223 Emma
E 223 James 126 Josiah C 223
TAYLOR, --- 197 Abigail 73
Amanda 197 Anna C 164 Anthony
177 Betsey 245 Bettie 134
Deborah 257 Ella M 15 Gilman R
12 Gratia 134 Harriet N 180
Joanna 97 John 45 73 Joseph L
109 Mrs Julia A 150 Laura 109
Lydia 177 274 Margaret 186 187

Martha 206 Mary 197 Mary A 4
Matilda R 45 Molly 232 Mrs 4
Nellie 156 Nelly 157 Patience
115 218 Polly 12 180 Rachel 187
Sally 45 Sarah 266 Sarah J 187
TEAD, Sarah E 105
TEBBETS, Jeremy 37 Judith 64
Mary 37 Capt Thomas 64
TEEL, Asenath 253
TEMPLE, Charles 52 Hannah D 273
Josie 52 Roxana 52
TENNANT, --- 4 Betsy 4
TENNEY, Betsey A 30 Emeline 149
Emma 149 Eunice 42 John 42
Lucinda 145 230 Lydia 274
Marinda 170 Nancy 208 Dea
William 149 178
TENNY, Charles 192 Eliza 192
Lydia 192 Mary 192
TERRETT, Eleanor 167 William R
167
TERRILL, Emily 227
TERRY, Asa 57 Content 57 Rev
Joel 54 Lydia 4 Martha 189 Mary
189 Susan F 54
TEWKSBURY, Mary 77 Mary A 71
Olive 182 Sally 188
THATCHER, E 204 Mary 149 150
Sally 204
THAYER, Annie Laurie 234
Augustus MD 234 Rev Elihu DD 36
216 Ephraim 96 Esther 95 96
Hannah 36 Mary 216 Sarah 96
THAYERS, Lucy H 118
THEMBER, Joanna 51
THING, Hannah 193 John 54
Mehitable 54
THINK, --- 54 Mehetable 54
THISELL, Charles 263 Susan J 263
THISSELL, Seba A 175
THOM, Juliette 44 Martha S 224
Persis 21 Richard 224 William H
44
THOMAS, Amanda 87 Imogene 87
John 235 L B 87 Mary 172 Meriel
235 Nancy N 56 William 56
THOMKINS, Elizabeth Bagshaw 189
THOMPSON, --- 37 Rev A C
127 Abigail 83 Albert H 118
Alvin R 217 Ann Dorothy 153
Anne Eliza 8 Annie 50 Benjamin
263 Clara H 217 Deborah 200 Col
E 46 Eliza 208 Eliza J 200
Elizabeth 49 52 127 190 Ella M
187 188 Ellen 242 Eunice 43
Flora 204 Hannah 19 37 45 234
Harriet 155 Henry M 242 Hiram
19 Joanna 19 John 45 204
Jonathan 270 Jonathan R 127
Joseph 116 Mrs Laura A 92 Rev
Leander 8 Lucia Annette 12 Mary

11 46 127 204 Moses Esq 187
Noah 234 Polly 27 270 Robert R
12 Sabrina 19 Samuel W 208
Sarah 263 Silas M 241 Sophronia
241 Theodore 19 37 Washington
19 William 200
THOMSON, Florence E 74 Maria 43
Mary A 89 Robert C 89
THORN, Elizabeth 173 Mary 173
Nathan 173 Zilpha 147
THORNDIKE, --- 218 Mary E 220
THORNDYKE, Mary D 109 Thomas W
109
THORNTON, --- 22 Emma Elizabeth
142 Hannah 111 James 111 Joshua
55 Mary 111 Hon Matthew 22
Polly 46 Sally 55 William 142
THRESHER, Sally C 185
THURBER, Ellen 153 Lester 153
Lydia 100
THURSON, Abigail 173 Elijah 173
THURSTON, Benjamin F 178 Betsey
205 Ebenezer 212 Emma L 85
Josiah 249 Martha B 177 178
Mary 182 247 Mary Ann 247 248
Moses 182 Phebe 182 Sally K 212
Sarah A 249 Velorus 85 William
247
THYNG, Abbie S 141 Aphia 151
Betsey 151 Dorothy E 148 Dudley
151 Gilman 220 Jonathan Esq 148
Lydia Swasey 204 Sally 220
Sarah 220
TIBBETS, Betsey 29
TIBBETTS, --- 265 Anetta A 268
268 Betsey 29 Lucinda 265 Lydia
20 Phoebe 213 Samuel 20 Sarah
40 Sophia 178
TIDD, Joseph 63 Mary 63
TIFFANY, --- 13
TILDEN, Achsah 272
TILTON, --- 136 Abigail 24 209
215 216 Abraham 215 Alice 60
Betsey 18 19 Caleb 218 Elbridge
60 Elizabeth 136 272 Emma 160
Emma M 196 Esther D 117 Henry W
117 Ida B 218 James S 218
Joanna 215 John F 215 Louisa A
24 Mahala 7 57 Mary 81
Mehetable 7 Sarah 217 218 Sarah
Jane 215 Susan 108 148 149
Susan French 77 Timothy 96
William 108 William Jr 24
TINKER, Josiah 98
TINKHAM, --- 232 Mary 232
TIRELL, Mary 24
TIRRELL, Inez 210
TITCOMB, Emily 130 Margaret 73
Sally Hale 258 Simeon C 258
TITHER, Elizabeth S 63 Hon
Samuel 63

TODD, Col Andrew 75 Rachel 174
Sarah 75 243
TOLEMAN, Mary S 266
TOLFORD, Mary 179
TOLLE, James H 236 Mary G 236
TOLMAN, Mary S 266
TOPPAN, Elizabeth 47 48 Jane 48
Dr Peter 48
TORR, Abigail 157 159 Sarah 112
157 Simon 112 157
TORRY, Hannah 152
TORY, Sabra 204
TOURTILLOTTE, Josiah 16 Lula 16
TOWER, Betsey 271 Henry 271
TOWLE, Anna 186 Annie L 51
Benjamin 251 Caroline 118
Charles P 51 Edwin 247 Eleanor
H 42 Frank C 101 Hannah 68 Mary
207 Nellie 118 Patience 73
Ransellear 118 Samuel 186 Sarah
251 Sarah A 247 Tabitha 251
TOWNE, Barton G 32 Dr Frank 32
Maria P 32 Sarah 13
TOWNSEND, --- 64 Abigail 16
Charles 232 Eliza 64 Sarah H
232
TOZZER, Carrie B 163 Samuel C
163
TRASK, James 273 Lydia 174
TRAVIS, Aaron 191 Betsy 191
Bridget 255 256 Henry 255 256
Priscilla 130 Sarah 255 256
TREADWELL, Capt Charles 2
Elizabeth 2 Sarah 259 Sarah W 2
TRICKEY, Eunice 81 Francis 272
Georgia A 262 J Colman 262
James 169 James C 81 Joanna 44
Joseph 44 Capt Joshua 169 262
Luceba W 262 Martha P 169 262
Mary 201 Ruth 78 81 Sally 169
Sarah 272
TRIPP, Ann 158 Richard 157
TROTTER, Jane 180
TROW, Betsy 131 Levi 131 Mary 94
131
TROWBRIDGE, Elizabeth 252 George
G 157 Hannah 152
TROY, Daniel 110 Phoebe C 110
TRUE, --- 9 131 Abigail 30 Emily
B 229 Miriam 195 196 Nellie A
140 141 Rachel 8 9 Ruth 12 131
Samuel M 9 Sarah T 246
TRUMBULL, Frances 243 Sarah 261
TRUSCOTT, Olive 120 121
TRUSSELL, --- 217 Asenath 83
Benjamin 83 Mary 19
TUBBS, Alice 191 Sarah 66
TUCK, John 219 Mary 218 219 Mary
Ann 174 Robert 218
TUCKER, Alice 40 Ezra 40 Harriet
W 218 Henry 78 Judith 40 Kezia

78 Luther 171 Lydia 31 Mary 171
Mary C 84 Mary J 171 Sally 157
Sarah 256
TUFTS, Harriet 70 208 Jefferson
70
TURNER, --- 32 Betsey 129
Charlotte 43 Eliza 264 Lucinda
32 Mrs Mary 188 Rachel G 82 Rev
Sydney 129
TUTHERLY, Hannah 91 Lydia 91
Rufus 91 Samuel 91
TUTON, Henry 231 Mary 231 Robert
231
TUTTLE, --- 33 Alonzo 139
Benjamin 215 241 Betsey 224
Catherine 129 Charlotte 139
Eliza 115 Lt George 129 Hon
Jacob 224 Jane 215 241 Judge
John 255 Louisa 215 Lydia 168
169 Martha 241 Mary 34 201 253
255 256 Mary E 224 Robert 215
Sarah 129 Sophronia 215 William
P 253
TWISS, Hannah T 80 Jeremiah 103
Julia 103 Marion 103
TWIST, Almira 170
TWITCHELL, Adams 84 Alice 246
Helen Mar 84 Hiram 246 Lusylvia
84 Mrs Sarah E Swasey 44
TWOMBLY, --- 130 Ann H 253
Daniel 72 Elvira 245 Fannie H
72 Fanny W 202 Frozilla 72 Dr J
H 202 John 27 Julia 27 Mary 220
Mercy 37 Nathaniel 220 Nehemiah
Caverly 245 Polly 220 Sarah 183
TYLER, Austin 262 Louise 262
TYNER, Mrs Hannah W 196

UNDERWOOD, Clara A 204 John 204
Mehitabel 98 Sally 188 Thomas
98
UPHAM, Catherine 50 John H 50
Judith 21 Julia 185 Mary 267
Hon Peter 75 Sarah Miller 75

VALENTINE, Augusta L 227
VALLEY, Joseph 179 Maria 179
VAN ALSTINE, --- 266 Maria 266
VANCE, Olive E 15
VARNEY, Abigail 223 253 Anna 253
Elizabeth 91 Enoch 253 Mrs
Hannah E 43 Humphrey 237 Joseph
20 Judith 268 Laura C 265 Mary
20 Richard 20 Sarah 20 Timothy
223 265
VARNUM, Abigail 15 Mary 61
VEASEY, Adelaide H 142 Aurelia 4
Lewis R 142 Olive 65 Simeon 65
VEASIE, Mahala 12
VERY, Lydia 207
VICKERY, Hannah Gilman 90

VIETS, Herbert Allen 270 Marian
270
VIRGIN, --- 65 Sarah A 65
VITTUM, Ruth 137 138
VORE, Richard 189 Sarah 189 190
VOSE, Emily 72 John 72 Joshua
225 Minnie E 228 Nancy 225
Nellie 72

WADLEIGH, --- 19 84 Anna 228
Annie S 150 Benjamin 200
Benjamin Esq 240 Benjamin E 162
Charles F 150 Ellen E 219
Ephraim S 231 Hannah M 214
Harriet 140 232 Henry 259 Capt
John S 219 Joseph 228 Joseph N
172 Judge 104 Martha J 162 Mary
137 157 219 Mary E 230 232 Mary
Elizabeth 231 Myra 172 Oliver
162 Sally 68 259 Samuel 232
Susan 61 200
WADLEY, Harriet Elizabeth 61
Mary E 249 Moses D 61
WADROBE, Jennie 245
WADSWORTH, George G 131 Martha E
131
WAGNER, Ella 146
WAIT, Mary 257
WAITE, Deborah 103 Elizabeth 262
Mary 162 Sarah D 232
WAKEFIELD, David 99 Kate J 99
WALBRIDGE, Isaac 233
WALCH, Ella Frances 258 Frank A
258
WALDA, Irene 6
WALDEY, Deborah 55
WALDO, Irene 5 Mary 63
WALDRON, Aaron 92 George 268
Mary 268 Sarah 92 93
WALES, Mary F C 274 Samuel Esq
274
WALKER, --- 11 82 108 232 270
Abbie 82 Abbie M 106 120 Alden
114 Ann 173 Annie 270 Betsey 45
C B 245 Daniel 101 Delia A 166
Eliza 42 Frances 188 Hannah 101
Harriet N 17 Hattie 232 Mrs
Huldah B 215 Jane 129 130
Joseph B 253 Laura 15 16
Leonard 188 Lydia 11 175 Lydia
B 231 Mary 140 Miranda H 54 55
Nathan 17 Nellie F 104 Ruth 101
Sally 210 Sarah 28 213 Sophia
177 Susan 114 Suunnah 257
Tamson 222 Rev Timothy 108 213
W E 104 William 166 William B
42
WALLACE, Mrs Ann 1 Ann M 76
Annie 46 47 Betsey 127 197
Catherine S 148 149 Cleora J 43
Danfort 57 E G 112 Edward 197

Mrs Eliza Burns 66 67 Elizabeth 75 191 Emeline 56 George W 258 Henry 43 Jane 111 Jennie 50 John 76 Dr John 66 Julia M 258 Lydia 106 Lydia M 258 Margaret 158 197 238 Mary 108 Nathaniel 75 Ruth 57 Dea Samuel 157 Sarah 91 197 Mrs Sarah C 268 Sarah E 112 William 91 William Esq 149

WALLINGFORD, Elvira 124 Mary B 202 Samuel W 202

WALLINGTON, Nicholas 255

WALLIS, Benjamin 181 Rebecca 46 47 181 S Augusta 181

WALSWORTH, Harriet 225 226 James 225

WALTON, Nancy 28 151

WARD, Abigail 73 Abner 66 Arthur 217 Bagley 95 Betsey 66 Catharine 66 Deborah 18 19 219 Eliza 132 Ella J 4 Enoch 123 Hannah 217 Isaac 66 John 66 Martha C 217 Mary 68 123 Mehitable 232 Molly 66 Oscar 4 Phebe 95 96 Sally 66 Mrs Sarah Goodwell 45 Simon Jr 132 Stephen 66 Zilpha 134

WARDEN, A H 89 Alexander 89 Lucy A 89

WARE, Alfred F 253 Emily 124 Esther 161 Hannah E 253 J Q A 124

WARNER, --- 46 Addie J 105 J B 30 Martha 244 Mary 30 O H 105 Sally 47

WARREN, Ann 173 Asa 130 Caroline 173 Elizabeth 50 Georgia 9 Isaiah 173 Jane 45 John 44 Josiah 45 L D 247 Martha A 130 Mary 44 45 238 Nellie 247 Capt Robert 50 Submit 252 Zibiah 45

WASHBURN, A G 69 Abbie M 244 Abby M 44 Alden 117 Elijah 244 George 44 Hannah 99 Mary 244 Oliver 99 Paulina D 69 Sally 117

WASSON, Isabella 24

WATERHOUSE, Almeda E 117 Eli 42 Margaret 272 Martha J 42

WATERMAN, Chloe 146 Emma E 36 Oren H 36 Patty 106 Susan 122 Susan C 146

WATERS, Anna 243 Hannah 153

WATKINS, Desdemonia Fisk 1

WATSON, --- 4 Charles 233 Elsie 4 Hale 247 Lizzie 233 Martha 247 Mary 140 Nicodemus 140 Sarah 100 230 232

WATTS, Abigail 65

WAUGH, Achisa 35

WAY, Delia 103 104

WEARE, Abigail 73 244 Betsy 29 Jonathan 182 Joseph H 29 Mary Ann 29 30 Nancy 182

WEATHERBY, Catherine 110

WEBB, --- 48 Azariah 259 Eliza 67 Elizabeth 259 Mary 48 244 Mary Ann 151 Sarah M 125 126

WEBBER, Alvira 119 Betsey 74 75 Emily A 72

WEBER, Johanna 164

WEBSTER, --- 160 204 273 Angeline W 164 Bailey 86 Betsey 160 217 Charlotte Smith 242 Daniel 89 Dorothy 251 Ebenezer 18 Elisha A 65 Eliza 170 Elizabeth 65 Emeline M 118 Esther 230 233 Euhoit 218 George 216 Grace 89 Hannah 174 223 Harriet 86 Iddo 205 Jacob 70 154 James P 83 Prof James W 38 Joanna 154 John 153 Jonathan Ladd 251 Judith 67 Levina 154 Lizzie J 205 Lois 175 Louisa Augusta 217 Martha T 216 Mary Ann 149 218 Mary C 23 Nancy 70 153 Rebekah 83 Sally 197 205 Sarah 127 149 150 Sarah L 38 Susanna 18 170 Timothy 170

WEED, Betsey 260 Delia H 194 Phoebe 96

WEEK, Lizzie 49

WEEKS, Dr A G 219 Adaline B 273 Comfort 8 Comfort 171 172 David 177 204 Dudley 273 Elizabeth 78 210 272 Ellen Marie 121 123 Emily 170 Hannah 93 94 Harriet 21 Dr Ichabod 260 James 210 James Brackett 78 James Jr 78 Dr John 11 Maj John W 84 Lucie 204 Malinda 108 Marie 121 Martha 11 180 235 236 Mary 26 78 204 Mary J 166 167 Mary Nye 78 Mary Shackford 107 Mary W 26 Matilda 204 Minerva 177 Moses 21 Persis F 84 Persis Fayette 210 Sally Cotta 260 Samuel 272 Sarah 190 Sarah (Sally) 11 Sarah Cotton 260 Stephen 107 William 121

WELBRIDGE, Hannah 233

WELCH, Hannah 21

WELD, Jabez H 208 Mary Grace 208

WELLMAN, Emma P 261

WELLS, Aaron 99 Abiah 95 Anna 205 206 Arthur C 225 B F 187 Dr D E 107 Eliza A 40 Elizabeth 34 Emily R 225 Ephraim 88 George 176 Hannah 109 154 Hattie 187 Henry 154 Kiah 154 L C 176 Levina 154 Lois 8 9 Louise 107 Mary 74 Mary C S 167 Mary E 107

Moses 109 Nancy 99 172 Stephen
40 Theody 131
WENTHWORTH, Dorothy 100 Lydia
100
WENTWORTH, --- 99 Amy 129 Anna
199 Betsey 194 Caroline 203
David P 203 Dorothy 100 Eliza
202 224 Eliza D 202 Elmza 157
Elvira C 10 237 Georgia A 250
Dea Gershom 122 Hannah 122 J T
202 Joanna 213 John 224 Col
Joseph 246 Louisa 99 Lydia 100
Gen Marshall 249 Martha E 69
Mrs Mary 72 Mary Ann 254 Nancy
99 Roxannah C 140 Sally 129 152
217 Sarah 100 152 Sarah Clarke
246 Tamsen 122 Lt Timothy 129
William 69 122
WEST,--- 24 214 Alice D 237
Ellen E 214 John 214 William
237
WESTCOTT,Abbie A 97 Stephen 97
WESTON,--- 201 Eliza A 270 271
Mary Bartlett 201 Sutheric 270
WESTWORK, Abigail 90
WETHERBEE, Laura G 99 Mary J 59
178 179 Sarah 179 180 Solomon
179
WETHERBY, Smith 137
WHEAT, Allen H 101 Dr Asa 101
Huldah 230 Jane E 101 Joshua R
230 Sarah A 230
WHEELER, Amos 198 Betsey 88
Betsey Jane 88 Daphne 41 Dexter
128 223 Elizabeth F 223 Ellen
155 Genette 10 Gillman 138
Hannah 7 163 Hazen 155 John 188
John Brooks 269 John Esq 45
John H Esq 205 Judith 192 Lucy
80 Lydia 7 Lydia G 197 Marietta
188 Mary Ann 263 Mary C 182
Mary L 35 Meriel 269 Polly 47
53 111 112 128 Reuben H 41
Sally 111 138 Samuel 7 Sara E
223 Sarah 270 Sarah E 205 Sarah
S 36 Thomas 111 William 88
William T 10
WHEELOCK, Jonathan 73 Lucy 73
Mary 175 Nancy 175 176 Rhoda H
32
WHEET, Caroline B 115 Elvira 216
Huldah 115 Joshua R 115 Sarah
25 59
WHICHER, Lydia 160
WHIDDEN, Mary P 248 Parson 248
WHIPPLE, Alma C 104 Betsey 165
Mrs Clemantine 71 Elizabeth 102
Hannah 146 Hannah Dane 34 Mrs
Helen L 239 240 Irena 215 James
B 71 Joel 165 John 240 Lucy B
101 Martha W 71 Sally 126

Stephen 146 Mrs Susanna 200 201
WHITAKER, Betsey 208 Charles 70
Charles S 208 Ebenezer 137
Hannah 113 James 43 Jesse 264
John 43 Luther 208 Lydia 43 191
Martha 70 Mary 43 Peter 3 Phebe
16 17 137 Sally 3 Susan 208
Susannah 264
WHITAMORE, Amos 32 John 32 Ruth
32 Sally 32
WHITCHER, Cynthia J 264 Ida M 15
John 26 Louisa 79 Mary 42
Nathaniel 42
WHITCOMB Clark 166 Esther 63
Harriet Maria 166 L T 175
Lucinda 35 Martha L 175 Nancy
47 Oliver 47 Rosanna 32
WHITE, --- 24 133 A J 233
Armenia S 265 Caroline 199 Dr
Charles 95 Clarissa 113 Dana 35
David 220 Electa 55 Mrs Eliza P
73 Elizabeth 35 Emily 3 Fanny
159 Frances 114 Frank P 52
Hannah 96 Hannah Libbey 97
Harriet A 93 Helen A 245 Helen
H 85 Hope 16 James 5 John 113
265 Jonathan 44 Judith 11 Mrs
Letitia Stinson 3 Mahala 3
Martha 170 172 Mary 24 81 Mary
Ann 220 Mary E 81 Mrs Nancy 264
Nancy A 220 Nejmain 81 Nellie H
233 Nettie A 52 P 96 Phebe 87
Polly 5 Ruth 243 Sally 95 Sarah
95 116 133 Sarah P 153 Susannah
113
WHITEHOUSE, Abbie McD 42 43
George L 86 John McDuffee 42
Laura Ann 86 Liberty N 86
Lizzie 248 Susan R 255 Thomas
203 William 255
WHITEMORE, Hannah 47
WHITFORD, --- 270 Anna M 116
Elizabeth 115 Elliot 115
Josephine 270 Maria K 115 Mary
99
WHITING, Elizabeth 41 Emily J
111 Horace 111 Lucy 226 Mary 74
Nellie S 142 W H 142
WHITMAN, Azubah 131 Ford 131
WHITMORE, Ebenezer 182 Elizabeth
182 Susan C 182 183
WHITNEY, --- 8 9 Alexander 54 C
R 186 Caroline 15 Elvira A 9
Hannah 54 222 Harriet 46
Hepsabeth 222 223 Jeremiah 15
Lois 54 Martha A 185 Mary 15 92
Mary S 57 Nancy Fisher 77
Orlando 57 Ruth 266 Sally 115
Sarah 157 Sarah F 116
WHITTAKER, Anne 76 Laura Ann 175
Peter 175

WHITTEMORE, Hon Aaron 224 Albert
C 197 Alma 118 Arieannah S 224
George R 113 H H 118 Harriet M
A 93 Helen D 113 Judith 11 12
Sophia F 224 Sylvia C 197
WHITTEN, Hepsibath 170
WHITTER, Mary 31 Ruth 81
WHITTIER, Hannah 149 Lucy 239
Lydia 160 Reuben 204 Ruth 81
204 Sarah 42
WHITTLE, Eliza 109 Elizabeth 156
Emma J 105 Josephine 231 Martha
156 Mary 91 Thomas 91 William
109
WHITTON, Elizabeth 64
WICKS, --- 168 Laura 168
WICOM, Marinda L 243 Thomas H
243
WIDDEN, Sarah 150
WIDDRINGTON, Elizabeth 130
WIGGIN, --- 33 Aaron 193 Ancie 9
Hon Andrew 33 Anna M 204
Augustus 181 Benjamin 42 Betsey
51 Daniel 184 Dolly 268
Elizabeth 46 Ellen 42 137 Ellen
C 112 Emily J 192 Grace 1 Hon H
B 137 Hannah 33 Jacob C 51
James J 204 Joseph 9 Margaret 1
Mary 13 14 149 184 Mary F 193
Mary Jane 181 Mary Sargeant 51
Minnie Parker 181 182 Nancy 120
Nancy P 204 Russell B 192 Sarah
184 Sarah Ann 8 Sarah E 184
Sarah M 216 Sherburne 1 Thomas
B 216
WIGGINS, M Jane 185 Mary 15 Mrs
215 Philena 154 Timothy 154
WIGHT, Mary L 25 Nathaniel 25
WIKINS, Sarah 170
WILBUR, Mary Ann 94 96
WILCOMB, Sarah 58
WILDER, Edmund C 259 Maj Jonas
84 195 Lucy 195 Lydia A 144
Nancy 145 Persis 84 Sarah
Stanley 259
WILEY, Fannie M 176 Martha L 176
WILKINS, Abigail 43 82 154 191
Alexander 88 98 Mrs Almira P 75
Amos A 269 Andrew 157 211 Anna
168 Augustus 170 Betsy 119 145
170 Charles F 240 David 109 191
E Abbie 111 Elizabeth 192
Esther 239 Fanny 71 88 Harriet
L 82 Isaac 43 79 James 43
Joseph C 93 Judith Ann 109
Julia 94 Julia A 93 Lucinda 167
Lydia 88 98 Martha H 269 Mary
92 93 Mary Ann 240 Mrs Mary J
153 Mehitable 157 Nancy 43
Phineas 82 Rebecca 113 Rodney
82 Roxanna 79 Ruth 105 106

Sally 98 159 Sarah 201 211
WILKINSON, Jane 61
WILLARD, Emily 272 Hannah W 89
Mary 239 240 Mary Wilder 120
Phebe 43 Maj Simeon 239 Sophia
93 Steadman 120 William 102
WILLETS, Anna 190
WILLEY, Abigail 194 Alfred S 50
Betsey Emeline 28 29 Hannah L
174 Henry 174 Honor 119 James
119 James C 194 Lois 168 Mary
270 Mary J 50 Mary R 8 Polly
119 156 246 247 Samuel 156 246
Samuel Esq 119 Susan 50
WILLIAMS, Clarissa S 249 Emma F
162 Eveline 164 Fanny 15 George
L 162 Horace B 164 James 273
Jane 15 114 115 Lettice 249
Lydia B 46 83 Mary 265 Mary J
273 Melaney 15 N P 181 Nancy 24
Rebecca 114 Rufus 249 Sally 107
Sarah 181 Susan L 77
WILLIAMSON, Elvira 142
WILLIE, --- 84
WILLIS, Fanny 145 Harriet 180
Lucinda W 62 Mary Emma 89
WILLOUGHBY, Almira E 143 Dorothy
143 S K 143
WILLS, F E 171 Josephine R 171
WILLY, Esther 131
WILMOT, Sarah 23
WILSON, --- 63 113 133 Abbie 229
Mrs Abigal 236 Abigail Johnson
236 Abraham 133 Alexander 11
Ann 15 Ann A 77 78 Annis 180
Betsy 113 114 262 Charles 59
Crisel 191 David 3 David 69
Capt David 21 Dorcas 265 Edna
111 Elbridge 32 Electa 3 Eliza
32 38 Elizabeth 77 110 113 114
254 Emily 88 Rev Geo P 88
George 200 Hannah 126 Ida 59
Isaac R 230 J L 111 James 32
262 James M 151 Jane 133 134
Jennie 69 John 147 Joseph 38
Judith 184 Laura A 32 Lavinia
168 Capt Leonard 77 Lydia 239
Mary 69 87 111 265 Mary A 97 98
Mary L 151 Mehitable 11 Moody K
174 Nancy 13 21 Persis 106 Col
Robert 262 Sally 4 170 Samuel
106 Sarah 80 81 145 Sarah C 21
Sarah F 43 Sophia 131 William
43
WINCH, Almira 222 Fanny 222
Francis 222 Maria 77
WINCHESTER, Deborah 44
WINDRAM, Harold W 89 Mary
Adelaide 89
WINGATE, Adnah 201 Charles E 201
Elizabeth 122 Enoch 43 John 123

Martha 11 259 260 Mary 63 122
Hon Paine 259 Samuel 122 Sarah
42 43 122 123
WINKLEY, Abiah 213 214
WINN, Elizabeth 80 81 F P 207
Nellie M 207 Persis A 166 167
Persis G 167 William 167
WINSLOW, Anna 133 268 George 217
Mrs Harriet 217
WISE, Humphrey 195 Mary 195
Sadie L 101 Susan 101 Susannah
195 Willard W 101
WISWALL, Betsey 143 J P 143
Sarah Clark 100 143 144 176 187
WITCHER, Susan M 161
WITHERELL, Ann 17
WITHINGTON, --- 160 Mary 160
WNETWORTH, Susan 202
WOLCOTT, Sally 179
WOOD, --- 126 247 Abigail 96 192
Betsey 238 Clara P 264 Delia 43
Eliza 74 Elizabeth 67 Emma 181
Hannah 43 Rev Henry 247
Hortensia A 27 John 228
Jonathan 192 Lucy 154 Lucy M
134 Martha 35 Mary P 55 Moses
55 Patience 83 Persis A 56
Rosamond 229 Sally 228 Samuel
264
WOODARD, Eliza 199 Elvina 181
Henry H 181 Horace 199
WOODBRIDGE, --- 184 Rev Benjamin
184 Rev John 184
WOODBURY, --- 146 Alice A 98
Betsy A 98 193 Eliza H 193
Eliza S 64 Emaline 196 Harriet
70 71 Capt Israel 272 Jane 226
John 98 193 John B 191 Josiah A
147 Lois 272 Lydia A 237 Mary
138 Mary A 138 Mary Jane 164
Nathaniel 138 Hon Peter 71
Polly 147 Dr Robert 164 Sabrina
45 Susan 146 William Esq 237
WOODICE, Ruth 32
WOODLOCK, Mary 150
WOODMAN, Abigail 48 231 Abner 84
Apphia 146 Hon Charles 45 Mrs
Dorothy Dix 45 Eliza A 126
Esther 266 Hannah 84 James 166
Rev Joseph 266 Lucy 166 Mary A
203 Samuel 126 Sarah 166 168
WOODRAGE, Ruth 136
WOODS, Frances 6 Mary W 143
WOODWARD, Abigail 262 Aurora O
37 Charles R 37 J M 234 Jacob
60 262 Judge James 60 262
Jonathan 207 Katuria 65 66
Lydia 60 234 Lydia A 207
Lysander T 273 Mary A 36 Oliver
P 36 Orange 245 Susan 245
WOOLSON, Mrs Emma M 85

WOOSTER, Sallie 255 256
WORCESTER, Horace L 112 205
Millie A 112 Susannah 33
WORDSWORTH, Aurelia 108
WORSTER, Dorcas 183
WORTH, Anna 44 Elizabeth 38
Emeline M 244 Hannah 39 Samuel
87 Sarah 87
WORTHEN, --- 61 Ada 61 Eliza 95
96 Ezekiel 96 Judith 191 Lucia
N 263 Lydia 267 Mary J 86
Samuel 263
WORTHIN, Judith 107
WORTHING, Mehetable 233
WORTHLEY, Betsey 85 Sally 101
WRIGHT, Abel 63 Anna 170 Austin
36 Betsey 75 Charles W 33 David
170 Eben 166 Elizabeth 149 166
Emily 262 Hester 149 Irene 230
James N 4 John 230 Dea John 71
Joshua 262 Julia S 36 Mrs Lydia
63 Mary Ann 149 Mary Elizabeth
33 Melinda 63 Miriam 126 Nathan
126 Olive Atwood 105 106 Oliver
P 36 Polly 262 Sally 71 113 Dr
Samuel 149 Sarah R 4 Solon 75
Susan A 21 Zilpha 63
WYATT, --- 11 12 Dea Daniel 11
Eva L 96 Hannah 186 Mattie L
118 Molly 11 12 55 Polly 246
Sally L 133 Sarah 118 Thomas
118 Rev Thomas 117
WYMAN, Abby 113 Abigail 74 209
Laura 223 Martha P 169 Mary 10
Merrill 169 Nancy 129 Susan 41
Timothy Jr 74

YATES, Orpheia 56
YEATON, Annie R 58 Frances H 100
Sally 108
YEAW, Mary E 218
YEMMONS, Hannah 97
YOLPY, Adeline 77
YORK, Abigail 183 Betsey P 104
Daniel G 104 Diodama 224 Joseph
183 Mary A 104 Mary Elizabeth
182 183
YOUNG, --- 18 60 105 106 126 249
Aaron B 157 Benjamin Esq 150
Betsey 143 249 Mrs Caroline 114
Catharine 44 Daniel 182 David
249 Electa 56 Hannah 146 Jasper
S 18 Josiah 157 Louis A 13
Louisa 157 263 Lucy M 13 Mary
100 Mary Ann 117 Mary J 60
Mehitable 105 106 Mehitable
Clark 150 Minnie E 13 Nancy 8 9
Nancy A 157 Olivia 126 Peter
100 Sally Ann 60 Mrs Sarah 121
Violetta 182